C000300681

Mitsubishi Pajero Automotive Repair Manual

by Larry Warren and John H Haynes
Member of the Guild of Motoring Writers

Models covered:

All Mitsubishi Pajero models
1983 through 1996

(8D2 - 68765)

ABCDE
FGHIJ
KLM

Haynes Publishing Group
Sparkford Nr Yeovil
Somerset BA22 7JJ England

Haynes North America, Inc
861 Lawrence Drive
Newbury Park
California 91320 USA

Haynes Manuals, Inc
34 Jellico Drive
Scoresby, Victoria 3179 Australia

Acknowledgements

Technical writers who contributed to this project include Tim Imhoff and Jeff Killingsworth. Wiring diagrams provided exclusively for Haynes North America, Inc. by Valley Forge Technical Communications.

© **Haynes North America, Inc. 1997, 2000**

With permission from J.H. Haynes & Co. Ltd.

A book in the Haynes Automotive Repair Manual Series

Printed in the U.S.A.

All rights reserved. No part of this book may be reproduced or transmitted in any form or by any means, electronic or mechanical, including photocopying, recording or by any information storage or retrieval system, without permission in writing from the copyright holder.

ISBN 1 56392 382 3

Library of Congress Catalogue Card Number 97-80265

While every attempt is made to ensure that the information in this manual is correct, no liability can be accepted by the authors or publishers for loss, damage or injury caused by any errors in, or omissions from, the information given.

00-336

Contents

Haynes photographer, mechanic and author with 1987 model

About this manual

Its purpose

The purpose of this manual is to help you get the best value from your vehicle. It can do so in several ways. It can help you decide what work must be done, even if you choose to have it done by a dealer service department or a repair shop; it provides information and procedures for routine maintenance and servicing; and it offers diagnostic and repair procedures to follow when trouble occurs.

We hope you use the manual to tackle the work yourself. For many simpler jobs, doing it yourself may be quicker than arranging an appointment to get the vehicle into a shop and making the trips to leave it and pick it up. More importantly, a lot of money can be saved by avoiding the expense the shop must pass on to you to cover its labor and overhead costs. An added benefit is the sense of satisfaction and accomplishment that you feel after doing the job yourself.

Using the manual

The manual is divided into Chapters. Each Chapter is divided into numbered Sections, which are headed in bold type between horizontal lines. Each Section consists of consecutively numbered paragraphs.

At the beginning of each numbered Section you will be referred to any illustrations which apply to the procedures in that Section. The reference numbers used in illustration captions pinpoint the pertinent Section and the Step within that Section. That is, illustration 3.2 means the illustration refers to Section 3 and Step (or paragraph) 2 within that Section.

Procedures, once described in the text, are not normally repeated. When it's necessary to refer to another Chapter, the reference will be given as Chapter and Section number. Cross references given without use of the word "Chapter" apply to Sections and/or paragraphs in the same Chapter. For example, "see Section 8" means in the same Chapter.

References to the left or right side of the vehicle assume you are sitting in the driver's seat, facing forward.

Even though we have prepared this manual with extreme care, neither the publisher nor the author can accept responsibility for any errors in, or omissions from, the information given.

NOTE

A **Note** provides information necessary to properly complete a procedure or information which will make the procedure easier to understand.

CAUTION

A **Caution** provides a special procedure or special steps which must be taken while completing the procedure where the Caution is found. Not heeding a Caution can result in damage to the assembly being worked on.

WARNING

A **Warning** provides a special procedure or special steps which must be taken while completing the procedure where the Warning is found. Not heeding a Warning can result in personal injury.

Introduction to the Mitsubishi Pajero

Pajero models are available in two- and four-door body styles. The chassis design on these models features a separate body mounted on a boxed steel frame.

These models are equipped with either a 2.6L four-cylinder, a 3.0L SOHC or 3.5L DOHC petrol engine. The four-cylinder models are equipped with carburettors while V6 engines use port fuel injection. In addition, four-cylinder 2.5L and 2.8L diesel engines are available. Both diesel engines are available with a turbocharger and an intercooler.

The engine drives the rear wheels through either a five-speed manual or three- or four-speed automatic transmission via a driveshaft, differential and axles mounted in an axles housing. A transfer case and driveshaft are used to drive the front differential and driveaxles.

The front suspension is composed of upper and lower control arms, shock absorbers and torsion bars. The solid rear axle is suspended by leaf springs and shock absorbers on earlier models. Later models use coil spring rear suspension with the axle located by trailing arms and a track rod.

The steering box is located to the right of the engine and is connected to the steering arms by a series of rods. Power assist is available as an option.

The brakes are either disc on the front and drum on the rear wheels or four wheel disc, depending on model. Power assist is standard on most models.

Vehicle Identification Numbers

Modifications are a continuing and unpublicised process in vehicle manufacturing. Since spare parts manuals and lists are compiled on a numerical basis, the individual vehicle numbers are essential to correctly identify the component required.

Vehicle identification plate

The identification plate is located on the underside of the bonnet on earlier models and on the left (passenger) side of the engine compartment on the inner fender on later models. It contains information such as paint and trim, as well as engine, transmission and axle information.

Vehicle Identification Number

The Vehicle Identification Number (VIN) is found on a the right side of the frame, near the rear shock absorber **(see illustration)**.

Compliance plate

The identification plate is located on the underside of the bonnet on earlier models and on the left (passenger) side of the engine compartment on the inner fender on later models.

Engine identification number

The engine ID number consists of two parts: a model number and a serial number. On four-cylinder engines, it is located on the right side of the engine in one of two places: 1) on a machined surface at the front corner of the block, just below the number one spark plug (2.6L engine) or 2) at the lower right front corner of block (2.0L and 2.4L engine) **(see illustrations)**. On V6 engines, the ID number is located on a pad at the right side of the block **(see illustration)**.

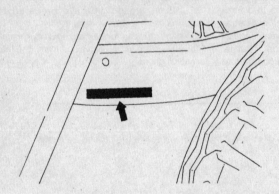

The Vehicle Identification Number (arrow) is located on the right side frame rail, near the shock absorber

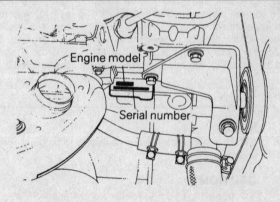

On four-cylinder petrol engines, the identification number is located on a machined surface at the right front corner of the block, just below the cylinder head

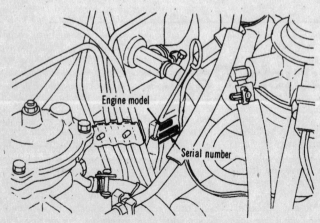

On four-cylinder diesel engines, the identification is located on the rear of the block

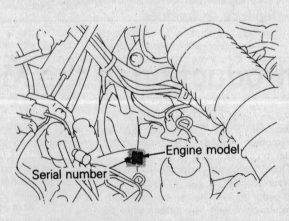

V6 engine identification number location

Buying parts

Spare parts are available from many sources, which generally fall into one of two categories - authorised dealer parts departments and independent retail auto parts stores. Our advice concerning these parts is as follows:

Retail auto parts stores: Good auto parts stores will stock frequently needed components which wear out relatively fast, such as clutch components, exhaust systems, brake parts, tune-up parts, etc. These stores often supply new or reconditioned parts on an exchange basis, which can save a considerable amount of money. Discount auto parts stores are often very good places to buy materials and parts needed for general vehicle maintenance such as oil, grease, filters, spark plugs, belts, touch-up paint, bulbs, etc. They also usually sell tools and general accessories, have convenient hours, charge lower prices and can often be found not far from home.

Authorised dealer parts department: This is the best source for parts which are unique to the vehicle and not generally available elsewhere (such as major engine parts, transmission parts, trim pieces, etc.).

Warranty information: If the vehicle is still covered under warranty, be sure that any spare parts purchased - regardless of the source - do not invalidate the warranty!

To be sure of obtaining the correct parts, have engine and chassis numbers available and, if possible, take the old parts along for positive identification.

Maintenance techniques, tools and working facilities

Maintenance techniques

There are a number of techniques involved in maintenance and repair that will be referred to throughout this manual. Application of these techniques will enable the home mechanic to be more efficient, better organised and capable of performing the various tasks properly, which will ensure that the repair job is thorough and complete.

Fasteners

Fasteners are nuts, bolts, studs and screws used to hold two or more parts together. There are a few things to keep in mind when working with fasteners. Almost all of them use a locking device of some type, either a lockwasher, locknut, locking tab or thread adhesive. All threaded fasteners should be clean and straight, with undamaged threads and undamaged corners on the hex head where the wrench fits. Develop the habit of renewing all damaged nuts and bolts. Special locknuts with nylon or fibre inserts can only be used once. If they are removed, they lose their locking ability and must be renewed.

Rusted nuts and bolts should be treated with a penetrating fluid to ease removal and prevent breakage. Some mechanics use turpentine in a spout-type oil can, which works quite well. After applying the rust penetrant, let it work for a few minutes before trying to loosen the nut or bolt. Badly rusted fasteners may have to be chiseled or sawed off or removed with a special nut breaker, available at tool stores.

If a bolt or stud breaks off in an assembly, it can be drilled and removed with a special tool commonly available for this purpose. Most automotive machine shops can perform this task, as well as other repair procedures, such as the repair of threaded holes that have been stripped out.

Flat washers and lockwashers, when removed from an assembly, should always be refitted exactly as removed. Renew any damaged washers. Never use a lockwasher on any soft metal surface (such as aluminium), thin sheet metal or plastic.

Fastener sizes

For a number of reasons, automobile manufacturers are making wider and wider use of metric fasteners. Therefore, it is important to be able to tell the difference between standard (sometimes called U.S. or SAE) and metric hardware, since they cannot be interchanged.

All bolts, whether standard or metric, are sized according to diameter, thread pitch and length. For example, a standard M12 - 1.75 x 25 metric bolt is 12 mm in diameter, has a thread pitch of 1.75 mm (the distance between threads) and is 25 mm long. The two bolts are nearly identical, and easily confused, but they are not interchangeable.

In addition to the differences in diameter, thread pitch and length, metric and standard bolts can also be distinguished by examining the bolt heads. To begin with, the distance across the flats on a standard bolt head is measured in inches, while the same dimension on a metric bolt is sized in millimetres (the same is true for nuts). As a result, a standard spanner should not be used on a metric bolt and a metric spanner should not be used on a standard bolt. Also, most standard bolts have slashes radiating out from the centre of the head to denote the grade or strength of the bolt, which is an indication of the amount of torque that can be applied to it. The greater the number of slashes, the greater the strength of the bolt. Grades 0 through 5 are commonly used on automobiles. Metric bolts have a property class (grade) number, rather than a slash, moulded into their heads to indicate bolt strength. In this case, the higher the number, the stronger the bolt. Property class numbers 8.8, 9.8 and 10.9 are commonly used on automobiles.

Strength markings can also be used to distinguish standard hex nuts from metric hex nuts. Many standard nuts have dots stamped into one side, while metric nuts are marked with a number. The greater the number of dots, or the higher the number, the greater the strength of the nut.

Metric studs are also marked on their ends according to property class (grade). Larger studs are numbered (the same as metric bolts), while smaller studs carry a geometric code to denote grade.

It should be noted that many fasteners, especially Grades 0 through 2, have no distinguishing marks on them. When such is the case, the only way to determine whether it is standard or metric is to measure the thread pitch or compare it to a known fastener of the same size.

Standard fasteners are often referred to as SAE, as opposed to metric. However, it should be noted that SAE technically refers to a non-metric fine thread fastener only. Coarse thread non-metric fasteners are referred to as USS sizes.

Since fasteners of the same size (both

Grade 1 or 2   Grade 5   Grade 8

Bolt strength marking (standard/SAE/USS; bottom - metric)

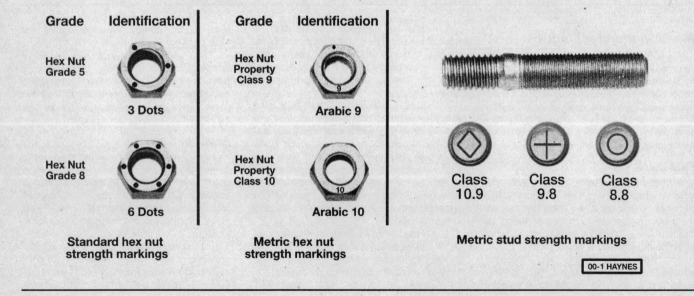

Grade	Identification
Hex Nut Grade 5	3 Dots
Hex Nut Grade 8	6 Dots

Standard hex nut strength markings

Grade	Identification
Hex Nut Property Class 9	Arabic 9
Hex Nut Property Class 10	Arabic 10

Metric hex nut strength markings

Class 10.9   Class 9.8   Class 8.8

Metric stud strength markings

00-1 HAYNES

standard and metric) may have different strength ratings, be sure to reinstall any bolts, studs or nuts removed from your vehicle in their original locations. Also, when renewing a fastener with a new one, make sure that the new one has a strength rating equal to or greater than the original.

Tightening sequences and procedures

Most threaded fasteners should be tightened to a specific torque value (torque is the twisting force applied to a threaded component such as a nut or bolt). Overtightening the fastener can weaken it and cause it to break, while undertightening can cause it to eventually come loose. Bolts, screws and studs, depending on the material they are made of and their thread diameters, have specific torque values, many of which are noted in the Specifications at the beginning of each Chapter. Be sure to follow the torque recommendations closely. For fasteners not assigned a specific torque, a general torque value chart is presented here as a guide. These torque values are for dry (unlubricated) fasteners threaded into steel or cast iron (not aluminium). As was previously mentioned, the size and grade of a fastener determine the amount of torque that can safely be applied to it. The figures listed here are approximate for Grade 2 and Grade 3 fasteners. Higher grades can tolerate higher torque values.

Fasteners laid out in a pattern, such as cylinder head bolts, sump bolts, differential cover bolts, etc., must be loosened or tightened in sequence to avoid warping the component. This sequence will normally be shown in the appropriate Chapter. If a specific pattern is not given, the following procedures can be used to prevent warping.

Initially, the bolts or nuts should be assembled finger-tight only. Next, they should be tightened one full turn each, in a

Metric thread sizes	Nm	Ft-lbs
M-6	9 to 12	6 to 9
M-8	19 to 28	14 to 21
M-10	38 to 54	28 to 40
M-12	68 to 96	50 to 71
M-14	109 to 154	80 to 140
Pipe thread sizes		
1/8	7 to 10	5 to 8
1/4	17 to 24	12 to 18
3/8	30 to 44	22 to 33
1/2	34 to 47	25 to 35
U.S. thread sizes		
1/4 - 20	9 to 12	6 to 9
5/16 - 18	17 to 24	12 to 18
5/16 - 24	19 to 27	14 to 20
3/8 - 16	30 to 43	22 to 32
3/8 - 24	37 to 51	27 to 38
7/16 - 14	55 to 74	40 to 55
7/16 - 20	55 to 81	40 to 60
1/2 - 13	75 to 108	55 to 80

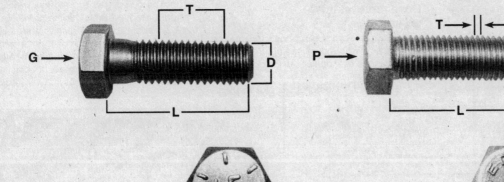

Standard (SAE and USS) bolt dimensions/grade marks

    G   *Grade marks (bolt strength)*
    L   *Length (in inches)*
    T   *Thread pitch (number of threads per inch)*
    D   *Nominal diameter (in inches)*

Metric bolt dimensions/grade marks

    P   *Property class (bolt strength)*
    L   *Length (in millimetres)*
    T   *Thread pitch (distance between threads in millimetres)*
    D   *Diameter*

criss-cross or diagonal pattern. After each one has been tightened one full turn, return to the first one and tighten them all one-half turn, following the same pattern. Finally, tighten each of them one-quarter turn at a time until each fastener has been tightened to the proper torque. To loosen and remove the fasteners, the procedure would be reversed.

Component disassembly

Component disassembly should be done with care and purpose to help ensure that the parts go back together properly. Always keep track of the sequence in which parts are removed. Make note of special characteristics or marks on parts that can be refitted more than one way, such as a grooved thrust washer on a shaft. It is a good idea to lay the disassembled parts out on a clean surface in the order that they were removed. It may also be helpful to make sketches or take instant photos of components before removal.

When removing fasteners from a component, keep track of their locations. Sometimes threading a bolt back in a part, or putting the washers and nut back on a stud, can prevent mix-ups later. If nuts and bolts cannot be returned to their original locations, they should be kept in a compartmented box or a series of small boxes. A cupcake or muffin tin is ideal for this purpose, since each cavity can hold the bolts and nuts from a particular area (i.e. sump bolts, valve cover bolts, engine mount bolts, etc.). A pan of this type is especially helpful when working on assemblies with very small parts, such as the carburettor, alternator, valve train or interior dash and trim pieces. The cavities can be marked with paint or tape to identify the contents.

Whenever wiring looms, harnesses or connectors are separated, it is a good idea to identify the two halves with numbered pieces of masking tape so they can be easily reconnected.

Gasket sealing surfaces

Throughout any vehicle, gaskets are used to seal the mating surfaces between two parts and keep lubricants, fluids, vacuum or pressure contained in an assembly.

Many times these gaskets are coated with a liquid or paste-type gasket sealing compound before assembly. Age, heat and pressure can sometimes cause the two parts to stick together so tightly that they are very difficult to separate. Often, the assembly can be loosened by striking it with a soft-face hammer near the mating surfaces. A regular hammer can be used if a block of wood is placed between the hammer and the part. Do not hammer on cast parts or parts that could be easily damaged. With any particularly stubborn part, always recheck to make sure that every fastener has been removed.

Avoid using a screwdriver or bar to prise apart an assembly, as they can easily mar the gasket sealing surfaces of the parts, which must remain smooth. If levering is absolutely necessary, use an old broom handle, but keep in mind that extra clean up will be necessary if the wood splinters.

After the parts are separated, the old gasket must be carefully scraped off and the gasket surfaces cleaned. Stubborn gasket material can be soaked with rust penetrant or treated with a special chemical to soften it so it can be easily scraped off. A scraper can be fashioned from a piece of copper tubing by flattening and sharpening one end. Copper is recommended because it is usually softer than the surfaces to be scraped, which reduces the chance of gouging the part. Some gaskets can be removed with a wire brush, but regardless of the method used, the mating surfaces must be left clean and smooth. If for some reason the gasket surface is gouged, then a gasket sealer thick enough to fill scratches will have to be used during reassembly of the components. For most applications, a non-drying (or semi-drying) gasket sealer should be used.

Hose removal tips

Warning: *If the vehicle is equipped with air conditioning, do not disconnect any of the A/C hoses without first having the system depressurised by a dealer service department or a service station.*

Hose removal precautions closely parallel gasket removal precautions. Avoid scratching or gouging the surface that the hose mates against or the connection may leak. This is especially true for radiator hoses. Because of various chemical reactions, the rubber in hoses can bond itself to the metal spigot that the hose fits over. To remove a hose, first loosen the hose clamps that secure it to the spigot. Then, with slip-joint pliers, grab the hose at the clamp and rotate it around the spigot. Work it back and forth until it is completely free, then pull it off. Silicone or other lubricants will ease removal if they can be applied between the hose and the outside of the spigot. Apply the same lubricant to the inside of the hose and the outside of the spigot to simplify fitting.

As a last resort (and if the hose is to be renewed with a new one anyway), the rubber can be slit with a knife and the hose peeled from the spigot. If this must be done, be careful that the metal connection is not damaged.

If a hose clamp is broken or damaged, do not reuse it. Wire-type clamps usually weaken with age, so it is a good idea to renew them with screw-type clamps whenever a hose is removed.

Tools

A selection of good tools is a basic requirement for anyone who plans to maintain and repair his or her own vehicle. For the owner who has few tools, the initial investment might seem high, but when compared to the spiraling costs of professional auto maintenance and repair, it is a wise one.

To help the owner decide which tools are needed to perform the tasks detailed in this manual, the following tool lists are offered: *Maintenance and minor repair, Repair/overhaul* and *Special*. The newcomer to practical mechanics should start off with the *maintenance and minor repair* tool kit, which is adequate for the simpler jobs performed on a vehicle. Then, as confidence and experience grow, the owner can tackle more difficult tasks, buying additional tools as they are needed.

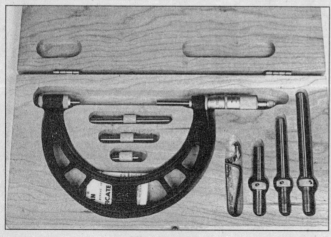

Micrometer set

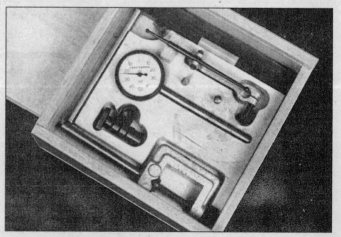

Dial indicator set

Dial caliper

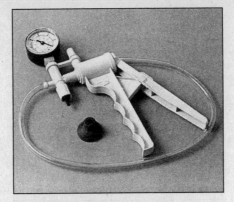

Hand-operated vacuum pump

Timing light

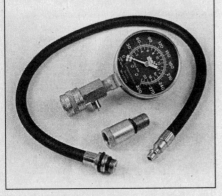

Compression gauge with spark plug hole adaptor

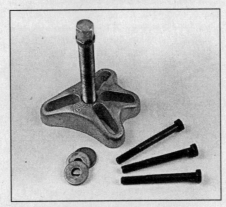

Damper/steering wheel puller

General purpose puller

Hydraulic lifter removal tool

Valve spring compressor

Valve spring compressor

Ridge reamer

Piston ring groove cleaning tool

Ring removal/installation tool

Ring compressor

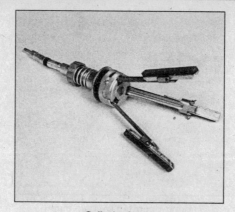

Cylinder hone

Brake hold-down spring tool

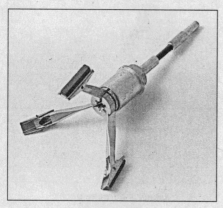

Brake cylinder hone

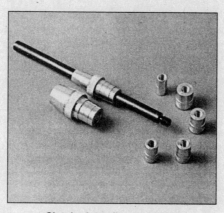

Clutch plate alignment tool

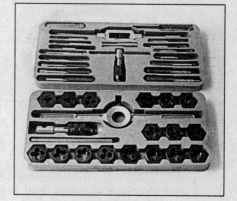

Tap and die set

Eventually the basic kit will be expanded into the *repair and overhaul* tool set. Over a period of time, the experienced do-it-yourselfer will assemble a tool set complete enough for most repair and overhaul procedures and will add tools from the special category when it is felt that the expense is justified by the frequency of use.

Maintenance and minor repair tool kit

The tools in this list should be considered the minimum required for performance of routine maintenance, servicing and minor repair work. We recommend the purchase of combination spanners (box-end and open-end combined in one spanner). While more expensive than open end spanners, they offer the advantages of both types of spanners.

Combination spanner set (6 mm to 19 mm)
Adjustable spanner
Spark plug socket with rubber insert
Spark plug gap adjusting tool
Feeler gauge set
Brake bleeder spanner
Standard screwdriver
Phillips screwdriver
Combination pliers
Hacksaw and assortment of blades
Tyre pressure gauge

Grease gun
Oil can
Fine emery cloth
Wire brush
Battery post and cable cleaning tool
Oil filter wrench
Funnel (medium size)
Safety goggles
Jackstands (2)
Drain pan

Note: *If basic tune-ups are going to be part of routine maintenance, it will be necessary to purchase a good quality stroboscopic timing light and combination tachometer/dwell meter. Although they are included in the list of special tools, it is mentioned here because they are absolutely necessary for tuning most vehicles properly.*

Repair and overhaul tool set

These tools are essential for anyone who plans to perform major repairs and are in addition to those in the maintenance and minor repair tool kit. Included is a comprehensive set of sockets which, though expensive, are invaluable because of their versatility, especially when various extensions and drives are available. We recommend the 1/2-inch drive over the 3/8-inch drive. Although the larger drive is bulky and more expensive, it has the capacity of accepting a very wide range of large sockets. Ideally, however, the mechanic should have a 3/8-inch drive set and a 1/2-inch drive set.

Socket set(s)
Reversible ratchet
Extension
Universal joint
Torque wrench (same size drive as sockets)
Ball peen hammer
Soft-face hammer (plastic/rubber)
Standard screwdriver
Standard screwdriver (stubby)
Phillips screwdriver
Phillips screwdriver (stubby - No. 2)
Pliers - vice grip
Pliers - lineman's
Pliers - needle nose
Pliers - snap-ring (internal and external)
Cold chisel
Scribe
Scraper (made from flattened copper tubing)
Centerpunch
Pin punches
Steel rule/straightedge
Allen wrench set (4 mm to 10 mm)
A selection of files
Wire brush (large)
Jackstands (second set)
Jack (scissors or hydraulic type)

Note: *Another tool which is often useful is an electric drill with a chuck capacity of 10 mm and a set of good quality drill bits.*

Special tools

The tools in this list include those which are not used regularly, are expensive to buy, or which need to be used in accordance with their manufacturer's instructions. Unless these tools will be used frequently, it is not very economical to purchase many of them. A consideration would be to split the cost and use between yourself and a friend or friends. In addition, most of these tools can be obtained from a tool rental shop on a temporary basis.

This list primarily contains only those tools and instruments widely available to the public, and not those special tools produced by the vehicle manufacturer for distribution to dealer service departments. Occasionally, references to the manufacturer's special tools are included in the text of this manual. Generally, an alternative method of doing the job without the special tool is offered. However, sometimes there is no alternative to their use. Where this is the case, and the tool cannot be purchased or borrowed, the work should be turned over to the dealer service department or an automotive repair shop.

> *Valve spring compressor*
> *Piston ring groove cleaning tool*
> *Piston ring compressor*
> *Piston ring installation tool*
> *Cylinder compression gauge*
> *Cylinder ridge reamer*
> *Cylinder surfacing hone*
> *Cylinder bore gauge*
> *Micrometers and/or dial calipers*
> *Hydraulic lifter removal tool*
> *Balljoint separator*
> *Universal-type puller*
> *Impact screwdriver*
> *Dial indicator set*
> *Stroboscopic timing light (inductive pick-up)*
> *Hand operated vacuum/pressure pump*
> *Tachometer/dwell meter*
> *Universal electrical multimeter*
> *Cable hoist*
> *Brake spring removal and installation tools*
> *Floor jack*

Buying tools

For the do-it-yourselfer who is just starting to get involved in vehicle maintenance and repair, there are a number of options available when purchasing tools. If maintenance and minor repair is the extent of the work to be done, the purchase of individual tools is satisfactory. If, on the other hand, extensive work is planned, it would be a good idea to purchase a modest tool set from one of the large retail chain stores. A set can usually be bought at a substantial savings over the individual tool prices, and they often come with a tool box. As additional tools are needed, add-on sets, individual tools and a larger tool box can be purchased to expand the tool selection. Building a tool set gradually allows the cost of the tools to be spread over a longer period of time and gives the mechanic the freedom to choose only those tools that will actually be used.

Tool stores will often be the only source of some of the special tools that are needed, but regardless of where tools are bought, try to avoid cheap ones, especially when buying screwdrivers and sockets, because they won't last very long. The expense involved in renewing cheap tools will eventually be greater than the initial cost of quality tools.

Care and maintenance of tools

Good tools are expensive, so it makes sense to treat them with respect. Keep them clean and in useable condition and store them properly when not in use. Always wipe off any dirt, grease or metal chips before putting them away. Never leave tools lying around in the work area. Upon completion of a job, always check closely under the bonnet for tools that may have been left there so they won't get lost during a test drive.

Some tools, such as screwdrivers, pliers, spanners and sockets, can be hung on a panel mounted on the garage or workshop wall, while others should be kept in a tool box or tray. Measuring instruments, gauges, metres, etc. must be carefully stored where they cannot be damaged by weather or impact from other tools.

When tools are used with care and stored properly, they will last a very long time. Even with the best of care, though, tools will wear out if used frequently. When a tool is damaged or worn out, renew it. Subsequent jobs will be safer and more enjoyable if you do.

How to repair damaged threads

Sometimes, the internal threads of a nut or bolt hole can become stripped, usually from overtightening. Stripping threads is an all-too-common occurrence, especially when working with aluminium parts, because aluminium is so soft that it easily strips out.

Usually, external or internal threads are only partially stripped. After they've been cleaned up with a tap or die, they'll still work. Sometimes, however, threads are badly damaged. When this happens, you've got three choices:

1) *Drill and tap the hole to the next suitable oversize and install a larger diameter bolt, screw or stud.*
2) *Drill and tap the hole to accept a threaded plug, then drill and tap the plug to the original screw size. You can also buy a plug already threaded to the original size. Then you simply drill a hole to the specified size, then run the threaded plug into the hole with a bolt and jam nut. Once the plug is fully seated, remove the jam nut and bolt.*
3) *The third method uses a patented thread repair kit like Heli-Coil or Slimsert. These easy-to-use kits are designed to repair damaged threads in straight-through holes and blind holes. Both are available as kits which can handle a variety of sizes and thread patterns. Drill the hole, then tap it with the special included tap. Install the Heli-Coil and the hole is back to its original diameter and thread pitch.*

Regardless of which method you use, be sure to proceed calmly and carefully. A little impatience or carelessness during one of these relatively simple procedures can ruin your whole day's work and cost you a bundle if you wreck an expensive part.

Working facilities

Not to be overlooked when discussing tools is the workshop. If anything more than routine maintenance is to be carried out, some sort of suitable work area is essential.

It is understood, and appreciated, that many home mechanics do not have a good workshop or garage available, and end up removing an engine or doing major repairs outside. It is recommended, however, that the overhaul or repair be completed under the cover of a roof.

A clean, flat workbench or table of comfortable working height is an absolute necessity. The workbench should be equipped with a vice that has a jaw opening of at least 10 centimetres.

As mentioned previously, some clean, dry storage space is also required for tools, as well as the lubricants, fluids, cleaning solvents, etc. which soon become necessary.

Sometimes waste oil and fluids, drained from the engine or cooling system during normal maintenance or repairs, present a disposal problem. To avoid pouring them on the earth or into a sewage system, pour the used fluids into large containers, seal them with caps and take them to an authorised disposal site or recycling centre. Plastic jugs, such as old antifreeze containers, are ideal for this purpose.

Always keep a supply of old newspapers and clean rags available. Old towels are excellent for mopping up spills. Many mechanics use rolls of paper towels for most work because they are readily available and disposable. To help keep the area under the vehicle clean, a large cardboard box can be cut open and flattened to protect the garage or shop floor.

Whenever working over a painted surface, such as when leaning over a fender to service something under the bonnet, always cover it with an old blanket or bedspread to protect the finish. Vinyl covered pads, made especially for this purpose, are available at auto parts stores.

Jacking and towing

Jacking

The jack supplied with the vehicle should only be used for raising the vehicle when changing a tyre or placing jackstands under the frame. **Warning:** *Never work under the vehicle or start the engine while this jack is being used as the only means of support.*

The vehicle should be on level ground with the hazard flashers on, the wheels blocked, the parking brake applied and the transmission in Park (automatic) or Reverse (manual). If a tyre is being changed, loosen the lug nuts one-half turn and leave them in place until the wheel is raised off the ground. Place the jack under the vehicle suspension in the indicated position **(see illustration).** Operate the jack with a slow, smooth motion until the wheel is raised off the ground. Remove the lug nuts, pull off the wheel, install the spare and thread the lug nuts back on with the beveled sides facing in. Tighten them snugly, but wait until the vehicle is lowered to tighten them completely. Lower the vehicle, remove the jack and tighten the nuts (if loosened or removed) in a criss-cross pattern.

Towing

As a general rule, vehicles may be towed with all four wheels on the ground. If necessary, the front or rear wheels may be raised for towing. On vehicles with an automatic transmission, do not exceed 50 KPH or tow the vehicle farther than 25 kilometres (there are no speed or distance limitations on vehicles with a manual transmission).

Equipment specifically designed for towing should be used and should be attached to the main structural members of the vehicle, not the bumper or brackets. Tow hooks are attached to the frame at both ends of the vehicle. However, they are for emergency use only and should not be used for highway towing. Stand clear of vehicles when using the tow hooks - tow straps and chains may break, causing serious injury.

Safety is a major consideration when towing and all applicable state and local laws must be obeyed. A safety chain must be used for all towing (in addition to the tow bar).

While towing, the parking brake must be released, the transmission must be in Neutral and the transfer case must be in 2H. The steering must be unlocked (ignition switch in the Off position). If you're towing with the front wheels on the ground, the front hubs must be unlocked. Remember that power steering and power brakes will not work with the engine off.

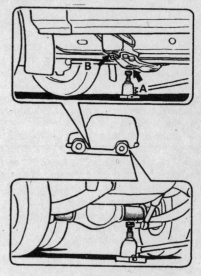

Jacking points

Booster battery (jump) starting

Observe these precautions when using a booster battery to start a vehicle:

a) *Before connecting the booster battery, make sure the ignition switch is in the Off position.*

b) *Turn off the lights, heater and other electrical loads.*

c) *Your eyes should be shielded. Safety goggles are a good idea.*

d) *Make sure the booster battery is the same voltage as the dead one in the vehicle.*

e) *The two vehicles MUST NOT TOUCH each other!*

f) *Make sure the transmission is in Neutral (manual) or Park (automatic).*

g) *If the booster battery is not a maintenance-free type, remove the vent caps and lay a cloth over the vent holes.*

Connect the red jumper cable to the positive (+) terminals of each battery.

Connect one end of the black jumper cable to the negative (-) terminal of the booster battery. The other end of this cable should be connected to a good earthing point on the vehicle to be started, such as a bolt or bracket on the engine block **(see illustration).** Make sure the cable will not come into contact with the fan, drivebelts or other moving parts of the engine.

Start the engine using the booster battery, then, with the engine running at idle speed, disconnect the jumper cables in the reverse order of connection.

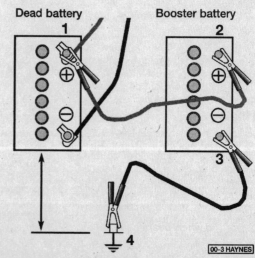

Make the booster battery cable connections in the numerical order shown (note that the negative cable of the booster battery is NOT attached to the negative terminal of the dead battery)

Automotive chemicals and lubricants

A number of automotive chemicals and lubricants are available for use during vehicle maintenance and repair. They include a wide variety of products ranging from cleaning solvents and degreasers to lubricants and protective sprays for rubber, plastic and vinyl.

Cleaners

Carburettor cleaner and choke cleaner is a strong solvent for gum, varnish and carbon. Most carburettor cleaners leave a dry-type lubricant film which will not harden or gum up. Because of this film it is not recommended for use on electrical components.

Brake system cleaner is used to remove grease and brake fluid from the brake system, where clean surfaces are absolutely necessary. It leaves no residue and often eliminates brake squeal caused by contaminants.

Electrical cleaner removes oxidation, corrosion and carbon deposits from electrical contacts, restoring full current flow. It can also be used to clean spark plugs, carburettor jets, voltage regulators and other parts where an oil-free surface is desired.

Demoisturants remove water and moisture from electrical components such as alternators, voltage regulators, electrical connectors and fuse blocks. They are non-conductive, non-corrosive and non-flammable.

Degreasers are heavy-duty solvents used to remove grease from the outside of the engine and from chassis components. They can be sprayed or brushed on and, depending on the type, are rinsed off either with water or solvent.

Lubricants

Motor oil is the lubricant formulated for use in engines. It normally contains a wide variety of additives to prevent corrosion and reduce foaming and wear. Motor oil comes in various weights (viscosity ratings) from 5 to 80. The recommended weight of the oil depends on the season, temperature and the demands on the engine. Light oil is used in cold climates and under light load conditions. Heavy oil is used in hot climates and where high loads are encountered. Multi-viscosity oils are designed to have characteristics of both light and heavy oils and are available in a number of weights from 5W-20 to 20W-50.

Gear oil is designed to be used in differentials, manual transmissions and other areas where high-temperature lubrication is required.

Chassis and wheel bearing grease is a heavy grease used where increased loads and friction are encountered, such as for wheel bearings, balljoints, tie-rod ends and universal joints.

High-temperature wheel bearing grease is designed to withstand the extreme temperatures encountered by wheel bearings in disc brake equipped vehicles. It usually contains molybdenum disulfide (moly), which is a dry-type lubricant.

White grease is a heavy grease for metal-to-metal applications where water is a problem. White grease stays soft under both low and high temperatures (usually from -56 to +106-degrees C), and will not wash off or dilute in the presence of water.

Assembly lube is a special extreme pressure lubricant, usually containing moly, used to lubricate high-load parts (such as main and rod bearings and cam lobes) for initial start-up of a new engine. The assembly lube lubricates the parts without being squeezed out or washed away until the engine oiling system begins to function.

Silicone lubricants are used to protect rubber, plastic, vinyl and nylon parts.

Graphite lubricants are used where oils cannot be used due to contamination problems, such as in locks. The dry graphite will lubricate metal parts while remaining uncontaminated by dirt, water, oil or acids. It is electrically conductive and will not foul electrical contacts in locks such as the ignition switch.

Moly penetrants loosen and lubricate seized, rusted and corroded fasteners and prevent future rusting or freezing.

Heat-sink grease is a special electrically non-conductive grease that is used for mounting electronic ignition modules where it is essential that heat is transferred away from the module.

Sealants

RTV sealant is one of the most widely used gasket compounds. Made from silicone, RTV is air curing, it seals, bonds, waterproofs, fills surface irregularities, remains flexible, doesn't shrink, is relatively easy to remove, and is used as a supplementary sealer with almost all low and medium temperature gaskets.

Anaerobic sealant is much like RTV in that it can be used either to seal gaskets or to form gaskets by itself. It remains flexible, is solvent resistant and fills surface imperfections. The difference between an anaerobic sealant and an RTV-type sealant is in the curing. RTV cures when exposed to air, while an anaerobic sealant cures only in the absence of air. This means that an anaerobic sealant cures only after the assembly of parts, sealing them together.

Thread and pipe sealant is used for sealing hydraulic and pneumatic fittings and vacuum lines. It is usually made from a Teflon compound, and comes in a spray, a paint-on liquid and as a wrap-around tape.

Chemicals

Anti-seize compound prevents seizing, galling, cold welding, rust and corrosion in fasteners. High-temperature ant-seize, usually made with copper and graphite lubricants, is used for exhaust system and exhaust manifold bolts.

Anaerobic locking compounds are used to keep fasteners from vibrating or working loose and cure only after installation, in the absence of air. Medium strength locking compound is used for small nuts, bolts and screws that may be removed later. High-strength locking compound is for large nuts, bolts and studs which aren't removed on a regular basis.

Oil additives range from viscosity index improvers to chemical treatments that claim to reduce internal engine friction. It should be noted that most oil manufacturers caution against using additives with their oils.

Fuel additives perform several functions, depending on their chemical makeup. They usually contain solvents that help dissolve gum and varnish that build up on carburettor, fuel injection and intake parts. They also serve to break down carbon deposits that form on the inside surfaces of the combustion chambers. Some additives contain upper cylinder lubricants for valves and piston rings, and others contain chemicals to remove condensation from the fuel tank.

Miscellaneous

Brake fluid is specially formulated hydraulic fluid that can withstand the heat and pressure encountered in brake systems. Care must be taken so this fluid does not come in contact with painted surfaces or plastics. An opened container should always be resealed to prevent contamination by water or dirt.

Weatherstrip adhesive is used to bond weatherstripping around doors, windows and luggage compartment lids. It is sometimes used to attach trim pieces.

Undercoating is a petroleum-based, tar-like substance that is designed to protect metal surfaces on the underside of the vehicle from corrosion. It also acts as a sound-deadening agent by insulating the bottom of the vehicle.

Waxes and polishes are used to help protect painted and plated surfaces from the weather. Different types of paint may require the use of different types of wax and polish. Some polishes utilise a chemical or abrasive cleaner to help remove the top layer of oxidised (dull) paint on older vehicles. In recent years many non-wax polishes that contain a wide variety of chemicals such as polymers and silicones have been introduced. These non-wax polishes are usually easier to apply and last longer than conventional waxes and polishes.

Conversion factors

Length (distance)

Inches (in)	X	25.4	= Millimetres (mm)	X 0.0394	= Inches (in)
Feet (ft)	X	0.305	= Metres (m)	X 3.281	= Feet (ft)
Miles	X	1.609	= Kilometres (km)	X 0.621	= Miles

Volume (capacity)

Cubic inches (cu in; in³)	X	16.387	= Cubic centimetres (cc; cm³)	X 0.061	= Cubic inches (cu in; in³)
Imperial pints (Imp pt)	X	0.568	= Litres (l)	X 1.76	= Imperial pints (Imp pt)
Imperial quarts (Imp qt)	X	1.137	= Litres (l)	X 0.88	= Imperial quarts (Imp qt)
Imperial quarts (Imp qt)	X	1.201	= US quarts (US qt)	X 0.833	= Imperial quarts (Imp qt)
US quarts (US qt)	X	0.946	= Litres (l)	X 1.057	= US quarts (US qt)
Imperial gallons (Imp gal)	X	4.546	= Litres (l)	X 0.22	= Imperial gallons (Imp gal)
Imperial gallons (Imp gal)	X	1.201	= US gallons (US gal)	X 0.833	= Imperial gallons (Imp gal)
US gallons (US gal)	X	3.785	= Litres (l)	X 0.264	= US gallons (US gal)

Mass (weight)

Ounces (oz)	X	28.35	= Grams (g)	X 0.035	= Ounces (oz)
Pounds (lb)	X	0.454	= Kilograms (kg)	X 2.205	= Pounds (lb)

Force

Ounces-force (ozf; oz)	X	0.278	= Newtons (N)	X 3.6	= Ounces-force (ozf; oz)
Pounds-force (lbf; lb)	X	4.448	= Newtons (N)	X 0.225	= Pounds-force (lbf; lb)
Newtons (N)	X	0.1	= Kilograms-force (kgf; kg)	X 9.81	= Newtons (N)

Pressure

Pounds-force per square inch (psi; lbf/in²; lb/in²)	X	0.070	= Kilograms-force per square centimetre (kgf/cm²; kg/cm²)	X 14.223	= Pounds-force per square inch (psi; lbf/in²; lb/in²)
Pounds-force per square inch (psi; lbf/in²; lb/in²)	X	0.068	= Atmospheres (atm)	X 14.696	= Pounds-force per square inch (psi; lbf/in²; lb/in²)
Pounds-force per square inch (psi; lbf/in²; lb/in²)	X	0.069	= Bars	X 14.5	= Pounds-force per square inch (psi; lbf/in²; lb/in²)
Pounds-force per square inch (psi; lbf/in²; lb/in²)	X	6.895	= Kilopascals (kPa)	X 0.145	= Pounds-force per square inch (psi; lbf/in²; lb/in²)
Kilopascals (kPa)	X	0.01	= Kilograms-force per square centimetre (kgf/cm²; kg/cm²)	X 98.1	= Kilopascals (kPa)

Torque (moment of force)

Pounds-force inches (lbf in; lb in)	X	1.152	= Kilograms-force centimetre (kgf cm; kg cm)	X 0.868	= Pounds-force inches (lbf in; lb in)
Pounds-force inches (lbf in; lb in)	X	0.113	= Newton metres (Nm)	X 8.85	= Pounds-force inches (lbf in; lb in)
Pounds-force inches (lbf in; lb in)	X	0.083	= Pounds-force feet (lbf ft; lb ft)	X 12	= Pounds-force inches (lbf in; lb in)
Pounds-force feet (lbf ft; lb ft)	X	0.138	= Kilograms-force metres (kgf m; kg m)	X 7.233	= Pounds-force feet (lbf ft; lb ft)
Pounds-force feet (lbf ft; lb ft)	X	1.356	= Newton metres (Nm)	X 0.738	= Pounds-force feet (lbf ft; lb ft)
Newton metres (Nm)	X	0.102	= Kilograms-force metres (kgf m; kg m)	X 9.804	= Newton metres (Nm)

Vacuum

Inches mercury (in. Hg)	X	3.377	= Kilopascals (kPa)	X 0.2961	= Inches mercury
Inches mercury (in. Hg)	X	25.4	= Millimetres mercury (mm Hg)	X 0.0394	= Inches mercury

Power

Horsepower (hp)	X	745.7	= Watts (W)	X 0.0013	= Horsepower (hp)

Velocity (speed)

Miles per hour (miles/hr; mph)	X	1.609	= Kilometres per hour (km/hr; kph)	X 0.621	= Miles per hour (miles/hr; mph)

Fuel consumption*

Miles per gallon, Imperial (mpg)	X	0.354	= Kilometres per litre (km/l)	X 2.825	= Miles per gallon, Imperial (mpg)
Miles per gallon, US (mpg)	X	0.425	= Kilometres per litre (km/l)	X 2.352	= Miles per gallon, US (mpg)

Temperature

Degrees Fahrenheit = (°C x 1.8) + 32

Degrees Celsius (Degrees Centigrade; °C) = (°F - 32) x 0.56

*It is common practice to convert from miles per gallon (mpg) to litres/100 kilometres (l/100km),
where mpg (Imperial) x l/100 km = 282 and mpg (US) x l/100 km = 235

Safety first!

Regardless of how enthusiastic you may be about getting on with the job at hand, take the time to ensure that your safety is not jeopardised. A moment's lack of attention can result in an accident, as can failure to observe certain simple safety precautions. The possibility of an accident will always exist, and the following points should not be considered a comprehensive list of all dangers. Rather, they are intended to make you aware of the risks and to encourage a safety conscious approach to all work you carry out on your vehicle.

Essential DOs and DON'Ts

DON'T rely on a jack when working under the vehicle. Always use approved jackstands to support the weight of the vehicle and place them under the recommended lift or support points.

DON'T attempt to loosen extremely tight fasteners (i.e. wheel lug nuts) while the vehicle is on a jack - it may fall.

DON'T start the engine without first making sure that the transmission is in Neutral (or Park where applicable) and the parking brake is set.

DON'T remove the radiator cap from a hot cooling system - let it cool or cover it with a cloth and release the pressure gradually.

DON'T attempt to drain the engine oil until you are sure it has cooled to the point that it will not burn you.

DON'T touch any part of the engine or exhaust system until it has cooled sufficiently to avoid burns.

DON'T siphon toxic liquids such as petrol, antifreeze and brake fluid by mouth, or allow them to remain on your skin.

DON'T inhale brake lining dust - it is potentially hazardous (see *Asbestos* below).

DON'T allow spilled oil or grease to remain on the floor - wipe it up before someone slips on it.

DON'T use loose fitting spanners or other tools which may slip and cause injury.

DON'T push on spanners when loosening or tightening nuts or bolts. Always try to pull the spanner toward you. If the situation calls for pushing the spanner away, push with an open hand to avoid scraped knuckles if the spanner should slip.

DON'T attempt to lift a heavy component alone - get someone to help you.

DON'T rush or take unsafe shortcuts to finish a job.

DON'T allow children or animals in or around the vehicle while you are working on it.

DO wear eye protection when using power tools such as a drill, sander, bench grinder, etc. and when working under a vehicle.

DO keep loose clothing and long hair well out of the way of moving parts.

DO make sure that any hoist used has a safe working load rating adequate for the job.

DO get someone to check on you periodically when working alone on a vehicle.

DO carry out work in a logical sequence and make sure that everything is correctly assembled and tightened.

DO keep chemicals and fluids tightly capped and out of the reach of children and pets.

DO remember that your vehicle's safety affects that of yourself and others. If in doubt on any point, get professional advice.

Asbestos

Certain friction, insulating, sealing, and other products - such as brake linings, brake bands, clutch linings, torque converters, gaskets, etc. - may contain asbestos. Extreme care must be taken to avoid inhalation of dust from such products, since it is hazardous to health. If in doubt, assume that they do contain asbestos.

Fire

Remember at all times that petrol is highly flammable. Never smoke or have any kind of open flame around when working on a vehicle. But the risk does not end there. A spark caused by an electrical short circuit, by two metal surfaces contacting each other, or even by static electricity built up in your body under certain conditions, can ignite petrol vapours, which in a confined space are highly explosive. Do not, under any circumstances, use petrol for cleaning parts. Use an approved safety solvent.

Always disconnect the battery negative (-) cable at the battery before working on any part of the fuel system or electrical system. Never risk spilling fuel on a hot engine or exhaust component. It is strongly recommended that a fire extinguisher suitable for use on fuel and electrical fires be kept handy in the garage or workshop at all times. Never try to extinguish a fuel or electrical fire with water.

Fumes

Certain fumes are highly toxic and can quickly cause unconsciousness and even death if inhaled to any extent. Petrol vapour falls into this category, as do the vapours from some cleaning solvents. Any draining or pouring of such volatile fluids should be done in a well ventilated area.

When using cleaning fluids and solvents, read the instructions on the container carefully. Never use materials from unmarked containers.

Never run the engine in an enclosed space, such as a garage. Exhaust fumes contain carbon monoxide, which is extremely poisonous. If you need to run the engine, always do so in the open air, or at least have the rear of the vehicle outside the work area.

If you are fortunate enough to have the use of an inspection pit, never drain or pour petrol and never run the engine while the vehicle is over the pit. The fumes, being heavier than air, will concentrate in the pit with possibly lethal results.

The battery

Never create a spark or allow a bare light bulb near a battery. They normally give off a certain amount of hydrogen gas, which is highly explosive.

Always disconnect the battery negative (-) cable at the battery before working on the fuel or electrical systems.

If possible, loosen the filler caps or cover when charging the battery from an external source (this does not apply to sealed or maintenance-free batteries). Do not charge at an excessive rate or the battery may burst.

Take care when adding water to a non maintenance-free battery and when carrying a battery. The electrolyte, even when diluted, is very corrosive and should not be allowed to contact clothing or skin.

Always wear eye protection when cleaning the battery to prevent the caustic deposits from entering your eyes.

Household current

When using an electric power tool, inspection light, etc., which operates on household current, always make sure that the tool is correctly connected to its plug and that, where necessary, it is properly earthed. Do not use such items in damp conditions and, again, do not create a spark or apply excessive heat in the vicinity of fuel or fuel vapour.

Secondary ignition system voltage

A severe electric shock can result from touching certain parts of the ignition system (such as the spark plug wires) when the engine is running or being cranked, particularly if components are damp or the insulation is defective. In the case of an electronic ignition system, the secondary system voltage is much higher and could prove fatal.

Troubleshooting

Contents

This Section provides an easy reference guide to the more common problems that may occur during the operation of your vehicle. Various symptoms and their probable causes are grouped under headings denoting components or systems, such as Engine, Cooling system, etc. They also refer to the Chapter and/or Section that deals with the problem.

Remember that successful troubleshooting isn't a mysterious black art practiced only by professional mechanics; it's simply the result of knowledge combined with an intelligent, systematic approach to a problem. Always use a process of elimination starting with the simplest solution and working through to the most complex - and never overlook the obvious. Anyone can run the fuel tank dry or leave the lights on overnight, so don't assume that you're exempt from such oversights.

Finally, always establish a clear idea why a problem has occurred and take steps to ensure that it doesn't happen again. If the electrical system fails because of a poor connection, check all other connections in the system to make sure they don't fail as well. If a particular fuse continues to blow, find out why - don't just go on renewing fuses. Remember, failure of a small component can often be indicative of potential failure or incorrect functioning of a more important component or system.

Engine and performance

1 Engine will not rotate when attempting to start

1 Battery terminal connections loose or corroded. Check the cable terminals at the battery; tighten cable clamp and/or clean off corrosion as necessary (see Chapter 1).
2 Battery discharged or faulty. If the cable ends are clean and tight on the battery posts, turn the key to the On position and switch on the headlights or windscreen wipers. If they won't run, the battery is discharged.
3 Automatic transmission not engaged in park (P) or Neutral (N).
4 Broken, loose or disconnected wires in the starting circuit. Inspect all wires and connectors at the battery, starter solenoid and ignition switch (on steering column).
5 Starter motor pinion jammed in flywheel ring gear. If manual transmission, place transmission in gear and rock the vehicle to manually turn the engine. Remove starter (Chapter 5) and inspect pinion and flywheel (Chapter 2) at earliest convenience.
6 Starter solenoid faulty (Chapter 5).
7 Starter motor faulty (Chapter 5).
8 Ignition switch faulty (Chapter 12).
9 Engine seized. Try to turn the crankshaft with a large socket and breaker bar on the pulley bolt.

2 Engine rotates but will not start

1 Fuel tank empty.
2 Battery discharged (engine rotates slowly). Check the operation of electrical components as described in previous Section.
3 Battery terminal connections loose or corroded. See previous Section.
4 Fuel not reaching carburettor or fuel injector. Check for clogged fuel filter or lines and defective fuel pump. Also make sure the tank vent lines aren't clogged (Chapter 4).
5 Choke not operating properly (Chapter 1).
6 Faulty distributor components. Check the cap and rotor (Chapter 1).
7 Low cylinder compression. Check as described in Chapter 2.
8 Valve clearances not properly adjusted - Chapter 1 (four-cylinder engines).
9 Water in fuel. Drain tank and fill with new fuel.
10 Defective ignition coil (Chapter 5).
11 Dirty or clogged carburettor jets or fuel injector. Carburettor out of adjustment. Check the float level (Chapter 4).
12 Wet or damaged ignition components (Chapters 1 and 5).
13 Worn, faulty or incorrectly gapped spark plugs (Chapter 1).
14 Broken, loose or disconnected wires in the starting circuit (see previous Section).
15 Loose distributor (changing ignition timing). Turn the distributor body as necessary to start the engine, then adjust the ignition timing as soon as possible (Chapter 1).
16 Broken, loose or disconnected wires at the ignition coil or faulty coil (Chapter 5).
17 Timing chain or belt failure or wear affecting valve timing (Chapter 2).
18 Diesel fuel cut-off solenoid faulty.
19 Diesel fuel contamination. Refer to Chapter 4.
20 Defective diesel injection pump.
21 Incorrect diesel injector pump timing.

3 Starter motor operates without turning engine

1 Starter pinion sticking. Remove the starter (Chapter 5) and inspect.
2 Starter pinion or flywheel/driveplate teeth worn or broken. Remove the inspection cover and inspect.

4 Engine hard to start when cold

1 Battery discharged or low. Check as described in Chapter 1.
2 Fuel not reaching the carburettor or fuel injectors. Check the fuel filter, lines and fuel pump (Chapters 1 and 4).
3 Choke inoperative (Chapters 1 and 4).
4 Defective spark plugs (Chapter 1).
5 Diesel pre-heating system not operating properly.

5 Engine hard to start when hot

1 Air filter dirty (Chapter 1).
2 Fuel not reaching carburettor or fuel injectors (see Section 4). Check for a vapour lock situation, brought about by clogged fuel tank vent lines.
3 Bad engine earthing point connection.
4 Choke sticking (Chapter 1).
5 Defective pick-up coil in distributor (Chapter 5).
6 Float level too high (Chapter 4).
7 Air in the fuel system, defective diesel injection pump or pump timing.

6 Starter motor noisy or engages roughly

1 Pinion or flywheel/driveplate teeth worn or broken. Remove the inspection cover on the left side of the engine and inspect.
2 Starter motor mounting bolts loose or missing.

7 Engine starts but stops immediately

1 Loose or damaged wire harness connections at distributor, coil or alternator.
2 Inlet manifold vacuum leaks. Make sure all mounting bolts/nuts are tight and all vacuum hoses connected to the manifold are attached properly and in good condition.
3 Insufficient fuel flow (see Chapter 4).
4 Air in the fuel system, defective diesel injection pump or pump timing.

8 Engine 'lopes' while idling or idles erratically

1 Vacuum leaks. Check mounting bolts at the inlet manifold for tightness. Make sure that all vacuum hoses are connected and in good condition. Use a stethoscope or a length of fuel hose held against your ear to listen for vacuum leaks while the engine is running. A hissing sound will be heard. A soapy water solution will also detect leaks. Check the inlet manifold gasket surfaces.
2 Leaking EGR valve or plugged PCV valve (see Chapters 1 and 6).
3 Air filter clogged (Chapter 1).
4 Fuel pump not delivering sufficient fuel (Chapter 4).
5 Leaking head gasket. Perform a cylinder compression check (Chapter 2).
6 Timing chain or belt worn (Chapter 2).
7 Camshaft lobes worn (Chapter 2).
8 Valve clearance out of adjustment - Chapter 1 (four-cylinder engine).
9 Valves burned or otherwise leaking (Chapter 2).
10 Ignition timing out of adjustment (Chapter 1).

11 Ignition system not operating properly (Chapters 1 and 5).
12 Thermostatic air cleaner not operating properly (Chapter 1).
13 Choke not operating properly (Chapters 1 and 4).
14 Dirty or clogged injector(s). Carburettor dirty, clogged or out of adjustment. Check the float level (Chapter 4).
15 Idle speed out of adjustment (Chapter 1).
16 Air in the fuel system, defective diesel injection pump or pump timing.

9 Engine misses at idle speed

1 Spark plugs faulty or not gapped properly (Chapter 1).
2 Faulty spark plug wires (Chapter 1).
3 Wet or damaged distributor components (Chapter 1).
4 Short circuits in ignition, coil or spark plug wires.
5 Sticking or faulty emissions systems (see Chapter 6).
6 Clogged fuel filter and/or foreign matter in fuel. Remove the fuel filter (Chapter 1) and inspect.
7 Vacuum leaks at inlet manifold or hose connections. Check as described in Section 8.
8 Incorrect idle speed (Chapter 1) or idle mixture (Chapter 4).
9 Incorrect ignition timing (Chapter 1).
10 Low or uneven cylinder compression. Check as described in Chapter 2.
11 Choke not operating properly (Chapter 1).
12 Clogged or dirty fuel injectors (Chapter 4).
13 Air in the fuel system, defective diesel injection pump or pump timing.

10 Excessively high idle speed

1 Sticking throttle linkage (Chapter 4).
2 Choke opened excessively at idle (Chapter 4).
3 Idle speed incorrectly adjusted (Chapter 1).
4 Valve clearances incorrectly adjusted - Chapter 1 (some four-cylinder engines).

11 Battery will not hold a charge

1 Alternator drivebelt defective or not adjusted properly (Chapter 1).
2 Battery cables loose or corroded (Chapter 1).
3 Alternator not charging properly (Chapter 5).
4 Loose, broken or faulty wires in the charging circuit (Chapter 5).
5 Short circuit causing a continuous drain on the battery.
6 Battery defective internally.

12 Alternator light stays on

1 Fault in alternator or charging circuit (Chapter 5).
2 Alternator drivebelt defective or not properly adjusted (Chapter 1).

13 Alternator light fails to come on when key is turned on

1 Faulty bulb (Chapter 12).
2 Defective alternator (Chapter 5).
3 Fault in the printed circuit, dash wiring or bulb holder (Chapter 12).

14 Engine misses throughout driving speed range

1 Fuel filter clogged and/or impurities in the fuel system. Check fuel filter (Chapter 1) or clean system (Chapter 4).
2 Faulty or incorrectly gapped spark plugs (Chapter 1).
3 Incorrect ignition timing (Chapter 1).
4 Cracked distributor cap, disconnected distributor wires or damaged distributor components (Chapter 1).
5 Defective spark plug wires (Chapter 1).
6 Emissions system components faulty (Chapter 6).
7 Low or uneven cylinder compression pressures. Check as described in Chapter 2.
8 Weak or faulty ignition coil (Chapter 5).
9 Weak or faulty ignition system (Chapter 5).
10 Vacuum leaks at inlet manifold or vacuum hoses (see Section 8).
11 Dirty or clogged carburettor or fuel injector (Chapter 4).
12 Leaky EGR valve (Chapter 6).
13 Carburettor out of adjustment (Chapter 4).
14 Idle speed out of adjustment (Chapter 1).
15 Air in the fuel system, defective diesel injection pump or pump timing.

15 Hesitation or stumble during acceleration

1 Ignition timing incorrect (Chapter 1).
2 Ignition system not operating properly (Chapter 5).
3 Dirty or clogged carburettor or fuel injector (Chapter 4).
4 Low fuel pressure. Check for proper operation of the fuel pump and for restrictions in the fuel filter and lines (Chapter 4).
5 Carburettor out of adjustment (Chapter 4).
6 Air in the fuel system, defective diesel injection pump or pump timing.

16 Engine stalls

1 Idle speed incorrect (Chapter 1).
2 Fuel filter clogged and/or water and impurities in the fuel system (Chapter 1).
3 Choke not operating properly (Chapter 1).
4 Damaged or wet distributor cap and wires.
5 Emissions system components faulty (Chapter 6).
6 Faulty or incorrectly gapped spark plugs (Chapter 1). Also check the spark plug wires (Chapter 1).
7 Vacuum leak at the carburettor, inlet manifold or vacuum hoses. Check as described in Section 8.
8 Valve clearances incorrect - Chapter 1 (four-cylinder engine).
9 Air in the fuel system, defective diesel injection pump or pump timing.

17 Engine lacks power

1 Incorrect ignition timing (Chapter 1).
2 Excessive play in distributor shaft. At the same time check for faulty distributor cap, wires, etc. (Chapter 1).
3 Faulty or incorrectly gapped spark plugs (Chapter 1).
4 Air filter dirty (Chapter 1).
5 Faulty ignition coil (Chapter 5).
6 Brakes binding (Chapters 1 and 10).
7 Automatic transmission fluid level incorrect, causing slippage (Chapter 1).
8 Clutch slipping (Chapter 8).
9 Fuel filter clogged and/or impurities in the fuel system (Chapters 1 and 4).
10 EGR system not functioning properly (Chapter 6).
11 Use of sub-standard fuel. Fill tank with proper octane fuel.
12 Low or uneven cylinder compression pressures. Check as described in Chapter 2.
13 Air leak at carburettor or inlet manifold (check as described in Section 8).
14 Dirty or clogged carburettor jets or malfunctioning choke (Chapters 1 and 4).
15 Incorrect diesel injection pump timing.

18 Engine backfires

1 EGR system not functioning properly (Chapter 6).
2 Ignition timing incorrect (Chapter 1).
3 Thermostatic air cleaner system not operating properly (Chapter 6).
4 Vacuum leak (refer to Section 8).
5 Valve clearances incorrect - Chapter 1 (some four-cylinder engines).
6 Damaged valve springs or sticking valves (Chapter 2).
7 Intake air leak (see Section 8).
8 Carburettor float level out of adjustment (Chapter 4).
9 Incorrect diesel injection pump timing.

19 Engine surges while holding accelerator steady

1 Intake air leak (see Section 8).
2 Fuel pump not working properly (Chapter 4).
3 Internal diesel injection pump fault or air in the fuel system (Chapter 4).

20 Pinging or knocking engine sounds when engine is under load

1 Incorrect grade of fuel. Fill tank with fuel of the proper octane rating.
2 Ignition timing incorrect (Chapter 1).
3 Carbon build-up in combustion chambers. Remove cylinder head(s) and clean combustion chambers (Chapter 2).
4 Incorrect spark plugs (Chapter 1).
5 Incorrect diesel injection pump timing.

21 Engine continues to run after being turned off

1 Idle speed too high (Chapter 1).
2 Ignition timing incorrect (Chapter 1).
3 Incorrect spark plug heat range (Chapter 1).
4 Intake air leak (see Section 8).
5 Carbon build-up in combustion chambers. Remove the cylinder head(s) and clean the combustion chambers (Chapter 2).
6 Valves sticking (Chapter 2).
7 Valve clearances incorrect - Chapter 1 (some four-cylinder engines).
8 EGR system not operating properly (Chapter 6).
9 Fuel shut-off system not operating properly (Chapter 6).
10 Check for causes of overheating (Section 27).
11 Faulty diesel fuel cut-off solenoid.

22 Low oil pressure

1 Improper grade of oil.
2 Oil pump worn or damaged (Chapter 2).
3 Engine overheating (refer to Section 27).
4 Clogged oil filter (Chapter 1).
5 Clogged oil strainer (Chapter 2).
6 Oil pressure gauge not working properly (Chapter 2).

23 Excessive oil consumption

1 Loose oil drain plug.
2 Loose bolts or damaged oil sump gasket (Chapter 2).
3 Loose bolts or damaged front cover gasket (Chapter 2).

4 Front or rear crankshaft oil seal leaking (Chapter 2).
5 Loose bolts or damaged rocker arm cover gasket (Chapter 2).
6 Loose oil filter (Chapter 1).
7 Loose or damaged oil pressure switch (Chapter 2).
8 Pistons and cylinders excessively worn (Chapter 2).
9 Piston rings not refitted correctly on pistons (Chapter 2).
10 Worn or damaged piston rings (Chapter 2).
11 Inlet and/or exhaust valve oil seals worn or damaged (Chapter 2).
12 Worn valve stems.
13 Worn or damaged valves/guides (Chapter 2).

24 Excessive fuel consumption

1 Dirty or clogged air filter element (Chapter 1).
2 Incorrect ignition timing (Chapter 1).
3 Incorrect idle speed (Chapter 1).
4 Low tyre pressure or incorrect tyre size (Chapter 11).
5 Fuel leakage. Check all connections, lines and components in the fuel system (Chapter 4).
6 Choke not operating properly (Chapter 4).
7 Dirty or clogged carburettor jets or fuel injectors (Chapter 4).
8 Air in the fuel system, defective diesel injection pump or pump timing.

25 Fuel odour

1 Fuel leakage. Check all connections, lines and components in the fuel system (Chapter 4).
2 Fuel tank overfilled. Fill only to automatic shut-off.
3 Charcoal canister filter in Evaporative Emissions Control system clogged (Chapter 1).
4 Vapour leaks from Evaporative Emissions Control system lines (Chapter 6).

26 Miscellaneous engine noises

1 A strong dull noise that becomes more rapid as the engine accelerates indicates worn or damaged crankshaft bearings or an unevenly worn crankshaft. To pinpoint the trouble spot on petrol models, remove the spark plug wire from one plug at a time and crank the engine over. If the noise stops, the cylinder with the removed plug wire indicates the problem area. Renew the bearing and/or service or renew the crankshaft (Chapter 2).
2 A similar (yet slightly higher pitched) noise to the crankshaft knocking described in the previous paragraph, that becomes more

rapid as the engine accelerates, indicates worn or damaged connecting rod bearings (Chapter 2). The procedure for locating the problem cylinder on petrol models is the same as described in Paragraph 1.
3 An overlapping metallic noise that increases in intensity as the engine speed increases, yet diminishes as the engine warms up indicates abnormal piston and cylinder wear (Chapter 2). To locate the problem cylinder on petrol models, use the procedure described in Paragraph 1.
4 A rapid clicking noise that becomes faster as the engine accelerates indicates a worn piston pin or piston pin hole. This sound will happen each time the piston hits the highest and lowest points in the stroke (Chapter 2). The procedure for locating the problem piston on petrol models is described in Paragraph 1.
5 A metallic clicking noise coming from the water pump indicates worn or damaged water pump bearings or pump. Renew the water pump with a new one (Chapter 3).
6 A rapid tapping sound or clicking sound that becomes faster as the engine speed increases indicates "valve tapping" or improperly adjusted valve clearances. This can be identified by holding one end of a section of hose to your ear and placing the other end at different spots along the rocker arm cover. The point where the sound is loudest indicates the problem valve. Adjust the valve clearance (Chapter 1). If the problem persists, you likely have a collapsed valve lifter or other damaged valve train component. Changing the engine oil and adding a high-viscosity oil treatment will sometimes cure a stuck lifter problem. If the problem still persists, the lifters and rocker arms must be removed for inspection (see Chapter 2).
7 A steady metallic rattling or rapping sound coming from the area of the timing chain cover indicates a worn, damaged or out-of-adjustment timing chain. Service or renew the chain and related components (Chapters 1 and 2).

Cooling system

27 Overheating

1 Insufficient coolant in system (Chapter 1).
2 Drivebelt defective or not adjusted properly (Chapter 1).
3 Radiator core blocked or radiator grille dirty or restricted (Chapter 3).
4 Thermostat faulty (Chapter 3).
5 Fan not functioning properly (Chapter 3).
6 Radiator cap not maintaining proper pressure. Have cap pressure tested by gas station or repair shop.
7 Ignition timing incorrect (Chapter 1).
8 Defective water pump (Chapter 3).
9 Improper grade of engine oil.
10 Inaccurate temperature gauge (Chapter 12).

28 Overcooling

1 Thermostat faulty (Chapter 3).
2 Inaccurate temperature gauge (Chapter 12).

29 External coolant leakage

1 Deteriorated or damaged hoses. Loose clamps at hose connections (Chapter 1).
2 Water pump seals defective. If this is the case, water will drip from the weep hole in the water pump body (Chapter 3).
3 Leakage from radiator core or header tank. This will require the radiator to be professionally repaired (see Chapter 3 for removal procedures).
4 Engine drain plugs or water jacket freeze plugs leaking (see Chapters 1 and 2).
5 Leak from coolant temperature switch (Chapter 3).
6 Leak from damaged gaskets or small cracks (Chapter 2).
7 Damaged head gasket. This can be verified by checking the condition of the engine oil as noted in Section 30.

30 Internal coolant leakage

Note: *Internal coolant leaks can usually be detected by examining the oil. Check the dipstick and inside the rocker arm cover for water deposits and an oil consistency like that of a milkshake.*
1 Leaking cylinder head gasket. Have the system pressure tested or remove the cylinder head (Chapter 2) and inspect.
2 Cracked cylinder bore or cylinder head. Dismantle engine and inspect (Chapter 2).
3 Loose cylinder head bolts (tighten as described in Chapter 2).

31 Abnormal coolant loss

1 Overfilling system (Chapter 1).
2 Coolant boiling away due to overheating (see causes in Section 27).
3 Internal or external leakage (see Sections 29 and 30).
4 Faulty radiator cap. Have the cap pressure tested.
5 Cooling system being pressurised by engine compression. This could be due to a cracked head or block or leaking head gasket(s).

32 Poor coolant circulation

1 Inoperative water pump. A quick test is to pinch the top radiator hose closed with your hand while the engine is idling, then release it. You should feel a surge of coolant if the pump is working properly (Chapter 3).

2 Restriction in cooling system. Drain, flush and refill the system (Chapter 1). If necessary, remove the radiator (Chapter 3) and have it reverse flushed or professionally cleaned.
3 Loose water pump drivebelt (Chapter 1).
4 Thermostat sticking (Chapter 3).
5 Insufficient coolant (Chapter 1).

33 Corrosion

1 Excessive impurities in the water. Soft, clean water is recommended. Distilled or rainwater is satisfactory.
2 Insufficient antifreeze solution (refer to Chapter 1 for the proper ratio of water to antifreeze).
3 Infrequent flushing and draining of system. Regular flushing of the cooling system should be carried out at the specified intervals as described in (Chapter 1).

Clutch

Note: *All clutch related service information is located in Chapter 8, unless otherwise noted.*

34 Fails to release (pedal pressed to the floor - shift lever does not move freely in and out of Reverse)

1 Freeplay incorrectly adjusted (see Chapter 1).
2 Clutch contaminated with oil. Remove clutch plate and inspect.
3 Clutch plate warped, distorted or otherwise damaged.
4 Diaphragm spring fatigued. Remove clutch cover/pressure plate assembly and inspect.
5 Leakage of fluid from clutch hydraulic system. Inspect master cylinder, operating cylinder and connecting lines.
6 Air in clutch hydraulic system. Bleed the system.
7 Insufficient pedal height. Check and adjust as necessary.
8 Piston seal in operating cylinder deformed or damaged.
9 Lack of grease on pilot bearing.

35 Clutch slips (engine speed increases with no increase in vehicle speed)

1 Worn or oil soaked clutch plate.
2 Clutch plate not broken in. It may take 30 or 40 normal starts for a new clutch to seat.
3 Diaphragm spring weak or damaged. Remove clutch cover/pressure plate assembly and inspect.
4 Flywheel warped (Chapter 2).
5 Debris in master cylinder preventing the

piston from returning to its normal position.
6 Clutch hydraulic line damaged.
7 Binding in the release mechanism.

36 Grabbing (chattering) as clutch is engaged

1 Oil on clutch plate. Remove and inspect. Repair any leaks.
2 Worn or loose engine or transmission mounts. They may move slightly when clutch is released. Inspect mounts and bolts.
3 Worn splines on transmission input shaft. Remove clutch components and inspect.
4 Warped pressure plate or flywheel. Remove clutch components and inspect.
5 Diaphragm spring fatigued. Remove clutch cover/pressure plate assembly and inspect.
6 Clutch linings hardened or warped.
7 Clutch lining rivets loose.

37 Squeal or rumble with clutch engaged (pedal released)

1 Improper pedal adjustment. Adjust pedal freeplay (Chapter 1).
2 Release bearing binding on transmission shaft. Remove clutch components and check bearing. Remove any burrs or nicks, clean and relubricate before refitting.
3 Pilot bush worn or damaged.
4 Clutch rivets loose.
5 Clutch plate cracked.
6 Fatigued clutch plate torsion springs. Renew clutch plate.

38 Squeal or rumble with clutch disengaged (pedal depressed)

1 Worn or damaged release bearing.
2 Worn or broken pressure plate diaphragm fingers.

39 Clutch pedal stays on floor when disengaged

Binding linkage or release bearing. Inspect linkage or remove clutch components as necessary.

Manual transmission

Note: *All manual transmission service information is located in Chapter 7, unless otherwise noted.*

40 Noisy in Neutral with engine running

1 Input shaft bearing worn.

2   Damaged main drive gear bearing.
3   Insufficient transmission oil (Chapter 1).
4   Transmission oil in poor condition. Drain and fill with proper grade oil. Check old oil for water and debris (Chapter 1).
5   Noise can be caused by variations in engine torque. Change the idle speed and see if noise disappears.

41   Noisy in all gears

1   Any of the above causes, and/or:
2   Worn or damaged output gear bearings or shaft.

42   Noisy in one particular gear

1   Worn, damaged or chipped gear teeth.
2   Worn or damaged synchroniser.

43   Slips out of gear

1   Transmission loose on clutch housing.
2   Stiff shift lever seal.
3   Shift linkage binding.
4   Broken or loose input gear bearing retainer.
5   Dirt between clutch lever and engine housing.
6   Worn linkage.
7   Damaged or worn check balls, fork rod ball grooves or check springs.
8   Worn mainshaft or countershaft bearings.
9   Loose engine mounts (Chapter 2).
10   Excessive gear end play.
11   Worn synchronisers.

44   Oil leaks

1   Excessive amount of lubricant in transmission (see Chapter 1 for correct checking procedures). Drain lubricant as required.
2   Transfer case oil seal(s) or speedometer oil seal damaged.
3   To pinpoint a leak, first remove all built-up dirt and grime from the transmission. Degreasing agents and/or steam cleaning will achieve this. With the underside clean, drive the vehicle at low speeds so the air flow will not blow the leak far from its source. Raise the vehicle and determine where the leak is located.

45   Difficulty engaging gears

1   Clutch not releasing completely.
2   Loose or damaged shift linkage. Make a thorough inspection, renewing parts as necessary.
3   Insufficient transmission oil (Chapter 1).
4   Transmission oil in poor condition. Drain

and fill with proper grade oil. Check oil for water and debris (Chapter 1).
5   Worn or damaged striking rod.
6   Sticking or jamming gears.

46   Noise occurs while shifting gears

1   Check for proper operation of the clutch (Chapter 8).
2   Faulty synchroniser assemblies.

Automatic transmission

Note: *Due to the complexity of the automatic transmission, it's difficult for the home mechanic to properly diagnose and service. For problems other than the following, the vehicle should be taken to a reputable mechanic.*

47   Fluid leakage

1   Automatic transmission fluid is a deep red colour, and fluid leaks should not be confused with engine oil which can easily be blown by air flow to the transmission.
2   To pinpoint a leak, first remove all built-up dirt and grime from the transmission. Degreasing agents and/or steam cleaning will achieve this. With the underside clean, drive the vehicle at low speeds so the air flow will not blow the leak far from its source. Raise the vehicle and determine where the leak is located. Common areas of leakage are:
a) *Fluid pan: tighten mounting bolts and/or renew pan gasket as necessary (Chapter 1). Some models have a drain plug; make sure it's tight.*
b) *Rear extension: tighten bolts and/or renew oil seal as necessary.*
c) *Filler pipe: renew the rubber oil seal where pipe enters transmission case.*
d) *Transmission oil lines: tighten fittings where lines enter transmission case and/or renew lines.*
e) *Vent pipe: transmission overfilled and/or water in fluid (see checking procedures, Chapter 1).*
f) *Speedometer connector: renew the O-ring where speedometer cable enters transmission case.*

48   General shift mechanism problems

Chapter 7 deals with checking and adjusting the shift linkage on automatic transmissions. Common problems which may be caused by out of adjustment linkage are:
a) *Engine starting in gears other than P (park) or N (Neutral).*
b) *Indicator pointing to a gear other than the one actually engaged.*
c) *Vehicle moves with transmission in P (Park) position.*

49   Transmission will not downshift with the accelerator pedal pressed to the floor

Chapter 7 deals with adjusting the TV linkage to enable the transmission to downshift properly.

50   Engine will start in gears other than Park or Neutral

Chapter 7 deals with adjusting the Neutral start switch installed on automatic transmissions.

51   Transmission slips, shifts rough, is noisy or has no drive in forward or Reverse gears

1   There are many probable causes for the above problems, but the home mechanic should concern himself only with one possibility: fluid level.
2   Before taking the vehicle to a shop, check the fluid level and condition as described in Chapter 1. Add fluid, if necessary, or change the fluid and filter if needed. If problems persist, have a professional diagnose the transmission.

Driveshaft

Note: *Refer to Chapter 8, unless otherwise specified, for service information.*

52   Leaks at front of driveshaft

Defective transfer case rear seal. See Chapter 7 for renewal procedure. As this is done, check the splined yoke for burrs or roughness that could damage the new seal. Remove burrs with a fine file or whetstone.

53   Knock or clunk when transmission is under initial load (just after transmission is put into gear)

1   Loose or disconnected rear suspension components. Check all mounting bolts and bushes (Chapters 7 and 10).
2   Loose driveshaft bolts. Inspect all bolts and nuts and tighten them securely.
3   Worn or damaged universal joint bearings. Inspect the universal joints (Chapter 8).
4   Worn sleeve yoke and mainshaft spline.

54   Metallic grating sound consistent with vehicle speed

Pronounced wear in the universal joint bearings. Renew U-joints or renew driveshafts, as necessary.

55 Vibration

Note: *Before blaming the driveshaft, make sure the tyres are perfectly balanced and perform the following test.*

1   Install a tachometer inside the vehicle to monitor engine speed as the vehicle is driven. Drive the vehicle and note the engine speed at which the vibration (roughness) is most pronounced. Now shift the transmission to a different gear and bring the engine speed to the same point.

2   If the vibration occurs at the same engine speed (rpm) regardless of which gear the transmission is in, the driveshaft is NOT at fault since the driveshaft speed varies.

3   If the vibration decreases or is eliminated when the transmission is in a different gear at the same engine speed, refer to the following probable causes.

4   Bent or dented driveshaft. Inspect and renew as necessary.

5   Undercoating or built-up dirt, etc. on the driveshaft. Clean the shaft thoroughly.

6   Worn universal joint bearings. Renew the U-joints or renew the driveshaft as necessary.

7   Driveshaft and/or companion flange out of balance. Check for missing weights on the shaft. Remove driveshaft and reinstall 180-degrees from original position, then recheck. Have the driveshaft balanced if problem persists.

8   Loose driveshaft mounting bolts/nuts.

9   Worn transfer case seal(s) (Chapter 7).

56 Scraping noise

Make sure the dust cover on the sleeve yoke isn't rubbing on the transmission extension housing.

57 Whining or whistling noise

Rear axle and differential

Note: *For differential servicing information, refer to Chapter 8, unless otherwise specified.*

58 Noise - same when in drive as when vehicle is coasting

1   Road noise. No corrective action available.

2   Tyre noise. Inspect tyres and check tyre pressures (Chapter 1).

3   Front wheel bearings loose, worn or damaged (Chapter 1).

4   Insufficient differential oil (Chapter 1).

5   Defective differential.

59 Knocking sound when starting or shifting gears

Defective or incorrectly adjusted differential.

60 Noise when turning

Defective differential.

61 Vibration

See probable causes under Driveshaft. Proceed under the guidelines listed for the driveshaft. If the problem persists, check the rear wheel bearings by raising the rear of the vehicle and spinning the wheels by hand. Listen for evidence of rough (noisy) bearings. Remove and inspect (Chapter 8).

62 Oil leaks

1   Pinion oil seal damaged (Chapter 8).

2   Axleshaft oil seals damaged (Chapter 8).

3   Differential cover leaking. Tighten mounting bolts or renew the gasket as required.

4   Loose filler or drain plug on differential (Chapter 1).

5   Clogged or damaged breather on differential.

Transfer case

Note: *Unless otherwise specified, refer to Chapter 7C for service and repair information.*

63 Gear jumping out of mesh

1   Incorrect control lever freeplay.

2   Interference between the control lever and the console.

3   Play or fatigue in the transfer case mounts.

4   Internal wear or incorrect adjustments.

64 Difficult shifting

1   Lack of oil.

2   Internal wear, damage or incorrect adjustment.

65 Noise

1   Lack of oil in transfer case.

2   Noise in 4H and 4L, but not in 2H indicates cause is in the front differential or front axle.

3   Noise in 2H, 4H and 4L indicates cause is in rear differential or rear axle.

4   Noise in 2H and 4H but not in 4L, or in 4L only, indicates internal wear or damage in transfer case.

Brakes

Note: *Before assuming a brake problem exists, make sure the tyres are in good condition and inflated properly, the front end alignment is correct and the vehicle is not loaded with weight in an unequal manner. All service procedures for the brakes are included in Chapter 9, unless otherwise noted.*

66 Vehicle pulls to one side during braking

1   Defective, damaged or oil contaminated brake pad on one side. Inspect as described in Chapter 1. Refer to Chapter 10 if renewal is required.

2   Excessive wear of brake pad material or disc on one side. Inspect and repair as necessary.

3   Loose or disconnected front suspension components. Inspect and tighten all bolts securely (Chapters 1 and 10).

4   Defective caliper assembly. Remove caliper and inspect for stuck piston or damage.

5   Scored or out of round rotor.

6   Loose caliper mounting bolts.

7   Incorrect wheel bearing adjustment.

67 Noise (high-pitched squeal)

1   Front brake pads worn out. This noise comes from the wear sensor rubbing against the disc. Renew pads immediately!

2   Glazed or contaminated pads.

3   Dirty or scored rotor.

4   Bent support plate.

68 Excessive brake pedal travel

1   Partial brake system failure. Inspect entire system (Chapter 1) and correct as required.

2   Insufficient fluid in master cylinder. Check (Chapter 1) and add fluid bleed system if necessary.

3   Air in system. Bleed system.

4   Excessive lateral rotor play.

5   Brakes out of adjustment. Check the operation of the automatic adjusters.

6   Defective proportioning valve. Renew valve and bleed system.

69 Brake pedal feels spongy when depressed

1   Air in brake lines. Bleed the brake system.

2 Deteriorated rubber brake hoses. Inspect all system hoses and lines. Renew parts as necessary.
3 Master cylinder mounting nuts loose. Inspect master cylinder bolts (nuts) and tighten them securely.
4 Master cylinder faulty.
5 Incorrect shoe or pad clearance.
6 Defective check valve. Renew valve and bleed system.
7 Clogged reservoir cap vent hole.
8 Deformed rubber brake lines.
9 Soft or swollen caliper seals.
10 Poor quality brake fluid. Bleed entire system and fill with new approved fluid.

70 Excessive effort required to stop vehicle

1 Power brake booster not operating properly.
2 Excessively worn linings or pads. Check and renew if necessary.
3 One or more caliper pistons seized or sticking. Inspect and rebuild as required.
4 Brake pads or linings contaminated with oil or grease. Inspect and renew as required.
5 New pads or linings fitted and not yet seated. It'll take a while for the new material to seat against the rotor or drum.
6 Worn or damaged master cylinder or caliper assemblies. Check particularly for seized pistons.
7 Also see causes listed under Section 69.

71 Pedal travels to the floor with little resistance

Little or no fluid in the master cylinder reservoir caused by leaking caliper piston(s) or loose, damaged or disconnected brake lines. Inspect entire system and repair as necessary.

72 Brake pedal pulsates during brake application

1 Wheel bearings damaged, worn or out of adjustment (Chapter 1).
2 Caliper not sliding properly due to improper refitting or obstructions. Remove and inspect.
3 Rotor not within specifications. Remove the rotor and check for excessive lateral runout and parallelism. Have the rotors resurfaced or renew them. Also make sure that all rotors are the same thickness.
4 Out of round rear brake drums. Remove the drums and have them turned or renew them with new ones.

73 Brakes drag (indicated by sluggish engine performance or wheels being very hot after driving)

1 Output rod adjustment incorrect at the brake pedal.
2 Obstructed master cylinder compensator. Disassemble master cylinder and clean.
3 Master cylinder piston seized in bore. Overhaul master cylinder.
4 Caliper assembly in need of overhaul.
5 Brake pads or shoes worn out.
6 Piston cups in master cylinder or caliper assembly deformed. Overhaul master cylinder.
7 Rotor not within specifications (Section 72).
8 Parking brake assembly will not release.
9 Clogged brake lines.
10 Wheel bearings out of adjustment (Chapter 1).
11 Brake pedal height improperly adjusted.
12 Wheel cylinder needs overhaul.
13 Improper shoe to drum clearance. Adjust as necessary.

74 Rear brakes lock up under light brake application

1 Tyre pressures too high.
2 Tyres excessively worn (Chapter 1).

75 Rear brakes lock up under heavy brake application

1 Tyre pressures too high.
2 Tyres excessively worn (Chapter 1).
3 Front brake pads contaminated with oil, mud or water. Clean or renew the pads.
4 Front brake pads excessively worn.
5 Defective master cylinder or caliper assembly.

Suspension and steering
Note: *All service procedures for the suspension and steering systems are included in Chapter 10, unless otherwise noted.*

76 Vehicle pulls to one side

1 Tyre pressures uneven (Chapter 1).
2 Defective Tyre (Chapter 1).
3 Excessive wear in suspension or steering components (Chapter 1).
4 Wheel alignment incorrect.
5 Front brakes dragging. Inspect as described in Section 73.
6 Wheel bearings improperly adjusted (Chapter 1 or 8).
7 Wheel lug nuts loose.

77 Shimmy, shake or vibration

1 Tyre or wheel out of balance or out of round. Have them balanced on the vehicle.
3 Shock absorbers and/or suspension components worn or damaged. Check for worn bushes in the upper and lower links.
4 Wheel lug nuts loose.
5 Incorrect tyre pressures.
6 Excessively worn or damaged tyre.
7 Loosely mounted steering gear housing.
8 Steering gear improperly adjusted.
9 Loose, worn or damaged steering components.
10 Damaged idler arm.
11 Worn balljoint.

78 Excessive pitching and/or rolling around corners or during braking

1 Defective shock absorbers. Renew as a set.
2 Broken or weak leaf springs and/or suspension components.
3 Worn or damaged stabiliser bar or bushes.

79 Wandering or general instability

1 Improper tyre pressures.
2 Worn or damaged upper and lower link or tension rod bushes.
3 Incorrect front end alignment.
4 Worn or damaged steering linkage or suspension components.
5 Improperly adjusted steering gear.
6 Out of balance wheels.
7 Loose wheel lug nuts.
8 Worn rear shock absorbers.
9 Fatigued or damaged rear leaf springs.

80 Excessively stiff steering

1 Lack of lubricant in power steering fluid reservoir, where appropriate (Chapter 1).
2 Incorrect tyre pressures (Chapter 1).
3 Lack of lubrication at balljoints (Chapter 1).
4 Front end out of alignment.
5 Steering gear out of adjustment or lacking lubrication.
6 Improperly adjusted wheel bearings.
7 Worn or damaged steering gear.
8 Interference of steering column with turn signal switch.
9 Low tyre pressures.
10 Worn or damaged balljoints.
11 Worn or damaged steering linkage.
12 See also Section 79.

81   Excessive play in steering

1   Loose wheel bearings (Chapter 8).
2   Excessive wear in suspension bushes (Chapter 1).
3   Steering gear improperly adjusted.
4   Incorrect wheel alignment.
5   Steering gear mounting bolts loose.
6   Worn steering linkage.

82   Lack of power assistance

1   Steering pump drivebelt faulty or not adjusted properly (Chapter 1).
2   Fluid level low (Chapter 1).
3   Hoses or pipes restricting the flow. Inspect and renew parts as necessary.
4   Air in power steering system. Bleed system.
5   Defective power steering pump.

83   Steering wheel fails to return to straight-ahead position

1   Incorrect front end alignment.
2   Tyre pressures low.
3   Steering gears improperly engaged.
4   Steering column out of alignment.
5   Worn or damaged balljoint.
6   Worn or damaged steering linkage.
7   Improperly lubricated idler arm.
8   Insufficient oil in steering gear.
9   Lack of fluid in power steering pump.

84   Steering effort not the same in both directions (power system)

1   Leaks in steering gear.
2   Clogged fluid passage in steering gear.

85   Noisy power steering pump

1   Insufficient oil in pump.
2   Clogged hoses or oil filter in pump.
3   Loose pulley.
4   Improperly adjusted drivebelt (Chapter 1).
5   Defective pump.

86   Miscellaneous noises

1   Improper tyre pressures.
2   Insufficiently lubricated balljoint or steering linkage.
3   Loose or worn steering gear, steering linkage or suspension components.
4   Defective shock absorber.
5   Defective wheel bearing.
6   Worn or damaged suspension bushes.
7   Damaged leaf spring.
8   Loose wheel lug nuts.
9   Worn or damaged rear axleshaft spline.
10   Worn or damaged rear shock absorber mounting bushes.
11   Incorrect rear axle end play.
12   See also causes of noises at the rear axle and driveshaft.

87   Excessive tyre wear (not specific to one area)

1   Incorrect tyre pressures.
2   Tyres out of balance. Have them balanced on the vehicle.
3   Wheels damaged. Inspect and renew as necessary.
4   Suspension or steering components worn (Chapter 1).

88   Excessive tyre wear on outside edge

1   Incorrect tyre pressure.
2   Excessive speed in turns.
3   Front end alignment incorrect (excessive toe-in).

89   Excessive tyre wear on inside edge

1   Incorrect tyre pressure.
2   Front end alignment incorrect (toe-out).
3   Loose or damaged steering components (Chapter 1).

90   Tyre tread worn in one place

1   Tyres out of balance. Have them balanced on the vehicle.
2   Damaged or buckled wheel. Inspect and renew if necessary.
3   Defective tyre.

Chapter 1
Tune-up and routine maintenance

Contents

Specifications

Recommended lubricants and fluids*

Note: *Listed here are manufacturer recommendations at the time this manual was written. Manufacturers occasionally upgrade their fluid and lubricant specifications, so check with your local auto parts store for current recommendations*

Engine oil

    Type

        Petrol engines .... API grade SG

        Diesel engines .... API grade CD or higher

    Viscosity .... See accompanying chart

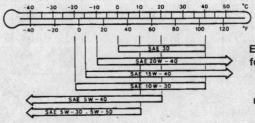

<Petrol-powered vehicles>

<Diesel-powered vehicles>

Barometric temperature

Barometric temperature

Engine oil viscosity chart - for best fuel economy and cold starting, select the lowest SAE viscosity number for the expected temperature range

Recommended lubricants and fluids* (continued)

Engine oil (continued)
  Capacity (with new oil filter)
    Four-cylinder petrol engine... 4.5 litres
    V6 engine .... 5.0 litres
    2.5L diesel engine .... 6.7 litres
    2.8L diesel engine .... 7.8 litres
Automatic transmission fluid
  Type... Dexron II or Mercon Automatic Transmission Fluid (ATF)
  Capacity (approximate)**
    1986 and earlier models .... 3.7 litres
    1987 and later models .... 5.1 litres
Manual transmission lubricant
  Type... SAE 80/90W GL-5 gear lubricant
  Capacity (approximate) .... 2.4 litres
Differential lubricant
  Type... SAE 80/90W GL-5 gear lubricant
  Capacity (approximate) .... 2.6 litres
Transfer case lubricant
  Type... SAE 80/90W GL-5 gear lubricant
  Capacity (approximate) .... 2.4 litres
Power steering fluid type .... Dexron II or Mercon Automatic Transmission Fluid (ATF)
Brake fluid type .... DOT 3 brake fluid
Clutch fluid type .... DOT 3 brake fluid
Coolant
  Type... 50/50 mixture of ethylene glycol-based antifreeze and demineralised water
  Capacity (approximate) .... 8.5 litres
Chassis grease .... NLGI no. 2 chassis grease
Bonnet and door hinges .... Engine oil

* All capacities approximate. Add as necessary to bring to appropriate level

**When refilling with automatic transmission fluid after overhaul or removing the pan, add fluid a little at a time, checking the fluid level after each addition. Do not drive the vehicle until you're certain the fluid level is correct. Normally, much more fluid is required after an overhaul than after a fluid change, since the torque converter is drained during an overhaul, but not during a normal fluid change.*

Tune-up information

Firing order
  Four-cylinder engines... 1-3-4-2
  V6 engine 1-2-3-4-5-6
Idle speed
  2.5L diesel engine .... 650 to 850 RPM
  2.8L diesel engine .... 700 to 900 RPM

Spark plug type and gap*

Four-cylinder engine.. NGK BP5ES or BP6ES or equivalent @ 0.08 mm
3.0L V6 engine .... NGK BP5ES-11 or equivalent @ 1.1 mm
3.5L V6 engine .... NGK PFR5J-11 or equivalent @ 1.1 mm
Ignition timing*
  Four-cylinder .... 6-degrees to 8-degrees BTDC
  V6 engine... 5-degrees to 8-degrees BTDC

Refer to the Vehicle Emission Control Information label in the engine compartment: use the information there if it differs from that listed here

**2.6L
4-cylinder engine**

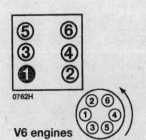

V6 engines

**Cylinder location and
distributor rotation**

*The blackened terminal shown on the
distributor cap indicates the Number
One spark plug wire position*

Valve clearances (engine at normal operating temperature)

Four-cylinder petrol models through 1990 only

Inlet valves	0.15 mm
Exhaust valves	0.25 mm
2.5L diesel engines	0.25 mm

2.8L diesel engines

Inlet valves	0.25 mm
Exhaust valves	0.35 mm

Clutch

Pedal freeplay	8 to 16 mm
Pedal height	186 to 191 mm

Brake

Parking brake adjustment	4 to 6 clicks

Pedal height

1989 and earlier	191 to 196 mm
1990-on	186 to 191 mm
Pedal freeplay	3 to 8 mm
Brake shoe lining wear limit	1 mm
Brake pad lining wear limit	2 mm

Torque specifications

	Nm
Spark plugs	
Four-cylinder	5 to 7
V6	9
Engine oil drain plug	
Four-cylinder (petrol)	8 to 9
V6 (petrol)	10 to 12
2.5L diesel	40
2.8L diesel	78
Valve cover bolts	
Four-cylinder	5 to 6
V6	9
Manual transmission check/fill plug	59
Manual transmission drain plug	33
Differential check/fill and drain plugs	60
Transfer case check/fill and drain plugs	33
Oxygen sensor	40 to 50
Wheel lug nuts	100 to 120

1

Typical four-cylinder petrol engine compartment checking points

1	Battery	5	Radiator hose	9	Engine oil dipstick
2	Air cleaner	6	Engine oil filler cap	10	Evaporative emissions canister
3	Brake master cylinder fluid reservoir	7	Radiator cap	11	Coolant reservoir
4	Clutch master cylinder fluid reservoir	8	Engine oil filter	12	Windscreen washer fluid reservoir

Typical V6 engine compartment checking points

1	Evaporative emissions canister	6	Engine oil dipstick	10	Engine oil filler cap
2	Engine compartment fuse block	7	Radiator hose	11	Brake master cylinder fluid reservoir
3	Windscreen washer fluid reservoir	8	Radiator cap	12	Air cleaner
4	Coolant reservoir	9	Air conditioning compressor drivebelt	13	Power steering pump reservoir
5	Battery				

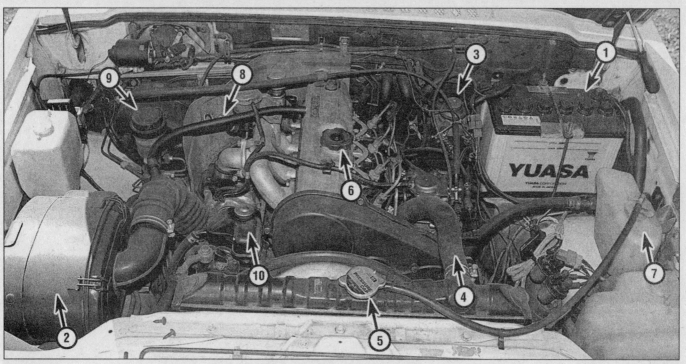

Typical 2.5L four-cylinder diesel engine compartment checking points

1	Battery	5	Radiator cap	9	Brake master cylinder fluid reservoir
2	Air cleaner	6	Engine oil filler cap	10	Power steering fluid reservoir
3	Water separator	7	Coolant reservoir		
4	Radiator hose	8	Engine oil dipstick		

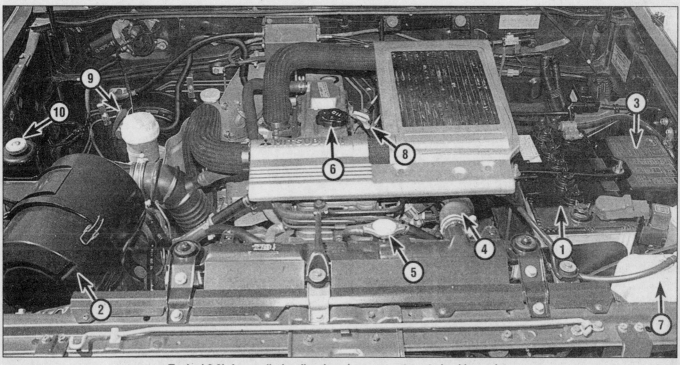

Typical 2.8L four-cylinder diesel engine compartment checking points

1	Battery	5	Radiator cap	9	Brake master cylinder fluid reservoir
2	Air cleaner	6	Engine oil filler cap	10	Power steering fluid reservoir
3	Fuse box	7	Coolant reservoir		
4	Radiator hose	8	Engine oil dipstick		

Typical engine compartment underside checking points

1	Engine drivebelt	4	Differential drain plug	7	Manual transmission drain plug
2	Radiator	5	Brake disc	8	Exhaust pipe
3	Differential check/fill plug	6	Driveshaft	9	Driveaxle boot

Typical rear underside components

1	Fuel tank	3	Disc brake	5	Differential drain plug
2	Shock absorber	4	Muffler	6	Driveshaft

1 Mitsubishi Pajero Maintenance schedule

The following maintenance intervals are based on the assumption that the vehicle owner will be doing the maintenance or service work, as opposed to having a dealer service department do the work. Although the time/number of kilometres intervals are loosely based on factory recommendations, most have been shortened to ensure, for example, that such items as lubricants and fluids are checked/changed at intervals that promote maximum engine/driveline service life. Also, subject to the preference of the individual owner interested in keeping his or her vehicle in peak condition at all times, and with the vehicle's ultimate resale in mind, many of the maintenance procedures may be performed more often than recommended in the following schedule. We encourage such owner initiative.

When the vehicle is new it should be serviced initially by a factory authorised dealer service department to protect the factory warranty. In many cases the initial maintenance check is done at no cost to the owner (check with your dealer service department for more information).

Every 400 kilometres or weekly, whichever comes first

Check the engine oil level (Section 4)
Check the engine coolant level (Section 4)
Check the windscreen washer fluid level (Section 4)
Check the brake and clutch fluid levels (Section 4)
Check the automatic transmission fluid level (Section 5)
Check the power steering fluid level (Section 6)
Check the tyres and tyre pressures (Section 7)

Every 5,000 kilometres or 3 months, whichever comes first

All items listed above plus:
Check and service the battery (Section 8)
Check the cooling system (Section 9)
Inspect and renew if necessary the windscreen wiper blades (Section 10)
Inspect and renew if necessary all underbonnet hoses (Section 11)
Check and lubricate the accelerator linkage (Section 12)
Change the engine oil and filter (Section 13)*
Rotate the tyres (Section 14)

Every 10,000 kilometres or 6 months, whichever comes first

All items listed above plus:
Adjust the valves (four-cylinder models) (Section 15)
Lubricate the chassis components (Section 16)
Inspect the suspension and steering components (Section 17)*
Inspect the exhaust system (Section 18)*
Check and adjust if necessary, the clutch pedal freeplay (Section 19)
Check the manual transmission lubricant (Section 20)*
Check the transfer case lubricant level (Section 21)*
Check the differential lubricant level (Section 22)*

Check the brakes (Section 23)*
Check/adjust the four-cylinder petrol engine balance shaft chain tension (Section 24)*
Inspect the fuel system (Section 25)
Check the operation of the thermostatic air cleaner system (Section 26)
Check the engine drivebelts (Section 27)
Check the seat belts (Section 28)
Check and adjust, if necessary, the idle speed - four-cylinder engines (see Chapter 4)

Every 25,000 kilometres or 12 months, whichever comes first

Check the carburettor/fuel injection throttle body nut/bolt torque (Section 29)
Renew the air filter (Section 30)
Service the fuel filter (Section 31)
Check and adjust, if necessary, the brake pedal height (Section 32)
Check the distributor advance mechanism (Chapter 6)
Inspect the evaporative emissions system (Section 33)
Check the operation of the carburettor choke (Section 34)
Check and adjust, if necessary, the engine idle speed (carburetted and diesel models only) (Section 35)
Change the transfer case lubricant (Section 36)**
Change the manual transmission lubricant (Section 37)
Change the differential lubricant (Section 38)**
Change the automatic transmission fluid and filter (Section 39)**
Service the cooling system (drain, flush and refill) (Section 40)
Inspect the Positive Crankcase Ventilation (PCV) system (Section 41)
Renew the spark plugs (Section 42)
Inspect the spark plug wires, distributor cap and rotor (Section 43)
Check and adjust, if necessary, the ignition timing (Section 44)
Check the Exhaust Gas Recirculation (EGR) system (Section 45)

Every 50,000 kilometres or 24 months, whichever comes first

Renew the oxygen sensor (1988 and earlier models so equipped) (Section 46)

Renew the EGR Valve (four-cylinder models) (see Chapter 6)

Every 100,000 kilometres

Renew the timing belt (Chapter 2)

Renew the oxygen sensor (1989 and later models) (Section 46)

* This item is affected by "severe" operating conditions as described below. If your vehicle is operated under severe conditions, perform all maintenance indicated with an asterisk (*) at 4,500 kilometres/3 month intervals.

Severe conditions are indicated if you mainly operate your vehicle under one or more of the following:

In dusty areas
Off road use
Towing a trailer
Idling for extended periods and/or low speed operation
When outside temperatures remain below freezing and most trips are less than 6 kilometres

**If operated under one or more of the following conditions, perform the indicated maintenance item every 22,500 kilometres:

In heavy city traffic where the outside temperature regularly reaches 32-degrees C or higher
In hilly or mountainous terrain
Frequent trailer pulling
Frequent off road use

2   Introduction

This Chapter is designed to help the home mechanic maintain the Mitsubishi Pajero with the goals of maximum performance, economy, safety and reliability in mind.

Included is a master maintenance schedule, followed by procedures dealing specifically with every item on the schedule. Visual checks, adjustments, component renewal and other helpful items are included. Refer to the **accompanying illustrations** of the engine compartment and the under side of the vehicle for the locations of various components.

Servicing your vehicle in accordance with the planned number of kilometres/time maintenance schedule and the step-by-step procedures should result in maximum reliability and extend the life of your vehicle. Keep in mind that it's a comprehensive plan - maintaining some items but not others at the specified intervals will not produce the same results.

As you perform routine maintenance procedures, you'll find that many can, and should, be grouped together because of the nature of the procedures or because of the proximity of two otherwise unrelated components or systems.

For example, if the vehicle is raised for chassis lubrication, you should inspect the exhaust, suspension, steering and fuel systems while you're under the vehicle. When you're rotating the tyres, it makes good sense to check the brakes since the wheels are already removed. Finally, let's suppose you have to borrow or rent a torque wrench. Even if you only need it to tighten the spark plugs, you might as well check the torque of as many critical fasteners as time allows.

The first step in this maintenance program is to prepare yourself before the actual work begins. Read through all the procedures you're planning to do, then gather up all the parts and tools needed. If it looks like you might run into problems during a particular job, seek advice from a mechanic or experienced do-it-yourselfer.

3   Tune-up general information

The term tune-up is used in this manual to represent a combination of individual operations rather than one specific procedure.

If, from the time the vehicle is new, the routine maintenance schedule is followed closely and frequent checks are made of fluid levels and high wear items, as suggested throughout this manual, the engine will be kept in relatively good running condition and the need for additional work will be minimised.

More likely than not, however, there will be times when the engine is running poorly due to lack of regular maintenance. This is even more likely if a used vehicle, which has not received regular and frequent maintenance checks, is purchased. In such cases, an engine tune-up will be needed outside of the regular routine maintenance intervals.

The first step in any tune-up or diagnostic procedure to help correct a poor running engine is a cylinder compression check. A compression check (see Chapter 2 Part C) will help determine the condition of internal engine components and should be used as a guide for tune-up and repair procedures. If, for instance, a compression check indicates serious internal engine wear, a conventional tune-up will not improve the performance of the engine and would be a waste of time and money. Because of its importance, the compression check should be done by someone with the right equipment and the knowledge to use it properly.

The following procedures are those most often needed to bring a generally poor running engine back into a proper state of tune.

Minor tune-up

Check all engine related fluids
Clean and check the battery (Section 8)
Check and adjust the drivebelts (Section 27)
Renew the spark plugs (Section 42)
Check the cylinder compression (Chapter 2)
Inspect the distributor cap and rotor (Section 43)
Inspect the spark plug and coil wires (Section 43)
Renew the air filter (Section 30)
Check and adjust the idle speed (Section 35)
Check and adjust the ignition timing (Section 44)
Renew the fuel filter (Section 31)
Check the PCV system (Section 41)
Adjust the valve clearances (Section 15)
Check and service the cooling system (Section 40)

Major tune-up

All items listed under Minor tune-up plus . . .

Check the EGR system (Section 45 and Chapter 6)
Check the charging system (Chapter 5)
Check the ignition system (Chapter 5)
Check the fuel system (Section 25 and Chapter 4)
Renew the spark plugs (Section 42)
Renew the spark plug wires, distributor cap and rotor (Section 43)

4   Fluid level checks (400 kilometres or weekly)

Note: *The following are fluid level checks to be done on a 400 kilometre or weekly basis. Additional fluid level checks can be found in specific maintenance procedures which follow. Regardless of how often the fluid levels are checked, watch for puddles under the*

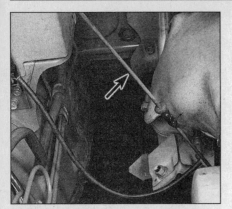

4.2 The engine oil dipstick (arrow) is located on the right (driver's) side of the engine compartment

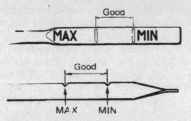

4.4 The oil level should be between the upper and lower notches - if it isn't, add enough oil to bring the level to or near the upper notch mark

vehicle - if leaks are noted, make repairs immediately.

1   Fluids are an essential part of the lubrication, cooling, brake, clutch and windscreen washer systems. Because the fluids gradually become depleted and/or contaminated during normal operation of the vehicle, they must be periodically replenished. See *Recommended lubricants and fluids* at the beginning of this Chapter before adding fluid to any of the following components. **Note:** *The vehicle must be on level ground when fluid levels are checked.*

Engine oil

Refer to illustrations 4.2, 4.4 and 4.6

2   The engine oil level is checked with a dipstick that extends through a tube and into the sump at the bottom of the engine **(see illustration)**.

3   The oil level should be checked before the vehicle has been driven, or about 15 minutes after the engine has been shut off. If the oil is checked immediately after driving the vehicle, some of the oil will remain in the upper engine components, resulting in an inaccurate reading on the dipstick.

4   Pull the dipstick from the tube and wipe all the oil from the end with a clean rag or paper towel. Insert the clean dipstick all the way back into the tube, then pull it out again. Note the oil at the end of the dipstick. Add oil as necessary to keep the level between the MAX and MIN marks or within the hatched area on the dipstick **(see illustration)**.

5   Don't overfill the engine by adding too much oil since this may result in oil fouled spark plugs, oil leaks or oil seal failures.

6   Oil is added to the engine after removing a threaded cap from the valve cover **(see illustration)**. An oil can spout or funnel may help to reduce spills.

7   Checking the oil level is an important preventive maintenance step. A consistently low oil level indicates oil leakage through damaged seals, defective gaskets or past worn rings or valve guides. If the oil looks milky in colour or has water droplets in it, the cylinder head gasket(s) may be blown or the head(s) or block may be cracked. The engine should be checked immediately. The condition of the oil should also be checked. Whenever you check the oil level, slide your thumb and index finger up the dipstick before wiping off the oil. If you see a small amount of dirt or metal particles clinging to the dipstick, the oil should be changed (Section 13).

Engine coolant

Refer to illustration 4.8

Warning: *Don't allow antifreeze to come in contact with your skin or painted surfaces of the vehicle. Flush contaminated areas immediately with plenty of water. Don't store new coolant or leave old coolant lying around where it's accessible to children or pets - they're attracted by its sweet taste. Ingestion of even a small amount of coolant can be fatal! Wipe up garage floor and drip pan coolant spills immediately. Keep antifreeze containers covered and repair leaks in your cooling system immediately.*

8   All vehicles covered by this manual are equipped with a pressurised coolant recovery system. A white plastic coolant reservoir located in the engine compartment is connected by a hose to the radiator filler neck **(see illustration)**. If the engine overheats, coolant escapes through a valve in the radiator cap and travels through the hose into the reservoir. As the engine cools, the coolant is automatically drawn back into the cooling system to maintain the correct level.

9   The coolant level in the reservoir should be checked regularly. **Warning:** *Do not remove the radiator cap to check the coolant level when the engine is warm. The level in the reservoir varies with the temperature of the engine. When the engine is cold, the coolant level should be at or slightly above the lower mark on the reservoir. Once the engine has warmed up, the level should be at or near the upper mark. If it isn't, allow the engine to cool, then remove the cap from the reservoir and add a 50/50 mixture of ethylene glycol-based antifreeze and demineralised water.*

10   Drive the vehicle and recheck the coolant level. If only a small amount of coolant is required to bring the system up to the proper level, water can be used. However, repeated additions of water will dilute the antifreeze and water solution. In order to maintain the proper ratio of antifreeze and water, always top up the coolant level with the correct mixture. An empty plastic milk jug or bleach bottle makes an excellent container for mixing coolant. Do not use rust inhibitors or additives.

11   If the coolant level drops consistently, there may be a leak in the system. Inspect the radiator, hoses, filler cap, drain plugs and water pump (see Section 9). If no leaks are noted, have the radiator cap pressure tested by a service station.

12   If you have to remove the radiator cap, wait until the engine has cooled, then wrap a thick cloth around the cap and turn it to the first stop. If coolant or steam escapes, let the engine cool down longer, then remove the cap.

13   Check the condition of the coolant as well. It should be relatively clear. If it's brown or rust coloured, the system should be drained, flushed and refilled. Even if the coolant appears to be normal, the corrosion inhibitors wear out, so it must be renewed at the specified intervals.

Windscreen, headlight and rear washer fluid

Refer to illustrations 4.14a, 4.14b and 4.14c

14   Fluid for the windscreen washer system is stored in a plastic reservoir located on the

4.6 Rotate the oil filler cap counterclockwise remove it - always make sure the area around the opening is clean before removing the cap; this prevents dirt from contaminating the engine

4.8 The coolant reservoir is located in the front corner of the engine compartment - the level must be maintained between the upper and lower marks

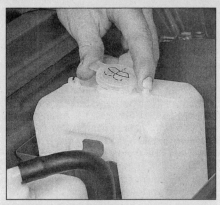

4.14a The windscreen washer fluid reservoir is located next to the coolant reservoir on most models

passenger's side of the engine compartment **(see illustration)**. If necessary, refer to the **underbonnet component illustration(s)** at the beginning of this Chapter to locate the reservoir. Some models are equipped with headlight washers. The fluid reservoir is located on the left side of the engine compartment and should be kept filled the upper mark **(see illustration)**. On vehicles with rear window washers, the fluid reservoir is located under a cover on the right side of the cargo area **(see illustration)**.

15   In milder climates, plain water can be used in the reservoir, but it should be kept no more than 2/3 full to allow for expansion if the water freezes. In colder climates, use wind-

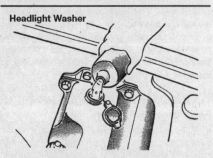

4.14b On headlight washer-equipped models, flip up the cap to add more fluid

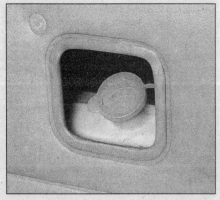

4.14c The rear washer fluid reservoir is located in the cargo area, behind a cover

screen washer system antifreeze, available at any auto parts store, to lower the freezing point of the fluid. Mix the antifreeze with water in accordance with the manufacturer's directions on the container. **Caution:** *Don't use cooling system antifreeze - it will damage the vehicle's paint.*

16   To help prevent icing in cold weather, warm the windscreen with the defroster before using the washer.

Battery electrolyte

17   To check the electrolyte level in the battery on conventional batteries, remove all of the cell caps. If the level is low, add distilled water until it's above the plates. Most aftermarket renewal batteries have a split-ring indicator in each cell to help you judge when enough water has been added - don't overfill the cells!

Brake and clutch fluid

Refer to illustration 4.19

18   The brake master cylinder is mounted on the front of the power booster unit in the engine compartment. The clutch cylinder used on some models with manual transmissions is mounted adjacent to it on the firewall.

19   The fluid inside is readily visible. The level should be between the upper and lower marks on the reservoirs **(see illustration)**. If a low level is indicated, be sure to wipe the top of the reservoir cover with a clean rag to prevent contamination of the brake and/or clutch system before removing the cover.

20   When adding fluid, pour it carefully into the reservoir to avoid spilling it onto surrounding painted surfaces. Be sure the specified fluid is used, since mixing different types of brake fluid can cause damage to the system. See *Recommended lubricants and fluids* at the front of this Chapter or your owner's manual. **Warning:** *Brake fluid can harm your eyes and damage painted surfaces, so be very careful when handling or pouring it. Don't use brake fluid that's been standing open or is more than one year old. Brake fluid absorbs moisture from the air. Excess mois-*

4.19 Keep the brake and clutch fluid levels near the upper or MAX marks on the reservoir - fluid can be added after unscrewing the cap

ture can cause a dangerous loss of brake efficiency.

21   At this time the fluid and master cylinder can be inspected for contamination. The system should be drained and refilled if deposits, dirt particles or water droplets are seen in the fluid.

22   After filling the reservoir to the proper level, make sure the cover is on tight to prevent fluid leakage.

23   The brake fluid level in the master cylinder will drop slightly as the pads and the brake shoes at each wheel wear down during normal operation. If the master cylinder requires repeated additions to keep it at the proper level, it's an indication of leakage in the brake system, which should be corrected immediately. Check all brake lines and connections (see Section 23 for more information).

24   If, upon checking the master cylinder fluid level, you discover one or both reservoirs empty or nearly empty, the brake system should be bled (Chapter 9).

---

5   Automatic transmission fluid level check (400 kilometres or weekly)

Refer to illustration 5.6

1   The automatic transmission fluid level should be carefully maintained. Low fluid level can lead to slipping or loss of drive, while overfilling can cause foaming and loss of fluid.

2   With the parking brake set, start the engine, then move the shift lever through all the gear ranges, ending in Neutral. The fluid level must be checked with the vehicle level and the engine running at idle. **Note:** *Incorrect fluid level readings will result if the vehicle has just been driven at high speeds for an extended period, in hot weather in city traffic, or if it has been pulling a trailer. If any of these conditions apply, wait until the fluid has cooled (about 30 minutes).*

3   With the transmission at normal operating temperature, remove the dipstick from the filler tube. The dipstick is located at the rear of the engine compartment on the passenger's side.

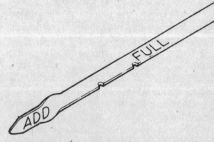

5.6 The automatic transmission fluid level must be between the two notches or marks on the dipstick with the engine at normal operating temperature

4   Wipe the fluid from the dipstick with a clean rag and push it back into the filler tube until the cap seats.

5   Pull the dipstick out again and note the fluid level.

6   The level should be between the two notches **(see illustration)**.

7   If additional fluid is required, add it directly into the tube using a funnel. It takes about .5 litre to raise the level from the lower notch to the FULL notch with a hot transmission, so add the fluid a little at a time and keep checking the level until it's correct.

8   The condition of the fluid should also be checked along with the level. If the fluid at the end of the dipstick is a dark reddish-brown colour, or if it smells burned, it should be changed. If you are in doubt about the condition of the fluid, purchase some new fluid and compare the two for colour and smell.

6   Power steering fluid level check (400 kilometres or weekly)

Refer to illustration 6.5

1   Unlike manual steering, the power steering system relies on fluid which may, over a period of time, require replenishing.

2   The fluid reservoir for the power steering pump is located remotely from the pump on the passenger's side of the engine compartment.

3   For the check, the front wheels should be pointed straight ahead and the engine should be off. The power steering fluid should be checked after the vehicle has been driven and the fluid is at normal operating temperature.

4   Clean the cap and the area around the to prevent contamination of the fluid.

5   Twist off the reservoir cap which has a built-in dipstick attached to it **(see illustration)**. Wipe off the dipstick with a clean rag, reinstall it and remove it to get an accurate reading. The fluid level should be between the MIN and MAX marks on the dipstick.

6   If additional fluid is required, pour the specified type directly into the reservoir, using a funnel to prevent spills.

7   If the reservoir requires frequent fluid additions, all power steering hoses, hose connections and the power steering pump should be carefully checked for leaks.

7   Tyre and tyre pressure checks (400 kilometres or weekly)

Refer to illustrations 7.2, 7.3, 7.4a, 7.4b and 7.8

1   Periodic inspection of the tyres may spare you the inconvenience of being stranded with a flat tyre. It can also provide you with vital information regarding possible problems in the steering and suspension systems before major damage occurs.

2   The original tyres on this vehicle are equipped with 12.7 mm wear indicator bars that will appear when tread depth reaches a predetermined limit, usually 1.6 mm, but they don't appear until the tyres are worn out. Tread wear can be monitored with a simple, inexpensive device known as a tread depth indicator **(see illustration)**.

3   Note any abnormal tread wear **(see illustration)**. Tread pattern irregularities such as cupping, flat spots and more wear on one side than the other are indications of front end alignment and/or balance problems. If any of these conditions are noted, take the

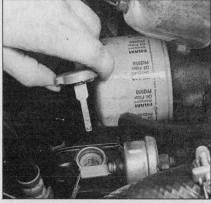

6.5 Unscrew the cap on the power steering fluid reservoir and check the fluid level on the dipstick

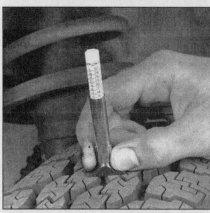

7.2 Use a tyre tread depth indicator to monitor tyre wear - they are available at auto parts stores and service stations and cost very little

UNDERINFLATION

CUPPING

Cupping may be caused by:
- Underinflation and/or mechanical irregularities such as out-of-balance condition of wheel and/or tyre, and bent or damaged wheel.
- Loose or worn steering tie-rod or steering idler arm.
- Loose, damaged or worn front suspension parts.

OVERINFLATION

7.3 This chart will help you determine the condition of the tyres, the probable cause(s) of abnormal wear and the corrective action necessary

INCORRECT TOE-IN OR EXTREME CAMBER

FEATHERING DUE TO MISALIGNMENT

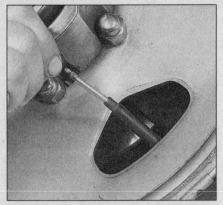

7.4a If a tyre loses air on a steady basis, check the valve core first to make sure it's snug (special inexpensive spanners are commonly available at auto parts stores)

7.4b If the valve core is tight, raise the corner of the vehicle with the low tyre and spray a soapy water solution onto the tread as the tyre is turned slowly - leaks will cause small bubbles to appear

7.8 To extend the life of the tyres, check the air pressure at least once a week with an accurate gauge (don't forget the spare!)

vehicle to a tyre shop or service station to correct the problem.

4   Look closely for cuts, punctures and embedded nails or tacks. Sometimes a tyre will hold air pressure for a short time or leak down very slowly after a nail has embedded itself in the tread. If a slow leak persists, check the valve stem core to make sure it's tight **(see illustration)**. Examine the tread for an object that may have embedded itself in the tyre or for a "plug" that may have begun to leak (radial tyre punctures are repaired with a plug that's refitted in a puncture). If a puncture is suspected, it can be easily verified by spraying a solution of soapy water onto the puncture area **(see illustration)**. The soapy solution will bubble if there's a leak. Unless the puncture is unusually large, a tyre shop or service station can usually repair the tyre.

5   Carefully inspect the inner sidewall of each tyre for evidence of brake fluid leakage.

If you see any, inspect the brakes immediately.

6   Correct air pressure adds wear to the lifespan of the tyres, improves performance and enhances overall ride quality. Tyre pressure cannot be accurately estimated by looking at a tyre, especially if it's a radial. A tyre pressure gauge is essential. Keep an accurate gauge in the vehicle. The pressure gauges attached to the nozzles of air hoses at petrol stations are often inaccurate.

7   Always check tyre pressure when the tyres are cold. Cold, in this case, means the vehicle has not been driven over a kilometre in the three hours preceding a tyre pressure check. A pressure rise of four to eight pounds is not uncommon once the tyres are warm.

8   Unscrew the valve cap protruding from the wheel or hub cap and push the gauge firmly onto the valve stem **(see illustration)**. Note the reading on the gauge and compare

the figure to the recommended tyre pressure shown on the placard on the glove compartment door. Be sure to reinstall the valve cap to keep dirt and moisture out of the valve stem mechanism. Check all four tyres and, if necessary, add enough air to bring them up to the recommended pressure.

9   Don't forget to keep the spare tyre inflated to the specified pressure (refer to your owner's manual or the tyre sidewall).

8   Battery check, maintenance and charging (5,000 kilometres or 3 months)

Refer to illustrations 8.1, 8.6, 8.7a, 8.7b and 8.7c

Warning: *Certain precautions must be followed when checking and servicing the battery. Hydrogen gas, which is highly flam-*

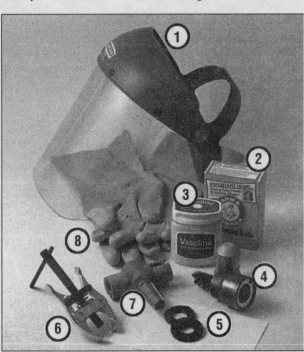

8.1 Tools and materials required for battery maintenance

1   *Face shield/safety goggles - When removing corrosion with a brush, the acidic particles can easily fly up into your eyes*

2   *Baking soda - A solution of baking soda and water can be used to neutralise corrosion*

3   *Petroleum jelly - A layer of this on the battery posts will help prevent corrosion*

4   *Battery post/cable cleaner - This wire brush cleaning tool will remove all traces of corrosion from the battery posts and cable clamps*

5   *Treated felt washers - Placing one of these on each post, directly under the cable clamps, will help prevent corrosion*

6   *Puller - Sometimes the cable clamps are very difficult to pull off the posts, even after the nut/bolt has been completely loosened. This tool pulls the clamp straight up and off the post without damage.*

7   *Battery post/cable cleaner - Here is another cleaning tool which is a slightly different version of number 4 above, but it does the same thing*

8   *Rubber gloves - Another safety item to consider when servicing the battery; remember that's acid inside the battery!*

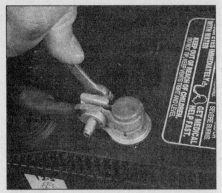

8.6 Use a spanner to check the tightness of the battery cable bolts; when removing corroded bolts, it may be necessary to use special battery pliers

mable, is always present in the battery cells, so keep lighted tobacco and all other open flames and sparks away from the battery. The electrolyte inside the battery is actually dilute sulfuric acid, which will cause injury if splashed on your skin or in your eyes. It will also ruin clothes and painted surfaces. When removing the battery cables, always detach the negative cable first and hook it up last!

Check and maintenance

1   Battery maintenance is an important procedure which will help ensure that you aren't stranded because of a dead battery. Several tools are required for this procedure **(see illustration)**.

2   When checking/servicing the battery, always turn the engine and all accessories off.

3   A sealed (sometimes called maintenance-free), battery is standard equipment on some vehicles. The cell caps cannot be removed, no electrolyte checks are required and water cannot be added to the cells. However, if a standard aftermarket battery has been refitted, the following maintenance procedure can be used.

4   Remove the caps and check the electrolyte level in each of the battery cells (see Section 4). It must be above the plates. There's usually a split-ring indicator in each cell to indicate the correct level. If the level is low, add distilled water only, then reinstall the cell caps. **Caution:** *Overfilling the cells may cause electrolyte to spill over during periods of heavy charging, causing corrosion and damage to nearby components.*

5   The external condition of the battery should be checked periodically. Look for damage such as a cracked case.

6   Check the tightness of the battery cable bolts **(see illustration)** to ensure good electrical connections. Inspect the entire length of each cable, looking for cracked or abraded insulation and frayed conductors.

7   If corrosion (visible as white, fluffy deposits) **(see illustration)** is evident, remove the cables from the terminals, clean them with a battery brush and reinstall them **(see illustrations)**. Corrosion can be kept to a minimum by applying a layer of petroleum jelly or grease to the terminals.

8   Make sure the battery carrier is in good condition and the hold-down clamp is tight. If the battery is removed (see Chapter 5 for the removal and refitting procedure), make sure that no parts remain in the bottom of the carrier when it's reinstalled. When refitting the hold-down clamp, don't overtighten the nuts.

9   Corrosion on the carrier, battery case and surrounding areas can be removed with a solution of water and baking soda. Apply the mixture with a small brush, let it work, then rinse it off with plenty of clean water.

10   Any metal parts of the vehicle damaged by corrosion should be coated with a zinc-based primer, then painted.

11   Additional information on the battery and jump starting can be found in the front of this manual and in Chapter 5.

Charging

12   Remove all of the cell caps (if equipped) and cover the holes with a clean cloth to prevent spattering electrolyte. Disconnect the negative battery cable and hook the battery charger leads to the battery posts (positive to positive, negative to negative), then plug in the charger. Make sure it is set at 12 volts if it has a selector switch.

13   If you're using a charger with a rate higher than two amps, check the battery regularly during charging to make sure it doesn't overheat. If you're using a trickle charger, you can safely let the battery charge overnight after you've checked it regularly for the first couple of hours.

14   If the battery has removable cell caps, measure the specific gravity with a hydrometer every hour during the last few hours of the charging cycle. Hydrometers are available inexpensively from auto parts stores - follow the instructions that come with the hydrometer. Consider the battery charged when there's no change in the specific gravity reading for two hours and the electrolyte in the cells is gassing (bubbling) freely. The specific gravity reading from each cell should be very close to the others. If not, the battery probably has a bad cell(s).

15   Some batteries with sealed tops have built-in hydrometers on the top that indicate the state of charge by the colour displayed in the hydrometer window. Normally, a bright-coloured hydrometer indicates a full charge and a dark hydrometer indicates the battery still needs charging. Check the battery manufacturer's instructions to be sure you know what the colours mean.

16   If the battery has a sealed top and no built-in hydrometer, you can hook up a digital voltmeter across the battery terminals to check the charge. A fully charged battery should read 12.6 volts or higher.

17   Further information on the battery and jump starting can be found in Chapter 5 and at the front of this manual.

9   Cooling system check (5,000 kilometres or 3 months)

Refer to illustration 9.4

1   Many major engine failures can be attributed to a faulty cooling system. If the vehicle is equipped with an automatic trans-

8.7a Battery terminal corrosion usually appears as light, fluffy powder

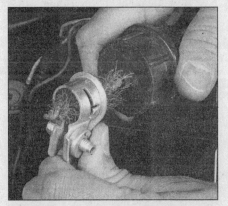

8.7b When cleaning the cable clamps, all corrosion must be removed (the inside of the clamp is tapered to match the taper on the post, so don't remove too much material)

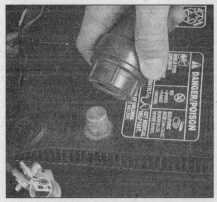

8.7c Regardless of the type of tool used on the battery posts, a clean, shiny surface should be the result

Check for a chafed area that could fail prematurely.

Check for a soft area indicating the hose has deteriorated inside.

Overtightening the clamp on a hardened hose will damage the hose and cause a leak.

Check each hose for swelling and oil-soaked ends. Cracks and breaks can be located by squeezing the hose.

9.4 Hoses, like drivebelts, have a habit of failing at the worst possible time - to prevent the inconvenience of a blown radiator or heater hose, inspect them carefully as shown here

mission, the cooling system also cools the transmission fluid, prolonging transmission life.

2   The cooling system should be checked with the engine cold. Do this before the vehicle is driven for the day or after it has been shut off for at least three hours.

3   Remove the radiator cap by turning it counterclockwise until it reaches a stop. If you hear a hissing sound (indicating there's still pressure in the system), wait until it stops. Now press down on the cap with the palm of your hand and continue turning until it can be removed. Thoroughly clean the cap, inside and out, with clean water. Also clean the filler neck on the radiator. All traces of corrosion should be removed. The coolant inside the radiator should be relatively transparent. If it's rust coloured, the system should be drained and refilled (Section 40). If the coolant level is not up to the top, add additional anti-freeze/coolant mixture (see Section 4).

4   Carefully check the large upper and

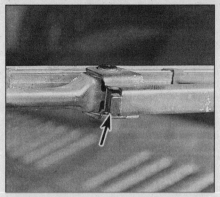

10.5 Depress the tab (arrow) and pull the blade assembly off the wiper arm

lower radiator hoses along with the smaller diameter heater hoses which run from the engine to the firewall. Inspect each hose along its entire length, renewing any hose that's cracked, swollen or deteriorated. Cracks may become more apparent if the hose is squeezed **(see illustration)**. Regardless of condition, it's a good idea to renew hoses with new ones every two years. Make sure that all hose connections are tight. A leak in the cooling system will usually show up as white or rust coloured deposits on the areas adjoining the leak. If wire-type clamps are used at the ends of the hoses, it may be a good idea to renew them with more secure screw-type clamps.

5   Use compressed air or a soft brush to remove bugs, leaves, etc. from the front of the radiator or air conditioning condenser. Be careful not to damage the delicate cooling fins or cut yourself on them.

6   Every other inspection, or at the first indication of cooling system problems, have the cap and system pressure tested. If you don't have a pressure tester, most petrol stations and repair shops will do this for a minimal charge.

10   Wiper blade inspection and renewal (5,000 kilometres or 3 months)

Refer to illustrations 10.5, 10.6a, 10.6b and 10.8

1   The windscreen wiper blades should be inspected periodically for damage, loose components and cracked or worn blade elements (the rubber portions).

2   Road film can build up on the blade elements and can affect their efficiency, so they should be washed regularly with a mild detergent solution.

3   The action of the wiping mechanism can loosen bolts, nuts and fasteners, so they should be checked and tightened, as necessary, at the same time the wiper blade elements are checked.

4   If the wiper blade elements are cracked, worn or warped, or no longer clean ade-

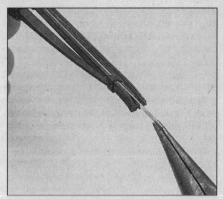

10.6a Use needle-nose pliers to pull the two support rods out of the blade element

10.6b With the rods out, it's an easy job to remove the element

quately, they should be renewed with new ones.

5   The wiper blade is removed by depressing the release tab at the centre of the wiper arm and pulling the blade off the arm **(see illustration)**.

6   Bend the element end out of the way, use needle-nose pliers to pull the two support rods out, then slide the element out of the wiper bridge **(see illustrations)**.

7   Slide the new element into place and insert the rods to lock it in place.

8   When fitting the wiper blade on the arm, place the plastic clip in position on the arm, then slide the blade into position over it until it locks **(see illustration)**.

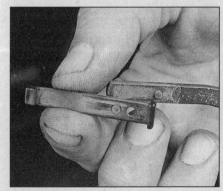

10.8 Place the plastic clip in position, then insert the blade onto the wiper arm

11 Underbonnet hose check and renewal (5,000 kilometres or 3 months)

General

Caution: *Renewal of air conditioning hoses must be left to a dealer service department or air conditioning shop that has the equipment to depressurise the system safely. Never remove air conditioning components or hoses until the system has been depressurised.*

1   High temperatures in the engine compartment can cause the deterioration of the rubber and plastic hoses used for engine, accessory and emission systems operation. Periodic inspection should be made for cracks, loose clamps, material hardening and leaks. Information specific to the cooling system hoses can be found in Section 9.

2   Some, but not all, hoses are secured to the fittings with clamps. Where clamps are used, check to be sure they haven't lost their tension, allowing the hose to leak. If clamps aren't used, make sure the hose has not expanded and/or hardened where it slips over the fitting, allowing it to leak.

Vacuum hoses

3   It's quite common for vacuum hoses, especially those in the emissions system, to be colour coded or identified by coloured stripes moulded into them. Various systems require hoses with different wall thicknesses, collapse resistance and temperature resistance. When renewing hoses, be sure the new ones are made of the same material.

4   Often the only effective way to check a hose is to remove it completely from the vehicle. If more than one hose is removed, be sure to label the hoses and fittings to ensure correct refitting.

5   When checking vacuum hoses, be sure to include any plastic T-fittings in the check. Inspect the fittings for cracks and the hose where it fits over the fitting for distortion, which could cause leakage.

6   A small piece of vacuum hose (6.35 mm inside diameter) can be used as a stethoscope to detect vacuum leaks. Hold one end of the hose to your ear and probe around vacuum hoses and fittings, listening for the "hissing" sound characteristic of a vacuum leak. **Warning:** *When probing with the vacuum hose stethoscope, be very careful not to come into contact with moving engine components such as the drivebelts, cooling fan, etc.*

Fuel hose

Warning: *There are certain precautions which must be taken when inspecting or servicing fuel system components. Work in a well ventilated area and don't allow open flames (cigarettes, appliance pilot lights, etc.) or bare light bulbs near the work area. Mop up any spills immediately and don't store fuel soaked rags where they could ignite. On vehicles equipped with fuel injection, the fuel system is under pressure, so if any fuel lines are*

to be disconnected, the pressure in the system must be relieved first (see Chapter 4 for more information).

7   Check all rubber fuel lines for deterioration and chafing. Check carefully for cracks in areas where the hose bends and where it's attached to fittings.

8   High quality fuel line should be used for fuel line renewal. **Warning:** *Never, under any circumstances, use unreinforced vacuum line, clear plastic tubing or water hose for fuel lines!*

9   Spring-type clamps are commonly used on fuel lines. They often lose their tension over a period of time, and can be "sprung" during removal. Renew all spring-type clamps with screw clamps whenever a hose is renewed.

Metal lines

10   Sections of metal line are often used for fuel line between the fuel pump and carburettor or fuel injection unit. Check carefully to be sure the line has not been bent or crimped and look for cracks.

11   If a section of metal fuel line must be renewed, only seamless steel tubing should be used, since copper and aluminium tubing don't have the strength necessary to withstand normal engine vibration.

12   Check the metal brake lines where they enter the master cylinder and brake proportioning unit (if used) for cracks in the lines and loose fittings. Any sign of brake fluid leakage means an immediate thorough inspection of the brake system should be done.

Turbocharger hoses and lines

13   Close attention must be paid to the condition of the vacuum and oil lines connected to the turbocharger (if so equipped). A deteriorated vacuum hose can lead to engine damage due to over-boosting and a damaged oil line can prevent lubrication from reaching the turbocharger. This will result in instant turbocharger failure.

14   Closely examine all hoses and steel lines. Renew any that are suspect. If the oil supply line to the turbocharger has been disconnected for any reason, allow the engine to idle for one minute after re-starting.

12 Accelerator linkage check and lubrication (5,000 kilometres or 3 months)

1   At the specified intervals, inspect the accelerator linkage and check it for free movement to make sure it is not binding.

2   Lubricate the linkage with a few drops of oil.

13 Engine oil and filter change (5,000 kilometres or 3 months)

Refer to illustrations 13.3, 13.9, 13.14 and 13.18

1   Frequent oil changes are the most

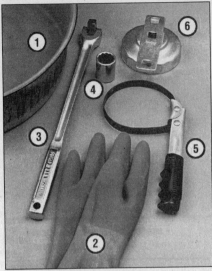

13.3 These tools are required when changing the engine oil and filter

1   ***Drain pan -*** *It should be fairly shallow in depth, but wide to prevent spills*

2   ***Rubber gloves -*** *When removing the drain plug and filter, you will get oil on your hands (the gloves will prevent burns)*

3   ***Breaker bar -*** *Sometimes the oil drain plug is tight and a long breaker bar is needed to loosen it*

4   ***Socket -*** *To be used with the breaker bar or a ratchet (must be the correct size to fit the drain plug - six-point preferred)*

5   ***Filter wrench -*** *This is a metal band-type wrench, which requires clearance around the filter to be effective*

6   ***Filter spanner -*** *This type fits on the bottom of the filter and can be turned with a ratchet or breaker bar (different size spanners are available for different types of filters)*

important preventive maintenance procedures that can be done by the home mechanic. As engine oil ages, it becomes diluted and contaminated, which leads to premature engine wear.

2   Although some sources recommend oil filter changes every other oil change, the minimal cost of an oil filter and the fact that it's easy to Refit dictate that a new filter be used every time the oil is changed.

3   Gather all necessary tools and materials before beginning this procedure **(see illustration)**.

4   You should have plenty of clean rags and newspapers handy to mop up any spills. Access to the underside of the vehicle is greatly improved if the vehicle can be lifted on a hoist, driven onto ramps or supported by jackstands. **Warning:** *Do not work under a vehicle which is supported only by a bumper, hydraulic or scissors-type jack!*

5   If this is your first oil change, get under the vehicle and familiarise yourself with the locations of the oil drain plug and the oil filter.

13.9 Use the proper size box-end spanner or six-point socket to remove the oil drain plug to avoid rounding it off

13.14 The oil filter is usually on very tight and will require a special wrench for removal - DO NOT use the wrench to tighten the new filter

13.18 Lubricate the oil filter gasket with clean engine oil before fitting the filter on the engine

The engine and exhaust components will be warm during the actual work, so note how they're situated to avoid touching them when working under the vehicle.

6   Warm the engine to normal operating temperature. If the new oil or any tools are needed, use the warm-up time to obtain everything necessary for the job. The correct oil for your application can be found in *Recommended lubricants and fluids* at the beginning of this Chapter.

7   With the engine oil warm (warm engine oil will drain better and more built-up sludge will be removed with it), raise and support the vehicle. Make sure it's safely supported!

8   Move all necessary tools, rags and newspapers under the vehicle. Set the drain pan under the drain plug. Keep in mind that the oil will initially flow from the pan with some force; position the pan accordingly.

9   Being careful not to touch any of the hot exhaust components, use a wrench to remove the drain plug near the bottom of the sump **(see illustration)**. Depending on how hot the oil is, you may want to wear gloves while unscrewing the plug the final few turns.

10   Allow the old oil to drain into the pan. It may be necessary to move the pan as the oil flow slows to a trickle.

11   After all the oil has drained, wipe off the drain plug with a clean rag. Small metal particles may cling to the plug and would immediately contaminate the new oil.

12   Clean the area around the drain plug opening and reinstall the plug. Tighten the plug securely with the wrench. If a torque wrench is available, use it to tighten the plug.

13   Move the drain pan into position under the oil filter.

14   Use the filter wrench to loosen the oil filter **(see illustration)**. Chain or metal band filter wrenches may distort the filter canister, but it doesn't matter since the filter will be discarded anyway.

15   Completely unscrew the old filter. Be careful; it's full of oil. Empty the oil inside the filter into the drain pan.

16   Compare the old filter with the new one to make sure they're the same type.

17   Use a clean rag to remove all oil, dirt and sludge from the area where the oil filter mounts to the engine. Check the old filter to make sure the rubber gasket isn't stuck to the engine. If the gasket is stuck to the engine, remove it.

18   Apply a light coat of clean oil to the rubber gasket on the new oil filter **(see illustration)**.

19   Attach the new filter to the engine, following the tightening directions printed on the filter canister or packing box. Most filter manufacturers recommend against using a filter wrench due to the possibility of over-tightening and damage to the seal.

20   Remove all tools, rags, etc. from under the vehicle, being careful not to spill the oil in the drain pan, then lower the vehicle.

21   Move to the engine compartment and locate the oil filler cap.

22   Pour the fresh oil into the filler opening. A funnel may be used.

23   Pour three or four litres of fresh oil into the engine. Wait a few minutes to allow the oil to drain into the pan, then check the level on the oil dipstick (see Section 4 if necessary). If the oil level is above the L mark, start the engine and allow the new oil to circulate.

24   Run the engine for only about a minute and then shut it off. Immediately look under the vehicle and check for leaks at the sump drain plug and around the oil filter. If either one is leaking, tighten it a little more.

25   With the new oil circulated and the filter now completely full, recheck the level on the dipstick and add more oil as necessary.

26   During the first few trips after an oil change, make it a point to check frequently for leaks and correct oil level.

27   The old oil drained from the engine cannot be reused in its present state and should be disposed of. Oil reclamation facilities, auto repair shops and petrol stations will normally accept the oil, which can be refined and used again. After the oil has cooled it can be poured into a container (capped plastic jugs or bottles, milk cartons, etc.) for transport to a disposal site.

14   Tyre rotation (5,000 kilometres or 3 months)

Refer to illustration 14.2

1   The tyres should be rotated at the specified intervals and whenever uneven wear is noticed.

2   Refer to the **accompanying illustration** for the preferred tyre rotation pattern.

3   Refer to the information in *Jacking and towing* at the front of this manual for the proper procedures to follow when raising the vehicle and changing a tyre. If the brakes are to be checked, don't apply the parking brake as stated. Make sure the tyres are blocked to prevent the vehicle from rolling as it's raised.

4   Preferably, the entire vehicle should be raised at the same time. This can be done on a hoist or by jacking up each corner and then lowering the vehicle onto jackstands placed under the frame rails. Always use four jackstands and make sure the vehicle is safely supported.

5   After rotation, check and adjust the tyre

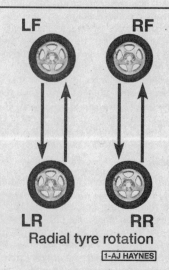

14.2 The recommended tyre rotation pattern for these vehicles

15.1 The rocker arms on petrol engines that do not require valve adjustment look like this (arrows) - they don't have adjustment screws (if the rocker arms do have adjustment screws, follow the procedure in the text)

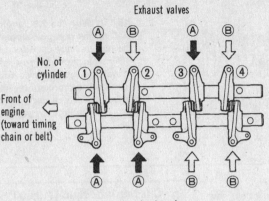

15.5 With the number one piston at Top Dead Centre (TDC), adjust the valves marked A - with the number four piston at TDC, adjust the valves marked B (2.5L petrol engines)

pressures as necessary and be sure to check the lug nut tightness.

6   For additional information on the wheels and tyres, refer to Chapter 11.

15 Valve clearance check and adjustment (four-cylinder engines only) (10,000 kilometres or 6 months)

Petrol and 2.5L diesel engines

Refer to illustrations 15.1, 15.5 and 15.10

1   The valve clearances must be checked and adjusted at the specified intervals with the engine at normal operating temperature. Generally speaking, later vehicles starting with the ND automatic transmission models don't require valve adjustment. Consult your owner's manual or dealer to determine if your vehicle requires valve adjustment. If this information is not readily available, the only

15.10 To make sure the adjusting screw doesn't move when the locknut is tightened, use a box-end spanner and have a good grip on the screwdriver

sure way to tell that adjustment is required is to remove the engine valve cover. Valves that do not require adjustment have no adjusting screws (see illustration).

2   Remove the air cleaner assembly (see Chapter 4).

3   Remove the valve cover (see Chapter 2).

4   Place the number one piston at Top Dead Centre (TDC) on the compression stroke (see Chapter 2). The number one cylinder rocker arms (closest to the timing chain end of the engine) should be loose (able to move up and down slightly) and the camshaft lobes should be facing away from the rocker arms.

5   With the crankshaft in this position the valves labeled can be checked and adjusted (see illustration).

6   The valve adjusting screws are located on the rocker arms.

7   Back off the inlet valve locknut two full turns. Turn the adjusting screw counterclockwise and insert the appropriate size feeler gauge (see this Chapter's Specifications) between the valve stem and the adjusting screw. Carefully tighten the adjusting screw until you can feel a slight drag on the feeler gauge as you withdraw it from between the stem and adjusting screw.

8   Hold the adjusting screw with a screwdriver (to keep it from turning) and tighten the locknut. Recheck the clearance to make sure it hasn't changed.

9   After checking the inlet valves, loosen the locknut on the exhaust valve adjusting screw. Turn the adjusting screw counterclockwise and insert the appropriate size feeler gauge between the valve stem and the adjusting screw. Carefully tighten the adjusting screw until you can feel a slight drag on the feeler gauge as you withdraw it from between the stem and adjusting screw.

10   Hold the adjusting screw with a screwdriver (to keep it from turning) and tighten the locknut (see illustration). Recheck the clearance to make sure it hasn't changed.

11   Rotate the crankshaft until the number four piston is at TDC on the compression stroke. The number four cylinder rocker arms (closest to the rear end of the engine) should be loose with the camshaft lobes facing away

from the rocker arms.

12   Adjust the valves labeled B as described above (see illustration 15.5a and 15.5b).

13   Refit the valve cover and the air cleaner assembly.

2.8L diesel engines

Refer to illustrations 15.17a, 15.17b and 15.18

14   Allow the engine to run until it has reached normal operating temperature. Remove the valve cover (refer to Chapter 2).

15   Remove the glow plug plate and the glow plugs (refer to Chapter 4).

16   Set the manual transmission in Neutral or the automatic transmission in PARK. With the parking brake set, rotate the crankshaft clockwise with a large ratchet and socket until the engine is at TDC on the compression stroke (refer to Chapter 2). There is a protrusion on the camshaft which should be pointing upward when TDC on cylinder number one has been reached (refer to Chapter 2D).

17   Use a feeler gauge to check the valve clearances shown (see illustrations). Make note of all clearances measured. If any are outside of the allowable specifications, new shims will have to be purchased and refitted. Refer to the values listed in this Chapter's Specifications. Rotate the crankshaft one full revolution and check the valve clearances on

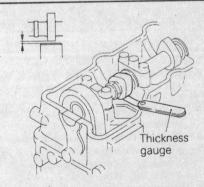

15.17a On 2.8L engines, the valve clearance is measured directly below each cam

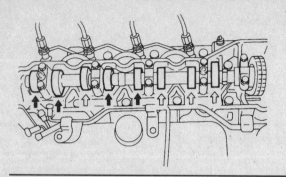

15.17b With the 2.8L engine at TDC on the compression stroke for number one cylinder, check the clearances for the valves indicated with dark arrows. Rotate the crankshaft one full revolution to check the valves with light arrows

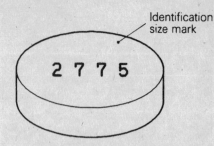

15.18 Each valve shim used on 2.8L diesel engines is marked with its thickness - this one is 2.775 mm thick

the remaining four valves.

18   Perform the calculations to select new shims: The thickness of the new shim will be equal to the thickness of the existing shims, plus the clearance measured in Step 17, less the required clearance. Shims are made in 0.025 mm thickness differences. Their thickness is stamped on them ("2525" is equal to a thickness of 2.525 mm) **(see illustration)**.

19   After selecting the appropriate shims, remove the camshaft (refer to Chapter 2). Refit the shims needed, refit the camshaft and recheck the valve clearances.

20   Rotate the crankshaft one full revolution and perform the same operation on the remaining four valves **(see illustration 15.17)**.

21   After all valve clearances have been double checked, assemble the engine in the reverse order of disassembly.

16.1 Materials required for chassis and body lubrication

1   *Engine oil - Light engine oil in a can like this can be used for door and bonnet hinges*

2   *Graphite spray - Used to lubricate lock cylinders*

3   *Grease - Grease, in a variety of types and weights, is available for use in a grease gun. Check the Specifications for your requirements*

4   *Grease gun - A common grease gun, shown here with a detachable hose and nozzle, is needed for chassis lubrication. After use, clean it thoroughly*

16   Chassis lubrication (10,000 kilometres or 6 months)

Refer to illustrations 16.1 and 16.2

1   A grease gun and cartridge filled with the recommended grease are the only items required for chassis lubrication other than some clean rags and equipment needed to raise and support the vehicle safely **(see illustration)**.

2   There are several points on the vehicle's suspension, steering and drivetrain components that must be periodically lubricated with lithium-based multi-purpose grease, depending on model and year. Included are the upper and lower suspension balljoints, the swivel joints on the steering linkage and the front and rear driveshafts **(see illustration)**.

3   The grease point for each upper suspension balljoint (if equipped) is on top of the balljoint and is accessible by removing the front wheel and tyre. The steering linkage swivel joints on some models are designed to be lubricated and the driveshaft universal joints require lubrication as well.

4   For easier access under the vehicle, raise it with a jack and place jackstands under the frame. Make sure the vehicle is safely supported on the stands!

5   If grease fittings aren't already refitted, the plugs will have to be removed and fittings screwed into place.

6   Force a little of the grease out of the gun nozzle to remove any dirt, then wipe it clean with a rag.

7   Wipe the grease fitting and push the nozzle firmly over it. Squeeze the trigger on the grease gun to force grease into the component. Both the balljoints and swivel joints should be lubricated until the rubber reservoir is firm to the touch. Don't pump too much grease into the fittings or it could rupture the reservoir. If the grease seeps out around the grease gun nozzle, the fitting is clogged or the nozzle isn't seated all the way. Re-secure the gun nozzle to the fitting and try again. If necessary, renew the fitting.

8   Wipe excess grease from the components and the grease fittings.

9   While you're under the vehicle, clean and lubricate the parking brake cable along with the cable guides and levers. This can be done by smearing some of the chassis

grease onto the cable and its related parts with your fingers.

10   Lower the vehicle to the ground for the remaining body lubrication process.

11   Open the bonnet and rear gate and smear a little chassis grease on the latch mechanisms. Have an assistant pull the release knob from inside the vehicle as you lubricate the cable at the latch.

12   Lubricate all the hinges (door, bonnet, hatch) with a few drops of light engine oil to keep them in proper working order.

13   The key lock cylinders can be lubricated with spray-on graphite, which is available at auto parts stores.

17   Suspension and steering check (10,000 kilometres or 6 months)

Refer to illustration 17.11

1   Whenever the front of the vehicle is raised for any reason, it's a good idea to visually check the suspension and steering components for wear.

2   Indications of steering or suspension problems include excessive play in the steering wheel before the front wheels react, excessive swaying around corners or body movement over rough roads and binding at some point as the steering wheel is turned.

3   Before the vehicle is raised for inspection, test the shock absorbers by pushing down aggressively at each corner. If the vehicle doesn't come back to a level position within one or two bounces, the shocks are worn and should be renewed. As this is done listen for squeaks and other noises from the suspension components. Information on shock absorber and suspension components can be found in Chapter 10.

4   Raise the front end of the vehicle and support it on jackstands. Make sure it's safely supported!

5   Crawl under the vehicle and check for loose bolts, broken or disconnected parts and deteriorated rubber bushes on all suspension and steering components. Look for grease or fluid leaking from around the steering gear assembly and shock absorbers. If equipped, check the power steering hoses

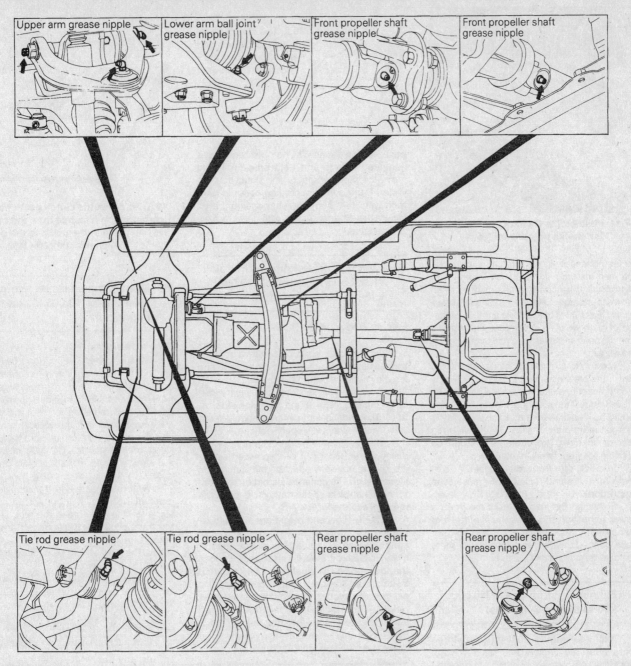

16.2 Typical chassis lubrication points

and connections for leaks.

6   The balljoint boots should be checked at this time. This includes not only the upper and lower suspension balljoints, but those connecting the steering linkage parts as well. After cleaning around the balljoints, inspect the seals for cracks and damage.

7   Grip the top and bottom of each wheel and try to move it in and out. It won't take a lot of effort to be able to feel any play in the wheel bearings. If the play is noticeable it would be a good idea to adjust it right away or it could confuse further inspections.

8   Grip each side of the wheel and try rocking it laterally. Steady pressure will, of course, turn the steering, but back-and-forth pres-

sure will reveal a loose steering joint. If some play is felt it would be easier to get assistance from someone so while one person rocks the wheel from side to side, the other can look at the joints, bushes and connections in the steering linkage. Generally speaking, there are eight places where the play may occur. The two outer balljoints on the tie-rods are the most likely, followed by the two inner joints on the same rods, where they join to the centre rod. Any play in them means renewal of the tie-rod end. Next are two swivel bushes, one at each end of the centre gear rod. Finally, check the steering gear arm balljoint and the one on the idler arm which supports the centre rod on the

side opposite the steering box. This unit is bolted to the side of the frame member and any play calls for renewal of the bushes.

9   To check the steering box, first make sure the bolts holding the steering box to the frame are tight. Then get another person to help examine the mechanism. One should look at, or hold onto, the arm at the bottom of the steering box while the other turns the steering wheel a little from side to side. The amount of lost motion between the steering wheel and the gear arm indicates the degree of wear in the steering box mechanism. This check should be carried out with the wheels first in the straight ahead position and then at nearly full lock on each side. If the play only

17.11 Push on the CV joint boot to check for cracks or lubricant leaks

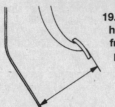

19.2 The clutch pedal height is measured from the top of the pedal to the floor

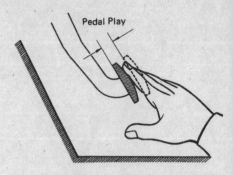

19.3 To check the clutch pedal freeplay, measure the distance from the natural resting place of the pedal to the point at which resistance is felt

occurs noticeably in the straight ahead position then the wear is most likely in the worm and/or nut. If it occurs at all positions, then the wear is probably in the sector shaft bearing. Oil leaks from the unit are another indication of such wear. In either case the steering box will need removal for closer examination and repair.

10   Moving to the vehicle interior, check the play in the steering wheel by turning it slowly in both directions until the wheels can just be felt turning. The steering wheel free play should be less than 35 mm. Excessive play is another indication of wear in the steering gear or linkage. The steering box can be adjusted for wear (see Chapter 10).

11   Inspect the front driveaxle CV joint boots for tears and leakage of grease **(see illustration)**.

12   Following the inspection of the front, a similar inspection should be made of the rear suspension components, again checking for loose bolts, damaged or disconnected parts and deteriorated rubber bushes.

18 Exhaust system check (10,000 kilometres or 6 months)

1   With the engine cold (at least three hours after the vehicle has been driven), check the complete exhaust system from the manifold to the end of the tailpipe. Be careful around the catalytic converter, which may be hot even after three hours. The inspection should be done with the vehicle on a hoist to permit unrestricted access. If a hoist isn't available, raise the vehicle and support it securely on jackstands.

2   Check the exhaust pipes and connections for signs of leakage and/or corrosion indicating a potential failure. Make sure that all brackets and hangers are in good condition and tight.

3   Inspect the underside of the body for holes, corrosion, open seams, etc. which may allow exhaust gases to enter the passenger compartment. Seal all body openings with silicone sealant or body putty.

4   Rattles and other noises can often be

traced to the exhaust system, especially the hangers, mounts and heat shields. Try to move the pipes, mufflers and catalytic converter. If the components can come in contact with the body or suspension parts, secure the exhaust system with new brackets and hangers.

19 Clutch pedal height and freeplay check and adjustment (10,000 kilometres or 6 months)

Refer to illustrations 19.2, 19.3, 19.4a and 19.4b

1   On vehicles equipped with a manual transmission, the clutch pedal height and freeplay must be correctly adjusted.

2   The height of the clutch pedal is the distance the pedal sits off the floor **(see illustration)**. The pedal height distance should be as listed in this Chapter's specifications.

3   The freeplay is the pedal slack, or the distance the pedal can be depressed before it begins to have any effect on the clutch **(see illustration)**. The distance should be as listed in this Chapter's specifications. If it isn't, it must be adjusted.

4   The freeplay and height are adjusted by turning the stopper bolt or cruise control clutch switch or adjustable clutch master cylinder pushrod **(see illustrations)**. Loosen the locknut on the pushrod, bolt or clutch switch. Turn the bolt, switch or pushrod to achieve the proper freeplay or height, then retighten the locknut. If the freeplay and height are not as specified after adjustment, it may mean there is air in the system and it should be bled (see Chapter 8).

20 Manual transmission lubricant level check (10,000 kilometres or 6 months)

Refer to illustration 20.1

1   Manual transmissions don't have a dipstick. The lubricant level is checked by removing a filler plug from the side of the transmission case **(see illustration)**. Locate the plug and use a rag to clean the plug and the area around it. If the vehicle is raised to gain access to the plug, be sure to support it safely on jackstands - DO NOT crawl under the vehicle when it's supported only by a jack!

2   With the engine and transmission cold, remove the plug. If lubricant immediately starts leaking out, thread the plug back into the transmission - the level is correct. If it doesn't, reach inside the hole with your little finger. The level should be even with the bottom of the plug hole.

3   If the transmission needs more lubricant, use a syringe or small pump to add it through the plug hole.

4   Thread the plug back into the transmission and tighten it securely. Drive the vehicle, then check for leaks around the plug.

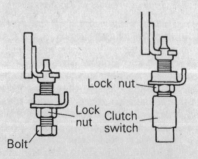

19.4a Adjust the pedal height and freeplay at the clutch pedal stopper bolt (left) or cruise control switch (right) - be careful not to push the pushrod toward the master cylinder during the adjustment

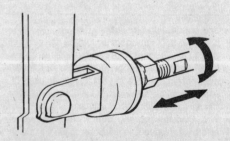

19.4b The pedal height and freeplay can also be adjusted at the pushrod - don't push it toward the master cylinder during the adjustment

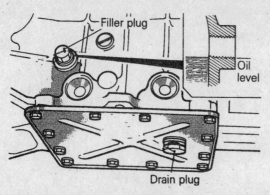

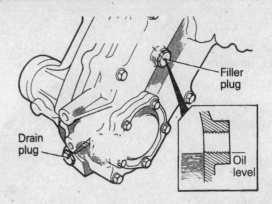

20.1 Manual transmission filler and drain plug locations

21.2 Transfer case filler and drain plug locations

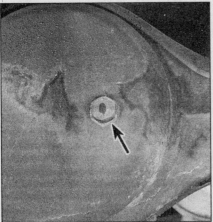

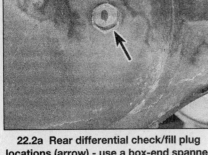

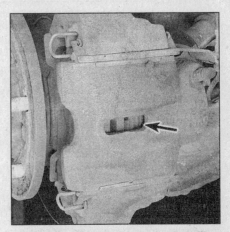

22.2a Rear differential check/fill plug locations (arrow) - use a box-end spanner or socket when removing or installing the plug to avoid rounding off the hex

22.2b Front differential check/fill plug (arrow)

23.6 You will find an inspection hole like this in each caliper - placing a steel ruler across the hole should enable you to determine the thickness of the remaining pad material for both inner and outer pads

22 Differential lubricant level check (10,000 kilometres or 6 months)

Refer to illustrations 22.2a and 22.2b

1   The differential has a check/fill plug which must be removed to check the lubricant level. If the vehicle is raised to gain access to the plug, be sure to support it safely on jackstands - DO NOT crawl under the vehicle when it's supported only by a jack.

2   Remove the check/fill plug from the differential **(see illustrations)**.

3   The lubricant level should be at the bottom of the plug opening. If not, use a syringe to add the recommended lubricant until it just starts to run out of the opening.

4   Refit the plug and tighten it securely.

23 Brake check (10,000 kilometres or 6 months)

Refer to illustrations 23.6, 23.13 and 23.15
Note: *For detailed photographs of the brake system, refer to Chapter 9.*
Warning: *Brake system dust may contain asbestos, which is hazardous to your health. DO NOT blow it out with compressed air and DO NOT inhale it. DO NOT use petrol or sol-*

21 Transfer case lubricant level check (10,000 kilometres or 6 months)

Refer to illustration 21.2

1   If necessary, remove the transfer case rock guard (if equipped). The lubricant level is checked by removing a filler plug from the side of the case. If the vehicle is raised to gain access to the plug, be sure to support it safely on jackstands - DO NOT crawl under the vehicle when it's supported only by a jack!

2   With the engine and transfer case cold, remove the plug **(see illustration)**. If lubricant immediately starts leaking out, thread the plug back into the case - the level is correct. If it doesn't, completely remove the plug and reach inside the hole with your little finger. The level should be even with the bottom of the plug hole.

3   If more lubricant is needed, use a syringe or small pump to add it through the opening.

4   Thread the plug back into the case and tighten it securely. Drive the vehicle, then check for leaks around the plug. Refit the rock guard.

vents to remove the dust. Use brake system cleaner or denatured alcohol only!

1   In addition to the specified intervals, the brakes should be inspected every time the wheels are removed or whenever a defect is suspected.

2   To check the brakes, the vehicle must be raised and supported securely on jackstands.

Disc brakes

3   Disc brakes are used on the front wheels. Extensive rotor damage can occur if the pads are allowed to wear beyond the specified limit.

4   Raise the vehicle and support it securely on jackstands, then remove the wheels (see *Jacking and Towing* at the front of the manual if necessary).

5   The disc brake calipers, which contain the pads, are visible with the wheels removed. There's an outer pad and an inner pad in each caliper. All pads should be inspected.

6   Each caliper has an opening, which allows you to inspect the pads **(see illustration)**. If the pad material has worn below the limit listed in this Chapter's Specifications, the pads should be renewed.

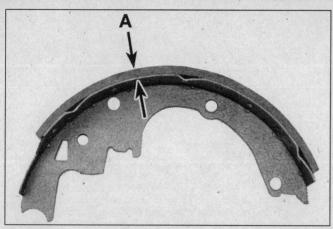

23.13 If the lining is bonded to the brake shoe, measure the lining thickness from the outer surface to the metal shoe, as shown here; if the lining is riveted to the shoe, measure from the lining outer surface to the rivet head

23.15 Prise the wheel cylinder boot back carefully to check for fluid leakage at both ends

7   If you're unsure about the exact thickness of the remaining lining material, remove the pads for further inspection or renewal (refer to Chapter 9).

8   Before installing the wheels, check for leakage and/or damage (cracks, splitting, etc.) around the brake hose connections. Renew the hose or fittings as necessary, referring to Chapter 9.

9   Check the condition of the rotor. Look for score marks, deep scratches and burned spots. If these conditions exist, the hub/rotor assembly should be removed for servicing (Chapter 9).

Drum brakes

10   On rear brakes, remove the drum (see Chapter 9). If it's stuck, make sure the parking brake is released, then squirt penetrating oil into the joint between the hub and drum. Allow the oil to soak in and try to pull the drum off again.

11   If the drum still can't be pulled off, the brake shoes will have to be adjusted. This is done by first removing the cover in the backing plate, inserting a screwdriver into the opening and lifting the adjustment lever off the star wheel adjuster and backing the adjuster off to move the shoes away from the drum.

12   With the drum removed, be careful not to touch any brake dust (see the **Warning** at the beginning of this Section).

13   Note the thickness of the lining material on both the front and rear brake shoes. If the material has worn away to below the specified thickness above the recessed rivets or metal shoe, the shoes should be renewed **(see illustration)**. The shoes should also be renewed if they're cracked, glazed (shiny surface) or contaminated with brake fluid.

14   Make sure that all the brake assembly springs are connected and in good condition.

15   Check the brake components for signs of fluid leakage. Carefully prise back the rubber cups on the wheel cylinders located at the top of the brake shoes with your finger or

24.1 Location of the balance shaft chain access cover (arrow)

a small screwdriver **(see illustration)**. Any leakage is an indication that the wheel cylinders should be overhauled immediately (see Chapter 9). Also check brake hoses and connections for leakage.

16   Wipe the inside of the drum with a clean rag and brake cleaner or denatured alcohol. Again, be careful not to breathe the asbestos dust.

17   Check the inside of the drum for cracks, score marks, deep scratches and hard spots, which will appear as small discolourations. If imperfections cannot be removed with fine emery cloth, the drum must be taken to a machine shop equipped to turn the drums.

18   If after the inspection process all parts are in good working condition, reinstall the brake drum.

19   Refit the wheels and lower the vehicle.

Parking brake

20   The parking brake is operated by a centre-mounted lever and locks the rear brake system. The easiest, and perhaps most obvious method of periodically checking the operation of the parking brake assembly is to

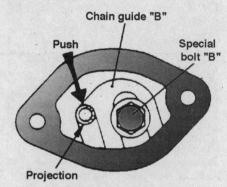

24.3 Balance shaft chain tension adjustment details

park the vehicle on a steep hill with the parking brake set and the transmission in Neutral. If the parking brake cannot prevent the vehicle from rolling within 4 to 6 (lever) clicks, it's in need of adjustment (see Chapter 9).

24   Balance shaft chain tension check and adjustment (four-cylinder engine) (10,000 kilometres or 6 months)

Refer to illustrations 24.1 and 24.3

1   With the engine off, open the bonnet and locate the access cover mounted on the front of the engine timing chain cover **(see illustration)**.

2   Remove the access cover and gasket.

3   Loosen bolt "B" and using your finger push the projection in the direction of the arrow **(see illustration).Note:** *Do not use a screwdriver or other implement to apply force. Excessive pressure will cause accelerated chain guide wear and excessive chain noise.*

4   Tighten bolt "B" and reinstall the access cover and gasket.

25 Fuel system check (10,000 kilometres or 6 months)

Warning: *Petrol is extremely flammable, so take extra precautions when you work on any part of the fuel system. Don't smoke or allow open flames or bare light bulbs near the work area, and don't work in a garage where a natural gas-type appliance (such as a water heater or clothes drier) with a pilot light is present. If you spill any fuel on your skin, rinse it off immediately with soap and water. When you perform any kind of work on the fuel tank, wear safety glasses and have a Class B type fire extinguisher on hand. On fuel-injected models, no components should be disconnected until the pressure has been relieved (see Chapter 4).*

1   The fuel tank is located at the rear of the vehicle.
2   The fuel system should be checked with the vehicle raised on a hoist so the components underneath the vehicle are readily visible and accessible.
3   If the smell of petrol is noticed while driving or after the vehicle has been in the sun, the system should be thoroughly inspected immediately.
4   Remove the fuel tank cap and check for damage, corrosion and an unbroken sealing imprint on the gasket. Renew the cap with a new one if necessary.
5   With the vehicle raised, check the fuel tank and filler neck for punctures, cracks and other damage. The connection between the filler neck and the tank is especially critical. Sometimes a rubber filler neck will leak due to loose clamps or deteriorated rubber, problems a home mechanic can usually rectify. **Warning:** *Do not, under any circumstances, try to repair a fuel tank yourself (except rubber components). A welding torch or any open flame can easily cause the fuel vapours to explode if the proper precautions are not taken!*
6   Carefully check all rubber hoses and metal lines leading away from the fuel tank. Look for loose connections, deteriorated hoses, crimped lines and other damage. Follow the lines to the front of the vehicle, carefully inspecting them all the way. Repair or renew damaged sections as necessary.
7   If a fuel odour is still evident after the inspection, refer to Section 33 and check the evaporative emissions system.

26 Thermostatic air cleaner check (carburetted models) (10,000 kilometres or 6 months)

1   Carburetted models are equipped with a thermostatically controlled air cleaner, which draws air to the carburettor from different locations depending on engine temperature.
2   This is a simple visual check. However, if access is tight, a small mirror may have to be used.
3   Open the bonnet and find the air control

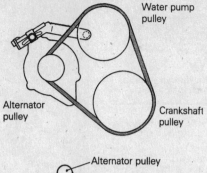

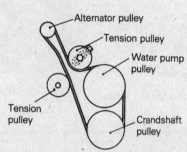

27.2 Drivebelt routing - top is for a typical four-cylinder engine; bottom is a typical V6 engine

valve on the air cleaner assembly. It's located inside the long snorkel portion of the metal air cleaner housing.
4   If there's a flexible air duct attached to the end of the snorkel, disconnect it so you can look through the end of the snorkel and see the air control valve inside. A mirror may be needed if you can't safely look directly into the end of the snorkel.
5   The check should be done when the engine and outside air are cold. Start the engine and watch the air control valve, which should move up and close off the snorkel air passage. With the valve closed, air can't enter through the end of the snorkel, but instead enters the air cleaner through the hot air duct attached to the exhaust manifold.
6   As the engine warms up to operating temperature, the valve should open to allow air through the snorkel end. Depending on outside air temperature, this may take 10 to 15 minutes. To speed up the check you can reconnect the snorkel air duct, drive the vehicle and then check the position of the valve.
7   If the thermostatic air cleaner isn't operating properly, see Chapter 6 for more information.

27 Drivebelt check, adjustment and renewal (10,000 kilometres or 6 months)

Refer to illustrations 27.2, 27.4a, 27.4b, 27.5, 27.7a and 27.7b

1   The accessory drivebelts are located at the front of the engine. The belts drive the water pump, alternator, power steering pump and air conditioning compressor. The condition and tension of the drivebelts are critical

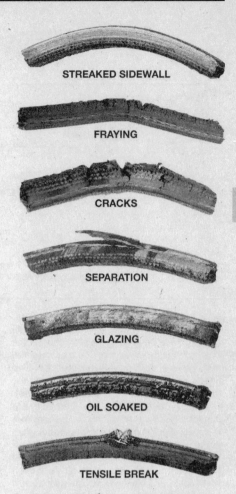

STREAKED SIDEWALL

FRAYING

CRACKS

SEPARATION

GLAZING

OIL SOAKED

TENSILE BREAK

27.4a Here are some of the more common problems associated with drivebelts ((check very carefully to prevent an untimely breakdown)

to the operation of the engine and accessories. Excessive tension causes bearing wear, while insufficient tension produces slippage, noise, component vibration and belt failure. Because of their composition and the high stress to which they are subjected, drivebelts stretch and continue to deteriorate as they get older. As a result, they must be periodically checked and adjusted.

Check

2   The number, type and routing of belts used on a particular vehicle depends on the engine, model year and accessories refitted **(see illustration)**.
3   Various types of drivebelts are used on these models. Some components are driven by V-belts (these are the conventional type). Others are driven by V-ribbed belts. Some models use a single V-ribbed belt to drive all of the accessories. This is known as a "serpentine" belt because of the winding path it follows between various drive, accessory and idler pulleys.
4   With the engine off, open the bonnet and locate the drivebelt(s) at the front of the

1

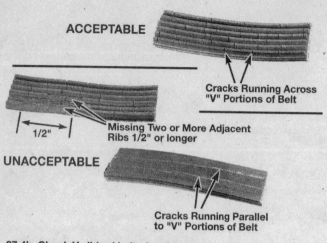

ACCEPTABLE

Cracks Running Across "V" Portions of Belt

1/2"

Missing Two or More Adjacent Ribs 1/2" or longer

UNACCEPTABLE

Cracks Running Parallel to "V" Portions of Belt

27.4b Check V-ribbed belts for signs of wear like these - if the belt looks worn, renew it

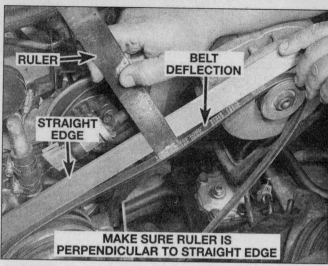

RULER

BELT DEFLECTION

STRAIGHT EDGE

MAKE SURE RULER IS PERPENDICULAR TO STRAIGHT EDGE

27.5 Measuring drivebelt deflection with a straightedge and ruler

engine. With a flashlight, check each belt for separation of the rubber plies from each side of the core, a severed core, separation of the ribs from the rubber, cracks, torn or worn ribs and cracks in the inner ridges of the ribs. Also check for fraying and glazing, which gives the belt a shiny appearance (see illustrations). Cracks in the rib side of V-ribbed belts are acceptable, as are small chunks missing from the ribs. If a V-ribbed belt has lost chunks bigger than 13 mm from two adjacent ribs, or if the missing chunks cause belt noise, the belt should be renewed. Both sides of each belt should be inspected, which means you'll have to twist them to check the undersides. Use your fingers to feel a belt where you can't see it. If any of the above conditions are evident, renew the belt as described below.

5   To check the tension of the belts, the following "rule of thumb" method is recommended. Lay a straightedge across the longest free span (the distance between two pulleys) of the belt. Push down firmly on the belt at a point half way between the pulleys and see how much the belt moves (deflects). Measure the deflection with a ruler (see illustration). The belt should deflect 6 to 8 mm if the distance from pulley centre-to-pulley centre is less than 300 mm; it should deflect from 9 to 12 mm if the distance from pulley centre-to-pulley centre is over 300 mm.

Adjustment

6   To adjust belt tension on serpentine belts, turn the adjusting screw on the tension pulley (see illustration 27.2). To adjust all except serpentine belts, move the belt-driven accessory on the bracket, as follows:

7   For each accessory, there will be a locking bolt and a pivot bolt or nut (see illustrations). Both must be loosened slightly to enable you to move the component.

8   After the two bolts have been loosened, move the component away from the engine (to tighten the belt) or toward the engine (to loosen the belt). Some models have an

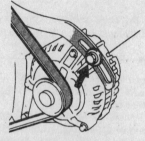

27.7a On earlier models, adjust the alternator belt by loosening the locking bolt (arrow) and the pivot bolt or nut at the bottom of the alternator

adjuster bolt which is turned to move the component. Some other accessories are equipped with a square hole designed to accept a 1/2-inch square drive breaker bar. The bar can be used to lever the component and tension the drivebelt. Others have a cast lug which is designed to accept an open-end spanner, which can be used to prise the accessory. **Caution:** *If it's necessary to prise against an accessory to tighten a drivebelt, be very careful not to damage the accessory or the point the lever rests against.*

9   Hold the accessory in position and check the belt tension. If it's correct, tighten the two bolts until snug, then recheck the tension. If it's all right, tighten the two bolts completely.

Renewal

10   Follow the above procedures for drivebelt adjustment, but loosen the belt until it will slip off the pulleys, then remove it. On some models, it may be necessary to remove forward belts to renew a rearward belt. Since belts tend to wear out at the same time, it's a good idea to renew all of them at the same time. Mark each belt and the corresponding pulley grooves so the belt can be reinstalled properly.

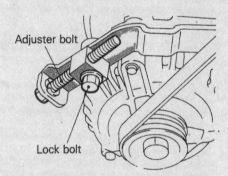

Adjuster bolt

Lock bolt

27.7b On later models, after loosening the locking bolt or nut at the bottom of the alternator, loosen the lock bolt and turn the adjuster bolt

28   Seat belt check (10,000 kilometres or 6 months)

1   Check the seat belts, buckles, latch plates and guide loops for any obvious damage or signs of wear.

2   Make sure the seat belt reminder light comes on when the key is turned on.

3   The seat belts are designed to lock up during a sudden stop or impact, yet allow free movement during normal driving. The retractors should hold the belt against your chest while driving and rewind the belt when the buckle is unlatched.

4   If any of the above checks reveal problems with the seat-belt system, renew parts as necessary.

29   Carburettor/throttle body mounting nut/bolt torque check (25,000 kilometres or 12 months)

1   Nuts or bolts attach the carburettor to the inlet manifold or the fuel injection system

30.3a Pull up on the clips to detach them

30.3b Remove the wing nut so the top cover can be lifted off

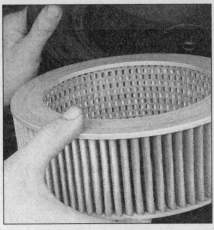

30.4 Lift out the air filter element and wipe out the inside of the air cleaner housing with a clean rag

throttle body to the air intake plenum. The bolts or nuts can sometimes work loose during normal engine operation and cause a vacuum leak.

2 To properly tighten the mounting bolts or nuts, a torque wrench is necessary. If you do not own one, they can usually be rented on a daily basis.

3 Remove the air cleaner or intake hose assembly (see Chapter 4).

4 Locate the mounting bolts/nuts at the base of the carburettor/throttle body. Decide what special tools or adaptors will be necessary, if any, to tighten the bolts/nuts with a socket and the torque wrench.

5 Tighten the bolts/nuts to the torque specified in Chapter 4. Do not overtighten the bolts/nuts, as the threads may strip.

6 If you suspect a vacuum leak exists at the bottom of the carburettor/throttle body obtain a short length of rubber hose. Start the engine and place one end of the hose next to your ear as you probe around the base of the carburettor/throttle body with the other end. You should hear a hissing sound if a leak exists.

7 If, after the bolts/nuts are properly tightened, a vacuum leak still exists, the carburet-

tor/throttle body must be removed and a new gasket refitted. See Chapter 4 for more information.

8 After tightening the bolts/nuts, reinstall the air cleaner housing or intake hose.

---

30 Air filter renewal (25,000 kilometres or 12 months)

1 At the specified intervals, the air filter should be renewed. A thorough program of preventive maintenance would also call for the filter to be inspected periodically between changes, especially if the vehicle is often driven in dusty conditions.

2 The air filter is located inside the air cleaner housing, which is mounted on top of the carburettor or at the right front corner of the engine compartment on fuel-injected models.

Carburetted models

Refer to illustrations 30.3a, 30.3b and 30.4

3 Release the clips, remove the wing nut and lift the top plate off the air cleaner hous-

ing (see illustrations).

4 Lift the air filter out of the housing (see illustration). If it's covered with dirt, it should be renewed.

5 Wipe the inside of the air cleaner housing with a rag.

6 Place the old filter (if in good condition) or the new filter (if renewal is necessary) into the air cleaner housing.

7 Reinstall the top plate on the air cleaner, then tighten the wing nut and snap the clips into place.

Fuel-injected models

Round filter housing

Refer to illustrations 30.9a, 30.9b and 30.10

8 Detach the air intake hose.

9 Release the clips and pull the air flow sensor out of the air cleaner housing (see illustrations).

10 Remove the old filter element (see illustration). If it is covered with dirt, it should be renewed.

11 Insert the filter element in the air cleaner housing and align the tabs, the Refit the air flow sensor body and secure it with the clips.

30.9a Detach the round filter housing clips by lifting up

30.9b Be careful when pulling the air flow sensor out of the air cleaner housing

30.10 Support the air flow sensor and lift the air filter element out

30.13 Rectangular filter housing clip locations (arrows)

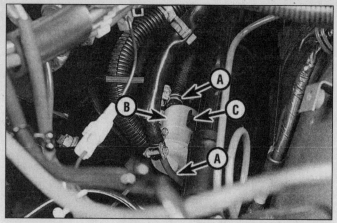

31.4 Disconnect the hoses (A), then detach the carburettor fuel filter (B) from the clip (C)

12 Connect the air intake hose securely, making sure there are no air leaks.

Rectangular filter housing

Refer to illustration 30.13

13 Detach the clips, pull the cover up and lift the filter out of the housing (see illustration). If the filter is covered with dirt, it should be renewed.

14 Wipe the inside of the air cleaner housing with a rag.

15 Place the old filter (if in good condition) or the new filter (if renewal is necessary) into the air cleaner housing. Set the cover in place and attach the clips.

31 Fuel filter service (25,000 kilometres or 12 months)

Warning: *Fuel is extremely flammable, so take extra precautions when you work on any part of the fuel system. Don't smoke or allow open flames or bare light bulbs near the work area, and don't work in a garage where a natural gas-type appliance (such as a water heater or clothes drier) with a pilot light is present. If you spill any fuel on your skin, rinse it off immediately with soap and water. When you perform any kind of work on the fuel tank, wear safety glasses and have a Class B type fire extinguisher on hand.*

1 This job should be done with the engine cold (after sitting at least three hours). Place a metal container, rags or newspapers under the filter to catch spilled fuel.

2 **Warning:** *Before attempting to remove the fuel filter, disconnect the negative cable from the battery and position it out of the way so it can't accidentally contact the battery post.*

Carburetted models

Refer to illustration 31.4

3 The fuel filter is located below the carburettor in the engine compartment. Clamp the inlet hose before disconnecting the filter, otherwise fuel will continue to drain from the tank.

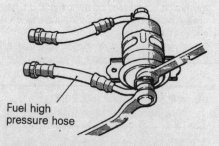

Fuel high pressure hose

31.9 On petrol engines, use two spanners when removing the fuel hoses - an open end to steady the filter and a box-end to loosen the bolt without rounding it off

4 Loosen the clamps and slide them down the hoses, past the fittings on the filter, then detach the filter from the clip (see illustration).

5 Carefully twist and pull on the hoses to separate them from the filter. If the hoses are in bad shape, now would be a good time to renew them.

6 Connect the filter to the hoses and tighten the clamps securely. If spring-type clamps were originally refitted, it would be a good idea to renew them with screw-type clamps. Push the filter back into the clip. Start the engine and check carefully for leaks at the filter hose connections.

Fuel-injected petrol models

Refer to illustration 31.9

7 Depressurise the fuel system (Chapter 4).

8 The fuel filter is located under the vehicle, adjacent to the fuel tank. Raise the vehicle and support it securely on jackstands. Remove the filter protector plate (if equipped).

9 Using two wrenches, remove the high-pressure hose (see illustration).

10 Loosen the output hose bolt or fitting and detach it. If the hoses are in bad shape, now would be a good time to renew them.

11 Remove the bolts and detach the filter,

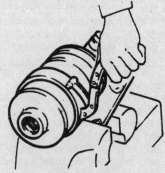

31.20 An oil filter wrench can be used to disassemble the fuel filter unit

noting the direction in which it was refitted.

12 Refit the new filter in the bracket, making sure the filter is properly oriented.

13 Connect the hoses to the new filter and tighten the bolts or fitting securely. On bolt-type (banjo) connections, use new sealing washers.

14 Start the engine and check carefully for leaks at the filter hose connections.

Diesel models

Fuel filter renewal

Refer to illustrations 31.20 and 31.21

15 Remove the cap from the fuel tank.

16 If the engine is turbocharged, remove the intercooler (refer to Chapter 4).

17 Disconnect the wiring from the water sensor.

18 Place rags around and beneath the fuel filter to catch fuel that may spray or leak. Disconnect the fuel hoses.

19 Remove the filter assembly and place it horizontally in a vice.

20 Using an oil filter wrench, remove the fuel filter canister (see illustration).

21 Place the canister vertically in the vice with the water sensor in the jaws. Manually screw the canister off of the water sensor (see illustration).

22 Refitting is the reverse of removal. Bleed the system (refer to Step 23).

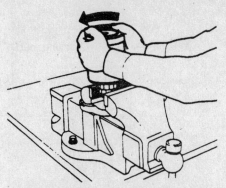

31.21 The assembly must be securely mounted in a vice in order to remove the fuel filter

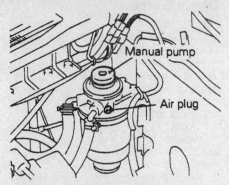

31.23 Locations of the fuel filter pump and air bleed plug

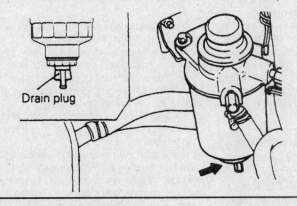

31.26 The water drain plug is at the bottom of the fuel filter

Bleeding the fuel system

Refer to illustration 31.23

23   Remove the small air plug located near the top of the filter assembly **(see illustration)**. Place rags under the filter.
24   Operate the manual pump until clear fuel with no bubbles runs from the bleed hole. Replace the air plug.
25   Operate the manual pump again until increased resistance is felt.

Draining water from the fuel filter

Refer to illustration 31.26
Note: *Drain the system any time the fuel filter lamp on the instrument panel lights.*

26   Place rags under the filter. Loosen the drain plug at the bottom of the fuel filter a few turns **(see illustration)**.
27   Operate the hand pump at the top of the filter assembly until clear fuel runs out. Hand tighten the drain plug.

32   Brake pedal height and freeplay check and adjustment (25,000 kilometres or 12 months)

Refer to illustrations 32.1a and 32.1b
1   Brake pedal height is the distance the pedal sits away from the floor **(see illustra-**

tion). The distance should be as specified (see this Chapter's Specifications). If the pedal height is not within the specified range, loosen the locking nut and back the stop light switch off until it doesn't contact the brake pedal arm. Loosen the brake booster operating rod locking nut and turn rod in or out until the pedal height is correct **(see illustration)**. Retighten the locking nut.
2   Brake pedal freeplay is the distance the pedal can be depressed before it begins to have any effect on the brakes. Measure the freeplay with the engine off after stepping on the brake pedal five times. The freeplay should be as specified. If it isn't, loosen the locknut, back off the brake light switch and adjust the brake booster rod until the freeplay is correct, then retighten the locknut.
3   After adjustment, turn the stop light switch until it contacts the brake pedal arm, then back it off about one turn and tighten the locknut.

33   Evaporative emissions system check (25,000 kilometres or 12 months)

Refer to illustration 33.2
1   The function of the evaporative emissions system is to draw fuel vapours from the fuel tank, store them in a charcoal canister and burn them during normal engine operation.
2   The most common symptom of a fault in the evaporative emissions system is a strong fuel odour in the engine compartment. If a fuel odour is detected, inspect the charcoal canister, located in the engine compartment. Check the canister and all hoses for damage and deterioration **(see illustration)**.
3   The canister is held to the fenderwell by a spring clip, secured around the outside of the canister body. The canister is removed by marking and disconnecting the hoses, disengaging the clamp and lifting the canister out.
4   The evaporative emissions control system is explained in more detail in Chapter 6.

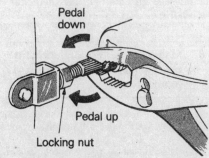

32.1b Use pliers to turn the brake booster operating rod to adjust the pedal height and freeplay

32.1a Brake pedal height adjustment details

33.2 The charcoal canister is attached to the fenderwell in the engine compartment - check the canister housing and hoses for damage

34 Carburettor choke check (25,000 kilometres or 12 months)

1   The choke operates only when the engine is cold, so this check should be performed before the engine has been started for the day.

2   Open the bonnet and remove the top plate of the air cleaner assembly. It's held in place by one or two wing nuts at the centre and several spring clips around the edge. If any vacuum hoses must be disconnected, tag them to ensure refitting in their original positions.

3   Look at the centre of the air cleaner housing. You'll notice a flat plate at the carburettor opening.

4   Have an assistant press the throttle pedal to the floor. The plate should close completely. Start the engine while you watch the plate at the carburettor. Don't position your face near the carburettor, as the engine could backfire, causing serious burns! When the engine starts, the choke plate should open slightly.

5   Allow the engine to continue running at an idle speed. As the engine warms up to operating temperature, the plate should slowly open, allowing more air to enter through the top of the carburettor.

6   After a few minutes, the choke plate should be completely open to the vertical position. Tap the accelerator to make sure the fast idle cam disengages.

7   You'll notice that engine speed corresponds to the plate opening. With the plate closed, the engine should run at a fast idle speed. As the plate opens and the throttle is moved to disengage the fast idle cam, the engine speed will decrease.

8   With the engine off and the throttle held half-way open, open and close the choke several times. Check the linkage to see if it's hooked up correctly and make sure it doesn't bind.

9   If the choke or linkage binds, sticks or works sluggishly, clean it with choke cleaner (an aerosol spray available at auto parts stores). If the condition persists after cleaning, renew the troublesome parts.

10   Visually inspect all vacuum hoses to be sure they're securely connected and look for cracks and deterioration. Renew as necessary.

11   If the choke fails to operate normally, but no mechanical causes can be found, check the choke electrical circuits.

35 Idle speed check and adjustment (carburetted and diesel models only) (25,000 kilometres or 12 months)

Carburetted models

Refer to the carburettor adjustment procedure in Chapter 4.

Diesel models

Refer to illustration 35.6

1   Idle speed is critical to the performance of the engine itself as well as many accessories. A special diesel tachometer must be used when adjusting idle speed. The connection for these meters depends on the manufacturer, so follow the directions included with the tachometer.

2   Apply the parking brake and block the rear wheels. Be sure the transmission is in Neutral (manual transmission) or Park (automatic).

3   Turn off the air conditioner and all other accessories.

4   Start the engine and bring it to normal operating temperature.

5   Check the idle speed with the tachometer and compare your reading with that listed in the Specifications in this Chapter.

6   If the idle speed is incorrect, loosen the lock-nut and then turn the idle speed screw on the fuel injection pump to change it **(see illustration)**. Tighten the lock-nut securely.

7   Make sure the accelerator cable still has the proper amount of slack in it. If it does not, adjust the cable (refer to Chapter 4).

36 Transfer case lubricant change (25,000 kilometres or 12 months)

1   Drive the vehicle for at least 15 minutes in 4WD to warm up the lubricant in the case.

2   Raise the vehicle and support it securely on jackstands.

3   Move a drain pan, rags, newspapers and tools under the vehicle.

4   Remove the filler plug (see Section 21).

5   Remove the drain plug from the lower part of the case and allow the old lubricant to drain completely.

6   Carefully clean and Refit the drain plug after the case is completely drained. Tighten the plug to the torque listed in this Chapter's Specifications.

7   Fill the case with the specified lubricant until it's level with the lower edge of the filler hole.

8   Refit the filler plug and tighten it securely.

9   Check carefully for leaks around the drain plug after the first few kilometres of driving.

37 Manual transmission lubricant change (25,000 kilometres or 12 months)

1   Drive the vehicle for a few kilometres to thoroughly warm up the transmission lubricant.

2   Raise the vehicle and support it securely on jackstands.

3   Move a drain pan, rags, newspapers and tools under the vehicle. With the drain pan and newspapers in position under the

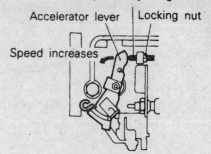

Idle speed adjusting screw
Accelerator lever   Locking nut
Speed increases

35.6 Idle speed adjustment details (diesel models)

transmission, loosen the drain plug located in the bottom of the transmission case.

4   Once loosened, carefully unscrew it with your fingers until you can remove it from the transmission. Allow all of the oil to drain into the pan. If the plug is too hot to touch, use the wrench to remove it.

5   Clean the drain plug, then reinstall it in the transmission and tighten it to the specified torque.

6   Remove the transmission lubricant filler plug (see Section 20). Using a hand pump or syringe, fill the transmission with the correct amount and grade of lubricant, until the level is just at the bottom of the plug hole.

7   Reinstall the filler plug and tighten it securely.

38 Differential lubricant change (25,000 kilometres or 12 months)

Note: *The following procedure can be used for the rear differential as well as the front differential.*

1   Drive the vehicle for several kilometres to warm up the differential lubricant, then raise the vehicle and support it securely on jackstands.

2   Move a drain pan, rags, newspapers and a 1/2-inch drive breaker bar or ratchet with an extension under the vehicle.

3   With the drain pan under the differential, use the breaker bar or ratchet and extension to loosen the drain plug. It's the lower of the two plugs.

4   Once loosened, carefully unscrew it with your fingers until you can remove it from the case.

5   Allow all of the lubricant to drain into the pan, then renew the drain plug and tighten it to the torque listed in this Chapter's Specifications.

6   Feel with your hands along the bottom of the drain pan for any metal bits that may have come out with the lubricant. If there are any, it's a sign of excessive wear, indicating that the internal components should be carefully inspected in the near future.

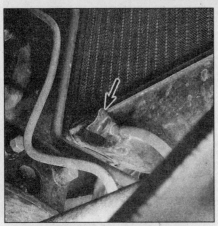

40.4 The radiator drain plug (arrow) is located at the bottom of the radiator

7   Using a hand pump, syringe or funnel, fill the differential with the correct amount and grade of lubricant until the level is just at the bottom of the fill plug hole.
8   Reinstall the plug and tighten it securely.
9   Lower the vehicle. Check for leaks after the first few kilometres of driving.

39 Automatic transmission fluid change (25,000 kilometres or 12 months)

1   At the specified time intervals, the transmission fluid should be drained and renewed. Since the fluid should be hot when it's drained, drive the vehicle for 15 or 20 minutes before proceeding.
2   Before beginning work, purchase the specified transmission fluid and filter (if equipped). Most models with drain plugs do not have filter, so it's important before starting the job to determine whether your model requires a renewal filter.
3   Other tools necessary for this job include jackstands to support the vehicle in a raised position, a drain pan capable of holding at least 4 litres, newspapers and clean rags.
4   Raise the vehicle and support it securely on jackstands.
5   Move the drain pan and necessary tools under the vehicle, being careful not to touch any of the hot exhaust components.
6   Place the pan under the drain plug in the transmission pan and remove the plug. Be sure the drain pan is in position, as fluid will come out with some force. Once the fluid is drained, reinstall the drain plug securely.
7   Lower the vehicle and add new automatic transmission fluid through the filler tube (Section 5). The amount should be slightly less than the amount of fluid that was drained (you don't want to overfill it).
8   With the transmission in Park and the parking brake set, run the engine at a fast idle, but don't race it.
9   Move the gear selector through each range and back to Park, then check the fluid level (Section 5). Add more fluid as required.

Add the fluid a little at a time, continually checking the level so you don't overfill the transmission.
10   Check under the vehicle for leaks during the first few kilometres of driving.

40 Cooling system servicing (draining, flushing and refilling) (25,000 kilometres or 12 months)

Refer to illustration 40.4
Warning: *Antifreeze is a corrosive and poisonous solution, so be careful not to spill any of the coolant mixture on the vehicle's paint or your skin. If you do, rinse it off immediately with plenty of clean water. Consult local authorities regarding proper disposal of antifreeze before draining the cooling system. In many areas, reclamation facilities have been established to collect used oil and coolant mixtures.*

1   Periodically, the cooling system should be drained, flushed and refilled to replenish the antifreeze mixture and prevent formation of rust and corrosion, which can impair the performance of the cooling system and cause engine damage. When the cooling system is serviced, all hoses and the radiator cap should be checked and renewed if necessary.
2   Apply the parking brake and block the wheels. If the vehicle has just been driven, wait several hours to allow the engine to cool down before beginning this procedure.
3   Once the engine is completely cool, remove the radiator cap. Place the heater temperature control in the maximum heat position.
4   Move a large container under the radiator drain to catch the coolant, then unscrew the drain plug (a pair of pliers may be required to turn it) **(see illustration)**.
5   After the coolant stops flowing out of the radiator, move the container under the engine block drain plug(s) (on four-cylinder engines there is one plug on the side of the block; on V6 engines there are two plugs, located on each side of the block). Remove the plug(s) and allow the coolant in the block to drain.
6   While the coolant is draining, check the condition of the radiator hoses, heater hoses and clamps (refer to Section 9 if necessary).
7   Renew any damaged clamps or hoses.
8   Once the system is completely drained, flush the radiator with fresh water from a garden hose until it runs clear at the drain. The flushing action of the water will remove sediments from the radiator but will not remove rust and scale from the engine and cooling tube surfaces.
9   These deposits can be removed with a chemical cleaner. Follow the procedure outlined in the manufacturer's instructions. If the radiator is severely corroded, damaged or leaking, it should be removed (Chapter 3) and taken to a radiator repair shop.
10   Remove the overflow hose from the coolant recovery reservoir. Drain the reservoir

and flush it with clean water, then reconnect the hose.
11   Reinstall and tighten the radiator drain plug. Refit and tighten the block drain plug(s).
12   Slowly add new coolant (a 50/50 mixture of water and antifreeze) to the radiator until it's full. Add coolant to the reservoir up to the lower mark.
13   Leave the radiator cap off and run the engine in a well-ventilated area until the thermostat opens (coolant will begin flowing through the radiator and the upper radiator hose will become hot).
14   Turn the engine off and let it cool. Add more coolant mixture to bring the level back up to the lip on the radiator filler neck.
15   Squeeze the upper radiator hose to expel air, then add more coolant mixture if necessary. Refit the radiator cap.
16   Start the engine, allow it to reach normal operating temperature and check for leaks.

41 Positive Crankcase Ventilation (PCV) system check (25,000 kilometres or 12 months)

Refer to illustrations 41.5 and 41.6
1   The Positive Crankcase Ventilation (PCV) system directs blowby gases from the crankcase back into the inlet manifold so they can be burned in the engine.
2   Rough idling or high idle speed and stalling are symptoms of faults in the PCV system.
3   The system on these models consists of a hose leading from the valve cover to the inlet manifold and a fresh air hose between the air cleaner assembly and the valve cover. Gases from the crankcase are carried by the hose through a PCV valve or orifice in the hose into the inlet manifold.
4   Check the system hoses for cracks, leaks and clogging. Clean the hoses if they are clogged and renew any which are damaged.
5   Remove PCV valve **(see illustration)**.

41.5 On models with a PCV valve, pull off the hose and use a spanner to unscrew the PCV valve from the engine valve cover

41.6 With the engine running, suction should be felt at the threaded end of the PCV valve

6   Start the engine and verify that air can be heard passing through the valve and a suction should be felt, indicating it is operating properly **(see illustration)**.
7   Shut off the engine and blow though the valve from the threaded end. If air will not pass through, renew the valve with a new one.
8   More information on the PCV system can be found in Chapter 6.

42   Spark plug renewal (25,000 kilometres or 12 months)

Refer to illustrations 42.2, 42.5a, 42.5b, 42.6, 42.8, 42.10a and 42.10b

1   Renew the spark plugs with new ones at the intervals recommended in the Maintenance schedule.
2   In most cases, the tools necessary for spark plug renewal include a spark plug socket which fits onto a ratchet (spark plug sockets are padded inside to prevent damage to the porcelain insulators on the new plugs), various extensions and a gap gauge

42.5b To change the gap, bend the *side* electrode only, as indicated by the arrows, and be very careful not to crack or chip the porcelain insulator surrounding the centre electrode

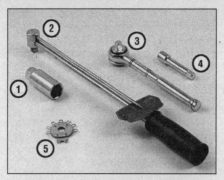

42.2 Tools required for renewing spark plugs

1   **Spark plug socket** - *This will have special padding inside to protect the spark plug's porcelain insulator*
2   **Torque wrench** - *Although not mandatory, using this tool is the best way to ensure the plugs are tightened properly*
3   **Ratchet** - *Standard hand tool to fit the spark plug socket*
4   **Extension** - *Depending on model and accessories, you may need special extensions and universal joints to reach one or more of the plugs*
5   **Spark plug gap gauge** - *This gauge for checking the gap comes in a variety of styles. Make sure the gap for your engine is included*

to check and adjust the gaps on the new plugs **(see illustration)**. A special plug wire removal tool is available for separating the wire boots from the spark plugs, but it isn't absolutely necessary. A torque wrench should be used to tighten the new plugs.
3   The best approach when renewing the spark plugs is to purchase the new ones in advance, adjust them to the proper gap and renew them one at a time. When buying the new spark plugs, be sure to obtain the correct plug type for your particular engine. This information can be found on the Emission Control Information label located under the bonnet and in the owner's manual. If differences exist between the plug specified on

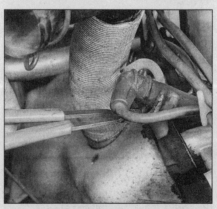

42.6 When removing the spark plug wires, pull only on the boot and use a twisting, pulling motion

42.5a Spark plug manufacturers recommend using a wire type gauge when checking the gap - if the wire does not slide between the electrodes with a slight drag, adjustment is required

the emissions label and in the owner's manual, assume the emissions label is correct.
4   Allow the engine to cool completely before attempting to remove any of the plugs. While you're waiting for the engine to cool, check the new plugs for defects and adjust the gaps.
5   The gap is checked by inserting the proper thickness gauge between the electrodes at the tip of the plug **(see illustration)**. The gap between the electrodes should be the same as the one specified on the Emissions Control Information label. The wire should just slide between the electrodes with a slight amount of drag. If the gap is incorrect, use the adjuster on the gauge body to bend the curved side electrode slightly until the proper gap is obtained **(see illustration)**. If the side electrode is not exactly over the centre electrode, bend it with the adjuster until it is. Check for cracks in the porcelain insulator (if any are found, the plug shouldn't be used).
6   With the engine cool, remove the spark plug wire from one spark plug. Pull only on the boot at the end of the wire - don't pull on the wire. A plug wire removal tool should be used if available **(see illustration)**.

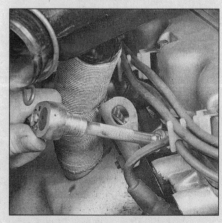

42.8 Use a socket wrench with a long extension to unscrew the spark plugs

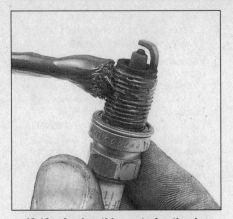

42.10a Apply a thin coat of anti-seize compound to the spark plug threads

42.10b A length of 10 mm ID rubber hose will save time and prevent damaged threads when fitting the spark plugs

7   If compressed air is available, use it to blow any dirt or foreign material away from the spark plug hole. A common bicycle pump will also work. The idea here is to eliminate the possibility of debris falling into the cylinder as the spark plug is removed.

8   Place the spark plug socket over the plug and remove it from the engine by turning it in a counterclockwise direction **(see illustration)**.

9   Compare the spark plug to those shown in the accompanying photos to get an indication of the general running condition of the engine.

10   Prior to refitting, apply a coat of anti-seize compound to the plug threads **(see illustration)**. Thread one of the new plugs into the hole until you can no longer turn it with your fingers, then tighten it with a torque wrench (if available) or the ratchet. It might be a good idea to slip a short length of rubber hose over the end of the plug to use as a tool to thread it into place **(see illustration)**. The hose will grip the plug well enough to turn it, but will start to slip if the plug begins to cross-thread in the hole - this will prevent damaged threads and the accompanying repair costs.

11   Before pushing the spark plug wire onto the end of the plug, inspect it following the procedures outlined in Section 43.

12   Attach the plug wire to the new spark plug, again using a twisting motion on the boot until it's seated on the spark plug.

13   Repeat the procedure for the remaining spark plugs, renewing them one at a time to prevent mixing up the spark plug wires.

43   Spark plug wire, distributor cap and rotor check and renewal (25,000 kilometres or 12 months)

Refer to illustrations 43.11 and 43.12

1   The spark plug wires should be checked whenever new spark plugs are renewed.

2   Begin this procedure by making a visual check of the spark plug wires while the engine is running. In a darkened garage (make sure there is ventilation) start the engine and observe each plug wire. Be careful not to come into contact with any moving engine parts. If there is a break in the wire, you will see arcing or a small spark at the damaged area. If arcing is noticed, make a note to obtain new wires, then allow the engine to cool and check the distributor cap and rotor.

3   The spark plug wires should be inspected one at a time to prevent mixing up the order, which is essential for proper engine operation. Each original plug wire should be numbered to help identify its location. If the number is illegible, a piece of tape can be marked with the correct number and wrapped around the plug wire.

4   Disconnect the plug wire from the spark plug. A removal tool can be used for this purpose or you can grasp the rubber boot, twist the boot half a turn and pull the boot free. Do not pull on the wire itself **(see illustration 42.6)**.

5   Check inside the boot for corrosion, which will look like a white crusty powder.

6   Push the wire and boot back onto the end of the spark plug. It should fit tightly onto the end of the plug. If it doesn't, remove the wire and use pliers to carefully crimp the metal connector inside the wire boot until the fit is snug.

7   Using a clean rag, wipe the entire length of the wire to remove built-up dirt and grease. Once the wire is clean, check for burns, cracks and other damage. Do not bend the wire sharply, because the conductor within the wire might break.

8   Disconnect the wire from the distributor. Again, pull only on the rubber boot. Check for corrosion and a tight fit. Press the wire back into the distributor.

9   Inspect the remaining spark plug wires, making sure that each one is securely fastened at the distributor and spark plug when the check is complete.

10   If new spark plug wires are required, purchase a set for your specific engine model. Pre-cut wire sets with the boots already refitted are available. Remove the wires one at a time to avoid mix-ups in the firing order.

11   Detach the distributor cap by levering off the two cap retaining clips or removing the two screws. Look inside it for cracks, carbon tracks and worn, burned or loose contacts **(see illustration)**.

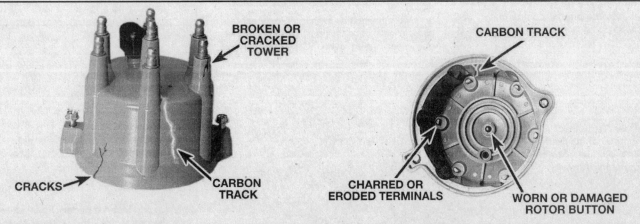

43.11 Shown here are some of the common defects to look for when inspecting the distributor cap (if in doubt about its condition, fit a new one)

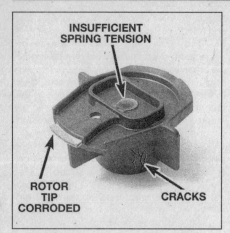

INSUFFICIENT SPRING TENSION

ROTOR TIP CORRODED

CRACKS

43.12 The ignition rotor should be checked for wear and corrosion as indicated here (if in doubt about its condition, buy a new one)

12   Remove the rotor from the distributor shaft. On some models there is a screw on the side of the rotor that must be removed. On other models, simply pull the rotor off the shaft. Examine the rotor for cracks and carbon tracks **(see illustration)**. Renew the cap and rotor if any damage or defects are noted.

13   It is common practice to Refit a new cap and rotor whenever new spark plug wires are refitted, but if you wish to continue using the old cap, clean the terminals first.

14   When fitting a new cap, remove the wires from the old cap one at a time and attach them to the new cap in the exact same location - do not simultaneously remove all the wires from the old cap or firing order mix-ups may occur.

44   Ignition timing check and adjustment (25,000 kilometres or 12 months)

Refer to illustrations 44.1, 44.6a, 44.6b, 44.7 and 44.10

Note: *If the information in this Section differs from the Vehicle Emission Control Information label in the engine compartment, the information on the label should be considered correct.*

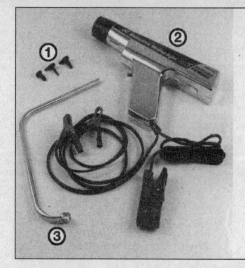

① ② ③

44.1 Tools needed to check and adjust the ignition timing

1   *Vacuum plugs* - *Vacuum hoses will, in most cases, have to be disconnected and plugged. Moulded plugs in various shapes and sizes are available for this*

2   *Inductive pick-up timing light* - *Flashes a bright, concentrated beam of light when the number one spark plug fires. Connect the leads according to the instructions supplied with the light*

3   *Distributor wrench* - *On some models, the hold-down bolt for the distributor is difficult to reach and turn with conventional wrenches or sockets. A special wrench like this must be used*

1   The proper ignition timing setting for your vehicle is printed on the VECI label located in the engine compartment. Some special tools will be required for this procedure **(see illustration)**.

2   Locate the timing plate on the front of the engine, near the crankshaft pulley. The T or 0 mark is Top Dead Centre (TDC). To locate which mark the notch in the pulley must line up with for the timing to be correct, count back from the T or 0 mark the number of degrees BTDC (Before Top Dead Centre) noted on the VECI label.

3   Locate the timing notch in the pulley and mark it with a dab of paint or chalk so it'll be visible under the strobe light. To locate the notch it may be necessary to have an assistant temporarily turn the ignition key to Start in short bursts to turn the crankshaft. **Warning:** *Stay clear of all moving engine components if the engine is turned in this manner!*

4   Connect a tachometer according to the manufacturer's instructions and make sure the idle speed is correct (carburetted models). Adjust it, if necessary, as described in Chapter 4.

5   Allow the engine to reach normal operating temperature. Be sure the air conditioner, if equipped, and all other accessories are off.

6   With the ignition switch off, connect the pick-up lead of the timing light to the number one spark plug wire. On four-cylinder

engines, it's the front one. On V6 engines it's the first spark plug on the right side as viewed from the driver's seat. Use either a jumper lead between the wire and plug or an inductive-type pick up. Don't pierce the wire or attempt to insert a wire between the boot and plug wire. Connect the timing light power leads according to the manufacturer's instructions. On V6 models, should it be necessary to connect a tachometer (to verify the idle speed is correct), insert a paper clip into the wire side of the fuel injector connector - without disconnecting it - **(see illustrations)**. Connect the tachometer between the paper clip and earth.

7   On V6 models, remove the waterproof cover from the ignition timing adjusting connector (in the engine compartment) and connect a wire with alligator clips between the terminal in the connector and earth **(see illustration)**. Do this before starting the engine to check the ignition timing.

8   Make sure the wiring for the timing light is clear of all moving engine components, then start the engine. Race the engine two or three times, then allow it to idle for a minute.

9   Point the flashing timing light at the timing marks, again being careful not to come in contact with moving parts. The marks you highlighted should appear stationary. If the

44.6a To connect a tachometer on V6 models, locate the fuel injector connector (arrow) . . .

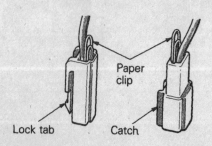

Paper clip

Lock tab   Catch

Female connector   Male connector

44.6b . . . and insert a paper clip as shown into the connector - the tachometer is then connected between the paper clip and earth

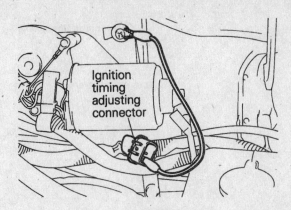

44.7 Connect a jumper wire between the ignition timing connector and earth

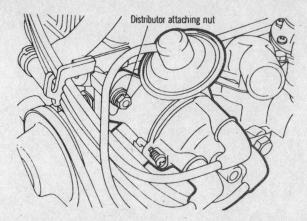

44.10 Loosen the distributor attaching/hold-down nut and turn the distributor to adjust the ignition timing

marks are in alignment, the timing is correct. If the marks aren't aligned, turn off the engine.

10   Loosen the distributor attaching/hold-down bolt/nut until the distributor can be rotated **(see illustration)**.

11   Start the engine and slowly rotate the distributor either left or right until the timing marks are aligned.

12   Shut off the engine and tighten the mounting bolt/nut, being careful not to move the distributor.

13   Restart the engine and recheck the timing to make sure the marks are still in alignment.

14   Disconnect the timing light and jumper wire.

15   Race the engine two or three times, then allow it to run at idle. Recheck the idle speed with the tachometer. If it has changed from the correct setting, readjust it (carburetted models only).

16   Drive the vehicle and listen for "pinging" noises. They'll be noticeable when the engine is hot and under load (climbing a hill, accelerating from a stop). If you hear engine pinging, the ignition timing is too far advanced (Before Top Dead Centre). Reconnect the timing light and turn the distributor to move the mark 1 or 2-degrees in the retard direction (counterclockwise). Road test the vehicle again to check for proper operation.

17   To keep "pinging" at a minimum, yet still allow you to operate the vehicle at the specified timing setting, use petrol of the same octane at all times. Switching fuel brands and octane levels can decrease performance and economy, and possibly damage the engine.

45   Exhaust Gas Recirculation (EGR) system check (25,000 kilometres or 12 months)

Refer to illustration 45.2

1   The EGR valve is located on the inlet manifold. Most of the time, when a problem develops in the emissions system, it is due to a stuck or corroded EGR valve.

2   With the engine cold to prevent burns, check the EGR valve hoses for damage **(see illustration)**. Pull the hoses off and inspect for clogging.

3   If the hoses are cracked or clogged, renew them with new ones.

4   Refer to Chapter 6 for more information on the EGR system.

46   Oxygen sensor renewal (50,000 kilometres or 24 months)

1   The oxygen (exhaust gas) sensor used on later models should be renewed at the specified intervals.

2   The sensor is threaded into the exhaust manifold and can be identified by the wire attached to it. Renewal consists of disconnecting the wire harness and unthreading the sensor from the manifold. Apply anti-seize compound to the threads of the new sensor (some new sensors may already have anti-seize compound on the threads). Tighten the new sensor to the torque listed in this Chapter's Specifications, then reconnect the wire harness.

3   Refer to the next section for the emissions maintenance reminder light resetting procedure.

45.2 Locate the EGR valve (arrow) and check the hoses leading to it for damage

Notes

Chapter 2 Part A
Four-cylinder petrol engine

Contents

Specifications

General

Firing order	1 - 3 - 4 - 2
Cylinder numbers (drivebelt end-to-transaxle end)	1 - 2 - 3 - 4
Bore and stroke	91.1 x 98.0 mm
Displacement	2.6 litres

Camshaft

Endplay	0.10 to 0.20 mm
Runout	0.020 mm
Journal diameter	34.0 mm
Bearing journal oil clearance	0.05 to 0.09 mm
Lobe height	
Intake	42.50 mm
Exhaust	42.56 mm
Lobe wear (maximum)	0.50 mm
Chain tensioner spring free length	65.71 mm

Cylinder location and distributor rotation

The blackened terminal shown on the distributor cap indicates the Number One spark plug wire position

Cylinder head

Warpage limit	0.2 mm
Inlet/exhaust manifold warpage limit	0.15 mm
Maximum allowable machining	0.2 mm

Oil pump

Gear-to-bearing clearance	0.020 to 0.046 mm
Driven gear rear bearing clearance	0.044 to 0.066 mm
Gear-to-housing clearance	0.105 to 0.150 mm
Gear endplay	0.06 to 0.012 mm
Relief spring free length	47.0 mm

Torque specifications

	Nm
Cylinder head bolts	90 to 100
Camshaft bearing cap bolts	
Long	19 to 21
Short	20 to 27
Camshaft sprocket bolt	50 to 60
Cylinder head cover bolts	5 to 7
Crankshaft pulley bolt	108 to 127
Flywheel/driveplate-to-crankshaft bolts	127 to 137
Oil pump sprocket bolt	60 to 70
Balance shaft sprocket bolt	59 to 69
Balance shaft thrust plate bolts	5 to 7
Chain guide B bolt	
Upper	8 to 10
Lower	15 to 22
Chain guide A and C bolt	10 to 12
Front cover bolts	12 to 15
Sump-to-engine block bolts	6 to 8
Sump drain plug	35 to 40
Oil pick-up tube bolts	14 to 21
Oil pump	
Sprocket bolt	59 to 69
Mounting bolts	8 to 10
Cover-to body screws	10 to 12
Relief valve cap	30 to 45
Exhaust manifold	
Manifold-to-cylinder head nuts	15 to 19
Manifold heat shield bolts	8 to 10
Manifold heat cowl screws	8 to 10
Manifold-to-exhaust pipe bolts	20 to 30
Oxygen sensor	40 to 50
Inlet manifold bolts	15 to 20
Rear main oil seal housing bolts	10 to 12
Timing chain guide bolts	18
Engine mounting	
Heat shield bolts	30 to 40
Heat shield nuts	6 to 10
Front insulator stopper bolts	30 to 40
Front insulator stopper nuts	13 to 20
Engine mounting front insulator plate bolts/nuts	18 to 25
Engine mounting front insulator bolts/nuts	18 to 25
Transfer mounting insulator bolts/nuts	18 to 25
Transfer mounting bracket bolts/nuts	18 to 25
No. 7 crossmember bolts	55 to 75
Rear mounting insulator bolts	18 to 25

1 General information

This Part of Chapter 2 is devoted to in-vehicle repair procedures for the 2.6L four-cylinder petrol engine. All information concerning engine removal and refitting and engine block and cylinder head overhaul can be found in Part E of this Chapter.

The following repair procedures are based on the assumption that the engine is refitted in the vehicle. If the engine has been removed from the vehicle and mounted on a stand, many of the steps outlined in this Part of Chapter 2 will not apply.

The Specifications included in this Part of Chapter 2 apply only to the procedures contained in this Part. Part E of Chapter 2 contains the Specifications necessary for cylinder head and engine block rebuilding.

The 2.6 litre engine is an inline vertical four, with a chain-driven overhead camshaft and a balance shaft counterbalancing system which cancels the engines power pulses and produces relatively vibration-free operation. The crankshaft rides in five renewable insert-type main bearings, with the centre bearing (the thrust bearing) assigned the additional task of controlling crankshaft endplay.

The pistons have two compression rings and one oil control ring. The semi-floating piston pins are press fitted into the small end of the connecting rod. The connecting rod big ends are also equipped with renewable insert-type plain bearings.

The engine is liquid-cooled, utilising a centrifugal impeller-type pump, driven by a belt from the camshaft, to circulate coolant around the cylinders and combustion chambers and through the inlet manifold.

Lubrication is handled by a gear-type oil pump mounted on the front of the engine under the timing chain cover. It is driven by the balance shaft chain. The oil is filtered continuously by a cartridge-type filter mounted on the right side of the engine.

2 Repair operations possible with the engine in the vehicle

Many major repair operations can be accomplished without removing the engine from the vehicle.

Clean the engine compartment and the exterior of the engine with some type of degreaser before any work is done. It will make the job easier and help keep dirt out of the internal areas of the engine.

Depending on the components involved, it may be helpful to remove the bonnet to improve access to the engine as repairs are performed (refer to Chapter 11 if necessary). Cover the fenders to prevent damage to the paint. Special pads are available, but an old bedspread or blanket will also work.

If vacuum, exhaust, oil or coolant leaks develop, indicating a need for gasket or seal renewal, the repairs can generally be made with the engine in the vehicle. The inlet and

3.8 Align the notch in the pulley with the T on the timing indicator

exhaust manifold gaskets, sump gasket, crankshaft oil seals and cylinder head gasket are all accessible with the engine in place.

Exterior engine components, such as the inlet and exhaust manifolds, the sump, the water pump, the starter motor, the alternator, the distributor and the fuel system components can be removed for repair with the engine in place.

Since the cylinder head can be removed without pulling the engine, camshaft and valve component servicing can also be accomplished with the engine in the vehicle. Renewal of the timing chain and sprockets is also possible with the engine in the vehicle.

In extreme cases caused by a lack of necessary equipment, repair or renewal of piston rings, pistons, connecting rods and rod bearings is possible with the engine in the vehicle. However, this practice is not recommended because of the cleaning and preparation work that must be done to the components involved.

3 Top Dead Centre (TDC) for number one piston - locating

Refer to illustrations 3.8 and 3.9
Note: *The following procedure is based on the assumption that the distributor is correctly refitted. If you are trying to locate TDC to refit the distributor correctly, piston position must be determined by feeling for compression at the number one spark plug hole, then aligning the ignition timing marks as described in Step 8.*

1   Top Dead Centre (TDC) is the highest point in the cylinder that each piston reaches as it travels up-and-down when the crankshaft turns. Each piston reaches TDC on the compression stroke and again on the exhaust stroke, but TDC generally refers to piston position on the compression stroke.

2   Positioning the number one piston at TDC is an essential part of many procedures, such as camshaft, timing chain or distributor removal.

3   Before beginning this procedure, be sure to place the transmission in Park (auto-

3.9 When the number one cylinder is at Top Dead Centre (TDC) on the compression stroke, the distributor rotor should point to the number one spark plug terminal

matic) or Neutral (manual) and apply the parking brake or block the rear wheels. Also, disable the ignition system by disconnecting the primary (low voltage) electrical connectors at the distributor) (see Chapter 5). Remove the spark plugs (see Chapter 1).

4   In order to bring any piston to TDC, the crankshaft must be turned using one of the methods outlined below. When looking at the front of the engine (timing chain end), normal crankshaft rotation is clockwise.

a) *The preferred method is to turn the crankshaft with a socket and ratchet attached to the bolt threaded into the front of the crankshaft.*

b) *A remote starter switch, which may save some time, can also be used. Follow the instructions included with the switch. Once the piston is close to TDC, use a socket and ratchet as described in the previous paragraph.*

c) *If an assistant is available to turn the ignition switch to the Start position in short bursts, you can get the piston close to TDC without a remote starter switch. Make sure your assistant is out of the vehicle, away from the ignition switch, then use a socket and ratchet as described in Paragraph a) to complete the procedure.*

5   Note the position of the terminal for the number one spark plug wire on the distributor cap. If the terminal isn't marked, follow the plug wire from the number one cylinder spark plug to the cap.

6   Use a felt-tip pen or chalk to make a mark on the distributor body directly under the number one terminal.

7   Detach the cap from the distributor and set it aside (see Chapter 1 if necessary).

8   Turn the crankshaft (see Step 4) until the notch in the crankshaft pulley is aligned with the T on the timing indicator located on the lower front chain cover **(see illustration)**.

9   Look at the distributor rotor - it should be pointing directly at the mark you made on the distributor body **(see illustration)**.

2A

4.9 Remove the two bolts (arrows) from the valve cover and lift the cover off the engine

4.13 Apply a small amount of RTV sealant to the corner of the cylinder head next to the camshaft bearing cap

10   If the rotor is 180-degrees off, the number one piston is at TDC on the exhaust stroke.

11   To get the piston to TDC on the compression stroke, turn the crankshaft one complete revolution (360-degrees) clockwise. The rotor should now be pointing at the mark on the distributor. When the rotor is pointing at the number one spark plug wire terminal in the distributor cap and the ignition timing marks are aligned, the number one piston is at TDC on the compression stroke. **Note:** *If it's impossible to align the ignition timing marks when the rotor is pointing at the mark on the distributor body, the timing chain may have jumped the teeth on the sprockets or may have been refitted incorrectly.*

12   After the number one piston has been positioned at TDC on the compression stroke, TDC for any of the remaining pistons can be located by turning the crankshaft and following the firing order. Mark the remaining spark plug wire terminals on the distributor body just like you did for the number one terminal, then number the marks to correspond with the cylinder numbers. As you turn the crankshaft, the rotor will also turn. When it's pointing directly at one of the marks on the distributor, the piston for that particular cylinder is at TDC on the compression stroke.

4   Valve cover - removal and refitting

Removal

Refer to illustration 4.9

1   Detach the cable from the negative battery terminal.

2   Remove the water pump pulley cover from the valve cover (see Chapter 3).

3   Remove the air cleaner inlet hose and housing assembly from the carburettor and the top of the valve cover (see Chapter 4A).

4   Disconnect the crankcase breather hose from the valve cover.

5   Disconnect the spark plug wires from the spark plugs, remove them from the hold-down clamps and position them aside. Be sure to mark each wire for correct refitting.

6   Remove any fuel lines or vent lines that will interfere with the removal of the valve cover.

7   Disconnect the accelerator cable from the valve cover and position it aside.

8   Wipe off the valve cover thoroughly to prevent debris from falling onto the exposed cylinder head or camshaft/valve train assembly.

9   Remove the valve cover bolts **(see illustration).**

10   Carefully lift off the valve cover and gasket. If the gasket is stuck to the cylinder head, tap it with a rubber mallet to break the seal. Do not prise between the cover and cylinder head or you'll damage the gasket mating surfaces.

Refitting

Refer to illustration 4.13

11   Use a gasket scraper to remove all traces of old gasket material from the gasket mating surfaces of the cylinder head and the valve cover. Clean the surfaces with a rag soaked in lacquer thinner or acetone.

12   Be sure to refit the semi-circular seal (camshaft plug) on top of the cylinder head near the camshaft sprocket. Apply beads of RTV sealant to the points where the seal meets the valve cover mating surfaces.

13   Refit a new gasket onto the valve cover. Refit the moulded rubber gasket onto the cover by pushing the new gasket into the slot that circles the valve cover perimeter. Apply a bead of RTV sealant where the cylinder head and camshaft bearing caps meet **(see illustration)**. Refit the valve cover and tighten the bolts to the torque listed in this Chapter's Specifications.

14   The remainder of refitting is the reverse of removal.

5.3 Remove the rocker arm assembly bolts (arrows)

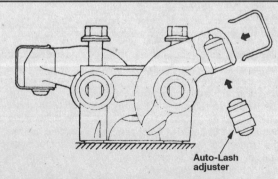

Auto-Lash adjuster

5.4 Before removing the rocker arm assembly, retain the hydraulic auto-lash adjusters to the rocker arms - If the special clips are not available, wrap them with electrical tape

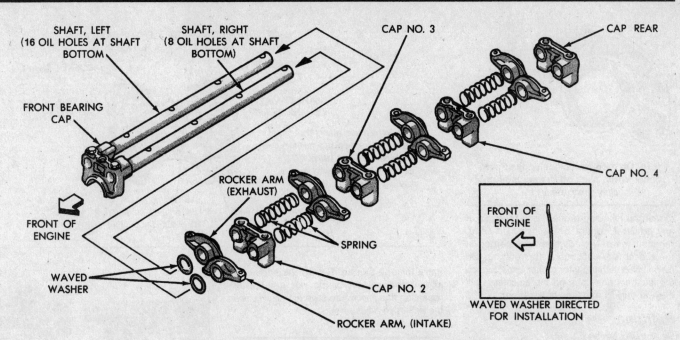

5.5 An exploded view of the rocker arms and shafts (typical)

5 Rocker arm assembly - removal, inspection and refitting

Note 1: *The camshaft bearing caps are removed together with the rocker arm assembly. To prevent the water pump end of the camshaft from popping up (from timing-chain tension) after the assembly is removed, have* an assistant hold the water pump end of the camshaft down, then reinstall the bearing cap on that end to hold it in place until reassembly.

Note 2: *While the camshaft bearing caps are off, inspect them, as well as the camshaft bearing journals, as described in Section 13.*

Removal

Refer to illustrations 5.3 and 5.4

1   Remove the valve cover (see Section 4).
2   Position the number one piston at Top Dead Centre (see Section 3).
3   Have an assistant hold down the water pump end of the camshaft, then loosen the camshaft bearing cap bolts 1/4-turn at a time each until the spring pressure is relieved **(see illustration)**. Do not remove the bolts.
4   On hydraulic lash adjuster-equipped engines, refit retaining clips (if available) onto

each rocker arm to retain the lash adjusters in the rocker arms as you lift the assembly off **(see illustration)**. If the clips are not available, tape the lash adjusters to the rocker arms with electrical tape or something similar. Lift the rocker arms and shaft assembly from the cylinder head. Reinstall the bearing cap at the water pump end to hold the camshaft in place.

Inspection

Refer to illustrations 5.5, 5.6a, 5.6b, 5.7a and 5.7b

5   To disassemble and inspect the rocker arm assembly, remove the retaining bolts and slip the rocker arms, springs and bearing caps off the shafts **(see illustration)**. Keep the parts in order so you can reassemble them in the same positions.
6   Thoroughly clean the parts and inspect them for wear and damage. Check the rocker arm faces that contact the camshaft **(see illustrations)**. Also, make sure the oil holes in the shafts are not plugged. Check the surfaces of the shafts that the rocker arms ride on, as well as the bearing surfaces inside the rocker arms, for scoring and excessive wear. Renew any parts that are damaged or excessively worn.
7   Remove the hydraulic lash adjusters from the rocker arms. Be sure to keep them in order so they can be returned to their original positions. Submerge each lash adjuster in a container filled with diesel fuel. Using a short section of rigid wire inserted into the hole at the top of the adjuster, lightly hold the steel ball down while you press the plunger in four or five times to bleed the air from the adjuster **(see illustration)**. Remove the wire and press down on the plunger, the plunger should not move (even slightly). If it moves,

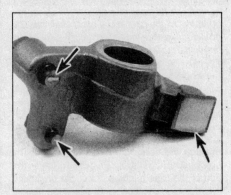

5.6a On mechanical adjuster rocker arms, check the contact faces and adjusting screw tips for wear or damage

5.6b Check the auto-lash-equipped rocker arm contact faces for wear or damage and make sure the oil hole is clear

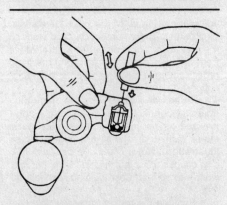

5.7a Submerge the lash adjuster in diesel fuel, press the ball off its seat with a section of wire and work the plunger up-and-down

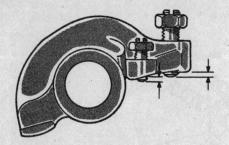

5.7b On mechanical lash adjustment rocker arms, back off the adjuster until they protrude 1 mm

IDENTIFICATION MARK (CENTER CAP ONLY)
(2: NO. 2, 3: NO. 3, 4: NO. 4)

ROCKER SHAFT, RIGHT

ROCKER SHAFT, LEFT

MATING MARK ON THE SHAFT

MATING MARK ON THE SHAFT

5.8 When installing the shafts in the bearing caps, align the mating mark on the bearing cap with the mating mark on the shaft

MATING MARK ON THE CAP

ARROW INDICATING THE FRONT

MATING MARK ON THE CAP

repeat the bleeding process and try again. If any adjuster cannot be pumped up solid, renew it. Keep the adjusters submerged in the diesel fuel until ready for refitting. On mechanical lash adjuster rocker arms, loosen the locknuts and back off the adjusters until they protrude 1 mm **(see illustration)**.

Refitting

Refer to illustration 5.8

8   Lubricate all components with engine assembly lube or engine oil and reassemble the shafts. When installing the rocker arms, shafts and springs, note the markings and the difference between the left and right side components and refit the waved washers in the correct direction **(see illustration 5.5)**. Place the marks in the end of the shaft directly in line with the marks on the bearing caps **(see illustration)** and keep them aligned until they are ready to be refitted onto the cylinder head.

9   Refit the lash adjusters into the rocker arms and secure them with clips or tape. Apply a thin coat of anaerobic sealant to the cylinder head mating surface of bearing cap number five and position the rocker arm assembly on the cylinder head. Make sure the camshaft oil seal is properly positioned and in good condition; renew it if necessary (see Section 11). Refit the mounting bolts finger tight. Check the numbered markings on the bearing caps to make sure the bearing caps are in the correct numerical sequence.

10   Tighten the camshaft bearing cap bolts on cap numbers 3, 2 and 4, 1/4 turn at a time and in sequence, to draw the camshaft down evenly. Tighten the bearing cap bolts on caps one and five. Tighten all the bolts, in sequence (3, 2, 4, 1, 5) to the torque listed in this Chapters Specifications.

11   On non-hydraulic lash adjuster models, adjust the valve clearances (cold) as described in Chapter 1. Temporarily reinstall the valve cover and run the engine until it is fully warmed up. Remove the valve cover and readjust the valves while the engine is still warm. Refit the valve cover.

12   On hydraulic valve adjuster-equipped models, refit the valve cover and run the engine until it is fully warmed up. Check for oil leaks and proper operation. If the lash adjusters are noisy, Increase the engine speed to approximately 3,000 rpm and hold it

there for one minute. Return the engine to idle, if the adjuster(s) do not quiet after repeating this procedure several times, renew the defective adjuster(s).

6   Valve springs, retainers and seals - renewal

Refer to illustrations 6.4, 6.9, 6.10 and 6.15
Note: *Broken valve springs and defective valve stem seals can be renewed without removing the cylinder heads. Two special tools and a compressed air source are normally required to perform this operation, so read through this Section carefully and rent or buy the tools before beginning the job. If compressed air isn't available, a length of nylon rope can be used to keep the valves from falling into the cylinder during this procedure.*

1   Refer to Section 4 and remove the valve cover from the cylinder head.

2   Remove the spark plug from the cylinder which has the defective component. If all of the valve stem seals are being renewed, all of the spark plugs should be removed.

3   Turn the crankshaft until the piston in the affected cylinder is at Top Dead Centre on the compression stroke (see Section 3). If you're renewing all of the valve stem seals, begin with cylinder number one and work on the valves for one cylinder at a time. Move from cylinder-to-cylinder following the firing order sequence (see this Chapter's Specifications).

4   Thread an adaptor into the spark plug hole and connect an air hose from a compressed air source to it. Most auto parts stores can supply the air hose adaptor **(see illustration)**. **Note:** *Many cylinder compression gauges utilise a screw-in fitting that may work with your air hose quick-disconnect fitting.*

5   Remove the rocker arm assembly (see Section 5).

6   Apply compressed air to the cylinder. **Warning:** *The piston may be forced down by compressed air, causing the crankshaft to*

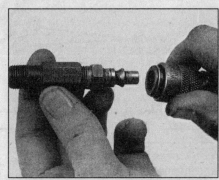

6.4 This is what the air hose adaptor that threads into the spark plug hole looks like - they're commonly available from auto parts stores

turn suddenly. If the spanner used when positioning the number one piston at TDC is still attached to the bolt in the crankshaft nose, it could cause damage or injury when the crankshaft moves.

7   The valves should be held in place by the air pressure.

8   If you don't have access to compressed air, an alternative method can be used. Position the piston at a point approximately 45-degrees before TDC on the compression stroke, then feed a long piece of nylon rope through the spark plug hole until it fills the combustion chamber. Be sure to leave the end of the rope hanging out of the engine so it can be removed easily. Use a large ratchet and socket to rotate the crankshaft in the normal direction of rotation until slight resistance is felt.

9   Stuff shop rags into the cylinder head holes around the valve spring area to prevent parts and tools from falling into the engine, then use a valve spring compressor to compress the spring. Remove the collets with small needle-nose pliers or a magnet **(see illustration)**.

10   Remove the spring retainer, shield and valve spring, then remove the valve guide seal **(see illustration)**. **Note:** *If air pressure fails to hold the valve in the closed position during this operation, the valve face or seat is probably damaged. If so, the cylinder head*

6.9 Compress the valve spring and remove the valve collets with a small magnet or needle-nose pliers

6.10 Remove the valve seal from the valve guide

6.15 Carefully tap the valve seal onto the valve guide with a seal refitting tool or a deep socket

will have to be removed for additional repair operations.

11 Wrap a rubber band or tape around the top of the valve stem so the valve won't fall into the combustion chamber, then release the air pressure. **Note:** *If a rope was used instead of air pressure, turn the crankshaft slightly in the direction opposite normal rotation.*

12 Inspect the valve stem for damage. Rotate the valve in the guide and check the end for eccentric movement, which would indicate that the valve is bent.

13 Move the valve up-and-down in the guide and make sure it doesn't bind. If the valve stem binds, either the valve is bent or the guide is damaged. In either case, the cylinder head will have to be removed for repair.

14 Reapply air pressure to the cylinder to retain the valve in the closed position, then remove the tape or rubber band from the valve stem. If a rope was used instead of air pressure, rotate the crankshaft in the normal direction of rotation until slight resistance is felt.

15 Lubricate the valve stem with engine oil and refit a new guide seal **(see illustration)**.

16 Refit the spring and retainer in position over the valve.

17 Compress the valve spring and carefully position the collets in the groove. Apply a small dab of grease to the inside of each collet to hold it in place.

18 Remove the pressure from the spring tool and make sure the collets are seated.

19 Disconnect the air hose and remove the adaptor from the spark plug hole. If a rope was used in place of air pressure, pull it out of the cylinder.

20 Refer to Section 5 and refit the rocker arm assembly.

21 Refit the spark plugs and connect the spark plug wires.

22 Refer to Section 4 and refit the valve cover.

23 Start and run the engine, then check for oil leaks and unusual sounds coming from the valve cover area.

7 Inlet manifold - removal and refitting

Warning: *Petrol is extremely flammable, so take extra precautions when you work on any part of the fuel system. Don't smoke or allow open flames or bare light bulbs near the work area, and don't work in a garage where a natural gas-type appliance (such as a water heater or clothes dryer) with a pilot light is present. If you spill any fuel on your skin, rinse it off immediately with soap and water. When you perform any kind of work on the fuel system, wear safety glasses and have a Class B type fire extinguisher on hand.*

Removal

Refer to illustration 7.8

1 Detach the cable from the negative battery terminal.

2 Drain the cooling system (see Chapter 1). Disconnect the upper radiator hose from the thermostat housing (see Chapter 3).

3 Remove the air cleaner (see Chapter 4A).

4 Clearly label, then detach all vacuum lines, electrical wiring and fuel lines from the carburettor and inlet manifold. Cap the fuel lines.

5 Detach the accelerator cable from the throttle linkage (see Chapter 4A).

6 Remove the carburettor from the inlet manifold, if desired (see Chapter 4A).

7 Remove the coolant hoses from the inlet manifold.

8 Remove the inlet manifold bolts **(see illustration)** and remove the manifold from the engine.

Refitting

9 Clean the inlet manifold and cylinder head surface, removing all traces of gasket material.

10 Check the mating surfaces of the manifold for flatness with a precision straightedge and feeler gauge. Refer to this Chapter's Specifications for the warpage limit.

11 Inspect the manifold for cracks and distortion.

12 If the manifold is cracked or warped, renew it or see if it can be resurfaced/repaired at an automotive machine shop.

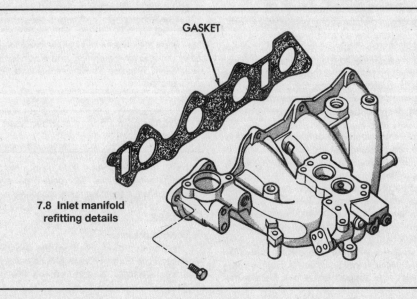

7.8 Inlet manifold refitting details

GASKET

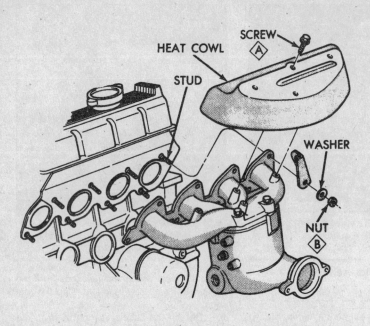

8.6 Exhaust manifold refitting details

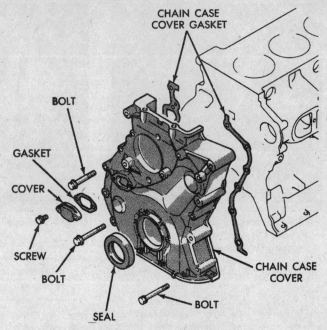

9.7 Front chain cover refitting details

13   Check carefully for any stripped or broken inlet manifold bolts. Renew any defective bolts.
14   Apply a thin coat of RTV sealant to both sides of the gasket, around the water passages. Place the gasket onto the cylinder head.
15   Refit the inlet manifold and tighten the bolts finger-tight. Starting at the centre and working out in both directions, tighten the bolts in a criss-cross pattern until the torque listed in this Chapter's Specifications is reached.
16   The remainder of the refitting procedure is the reverse of removal.

8   Exhaust manifold - removal and refitting

Removal

Refer to illustration 8.6
1   Disconnect the negative battery cable from the battery.
2   Remove the air cleaner (see Chapter 4). Remove the carburettor air heater from the exhaust manifold.
3   Remove the secondary air injection pipe from the exhaust manifold. Detach the air injection valve and position the valve and pipe aside.
4   Remove the heat cowl and the heat shield from the manifold. Be sure to soak the bolts and nuts with penetrating oil before attempting to remove them from the manifold.
5   Raise the front of the vehicle and support it securely on jackstands. Remove the exhaust pipe support brace bolt. Detach the

exhaust pipe from the exhaust manifold. Apply penetrating oil to the fastener threads if they are difficult to remove.
6   Remove the exhaust manifold nuts **(see illustration)** and detach the exhaust manifold.

Refitting

7   Inspect the exhaust manifold for cracks, damage or distortion.
8   Discard the old gaskets and use a scraper to clean the gasket mating surfaces on the exhaust manifold and cylinder head. Place a new gasket onto the cylinder head.
9   Place the exhaust manifold in position on the cylinder head and refit the nuts. Starting at the centre, tighten the nuts in a criss-cross pattern until the torque listed in this Chapter's Specifications is reached.
10   The remainder of refitting is the reverse of removal.
11   Start the engine and check for exhaust leaks between the manifold and the cylinder head and between the manifold and the exhaust pipe.

9   Front chain cover - removal and refitting

Note: *If the timing chain is to be removed, position the engine on TDC for number one cylinder before beginning this procedure.*

Removal

Refer to illustration 9.7
1   Disconnect the cable from the negative terminal of the battery. Drain the cooling system (see Chapter 1) and remove the air

cleaner assembly.
2   Remove the drivebelts. Remove the alternator, power steering pump and air conditioning compressor, it equipped, and lay them aside. **Warning:** *The air conditioning system is under high pressure - do not disconnect the hoses!*
3   Remove the valve cover (see Section 4). Remove the distributor (see Chapter 5) and remove the two front cylinder head-to-front chain cover bolts. **Caution:** *Do not loosen any other cylinder head bolts.*
4   Raise the vehicle and support it securely on jackstands. Remove the left-side splash shield. Drain the engine oil and remove the sump (see Section 15) and the oil pump pick-up tube.
5   Position a floor jack with a wood block on the jack head under the engine. Raise the engine slightly to support the weight and remove the left-side engine mount (see Section 19). Remove the engine mounting plate and any brackets attached to the front cover.
6   Lower the engine, remove the crankshaft pulley bolt and prise the pulley off. **Note:** *It may be necessary to remove the through-bolts from the front and rear roll insulators, allowing the engine to drop for sufficient clearance.*
7   Remove the bolts attaching the front cover to the engine block **(see illustration)**. Note the location of each bolt so they can be returned to the same location from which they were removed. Tap the cover with a soft-faced hammer to break the gasket seal, then remove the cover from the engine block. **Caution:** *Levering between the cover and the engine block can damage the gasket sealing surfaces. Do not damage the cylinder head gasket.*

2A

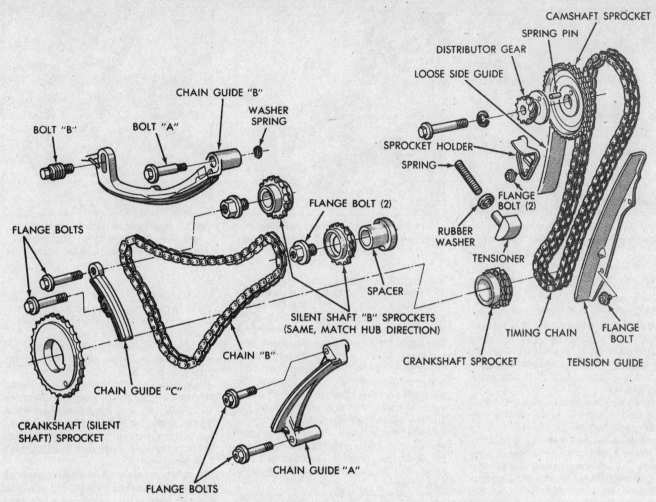

10.4 Balance shaft chain, timing chain, sprockets and guides refitting details

Refitting

8 Thoroughly clean the front cover and sump and remove all old gasket material and sealant from the front cover, sump and engine block. Clean the mating surfaces with lacquer thinner or acetone. Make sure the threaded holes in the engine block are clean and dry.

9 Renew the crankshaft front oil seal (see Section 12).

10 Using a new gasket and RTV-type sealant, fit the front chain cover onto the engine. Refit the bolts in a crisscross pattern and tighten them to the torque listed in this Chapter's Specifications. If the gasket protrudes beyond the top or bottom of the case and engine block, trim off the excess with a razor blade.

11 Refit the engine mounting plate onto the front chain cover.

12 Apply a thin layer of clean moly-based grease to the seal contact surface of the crankshaft pulley, then slide it onto the crankshaft. Refit the bolt and tighten it to the torque listed in this Chapter's Specifications.

13 The remainder of refitting is the reverse of removal.

10 Balance shaft chain, timing chain and sprockets - removal, inspection and refitting

Removal

Refer to illustration 10.4

1 Disconnect the cable from the negative terminal of the battery. Drain the cooling system (see Chapter 1) and remove the air cleaner assembly.

2 Position the engine on TDC for number one cylinder. Remove the distributor (see Chapter 5) and remove the front chain cover (see Section 9).

3 Loosen the balance shaft and oil pump sprocket bolts.

4 Loosen the balance shaft chain tension adjusting bolt, release the tension on the chain and remove the chain guides **(see illustration)**. Note the location of each bolt so that it can be returned to the same location from which it was removed.

5 Remove the balance shaft sprocket bolts and slide the crankshaft sprocket, the balance shaft sprockets and the chain off the engine as an assembly. Do not lose the keys that index the sprockets to the shafts.

6 Remove the camshaft sprocket bolt and distributor drive gear. Remove the sprocket holder and the right and left timing chain guides from the front of the engine block.

7 Depress the timing chain tensioner plunger on the oil pump and slide the camshaft sprocket, the crankshaft sprocket and the timing chain off the engine as an assembly. Do not lose the key that indexes the crankshaft. Remove the timing chain tensioner plunger and spring from the oil pump.

Inspection

8 Inspect the sprocket teeth for wear and damage. Check the sprocket cushion rings and ring guides (balance shaft sprockets only) for wear and damage. Rotate the cushion rings and check for smooth operation. Check the chains for cracked plates and pitted or worn rollers. Check the chain tensioner rubber shoe for wear and the tensioner spring for cracks and deterioration. Measure the free length of the tensioner spring and compare it to this Chapter's Specifications. Check the chain guides for wear and damage. Renew any defective parts.

10.10 Lubricate the timing chain tensioner plunger and refit it in the oil pump bore

10.11 Refit the timing chain sprocket on the end of the crankshaft with the wide shoulder facing out

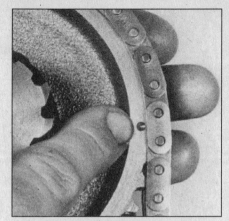

10.12 Mesh the camshaft sprocket and the timing chain with the mark on the sprocket directly opposite the plated link on the chain

Refitting

Refer to illustrations 10.10, 10.11, 10.12, 10.13a, 10.13b, 10.18a, 10.18b and 10.19

9   Refit the sprocket holder and the right and left timing chain guides onto the engine block. Tighten the bolts securely. Coat the entire length of the chain contact surfaces of the guides with clean, high-quality moly-based grease.

10   Make sure the crankshaft is positioned at Top Dead Centre (TDC) for number one cylinder (see Section 3). Apply a layer of clean moly-based grease or engine assembly lube to the timing chain tensioner plunger and refit the tensioner spring and plunger loosely into the oil pump body **(see illustration)**.

11   Position the timing chain crankshaft sprocket on the end of the crankshaft with the wide shoulder facing out **(see illustration)**. Align the keyway in the sprocket with the key on the crankshaft and press the sprocket on until it's flush with the end of the crankshaft only.

12   Refit the camshaft sprocket onto the chain, aligning the plated link on the chain with the marked tooth on the sprocket **(see illustration)**. Position the camshaft with the

dowel pin at 12 o'clock.

13   Lower the chain through the opening in the cylinder head and onto the crankshaft sprocket, aligning the plated link on the chain with the marked tooth on the sprocket **(see illustration)**. Press the crankshaft sprocket all the way onto the crankshaft while depressing the chain tensioner, so the chain fits into place in the guides and refit the camshaft sprocket onto the camshaft. Make sure the plated links and mating marks are properly aligned **(see illustration)**.

14   Refit the distributor drive gear aligning the hole in the gear with the camshaft dowel pin. Refit the camshaft sprocket bolt and tighten it to the torque listed in this Chapter's Specifications.

15   Press the balance shaft chain crankshaft sprocket onto the front of the crankshaft, aligning the keyway in the sprocket with the key on the shaft.

16   Place the balance shaft chain over the two small sprockets. The dished or chamfered side of the balance shaft sprocket must

face out while the dished or chamfered side of the oil pump sprocket must facing in. Align the plated links on the chain with the mating marks stamped into the sprockets.

17   Place the chain under the crankshaft sprocket, aligning the plated link with the mating mark in the crankshaft sprocket while simultaneously installing the small sprockets. Recheck the position of the mating marks on the chain and sprockets **(see illustration 10.19)**. Apply Loctite 242 to the threads, refit the balance shaft sprocket bolts and tighten them to the torque listed in this Chapter's Specifications.

18   Refit the balance shaft chain guides **(see illustrations)** and tighten the mounting bolts for chain guides A and C securely. Note the difference between the upper and lower chain guide B mounting bolts. Make sure they are refitted in the proper location. Leave the adjusting bolt for chain guide B loose, apply Loctite 242 to the pivot bolt threads, make sure the washer is in place and tighten the pivot to the torque listed in this Chapter's Specifications.

19   Adjust the chain slack as follows: rotate the balance shafts so the chain slack is col-

10.13a Installing the timing chain on the crankshaft sprocket with the plated link opposite the sprocket mark

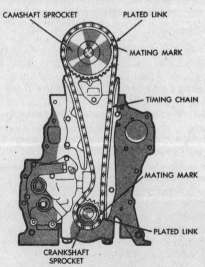

CAMSHAFT SPROCKET   PLATED LINK

MATING MARK

TIMING CHAIN

MATING MARK

PLATED LINK

CRANKSHAFT
SPROCKET

10.13b Correct timing chain and sprocket relationship

10.18a Refit the balance shaft chain guide C

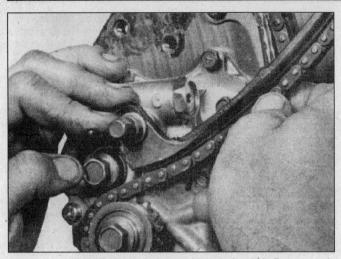

10.18b Refit the balance shaft chain guide B

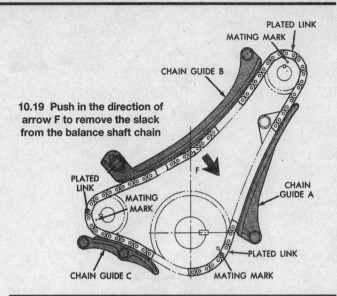

10.19 Push in the direction of arrow F to remove the slack from the balance shaft chain

lected between the sprockets. Press firmly on chain guide B with your finger tips in the direction of arrow F **(see illustration)**, then release the pressure and lightly press down on the chain guide while tightening the adjusting bolt. Do not use any tools to prise the chain guide, excessive tension will cause chain guide wear and chain noise.

20 Apply a coat of clean moly-based grease to the chain and chain guides.

21 Recheck the balance shaft chain and timing chain mating marks and the balance shaft chain tension; if all are correct, refit the front cover.

22 The remainder of refitting is the reverse of removal.

11 Camshaft oil seal - renewal

Refer to illustration 11.3

1 Remove the rocker arm assembly (see Section 5).

2 Remove the camshaft oil seal from the cylinder head.

3 Apply a thin coat of RTV sealant to the outer diameter of the new seal and refit the seal onto the cylinder head as shown **(see illustration)**.

4 Refit the rocker arm assembly (see Section 5).

5 Refit the valve cover (see Section 4).

12 Crankshaft front oil seal - renewal

Refer to illustration 12.3

1 Remove the drivebelts (see Chapter 1).

2 Remove the bolt in the centre of the crankshaft pulley and use two large screwdrivers to prise the pulley off. **Note:** *It may be necessary to remove the left-side engine mount (see Section 19) and lower the engine to gain clearance for pulley removal.*

3 Carefully prise the seal out of the front cover with a seal removal tool or a screwdriver **(see illustration)**. Don't scratch the seal bore or damage the crankshaft in the process (if the crankshaft is damaged, the new seal will end up leaking).

4 Clean the bore in the timing chain cover and coat the outer edge of the new seal with engine oil or multi-purpose grease. Using a socket with an outside diameter slightly smaller than the outside diameter of the seal, carefully drive the seal into place with a hammer. If a socket is not available, a short section of a large diameter pipe will work. Check the seal after refitting to be sure the spring did not pop out.

5 Refitting is the reverse of removal.

6 Run the engine and check for leaks.

13 Camshaft - removal, inspection and refitting

Removal

Refer to illustration 13.7

1 Disconnect the cable from the negative battery terminal.

2 Remove the valve cover (see Section 4).

3 Position the number one piston at Top Dead Centre (see Section 3).

4 Remove the distributor (see Chapter 5).

5 Remove the camshaft sprocket bolt and distributor drive gear. Using two large screwdrivers, carefully prise the camshaft sprocket off the camshaft and support it on the

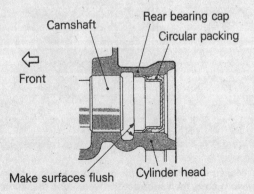

11.3 Camshaft oil seal refitting details

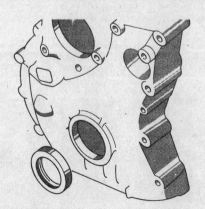

12.3 Crankshaft front oil seal refitting details

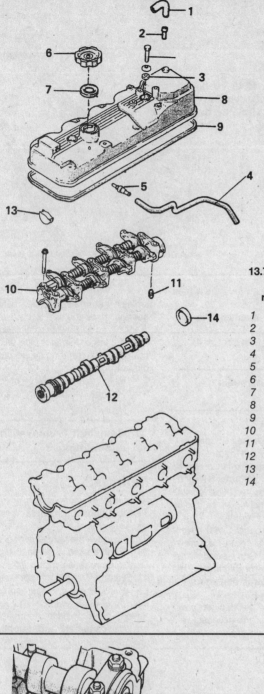

13.7 An exploded view of the camshaft and related components

1   Breather hose
2   Fitting
3   Oil seal
4   PCV hose
5   PCV valve
6   Oil filter cap
7   Oil filter cap seal
8   Valve cover
9   Valve cover gasket
10 Rocker arm assembly
11 Hydraulic lash adjuster
12 Camshaft
13 Semi-circular seal
14 Camshaft oil seal

sprocket holder. **Caution:** *Do not remove the timing chain from the camshaft sprocket or rotate the crankshaft with the camshaft sprocket removed from the camshaft.*

6   Remove the rocker arm assembly (see Section 5).

7   Lift the camshaft off the cylinder head **(see illustration)**. Remove and discard the seal.

Inspection

Refer to illustrations 13.8 and 13.11

8   To check camshaft endplay:

a)   *Refit the camshaft and secure it with bearing caps 1 and 5.*

b)   *Mount a dial indicator on the cylinder head* **(see illustration)**.

c)   *Using a large screwdriver as a lever at the opposite end, move the camshaft forward-and-backward and note the dial indicator reading.*

d)   *Compare the reading with the endplay listed in this Chapter's Specifications.*

e)   *If the indicated reading is higher, either the camshaft or the cylinder head is worn. Renew parts as necessary.*

9   To check camshaft runout:

a)   *Support the camshaft with a pair of V-blocks and attach a dial indicator with the stem resting against the centre bearing journal on the camshaft.*

b)   *Rotate the camshaft and note the indicated runout.*

c)   *Compare the results to the camshaft runout listed in this Chapter's Specifications.*

d)   *If the indicated runout exceeds the specified runout, renew the camshaft.*

10   Check the camshaft bearing journals and bearing caps for scoring and signs of wear. Check the bearing oil clearance as follows:

a)   *Measure and record the camshaft journals with a micrometer.*

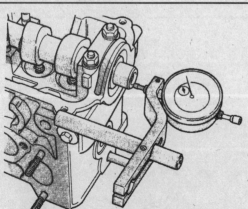

13.8 To check camshaft endplay, set up a dial indicator with the gauge plunger touching the nose of the camshaft

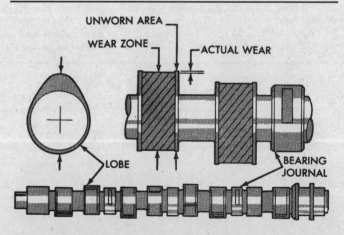

13.11 Measure the height of the camshaft lobes at the wear zone and unworn area, then subtract the wear zone measurement from the unworn area measurement to get the actual wear - compare the wear to the limit listed in this Chapter's Specifications

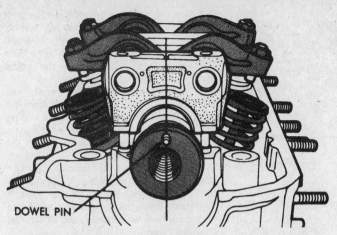

13.15 Refit the camshaft with the dowel pin at 12 o'clock

14.12 Use a gasket scraper to remove the cylinder head gasket

b) *Refit the bearing caps onto the cylinder head and measure and record the inside diameter of each journal using an inside micrometer.*

c) *Subtract the camshaft journal diameter from the bearing journal inside diameter to determine the oil clearance.*

If the oil clearance is greater than that listed in this Chapter's Specifications, renew the camshaft. If the bearing caps are worn, renew the cylinder head with a new or rebuilt unit.

11 Check the cam lobes for wear:

a) *Check the toe and ramp areas of each cam lobe for score marks and uneven wear. Also check for flaking and pitting.*

b) *If there's wear on the toe or the ramp, renew the camshaft, but first try to find the cause of the wear. Look for abrasive substances in the oil and inspect the oil pump and oil passages for blockage. Lobe wear is usually caused by inadequate lubrication or dirty oil.*

c) *Using a micrometer, calculate the lobe wear* **(see illustration)**. *If the lobe wear is greater than listed in this Chapter's Specifications, renew the camshaft.*

12 Inspect the rocker arms for wear, galling and pitting of the contact surfaces.

13 If any of the conditions described above are noted, the cylinder head is probably lacking sufficient lubrication, make sure you track down the cause of this problem (low oil level, low oil pump capacity, clogged oil passage, etc.) before installing a new cylinder head or camshaft.

Refitting

Refer to illustration 13.15

14 Thoroughly clean the camshaft, the bearing surfaces in the cylinder head and bearing caps and the rocker arms. Remove all sludge and dirt. Wipe off all components with a clean, lint-free cloth.

15 Lubricate the camshaft bearing surfaces in the cylinder head and the bearing journals and lobes on the camshaft with assembly lube or moly-base grease. Carefully lower the camshaft into position with the dowel pin pointing up **(see illustration)**. **Caution:** *Failure to adequately lubricate the camshaft and related components can cause serious damage to bearing and friction surfaces during the first few seconds after engine start-up, when the oil pressure is low or nonexistent.*

16 Refit a new oil seal onto the cylinder head (see Section 11).

17 Apply a thin coat of assembly lube or moly-base grease to the bearing surfaces of the camshaft bearing caps. Lubricate the contact surfaces on the top of the rocker arms with assembly lube or moly-base grease.

18 Refit the rocker arm assembly (see Section 5). Make sure you apply anaerobic-type sealant to bearing cap no. 5 and tighten the rocker arm assembly in sequence to the torque listed in this Chapter's Specifications.

19 Refit the camshaft sprocket, timing chain and distributor drive gear. Tighten the camshaft sprocket bolt to the torque listed in this Chapter's Specifications.

20 Refit the valve cover. The remainder of refitting is the reverse of removal.

14 Cylinder head - removal and refitting

Caution: *Allow the engine to cool completely before beginning this procedure.*

Removal

1 Disconnect the negative cable from the battery. Position the number one piston at Top Dead Centre (see Section 3).

2 Drain the cooling system and disconnect the upper radiator hose from the thermostat housing (see Chapter 3). Remove the spark plugs (see Chapter 1).

3 Disconnect the fuel lines from the carburettor and disconnect the throttle cable from the linkage (see Chapter 4).

4 Remove the inlet and exhaust manifolds (see Sections 7 and 8). **Note:** *If you're only renewing the cylinder head gasket, it isn't necessary to remove the manifolds. If you leave the manifolds attached, you may need an assistant to help lift the cylinder head off the engine, since it will be quite heavy. If the manifolds are to remain attached to the cylinder head, remove all vacuum hoses, coolant hoses and electrical connectors from the inlet manifold and cylinder head (be sure to mark the hoses and connectors.*

5 Disconnect the exhaust pipe from the exhaust manifold and remove the air injection pipe and valve (if equipped).

6 Remove the valve cover (see Section 4). Remove the distributor (see Chapter 5), including the cap and wires.

7 Remove the camshaft sprocket bolt and distributor drive gear. Prise the sprocket off the camshaft and support it on the sprocket holder (see Section 13).

8 Loosen the cylinder head bolts in 1/4-turn increments, following the reverse of the recommended tightening sequence **(see illustration 14.16)**, until they can be removed by hand. Note the location of each bolt so it can be returned to the same location on refitting.

9 Lift the cylinder head off the engine. If resistance is felt, don't prise between the cylinder head and engine block gasket mating surfaces - damage to the mating surfaces will result. Instead, prise against the casting protrusions on the sides of the cylinder head. Set the cylinder head on wood blocks to prevent damage to the gasket sealing surfaces. **Caution:** *Be careful not to disturb the timing chain and sprocket when lifting the cylinder head off. After the cylinder head is removed, secure the timing chain and sprocket to the sprocket support, keeping tension on the chain. If the timing chain is disturbed it will become necessary to remove the front cover to restore timing. Do not rotate the crankshaft with the sprocket and chain removed from the camshaft.*

10 Cylinder head disassembly and inspection procedures are covered in detail in Chapter 2, Part B. Check the cylinder head for warpage.

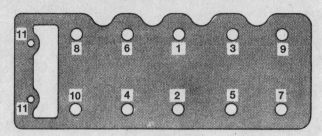

14.16 Cylinder head bolt TIGHTENING sequence

Refitting

Refer to illustrations 14.12 and 14.16

11   The mating surfaces of the cylinder head and engine block must be perfectly clean when the cylinder head is refitted.

12   Use a gasket scraper to remove all traces of carbon and old gasket material **(see illustration)**, then clean the mating surfaces with lacquer thinner or acetone. If there's oil on the mating surfaces when the cylinder head is refitted, the gasket may not seal correctly and leaks may develop. When working on the engine block, stuff the cylinders with clean shop rags to keep out debris. Use a vacuum cleaner to remove material that falls into the cylinders. Since the cylinder head is made of aluminium, aggressive scraping can cause damage. Be extra careful not to nick or gouge the mating surfaces with the scraper. Gasket removal solvents are available from most auto parts stores and may prove helpful.

13   Check the engine block and cylinder head mating surfaces for nicks, deep scratches and other damage. If damage is slight, it can be removed with a file; if it's excessive, machining may be the only alternative.

14   Use a tap of the correct size to chase the threads in the cylinder head bolt holes. Clean and dry each bolt hole, if any fluid remains in a bolt hole damage to the engine block may result when the bolts are tightened. Mount each cylinder head bolt in a vice and run a die down the threads to remove corrosion and restore the threads. Dirt, corrosion, sealant and damaged threads will affect torque readings.

15   Apply a dab of RTV sealant at the front cover-to-engine block junction and place a new gasket on the engine block. Check to see if there are any markings (such as "TOP") on the gasket that say how it is to be refitted. Set the cylinder head in position.

16   Lightly oil the cylinder head bolt threads and refit the bolts. Tighten the cylinder head bolts in three increments, following the recommended sequence **(see illustration)**, to the torque's listed in this Chapter's Specifications. Note that the cylinder head-to-front cover bolts are tightened to a different torque specification.

17   Refit the timing chain and sprocket. Refit the distributor drive gear and tighten the camshaft sprocket bolt to the torque listed in this Chapter's Specifications.

18   Reinstall the remaining parts in the reverse order of removal.

19   Be sure to refill the cooling system and check all fluid levels.

20   Rotate the crankshaft clockwise slowly by hand through two complete revolutions. Recheck the camshaft timing marks (see Section 10). **Caution:** *If you feel any resistance while turning the engine over, stop and recheck the camshaft timing. The valves may be hitting the pistons.*

21   Start the engine and check the ignition timing and idle speed (see Chapter 1).

22   Run the engine until normal operating temperature is reached. Check for leaks and proper operation.

15   Sump - removal and refitting

Note: *The following procedure is based on the assumption that the engine is in the vehicle.*

Removal

Refer to illustration 15.5

1   Detach the cable from the negative battery terminal.

2   Raise the vehicle and support it securely on jackstands.

3   Drain the oil and renew the oil filter (see Chapter 1).

4   Disconnect the exhaust pipe from the exhaust manifold, lower and support the exhaust pipe.

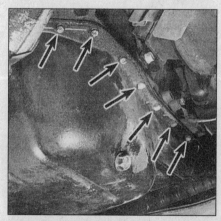

15.5 Remove the bolts from the sump

5   Remove the bolts securing the sump to the engine block **(see illustration)**. Tap on the sump with a soft-face hammer to break the gasket seal, then detach the sump from the engine. Don't prise between the engine block and sump mating surfaces.

6   Using a gasket scraper, remove all traces of old gasket and/or sealant from the engine block and sump. Clean the mating surfaces with lacquer thinner or acetone. Make sure the threaded bolt holes in the engine block are clean.

7   Clean the sump with solvent and dry it thoroughly. Check the gasket flanges for distortion, particularly around the bolt holes. If necessary, place the sump on a wood block and use a hammer to flatten and restore the gasket surfaces.

Refitting

8   Coat both sides of the sump gasket with gasket sealant and place the gasket on the engine block.

9   Carefully place the sump in position.

10   Refit the bolts and tighten them in 1/4-turn increments to the torque listed in this Chapter's Specifications. Start with the bolts closest to the centre of the sump and work out in a spiral pattern. Don't overtighten them or leakage may occur.

11   The remainder of refitting is the reverse of removal. Add oil, run the engine and check for oil leaks.

16   Oil pump - removal, inspection and refitting

Removal

Refer to illustration 16.3

1   Disconnect the cable from the negative battery terminal.

2   Remove the sump (see Section 15). Remove the front chain cover, the balance shaft chain and the timing chain (see Sections 9 and 10). **Note:** *Loosen the oil pump drive sprocket bolt and the balance shaft bolt before removing the balance shaft chain.*

3   Remove the oil pump mounting bolts and remove the oil pump assembly **(see illustration)**.

Inspection

Refer to illustrations 16.5, 16.6a 16.6b, 16.7, 16.8, 16.9 and 16.11

4   Remove the bolts and lift off the oil pump cover.

5   Check the oil pump bearing clearance on each gear **(see illustration)**.

6   Using a feeler gauge and a straightedge, check the endplay of the driven gear and the drive gear **(see illustrations)**.

7   Check the clearance between the driven gear and the pump housing with a feeler gauge **(see illustration)**.

8   Check the clearance between the drive gear and the pump housing with a feeler gauge **(see illustration)**.

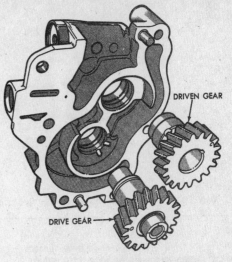

16.5 Check oil pump bearing clearance on each gear

2A

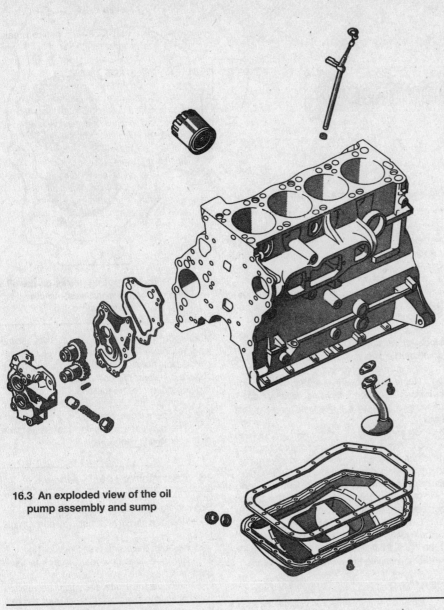

16.3 An exploded view of the oil pump assembly and sump

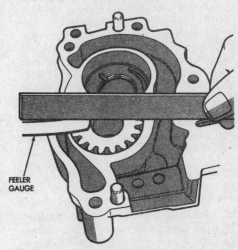

16.6a Use a straightedge and a feeler gauge to check the endplay on the driven gear

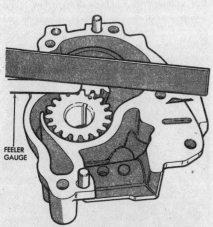

16.6b Use a straightedge and a feeler gauge to check the endplay on the drive gear

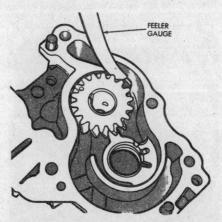

16.7 Check the driven gear-to-housing clearance

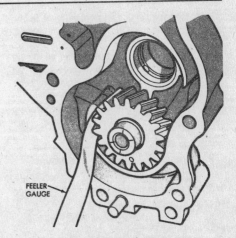

16.8 Check the drive gear-to-housing clearance

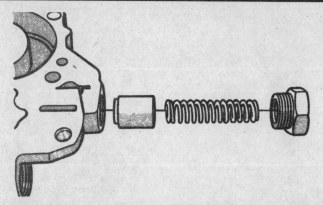

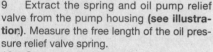

16.9 Remove the oil pressure relief valve spring and measure its free length

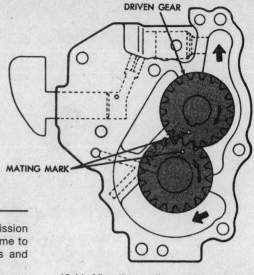

16.11 Align the mating marks on the oil pump gears when assembling the oil pump

9   Extract the spring and oil pump relief valve from the pump housing **(see illustration)**. Measure the free length of the oil pressure relief valve spring.
10   Compare the measurements to this Chapter's Specifications. If any of them are outside the limits, renew the pump.
11   Lubricate the gears and bearing surfaces with clean engine oil. Refit the gears into the body with the mating marks aligned **(see illustration)**. Lubricate the oil pressure relief valve and refit the relief valve and spring assembly. Tighten the relief valve cap to the torque listed in this Chapter's Specifications. Refit the cover onto the pump body and tighten the screws securely.
12   Check the tensioner plunger, spring and rubber damper for scoring, wear or damage. Lubricate the tensioner and make sure it slides smoothly in the bore.

Refitting

13   Thoroughly clean the gasket material from the pump cover and engine block. While holding the pump in a vertical position apply approximately 10 cc of engine oil into the delivery port. Refit the pump, with a new gasket, onto the engine block, engaging the balance shaft key with the oil pump driven gear.
14   While holding the pump securely in place, refit the bolts and tighten them to the torque listed in this Chapter's Specifications.
15   Refit a new gasket on the oil pick-up tube, if removed, **(see illustration 16.3)** and Refit the oil pick-up tube and screen. Tighten the bolts to the torque listed in this Chapter's Specifications.
16   The remainder of refitting is the reverse of removal.

17   Flywheel/driveplate - removal and refitting

Removal

Refer to illustrations 17.3
1   Raise the vehicle and support it securely on jackstands, then refer to Chapter 7 and remove the transmission.
2   Remove the pressure plate and clutch

disc (see Chapter 8) (manual transmission equipped vehicles). Now is a good time to check/renew the clutch components and pilot bearing.
3   Make alignment marks on the flywheel/driveplate and crankshaft **(see illustration)** to ensure correct alignment during reinstallation.
4   Remove the bolts that secure the flywheel/driveplate to the crankshaft. If the crankshaft turns, use an appropriate tool to hold the starter ring gear.
5   Remove the flywheel/driveplate from the crankshaft. Since the flywheel is fairly heavy, be sure to support it while removing the last bolt.
6   Clean the flywheel to remove grease and oil. Inspect the surface for cracks, rivet grooves, burned areas and score marks. Light scoring can be removed with emery cloth. Check for cracked and broken ring gear teeth. Lay the flywheel on a flat surface and use a straightedge to check for warpage.
7   Clean and inspect the mating surfaces of the flywheel/driveplate and the crankshaft. If the crankshaft rear seal is leaking, renew it before reinstalling the flywheel/driveplate.

Refitting

8   Position the flywheel/driveplate against the crankshaft. Be sure to align the marks

made during removal. Note that some engines have an alignment dowel or staggered bolt holes to ensure correct refitting. Before installing the bolts, apply thread locking compound to the threads.
9   Tighten the bolts to the torque listed in this Chapter's Specifications.
10   The remainder of refitting is the reverse of the removal procedure.

18   Rear main oil seal - renewal

Refer to illustrations 18.4, 18.5 and 18.6
1   Remove the transmission (see Chapter 7).
2   Remove the sump (see Section 15).
3   Remove the flywheel/driveplate (see Section 17).
4   Remove the bolts securing the rear oil seal retainer to the engine block and remove the retainer and seal **(see illustration)**. Clean the seal retainer and engine block of all gas-

17.3 Mark the relationship of the flywheel or driveplate to the crankshaft before removal

18.4 Remove the rear main oil seal retainer bolts (arrows)

18.5 Support the retainer on two wood blocks and drive out the seal from the backside

18.6 Drive the new seal into the retainer until it's flush - make sure it's square in the bore

ket material.

5   Support the retainer between two wood blocks and drive the seal out of the retainer from the backside **(see illustration)**.

6   Drive the new seal into the retainer from the front side until the seal face is flush with the retainer **(see illustration)**. Make sure you have the seal positioned correctly (with the seal lip facing in).

7   Lubricate the seal and crankshaft with clean engine oil. Refit the separator (if equipped) onto the retainer with the oil hole at the bottom and the lugs facing toward the engine.

8   Coat both sides of a new gasket with gasket sealant and place the gasket on the engine block. Place the retainer and seal onto the crankshaft, carefully working the seal lip onto the crankshaft.

9   Refit the bolts and tighten them securely. The remainder of refitting is the reverse of removal.

19 Engine mounts - check and renewal

1   Engine mounts seldom require attention, but broken or deteriorated mounts should be renewed immediately or the added strain placed on the driveline components may cause damage or wear.

Check

Refer to illustration 19.4

2   During the check, the engine must be raised slightly to remove the weight from the mounts.

3   Raise the vehicle and support it securely on jackstands, then position a jack under the engine sump. Place a large wood block between the jack head and the sump, then carefully raise the engine just enough to take the weight off the mounts. **Warning:** *DO NOT place any part of your body under the engine when it's supported only by a jack!*

4   Check the mount insulators **(see illustration)** to see if the rubber is cracked, hardened or separated from the metal plates. Sometimes the rubber will split right down the centre.

5   Check for relative movement between the mount plates and the engine or frame (use a large screwdriver or lever to attempt to move the mounts). If movement is noted,

2A

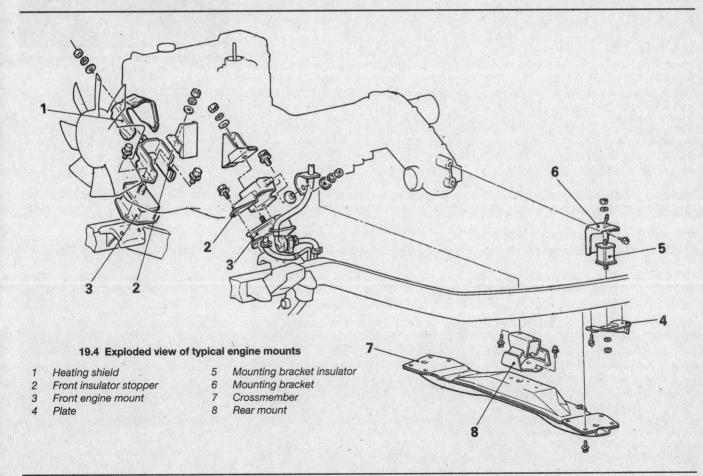

19.4 Exploded view of typical engine mounts

1 Heating shield	5 Mounting bracket insulator
2 Front insulator stopper	6 Mounting bracket
3 Front engine mount	7 Crossmember
4 Plate	8 Rear mount

19.8a Removing the mount - note the alignment pin (arrow)

19.8b Separating the roll restrictor and mount

lower the engine and tighten the mount fasteners.

6   Rubber preservative should be applied to the insulators to slow deterioration.

Renewal

Refer to illustrations 19.8a, 19.8b and 19.8c

7   Disconnect the negative battery cable from the battery, then raise the vehicle and support it securely on jackstands and support the engine with a floor jack as described above.

8   Raise the engine slightly and remove the insulator through-bolt **(see illustrations)**.

9   Remove the fasteners and detach the insulator from the frame or bracket.

10 Refitting is the reverse of removal. Use thread locking compound on the mount bolts and be sure to tighten them securely.

19.8c Removing the mount brackets from the engine block

Chapter 2 Part B
V6 engines

Contents

2B

Specifications

General

SOHC engine

Displacement	3.0 litres
Bore	91.1 mm
Stroke	76 mm
Compression ratio	8.9:1
Firing order	1-2-3-4-5-6

DOHC 6G74 engine

Displacement	3.5 litres
Bore	93 mm
Stroke	85.8 mm
Compression ratio	9.5:1
Firing order	1-2-3-4-5-6

Cylinder numbers (front to rear)

Right (driver's side)	1-3-5
Left (passenger's side)	2-4-6

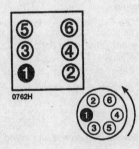

Cylinder location and distributor rotation

The blackened terminal shown on the distributor cap indicates the Number One spark plug wire position

Camshaft and related components

SOHC engine

Camshaft runout limit	0.10 mm
Lobe height	41.25 mm
Lobe wear limit	0.5 mm

DOHC engine

Camshaft runout limit	0.10 mm
Lobe height	
Intake	35.20 mm
Exhaust	34.91 mm
Lobe wear limit	0.5 mm

Camshaft journal diameter

SOHC	34 mm
DOHC	26 mm
Camshaft bearing oil clearance	0.05 to 0.09 mm
Camshaft endplay (all engines)	11 mm

Oil pump

Case-to-outer rotor clearance	0.06 to 0.18 mm
Rotor end clearance	0.04 to 0.010 mm
Case-to-inner rotor clearance (maximum wear limit)	0.18 mm

Torque specifications

	Nm
SOHC rocker arm shaft bolts	9 to 21
DOHC camshaft bearing cap bolts	
Front and rear	20
No. 2, 3, 4	11
Inlet manifold nuts/bolts	15
Distributor drive adaptor bolts	13
Engine mounts	
Stopper bolts	40
Front insulator bolts	40
Rear insulator-to-crossmember bolts	18 to 25
Heat shield bolts	30 to 40
Transfer support bracket bolts	18 to 25
Exhaust manifold nuts	15 to 22
Exhaust manifold heat shield bolts	12 to 15
Exhaust pipe-to-manifold bolts	30 to 40
Crankshaft vibration damper-to-crankshaft bolt	
SOHC engine	150 to 160
DOHC engine	177 to 180
Camshaft sprocket bolt	90
Timing belt cover bolts	10 to 12
Timing belt tensioner locking nut or bolt	
SOHC engine	25
DOHC engine	48
Cylinder head bolt	
SOHC engine	
1990 and earlier	65 to 72
1991 and later	76 to 83
DOHC engine	103 to 113
Flywheel/driveplate mounting bolts*	73 to 77
Sump mounting bolts	
SOHC engine	40
DOHC engine	
Upper	6
Lower	10 to 12
Oil pump assembly mounting bolts	12 to 15
Oil pump relief plug	40 to 50
Oil pick-up tube-to-pump bolts	15 to 22
Oil pump cover bolts	8 to 12
Valve cover bolts	
SOHC engine	9
DOHC engine	3 to 4

Apply a thread locking compound to the threads prior to refitting

1   General information

This Part of Chapter 2 is devoted to in-vehicle repair procedures for the SOHC 3.0L and DOHC 3.5L V6 engine. All information concerning engine removal and refitting and engine block and cylinder head overhaul can be found in Part E of this Chapter.

The following repair procedures are based on the assumption that the engine is refitted in the vehicle. If the engine has been removed from the vehicle and mounted on a stand, many of the steps outlined in this Part of Chapter 2 will not apply.

The Specifications included in this Part of Chapter 2 apply only to the procedures contained in this Part. Part E of Chapter 2 contains the Specifications necessary for cylinder head and engine block rebuilding.

The 60-degree V6 has a cast iron block and aluminium heads. The SOHC 3.0L engine has a camshaft in each head, while the DOHC 3.5L has two camshafts per cylinder head. The block has thin walled sections for light weight. A "cradle frame" main bearing casting - the main bearing caps are cast as a unit, with a bridge, or truss, connecting them - supports the cast ductile iron crankshaft.

Camshafts are driven off the crankshaft by a cog belt. A spring loaded tensioner, adjusted by an eccentric type locknut, maintains belt tension. On SOHC engines, each camshaft actuates two valves per cylinder through hydraulic lash adjusters and shaft-mounted forged aluminium rocker arms. On DOHC engines, each camshaft directly actuates two valves per cylinder through rocker arms and hydraulic lash adjusters.

Each cast aluminium three-ring piston has two compression rings and a three-piece oil control ring. The piston pins are pressed into forged steel connecting rods.

The distributor (or crank angle sensor), which is mounted on the drivebelt end of the front cylinder head, is driven by a helical gear on the camshaft. The water pump, which is bolted to the timing belt end of the block, is driven off the crankshaft by a drivebelt and pulley. The gear type oil pump is mounted in the oil pump case and attached to the timing belt cover. It is driven by the crankshaft.

From the oil pump, oil travels through the filter to the main oil gallery, from which it is routed either directly to the main bearings, crankshaft, connecting rod bearings and pistons and cylinder walls or to the cylinder heads.

2 Repair operations possible with the engine in the vehicle

Many major repair operations can be accomplished without removing the engine from the vehicle.

Clean the engine compartment and the exterior of the engine with some type of degreaser before any work is done. It will make the job easier and help keep dirt out of the internal areas of the engine.

Depending on the components involved, it may be helpful to remove the bonnet to improve access to the engine as repairs are performed (refer to Chapter 11 if necessary). Cover the fenders to prevent damage to the paint. Special pads are available, but an old bedspread or blanket will also work.

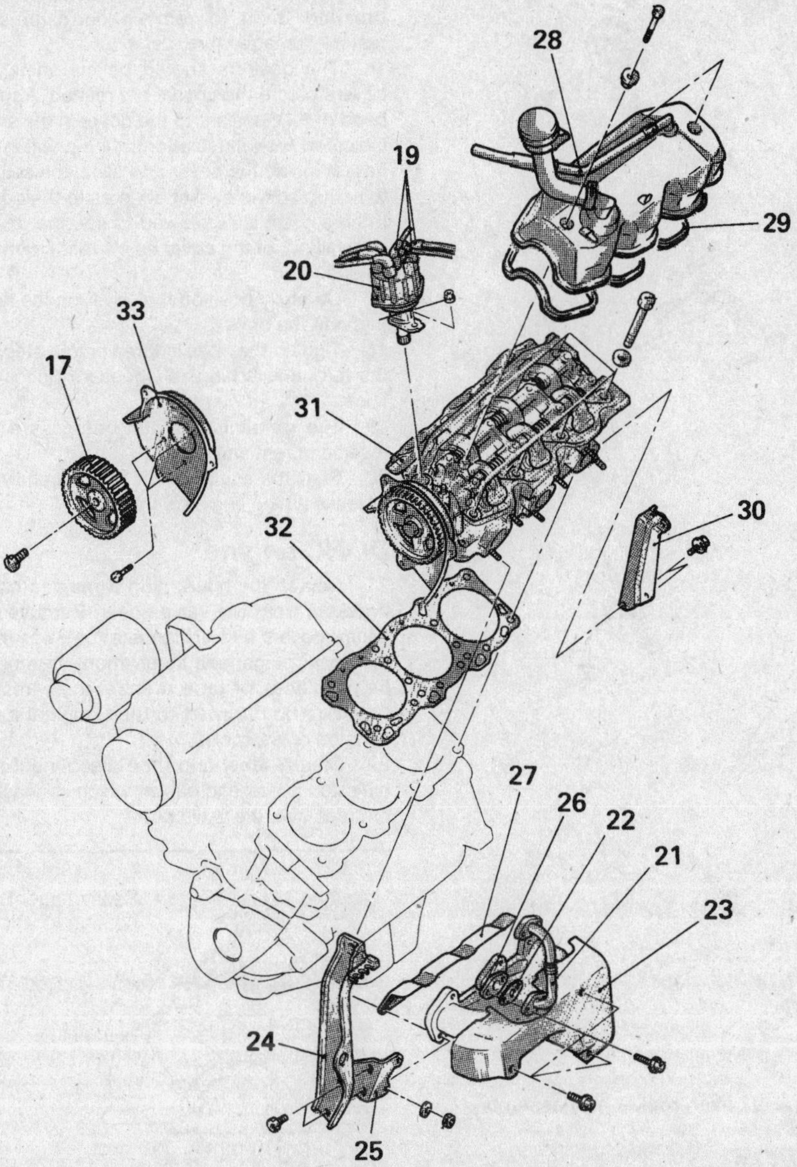

If vacuum, exhaust, oil or coolant leaks develop, indicating a need for gasket or seal renewal, the repairs can generally be made with the engine in the vehicle. The intake and exhaust manifold gaskets, sump gasket, camshaft and crankshaft oil seals and cylinder head gaskets are all accessible with the engine in place.

Exterior engine components, such as the intake and exhaust manifolds, the sump (and the oil pump), the water pump, the starter motor, the alternator, the distributor and the fuel system components can be removed for repair with the engine in place.

Since the cylinder heads can be removed without pulling the engine, camshaft and valve component servicing can also be accomplished with the engine in the vehicle. Renewal of the timing belt and sprockets is also possible with the engine in the vehicle.

In extreme cases caused by a lack of necessary equipment, repair or renewal of piston rings, pistons, connecting rods and rod bearings is possible with the engine in the vehicle. However, this practice is not recommended because of the cleaning and preparation work that must be done to the components involved.

3 Top Dead Centre (TDC) for number one piston - locating

This procedure is essentially the same for all engines. Refer to Chapter 2, Part A and follow the procedure outlined there.

4 Valve covers - removal and refitting

Refer to illustrations 4.3, 4.8, 4.16 and 4.21

SOHC engine

Removal

1 Relieve the fuel system pressure (see Chapter 4).
2 Disconnect the negative cable from the battery.

Left side cover

3 Remove the breather hose from the valve cover **(see illustration)**.
4 Remove the spark plug wires from the spark plugs. Mark them clearly with pieces of masking tape to prevent confusion during refitting.
5 Remove air intake plenum (see Chapter 4).
6 Remove the valve cover bolts and washers.
7 Detach the valve cover. **Caution:** *If the cover is stuck to the head, bump one end with a block of wood and a hammer to jar it loose. If that doesn't work, try to slip a flexible putty knife between the head and cover to break the gasket seal. Don't prise at the cover-to-head joint or damage to the sealing surfaces may occur (leading to oil leaks in the future).*

4.3 An exploded view of the SOHC engine left side valve cover, rocker arm assembly and cylinder head

19	Spark plug wire assembly	24	Air intake plenum bracket	29	Valve cover gasket
20	Distributor	25	Bracket	30	Air intake plenum gasket rear
21	EGR pipe	26	Exhaust manifold	31	Cylinder head
22	EGR gasket	27	Gasket	32	Cylinder head gasket
23	Heat protector	28	Valve cover	33	Timing belt rear cover

Right side cover

8   Remove the breather hose from the cover **(see illustration)**.
9   Tag and detach the spark plug wires.
10 Disconnect the electrical connectors and vacuum hoses necessary for removal. Label and move the wiring and hoses aside.

11 Remove the air cleaner assembly (see Chapter 4).
12 Remove the air intake plenum (see Chapter 4).
13 Remove the valve cover bolts and washers and lift off the valve cover. Read the Caution in Step 7.

Refitting

14 The mating surfaces of each cylinder head and valve cover must be perfectly clean when the covers are refitted. Use a gasket scraper to remove all traces of sealant and old gasket material, then clean the mating surfaces with lacquer thinner or acetone. If there's sealant or oil on the mating surfaces when the cover is refitted, oil leaks may develop.
15 If necessary, clean the mounting screw threads with a die to remove any corrosion and restore damaged threads. Make sure the threaded holes in the head are clean - run a tap into them to remove corrosion and restore damaged threads.
16 The gaskets should be mated to the covers before the covers are refitted. Apply a bead of RTV sealant to the cover in the areas indicated **(see illustration)**, then position the gasket inside the cover and allow the sealant to set up so the gasket adheres to the cover. If the sealant isn't allowed to set, the gasket may fall out of the cover as it's refitted on the engine.
17 Carefully position the cover on the head and refit the bolts.
18 Tighten the bolts in three or four steps to the torque listed in this Chapter's Specifications.
19 The remaining refitting steps are the reverse of removal.
20 Start the engine and check carefully for oil leaks as the engine warms up.

DOHC engine

21 Detach the spark plug wires and cable brackets from the valve cover. Remove the centre covers and disconnect the wires from the spark plugs **(see illustration)**. Use numbered pieces of tape to label the wires so they can be returned to their original locations on reassembly.
22 Clearly label and then disconnect any emission hoses and cables which connect to or cross over the valve cover.

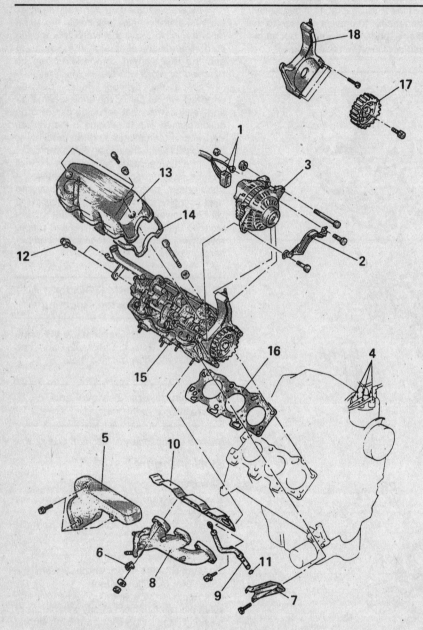

4.8 Exploded view of the SOHC engine right side valve cover, rocker arm assembly and cylinder head

1	Alternator connectors	10	Gasket
2	Alternator cover	11	O-ring
3	Alternator	12	Bolt
4	Spark plug wire connectors (Nos. 1, 3 and 5)	13	Valve cover
5	Heat shield	14	Valve cover gasket
6	Engine removal bracket	15	Cylinder head assembly
7	Alternator bracket	16	Cylinder head gasket
8	Exhaust manifold	17	Camshaft sprocket
9	Oil level gauge guide	18	Alternator bracket

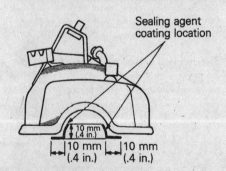

Sealing agent coating location

10 mm (.4 in.)
10 mm (.4 in.)   10 mm (.4 in.)

4.16 It's not necessary to use RTV gasket on the inside of the gasket if the gasket is a tight fit and does not budge once it is refitted inside the valve cover - it is necessary to apply RTV to the edges (arrows) on the outside of the gasket where it mates with the camshaft seals

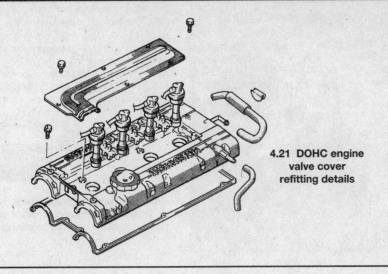

4.21 DOHC engine valve cover refitting details

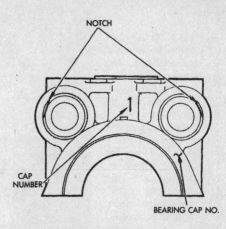

5.4 Check each bearing cap stamped numeral and the position of the notches to aid in correct assembly (SOHC engine)

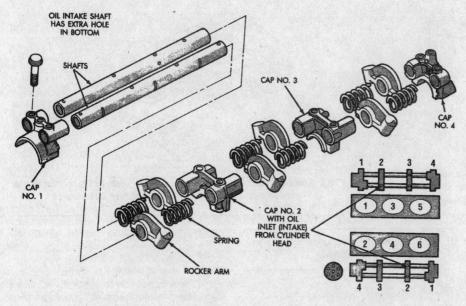

5.2 An exploded view of SOHC engine rocker arm assembly

3   Prior to removal, scribe or paint identifying marks on the rockers to ensure they will be refitted in their original locations.

4   Remove the bolts and lift off the rocker arm shaft assemblies one at a time. Lay them down on a nearby workbench in the same relationship to each other that they're in when refitted. They must be reinstalled on the same cylinder head. Note the location of the stamped bearing cap number and the position of the notches (see illustration).

5   Refitting is the reverse of the removal procedure. **Note:** *Be sure the arrows stamped into the cylinder head and the bearing caps (see illustration) are pointing in the same direction. Tighten the rocker arm shaft*

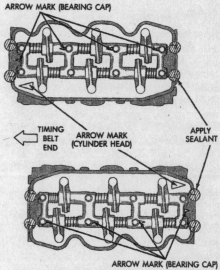

5.5 The arrows on the bearing caps should point in the same direction as the arrows on the cylinder heads (SOHC engine)

23   Remove the valve cover bolts and lift the covers off. If the cover sticks to the cylinder head, tap on it with a soft-face hammer or place a block of wood against the cover and tap on the wood with a hammer. **Caution:** *If you have to prise between the valve cover and the cylinder head, be extremely careful not to gouge or nick the gasket surfaces of either part. A leak could develop after reassembly.*

24   After cleaning the surfaces, degrease them with a rag soaked in lacquer thinner or acetone.

25   Refit a new gasket on the cover, using RTV to hold it in place **(see illustration 4.16)**. Place the cover on the engine and refit the cover bolts.

26   Tighten the bolts to the torque listed in this Chapter's Specifications. The remaining steps are the reverse of removal. When finished, run the engine and check for oil leaks.

5   Rocker arm components - removal and refitting

SOHC engine

Refer to illustrations 5.2, 5.4 and 5.5

1   Position the engine at TDC compression for the number 1 cylinder (see Section 3). Remove the valve cover (see Section 4).

2   Loosen the rocker arm shaft bolts **(see illustration)** in two or three stages, working your way from the ends toward the middle of the shafts. **Caution:** *Some of the valves will be open when you loosen the rocker arm shaft bolts and the rocker arm shafts will be under a certain amount of valve spring pressure. Therefore, the bolts must be loosened gradually. Loosening a bolt all at once near a rocker arm under spring pressure could bend or break the rocker arm shaft.*

5.7 On DOHC engines, once the camshaft has been removed, the rocker arms can be lifted off. If necessary, the lash adjuster below the rocker arm can also be removed - be sure to keep the rocker arms and lash adjusters in order so they can be returned to their original locations

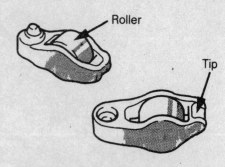

5.8 On DOHC engines, check the roller, tip and lash adjuster contact area for score marks and pitting

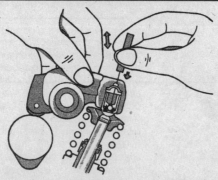

6.1 When performing the freeplay test, make sure the adjuster that is being tested has the corresponding camshaft lobe pointing away from the rocker arm (closed valve)

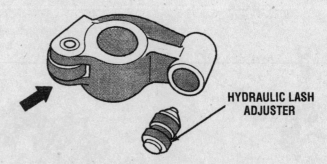

6.4 The hydraulic lash adjusters are precision units refitted in the machined openings in the rocker arm assemblies

bolts, in several steps, to the torque listed in this Chapter's Specifications. Work from the ends of the shafts toward the middle.

DOHC engine

Refer to illustrations 5.7 and 5.8

6   Remove the camshafts (see Section 15).
7   Once the camshafts have been removed, the rocker arms can be lifted off **(see illustration)**. **Caution:** *Each rocker arm must be placed back in the same location it was removed from, so mark each rocker arm or place them in a container (such as an egg carton) so they won't get mixed up. The lash adjusters can remain in the head at this time, unless they are being renewed (see Section 6).*

Inspection

8   Visually check the rocker arms for wear **(see illustration)**. Renew them if evidence of wear or damage is found.

Refitting

9   When reassembling the parts, be sure they all go back on in the same locations they were removed from.
10   The remainder of the reassembly is in the reverse order of disassembly. Run the engine and check for oil leaks and proper operation.

6   Hydraulic lash adjusters - check, removal and refitting

SOHC engine

Check

Refer to illustration 6.1

1   Check the hydraulic lash adjusters for freeplay by inserting a small wire through the air bleed hole in the rocker arm while lightly pushing the check ball down **(see illustration)**.
2   While lightly holding the check ball down, move the rocker arm up and down to check for freeplay. There should be a small amount of movement. If there is no freeplay, renew the adjuster.

Removal

Refer to illustration 6.4

3   Remove the valve cover(s) (see Section 4) and the rocker arm shaft components (see Section 5).
4   Pull the hydraulic lash adjuster(s) out of the rocker arm(s) **(see illustration)**. **Note:** *Be sure to label each rocker arm and adjuster and place them in a partitioned box or something suitable to keep them from getting mixed with each other.*
5   Refitting is the reverse of removal.

DOHC engine

Check

Refer to illustration 6.6

6   The simplest way to check the adjusters is to warm the engine up to normal operating temperature and listen for "tapping" noises. After warm-up, raise the speed of the engine from idle to 3,000 rpm for one minute. If the adjuster(s) do not become silent, renew the defective ones. Another simple check can be made by removing the valve cover and push-

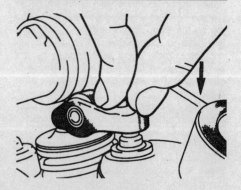

6.6 Push down on the hydraulic lash adjusters to make sure they resist movement

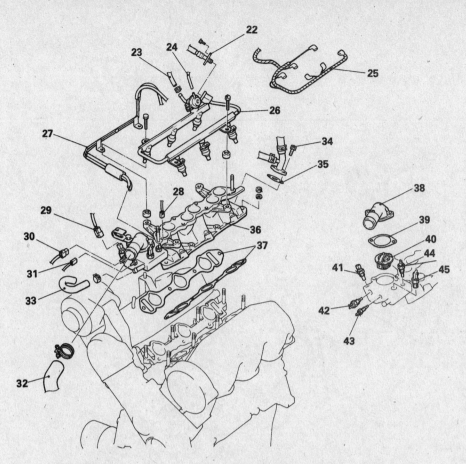

7.13 An exploded view of a typical inlet manifold and related components

22	Fuel connection	34	Heater pipe hose
23	Fuel return hose	35	Gasket
24	Vacuum hose	36	Inlet manifold
25	Fuel injector harness	37	Inlet manifold gasket
26	Fuel rail and injectors	38	Thermostat housing
27	Vacuum hose and pipe assembly	39	Gasket
28	Temperature sending unit connector	40	Thermostat
29	Coolant temperature switch connector (air conditioning)	41	Coolant temperature switch
30	Coolant temperature sensor connector	42	Coolant temperature sensor
31	Thermo switch connector (automatic transmission)	43	Thermo switch (automatic transmission
32	Upper hose	44	Coolant temperature sending unit
33	Water by-pass hose	45	Thermo valve assembly

ing down on each adjuster **(see illustration)**. The adjuster should feel solid and not "give". If an adjuster can be easily pushed down, it is faulty and should be renewed.

Removal

7   Remove the camshaft(s) (see Section 15).
8   Remove the rocker arms (see Section 5).
9   If the hydraulic lifters aren't already removed from the head, lift them out now. **Caution:** *Be sure to keep the lifters in order so they can be placed back on the same camshaft lobe it was removed from.*
10   Inspect each adjuster carefully for signs of wear and damage, particularly on the ball

tip that contacts the rocker arm. Since the lash adjusters frequently become clogged, we recommend renewing them if you're concerned about their condition or if the engine is exhibiting valve "tapping" noises.
11   Refitting is the reverse of removal.

---

7   Inlet manifold - removal and refitting

Removal

Refer to illustration 7.13

1   Relieve the fuel system pressure (see Chapter 4).

2   Disconnect the cable from the negative terminal of the battery.
3   Drain the cooling system (don't forget to drain the cylinder block) (see Chapter 1).
4   Remove the air cleaner-to-throttle body inlet hose (see Chapter 4).
5   Remove the spark plug wires and distributor cap. Be sure to mark the spark plug wires for proper reinstallation (see Chapter 1).
6   Remove the throttle cable and transmission kickdown linkage (see Chapter 4 and 7B).
7   Remove the Idle Speed Control (ISC) motor and throttle position sensor (TPS) electrical connectors from the throttle body.
8   Remove the EGR tube flange from the air intake plenum.
9   Label and detach any vacuum lines from the throttle body.
10   Detach the fuel lines from the fuel rail (see Chapter 4).
11   Remove the throttle body, air intake plenum and the fuel injectors (see Chapter 4).
12   Label and remove any remaining hoses, wires or cables attached to the inlet manifold or its components.
13   Loosen the manifold mounting bolts/nuts in 1/4-turn increments until they can be removed by hand. Loosen the outer bolts first, then the inner bolts **(see illustration)**.
14   The manifold will probably be stuck to the cylinder heads and force may be required to break the gasket seal. **Caution:** *Don't prise between the manifold and the heads or damage to the gasket sealing surfaces may occur, leading to vacuum leaks.*

Refitting

Note: *The mating surfaces of the cylinder heads and manifold must be perfectly clean when the manifold is refitted. Gasket removal solvents in aerosol cans are available at most auto parts stores and may be helpful when removing old gasket material that's stuck to the heads and manifold (since they're made of aluminium, aggressive scraping can cause damage). Be sure to follow the directions printed on the container.*

15   Use a gasket scraper to remove all traces of sealant and old gasket material, then clean the mating surfaces with lacquer thinner or acetone. If there's old sealant or oil on the mating surfaces when the manifold is refitted, oil or vacuum leaks may develop. Use a vacuum cleaner to remove any material that falls into the intake ports in the heads.
16   Use a tap of the correct size to chase the threads in the bolt holes, then use compressed air (if available) to remove the debris from the holes. **Warning:** *Wear safety glasses or a face shield to protect your eyes when using compressed air!*
17   Position the gaskets on the cylinder heads. No sealant is required; however, follow the instructions included with the new gaskets.
18   Make sure all intake port openings, coolant passage holes and bolt holes are

2B

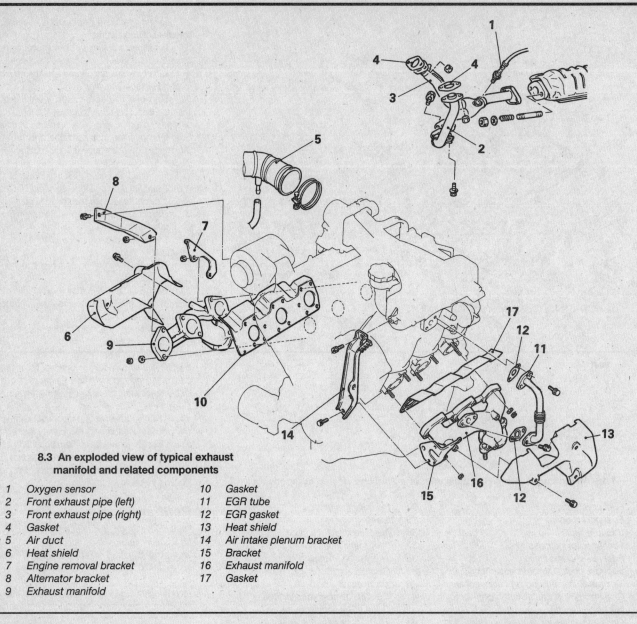

8.3 An exploded view of typical exhaust manifold and related components

1	Oxygen sensor	10	Gasket
2	Front exhaust pipe (left)	11	EGR tube
3	Front exhaust pipe (right)	12	EGR gasket
4	Gasket	13	Heat shield
5	Air duct	14	Air intake plenum bracket
6	Heat shield	15	Bracket
7	Engine removal bracket	16	Exhaust manifold
8	Alternator bracket	17	Gasket
9	Exhaust manifold		

aligned correctly.

19   Carefully set the manifold in place. Be careful not to disturb the gaskets.

20   Refit the nuts/bolts and tighten them to the torque listed in this Chapter's Specifications starting with the inner bolts and working your way to the outer bolts. Work up to the final torque in two steps.

21   Refit the air intake plenum (see Chapter 4).

22   The remaining refitting steps are the reverse of removal. Start the engine and check carefully for oil and coolant leaks at the inlet manifold joints.

8   Exhaust manifolds - removal and refitting

Refer to illustration 8.3
Note: *The engine must be completely cool*

when this procedure is done.

1   Disconnect the negative cable from the battery. Raise the vehicle and support it securely on jackstands.

2   Spray penetrating oil on the exhaust manifold fasteners and allow it to soak in. Disconnect the oxygen sensor electrical connector.

3   Remove the bolts and nuts that retain the front exhaust pipes to the manifolds **(see illustration)** and lower the pipes.

4   Remove the bolts and detach the EGR tube from the left manifold.

5   Remove the nuts retaining the heat shield(s) to the manifold(s) near the cylinder head and slip it off the mounting studs **(see illustration 8.3)**.

6   Remove the nuts that retain the manifold to the cylinder head and lift the exhaust manifold off.

7   Carefully inspect the manifolds and fasteners for cracks and damage.

8   Use a scraper to remove all traces of old gasket material and carbon deposits from the manifold and cylinder head mating surfaces. If the gasket was leaking, have the manifold checked for warpage at an automotive machine shop and resurfaced if necessary.

9   Position new gaskets over the cylinder head studs. **Note:** *If the new gasket is marked, refit the gasket with the numbers 1-3-5 on the top onto the right cylinder head and refit the gasket with the numbers 2-4-6 onto the left cylinder head.*

10   Refit the manifold and thread the mounting nuts into place.

11   Working from the centre out, tighten the nuts to the torque listed in this Chapter's Specifications in three or four equal steps.

12   Reinstall the remaining parts in the reverse order of removal. Use new gaskets when connecting the exhaust pipes.

13   Run the engine and check for exhaust leaks.

5   Wrap a cloth around the vibration damper to protect the belt surface and attach a chain wrench to the pulley. Hold the crankshaft from turning and use a socket wrench to loosen the bolt.

6   Refit a special tool (vibration damper/steering wheel puller) to the damper and slowly draw the vibration damper off.

Refitting

7   Lightly lubricate the seal contact surface with engine oil and position it on the nose of the crankshaft. Align the keyway in the pulley with the key in the crankshaft and push the pulley into place by hand. If necessary, tap lightly on the damper using a block of wood and a hammer.

8   Prevent the crankshaft from turning as described in Step 5, then refit the bolt and tighten it to the torque listed in this Chapter's Specifications.

9   Reinstall the remaining parts in the reverse order of removal.

2B

10   Timing belt - removal, refitting and adjustment

SOHC engine

Removal

Refer to illustration 10.9, 10.13 and 10.14

1   Disconnect the cable from the negative terminal of the battery.

2   If equipped, unbolt the cruise control servo and set it aside, without disconnecting the wires or cables.

3   Drain the coolant from the system (see Chapter 1) and remove the coolant reservoir (see Chapter 3).

4   Remove the radiator shroud and the radiator (see Chapter 3).

5   Raise the front of the vehicle and support it securely on jackstands.

6   Remove the splash pan from under the engine.

7   Remove the cooling fan and clutch assembly (see Chapter 3).

8   Position the number one piston at TDC on the compression stroke (see Section 3). Remove the spark plugs (see Chapter 1).

9   Remove the drivebelts (see Chapter 1) **(see illustration)**.

10   Remove the power steering pump (see Chapter 10) without disconnecting the lines. Also remove the power steering pump bracket and the belt tensioner bracket.

11   Remove the air conditioning compressor (see Chapter 3), bracket and idler pulley **(see illustration 10.9)**. Do not disconnect the refrigerant lines from the compressor. Remove the cooling fan bracket assembly.

12   Remove the crankshaft pulley (see Section 9), the vibration damper and crankshaft sprocket flange. **Note:** *Don't allow the crankshaft to rotate during removal of the pulley. If the crankshaft moves, the number one piston will no longer be at TDC.*

13   Remove the bolts securing the timing

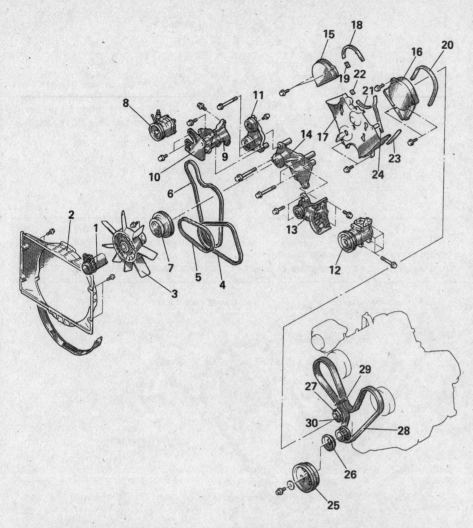

10.9 An exploded view of the SOHC engine timing belt, covers and related components

1	Upper radiator hose	15	Upper timing belt cover (right side)
2	Radiator upper shroud	16	Upper timing belt cover (left side)
3	Cooling fan clutch assembly	17	Lower timing belt cover
4	Air conditioning drivebelt	18	Gasket K
5	Power steering drivebelt	19	Gasket J
6	Alternator drivebelt	20	Gasket N
7	Cooling fan pulley	21	Gasket O
8	Power steering pump	22	Gasket J
9	Power steering pump bracket	23	Gasket P
10	Power steering pump mounting bracket	24	Gasket H
11	Belt tensioner bracket	25	crankshaft pulley
12	Air conditioning compressor	26	Front flange
13	Air conditioning compressor bracket and idler pulley	27	Timing belt tensioner bolt
14	Cooling fan bracket assembly	28	Timing belt
		29	Tensioner spring
		30	Timing belt tensioner

9   Crankshaft pulley/vibration damper - removal and refitting

Removal

1   Disconnect the negative cable from the battery.

2   Raise the front of the vehicle and support it securely on jackstands.

3   Remove the drivebelts (see Chapter 1).

4   Remove the bolts that retain the pulley to the vibration damper. Remove the pulley from the engine.

belt upper and lower covers **(see illustration)**. Note the various type and sizes of bolts by recording a diagram or making specific notes while the timing belt cover is being removed. The bolts must be reinstalled in their original locations.

14   Confirm that the number one piston is still at TDC on the compression stroke by verifying that the timing marks on all three timing belt sprockets are aligned with their respective stationary timing marks **(see illustration)**.

15   Relieve tension on the timing belt by loosening the nut or bolt on the timing belt tensioner **(see illustration 10.14)**.

16   Check to see that the timing belt is marked with an arrow as to which side faces out. If there isn't a mark, paint one on (only if the same belt will be reinstalled). Slide the timing belt off the sprockets. Check the condition of the tensioner.

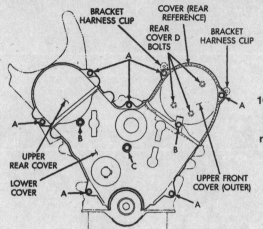

10.13 Be sure to mark each bolt with the correct size and location for proper reassembly (SOHC engine)

Refitting

Refer to illustrations 10.17a and 10.17b

17   Prepare to refit the timing belt by levering the tensioner away from the spring to the end of the adjustment slot **(see illustration)**, then temporarily tightening the locking nut or bolt. Make sure the tensioner spring is posi-

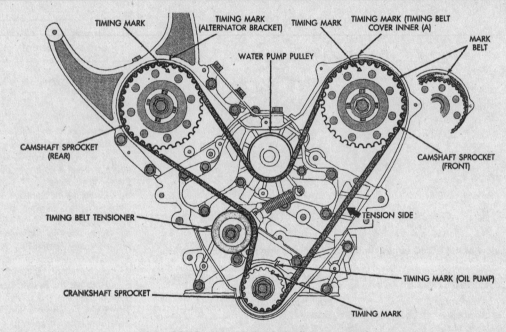

10.14 SOHC engine timing belt alignment marks

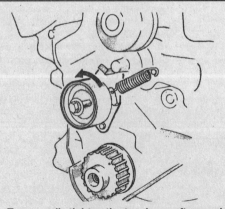

10.17a Temporarily tighten the tensioner after moving it to the end of the slot (SOHC engine)

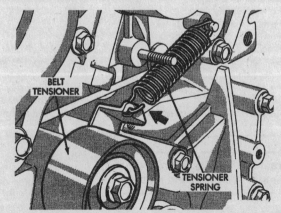

10.17b Correct spring position on the tensioner (SOHC engine)

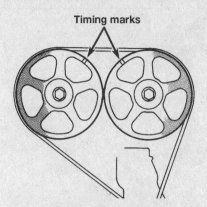

Timing marks

10.40a The timing belt sprockets must be aligned with the timing marks

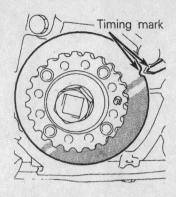

Timing mark

10.40b The crankshaft sprocket timing mark and pointer in proper alignment

tioned properly **(see illustration)**.

18 Refit the belt on the crankshaft sprocket first, and simultaneously keep the belt tight on the tension side **(see illustration 10.14)**.

19 Refit the belt on the left camshaft sprocket and then onto the water pump pulley and finally the right camshaft sprocket and timing belt tensioner. Be careful not to nudge the camshaft sprocket(s) or crankshaft gear off the timing marks. Refit the timing belt with the directional arrow pointing away from the engine.

20 Align the factory-made white lines on the timing belt with the punch mark on each of the camshaft sprockets and the crankshaft sprocket. Make sure all three sets of timing marks are properly aligned **(see illustration 10.14)**. **Note:** Be sure to refit the crankshaft sprocket flange onto the crankshaft sprocket **(see illustration 10.9)**.

Adjustment

21 Loosen the tensioner nut or bolt and let the tensioner assembly spring toward the belt - the spring tension will automatically apply the proper amount of tension to the belt.

22 Slowly turn the crankshaft clockwise two full revolutions, returning the number one piston to TDC on the compression stroke.

Caution: *If excessive resistance is felt wile turning the crankshaft, it's an indication that the pistons are coming into contact with the valves. Go back over the procedure to correct the situation before proceeding.*

23 Check to be sure all timing marks are still aligned **(see illustration 10.14)**. Tighten the tensioner nut or bolt to the torque listed in this Chapter's Specifications while keeping the tensioner steady with your hand.

24 Check the deflection of the timing belt by observing the force the tensioner pulley applies to the timing belt. If the belt seems loose, renew the tensioner spring.

25 Refit the various components removed during disassembly, referring to the appropriate Sections as necessary.

DOHC engine

Removal

Refer to illustrations 10.40a, 10.40b, 10.41, 10.42a, 10.42b, 10.48 and 10.53

26 Disconnect the cable from the negative terminal of the battery.

27 Position the number one piston at Top Dead Centre (see Section 3).

28 If equipped, unbolt the cruise control servo and set it aside, without disconnecting

the wires or cables.

29 Drain the coolant from the system (see Chapter 1) and remove the coolant reservoir (see Chapter 3).

30 Remove the radiator shroud and the radiator (see Chapter 3).

31 Remove the power steering pump (see Chapter 10) without disconnecting the lines.

32 Remove the air conditioning compressor (see Chapter 3), bracket and idler pulley. Do not disconnect the refrigerant lines from the compressor.

33 Raise the front of the vehicle and support it securely on jackstands.

34 Remove the splash pan from under the engine.

35 Position the number one piston at TDC on the compression stroke (see Section 3).

36 Remove the accessory mount, cooling fan and clutch assembly.

37 Remove the spark plugs (see Chapter 1).

38 Remove the crankshaft pulley (see Section 9), the vibration damper and crankshaft sprocket flange. **Note:** *Don't allow the crankshaft to rotate during removal of the pulley. If the crankshaft moves, the number one piston will no longer be at TDC.*

39 Remove the bolts securing the timing belt upper and lower covers. Note the various type and sizes of bolts by recording a diagram or making specific notes while the timing belt cover is being removed. The bolts must be reinstalled in their original locations.

40 Align the timing belt sprocket timing marks **(see illustrations)**.

41 Make a mark on the timing belt in the direction of rotation **(see illustration)** so it may be reinstalled in the same direction in the event the timing belt is reused. Loosen the centre bolt on tensioner pulley, then remove the timing belt. **Caution:** *Be sure that the timing marks are correctly aligned before removing the timing belt* **(see illustrations 10.40a and 10.40b)**.

42 If you plan to renew the camshaft(s) or camshaft oil seal(s), remove the camshaft sprocket(s). Using an adjustable wrench or

10.41 If you'll be reusing the timing belt, mark an arrow on the belt in the direction of rotation so it may be reinstalled in the same direction

10.42a When loosening the camshaft sprocket bolt, hold the camshaft at the hexagon with an open-end wrench . . .

10.42b ... and, if the bolt is very tight, position a wood block, as shown, to prevent damaging the cylinder head when the bolt breaks loose

10.48 Once the tensioner is compressed, place a small Allen wrench, or something similar, through the hole to keep the rod retracted for reassembly on the engine

an open-end wrench, hold the camshaft at the hexagon and remove the camshaft sprocket bolt **(see illustration)**. If the sprocket bolt cannot be loosened easily, place a block of wood between the head and the wrench **(see illustration)** to prevent damage to the head so more force can be used on the camshaft sprocket bolt. Remove the bolt and slide the sprocket off the camshaft.

Inspection

43　Rotate the tensioner pulley by hand and check for roughness and excessive play.

44　Inspect the timing belt for cracks, separation, wear, missing teeth and oil contamination. Renew the belt if it's in questionable condition.

45　Check the automatic tensioner for leaks or any obvious damage to the body. Also, check the rod end for wear or damage. Measure the rod protrusion for the correct length - it should extend 3.8 to 4.5 mm beyond the body of the tensioner.

Refitting

46　Reinstall the timing belt sprockets, if they were removed. Tighten the bolts to the values listed in this Chapter's Specifications.

47　Align the timing marks located on the camshaft, crankshaft and sprockets **(see illustrations 10.40a and 10.40b)**.

48　Prepare the automatic tensioner for refitting. Place the tensioner in a vice that is equipped with soft jaws (or put a shop rag over the jaws to prevent damage to the tensioner). If the rod is easily retracted, renew it. The tensioner should have a fair amount of strength or resistance. **Caution:** *Be sure the tensioner is in a level position when it is in the vice.* Once the tensioner is compressed place a small Allen wrench, pin or something similar, through the hole to keep the rod retracted for reassembly on the engine **(see illustration)**.

49　Refit the automatic tensioner onto the engine, keeping it in the compressed position.

50　Refit the tensioner pulley onto the tensioner arm. Position the two small holes in the tensioner pulley hub just to the left of the centre bolt. Tighten the centre bolt finger tight. Don't remove the Allen wrench from the tensioner yet.

51　Slide the sprocket onto the crankshaft and rotate it forward about three teeth, to slightly past the number 1 piston TDC mark. Then line up the timing marks on the left and right camshaft sprockets with the ones on the cylinder heads **(see illustrations 10.40a and 10.40b)**. Have an assistant hold the camshaft sprockets from moving with two spanners on the sprocket nuts.

52　Refit the timing belt in the following sequence:

a) *Refit the timing belt around the right bank camshaft sprockets, pull the timing belt onto the water pump pulley and hold it.*

b) *Pulling the belt with your right hand, refit it around the left bank sprockets.*

c) *Refit the belt around the idler pulley.*

d) *Align the crankshaft sprocket timing marks and turn the crankshaft sprocket one tooth anti-clockwise and refit the belt around the crankshaft sprocket.*

e) *Refit the belt on the tensioner pulley.*

f) *Turn the tensioner pulley so the pin hole faces up, press the pulley onto belt, then temporarily tighten the centre bolt. Make sure that all of the timing marks are now properly aligned* **(see illustrations 10.40a and 10.40b)**.

53　Adjust the timing belt tension in the following sequence:

a) *Turn the crankshaft 1/4 turn anti-clockwise, then clockwise to move all of the timing marks into alignment.*

b) *Loosen the tensioner centre bolt and attach Mitsubishi special socket tool no. MD998767 (or equivalent) to a torque wrench.* **Note:** *The torque wrench must be capable of measuring small increments between 0 and 3 Nm. Apply 9.4 Nm to the tensioner* **(see illustration)**.

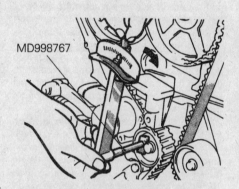

10.53 Apply the specified pressure on the tensioner and tighten the centre bolt to specified torque - be careful not to rotate the tensioner while tightening the bolt

c) *While holding the 9.4 Nm tension on the timing belt tensioner, tighten the centre bolt to the torque listed in this Chapter's Specifications. Be careful not to rotate the tensioner while tightening the centre bolt.*

d) *Remove the Allen wrench or pin from the tensioner.*

e) *Rotate the crankshaft two complete turns and wait five minutes.* **Caution:** *If you feel resistance while turning the crankshaft, the valves may be hitting the pistons from incorrect valve timing. Stop and re-check the valve timing. Measure how far the tensioner plunger protrudes from the tensioner body (the distance between the tensioner arm and the automatic tensioner body). It should be between 3.8 to 4.5 mm. Also, check that all timing marks are still aligned.*

54　If the tensioner protrusion is not as specified, repeat the belt adjustment procedure.

55　Refit the timing covers.

56　The remaining steps are the reverse of removal.

11.4 If the sprocket is stuck, drill and tap two holes and remove it with a bolt-type puller

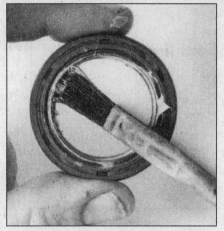

11.7 Apply a film of grease to the lips of the new seal before installing it (if you apply a small amount of grease to the outer edge, it will be easier to push into the bore

11.8a Fabricate a seal refitting tool from a piece of pipe and a large washer . . .

2B

11.8b . . . to push the seal into the bore - the pipe must bear against the outer edge of the seal as the bolt is tightened

11 Crankshaft front oil seal - renewal

Refer to illustrations 11.4, 11.7, 11.8a and 11.8b

1 Disconnect the negative cable from the battery.
2 Remove the drivebelts (see Chapter 1), crankshaft pulley and timing belt (see Sections 9 and 10).
3 Wedge two screwdrivers behind the crankshaft sprocket. Carefully prise the sprocket off the crankshaft. Some timing belt sprockets can be pried off easily with screwdrivers. Others are more difficult to remove because corrosion fuses them onto the nose of the crankshaft. If the pulley on your engine is difficult to prise off, don't damage the oil pump with the screwdrivers.
4 If the sprocket won't come loose, drill and tap two holes into the face of the sprocket (later modes already have these holes) and use a bolt-type puller to slip it off the crankshaft **(see illustration). Caution:** *Do not reuse a drilled sprocket - renew it.*
5 Turn the bolt of the puller until the pulley comes off. Remove the timing belt plate.
6 Carefully prise the old oil seal out with a screwdriver or seal removal tool. Don't scratch or nick the crankshaft in the process!
7 Before refitting, apply a coat of multi-purpose grease to the inside of the seal **(see illustration).**
8 Fabricate a seal refitting tool with a short length of pipe of equal or slightly smaller outside diameter than the seal itself. File the end of the pipe that will bear down on the seal until it's free of sharp edges. You'll also need a large washer, slightly larger in diameter than the pipe, on which the bolt head can seat **(see illustration).** Refit the oil seal by pressing it into position with the seal refitting tool **(see illustration).** When you see and feel the seal stop moving, don't turn the bolt any more or you'll damage the seal.
9 Slide the timing belt plate onto the nose

of the crankshaft.
10 Make sure the Woodruff key is in place in the crankshaft.
11 Apply a thin coat of assembly lube to the inside of the timing belt sprocket and slide it onto the crankshaft.
12 Refitting of the remaining components is the reverse of removal. Be sure to refer to Section 10 for the timing belt refitting and adjustment procedure. Tighten all bolts to the torque values listed in this Chapter's Specifications.

12 Camshaft oil seal - renewal

Refer to illustration 12.5

SOHC engine

Note: *The SOHC 3.0L engine is equipped with two camshaft oil seals on the front as well as two camshaft oil plugs on the rear of the engine. The DOHC 3.5L engine has four oil seals, one at the front of each camshaft.*
1 Disconnect the negative battery cable from the battery.
2 Remove the drivebelts (see Chapter 1), crankshaft pulley (see Section 9) and timing belt (see Section 10).

3 On SOHC engines, insert a screwdriver through a hole in the camshaft sprocket to lock it in place while loosening the mounting bolt. On DOHC engines, remove the sprocket as described in Section 10 **(see illustrations 10.42a and 10.42b).**
4 Once the bolt is out, the sprocket can be removed by hand. **Note:** *If you're removing more than one camshaft sprocket, don't mix them up. Mark each sprocket and keep them separate.*
5 Carefully remove the old oil seal with a screwdriver **(see illustration).** Don't nick or scratch the camshaft in the process. Refer to Steps 6, 7 and 8 in Section 11. A similar seal refitting tool to the one used for the crankshaft seal can be used for the camshaft seals.

12.5 The oil seal on the rear camshaft is located inside the distributor drive adaptor

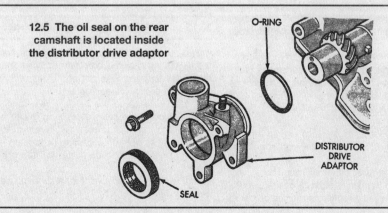

O-RING

DISTRIBUTOR DRIVE ADAPTOR

SEAL

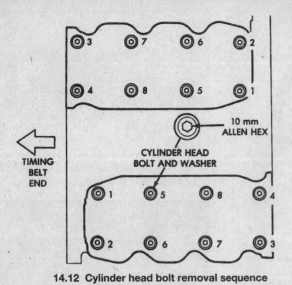

14.12 Cylinder head bolt removal sequence

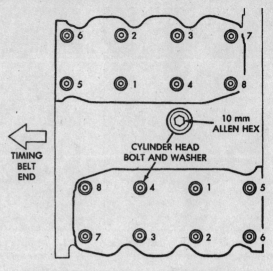

14.23a SOHC cylinder head bolt tightening sequence

6   Refit the sprocket. Make sure they are refitted in the original positions. On SOHC engines the sprockets are marked with an R or L and the side with the deep recess must face the engine, which means the shallow recess must face out.

7   Lock the sprocket in place while you tighten the bolt to the torque listed in this Chapter's Specifications.

8   Refitting of the remaining components is the reverse of removal.

13   Valve spring, retainer and seals - renewal

This procedure is essentially the same as for the 2.6 litre four-cylinder engine. Refer to Chapter 2A, Section 6 and follow the procedure outlined there.

14   Cylinder head(s) - removal and refitting

Note: *Allow the engine to cool completely before beginning this procedure.*

Removal

1   Position the engine at TDC on the compression stroke for the number 1 cylinder (see Section 3). Drain the engine coolant (see Chapter 1).

2   Remove the timing belt cover, timing belt, camshaft sprockets and camshafts (see Sections 10, 12 and 15). and any other components that will interfere with.

3   Remove the inlet manifold (see Section 7).

4   Remove the rocker arm components (see Section 5) and hydraulic lash adjusters (see Section 6).

5   Remove the exhaust manifold(s) as described in Section 8. **Note:** *If desired, each manifold may remain attached to the cylinder*

head until after the head is removed from the engine. However, the manifold must still be disconnected from the exhaust system.

Left (passenger's side) cylinder head

6   Remove the distributor (crank angle sensor) (see Chapter 5).

7   Remove the air conditioning compressor from the bracket without disconnecting any hoses (see Chapter 3) and set it aside. It may be helpful to secure the compressor to the vehicle with rope or wire to make sure it doesn't hang by its hoses.

8   Remove the air conditioning compressor bracket (if equipped).

Right (driver's side) cylinder head

9   Detach the heater hoses and brackets from the rear of the head.

10   Remove the air cleaner housing from the engine compartment (see Chapter 4).

11   Remove the alternator and bracket from the cylinder head (see Chapter 5).

Both sides

Refer to illustration 14.12

12   Loosen the cylinder head bolts with a 10 mm hex drive tool in 1/4-turn increments until they can be removed by hand. Be sure to follow the proper numerical sequence on SOHC engines **(see illustration)**.

13   Head bolts must be reinstalled in their original locations. To keep them from getting mixed up, store them in cardboard holders marked to indicate the bolt pattern. Mark the holders L (left) and R (right) and indicate the timing belt end of the engine.

14   Lift the head off the block. If resistance is felt, dislodge the head by striking it with a wood block and hammer. If levering is required, prise only on a casting protrusion - be very careful not to damage the head or block!

15   If necessary, remove the camshaft(s) as described in Section 15.

Refitting

Refer to illustrations 14.23a and 14.23b

16   Remove all traces of old gasket material from the cylinder heads and the engine block. The mating surfaces of the cylinder heads and block must be perfectly clean when the heads are refitted.

17   Use a gasket scraper to remove all traces of carbon and old gasket material, then clean the mating surfaces with lacquer thinner or acetone. If there's oil on the mating surfaces when the heads are refitted, the gaskets may not seal correctly and leaks may develop. Use a vacuum cleaner to remove any debris that falls into the cylinders.

18   Check the block and head mating surfaces for nicks, deep scratches and other damage. If damage is slight, it can be removed with a file - if it's excessive, machining may be the only alternative.

19   Use a tap of the correct size to chase the threads in the head bolt holes. Mount each bolt in a vice and run a die down the threads to remove corrosion and restore the threads. Dirt, corrosion, sealant and damaged threads will affect torque readings. Ensure that the threaded holes in the block are clean and dry.

20   Position the new gaskets over the dowel pins on the block with the identification mark facing up at the front (timing belt) side.

21   Carefully position the heads on the block without disturbing the gaskets.

22   Lightly oil the threads and refit the bolts in their original locations. Tighten them finger tight.

23   Follow the recommended sequence and tighten the bolts in three steps to the torque listed in this Chapter's Specifications **(see illustrations)**.

24   The remaining refitting steps are the reverse of removal.

25   Add coolant and change the engine oil and filter (see Chapter 1), then start the engine and check carefully for oil and coolant leaks.

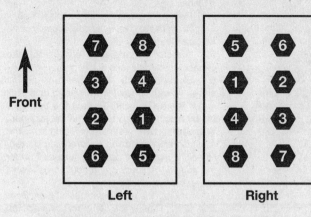

Front

Left   Right

14.23b DOHC cylinder head bolt tightening sequence

15.7 A dial indicator and V-blocks are needed to check camshaft runout

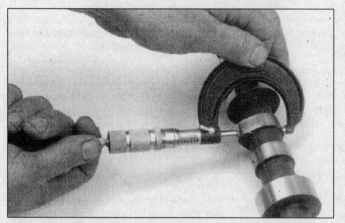

15.8 Measuring cam lobe height with a micrometer

15.15 If the bearing caps are difficult to remove, use the bolts as levers to help break the caps free

15 Camshaft - removal, inspection and refitting

SOHC engine

Removal

1   Position the engine at TDC on the compression stroke for the number 1 cylinder (see Section 3). Remove the timing belt and camshaft sprockets (see Sections 10 and 12). **Note:** *If you're only removing one camshaft and you want to save time by not removing and installing the timing belt and re-timing the engine, you can unfasten the camshaft sprocket and suspend it out of the way - with the belt still attached - by a piece of rope. Be sure the rope keeps firm tension on the belt so the belt won't become disengaged from any of the sprockets.*

2   If you're removing the left (driver's side) cylinder head, remove the bolts and gently prise off the distributor drive adaptor **(see illustration 12.5)**.

3   Remove the rocker arm assembly (see Section 5).

4   Carefully prise the camshaft plugs from the rear section of the cylinder head. Don't scratch or nick the camshaft in the process!

5   Carefully lift the camshaft from the cylin-

der head. Inspect the camshaft as described in the following subsection.

Inspection

Refer to illustrations 15.7 and 15.8

6   Visually check the camshaft bearing surfaces for pitting, score marks, galling and abnormal wear. If the bearing surfaces are damaged, the head will have to be renewed.

7   Check camshaft runout by placing the camshaft between two V-blocks and set up a dial indicator on the centre journal **(see illustration)**. Zero the dial indicator. Turn the camshaft slowly and note the total indicator reading. Record your readings and compare them with the specified runout in this Chapter. If the measured runout exceeds the runout specified in this Chapter, renew the camshaft.

8   Check the camshaft lobe height by measuring each lobe with a micrometer **(see illustration)**. Compare the measurement to the cam lobe height specified in this Chapter. Then subtract the measured cam lobe height from the specified height to compute wear on the cam lobes. Compare it to the specified wear limit. If it's greater than the specified wear limit, renew the camshaft.

9   Inspect the contact and sliding surfaces of each hydraulic lash adjuster for scoring or damage (see Section 6). renew any defective parts.

10   Check the rocker arms and shafts for abnormal wear, pits, galling, score marks and rough spots. Don't attempt to restore rocker arms by grinding the pad surfaces. Renew any defective parts.

Refitting

11   Lubricate the camshaft bearing journals and lobes with moly-base grease or engine assembly lube, then refit it carefully in the head. Don't scratch the bearing surfaces with the cam lobes!

12   Refit the distributor drive adaptor retaining bolts and tighten them to the torque listed in this Chapter's Specifications.

13   Check to make sure the mark on the crankshaft sprocket is still aligned with its mark on the oil pump. Slide the camshaft sprockets onto the camshafts and align the marks on the sprockets with their corresponding marks on the cylinder heads.

14   The remaining steps are the reverse of the removal procedure.

DOHC engine

Refer to illustration 15.15

Removal

15   Remove the timing belt and camshaft sprocket(s), then remove the camshaft bearing caps, loosening the bolts a little at a time

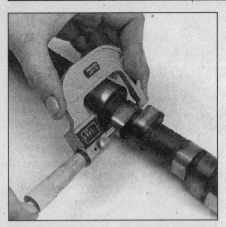

15.17 Measure the camshaft lobe heights with a micrometer

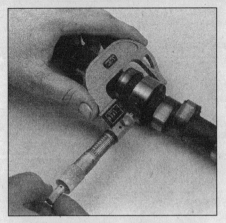

15.18 Measure the camshaft bearing journal diameters

to prevent distorting the camshaft(s) by loosening the caps from the ends of the shaft towards the centre. Once the bearing caps have all been loosened enough for removal, they may still be difficult to remove. Using the bearing cap bolts for extra leverage, move the cap back and forth to loosen the cap from the cylinder head **(see illustration)**. If they are still difficult to remove you can tap them gently with a soft face hammer so they can be lifted off. **Caution:** *Store them in order so they can be returned to their original locations, with the same side facing forward. It's a good idea to mark the caps so there's no possibility of making a mistake.* Carefully lift the camshaft(s) out of the cylinder head.

Inspection

Refer to illustrations 15.17 and 15.18

16   Remove the seal(s) from the camshaft(s) and thoroughly clean the camshaft(s) and the gasket surface. Visually inspect the camshaft for wear and/or damage to the distributor drive gear, lobe surfaces, bearing journals and seal contact surfaces. Visually inspect the camshaft bearing surfaces in the cylinder head for scoring and other damage.

17   Measure the camshaft lobe heights **(see illustration)** and compare them to this Chapter's Specifications.

18   Measure the camshaft bearing journal diameters **(see illustration)**, then temporarily refit the bearing caps and measure the inside diameter of the camshaft bearing surfaces in the cylinder head, using a telescoping gauge. Subtract the journal measurement from the bearing measurement to obtain the camshaft bearing oil clearance. Compare this clearance with this Chapter's Specifications.

19   Renew the camshaft if it fails any of the above inspections. *If the lobes are worn, renew the rocker arms along with the camshaft. Cylinder head renewal may be necessary if the camshaft bearing surfaces in the head are damaged or excessively worn.*

Refitting

20   Very carefully clean the camshaft and bearing journals/caps. Liberally coat the journals, lobes and thrust portions of the camshaft with assembly lube or engine oil.

21   Carefully refit the camshaft(s) in the cylinder head.

22   Refit the lash adjusters and rocker arms if they haven't been reinstalled yet. Next refit the camshaft and camshaft bearing caps. Tighten them a little at a time, working from the centre journals on out, doing one camshaft at a time, until the torque listed in this Chapter's Specifications is reached.

23   Coat a new camshaft oil seal with engine oil and press it into place with a hammer and deep socket.

24   Refit the camshaft sprocket(s) and tighten the bolts to the torque listed in this Chapter's Specifications.

25   Refit the timing belt (see Section 10).

26   Reinstall the remaining parts in the reverse order of removal.

27   Reinstall the valve cover and run the engine while checking for oil leaks.

---

16   Sump - removal and refitting

SOHC engine

Removal

1   Disconnect the negative cable from the battery.

2   Raise the vehicle and support it securely on jackstands.

3   Remove the under-vehicle splash pan.

4   Drain the engine oil and refit a new oil filter (see Chapter 1).

5   Unbolt the exhaust pipe from the exhaust manifolds (see Section 8).

6   Support the engine/transmission securely with a hoist from above or a jack under the bellhousing. Protect the bellhousing by placing a wood block on the jack pad. **Warning:** *Be absolutely certain the engine/transmission is securely supported! DO NOT place any part of your body under the engine/transmission - it could crush you if the jack or hoist fails!*

7   Unbolt the engine mounts (see Section 20). Raise the engine/transmission assembly to provide clearance for sump removal.

8   Remove the sump bolts.

9   Detach the sump. Don't prise between the pan and block or damage to the sealing surfaces may result and oil leaks could develop. If the pan is stuck, dislodge it with a hammer and a block of wood.

10   Use a gasket scraper to remove all traces of old gasket material and sealant from the block and pan. Clean the mating surfaces with lacquer thinner or acetone.

11   Unbolt the oil pick-up tube and screen assembly.

Refitting

Refer to illustrations 16.14 and 16.15

12   Renew the gasket on the flange of the oil pick-up tube and reinstall the tube. Tighten the pick-up tube bolts to the torque listed in this Chapter's Specifications.

13   Ensure that the threaded holes in the block are clean (use a tap to remove any sealant or corrosion from the threads).

14   Apply a small amount of RTV sealant (or equivalent) to the oil pump-to-block and rear seal retainer-to-block junctions **(see illustration)** and apply a thin continuous bead along the circumference of the sump flange. **Note:** *Allow the sealant to "set-up" (slightly harden) before installing the gasket.*

15   Refit the sump and tighten the bolts in three or four steps following the sequence shown **(see illustration)** to the torque listed in this Chapter's Specifications.

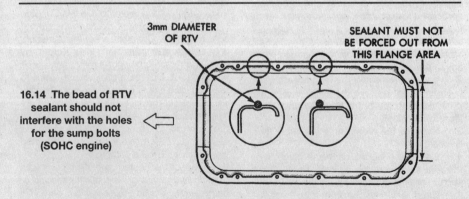

16.14 The bead of RTV sealant should not interfere with the holes for the sump bolts (SOHC engine)

3mm DIAMETER OF RTV

SEALANT MUST NOT BE FORCED OUT FROM THIS FLANGE AREA

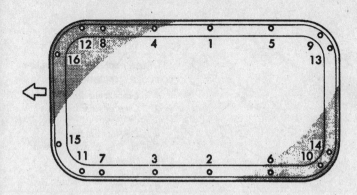

16.15 Oil pan bolt tightening sequence

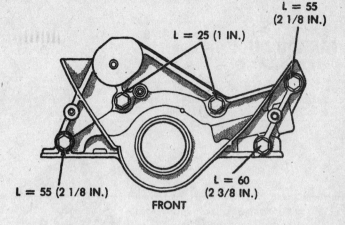

17.3 Be sure to mark the position of each bolt to aid in refitting

16   The remaining refitting steps are the reverse of removal.

17   Allow at least 30 minutes for the sealant to dry. Fill the crankcase with oil (see Chapter 1), start the engine and check for oil pressure and leaks.

DOHC engine

Removal

18   Disconnect the negative cable from the battery.

19   Raise the vehicle and support it securely on jackstands.

20   Remove the under-vehicle splash pan.

21   Drain the engine oil and refit a new oil filter (see Chapter 1).

22   Unbolt the exhaust pipe from the exhaust manifolds (see Section 8).

23   Support the engine/transmission securely with a hoist from above or a jack under the bellhousing. Protect the bellhousing by placing a wood block on the jack pad. **Warning:** *Be absolutely certain the engine/transmission is securely supported! DO NOT place any part of your body under the engine/transmission - it could crush you if the jack or hoist fails!*

24   If necessary, unbolt the engine mounts and raise the engine/transmission assembly to provide clearance for sump removal.

Lower sump

25   Remove the sump bolts.

26   Detach the sump. Don't prise between the upper and lower sump or damage to the sealing surfaces may result and oil leaks could develop. If the pan is stuck, dislodge it with a hammer and a block of wood.

Upper sump

27   Remove the lower sump (see above).

28   Remove the upper sump bolts.

29   Detach the sump. Don't prise between the sump and block or damage to the sealing surfaces may result and oil leaks could develop. If the pan is stuck, dislodge it with a hammer and a block of wood.

30   Unbolt the oil pick-up tube and screen assembly.

Refitting

Upper sump

31   Use a gasket scraper to remove all traces of old gasket material and sealant from the block and pan. Clean the mating surfaces with lacquer thinner or acetone.

32   Ensure that the threaded holes in the block are clean (use a tap to remove any sealant or corrosion from the threads).

33   Renew the gasket on the flange of the oil pick-up tube and reinstall the tube. Tighten the pick-up tube bolts to the torque listed in this Chapter's Specifications.

34   Apply a small amount of RTV sealant (or equivalent) to the oil pump-to-block and rear seal retainer-to-block junctions) and apply a thin continuous bead along the circumference of the sump flange. **Note:** *Allow the sealant to "set-up" (slightly harden) before installing the gasket.*

35   Refit the sump and tighten the bolts in three or four steps following the sequence shown to the torque listed in this Chapter's Specifications. Make sure that 38 mm long bolts (numbers 13 and 14 in the tightening sequence) are securely threaded into the engine block or transmission damage could result.

Lower sump

36   Use a gasket scraper to remove all traces of old gasket material and sealant from the upper sump to lower sump contact surfaces. Clean the mating surfaces with lacquer thinner or acetone.

37   Apply a small amount of RTV sealant in one continuous bead along the circumference of the sump flange. **Note:** *Allow the sealant to "set-up" (slightly harden) before installing the gasket.*

38   Refit the sump and tighten the bolts in three or four steps following the sequence shown to the torque listed in this Chapter's Specifications.

39   The remaining refitting steps are the reverse of removal.

40   Allow at least 30 minutes for the sealant to dry. Fill the crankcase with oil (see Chapter 1), start the engine and check for oil pressure and leaks.

---

17   Oil pump - removal, inspection and refitting

Removal

Refer to illustration 17.3

1   Remove the timing belt and the crankshaft sprocket (see Sections 10 and 11). Remove the sump and pick-up tube (see Section 17).

2   Unbolt the power steering pump (see Chapter 10) without disconnecting the hoses. Remove the power steering pump bracket.

3   Remove the oil pump-to-engine block bolts from the front of the engine **(see illustration)**.

4   Use a block of wood and a hammer to break the oil pump loose.

5   Pull out on the oil pump to remove it from the engine block.

6   Use a scraper to remove old gasket material and sealant from the oil pump and engine block mating surfaces. Clean the mating surfaces with lacquer thinner or acetone.

Inspection

Refer to illustrations 17.7, 17.10a, 17.10b and 17.10c

7   Remove the screws holding the rear cover to the oil pump **(see illustration on following page)**.

8   Clean all components with solvent, then inspect them for wear and damage.

9   Remove the oil pressure relief valve plug, washer, spring and valve (plunger). Check the oil pressure relief valve sliding surface and valve spring. If either the spring or the valve is damaged, they must be renewed as a set.

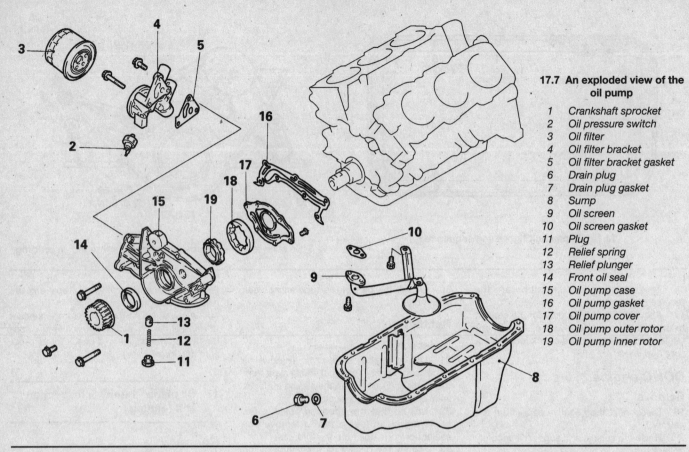

17.7 An exploded view of the oil pump

1   Crankshaft sprocket
2   Oil pressure switch
3   Oil filter
4   Oil filter bracket
5   Oil filter bracket gasket
6   Drain plug
7   Drain plug gasket
8   Sump
9   Oil screen
10 Oil screen gasket
11 Plug
12 Relief spring
13 Relief plunger
14 Front oil seal
15 Oil pump case
16 Oil pump gasket
17 Oil pump cover
18 Oil pump outer rotor
19 Oil pump inner rotor

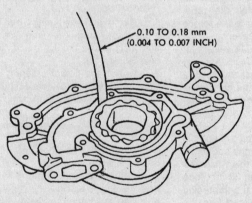

17.10a Checking case-to-outer rotor clearance with a feeler gauge

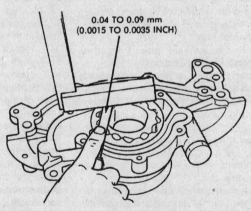

17.10b Checking rotor and clearance with a straightedge and a feeler gauge

10   Check the following clearances **(see illustrations)** and compare the measurements to the clearances listed in this Chapter's Specifications:

   Case-to-outer rotor
   Rotor end clearance
   Case-to-inner rotor

   If any of the clearances are excessive, renew the entire oil pump assembly.

11   Pack the cavities of the oil pump with petroleum jelly to prime it. Assemble the oil pump and tighten the screws to the torque listed in this Chapter's Specifications. Refit the oil pressure relief valve, spring and

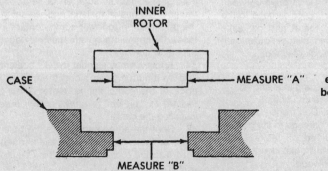

17.10c Check for excessive clearance between the case and inner rotor

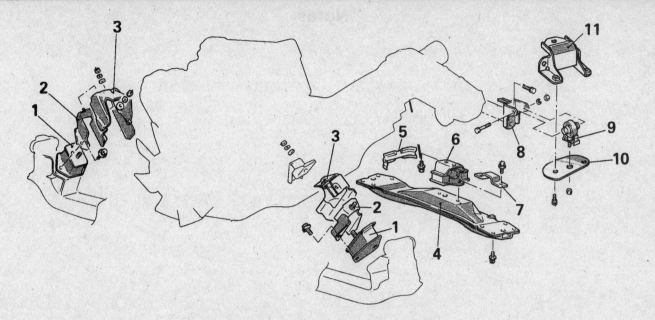

20.1 An exploded view of typical engine mounts

1	Front insulator	5	Heat shield	9	Transfer support insulator
2	Stopper	6	Rear insulator	10	Plate assembly
3	Heat shield	7	Stopper	11	Transfer support bracket
4	Number two crossmember	8	Transfer mounting bracket		

washer, then tighten the oil pressure relief valve plug to the torque listed in this Chapter's Specifications.

Refitting

12   Apply a thin film of RTV sealant to the new oil pump gasket.

13   Refitting is the reverse of the removal procedure. Align the flats on the crankshaft with the flats in the inner rotor of the oil pump. Tighten all fasteners to the torque values listed in this Chapter's Specifications.

18 Flywheel/driveplate - removal and refitting

This procedure is essentially the same for all engines. Refer to Part A and follow the procedure outlined there, but use the bolt torque listed in this Chapter's Specifications.

19 Rear main oil seal - renewal

This procedure is essentially the same for all engines. Refer to Part A and follow the procedure outlined there.

20 Engine mounts - check and renewal

Refer to illustration 20.1

This procedure is essentially the same for all engines. See Part A of this Chapter and follow the procedure outlined there, but use the torque values listed in this Chapter's Specifications. Use the accompanying exploded view for reference **(see illustration)**.

2B

Notes

Chapter 2 Part C
2.5L diesel engine

Contents

Specifications

General
Engine designation	4D56
Firing order	1 - 3 - 4 - 2
Cylinder numbers (drivebelt end-to-transmission end)	1 - 2 - 3 - 4
Bore and stroke	91.1 x 95.0 mm
Displacement	2,476 cc
Compression pressure	
Minimum	1,920 kPa
Maximum variation	300 kPa

Camshaft
Runout maximum	0.020 mm
Journal diameter	30 mm
Bearing journal oil clearance	0.05 to 0.09 mm
Lobe wear (maximum)	0.50 mm
Timing belt deflection	4 to 5 mm

Cylinder head
Warpage limit	0.1 mm

Oil pump
Gear-to-housing clearance	

Torque specifications
	Nm
Cylinder head bolts	115 to 125
Camshaft bearing cap bolts	17 to 20
Camshaft sprocket bolt	65 to 75
Valve cover bolts	6

Torque specifications (continued)

	Nm
Crankshaft pulley bolt	179 to 190
Crankshaft pulley bolts	10 to 12
Flywheel/driveplate-to-crankshaft bolts	130 to 140
Front cover bolts	10 to 12
Sump-to-engine block bolts	7
Oil cooler line banjo bolts	35
Oil cooler line-to-block banjo bolts	45
Sump drain plug	40
Exhaust manifold-to-cylinder head nuts	15 to 19
Exhaust manifold-to-exhaust pipe bolts	50
Front case bolts	12 to 14
Inlet manifold bolts	15 to 19
Rocker arm nuts	12 to 17
Rocker arm shaft bolts	35 to 39
Silent shaft chamber cover bolts	4 to 5
Silent shaft sprocket bolts	34 to 39
Timing belt tensioner fastener	22 to 29
Timing belt B tensioner pivot side bolt	24
Timing belt B slot side nut	26
Motor mount-to-frame bolts	35

1 General information

This Part of Chapter 2 is devoted to in-vehicle repair procedures for the 2.5L model 4D56 four-cylinder diesel engine. All information concerning engine removal and refitting and engine block and cylinder head overhaul can be found in Part E of this Chapter.

The following repair procedures are based on the assumption that the engine is refitted in the vehicle. If the engine has been removed from the vehicle and mounted on a stand, many of the steps outlined in this Part of Chapter 2 will not apply.

The Specifications included in this Part of Chapter 2 apply only to the procedures contained in this Part. Part E of Chapter 2 contains the Specifications necessary for cylinder head and engine block rebuilding.

The 2.5 litre engine is an inline vertical four, with a belt-driven overhead camshaft and a balance shaft counterbalancing system which cancels the engine's power pulses and produces relatively vibration-free operation. The crankshaft rides in five renewable insert-type main bearings, with the centre bearing (the thrust bearing) assigned the additional task of controlling crankshaft endplay.

The pistons have two compression rings and one oil control ring. The semi-floating piston pins are press fitted into the small end of the connecting rod. The connecting rod big ends are also equipped with renewable insert-type plain bearings.

The engine is liquid-cooled, utilising a centrifugal impeller-type pump, driven by a belt from the crankshaft, to circulate coolant around the cylinders and combustion chambers and through the inlet manifold.

Lubrication is handled by an oil pump mounted on the front of the engine. It is driven by the crankshaft through gears. The oil is filtered continuously by a cartridge-type filter mounted on the side of the engine.

2 Repair operations possible with the engine in the vehicle

Many major repair operations can be accomplished without removing the engine from the vehicle.

Clean the engine compartment and the exterior of the engine with some type of degreaser before any work is done. It will make the job easier and help keep dirt out of the internal areas of the engine.

Depending on the components involved, it may be helpful to remove the bonnet to improve access to the engine as repairs are performed (refer to Chapter 11 if necessary). Cover the fenders to prevent damage to the paint. Special pads are available, but an old bedspread or blanket will also work.

If vacuum, exhaust, oil or coolant leaks develop, indicating a need for gasket or seal renewal, the repairs can generally be made with the engine in the vehicle. The inlet and exhaust manifold gaskets, sump gasket, crankshaft oil seals and cylinder head gasket are all accessible with the engine in place.

Exterior engine components, such as the inlet and exhaust manifolds, the sump, the water pump, the starter motor, the alternator and the fuel system components can be removed for repair with the engine in place.

Since the cylinder head can be removed without pulling the engine, camshaft and valve component servicing can also be accomplished with the engine in the vehicle. Renewal of the timing belt and sprockets is also possible with the engine in the vehicle.

In extreme cases caused by a lack of necessary equipment, repair or renewal of piston rings, pistons, connecting rods and rod bearings is possible with the engine in the vehicle. However, this practice is not recommended because of the cleaning and preparation work that must be done to the components involved.

3 Top Dead Centre (TDC) for number one piston - locating

Refer to illustration 3.6

1   Top Dead Centre (TDC) is the highest point in the cylinder that each piston reaches as it travels up-and-down when the crankshaft turns. Each piston reaches TDC on the compression stroke and again on the exhaust stroke, but TDC generally refers to piston position on the compression stroke.

2   Positioning the number one piston at TDC is an essential part of many procedures, such as camshaft, timing chain or distributor removal.

3   Before beginning this procedure, be sure to place the transmission in Park (automatic) or Neutral (manual) and apply the parking brake or block the rear wheels.

4   In order to bring any piston to TDC, the crankshaft must be turned using one of the methods outlined below. When looking at the front of the engine (timing belt end), normal crankshaft rotation is clockwise.

a) *The preferred method is to turn the crankshaft with a socket and ratchet attached to the bolt threaded into the front of the crankshaft.*

b) *A remote starter switch, which may save some time, can also be used. Follow the instructions included with the switch. Once the piston is close to TDC, use a socket and ratchet as described in the previous paragraph.*

c) *If an assistant is available to turn the ignition switch to the Start position in short bursts, you can get the piston close to TDC without a remote starter switch. Make sure your assistant is out of the vehicle, away from the ignition switch, then use a socket and ratchet as described in Paragraph a) to complete the procedure.*

5   Remove the upper cover from the timing belt assembly.

6   Turn the crankshaft (see Step 4) until the mark on the crankshaft pulley is aligned with the"0" mark on the engine. The mark on the camshaft sprocket should be aligned with the mark on the front of the engine **(see illustration)**. **Caution:** *Always turn the crankshaft clockwise.* **Note:** *It may be necessary to remove the glow plugs in order to rotate the engine (refer to Chapter 4).*

7   If the mark on the camshaft sprocket is a half revolution away from the mark on the engine, rotate the crankshaft one additional turn. Until both marks are aligned.

8   To position the engine at TDC on number four cylinder (required when performing a valve adjustment), rotate the crankshaft one complete revolution until the mark on the camshaft sprocket is 180-degrees away from the mark on the front of the engine.

4   Valve cover - removal and refitting

Removal

Refer to illustration 4.6

1   Detach the cable from the negative battery terminal. Refer to Chapter 4 and remove any interfering turbocharger/intercooler components.

2   Disconnect the crankcase breather hose from the valve cover.

3   Disconnect any cables, air intake ducts or hoses which interfere with the valve cover removal.

4   Disconnect the accelerator cable from the valve cover and position it aside.

5   Wipe off the valve cover thoroughly to prevent debris from falling onto the exposed cylinder head or camshaft/valve train assembly.

6   Remove the valve cover bolts **(see illustration)**.

7   Carefully lift off the valve cover and gasket. If the cover is stuck to the cylinder head, tap it with a rubber mallet to break the seal. Do not prise between the cover and cylinder head or you'll damage the gasket mating surfaces.

Refitting

8   Use a gasket scraper to remove all traces of old gasket material from the gasket mating surfaces of the cylinder head and the valve cover. Clean the surfaces with a rag soaked in lacquer thinner or acetone.

9   Be sure to refit the semi-circular seal (camshaft plug) on top of the cylinder head near the camshaft sprocket. Apply beads of RTV sealant completely around the perimeter of the seal and also 10 mm on each side of it on the surface of the cylinder head.

10   Refit new seals on the valve cover bolts.

11   Refit a new gasket onto the valve cover. Refit the moulded rubber gasket onto the cover by pushing the new gasket into the slot that circles the valve cover perimeter. Apply a bead of RTV sealant where the cylinder head and camshaft bearing caps meet. Refit the valve cover and tighten the bolts to the torque listed in this Chapter's Specifications. **Caution:** *Do not overtighten the valve cover.*

12   The remainder of refitting is the reverse of removal.

5   Rocker arm assembly - removal, inspection and refitting

Removal

1   Remove the valve cover (see Section 4).

2   Position the number one piston at Top Dead Centre (see Section 3).

3   Remove the rocker shaft bolts and lift off the rocker shaft assembly **(see illustration)**.

Inspection

Refer to illustrations

4   To disassemble and inspect the rocker arm assembly, remove the retaining bolts and slip the rocker arms, springs and bearing caps off the shafts. **Caution:** *Keep the parts in order so you can reassemble them in the same positions.*

5   Thoroughly clean the parts and inspect them for wear and damage. Check the rocker arm faces that contact the camshaft. Also, make sure the oil holes in the shafts are not plugged. Check the surfaces of the shafts that the rocker arms ride on, as well as the bearing surfaces inside the rocker arms, for scoring and excessive wear. Renew any parts that are damaged or excessively worn.

Refitting

Refer to illustrations 5.6 and 5.7

6   Lubricate all components with engine assembly lube or engine oil and reassemble the shafts. When installing the rocker arms, shafts and springs, note the markings. Rockers for the inlet valves are marked with an "I". Rockers for the exhaust valves are marked with an "E" **(see illustration)**.

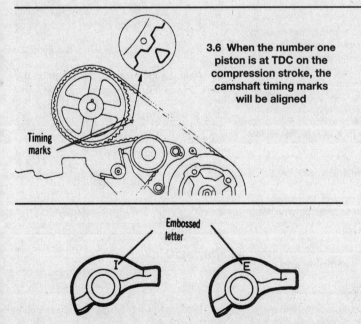

3.6 When the number one piston is at TDC on the compression stroke, the camshaft timing marks will be aligned

Timing marks

Embossed letter

For inlet   For exhaust

5.6 Inlet and exhaust rockers are clearly marked - keep them in order so each can be refitted on the valve from which it was removed

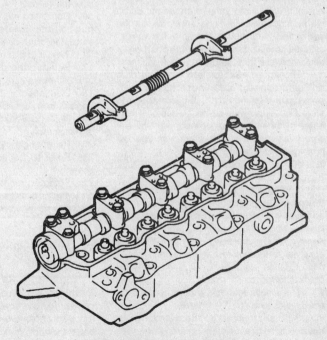

5.3 Rocker shaft refitting details

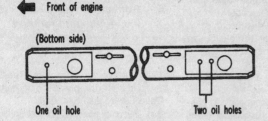

5.7 The rocker shaft must be refitted with the end with two oil holes at the rear

7   The rocker shaft must be refitted with the small oil feed holes down. The end of the shaft with only one oil hole should be at the front of the engine **(see illustration)**.

8   Adjust the valve clearances (cold) as described in Chapter 1. Temporarily reinstall the valve cover and run the engine until it is fully warmed up. Remove the valve cover and readjust the valves while the engine is still warm. Refit the valve cover permanently.

6   Valve springs, retainers and seals - renewal

Note: *Broken valve springs and defective valve stem seals can be renewed without removing the cylinder heads. Two special tools and a compressed air source are normally required to perform this operation, so read through this Section carefully and rent or buy the tools before beginning the job.*

1   Refer to Section 4 and remove the valve cover from the cylinder head.

2   Remove the glow plug from the affected cylinder. Refer to Chapter 4.

3   Turn the crankshaft until the piston in the affected cylinder is at Top Dead Centre on the compression stroke (see Section 3). If you're renewing all of the valve stem seals, begin with cylinder number one and work on the valves for one cylinder at a time. Move from cylinder-to-cylinder following the firing order sequence (see this Chapter's Specifications).

4   Thread an adaptor into the glow plug hole and connect an air hose from a compressed air source to it. Most auto parts stores can supply the air hose adaptor. **Note:** *Many cylinder compression gauges utilise a screw-in fitting that may work with your air hose quick-disconnect fitting.*

5   Remove the rocker arm assembly (see Section 5).

6   Apply compressed air to the cylinder. **Warning:** *The piston may be forced down by compressed air, causing the crankshaft to turn suddenly. If the spanner used when positioning the number one piston at TDC is still attached to the bolt in the crankshaft nose, it could cause damage or injury when the crankshaft moves.*

7   The valves should be held in place by the air pressure.

8   Stuff shop rags into the cylinder head holes around the valve spring area to prevent parts and tools from falling into the engine, then use a valve spring compressor to compress the spring. Remove the collets with small needle-nose pliers or a magnet.

9   Remove the spring retainer, shield and valve spring, then remove the valve guide seal. **Note:** *If air pressure fails to hold the valve in the closed position during this operation, the valve face or seat is probably damaged. If so, the cylinder head will have to be removed for additional repair operations.*

10   Wrap a rubber band or tape around the top of the valve stem so the valve won't fall into the combustion chamber, then release the air pressure.

11   Inspect the valve stem for damage. Rotate the valve in the guide and check the end for eccentric movement, which would indicate that the valve is bent.

12   Move the valve up-and-down in the guide and make sure it doesn't bind. If the valve stem binds, either the valve is bent or the guide is damaged. In either case, the cylinder head will have to be removed for repair.

13   Reapply air pressure to the cylinder to retain the valve in the closed position, then remove the tape or rubber band from the valve stem.

14   Lubricate the valve stem with engine oil and refit a new guide seal.

15   Refit the spring and retainer in position over the valve.

16   Compress the valve spring and carefully position the collets in the groove. Apply a small dab of grease to the inside of each collet to hold it in place.

17   Remove the pressure from the spring tool and make sure the collets are seated.

18   Disconnect the air hose and remove the adaptor from the spark plug hole.

19   Refer to Section 5 and refit the rocker arm assembly.

20   Refit the glow plugs.

21   Refer to Section 4 and refit the valve cover.

22   Start and run the engine, then check for oil leaks and unusual sounds coming from the valve cover area.

7   Inlet manifold - removal and refitting

Warning: *Diesel fuel is extremely flammable, so take extra precautions when you work on any part of the fuel system. Don't smoke or allow open flames or bare light bulbs near the work area, and don't work in a garage where a natural gas-type appliance (such as a water heater) with a pilot light is present. If you spill any fuel on your skin, rinse it off immediately with soap and water. When you perform any kind of work on the fuel system, wear safety glasses and have a Class B type fire extinguisher on hand.*

Removal

Note: *The following procedure applies to turbocharged models. Non-turbocharged models are similar.*

1   Detach the cable from the negative battery terminal.

2   Remove the intercooler and any other interfering ducts (see Chapter 4). Disconnect all interfering wiring and hoses.

3   Remove the boost hose from the waste gate and the inlet manifold. Depending on the model and options there may be other components which may need to be removed or disconnected

4   Remove the duct which connects the turbocharger or air cleaner to the inlet manifold.

5   Remove the inlet manifold bolts and remove the manifold from the engine.

Refitting

6   Clean the inlet manifold and cylinder head surface, removing all traces of gasket material.

7   Check the mating surfaces of the manifold for flatness with a precision straightedge and feeler gauge.

8   Inspect the manifold for cracks and distortion.

9   If the manifold is cracked or warped, renew it or see if it can be resurfaced/repaired at an automotive machine shop.

10   Check carefully for any stripped or broken inlet manifold bolts. Renew any defective bolts.

11   Place a new gasket onto the cylinder head.

12   Refit the inlet manifold and tighten the bolts finger-tight. Starting at the centre and working out in both directions, tighten the bolts in a criss-cross pattern until the torque listed in this Chapter's Specifications is reached.

13   The remainder of the refitting procedure is the reverse of removal.

8   Exhaust manifold - removal and refitting

Removal

Note: *The following procedure applies to turbocharged models. Non-turbocharged models are similar.*

1   Disconnect the negative battery cable from the battery.

2   Remove the inlet manifold (refer to Section 7).

3   If the vehicle is non-turbocharged, raise it and support it securely on jackstands. Disconnect the exhaust pipe from the exhaust

manifold. If it is turbocharged, disconnect the manifold from the turbocharger.

4   Remove the exhaust manifold fasteners and detach the exhaust manifold from the cylinder head and the turbocharger.

Refitting

5   Inspect the exhaust manifold for cracks, damage or distortion.

6   Discard the old gaskets and use a scraper to clean the gasket mating surfaces on the exhaust manifold, turbocharger and cylinder head. Place new gaskets onto the cylinder head and turbocharger.

7   Place the exhaust manifold in position on the cylinder head and refit the nuts. Starting at the centre, tighten the nuts in a criss-cross pattern until the torque listed in this Chapter's Specifications is reached.

8   The remainder of refitting is the reverse of removal.

9   Start the engine and check for exhaust leaks between the manifold and the cylinder head and between the manifold and the turbocharger.

9   Timing belt covers - removal and refitting

Removal

Refer to illustration 9.6

1   Disconnect the cable from the negative terminal of the battery. Remove the air cleaner assembly.

2   Remove the drivebelts. Remove the alternator, power steering pump and air conditioning compressor, if equipped, and lay them aside. **Warning:** *The air conditioning system is under high pressure - do not disconnect the hoses!*

3   Remove the water pump if necessary for clearance (refer to Chapter 3). Any other interfering components must be removed at this time.

4   Remove the crankshaft pulley bolt. **Note:** *This bolt is very tight. If a pneumatic impact wrench is not available, it will be necessary to remove the flywheel inspection plate and wedge a screwdriver in the starter ring gear teeth to prevent the crankshaft from turning.*

5   Remove the crankshaft pulley by levering it off. If it is stuck to the crankshaft, use a special puller to remove it. Do not use the type of puller that attaches to the belt groove.

6   Remove the upper front cover **(see illustration)**.

7   Remove the bolts attaching the lower front cover to the engine block. Note the location of each bolt so they can be returned to the same location from which they were removed. Tap the cover with a soft-faced hammer to break the gasket seal, then remove the cover from the engine block.

2C

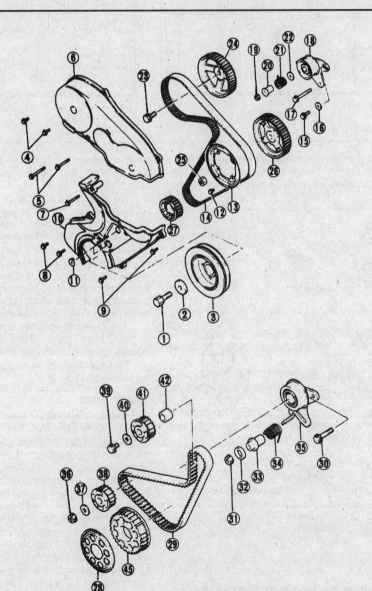

9.6 Timing component details

1	Bolt
2	Washer
3	Pulley
4	Bolt
5	Bolt
6	Upper cover
7	Bolt
8	Bolt
9	Bolt
10	Lower cover
11	Cover
12	Bolt
13	Flange
14	Timing belt
15	Bolt
16	Washer
17	Bolt
18	Tensioner assembly
19	Nut
20	Spacer
21	Spring
22	Washer
23	Bolt
24	Camshaft sprocket
25	Nut
26	Injection pump sprocket
27	Crankshaft sprocket
28	Flange
29	Timing belt "B"
30	Bolt
31	Nut
33	Spacer
34	Spring
35	Tensioner assembly
36	Nut
37	Washer
38	Silent shaft sprocket
39	Bolt
40	Washer
41	Silent shaft sprocket
42	Spacer
43	Crankshaft sprocket

Caution: *Levering between the cover and the engine block can damage the gasket sealing surfaces.*

Refitting

8   Thoroughly clean the front cover and engine block. Make sure the threaded holes in the engine block are clean and dry.

9   Fit the front cover onto the engine. Refit the bolts in a crisscross pattern and tighten them to the torque listed in this Chapter's Specifications.

10   Apply a thin layer of clean moly-based grease to the seal contact surface of the crankshaft pulley, then slide it onto the crankshaft. Refit the bolt and tighten it to the torque listed in this Chapter's Specifications.

11   The remainder of refitting is the reverse of removal.

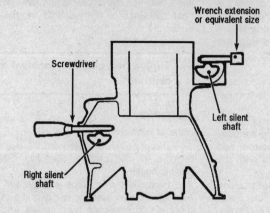

10.6 To remove the silent shaft sprockets, it is necessary to hold the shafts from turning using screwdrivers inserted through holes in the sides of the block

10   Balance shaft belt, timing belt and sprockets - removal, inspection, refitting and belt adjustment

Removal

Refer to illustration 10.6

1   Disconnect the cable from the negative terminal of the battery. Drain the cooling system (see Chapter 1).

2   Position the engine on TDC for number one cylinder (refer to Section 3). Remove the front belt covers (see Section 9).

3   Draw an arrow on each belt to indicate the direction of rotation.

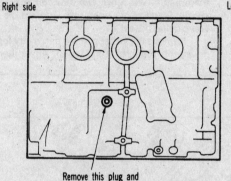

4   Loosen the timing belt tension adjusting bolt slightly, then slide the tensioner to the left to release tension on the belt. Tighten the tensioner temporarily in this position.

5   Perform the same operation with belt "B".

6   To remove the silent shaft sprockets, it will be necessary to hold the shafts from turning. There is a plug on the right side of the engine which can be removed for the insertion of a screwdriver to hold the right shaft. On the left side of the engine there is a small cover which can be removed in a similar manner **(see illustration)**. Both silent shafts must be positioned with their weights in the downward position in order to insert the screwdrivers.

7   The camshaft sprocket can be removed by first removing the valve cover and then using a spanner to hold the camshaft. There is a flat area cast into the camshaft for holding purposes.

Inspection

8   Inspect the sprocket teeth for wear and damage. Check the spacers (balance shaft sprockets only) for wear and damage. Check the tensioner spring for cracks and deterioration. Spin the tensioner rollers to check for free operation. Renew any defective parts.

9   The timing belts should be free of any obvious damage and wear. There should be no oil or grease on them. The belts must be renewed at the required intervals (refer to Chapter 1). Light dirt can be wiped off with a clean rag. **Note:** *Even though the belts may appear to be in good condition, they must still be renewed at the required intervals. Refer to the maintenance schedule in Chapter 1.*

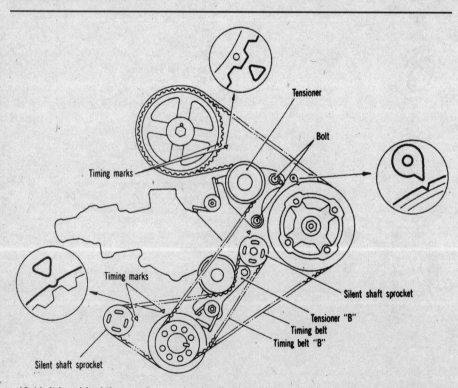

10.11 It is critical that each sprocket is aligned with its corresponding marks as shown

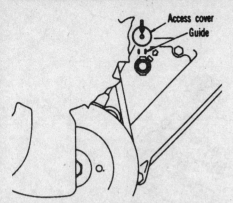

10.30 Slide the access cover to adjust the tension of timing belt "B"

Refitting

Refer to illustration 10.14

10 Make sure the crankshaft is positioned at Top Dead Centre (TDC) for number one cylinder (see Section 3).

11 Position the timing belt "B" sprocket, the flange which separates the two sprockets and the camshaft timing belt sprocket on the end of the crankshaft **(see illustration)**. The lip on the edge of the flange must face toward the front.

12 Refit both silent shaft sprockets. Use screwdrivers to lock the shafts while tightening the bolts to the value listed in the Specifications in this Chapter.

13 Refit the camshaft sprocket. Tighten the bolt to the value listed in the Specifications in this Chapter.

14 Make certain that the engine is still at TDC on number one cylinder. The mark on the crankshaft sprocket should be pointing directly at the mark on the front of the engine. Position both silent shaft sprockets so that their notches align with the marks on the front of the engine.

16 Refit timing belt "B" over the crankshaft sprocket, the tensioner and both silent shaft sprockets. The tension side of the belt should have no slack. Make sure that the arrow previously drawn is pointing the same direction.

17 Release the tensioner so that it snaps into position. Recheck the alignment of all marks. Tighten the tensioner bolts.

18 Press on the tension side of the belt with your thumb. The belt should deflect 4 to 5 mm.

19 Perform the same operation with the camshaft timing belt. Make certain that the timing marks on the crankshaft pulley, the camshaft pulley and the injection pump pulley are aligned with their respective marks **(see illustration 10.11)**. Check its tension by pressing on the belt midway between the injection pump sprocket and the camshaft sprocket.

20 Rotate the crankshaft by hand through two complete revolutions. Again check the alignment of all marks.

21 The remainder of refitting is the reverse of removal.

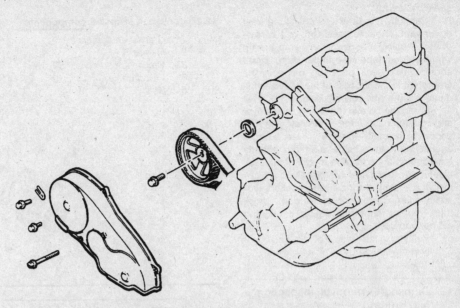

11.5 Camshaft sprocket refitting details

Timing belt adjustment

22 Remove the upper timing belt cover. Position the engine at TDC on the compression stroke for number one cylinder (refer to Section 3). Check that the camshaft sprocket marks are aligned.

23 Loosen both tensioner bolts. The tensioner will now adjust itself.

24 Make certain that the belt is tightly seated around the camshaft sprocket.

25 Smoothly turn the engine in the normal clockwise direction for a distance of exactly two camshaft sprocket teeth.

26 First, tighten the upper tensioner bolt. Next, tighten the lower bolt.

27 Turn the engine back in the reverse direction until the camshaft sprocket timing marks align again.

28 Press down on the uppermost portion of the timing belt. It should deflect 4 to 5 mm.

Silent shaft belt adjustment

Refer to illustration 10.30

29 Position the engine at TDC on the compression stroke of number one cylinder (refer to Section 3).

30 Slide up the lower timing inspection cover **(see illustration)**.

31 Loosen the nut and the bolt securing the lower tensioner. Loosen one turn on the upper bolt and two turns on the lower nut.

32 Tighten the lower nut first, followed by the upper bolt.

33 Lower the inspection cover.

11 Camshaft oil seal - renewal

Refer to illustration 11.5

1 Remove the intercooler assembly if so

equipped. Remove or disconnect any other interfering components.

2 Position the engine at TDC on number one cylinder (refer to Section 3).

3 Remove the upper timing belt cover. Slightly loosen the nut and bolt on the timing belt tensioner. Push the tensioner to the right of the engine to release some of the tension on the timing belt. Tighten the nut and bolt.

4 Make certain that the camshaft sprocket timing marks are aligned. Tightly tie the timing belt to the sprocket using a large plastic wire tie or a length of wire.

5 Remove the camshaft sprocket bolt **(see illustration)**. Place the sprocket (with the timing belt attached) on the timing belt lower cover. **Caution:** *Place a spacer of some sort under the camshaft sprocket/timing belt. The camshaft sprocket cannot be allowed to drop. Do not allow enough tension to be released from the timing belt that it will be allowed to drop off of the lower sprocket. Do not rotate the crankshaft after the sprocket has been removed.*

6 Prise the camshaft oil seal from the cylinder head using a sharp flat blade screwdriver.

7 Apply a thin coat of RTV sealant to the outer diameter of the new seal and refit the seal onto the cylinder head by carefully and evenly tapping it with a hammer and driver.

8 The remainder of refitting is the reverse of removal.

12 Crankshaft front oil seal - renewal

Refer to illustrations 12.2 and 12.3

1 Remove the drivebelts (see Chapter 1).

2 Remove the timing belts and the

2C

crankshaft sprockets (refer to Section 10 and **see illustration**).

3   Carefully prise the seal out of the front cover with a seal removal tool or a screwdriver. If using a screwdriver, wrap the tip with electrical tape **(see illustration)**. Don't scratch the seal bore or damage the crankshaft in the process (if the crankshaft is damaged, the new seal will leak).

4   Clean the bore in the timing chain cover and coat the outer edge of the new seal with engine oil or multi-purpose grease. Using a socket with an outside diameter slightly smaller than the outside diameter of the seal, carefully drive the seal into place with a hammer. If a socket is not available, a short section of a large diameter pipe will work. Check the seal after refitting to be sure the spring did not pop out.

5   Refitting is the reverse of removal.

6   Run the engine and check for leaks.

13   Camshaft - removal, inspection and refitting

Removal

Refer to illustration 13.6

1   Disconnect the cable from the negative battery terminal.

2   Remove the valve cover (see Section 4).

3   Position the number one piston at Top Dead Centre (see Section 3).

4   Remove the camshaft sprocket (refer to Section 11). **Caution: *Place a spacer of some sort under the camshaft sprocket/timing belt.* The camshaft sprocket cannot be allowed to drop. Do not allow enough tension to be released from the timing belt that it will be allowed to drop off of the lower sprocket. Do not rotate the crankshaft with the camshaft sprocket removed from the camshaft. If the timing belt falls slightly away from the lower sprocket, it will be necessary to reinstall the belt and verify its correct placement. Refer to Section 10 for this procedure.**

5   Remove the rocker shaft assembly (refer to Section 5).

6   Remove the five camshaft bearing caps **(see illustration)**.

7   Lift the camshaft off the cylinder head. Remove and discard the seal.

Inspection

8   To check camshaft runout:

a) *Support the camshaft with a pair of V-blocks and attach a dial indicator with the stem resting against the centre bearing journal on the camshaft.*

b) *Rotate the camshaft and note the indicated runout.*

c) *Compare the results to the camshaft runout listed in this Chapter's Specifications.*

d) *If the indicated runout exceeds the specified runout, renew the camshaft.*

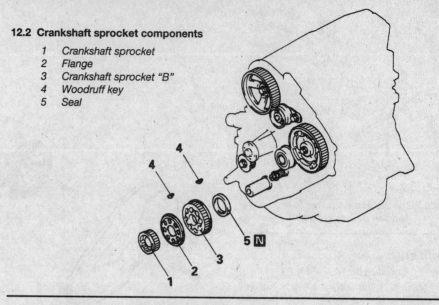

12.2 Crankshaft sprocket components

1   *Crankshaft sprocket*
2   *Flange*
3   *Crankshaft sprocket "B"*
4   *Woodruff key*
5   *Seal*

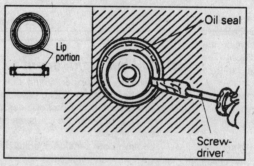

12.3 Be very careful to avoid nicking the shaft while removing the oil seal - wrap the end of the screwdriver with electrical tape

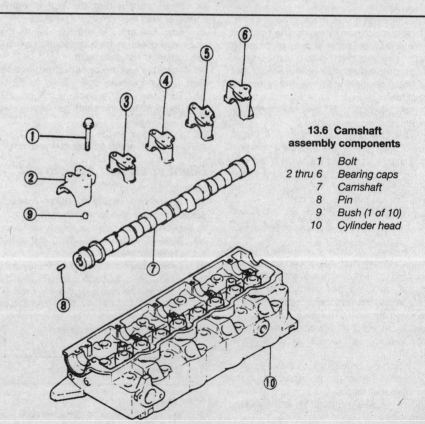

13.6 Camshaft assembly components

1	*Bolt*
2 thru 6	*Bearing caps*
7	*Camshaft*
8	*Pin*
9	*Bush (1 of 10)*
10	*Cylinder head*

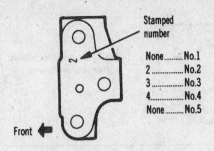

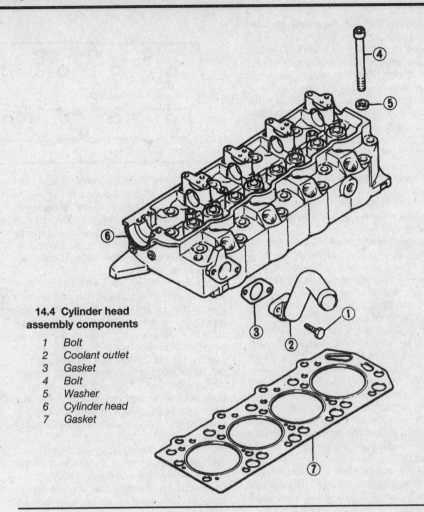

13.17 Each camshaft bearing cap is marked with an identifying number

9   Check the camshaft bearing journals and bearing caps for scoring and signs of wear.

10   Check the cam lobes for wear:

a) *Check the toe and ramp areas of each cam for score marks and uneven wear. Also check for flaking and pitting.*

b) *If there is wear on the toe or the ramp, renew the camshaft, but first try to find the cause of the wear. Look for abrasive substances in the oil and inspect the oil pump and oil passages for blockage. Cam wear is usually caused by inadequate lubrication or dirty oil.*

c) *Using a micrometer, calculate the lobe wear. If the lobe wear is greater than listed in this Chapter's Specifications, renew the camshaft.*

11   Inspect the rocker arms for wear, galling and pitting of the contact surfaces.

12   If any of the conditions described above are noted, the cylinder head is probably lacking sufficient lubrication, make sure you track down the cause of this problem (low oil level, low oil pump capacity, clogged oil passage, etc.) before installing a new cylinder head or camshaft.

Refitting

Refer to illustration 13.17

13   Thoroughly clean the camshaft, the bearing surfaces in the cylinder head and bearing caps and the rocker arms. Remove all sludge and dirt. Wipe off all components with a clean, lint-free cloth.

14   Lubricate the camshaft bearing surfaces in the cylinder head and the bearing journals and lobes on the camshaft with assembly lube or moly-base grease. Carefully lower the camshaft into position with the dowel pin pointing up. **Caution:** *Failure to adequately lubricate the camshaft and related components can cause serious damage to bearing and friction surfaces during the first few seconds after engine start-up, when the oil pressure is low or nonexistent.*

15   Refit a new oil seal onto the cylinder head (see Section 11).

16   Apply a thin coat of assembly lube or moly-base grease to the bearing surfaces of the camshaft bearing caps. Lubricate the

14.4 Cylinder head assembly components

1   Bolt
2   Coolant outlet
3   Gasket
4   Bolt
5   Washer
6   Cylinder head
7   Gasket

contact surfaces on the top of the rocker arms with assembly lube or moly-base grease.

17   Refit the camshaft bearing caps. They are numbered (the front and rear caps have no numbers) **(see illustration)**. Refit the rocker assembly.

18   Refit the camshaft sprocket/timing belt. Tighten the camshaft sprocket bolt to the torque listed in this Chapter's Specifications. Check the alignment of the injection pump sprocket and the camshaft sprocket after assembly.

19   Refit the valve cover. The remainder of refitting is the reverse of removal.

14   Cylinder head - removal and refitting

Caution: *Allow the engine to cool completely before beginning this procedure.*

Removal

Refer to illustration 14.4

1   Disconnect the negative cable from the battery. Position the number one piston at Top Dead Centre (see Section 3).

2   Remove the valve cover (refer to Section 4). This involves removal of the inter-

cooler/air inlet assembly, If so equipped.

3   Remove the power steering pump and lay it aside with out disconnecting the hoses.

4   Disconnect the accelerator cable and position it out of the way **(see illustration)**.

5   Remove the drivebelts (refer to Chapter 1).

6   Remove all interfering hoses. Be certain to label them as they are removed.

7   Remove the dipstick assembly.

8   Disconnect the alternator wiring harness, the oil pressure gauge wiring and all other interfering wiring.

9   Disconnect the turbocharger oil return hose if so equipped.

10   Drain the cooling system (refer to Chapter 1). Remove the radiator upper hose.

11   Remove the timing belt upper cover (refer to Section 9).

12   Disconnect the glow plug harness wiring, the coolant temperature sensor wiring and the earth cable.

13   Disconnect the fuel injection supply tubes and the return hose.

14   Disconnect the exhaust pipe from the exhaust manifold or turbocharger. If desired, the exhaust manifold/turbocharger assembly and the inlet manifold can be removed at this time.

15   Remove the camshaft sprocket (refer to Section 13). **Caution: Place a spacer of**

2C

some sort under the camshaft sprocket/timing belt. The camshaft sprocket cannot be allowed to drop. Do not allow enough tension to be released from the timing belt that it will be allowed to drop off of the lower sprocket. Do not rotate the crankshaft with the camshaft sprocket removed from the camshaft. If the timing belt falls slightly away from the lower sprocket, it will be necessary to reinstall the belt and verify its correct placement. Refer to Section 10 for this procedure.

16   Loosen the cylinder head bolts in 1/4-turn increments, following the reverse of the recommended tightening sequence, until they can be removed by hand **(see illustration 14.24)**.

17   Lift the cylinder head off the engine. If resistance is felt, don't prise between the cylinder head and engine block gasket mating surfaces - damage to the mating surfaces will result. Instead, prise against the casting protrusions on the sides of the cylinder head. Set the cylinder head on wood blocks to prevent damage to the gasket sealing surfaces. **Caution:** *Be careful not to disturb the timing belt and sprocket when lifting the cylinder head off. After the cylinder head is removed, secure the timing belt and sprocket to the engine, keeping tension on the belt. If the timing chain is disturbed it will become necessary to remove the front cover to restore timing. Do not rotate the crankshaft with the sprocket and chain removed from the camshaft.*

18   Cylinder head disassembly and inspection procedures are covered in detail in Chapter 2, Part E. Check the cylinder head for warpage.

Refitting

Refer to illustration 14.24

19   The mating surfaces of the cylinder head and engine block must be perfectly clean when the cylinder head is refitted.

20   Use a gasket scraper to remove all traces of carbon and old gasket material, then clean the mating surfaces with lacquer thinner or acetone. If there's oil on the mating surfaces when the cylinder head is refitted, the gasket may not seal correctly and leaks may develop. When working on the engine block, stuff the cylinders with clean shop rags to keep out debris. Use a vacuum cleaner to remove material that falls into the cylinders. Since the cylinder head is made of aluminium, aggressive scraping can cause damage. Be extra careful not to nick or gouge the mating surfaces with the scraper. Gasket removal solvents are available from most auto parts stores and may prove helpful.

21   Check the engine block and cylinder head mating surfaces for nicks, deep scratches and other damage. If damage is slight, it can be removed with a file; if it's excessive, machining may be the only alternative.

22   Use a tap of the correct size to chase the threads in the cylinder head bolt holes.

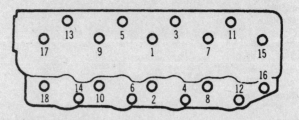

14.24 Cylinder head bolt tightening sequence

Clean and dry each bolt hole, if any fluid remains in a bolt hole damage to the engine block may result when the bolts are tightened. Mount each cylinder head bolt in a vice and run a die down the threads to remove corrosion and restore the threads. Dirt, corrosion, sealant and damaged threads will affect torque readings.

23   Apply a dab of RTV sealant at the front cover-to-engine block junction and place a new gasket on the engine block. The gasket must have the correct marking (56T). Check to see if there are any markings (such as "TOP") on the gasket that say how it is to be refitted. Set the cylinder head in position.

24   Lightly oil the cylinder head bolt threads and refit the bolts. Tighten the cylinder head bolts in three increments, following the recommended sequence, to the torque listed in this Chapter's Specifications **(see illustration)**.

25   Refit the timing chain and sprocket. Tighten the camshaft sprocket bolt to the torque listed in this Chapter's Specifications. Check to be certain that the camshaft sprocket and injection pump sprocket are aligned with their respective marks before proceeding.

26   Reinstall the remaining parts in the reverse order of removal.

27   Be sure to refill the cooling system and check all fluid levels.

28   Rotate the crankshaft clockwise slowly by hand through two complete revolutions. Recheck the camshaft timing marks (see Section 10). **Caution:** *If you feel any resistance while turning the engine over, stop and recheck the camshaft timing. The valves may be hitting the pistons.*

29   Start the engine and check the idle speed (see Chapter 1).

30   Run the engine until normal operating temperature is reached. Check for leaks and proper operation.

15   Sump - removal and refitting

Note: *The following procedure is based on the assumption that the engine is in the vehicle.*

Removal

1   Detach the cable from the negative battery terminal.

2   Raise the vehicle and support it securely on jackstands.

3   Drain the oil and renew the oil filter (see Chapter 1). Remove the skid plate.

4   Disconnect the exhaust pipe from the exhaust manifold or turbocharger, lower and support the exhaust pipe.

5   Remove the bolts securing the sump to the engine block. Tap on the sump with a soft-face hammer to break the gasket seal, then detach the sump from the engine. Don't prise between the engine block and sump mating surfaces.

6   Using a gasket scraper, remove all traces of old gasket and/or sealant from the engine block and sump. Clean the mating surfaces with lacquer thinner or acetone. Make sure the threaded bolt holes in the engine block are clean.

7   Clean the sump with solvent and dry it thoroughly. Check the gasket flanges for distortion, particularly around the bolt holes. If necessary, place the sump on a wood block and use a hammer to flatten and restore the gasket surfaces.

Refitting

8   Apply a 4 mm bead of RTV silicone sealant around the perimeter of the sump in the groove. Be certain to lay the sealant inboard of the bolt holes.

9   Carefully place the sump in position within 15 minutes of applying the silicone.

10   Refit the bolts and tighten them in 1/4-turn increments to the torque listed in this Chapter's Specifications. Start with the bolts closest to the centre of the sump and work out in a spiral pattern. Don't overtighten them or leakage may occur.

11   The remainder of refitting is the reverse of removal. Add oil, run the engine and check for oil leaks.

16   Oil pump, silent shafts and lower front case assembly - removal, inspection and refitting

Removal

Refer to illustration 16.5

1   Disconnect the cable from the negative battery terminal.

2   Remove both timing belts and the pulleys (refer to Section 10).

3   Remove the sump (refer to Section 15). Remove the oil screen and pick-up assembly.

4   Remove the front upper case and its gasket from the front of the engine block.

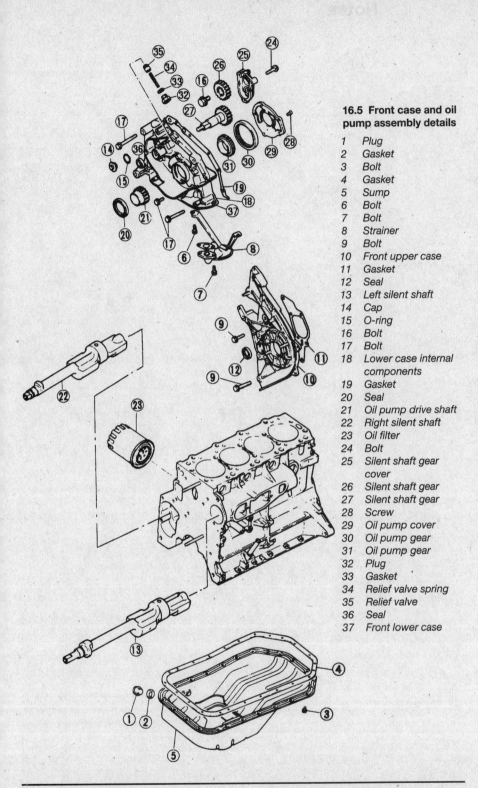

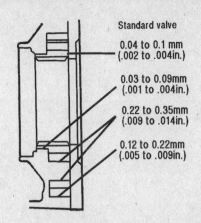

16.5 Front case and oil pump assembly details

1   Plug
2   Gasket
3   Bolt
4   Gasket
5   Sump
6   Bolt
7   Bolt
8   Strainer
9   Bolt
10 Front upper case
11 Gasket
12 Seal
13 Left silent shaft
14 Cap
15 O-ring
16 Bolt
17 Bolt
18 Lower case internal
     components
19 Gasket
20 Seal
21 Oil pump drive shaft
22 Right silent shaft
23 Oil filter
24 Bolt
25 Silent shaft gear
     cover
26 Silent shaft gear
27 Silent shaft gear
28 Screw
29 Oil pump cover
30 Oil pump gear
31 Oil pump gear
32 Plug
33 Gasket
34 Relief valve spring
35 Relief valve
36 Seal
37 Front lower case

Standard valve

0.04 to 0.1 mm
(.002 to .004in.)

0.03 to 0.09mm
(.001 to .004in.)

0.22 to 0.35mm
(.009 to .014in.)

0.12 to 0.22mm
(.005 to .009in.)

16.12 Oil pump clearance check points

2C

11 Extract the spring and oil pump relief valve.
12 Measure the side clearances between the inner and outer gears and the case **(see illustration)**. If any of the measurements are outside the limits, renew the pump.
13 Lubricate the gears and bearing surfaces with clean engine oil. Refit the gears into the body with the mating marks aligned. Lubricate the oil pressure relief valve and refit the relief valve and spring assembly. Tighten the relief valve cap to the torque listed in this Chapter's Specifications. Refit the cover onto the pump body and tighten the screws securely.
14 If the silent shafts, bearings or gear assemblies require service, consult a competent repair shop with the experience and special tools required.

Refitting

15 Refit the oil pump cover after making certain that the alignment marks on the inner and outer gears are aligned.
16 The remainder of refitting is the reverse of removal.

---

17 Flywheel/driveplate - removal and refitting

Refer to Chapter 2A.

---

18 Rear main oil seal - renewal

Refer to Chapter 2A. During refitting, make certain that the hole in the oil separator ring is refitted so that its hole is at the bottom (near the flat side of the housing).

---

19 Engine mounts - check and renewal

Refer to Chapter 2A.

---

5   Remove the left silent shaft oil seal and the left silent shaft **(see illustration)**. Refer to Section 10 if necessary.
6   Remove the plug cap and the O-ring from the lower case.
7   Remove the entire lower case assembly.
8   Remove the oil pump cover.
9   Use a center punch to make alignment marks on the oil pump inner and outer gears before removing them from the case if they do not already exist.

Inspection
Refer to illustration 16.12
10 Remove the bolts and lift off the oil pump cover.

Notes

Chapter 2 Part D
2.8L diesel engine

Contents

2D

Specifications

General

Firing order	1 - 3 - 4 - 2
Cylinder numbers (drivebelt end-to-transmission end)	1 - 2 - 3 - 4
Bore and stroke	95 x 100 mm
Displacement	2,835 cc
Compression pressure	
2.8L	
Standard	2,840 kPa
Minimum	2,250 kPa
Maximum variation	290 kPa

Camshaft

Endplay	
Standard	0.10 to 0.18 mm
Limit	0.30 mm
Runout maximum	0.020 mm
Bearing journal oil clearance	0.05 to 0.09 mm
Lobe lift	
Intake	9.89 mm
Exhaust	10.19 mm

Cylinder head

Warpage limit	0.2 mm
Inlet/exhaust manifold warpage limit	0.15 mm
Maximum allowable machining	0.2 mm

Oil pump

Gear -to-cover clearance	
Standard	0.05 to 0.10 mm
Limit	0.15 mm
Gear tip-to-case clearance	
Standard	0.15 to 0.26 mm
limit	0.27 mm
Shaft clearance	
Standard	0.03 to 0.05 mm
Limit	0.15 mm

Piston protrusion above block deck

Non-turbocharged .... 0.55 to 0.77 mm
Turbocharged .... 0.45 to 0.67 mm

Timing gears and balance shafts

Balance shaft-to-bush clearance
    Standard... 0.06 to 0.11 mm
    Limit .... 0.16 mm
Left idler shaft-to-bush clearance
    Standard... 0.02 to 0.05 mm
    Limit .... 0.1 mm
Right balance shaft gear and oil pump gear backlash
    Standard... 0.04 to 0.19 mm
    Limit .... 0.3 mm
Oil pump gear and crankshaft gear backlash
    Standard... 0.04 to 0.18 mm
    Limit .... 0.3 mm
Crankshaft gear and idler gear backlash
    Standard... 0.04 to 0.18 mm
    Limit .... 0.3 mm
Idler gear and left idler gear backlash
    Standard... 0.04 to 0.19 mm
    Limit .... 0.3 mm
Left idler gear and left balance shaft gear backlash
    Standard... 0.04 to 0.22 mm
    Limit .... 0.4 mm
Idler gear and injection pump gear backlash
    Standard... 0.04 to 0.21 mm
    Limit .... 0.4 mm
Balance shaft endplay
    Standard... 0.09 to 0.24 mm
    Limit .... 0.3 mm
Idler gear and sprocket
    Standard... 0.05 to 0.20 mm
    Limit .... 0.3 mm
Left idler gear
    Standard... 0.05 to 0.20 mm
    Limit .... 0.3 mm

Torque specifications

Nm

Large cylinder head bolts
    Step 1.. 100
    Step 2.. Fully loosen in reverse sequence
    Step 3.. 50
    Step 4.. Tighten an additional 90-degrees
    Step 5.. Tighten an additional 90-degrees
    Two small front cylinder head bolts 24
Balance shaft gear bolts.. 37
Camshaft bearing cap bolts .... 19 to 21
Camshaft sprocket bolt (left hand thread).............................. 90
Crankshaft pulley bolt... 240
Flywheel-to-crankshaft bolts 125
Flexplate-to crankshaft bolts.. 135
Oil cooler banjo bolts.. 29 to 34
Oil cooler hoses-to-block banjo bolts .... 39 to 44
Oil cooler plugs... 44
Oil cooler mounting nuts 20
Oil pump cover-to body screws 10
Exhaust manifold
    Manifold-to-cylinder head nuts.. 31
    Manifold heat shield bolts.. 12 to 15
    Manifold-to-exhaust pipe bolts.. 49
Inlet manifold bolts.. 18
Inlet manifold cover screws.. 10 to 12
Timing chain tension lever bolt 41
Valve cover bolts 4
Motor mount-to-frame bolts.. 44

1 General information

This Part of Chapter 2 is devoted to in-vehicle repair procedures for the 2.8L model 4M40 four-cylinder diesel engine. All information concerning engine removal and refitting and engine block and cylinder head overhaul can be found in Part E of this Chapter.

The following repair procedures are based on the assumption that the engine is refitted in the vehicle. If the engine has been removed from the vehicle and mounted on a stand, many of the steps outlined in this Part of Chapter 2 will not apply.

The Specifications included in this Part of Chapter 2 apply only to the procedures contained in this Part. Part E of Chapter 2 contains the Specifications necessary for cylinder head and engine block rebuilding.

The 2.8 litre engine is an inline vertical four, with a chain-driven overhead camshaft and a balance shaft counterbalancing system which cancels the engine's power pulses and produces relatively vibration-free operation. The crankshaft rides in renewable insert-type main bearings.

The pistons have two compression rings and one oil control ring. The semi-floating piston pins are press fitted into the small end of the connecting rod. The connecting rod big ends are also equipped with renewable insert-type plain bearings.

The engine is liquid-cooled, utilising a centrifugal impeller-type pump, driven by a belt from the camshaft, to circulate coolant around the cylinders and combustion chambers and through the inlet manifold.

Lubrication is handled by an oil pump mounted on the front of the engine. It is driven by the crankshaft. The oil is filtered continuously by a cartridge-type filter mounted on the side of the engine.

2 Repair operations possible with the engine in the vehicle

Many major repair operations can be accomplished without removing the engine from the vehicle.

Clean the engine compartment and the exterior of the engine with some type of degreaser before any work is done. It will make the job easier and help keep dirt out of the internal areas of the engine.

Depending on the components involved, it may be helpful to remove the bonnet to improve access to the engine as repairs are performed (refer to Chapter 11 if necessary). Cover the fenders to prevent damage to the paint. Special pads are available, but an old bedspread or blanket will also work.

If vacuum, exhaust, oil or coolant leaks develop, indicating a need for gasket or seal renewal, the repairs can generally be made with the engine in the vehicle. The inlet and exhaust manifold gaskets, oil sump gasket, crankshaft oil seals and cylinder head gasket

are all accessible with the engine in place.

Exterior engine components, such as the inlet and exhaust manifolds, the oil sump, the water pump, the starter motor, the alternator and the fuel system components can be removed for repair with the engine in place.

Since the cylinder head can be removed without pulling the engine, camshaft and valve component servicing can also be accomplished with the engine in the vehicle. Renewal of the timing belt and sprockets is also possible with the engine in the vehicle.

In extreme cases caused by a lack of necessary equipment, repair or renewal of piston rings, pistons, connecting rods and rod bearings is possible with the engine in the vehicle. However, this practice is not recommended because of the cleaning and preparation work that must be done to the components involved.

3 Top Dead Centre (TDC) for number one piston - locating

Refer to illustration 3.7

1   Top Dead Centre (TDC) is the highest point in the cylinder that each piston reaches as it travels up-and-down when the crankshaft turns. Each piston reaches TDC on the compression stroke and again on the exhaust stroke, but TDC generally refers to piston position on the compression stroke.
2   Positioning the number one piston at TDC is an essential part of many procedures, such as camshaft, timing chain or distributor removal.
3   Before beginning this procedure, be sure to place the transmission in Park (automatic) or Neutral (manual) and apply the parking brake or block the rear wheels.
4   In order to bring any piston to TDC, the crankshaft must be turned using one of the methods outlined below. When looking at the front of the engine (timing belt end), normal crankshaft rotation is clockwise.

   a) *The preferred method is to turn the crankshaft with a socket and ratchet attached to the bolt threaded into the front of the crankshaft.*
   b) *A remote starter switch, which may save some time, can also be used. Follow the instructions included with the switch. Once the piston is close to TDC, use a socket and ratchet as described in the previous paragraph.*
   c) *If an assistant is available to turn the ignition switch to the Start position in short bursts, you can get the piston close to TDC without a remote starter switch. Make sure your assistant is out of the vehicle, away from the ignition switch, then use a socket and ratchet as described in Paragraph a) to complete the procedure.* **Note:** *It may be necessary to remove the glow plugs in order to rotate the engine* (refer to Chapter 4).

5   Remove the valve cover (refer to Section 4).

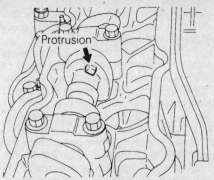

3.7 The protrusion indicated must face upward when the engine is correctly positioned at TDC for number one cylinder on the compression stroke

6   Rotate the engine until the notch on the crankshaft pulley is aligned with the "0" timing mark. **Caution:** *Always turn the crankshaft clockwise.*
7   Check that the protrusion on the camshaft is pointing up **(see illustration)**. If it is, then the engine is at TDC on the compression stroke for number one cylinder. If it is not, then rotate the crankshaft one full turn until the marks are aligned and the protrusion is up.
8   To position the engine at TDC on number four cylinder (required when performing a valve adjustment), rotate the crankshaft one complete revolution, again aligning the notch and the "0" mark.

4 Valve cover - removal and refitting

Removal

1   Detach the cable from the negative battery terminal. Refer to Chapter 4 and remove any interfering turbocharger/intercooler components.
2   Disconnect the crankcase breather hose from the valve cover.
3   Disconnect any cables, air intake ducts or hoses which interfere with the valve cover removal.
4   Disconnect the accelerator cable from the valve cover and position it aside.
5   Wipe off the valve cover thoroughly to prevent debris from falling onto the exposed cylinder head or camshaft/valve train assembly.
6   Remove the valve cover bolts.
7   Carefully lift off the valve cover and gasket. If the cover is stuck to the cylinder head, tap it with a rubber mallet to break the seal. Do not prise between the cover and cylinder head or you'll damage the gasket mating surfaces.

Refitting

8   Use a gasket scraper to remove all traces of old gasket material from the gasket

mating surfaces of the cylinder head and the valve cover. Clean the surfaces with a rag soaked in lacquer thinner or acetone.

9   Be sure to refit the semi-circular seals on top of the cylinder head. Apply beads of RTV sealant completely around the perimeter of the seals and also 10 mm on each side of them on the surface of the cylinder head.

10   Refit new seals on the valve cover bolts.

11   Refit a new gasket onto the valve cover. Refit the moulded rubber gasket onto the cover by pushing the new gasket into the slot that circles the valve cover perimeter. Refit new front and rear semi-circular seals with a bead of RTV sealant around them. Apply a bead of RTV sealant where the cylinder head and the front and rear semi-circular seals meet. Refit the valve cover and tighten the bolts to the torque listed in this Chapter's Specifications. **Caution:** *Do not overtighten the valve cover.*

12   The remainder of refitting is the reverse of removal.

5   Valve springs, retainers and seals - renewal

Refer to illustration 5.8

Note: *Broken valve springs and defective valve stem seals can be renewed without removing the cylinder heads. Two special tools and a compressed air source are normally required to perform this operation, so read through this Section carefully and rent or buy the tools before beginning the job.*

1   Refer to Section 4 and remove the valve cover from the cylinder head.

2   Remove the glow plug from the affected cylinder. Refer to Chapter 4.

3   Turn the crankshaft until the piston in the affected cylinder is at Top Dead Centre on the compression stroke (see Section 3). If you're renewing all of the valve stem seals, begin with cylinder number one and work on the valves for one cylinder at a time. Move from cylinder-to-cylinder following the firing order sequence (see this Chapter's Specifications).

4   Thread an adaptor into the glow plug hole and connect an air hose from a compressed air source to it. Most auto parts stores can supply the air hose adaptor. **Note:** *Many cylinder compression gauges utilise a screw-in fitting that may work with your air hose quick-disconnect fitting.*

5   Remove the camshaft (refer to Section 11. Remove the adjustment shim and the lifter.

6   Apply compressed air to the cylinder. **Warning:** *The piston may be forced down by compressed air, causing the crankshaft to turn suddenly. If the spanner used when positioning the number one piston at TDC is still attached to the bolt in the crankshaft nose, it could cause damage or injury when the crankshaft moves.*

7   The valves should be held in place by the air pressure.

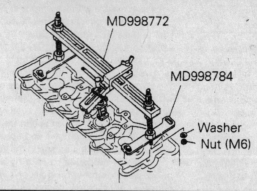

5.8 A special tool must be obtained or fabricated in order to compress the valve springs - Mitsubishi tool numbers are shown

8   Stuff shop rags into the cylinder head holes around the valve spring area to prevent parts and tools from falling into the engine, then use a valve spring compressor to compress the spring. **Note:** *A special valve spring compressor is required to perform this operation. Mitsubishi tools #MD998784 and MD998772 or their equivalents are needed* **(see illustration).** Remove the collets with small needle-nose pliers or a magnet.

9   Remove the spring retainer, the valve spring, the lower retainer and then remove the valve guide seal. **Note:** *If air pressure fails to hold the valve in the closed position during this operation, the valve face or seat is probably damaged. If so, the cylinder head will have to be removed for additional repair operations.*

10   Wrap a rubber band or tape around the top of the valve stem so the valve won't fall into the combustion chamber, then release the air pressure.

11   Inspect the valve stem for damage. Rotate the valve in the guide and check the end for eccentric movement, which would indicate that the valve is bent.

12   Move the valve up-and-down in the guide and make sure it doesn't bind. If the valve stem binds, either the valve is bent or the guide is damaged. In either case, the cylinder head will have to be removed for repair.

13   Reapply air pressure to the cylinder to retain the valve in the closed position, then remove the tape or rubber band from the valve stem.

14   Lubricate the valve stem with engine oil and refit a new guide seal.

15   Refit the spring and retainers in position over the valve.

16   Compress the valve spring and carefully position the collets in the groove. Apply a small dab of grease to the inside of each collet to hold it in place.

17   Remove the force from the spring tool and make sure the collets are seated.

18   Disconnect the air hose and remove the adaptor from the spark plug hole.

19   Refit the glow plugs.

20   Refer to Section 4 and refit the valve cover.

21   Start and run the engine, then check for oil leaks and unusual sounds coming from the valve cover area.

6   Inlet manifold - removal and refitting

Warning: *Diesel fuel is extremely flammable, so take extra precautions when you work on any part of the fuel system. Don't smoke or allow open flames or bare light bulbs near the work area, and don't work in a garage where a natural gas-type appliance (such as a water heater) with a pilot light is present. If you spill any fuel on your skin, rinse it off immediately with soap and water. When you perform any kind of work on the fuel system, wear safety glasses and have a Class B type fire extinguisher on hand.*

Removal

Refer to illustration 6.5

Note: *The following procedure applies to turbocharged models. Non-turbocharged models are similar.*

1   Detach the cable from the negative battery terminal.

2   Remove the intercooler and any other interfering ducts (refer to the turbocharger removal procedure in Chapter 4).

3   If the engine is equipped with EGR, remove the EGR hoses and tubes. The EGR valve can be left attached to the manifold if desired. Disconnect the boost hose from the waste gate and the inlet manifold.

4   Remove the duct which connects the turbocharger to the inlet manifold. Remove the wastegate.

5   Remove the inlet manifold bolts and remove the manifold from the engine **(see illustration).**

Refitting

6   Clean the inlet manifold and cylinder head surface, removing all traces of gasket material.

7   Check the mating surfaces of the manifold for flatness with a precision straightedge and feeler gauge.

8   Inspect the manifold for cracks and distortion.

9   If the manifold is cracked or warped, renew it or see if it can be resurfaced/repaired at an automotive machine shop.

10   Check carefully for any stripped or bro-

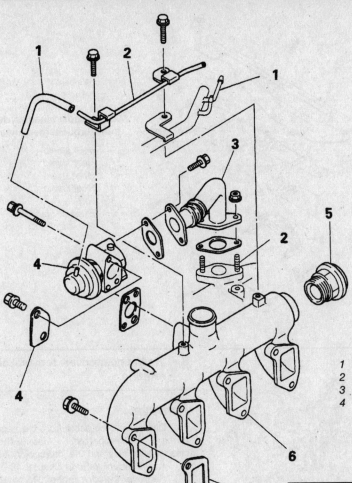

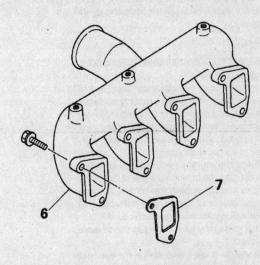

6.5 Inlet manifolds for turbocharged (left) and non-turbocharged engines

1	Hose	5	Relief valve
2	Tube	6	Inlet manifold
3	EGR tube	7	Gasket
4	EGR valve or cover plate		

ken inlet manifold bolts. Renew any defective bolts.

11　Place new gaskets onto the cylinder head.

12　Refit the inlet manifold and tighten the bolts finger-tight. Starting at the centre and working out in both directions, tighten the bolts in a criss-cross pattern until the torque listed in this Chapter's Specifications is reached.

13　The remainder of the refitting procedure is the reverse of removal.

7　Exhaust manifold - removal and refitting

Removal

Refer to illustrations 7.3a and 7.3b

Note: *The following procedure applies to tur-bocharged models. Non-turbocharged mod-els are similar.*

1　Disconnect the negative battery cable from the battery.

2　Remove the inlet manifold (refer to Sec-tion 7).

3　Remove the interfering heat shields from the exhaust manifold **(see illustrations)**.

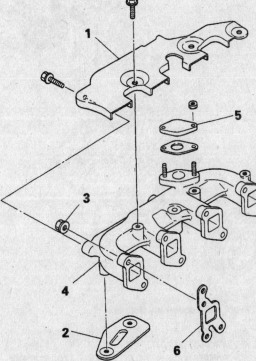

7.3a Exhaust manifold details (turbocharged engines)

1	Heat shield
2	Heat shield
3	Nut
4	Exhaust manifold
5	EGR block-off plate
6	Gasket

4   Disconnect the turbocharger from the exhaust manifold (refer to Chapter 4).
5   Remove the exhaust manifold nuts and detach the exhaust manifold from the cylinder head.

Refitting

6   Inspect the exhaust manifold for cracks, damage or distortion.
7   Discard the old gaskets and use a scraper to clean the gasket mating surfaces on the exhaust manifold, turbocharger (or exhaust pipe) and cylinder head. Place new gaskets onto the cylinder head and turbocharger (or exhaust pipe).
8   Place the exhaust manifold in position on the cylinder head and refit the nuts. Starting at the centre, tighten the nuts in a criss-cross pattern until the torque listed in this Chapter's Specifications is reached.
9   The remainder of refitting is the reverse of removal.
10 Start the engine and check for exhaust leaks between the manifold and the cylinder head and between the manifold and the turbocharger (or exhaust pipe).

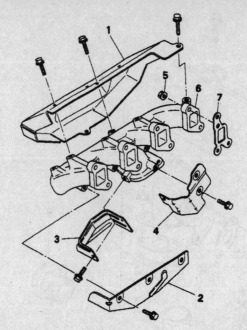

7.3b Exhaust manifold details (non-turbocharged engines)

1   Heat shield
2   Heat shield
3   Heat shield
4   Heat shield
5   Nut
6   Exhaust manifold
7   Gasket

8   Timing gear cover- removal and refitting

Removal

1   Disconnect the cable from the negative terminal of the battery. Remove the air cleaner assembly and the intercooler assembly if they interfere (refer to Chapter 4).
2   Remove the drivebelts. Remove the alternator, power steering pump and air conditioning compressor, it equipped, and lay them aside. **Warning:** *The air conditioning system is under high pressure - do not disconnect the hoses!*
3   Remove the water pump if necessary for clearance (refer to Chapter 3). Any other interfering components must be removed at this time.
4   Remove the crankshaft pulley bolt. **Note:** *This bolt is very tight. If a pneumatic impact wrench is not available, it will be necessary to remove the flywheel inspection plate and wedge a screwdriver in the starter ring gear*

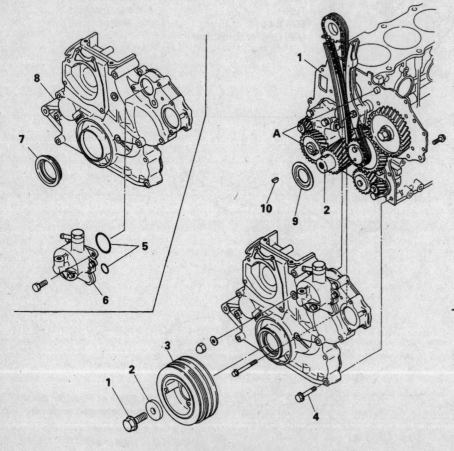

8.7 Front case assembly details

1	Bolt	5	O-ring	8	Case
2	Washer	6	Vacuum pump	9	Oil slinger
3	Pulley		assembly	10	Woodruff key
4	Bolt	7	Seal		

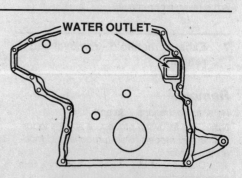

8.9 A continuous bead of RTV sealant must be applied around the entire case including the area which seals to the sump

teeth *to prevent the crankshaft from turning.*

5 Remove the crankshaft pulley by levering it off. If it is stuck to the crankshaft, use a special puller to remove it. Do not use the type of puller that attaches to the belt groove.

6 Disconnect the vacuum line and the wiring from the vacuum pump. Remove the vacuum pump and its O-rings from the timing cover.

7 Remove the bolts attaching the timing cover to the engine block and the oil sump **(see illustration)**. Note the location of the bolts so they can be returned to the same

locations from which they were removed. Tap the cover with a soft-faced hammer to break the gasket seal, then remove the cover from the engine block. **Caution:** *Levering between the cover and the engine block can damage the gasket sealing surfaces.*

Refitting

Refer to illustration 8.9

8 Thoroughly clean the front cover and engine block with acetone or lacquer thinner. Make sure the threaded holes in the engine block are clean and dry.

9 Apply a 3 mm bead of RTV sealant completely around the sealing surface of the cover, inboard of the bolt holes. Extend the bead to seal to the oil sump also.

10 Fit the front cover onto the engine. Refit the bolts in a crisscross pattern and tighten them.

11 Apply a thin layer of clean moly-based grease to the seal contact surface of the crankshaft pulley, then slide it onto the crankshaft. Refit the bolt and tighten it to the torque listed in this Chapter's Specifications. It may again be necessary to secure the crankshaft to prevent it from turning.

12 The remainder of refitting is the reverse of removal.

9 Timing chain, sprockets and gears - removal, inspection and refitting

Removal

Refer to illustration 9.4

1 Disconnect the cable from the negative terminal of the battery. Drain the cooling system (see Chapter 1).

2 Position the engine on TDC for number one cylinder (refer to Section 3). Remove the valve cover (refer to Section 4).

3 Remove the front cover (refer to Section 8).

4 Use a dial indicator to check the backlash of every pair of gears **(see illustration)**. Check each pair at three points around their circumference. Compare your readings with those listed in the Specifications in this Chapter. If any have excessive backlash, renew them.

5 Using the same dial indicator, check the endplay of each gear/shaft. Compare your

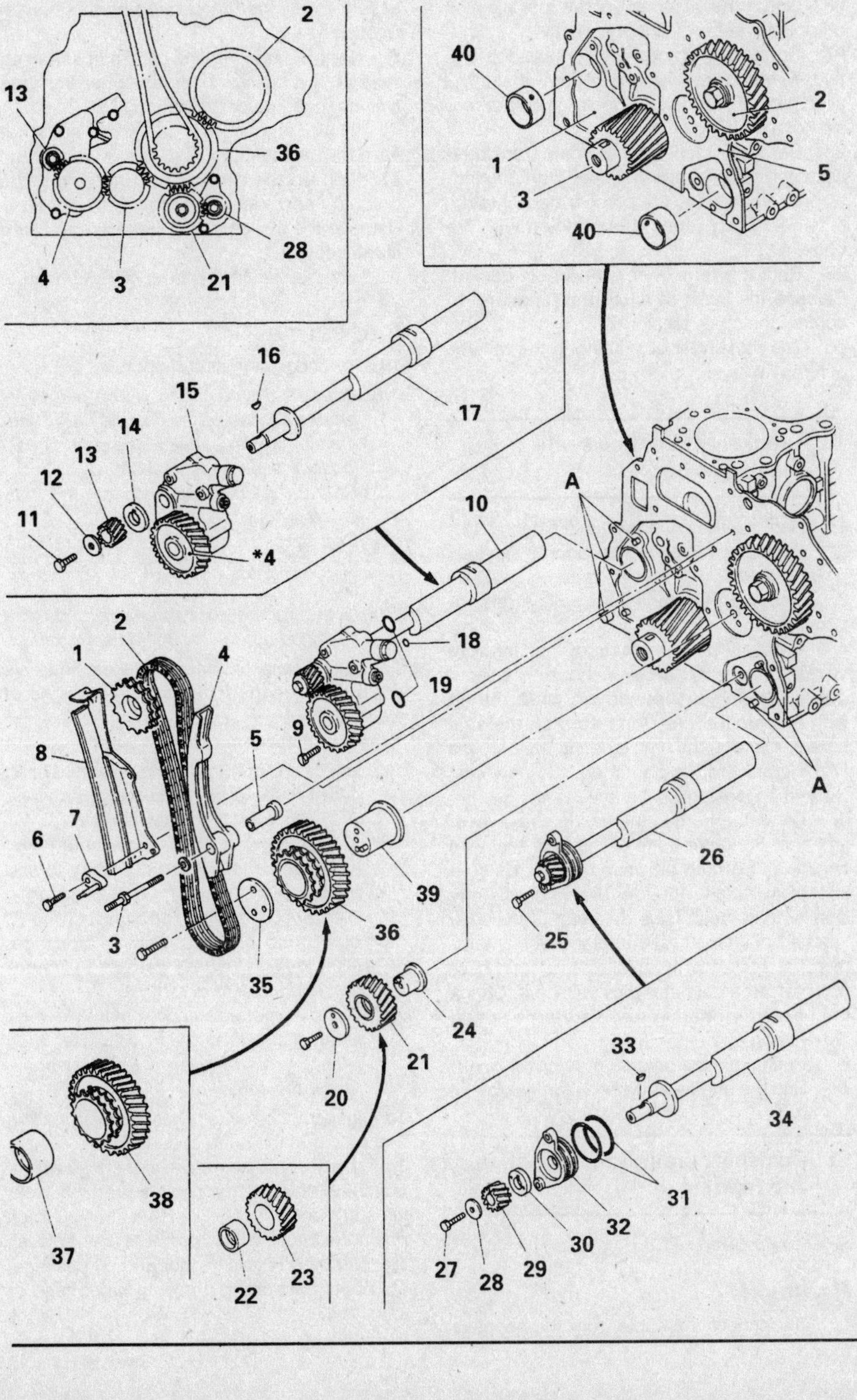

2D

9.4 Front case internal components

1	Block	22	Bush
2	Timing chain	23	Left idler gear
3	Bolt	24	Idler shaft A
4	Tension lever	25	Bolt
5	Shaft	26	Left silent shaft
6	Eyebolt		assembly
7	Oil jet assembly	27	Bolt
8	Guide plate	28	Washer
9	Bolt	29	Thrust washer
10	Right silent	30	O-ring
	shaft assembly	32	Thrust plate
11	Bolt	33	Key
12	Washer	34	Left silent shaft
13	Right silent	35	Idler washer
	shaft gear	36	Idler gear and
14	Thrust washer		sprocket
15	Oil pump		assembly
	assembly	37	Idler sprocket
16	Woodruff key		bush
17	Left silent shaft	38	Idler gear and
18	O-ring		sprocket
19	O-ring	39	Idler shaft
20	Washer	40	Bush

readings with those listed in the Specifications in this Chapter. If any have excessive endplay, renew the worn components.

6   Remove the timing chain tensioner assembly from the front of the cylinder head. Remove the camshaft sprocket. **Caution:** *Do not rotate the crankshaft after this point. Hold the camshaft by the hex section. The bolt has a left hand thread.* **Note:** *It is not necessary to remove the front cover in order to remove only the camshaft sprocket. Refer to the Section on camshaft removal.*

7   Remove the timing chain.

8   Remove the chain tensioner and guide plate assembly. The chain oil jet will be removed as part of this procedure.

9   Remove the oil pump/right balance shaft assembly.

10   Remove the left idler gear assembly.

11   Remove the two bolts securing the left idler shaft bearing retainer and slide the left balance shaft from the block.

12   Unbolt and remove the main idler gear assembly.

13   The fuel injection pump gear can be removed as part of the pump assembly.

14   Dismantle any assemblies which require further service.

Inspection

15   Check the chain tensioner components where they contact the chain for wear and damage. Also inspect the clearance at the tensioner lever shaft and its shaft. Renew any worn parts. Measure the clearance between the two sides of the timing chain as it is manually stretched. If the clearance is less than specified, renew it.

16   Check the fits of the balance shafts in their bushes. Special tools and expertise are required to renew the balance shaft bushes if they are excessively worn. The engine must be taken to a properly equipped repair shop. If the balance shafts are worn, they should be renewed at this time.

17   The other bushes in the idler gears can be renewed by a competent repair shop equipped with a hydraulic press.

Refitting

18   Make sure the crankshaft is positioned at Top Dead Centre (TDC) for number one cylinder (see Section 3).

19   Refit the idler gear and sprocket assembly. Align the "1" mark on the crankshaft gear between the two marks on the idler gear.

20   If the left balance shaft assembly has been dismantled, make certain that "O" mark on the gear is facing the front. Refit the left balance shaft assembly. **Caution:** *Several of these components use washers under the bolt heads which have an outer rounded edge. Make certain that this rounded edge faces toward the bolt head upon refitting.*

21   Refit the left idler gear assembly. Align the "3" and "O" marks on it with those on the two mating gears. Refit the bolt - make certain that the bolt's washer has the "F" facing the front.

22   Refit the right balance shaft/oil pump

assembly. Make certain that the "O" mark o the balance shaft gear is mated with the "6" mark on the oil pump gear. Align the "5" mark on the oil pump gear with the "5" mark on the crankshaft gear.

23   Make certain that the "1" marks on the crankshaft gear and idler gear are still aligned. Place the timing chain over the lower drive sprocket, aligning the single bright white link with the "O" mark.

24   Put the other end of the timing chain around the camshaft sprocket, aligning the two bright white links with the two "O" marks.

25   Refit the upper sprocket to the camshaft. Refit both tensioner assemblies.

26   Check the alignment of the fuel injection pump gear (refer to Chapter 4).

27   Rotate the crankshaft by hand through two complete revolutions. Again check the alignment of all marks. Check for proper tension of the timing chain.

28   Before installing the chain tensioner assembly into the cylinder head, turn the tensioner cam to force the plunger back into the tensioner body. Lock it in position with the hook.

29   Refit the tensioner with a new gasket. Release the hook to allow the tensioner to contact the chain tensioner.

30   The remainder of refitting is the reverse of removal.

---

10   Crankshaft front oil seal - renewal

---

1   Remove the drivebelts (see Chapter 1).

2   Raise the vehicle and support it securely on jackstands.

3   Remove the crankshaft pulley (refer to Section 8).

4   Carefully prise the seal out of the front cover with a seal removal tool or a screwdriver. If using a screwdriver, wrap the tip with electrical tape. Don't scratch the seal bore or damage the crankshaft in the process (if the crankshaft is damaged, the new seal will end up leaking).

5   Clean the bore in the timing chain cover and coat the outer edge of the new seal with engine oil or multi-purpose grease. Using a socket with an outside diameter slightly smaller than the outside diameter of the seal, carefully drive the seal into place with a hammer. If a socket is not available, a short section of a large diameter pipe will work. Check the seal after refitting to be sure the spring did not pop out.

6   Refitting is the reverse of removal.

7   Run the engine and check for leaks.

---

11   Camshaft - removal, inspection and refitting

Refer to illustration 11.8

Removal

1   Disconnect the cable from the negative

battery terminal.

2   Remove the valve cover (see Section 4).

3   Position the number one piston at Top Dead Centre (see Section 3).

4   Use an electrician's plastic wire tie or a length of wire to tightly secure the timing chain to the camshaft sprocket.

5   Remove the camshaft sprocket bolt (refer to Section 11). **Caution:** *Do not rotate the crankshaft after this point. Hold the camshaft by the hex section. The bolt has a left hand thread. Support the sprocket and chain with a fabricated holding device so they do not fall into the timing cover or off of the lower sprocket. If this happens, it will be necessary to reinstall the timing chain (refer to Section 9).*

6   Before removing the camshaft sprocket, remove the timing chain tensioner from the cylinder head (refer to Section 9).

7   Now remove the camshaft sprocket from the camshaft.

8   Loosen the camshaft bearing cap bolts gradually and evenly a quarter turn at a time. Remove the five camshaft bearing caps **(see illustration)**.

9   Lift the camshaft off the cylinder head.

Inspection

10   To check camshaft runout:

a) *Support the camshaft with a pair of V-blocks and attach a dial indicator with the stem resting against the centre bearing journal on the camshaft.*

b) *Rotate the camshaft and note the indicated runout.*

c) *Compare the results to the camshaft runout listed in this Chapter's Specifications.*

d) *If the indicated runout exceeds the specified runout, renew the camshaft.*

11   Check the camshaft bearing journals and bearing caps for scoring and signs of wear.

12   Check the cam lobes for wear:

a) *Check the toe and ramp areas of each cam for score marks and uneven wear. Also check for flaking and pitting.*

b) *If there is wear on the toe or the ramp, renew the camshaft, but first try to find the cause of the wear. Look for abrasive substances in the oil and inspect the oil pump and oil passages for blockage. Cam wear is usually caused by inadequate lubrication or dirty oil.*

c) *Using a micrometer, calculate the lobe wear. If the lobe wear is greater than listed in this Chapter's Specifications, renew the camshaft.*

13   Inspect the rocker arms for wear, galling and pitting of the contact surfaces.

14   If any of the conditions described above are noted, the cylinder head is probably lacking sufficient lubrication, make sure you track down the cause of this problem (low oil level, low oil pump capacity, clogged oil passage, etc.) before installing a new cylinder head or camshaft.

Refitting

15 Thoroughly clean the camshaft, the bearing surfaces in the cylinder head and bearing caps and the rocker arms. Remove all sludge and dirt. Wipe off all components with a clean, lint-free cloth.

16 Lubricate the camshaft bearing surfaces in the cylinder head and the bearing journals and lobes on the camshaft with assembly lube or moly-base grease. Carefully lower the camshaft into position with the dowel pin pointing up. **Caution:** *Failure to adequately lubricate the camshaft and related components can cause serious damage to bearing and friction surfaces during the first few seconds after engine start-up, when the oil pressure is low or nonexistent.*

17 Apply a thin coat of assembly lube or moly-base grease to the bearing surfaces of the camshaft bearing caps.

18 Refit the camshaft bearing caps. They are numbered with number one being closest to the front of the engine. They also have arrows pointing to the front of the engine. Tighten the bolts evenly and gradually to the torque listed in the Specifications in this Chapter.

19 Refit the camshaft sprocket/timing chain. Tighten the camshaft sprocket bolt to the torque listed in this Chapter's Specifications.

20 Refit the timing chain tensioner assembly with a new gasket (refer to Section 9).

21 Refit the valve cover. The remainder of refitting is the reverse of removal.

12 Cylinder head - removal and refitting

Caution: *Allow the engine to cool completely before beginning this procedure.*

Removal

Refer to illustrations 12.15, 12.20 and 12.21

1 Disconnect the negative cable from the battery.

2 Remove the intercooler and turbocharger on vehicles so equipped, (refer to Chapter 4).

3 Remove the inlet manifold (refer to Section 6).

4 Remove the exhaust manifold (refer to Section 7).

5 Disconnect the wiring, including the alternator wiring harness, and the oil pressure gauge wiring.

6 Remove the radiator upper hose and the other interfering coolant hoses. Disconnect the power steering line from the cylinder head bracket.

7 Remove the injection tube assembly (refer to Chapter 4).

8 Remove the interfering fuel hoses.

9 Remove the dipstick tube assembly.

10 Disconnect the vacuum/boost tubes and their brackets.

11 Drain the engine coolant (refer to Chapter 1).

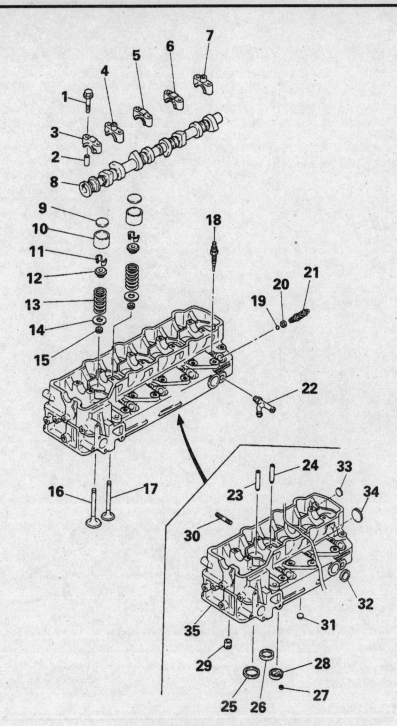

11.8 Camshaft and valve components

1	Bolt	13	Valve spring	25	Valve seat
2	Knock bush	14	Lower retainer	26	Valve seat
3	Camshaft bearing cap	15	Seal	27	Tablet
4	Camshaft bearing cap	16	Inlet valve	28	Combustion jet
5	Camshaft bearing cap	17	Exhaust valve	29	Coolant director
6	Camshaft bearing cap	18	Glow plug	30	Stud
7	Camshaft bearing cap	19	gasket	31	Sealing cap
8	Camshaft	20	Gasket support	32	Sealing cap
9	Lifter shim	21	Fuel injector	33	Sealing cap
10	Lifter	22	Coolant joint	34	Sealing cap
11	Collets	23	Valve guide	35	Cylinder head
12	Retainer	24	Valve guide		

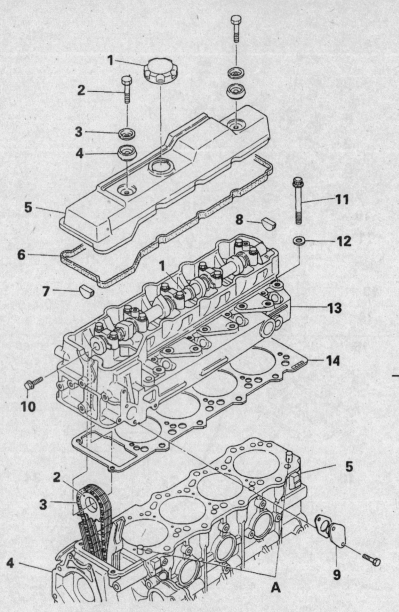

12.15 Cylinder head and valve cover details

1	Cap	6	Gasket	11	Bolt
2	Bolt	7	Front seal	12	Washer
3	Plate	8	Rear seal	13	Cylinder head
4	Seal	9	Tensioner	14	Gasket
5	Valve cover	10	Bolt		

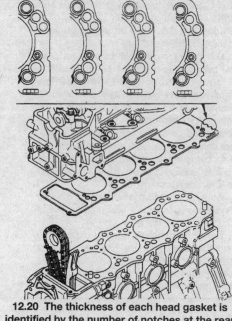

12.20 The thickness of each head gasket is identified by the number of notches at the rear

12   Remove the valve cover (refer to Section 4).

13   Remove the timing chain tensioner and the camshaft sprocket (refer to Section 11). **Caution:** *Do not rotate the crankshaft after this point. Hold the camshaft by the hex section when removing the sprocket bolt. The bolt has a left hand thread. Support the sprocket and chain with a fabricated holding device so they do not fall into the timing cover or off of the lower sprocket. If this happens, it will be necessary to reinstall the timing chain (refer to Section 9).*

14   Disconnect the glow plug harness wiring, the coolant temperature sensor and the earth cable.

15   Loosen the cylinder head bolts in 1/4-turn increments, following the reverse of the recommended tightening sequence, until they can be removed by hand **(see illustration)**.

16   Lift the cylinder head off the engine. If resistance is felt, don't prise between the cylinder head and engine block gasket mating surfaces - damage to the mating surfaces will result. Instead, prise against the casting protrusions on the sides of the cylinder head. **Caution:** *Support the timing chain/sprocket*

so they do not fall and so the chain does not lose its mating with the lower sprocket.

17   Set the cylinder head on wood blocks to prevent damage to the gasket sealing surfaces. **Caution:** *Be careful not to disturb the timing belt and sprocket when lifting the cylinder head off. After the cylinder head is removed, secure the timing belt and sprocket to the engine, keeping tension on the belt. If the timing chain is disturbed it will become necessary to remove the front cover to restore timing. Do not rotate the crankshaft with the sprocket and chain removed from the camshaft.*

18   Cylinder head disassembly and inspection procedures are covered in detail in Chapter 2, Part E. Check the cylinder head for warpage.

Refitting

Refer to illustration 12.26

19   A head gasket of the correct compressed thickness must be chosen prior to installing the cylinder head. If no changes have been made which would change the distance that the pistons protrude above the block deck surface, then refit a new gasket of the same grade as the one removed. (These changes include a new connecting rod or piston). The classification mark is stamped on the top rear of the block deck. **Note:** *If there is no mark stamped on the block, use a "C" gasket.*

20   The various head gasket thicknesses are identified by the number of notches **(see illustration)**.

21   If a new piston or connecting rod have been refitted, have a very competent machine shop measure the piston protru-

Piston Protrusion		Cylinder head gasket	
Average piston protusion	Crankcase identification Mark	Classification	Thickness when tightened
0.475 ± 0.028 mm (0.0187 ± 0.011 in.)	A	A (1 notch)	1.35± 0.03 mm (0.0531 ± 0.0012 in.)
0.532 ± 0.028 mm (0.0209 ± 0.011 in.)	B	B (2 notches)	1.40± 0.03 mm (0.0551 ± 0.0012 in.)
0.589 ± 0.028 mm (0.0232 ± 0.011 in.)	C	C (3 notches)	1.45± 0.03 mm (0.0571 ± 0.0012 in.)
0.646 ± 0.03 mm (0.0254 ± 0.011 in.)	D	D (4 notches)	1.50± 0.03 mm (0.0591 ± 0.0012 in.)

12.21 Head gasket selection chart for various average piston protrusions

sions and calculate the average. The chart can then be used to select the new gasket (see illustration). Note: *If one piston protrudes 0.03 mm or more than the average, use the next size thicker gasket.*

22   The mating surfaces of the cylinder head and engine block must be perfectly clean when the cylinder head is refitted.

23   Use a gasket scraper to remove all traces of carbon and old gasket material, then clean the mating surfaces with lacquer thinner or acetone. If there's oil on the mating surfaces when the cylinder head is refitted, the gasket may not seal correctly and leaks may develop. When working on the engine block, stuff the cylinders with clean shop rags to keep out debris. Use a vacuum cleaner to remove material that falls into the cylinders. Since the cylinder head is made of aluminium, aggressive scraping can cause damage. Be extra careful not to nick or gouge the mating surfaces with the scraper. Gasket removal solvents are available from most auto parts stores and may prove helpful.

24   Use a tap of the correct size to chase the threads in the cylinder head bolt holes. Clean and dry each bolt hole, if any fluid remains in a bolt hole damage to the engine block may result when the bolts are tightened. Mount each cylinder head bolt in a vice and run a die down the threads to remove corrosion and restore the threads. Dirt, corrosion, sealant and damaged threads will affect torque readings.

25   Apply a dab of RTV sealant at each front cover-to-engine block joint and place a new gasket on the engine block. The gasket must have the correct marking. Check to see if there are any markings (such as "TOP") on the gasket that say how it is to be refitted. Set the cylinder head in position.

26   Lightly oil the cylinder head bolt threads and refit the bolts. Tighten the cylinder head bolts in several increments, following the recommended sequence, to the torque listed in this Chapter's Specifications (see illustration).

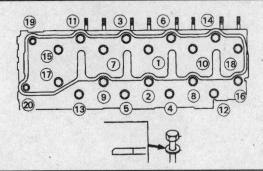

12.26 Head bolt tightening sequence. The head bolt washers must be refitted with their rounded edges up

27   Refit the timing chain and camshaft sprocket. Tighten the camshaft sprocket bolt to the torque listed in this Chapter's Specifications.

28   Reinstall the remaining parts in the reverse order of removal.

29   Be sure to refill the cooling system and check all fluid levels.

30   Rotate the crankshaft clockwise slowly by hand through two complete revolutions. **Caution:** *If you feel any resistance while turning the engine over, stop and recheck the camshaft timing. The valves may be hitting the pistons.*

31   Start the engine and check the idle speed (see Chapter 1).

32   Run the engine until normal operating temperature is reached. Check for leaks and proper operation.

13   Oil sump - removal and refitting

Note: *The following procedure is based on the assumption that the engine is in the vehicle.*

Removal

1   Detach the cable from the negative battery terminal.

2   Raise the vehicle and support it securely on jackstands.

3   Drain the oil and renew the oil filter (see Chapter 1). Remove the skid plate.

4   Disconnect the exhaust pipe from the exhaust manifold or turbocharger, lower and support the exhaust pipe.

5   Remove the bolts securing the oil sump to the engine block. Tap on the sump with a soft-face hammer to break the gasket seal, then detach the oil sump from the engine. Don't prise between the engine block and oil sump mating surfaces. **Note:** *If the sump is stuck to the crankcase, drive a short, stout knife blade between the two and then hammer it along the sump to break the seal.*

6   Using a gasket scraper, remove all traces of old gasket and/or sealant from the engine block and oil sump. Clean the mating surfaces with lacquer thinner or acetone. Make sure the threaded bolt holes in the engine block are clean.

7   Clean the oil sump with solvent and dry it thoroughly. Check the gasket flanges for distortion, particularly around the bolt holes. If necessary, place the sump on a wood block and use a hammer to flatten and restore the gasket surfaces.

Refitting

8   Apply a 4 mm bead of RTV silicone sealant around the perimeter of the sump in the groove. Be certain to lay the sealant inboard of the bolt holes.

9   Carefully place the oil sump in position within 15 minutes of applying the silicone.

10   Refit the bolts and tighten them in 1/4-

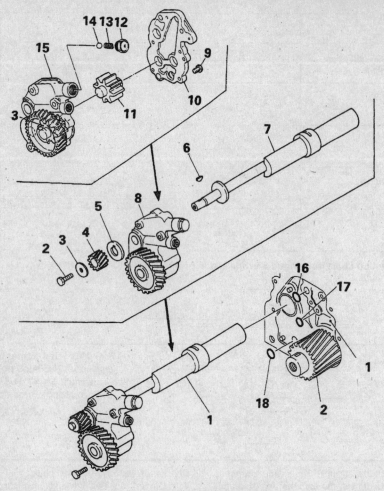

14.3 Oil pump assembly details

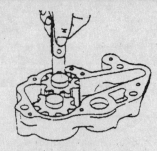

14.6 The gear tip-to-case clearance is checked in this manner

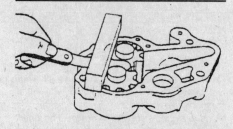

14.7 Check the gear-to-cover clearance in this manner

1	Right silent shaft	7	Right silent shaft	14	Ball
2	Bolt	8	Oil pump assembly	15	Gear and body
3	Washer	9	Screw		assembly
4	Right silent shaft gear	10	Oil pump cover	16	O-ring
5	Thrust washer	12	Plug	17	O-ring
6	Woodruff key	13	Relief valve spring	18	O-ring

turn increments to the torque listed in this Chapter's Specifications. Start with the bolts closest to the centre of the sump and work out in a spiral pattern. Don't overtighten them or leakage may occur.

11   The remainder of refitting is the reverse of removal. Add oil, run the engine and check for oil leaks.

14   Oil pump - removal, inspection and refitting

Removal

Refer to illustration 14.3

1   Disconnect the cable from the negative battery terminal.

2   Refer to Section 9 for the entire oil pump assembly removal procedure. The oil pump is removed as part of the right balance shaft/oil pump assembly.

3   To remove the balance shaft and dismantle the oil pump, place the assembly on a clean work bench. Remove the bolt from the smaller balance shaft drive gear and then remove the balance shaft **(see illustration)**.

4   Remove the screws from the rear of the oil pump housing. Remove the cover.

5   Remove the relief plug. Extract the small spring and the relief ball.

Inspection

Refer to illustrations 14.6 and 14.7

6   Use a marker to mark the mating gear teeth before removing the driven gear. Use a feeler gauge to check the clearance between the tips of the gear teeth and the case **(see illustration)**.

7   Lay a straightedge across the pump case and use a feeler gauge to check the clearance between the gears and the cover **(see illustration)**. Compare your readings with those listed in the Specifications in this

Chapter. Renew the oil pump if required.

8   Inspect the relief spring, bore and ball for signs of wear and damage. Renew any defective parts.

9   Lubricate the gears and bearing surfaces with clean engine oil. Refit the gears into the body with the mating marks aligned. Lubricate the oil pressure relief valve and refit the relief valve and spring assembly. Tighten the relief valve cap to the torque listed in this Chapter's Specifications. Refit the cover onto the pump body and tighten the screws securely.

Refitting

15   Pack the inner oil pump with petroleum jelly to assist in priming. Refit the oil pump cover after making certain that the alignment marks on the two gears are aligned. Tighten all fasteners to the torque listed in the Specifications in this Chapter.

16   The remainder of refitting is the reverse of removal.

15   Flywheel/driveplate - removal and refitting

Refer to Chapter 2A.

16   Rear main oil seal - renewal

Refer to Chapter 2A.

17   Engine mounts - check and renewal

Refer to Chapter 2A.

Chapter 2 Part E
General engine overhaul procedures

Contents

Specifications

Four-cylinder petrol engine

General
Displacement	2.6 litres
Bore and stroke	91.1 x 98.0 mm
Cylinder compression pressure	1250 kPa
Oil pressure (at idle)	147 kPa

Engine block
Bore diameter	91.1 mm
Cylinder taper limit	0.12 mm
Cylinder out-of-round limit	0.12 mm
Maximum bore wear	0.2 mm
Maximum bore oversize	1.20 mm

Pistons and rings
Piston diameter	
Grade A	91.07 to 91.08 mm
Grade B	91.08 to 91.09 mm
Grade C	91.09 to 91.10 mm
Grade D	91.11 to 91.12 mm
Grade E	91.12 to 91.13 mm
Piston-to-bore clearance	0.02 to 0.04 mm
Piston ring side clearance	
Top compression ring	
Standard	0.061 to 0.100 mm
Service limit	0.15 mm
Second compression ring	
Standard	0.020 to 0.061 mm
Service limit	0.12 mm
Piston ring end gap	
Top compression ring	
Standard	0.249 to 0.399 mm
Service limit	1.0 mm
Second compression ring and oil ring	
Standard	0.249 to 0.449 mm
Service limit	1.0 mm

Crankshaft and connecting rods

Crankshaft endplay (standard)	0.050 to 0.178 mm
Main bearing journal	
Diameter	60.0 mm
Taper limit	0.01 mm
Out-of-round limit	0.01 mm
Connecting rod journal	
Diameter	53.0 mm
Out-of-round/taper limits	0.01 mm
Main bearing oil clearance	
Journal no. 1, 2 and 4	0.016 to 0.045 mm
Journal no. 3	0.028 to 0.057 mm
Connecting rod bearing oil clearance	0.015 to 0.056 mm
Connecting rod endplay (side clearance)	0.10 to 0.25 mm

Counter-balance shafts

Front bearing journal diameter	23.0 mm
Front bearing oil clearance	0.02 to 0.06 mm
Rear bearing journal diameter	43.0 mm
Rear bearing oil clearance	0.043 to 0.086 mm

Cylinder head and valves

Head warpage limit	0.2 mm
Valve seat angle	45-degrees
Valve face angle	45-degrees
Valve length	
Intake	107.96 mm
Exhaust	105.86 mm
Valve stem diameter	
Standard	8.0 mm
Wear limit	
Intake	0.10 mm
Exhaust	0.15 mm
Valve guide inside diameter	8.0 to 8.018 mm
Valve stem-to-guide clearance	
Intake	0.025 to 0.055 mm
Exhaust	0.050 to 0.085 mm
Valve margin width (minimum)	0.100 mm
Valve spring free length	47.5 to 46.3 mm
Valve spring fitted height	40.40 mm ± 1.0 mm
Valve spring out of square	not available

Torque specifications*

	Nm
Balance shaft sprocket bolts	59 to 69
Balance shaft thrust plate bolts	10 to 12
Connecting rod bearing cap nuts	44 to 47
Main bearing cap bolts	78 to 83

* **Note:** *Refer to Part A for additional torque specifications.*

V6 engines

SOHC

Displacement	3.0 litres
Bore	91.1 mm
Stroke	76.0 mm

DOHC

Displacement	3.5 litres
Bore	93 mm
Stroke	85.8 mm
Cylinder compression pressure	840 kPa at 250 rpm
Oil pressure	80 kPa at idle

Engine block

Inside diameter	
SOHC engine	91.1 mm
DOHC engine	93.0 mm
Cylinder taper limit	0.02 mm
Cylinder out-of-round limit	0.02 mm

Pistons and rings

Piston diameter
    SOHC engine .... 91.1 mm
    DOHC engine .... 93.0 mm
Piston-to cylinder clearance
    SOHC engine .... 0.03 to 0.05 mm
    DOHC engine .... 0.02 to 0.04 mm
Piston ring side clearance
    Top compression ring
        Standard .... 0.03 to 0.09 mm
        Service limit.. 0.1 mm
    Second compression ring
        Standard .... 0.2 to 0.06 mm
        Service limit.. 0.1 mm
Piston ring end gap
    Top compression ring
        Standard .... 0.30 to 0.45 mm
        Service limit.. 0.01 mm
    Second compression ring
        Standard .... 0.25 to 0.40 mm
        Service limit.. 0.8 mm
    Oil ring
        Standard .... 0.20 to 0.70 mm
        Service limit.. 1.0 mm

Crankshaft and connecting rods

Endplay
    Standard.. 0.05 to 0.25 mm
    Service limit .... 0.3 mm
Main bearing journal
    Diameter
        SOHC engine .... 60 mm
        DOHC engine .... 64 mm
    Taper limit.. 0.005 mm
Connecting rod journal
    Diameter
        SOHC engine .... 50 mm
        DOHC engine .... 55 mm
    Taper limit.. 0.005 mm
    Out-of-round limit
        SOHC engine .... 0.05 mm
        DOHC engine .... 0.03 mm
Main bearing oil clearance .... 0.02 to 0.048 mm
Connecting rod bearing oil clearance............................ 0.016 to 0.046 mm
Connecting rod endplay (side clearance)
    Standard .... 0.10 to 0.25 mm
    Service limit .... 0.4 mm

Cylinder head and valves

Head warpage limit.. 0.05 mm
Valve seat angle.. 45-degrees
Valve face angle.. 45-degrees
Valve margin width
    SOHC engine
        Intake
            Standard.. 1.2 mm
            Service limit .... 0.7 mm
        Exhaust
            Standard.. 2.0 mm
            Service limit .... 1.5 mm
    DOHC engine
        Intake
            Standard.. 1.0 mm
            Service limit .... 0.5 mm
        Exhaust
            Standard.. 1.2 mm
            Service limit .... 0.7 mm

2E

Cylinder head and valves (continued)

Valve stem-to-guide clearance
  SOHC engine
    Intake
      Standard .... 0.02 to 0.06 mm
      Service limit .... 0.10 mm
    Exhaust
      Standard .... 0.05 to 0.09 mm
      Service limit .... 0.15 mm
  DOHC engine
    Intake
      Standard .... 0.02 to 0.04 mm
      Service limit .... 0.10 mm
    Exhaust
      Standard .... 0.03 to 0.06 mm
      Service limit .... 0.15 mm
Valve spring free length
  SOHC engine
    Standard .... 49.8 mm
    Service limit .... 48.8 mm
  DOHC engine
    Standard .... 51 mm
    Service limit .... 50 mm
Valve spring fitted height
  SOHC engine
    Standard .... 40.4 mm
    Service limit .... 41.4 mm
  DOHC engine
    Standard .... 37.9 mm
    Service limit .... 38.9 mm
Valve stem diameter
  SOHC engine
    Intake .... 7.960 to 7.975 mm
    Exhaust .... 7.930 to 7.950 mm
  DOHC engine
    Intake .... 6.57 to 6.58 mm
    Exhaust .... 6.63 to 6.55 mm

Torque specifications   **Nm**

Main bearing cap bolts .... 75 to 85
Connecting rod bearing cap nuts 52

***Note:** Refer to Part B for additional torque specifications.*

4D56 2.5 litre four cylinder diesel

General

Displacement .... 2.5 litres, 2,476 cc
Bore and stroke .... 91.1 x 95.0 mm
Cylinder compression pressure
  Minimum .... 1,920 kPa
  Maximum variation .... 300 kPa
Oil pressure (at idle) .... 49 kPa

Engine block

Bore diameter .... 91.1 mm
Cylinder taper limit .... 0.02 mm
Cylinder out-of-round limit .... 0.02 mm
Maximum bore wear .... 0.2 mm
Maximum bore oversize .... 1.00 mm

Pistons and rings

Piston diameter .... 91.1 mm
Piston-to-bore clearance .... 0.04 to 0.06 mm
Piston ring side clearance
  Top compression ring .... 0.02 to 0.04 mm
  Second compression ring .... 0.03 to 0.07 mm
  Oil ring .... 0.02 to 0.07 mm
Piston ring end gap
  Top compression ring .... 0.25 to 0.40 mm
  Second compression ring and oil ring .... 0.25 to 0.40 mm
  Oil ring .... 0.25 to 0.45 mm

Crankshaft and connecting rods

Crankshaft endplay (standard)	0.02 to 0.05 mm
Main bearing journal	
Diameter	66.0 mm
Taper limit	0.01 mm
Out-of-round limit	0.01 mm
Connecting rod journal	
Diameter	53.0 mm
Out-of-round/taper limits	0.01 mm
Main bearing oil clearance	0.02 to 0.05 mm
Connecting rod bearing oil clearance	0.02 to 0.06 mm
Connecting rod endplay (side clearance)	0.10 to 0.25 mm

Left silent shaft

Front bearing journal diameter	19.0 mm
Front bearing oil clearance	0.02 to 0.05 mm
Rear bearing journal diameter	43.0 mm
Rear bearing oil clearance	0.05 to 0.09 mm

Right silent shaft

Front bearing journal diameter	18.5 mm
Front bearing oil clearance	0.02 to 0.06 mm
Rear bearing journal diameter	43.0 mm
Rear bearing oil clearance	0.06 to 0.10 mm

Cylinder head and valves

Head warpage limit	0.1 mm
Valve stem diameter	8.0 mm
Valve stem-to-guide clearance	
Intake	0.03 to 0.06 mm
Exhaust	0.05 to 0.09 mm
Valve margin width	
Standard	2.0 mm
Minimum	0.5 mm
Valve spring free length	49.1 mm
Valve spring out of square maximum	1.5-degrees

Torque specifications*

	Nm
Connecting rod bearing cap nuts	45 to 47
Main bearing cap bolts	74 to 83

*Note: Refer to Part C for additional torque specifications.

4M40 2.8 litre four cylinder diesel

General

Displacement	2.8 litres, 2.835 cc
Bore and stroke	95 x 100 mm
Cylinder compression pressure	
Minimum	1250 kPa
Maximum variation	290 kPa

Engine block

Bore diameter	95.00 to 95.03 mm
Cylinder taper limit	0.15 mm
Cylinder out-of-round limit	0.15 mm
Maximum bore wear	0.2 mm

Pistons and rings

Piston protrusion above deck	
Non-turbo	0.55 to 0.77 mm
Turbo	0.45 to 0.67 mm
Piston-to-bore clearance	
Standard	
Non-turbo	0.04 to 0.05 mm
Turbo	0.07 to 0.08 mm
Limit	0.15 mm

Pistons and rings (continued)

Piston ring side clearance
  Top compression ring
    Standard
      Non-turbo .... 0.06 to 0.11 mm
      Turbo .... 0.03 to 0.08 mm
    Service limit.. 0.15 mm
  Second compression ring
    Standard
      Non-turbo .... 0.05 to 0.08 mm
      Turbo .... 0.07 to 0.10 mm
    Service limit.. 0.15 mm
  Oil ring
    Standard .... 0.03 to 0.06 mm
    Service limit.. 0.15 mm
Piston ring end gap
  Both compression rings
    Standard .... 0.3 to 0.45 mm
    Service limit.. 0.8 mm
  Oil ring
    Standard
      Non-turbo .... 0.3 to 0.5 mm
      Turbo .... 0.25 to 0.45 mm
    Service limit.. 0.8 mm

Crankshaft and connecting rods

Crankshaft endplay
  Standard... 0.10 to 0.28 mm
  Limit... 0.4 mm
Bend limit... 0.05 mm
Main bearing journal
  Taper limit.. 0.006 mm
  Out-of-round limit... 0.01 mm
Connecting rod journal
  Taper limit.. 0.006 mm
  Out-of-round limit... 0.01 mm
Main bearing oil clearance
  Journal no. 1, 2, 4 and 5
    Standard .... 0.04 to 0.06 mm
    Limit... 0.1 mm
  Journal no. 3
    Standard .... 0.06 to 0.08 mm
    Limit... 0.1 mm
Connecting rod bearing oil clearance
  Standard... 0.03 to 0.05 mm
  Limit... 0.1 mm
Connecting rod endplay (side clearance)
  Standard... 0.15 to 0.45 mm
  Limit... 0.6 mm

Balance shafts

Refer to Chapter 2D

Cylinder head and valves

Head warpage limit... 0.2 mm
Valve seat angle... 45-degrees
Valve stem diameter
  Intake
    Standard .... 7.96 to 7.97 mm
    Limit .... 7.85 mm
  Exhaust
    Standard .... 7.93 to 7.95 mm
    Limit .... 7.85 mm
Valve stem-to-guide clearance
  Intake
    Standard .... 0.03 to 0.05 mm
    Limit .... 0.10 mm
  Exhaust... 0.05 to 0.08 mm
    Standard .... 0.05 to 0.08 mm
    Limit .... 0.15 mm

Valve margin width (minimum)	0.8 mm
Valve spring free length	
Standard	48.8 mm
Limit	47.8 mm
Valve spring fitted height	38.67 mm
Valve spring force at fitted height	
Standard	280 N
Limit	238 N

Torque specifications*

	Nm
Connecting rod bearing cap nuts	
Step 1	30
Step 2	50
Step 3	Tighten an additional 40 to 50-degrees
Step 4	Tighten an additional 40 to 50-degrees
Main bearing cap bolts	
Step 1	20
Step 2	Tighten an additional 90-degrees
Step 3	Tighten an additional 90-degrees
Oil jet banjo bolts	33
Outer lower crankcase bolts	25

*Note: Refer to Part D for additional torque specifications.

1 General information

Included in this portion of Chapter 2 are the general overhaul procedures for the cylinder head(s) and internal engine components.

The information ranges from advice concerning preparation for an overhaul and the purchase of renewal parts to detailed, step-by-step procedures covering removal and refitting of internal engine components and the inspection of parts.

The following Sections have been written based on the assumption the engine has been removed from the vehicle. For information concerning in-vehicle engine repair, as well as removal and refitting of the external components necessary for the overhaul, see Part A through Part D of this Chapter.

The Specifications included in this Part are only those necessary for the inspection and overhaul procedures which follow. Refer to Parts A, B, C and D for additional Specifications.

2 Engine overhaul - general information

Refer to illustrations 2.4a and 2.4b

It's not always easy to determine when, or if, an engine should be completely overhauled, as a number of factors must be considered.

A high number of kilometres isn't necessarily an indication an overhaul is needed, while a low number of kilometers doesn't preclude the need for an overhaul. Frequency of servicing is probably the most important consideration. An engine that's had regular and frequent oil and filter changes, as well as other required maintenance, will most likely give many thousands of kilometres of reliable service. Conversely, a neglected engine may require an overhaul very early in its life.

Excessive oil consumption is an indication that piston rings, valve seals and/or valve guides are in need of attention. Make sure oil leaks aren't responsible before deciding the rings and/or guides are bad. Perform a cylinder compression check to determine the extent of the work required (see Section 3).

Remove the oil pressure sending unit and check the oil pressure with a gauge refitted in its place (see illustrations). Compare the results to this Chapter's Specifications. As a general rule, engines should have 70 kPa of oil pressure for every 1,000 rpm's. If the pressure is extremely low, the bearings and/or oil pump are probably worn out.

Loss of power, rough running, knocking or metallic engine noises, excessive valve train noise and high fuel consumption rates may also point to the need for an overhaul, especially if they're all present at the same time. If a complete tune-up doesn't remedy the situation, major mechanical work is the only solution.

An engine overhaul involves restoring the internal parts to the specifications of a new engine. During an overhaul, the piston rings are renewed and the cylinder walls are reconditioned (rebored and/or honed). If a

2E

2.4a Remove the oil pressure sending unit (switch) and refit a pressure gauge in its place (four-cylinder engine shown)

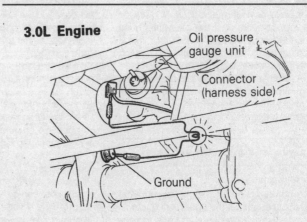

2.4b Location of the oil pressure sending unit on V6 engines

rebore is done by an automotive machine shop, new oversize pistons will also be fitted. The main bearings, connecting rod bearings and camshaft bearings are generally renewed and, if necessary, the crankshaft may be reground to restore the journals. Generally, the valves are serviced as well, since they're usually in less-than-perfect condition at this point. While the engine is being overhauled, other components, such as the starter and alternator, can be rebuilt as well. The end result should be a like-new engine that will give many trouble free kilometres. **Note:** *Critical cooling system components such as the hoses, drivebelts, thermostat and water pump MUST be renewed when an engine is overhauled. The radiator should be checked carefully to ensure it isn't clogged or leaking* (see Chapter 3). *Also, we don't recommend overhauling the oil pump - always fit a new one when an engine is rebuilt.*

Before beginning the engine overhaul, read through the entire procedure to familiarise yourself with the scope and requirements of the job. Overhauling an engine isn't particularly difficult, if you follow all of the instructions carefully, have the necessary tools and equipment and pay close attention to all specifications; however, it can be time consuming. Plan on the vehicle being tied up for a minimum of two weeks, especially if parts must be taken to an automotive machine shop for repair or reconditioning. Check on availability of parts and make sure any necessary special tools and equipment are obtained in advance. Most work can be done with typical hand tools, although a number of precision measuring tools are required for inspecting parts to determine if they must be renewed. Often an automotive machine shop will handle the inspection of parts and offer advice concerning reconditioning and renewal. **Note:** *Always wait until the engine has been completely disassembled and all components, especially the engine block, have been inspected before deciding what service and repair operations must be performed by an automotive machine shop.* Since the block's condition will be the major factor to consider when determining whether to overhaul the original engine or buy a rebuilt one, never purchase parts or have machine work done on other components until the block has been thoroughly inspected. As a general rule, time is the primary cost of an overhaul, so it doesn't pay to fit worn or substandard parts.

As a final note, to ensure maximum life and minimum trouble from a rebuilt engine, everything must be assembled with care in a spotlessly clean environment.

3 Cylinder compression check

Refer to illustration 3.6

1   A compression check will tell you what mechanical condition the upper end (pistons, rings, valves, head gaskets) of the engine is in. Specifically, it can tell you if the compression is down due to leakage caused by worn

piston rings, defective valves and seats or a blown head gasket. **Note:** *The engine must be at normal operating temperature and the battery must be fully charged for this check.*

2   Begin by cleaning the area around the spark plugs or glow plugs before you remove them. Compressed air should be used, if available, otherwise a small brush or even a bicycle tyre pump will work. The idea is to prevent dirt from getting into the cylinders as the compression check is being done.

3   Remove all of the spark plugs or glow plugs from the engine (see Chapter 1).

4   Block the throttle wide open on petrol models.

5   Disable the fuel system on petrol models by removing the fuel pump fuse (see Chapter 4).

6   Fit the compression gauge in the number one spark plug or glow plug hole **(see illustration)**.

7   Crank the engine over at least seven compression strokes and watch the gauge. The compression should build up quickly in a healthy engine. Low compression on the first stroke, followed by gradually increasing pressure on successive strokes, indicates worn piston rings. A low compression reading on the first stroke, which doesn't build up during successive strokes, indicates leaking valves or a blown head gasket (a cracked head could also be the cause). Deposits on the undersides of the valve heads can also cause low compression. Record the highest gauge reading obtained.

8   Repeat the procedure for the remaining cylinders and compare the results to this Chapter's Specifications.

9   If the readings are below normal, add some engine oil (about three squirts from a plunger-type oil can) to each cylinder, through the spark plug hole, and repeat the test.

10   If the compression increases after the oil is added, the piston rings are definitely worn. If the compression doesn't increase significantly, the leakage is occurring at the valves or head gasket. Leakage past the valves may be caused by burned valve seats and/or faces or warped, cracked or bent valves.

11   If two adjacent cylinders have equally low compression, there's a strong possibility the head gasket between them is blown. The appearance of coolant in the combustion chambers or the crankcase would verify this condition.

12   If one cylinder is about 20-percent lower than the others, and the engine has a slightly rough idle, a worn exhaust lobe on the camshaft could be the cause.

13   If the compression is unusually high, the combustion chambers are probably coated with carbon deposits. If that's the case, the cylinder head(s) should be removed and decarbonised.

14   If compression is way down or varies greatly between cylinders, it would be a good idea to have a leak-down test performed by an automotive repair shop. This test will pinpoint exactly where the leakage is occurring and how severe it is.

3.6 A compression gauge with a threaded fitting for the spark plug or glow plug hole is preferred over the type that requires hand pressure to maintain the seal

4 Engine removal - methods and precautions

If you've decided the engine must be removed for overhaul or major repair work, several preliminary steps should be taken.

Locating a suitable place to work is extremely important. Adequate work space, along with storage space for the vehicle, will be needed. If a shop or garage isn't available, at the very least a flat, level, clean work surface made of concrete or asphalt is required.

Cleaning the engine compartment and engine before beginning the removal procedure will help keep tools clean and organised.

An engine hoist or A-frame will also be necessary. Make sure the equipment is rated in excess of the combined weight of the engine and its accessories. Safety is of primary importance, considering the potential hazards involved in lifting the engine out of the vehicle.

If the engine is being removed by a novice, a helper should be available. Advice and aid from someone more experienced would also be helpful. There are many instances when one person cannot simultaneously perform all of the operations required when lifting the engine out of the vehicle.

Plan the operation ahead of time. Arrange for or obtain all of the tools and equipment you'll need prior to beginning the job. Some of the equipment necessary to perform engine removal and refitting safely and with relative ease are (in addition to an engine hoist) a heavy duty floor jack, complete sets of wrenches and sockets as described in the front of this manual, wooden blocks and plenty of rags and cleaning solvent for mopping up spilled oil, coolant and petrol. If the hoist must be rented, be sure to arrange for it in advance and perform all of the operations possible without it beforehand. This will save you money and time.

Plan for the vehicle to be out of use for quite a while. A machine shop will be

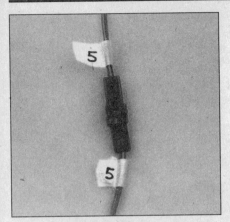

5.5 Label each wire before unplugging the connector

required to perform some of the work which the do-it-yourselfer can't accomplish without special equipment. These shops often have a busy schedule, so it would be a good idea to consult them before removing the engine in order to accurately estimate the amount of time required to rebuild or repair components that may need work.

Always be extremely careful when removing and refitting the engine. Serious injury can result from careless actions. Plan ahead, take your time and a job of this nature, although major, can be accomplished successfully.

5 Engine - removal and refitting

Refer to illustration 5.5

Warning: *Petrol is extremely flammable, so take extra precautions when you work on any part of the fuel system. Don't smoke or allow open flames or bare light bulbs near the work area, and don't work in a garage where a natural gas-type appliance (such as a water heater or clothes dryer) with a pilot light is present. If you spill any fuel on your skin, rinse it off immediately with soap and water. When you perform any kind of work on the fuel system, wear safety glasses and have a Class B type fire extinguisher on hand. Also, the air conditioning system is under high pressure - have a dealer service department or service station discharge the system before disconnecting any of the hoses or fittings.*

Note: *Read through the following steps carefully and familiarise yourself with the procedure before beginning work.*

Removal

1　On air-conditioned models only, have the air conditioning system discharged by a dealer service department or service station.
2　Refer to Chapter 4 and relieve the fuel system pressure, then disconnect the negative cable from the battery.
3　Cover the fenders and cowl and remove the bonnet (see Chapter 11). Special pads are available to protect the fenders, but an

old bedspread or blanket will also work.
4　Remove the air cleaner assembly (see Chapter 4).
5　Label the vacuum lines, emissions system hoses, electrical connectors, earth straps and fuel lines to ensure correct refitting, then detach them. Pieces of masking tape with numbers or letters written on them work well **(see illustration)**. If there's any possibility of confusion, make a sketch of the engine compartment and clearly label the lines, hoses and wires.
6　Raise the vehicle and support it securely on jackstands. Drain the cooling system (see Chapter 1).
7　Label and detach all coolant hoses from the engine.
8　Remove the coolant reservoir, cooling fan, shroud and radiator (see Chapter 3).
9　Remove the drivebelt(s) and idler, if equipped (see Chapter 1).
10　Disconnect the fuel lines running from the engine to the chassis (see Chapter 4). Plug or cap all open fittings/lines.
11　Disconnect the throttle linkage (and TV linkage/cruise control cable, if equipped) from the engine (see Chapters 4 and 7).
12　Unbolt the power steering pump and set it aside (see Chapter 10). Leave the lines/hoses attached and make sure the pump is kept in an upright position in the engine compartment.
13　Unbolt the air conditioning compressor (see Chapter 3) and set it aside. Do not disconnect the hoses.
14　Drain the engine oil and remove the filter (see Chapter 1).
15　Remove the starter and the alternator (see Chapter 5).
16　Check for clearance and remove the brake master cylinder, if necessary, to allow clearance for the engine (see Chapter 9).
17　Disconnect the exhaust system from the engine (see Chapter 4).
18　If the vehicle is equipped with an automatic transmission, remove the torque converter bolts (see Chapter 7, Part B). Do not remove any of the transmission-to-engine mounting bolts.
19　Support the transmission with a jack. Position a block of wood on the jack head to prevent damage to the transmission.
20　Attach an engine sling or a length of chain to the lifting brackets on the engine.
21　Roll the hoist into position and connect the sling to it. Take up the slack in the sling or chain, but don't lift the engine. **Warning:** *DO NOT place any part of your body under the engine when it's supported only by a hoist or other lifting device.*
22　Remove the driveshaft(s) (see Chapter 8).
23　Remove the engine mount-to-chassis bolts. Refer to the appropriate Chapter (2A or 2B) for the complete illustrations of the engine mounts.
24　Remove the engine-to-transmission bellhousing bolts.
25　Recheck to be sure nothing is still connecting the engine to the transmission. Dis-

connect anything still remaining.
26　Raise the engine slightly to disengage the mounts. Also, slightly raise the jack supporting the transmission. Move the engine forward, disengaging it from the transmission. If the vehicle is equipped with a manual transmission, be sure the clutch pressure plate is clear of the transmission input shaft. If the vehicle is equipped with an automatic transmission, make sure the torque converter stays with the transmission and doesn't stick to the driveplate. Slowly raise the engine out of the vehicle. Check carefully to make sure nothing is hanging up as the hoist is raised.
27　Once the engine assembly is out of the vehicle, be sure the torque converter (automatic transmission) stays in place (clamp a pair of vice-grips to the housing to keep the converter from sliding out).
28　Lower the engine to the ground and support it with blocks of wood. Remove the clutch and flywheel or driveplate and mount the engine on an engine stand.

Refitting

29　Check the engine and transmission mounts. If they're worn or damaged, renew them.
30　If you're working on a manual transmission equipped vehicle, fit the clutch and pressure plate (see Chapter 7). Now is a good time to fit a new clutch. Apply a dab of high-temperature grease to the input shaft.
31　Carefully lower the engine into the engine compartment and mate it to the transmission. **Caution:** *DO NOT use the bellhousing bolts to force the transmission and engine together.* If you're working on an automatic transmission equipped vehicle, take great care when fitting the torque converter, following the procedure outlined in Chapter 7B. Line up the holes in the engine mounts with the holes in the frame and fit the bolts, tightening them securely.
32　Add coolant, oil, power steering and transmission fluid as needed. If the brake master cylinder was removed, bleed the brakes (see Chapter 9). Recheck the fluid level and test the brakes.
33　Run the engine and check for leaks and proper operation of all accessories, then fit the bonnet and test drive the vehicle.
34　If the air conditioning system was discharged, have it evacuated, recharged and leak tested by the shop that discharged it.

6 Engine rebuilding alternatives

The home mechanic is faced with a number of options when performing an engine overhaul. The decision to renew the engine block, piston/connecting rod assemblies and crankshaft depends on a number of factors, with the number one consideration being the condition of the block. Other considerations are cost, access to machine shop facilities, parts availability, time required to complete the project and the extent of prior mechanical experience.

2E

Some of the rebuilding alternatives include:

Individual parts - If the inspection procedures reveal the engine block and most engine components are in reusable condition, purchasing individual parts may be the most economical alternative. The block, crankshaft and piston/connecting rod assemblies should all be inspected carefully. Even if the block shows little wear, the cylinder bores should be surface honed.

Short block - A short block consists of an engine block with a crankshaft and piston/connecting rod assemblies already fitted. All new bearings are incorporated and all clearances will be correct. The existing camshaft, valve train components, cylinder head(s) and external parts can be bolted to the short block with little or no machine shop work necessary.

Long block - A long block consists of a short block plus an oil pump, sump, cylinder head(s), valve cover(s), camshaft and valve train components, timing sprockets and chain and timing chain cover. All components are fitted with new bearings, seals and gaskets incorporated throughout. The refitting of manifolds and external parts is all that's necessary.

Give careful thought to which alternative is best for you and discuss the situation with local automotive machine shops, auto parts dealers and experienced rebuilders before ordering or purchasing renewal parts.

7   Engine overhaul - disassembly sequence

Refer to illustrations 7.5a and 7.5b

1   It's much easier to disassemble and work on the engine if it's mounted on a portable engine stand. A stand can often be rented quite cheaply from an equipment rental yard. Before it's mounted on a stand, the flywheel/driveplate should be removed from the engine.

2   If a stand isn't available, it's possible to disassemble the engine with it blocked up on the floor. Be extra careful not to tip or drop the engine when working without a stand.

3   If you're going to obtain a rebuilt engine, all external components must come off first, to be transferred to the renewal engine, just as they will if you're doing a complete engine overhaul yourself. These include:

Alternator and brackets
Emissions control components
Ignition coil/module assembly, spark plug wires and spark plugs
Thermostat and housing cover
Water pump
Carburettor/EFI components
Intake/exhaust manifolds
Oil filter
Engine mounts
Clutch and flywheel/driveplate

Note: *When removing the external components from the engine, pay close attention to*

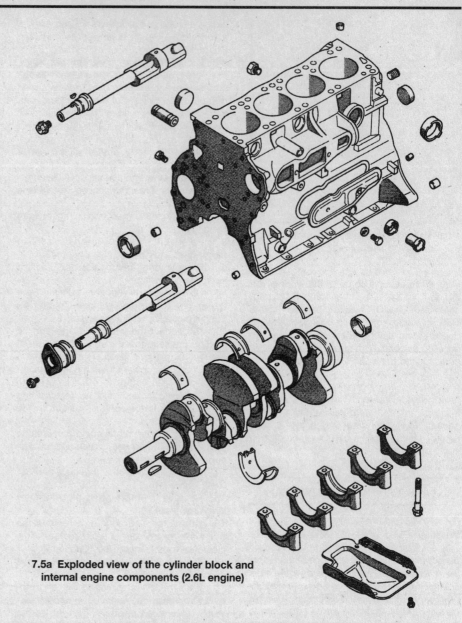

7.5a Exploded view of the cylinder block and internal engine components (2.6L engine)

details that may be helpful or important during refitting. Note the refitted position of gaskets, seals, spacers, pins, brackets, washers, bolts and other small items.

4   If you're obtaining a short block, which consists of the engine block, crankshaft, pistons and connecting rods all assembled, then the cylinder head(s), sump and oil pump will have to be removed as well. See Engine rebuilding alternatives for additional information regarding the different possibilities to be considered.

5   If you're planning a complete overhaul, the engine must be disassembled and the internal components removed in the following general order **(see illustrations on following pages):**

Four-cylinder petrol engine
Valve cover
Cylinder head and camshaft
Timing chain housing
Silent shaft chain and sprockets
Timing chain and sprockets
Sump
Oil pump
Piston/connecting rod assemblies
Rear main oil seal housing
Crankshaft and main bearings

V6 engines
Valve covers
Exhaust manifolds
Rocker arm assemblies and camshafts
Rocker arms
Inlet manifold
Timing belt cover
Timing belt and sprockets
Cylinder heads
Sump
Oil pump
Piston/connecting rod assemblies
Rear main oil seal housing
Crankshaft and main bearings

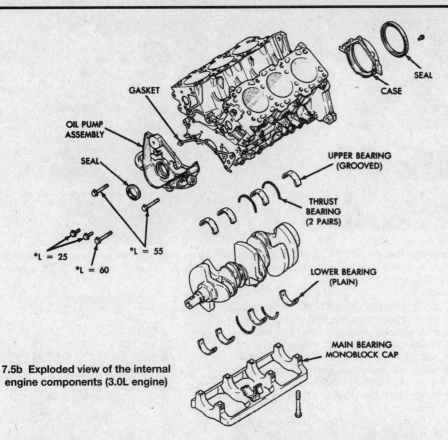

7.5b Exploded view of the internal engine components (3.0L engine)

8.2 A small plastic bag, with an appropriate label, can be used to store the valve train components so they can be kept together and refitted in the original location

8.3 Use a valve spring compressor to compress the spring, then remove the collets from the valve stem

8.4 If the valve won't pull through the guide, deburr the edge of the stem end and the area around the top of the collet groove with a file or whetstone

Four-cylinder diesel engines

  Valve cover
  Timing belt covers
  Cylinder head and camshaft
  Timing belt and sprockets
  Silent shaft belt and sprockets
  Sump
  Oil pump and front cover assembly
  Oil filter bracket assembly
  Piston/connecting rod assemblies
  Rear main oil seal housing
  Crankshaft and main bearings
  Piston cooling jets

6   Before beginning the disassembly and overhaul procedures, make sure the following items are available. Also, refer to Engine overhaul - reassembly sequence for a list of tools and materials needed for engine reassembly.

  Common hand tools
  Small cardboard boxes or plastic bags
    for storing parts
  Gasket scraper
  Ridge reamer
  Vibration damper puller
  Micrometers
  Telescoping gauges
  Dial indicator set
  Valve spring compressor
  Cylinder surfacing hone
  Piston ring groove cleaning tool
  Electric drill motor
  Tap and die set
  Wire brushes
  Oil gallery brushes
  Cleaning solvent

8 Cylinder head - disassembly

Refer to illustrations 8.2, 8.3 and 8.4
Note 1: *New and rebuilt cylinder heads are commonly available for most engines at dealerships and auto parts stores. Due to the fact that some specialised tools are necessary for the disassembly and inspection procedures, and renewal parts aren't always readily available, it may be more practical and economical for the home mechanic to purchase renewal head(s) rather than taking the time to disassemble, inspect and recondition the original(s).*
Note 2: *Diesel engines in particular use combustion jets, coolant diverters and/or removable combustion chambers which require special expertise and equipment for proper service. A machine shop specializing in diesel repair is needed.*

1   Cylinder head disassembly involves removal of the intake and exhaust valves and related components. The rocker arm assemblies and camshaft(s) must be removed before beginning the cylinder head disassembly procedure (see Part A, B, C or D of this Chapter). Label the parts or store them separately so they can be refitted in their original locations.

2   Before the valves are removed, arrange to label and store them, along with their related components, so they can be kept separate and refitted in their original locations **(see illustration)**.

3   Compress the springs on the first valve with a spring compressor and remove the collets **(see illustration)**. Carefully release

the valve spring compressor and remove the retainer, the spring and the spring seat (if used).

4   Pull the valve out of the head, then remove the oil seal from the guide. If the valve binds in the guide (won't pull through), push it back into the head and deburr the area around the collet groove with a fine file or whetstone **(see illustration)**.

2E

9.12 Check the cylinder head gasket surface for warpage by trying to slip a feeler gauge under the straightedge (see this Chapter's Specifications for the maximum warpage allowed and use a feeler gauge of that thickness)

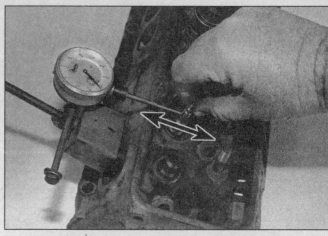

9.14 A dial indicator can be used to determine the valve stem-to-guide clearance (move the valve stem as indicated by the arrows)

5   Repeat the procedure for the remaining valves. Remember to keep all the parts for each valve together so they can be refitted in the same locations.

6   Once the valves and related components have been removed and stored in an organised manner, the head should be thoroughly cleaned and inspected. If a complete engine overhaul is being done, finish the engine disassembly procedures before beginning the cylinder head cleaning and inspection process.

9   Cylinder head - cleaning and inspection

1   Thorough cleaning of the cylinder head(s) and related valve train components, followed by a detailed inspection, will enable you to decide how much valve service work must be done during the engine overhaul. **Note:** *If the engine was severely overheated, the cylinder head is probably warped.*

Cleaning

2   Scrape all traces of old gasket material and sealant off the head gasket, inlet manifold and exhaust manifold mating surfaces. Be very careful not to gouge the cylinder head. Special gasket removal solvents that soften gaskets and make removal much easier are available at auto parts stores.

3   Remove all built-up scale from the coolant passages.

4   Run a stiff wire brush through the various holes to remove deposits that may have formed in them.

5   Run an appropriate size tap into each of the threaded holes to remove corrosion and thread sealant that may be present. If compressed air is available, use it to clear the holes of debris produced by this operation. **Warning:** *Wear eye protection when using compressed air!*

6   Clean the camshaft bearing cap bolt threads with a wire brush.

7   Clean the cylinder head with solvent and

dry it thoroughly. Compressed air will speed the drying process and ensure that all holes and recessed areas are clean. **Note:** *Decarbonising chemicals are available and may prove very useful when cleaning cylinder heads and valve train components. They're very caustic and should be used with caution. Be sure to follow the instructions on the container.*

8   Clean the rocker arms and bearing caps with solvent and dry them thoroughly (don't mix them up during the cleaning process). Compressed air will speed the drying process and can be used to clean out the oil passages.

9   Clean all the valve springs, spring seats, collets and retainers with solvent and dry them thoroughly. Do the components from one valve at a time to avoid mixing up the parts.

10   Scrape off any heavy deposits that may have formed on the valves, then use a motorised wire brush to remove deposits from the valve heads and stems. Again, make sure the valves don't get mixed up.

Inspection

Refer to illustrations 9.12, 9.14, 9.15, 9.16, 9.17 and 9.18

Note: *Be sure to perform all of the following inspection procedures before concluding machine shop work is required. Make a list of the items that need attention.*

Cylinder head

11   Inspect the head very carefully for cracks, evidence of coolant leakage and other damage. If cracks are found, check with an automotive machine shop concerning repair. If repair isn't possible, a new cylinder head should be obtained.

12   Using a straightedge and feeler gauge, check the head gasket mating surface for warpage **(see illustration)**. If the warpage exceeds the limit in this Chapter's Specifications, it can be resurfaced at an automotive machine shop. **Note:** *If the V6 engine heads are resurfaced, the inlet manifold flanges will also require machining.*

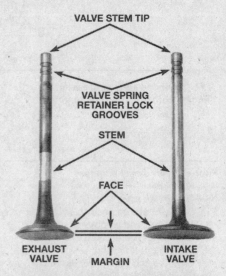

9.15 Check for valve wear at the points shown here

13   Examine the valve seats in each of the combustion chambers. If they're pitted, cracked or burned, the head will require valve service that's beyond the scope of the home mechanic.

14   Check the valve stem-to-guide clearance by measuring the lateral movement of the valve stem with a dial indicator attached securely to the head **(see illustration)**. The valve must be in the guide and approximately 1.6 mm off the seat. The total valve stem movement indicated by the gauge needle must be divided by two to obtain the actual clearance. After this is done, if there's still some doubt regarding the condition of the valve guides, they should be checked by an automotive machine shop (the cost should be minimal).

Valves

15   Carefully inspect each valve face for uneven wear, deformation, cracks, pits and burned areas. Check the valve stem for scuffing and galling and the neck for cracks. Rotate the valve and check for any obvious

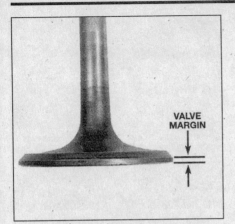

9.16 The valve margin width on each valve must be as specified (if no margin exists, the valve cannot be reused)

9.17 Measure each valve spring length

9.18 Check each valve spring for squareness

indication that it's bent. Look for pits and excessive wear on the end of the stem. The presence of any of these conditions **(see illustration)** indicates the need for valve service by an automotive machine shop.

16   Measure the margin width on each valve **(see illustration)**. Any valve with a margin narrower than specified in this Chapter will have to be renewed.

Valve components

17   Check each valve spring for wear (on the ends) and pits. Measure the free length and compare it to this Chapter's Specifications **(see illustration)**. Any springs that are shorter than specified have sagged and shouldn't be reused. The tension of all springs should be checked with a special fixture before deciding they're suitable for use in a rebuilt engine (take the springs to an automotive machine shop for this check).

18   Stand each spring on a flat surface and check it for squareness **(see illustration)**. If any of the springs are distorted or sagged, renew all of them.

19   Check the spring retainers and collets for obvious wear and cracks. Any questionable parts should be renewed, as extensive damage will occur if they fail during engine operation.

20   If the inspection process indicates the valve components are in generally poor condition and worn beyond the limits specified, which is usually the case in an engine that's being overhauled, reassemble the valves in the cylinder head and refer to Section 10 for valve servicing recommendations.

10   Valves - servicing

1   Because of the complex nature of the job and the special tools and equipment needed, servicing of the valves, the valve seats and the valve guides, commonly known as a valve job, should be done by a professional.

2   The home mechanic can remove and disassemble the head, do the initial cleaning and inspection, then reassemble and deliver it to a dealer service department or an automotive machine shop for the actual service work. Doing the inspection will enable you to see what condition the head and valvetrain components are in and will ensure that you know what work and new parts are required when dealing with an automotive machine shop.

3   The dealer service department, or automotive machine shop, will remove the valves and springs, recondition or renew the valves and valve seats, recondition the valve guides, check and renew the valve springs, rotators, spring retainers and collets (as necessary), renew the valve seals, reassemble the valve components and make sure the fitted spring height is correct. The cylinder head gasket surface will also be resurfaced if it's warped.

4   After the valve job has been performed by a professional, the head will be in like new condition. When the head is returned, be sure to clean it again before refitting on the engine to remove any metal particles and abrasive grit that may still be present from the valve service or head resurfacing operations. Use compressed air, if available, to blow out all the oil holes and passages.

11   Cylinder head - reassembly

Refer to illustrations 11.4, 11.6 and 11.8

1   Regardless of whether or not the head was sent to an automotive repair shop for valve servicing, make sure it's clean before beginning reassembly.

2   If the head was sent out for valve servicing, the valves and related components will already be in place. Begin the reassembly procedure with Step 8.

3   Fit the spring seats or valve rotators (if equipped) before the valve seals.

4   Fit new seals on each of the valve guides. Using a hammer and a deep socket or seal refitting tool, gently tap each seal into place until it's completely seated on the guide **(see illustration)**. Don't twist or cock the seals during refitting or they won't seal properly on the valve stems.

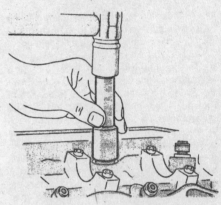

11.4 Make sure the valve stem seals are refitted evenly and carefully to avoid damage

11.6 Apply a small dab of grease to each collet as shown here before refitting - it'll hold them in place on the valve stem as the spring is released

5   Beginning at one end of the head, lubricate and fit the first valve. Apply moly-base grease or clean engine oil to the valve stem.

6   Position the valve springs (and shims, if used) over the valves. Compress the springs with a valve spring compressor and carefully refit the collets in the groove, then slowly release the compressor and make sure the collets seat properly. Apply a small dab of grease to each collet to hold it in place if necessary **(see illustration)**.

2E

11.8 Be sure to check the valve spring fitted height (the distance from the top of the seat/shims to the top of the spring)

12.1 A ridge reamer is required to remove the ridge from the top of each cylinder - do this before removing the pistons!

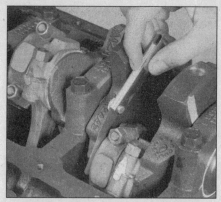

12.3 Check the connecting rod side clearance with a feeler gauge as shown

7   Repeat the procedure for the remaining valves. Be sure to return the components to their original locations - don't mix them up!
8   Check the fitted valve spring height with a ruler graduated in 1 mm increments or a dial caliper. If the head was sent out for service work, the fitted height should be correct (but don't automatically assume it is). The measurement is taken from the top of each spring seat to the bottom of the retainer (see illustration). If the height is greater than listed in this Chapter's Specifications, shims can be added under the springs to correct it. **Caution:** *Do not, under any circumstances, shim the springs to the point where the fitted height is less than specified.*
9   Apply moly-base grease to the rocker arm faces, the camshaft and the rocker shafts, then fit the camshaft, rocker arms and shafts (refer to Part A).
10   the camshafts, hydraulic lash adjusters and rocker arm assemblies onto the head.
11   Apply moly-base grease to the rocker arm faces and the pivot balls, then refit the rocker arm assembly on the cylinder head.

12 Pistons and connecting rods - removal

Refer to illustrations 12.1, 12.3 and 12.6
Note: *Prior to removing the piston/connecting rod assemblies, remove the cylinder head(s), the sump and the oil pump by referring to the appropriate Sections in Parts A or B of Chapter 2.*
1   Use your fingernail to feel if a ridge has formed at the upper limit of ring travel (about 5 mm down from the top of each cylinder). If carbon deposits or cylinder wear have produced ridges, they must be completely removed with a special tool (see illustration). Follow the manufacturer's instructions provided with the tool. Failure to remove the ridges before attempting to remove the piston/connecting rod assemblies may result in piston breakage.
2   After the cylinder ridges have been removed, turn the engine upside-down so the crankshaft is facing up.

3   Before the connecting rods are removed, check the endplay with feeler gauges. Slide them between the first connecting rod and the crankshaft throw until the play is removed (see illustration). The endplay is equal to the thickness of the feeler gauge(s). If the endplay exceeds the service limit, new connecting rods will be required. If new rods (or a new crankshaft) are fitted, the endplay may fall under the minimum listed in this Chapter's Specifications (if it does, the rods will have to be machined to restore it - consult an automotive machine shop for advice if necessary). Repeat the procedure for the remaining connecting rods.
4   Check the connecting rods and caps for identification marks. If they aren't plainly marked, use a small centre punch to make the appropriate number of indentations on each rod and cap (1, 2, 3, etc., depending on the engine type and cylinder they're associated with).
5   Loosen each of the connecting rod cap nuts 1/2-turn at a time until they can be removed by hand. Remove the number one connecting rod cap and bearing insert. Don't drop the bearing insert out of the cap.
6   Slip a short length of plastic or rubber hose over each connecting rod cap bolt to protect the crankshaft journal and cylinder wall as the piston is removed (see illustration).
7   Remove the bearing insert and push the connecting rod/piston assembly out through the top of the engine. Use a wooden or plastic hammer handle to push on the upper bearing surface in the connecting rod. If resistance is felt, double-check to make sure all of the ridge was removed from the cylinder.
8   Repeat the procedure for the remaining cylinders.
9   After removal, reassemble the connecting rod caps and bearing inserts in their respective connecting rods and fit the cap nuts finger tight. Leaving the old bearing inserts in place until reassembly will help prevent the connecting rod bearing surfaces from being accidentally nicked or gouged.
10   Don't separate the pistons from the connecting rods (see Section 17 for additional information).

12.6 To prevent damage to the crankshaft journals and cylinder walls, slip sections of rubber or plastic hose over the rod bolts before removing the pistons

13 Crankshaft - removal

Refer to illustrations 13.1, 13.3, 13.4a and 13.4b
Note: *The crankshaft can be removed only after the engine has been removed from the vehicle. It's assumed the flywheel or driveplate, crankshaft balancer/vibration damper, timing chain or belt, sump, oil pump and piston/connecting rod assemblies have already been removed. The rear main oil seal housing must be unbolted and separated from the block before proceeding with crankshaft removal.*
1   Before the crankshaft is removed, check the endplay. Mount a dial indicator with the stem in line with the crankshaft and touching one of the crank throws (see illustration).
2   Push the crankshaft all the way to the rear and zero the dial indicator. Next, prise the crankshaft to the front as far as possible and check the reading on the dial indicator. The distance it moves is the endplay. If it's greater than specified in this Chapter, check the crankshaft thrust surfaces for wear. If no wear is evident, new main bearings should correct the endplay.
3   If a dial indicator isn't available, feeler gauges can be used. Gently prise or push the crankshaft all the way to the front of the

13.1 Checking crankshaft endplay with a dial indicator

13.3 Checking crankshaft endplay with a feeler gauge

13.4a Use a centre-punch or number stamping dies to mark the main bearing caps to ensure refitting in their original locations on the block (make the punch marks near one of the bolt heads)

engine. Slip feeler gauges between the crankshaft and the front face of the thrust main bearing to determine the clearance **(see illustration)**.

4   Check the main bearing caps to see if they're marked to indicate their locations. They should be numbered consecutively from the front of the engine to the rear. If they aren't, mark them with number stamping dies or a centre punch **(see illustrations)**. Main bearing caps generally have a cast-in arrow, which points to the front of the engine. Loosen the main bearing cap bolts 1/4-turn at a time each, until they can be removed by hand. Note if any stud bolts are used and make sure they're returned to their original locations when the crankshaft is refitted.

5   Gently tap the caps with a soft-face hammer, then separate them from the engine block. If necessary, use the bolts as levers to remove the caps. Try not to drop the bearing inserts if they come out with the caps.

6   Carefully lift the crankshaft out of the engine. It may be a good idea to have an assistant available, since the crankshaft is quite heavy. With the bearing inserts in place in the engine block and main bearing caps, return the caps to their respective locations on the engine block and tighten the bolts finger tight.

14 Engine block - cleaning

Refer to illustrations 14.4, 14.8 and 14.10

1   Remove the main bearing caps and separate the bearing inserts from the caps and the engine block. Tag the bearings, indicating which cylinder they were removed from and whether they were in the cap or the block, then set them aside.

2   Using a gasket scraper, remove all traces of gasket material from the engine block. Be very careful not to nick or gouge the gasket sealing surfaces.

3   Remove all of the covers and threaded oil gallery plugs from the block. The plugs are usually very tight - they may have to be drilled out and the holes retapped. Use new plugs when the engine is reassembled.

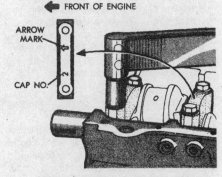

← FRONT OF ENGINE

13.4b The main bearing caps on four cylinder engines have arrows that point to the front of the engine

4   Remove the core plugs from the engine block. To do this, knock one side of the plugs into the block with a hammer and punch, then grasp the edge of the plug with large pliers and pull it out of the block **(see illustration)**. **Caution:** *The core plugs (also known as freeze or soft plugs) may be difficult or impossible to retrieve if they're driven into the block coolant passages.*

5   If the engine is extremely dirty, it should be taken to an automotive machine shop to be steam cleaned or hot tanked.

6   After the block is returned, clean all oil holes and oil galleries one more time. Brushes specifically designed for this purpose are available at most auto parts stores. Flush the passages with warm water until the water runs clear, dry the block thoroughly and wipe all machined surfaces with a light, rust preventive oil. If you have access to compressed air, use it to speed the drying process and blow out all the oil holes and galleries. **Warning:** *Wear eye protection when using compressed air!*

7   If the block isn't extremely dirty or sludged up, you can do an adequate cleaning job with hot soapy water and a stiff brush. Take plenty of time and do a thorough job. Regardless of the cleaning method used, be sure to clean all oil holes and galleries very thoroughly, dry the block completely and coat all machined surfaces with light oil.

14.4 Knock the core plugs sideways, then pull them out of the block with pliers

8   The threaded holes in the block must be clean to ensure accurate torque readings during reassembly. Run the proper size tap into each of the holes to remove rust, corrosion, thread sealant or sludge and restore damaged threads **(see illustration)**. If possible, use compressed air to clear the holes of

14.8 All bolt holes in the block - particularly the main bearing cap and head bolt holes - should be cleaned and restored with a tap (be sure to remove debris from the holes after this is done)

2E

14.10 A large socket on an extension can be used to drive the new core into the bores

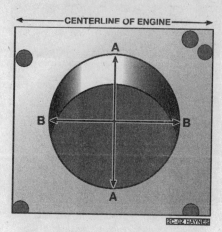

15.4a Measure the diameter of each cylinder at a right angle to the engine centerline (A), and parallel to the engine centreline (B) - out-of-round is the difference between A and B; taper is the difference between A and B at the top of the cylinder and A and B at the bottom of the cylinder

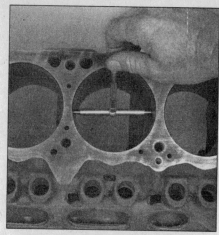

15.4b The ability to "feel" when the telescoping gauge is at the correct point will be developed over time, so work slowly and repeat the check until you're satisfied the bore measurement is accurate

debris produced by this operation. Now is a good time to clean the threads on the head bolts and the main bearing cap bolts as well.

9   Refit the main bearing caps and tighten the bolts finger tight.

10   After coating the sealing surfaces of the new core plugs with Permatex no. 2 sealant, fit them in the engine block **(see illustration)**. Make sure they're driven in straight and seated properly or leakage could result. Special tools are available for this purpose, but a large socket, with an outside diameter that will just slip into the core plug, a 1/2-inch drive extension and a hammer will work just as well.

11   Apply non-hardening sealant (such as Permatex no. 2 or Teflon pipe sealant) to the new oil gallery plugs and thread them into the holes in the block. Make sure they're tightened securely.

12   If the engine isn't going to be reassembled right away, cover it with a large plastic trash bag to keep it clean.

13   The complete oil filter bracket assembly should be removed from the block, thoroughly cleaned and checked for smooth operation of the bypass valve. Any damaged components such as deformed springs should be renewed at this time. Refer to Chapter 3 for more information on this procedure.

15   Engine block - inspection

Refer to illustrations 15.4a, 15.4b, 15.4c and 15.13

1   Before the block is inspected, it should be cleaned as described in Section 14.

2   Visually check the block for cracks, rust and corrosion. Look for stripped threads in the threaded holes. It's also a good idea to have the block checked for hidden cracks by an automotive machine shop that has the special equipment to do this type of work. If defects are found, have the block repaired, if possible, or renewed.

3   Check the cylinder bores for scuffing and scoring.

4   Measure the diameter of each cylinder at the top (just under the ridge area), centre and bottom of the cylinder bore, parallel to the crankshaft axis **(see illustrations)**. **Note:** *These measurements should not be made with the bare block mounted on an engine stand - the cylinders will be distorted and the measurements will be inaccurate.*

5   Next, measure each cylinder's diameter at the same three locations across the crankshaft axis. Compare the results to this Chapter's Specifications.

6   If the required precision measuring tools aren't available, the piston-to-cylinder clearances can be obtained, though not quite as accurately, using feeler gauge stock. Feeler gauge stock comes in various thicknesses and is generally available at auto parts stores.

7   To check the clearance, select a feeler gauge and slip it into the cylinder along with the matching piston. The piston must be positioned exactly as it normally would be. The feeler gauge must be between the piston and cylinder on one of the thrust faces (90-degrees to the piston pin bore).

8   The piston should slip through the cylinder (with the feeler gauge in place) with moderate pressure.

9   If it falls through or slides through easily, the clearance is excessive and a new piston will be required. If the piston binds at the lower end of the cylinder and is loose toward the top, the cylinder is tapered. If tight spots are encountered as the piston/feeler gauge is rotated in the cylinder, the cylinder is out-of-round.

10   Repeat the procedure for the remaining pistons and cylinders.

11   If the cylinder walls are badly scuffed or scored, or if they're out-of-round or tapered

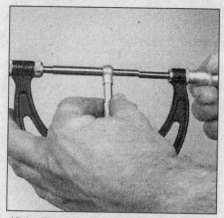

15.4c The gauge is then measured with a micrometer to determine the bore size

beyond the limits given in this Chapter's Specifications, have the engine block rebored and honed at an automotive machine shop. If a rebore is done, oversize pistons and rings will be required.

12   If the cylinders are in reasonably good condition and not worn to the outside of the limits, and if the piston-to-cylinder clearances can be maintained properly, they don't have to be rebored. Honing is all that's necessary (see Section 16).

13   Diesel engines should have their piston-cooling oil jets and check valves removed, cleaned, examined and refitted after the block has been prepared for assembly **(see illustration)**. Make certain that all components are undamaged and that all gaskets and seals have been renewed. The jets must be refitted so that their oil discharge strikes the bottoms of the piston dome and so that there is no interference with the movement of the pistons. Refer to Chapter 2C or 2D for additional information.

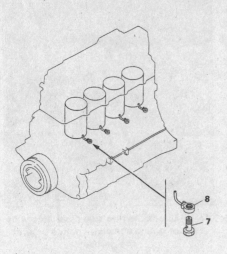

15.13 The piston-cooling oil jets are a critical part of diesel engines - make certain that they are clean and positioned properly

16.3a A "bottle brush" hone is the best choice if you've never honed cylinders before

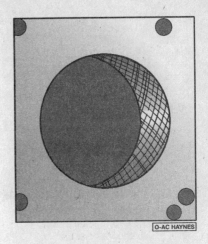

16.3b The cylinder hone should leave a smooth, crosshatch pattern with the lines intersecting at appropriately a 60-degree angle

2E

16 Cylinder honing

Refer to illustrations 16.3a and 16.3b

1   Prior to engine reassembly, the cylinder bores must be honed so the new piston rings will seat correctly and provide the best possible combustion chamber seal. **Note:** *If you don't have the tools or don't want to tackle the honing operation, most automotive machine shops will do it for a reasonable fee.*
2   Before honing the cylinders, fit the main bearing caps and tighten the bolts to the specified torque.
3   Two types of cylinder hones are commonly available - the flex hone or "bottle brush" type and the more traditional surfacing hone with spring-loaded stones. Both will do the job, but for the less experienced mechanic the "bottle brush" hone will probably be easier to use. You'll also need some honing oil (kerosene will work if honing oil isn't available), rags and an electric drill motor. Proceed as follows:

a) *Mount the hone in the drill motor, compress the stones and slip it into the first cylinder* **(see illustration)**. *Be sure to wear safety goggles or a face shield!*
b) *Lubricate the cylinder with plenty of honing oil, turn on the drill and move the hone up-and-down in the cylinder at a pace that will produce a fine crosshatch pattern on the cylinder walls. Ideally, the crosshatch lines should intersect at approximately a 60-degree angle* **(see illustration)**. *Be sure to use plenty of lubricant and don't take off any more material than is absolutely necessary to produce the desired finish.* **Note:** *Piston ring manufacturers may specify a smaller crosshatch angle than the traditional 60-degrees - read and follow any instructions included with the new rings.*

c) *Don't withdraw the hone from the cylinder while it's running. Instead, shut off the drill and continue moving the hone up-and-down in the cylinder until it comes to a complete stop, then compress the stones and withdraw the hone. If you're using a "bottle brush" type hone, stop the drill motor, then turn the chuck in the normal direction of rotation while withdrawing the hone from the cylinder.*
d) *Wipe the oil out of the cylinder and repeat the procedure for the remaining cylinders.*

4   After the honing job is complete, chamfer the top edges of the cylinder bores with a small file so the rings won't catch when the pistons are fitted. Be very careful not to nick the cylinder walls with the end of the file.
5   The entire engine block must be washed again very thoroughly with warm, soapy water to remove all traces of the abrasive grit produced during the honing operation. **Note:** *The bores can be considered clean when a lint-free white cloth - dampened with clean engine oil - used to wipe them out doesn't pick up any more honing residue, which will show up as gray areas on the cloth. Be sure to run a brush through all oil holes and galleries and flush them with running water.*
6   After rinsing, dry the block and apply a coat of light rust preventive oil to all machined surfaces. Wrap the block in a plastic trash bag to keep it clean and set it aside until reassembly.

17 Pistons and connecting rods - inspection

Refer to illustrations 17.2, 17.4a, 17,4b, 17.10 and 17.11

1   Before the inspection process can be carried out, the piston/connecting rod assemblies must be cleaned and the original piston rings removed from the pistons. **Note:** *Always use new piston rings when the engine is reassembled.*

17.2 Use a special tool to remove the piston rings from the piston

2   Using a piston ring refitting tool **(see illustration)**, carefully remove the rings from the pistons. Be careful not to nick or gouge the pistons in the process.
3   Scrape all traces of carbon from the top of the piston. A hand held wire brush or a piece of fine emery cloth can be used once the majority of the deposits have been scraped away. Do not, under any circumstances, use a wire brush mounted in a drill motor to remove deposits from the pistons. The piston material is soft and may be eroded away by the wire brush.
4   Use a piston ring groove cleaning tool to remove carbon deposits from the ring grooves. If a tool isn't available, a piece broken off the old ring will do the job. Be very careful to remove only the carbon deposits - don't remove any metal and do not nick or scratch the sides of the ring grooves **(see illustrations)**.
5   Once the deposits have been removed, clean the piston/rod assemblies with solvent

17.4a The piston ring grooves can be cleaned with a special tool, as shown here . . .

17.4b . . . or a section of a broken ring

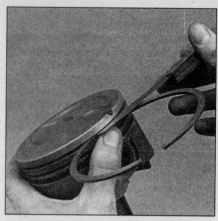

17.10 Check the ring side clearance with a feeler gauge at several points around the groove

and dry them with compressed air (if available). **Warning:** *Wear eye protection. Make sure the oil return holes in the back sides of the ring grooves are clear.*

6   If the pistons and cylinder walls aren't damaged or worn excessively, and if the engine block isn't rebored, new pistons won't be necessary. Normal piston wear appears as even vertical wear on the piston thrust surfaces and slight looseness of the top ring in its groove. New piston rings, however, should always be used when an engine is rebuilt.

7   Carefully inspect each piston for cracks around the skirt, at the pin bosses and at the ring lands.

8   Look for scoring and scuffing on the thrust faces of the skirt, holes in the piston crown and burned areas at the edge of the crown. If the skirt is scored or scuffed, the engine may have been suffering from overheating and/or abnormal combustion, which caused excessively high operating temperatures. The cooling and lubrication systems should be checked thoroughly. A hole in the piston crown is an indication that abnormal combustion (preignition) was occurring. Burned areas at the edge of the piston crown are usually evidence of spark knock (detonation). If any of the above problems exist, the causes must be corrected or the damage will occur again. The causes may include intake air leaks, incorrect fuel/air mixture, low octane fuel, ignition timing and EGR system malfunctions.

9   Corrosion of the piston, in the form of small pits, indicates coolant is leaking into the combustion chamber and/or the crankcase. Again, the cause must be corrected or the problem may persist in the rebuilt engine.

10   Measure the piston ring side clearance by laying a new piston ring in each ring groove and slipping a feeler gauge in beside it **(see illustration)**. Check the clearance at three or four locations around each groove. Be sure to use the correct ring for each groove - they are different. If the side clearance is greater than specified in this Chapter, new pistons will have to be used.

11   Check the piston-to-bore clearance by measuring the bore (see Section 15) and the piston diameter. Make sure the pistons and bores are correctly matched. Measure the piston across the skirt, at a 90-degree angle to the piston pin **(see illustration)** below the axis of the piston pin.

12   Subtract the piston diameter from the bore diameter to obtain the clearance. If it's greater than listed in this Chapter's Specifications, the block will have to be rebored and new pistons and rings fitted.

13   Check the piston-to-rod clearance by twisting the piston and rod in opposite directions. Any noticeable play indicates excessive wear, which must be corrected. The piston/connecting rod assemblies should be taken to an automotive machine shop to have the pistons and rods resized and new pins fitted.

14   If the pistons must be removed from the connecting rods for any reason, they should be taken to an automotive machine shop. While they are there have the connecting rods checked for bend and twist, since automotive machine shops have special equipment for this purpose. **Note:** *Unless new pistons and/or connecting rods must be fitted, do not disassemble the pistons and connecting rods.*

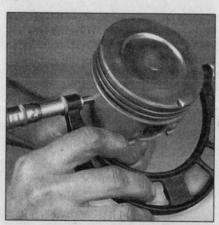

17.11 Measure the piston diameter at a 90-degree angle to the piston pin and in line with it

15   Check the connecting rods for cracks and other damage. Temporarily remove the rod caps, lift out the old bearing inserts, wipe the rod and cap bearing surfaces clean and inspect them for nicks, gouges and scratches. After checking the rods, renew the old bearings, slip the caps into place and tighten the nuts finger tight. **Note:** *If the engine is being rebuilt because of a connecting rod knock, be sure to fit new rods.*

16   2.5 litre diesel engine pistons and rods must be assembled with the notch on the piston crown and the letter mark on the side of the connecting rod facing the same direction. During refitting into the block, they will face toward the front of the engine.

18 Crankshaft - inspection

Refer to illustrations 18.1, 18.2, 18.4, 18.6 and 18.8

1   Remove all burrs from the crankshaft oil holes with a stone, file or scraper **(see illustration)**.

2   Clean the crankshaft with solvent and dry it with compressed air (if available). **Warning:** *Wear eye protection when using*

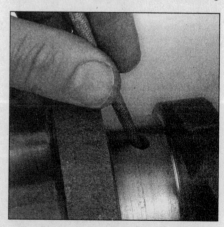

18.1 The oil holes should be chamfered so sharp edges don't gouge or scratch the new bearings

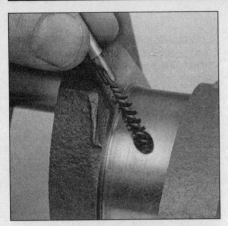

18.2 Use a wire or stiff plastic bristle brush to clean the oil passages in the crankshaft

18.4 Rubbing a penny lengthwise on each journal will reveal its condition - if copper rubs off and is embedded in the crankshaft, the journals should be reground

compressed air. Be sure to clean the oil holes with a stiff brush **(see illustration)** and flush them with solvent.

3   Check the main and connecting rod bearing journals for uneven wear, scoring, pits and cracks.

4   Rub a penny across each journal several times **(see illustration)**. If a journal picks up copper from the penny, it's too rough and must be reground.

5   Check the rest of the crankshaft for cracks and other damage. It should be magnafluxed to reveal hidden cracks - an automotive machine shop will handle the procedure.

6   Using a micrometer, measure the diameter of the main and connecting rod journals and compare the results to this Chapter's Specifications **(see illustration)**. By measuring the diameter

at a number of points around each journal's circumference, you'll be able to determine whether or not the journal is out-of-round. Take the measurement at each end of the journal, near the crank throws, to determine if the journal is tapered.

7   If the crankshaft journals are damaged, tapered, out-of-round or worn beyond the limits given in the Specifications, have the crankshaft reground by an automotive machine shop. Be sure to use the correct size bearing inserts if the crankshaft is reconditioned.

8   Check the oil seal journals at each end of the crankshaft for wear and damage. If the seal has worn a groove in the journal, or if it's nicked or scratched **(see illustration)**, the new seal may leak when the engine is reassembled. In some cases, an automotive machine shop may be able to repair the journal by pressing on a thin sleeve. If repair isn't feasible, a new or different crankshaft should be fitted.

9   Refer to Section 19 and examine the main and rod bearing inserts.

19 Main and connecting rod bearings - inspection

Refer to illustration 19.1

1   Even though the main and connecting

2E

18.6 Measure the diameter of each crankshaft journal at several points to detect taper and out-of-round conditions

18.8 If the seals have worn grooves in the crankshaft journals, or if the seal contact surfaces are nicked or scratched, the new seals will leak

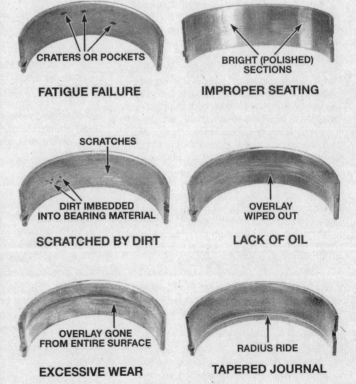

CRATERS OR POCKETS
FATIGUE FAILURE

BRIGHT (POLISHED) SECTIONS
IMPROPER SEATING

SCRATCHES
DIRT IMBEDDED INTO BEARING MATERIAL
SCRATCHED BY DIRT

OVERLAY WIPED OUT
LACK OF OIL

OVERLAY GONE FROM ENTIRE SURFACE
EXCESSIVE WEAR

RADIUS RIDE
TAPERED JOURNAL

19.1 Typical bearing failures

rod bearings should be renewed during the engine overhaul, the old bearings should be retained for close examination, as they may reveal valuable information about the condition of the engine **(see illustration)**.

2   Bearing failure occurs because of lack of lubrication, the presence of dirt or other foreign particles, overloading the engine and corrosion. Regardless of the cause of bearing failure, it must be corrected before the engine is reassembled to prevent it from happening again.

3   When examining the bearings, remove them from the engine block, the main bearing caps, the connecting rods and the rod caps and lay them out on a clean surface in the same general position as their location in the engine. This will enable you to match any bearing problems with the corresponding crankshaft journal.

4   Dirt and other foreign particles get into the engine in a variety of ways. It may be left in the engine during assembly, or it may pass through filters or the PCV system. It may get into the oil, and from there into the bearings. Metal chips from machining operations and normal engine wear are often present. Abrasives are sometimes left in engine components after reconditioning, especially when parts aren't thoroughly cleaned using the proper cleaning methods. Whatever the source, these foreign objects often end up embedded in the soft bearing material and are easily recognised. Large particles won't embed in the bearing and will score or gouge the bearing and journal. The best prevention for this cause of bearing failure is to clean all parts thoroughly and keep everything spotlessly clean during engine assembly. Frequent and regular engine oil and filter changes are also recommended.

5   Lack of lubrication (or lubrication breakdown) has a number of interrelated causes. Excessive heat (which thins the oil), overloading (which squeezes the oil from the bearing face) and oil leakage or throw off (from excessive bearing clearances, worn oil pump or high engine speeds) all contribute to lubrication breakdown. Blocked oil passages, which usually are the result of misaligned oil holes in a bearing shell, will also oil starve a bearing and destroy it. When lack of lubrication is the cause of bearing failure, the bearing material is wiped or extruded from the steel backing of the bearing. Temperatures may increase to the point where the steel backing turns blue from overheating.

6   Driving habits can have a definite effect on bearing life. Full throttle, low speed operation (lugging the engine) puts very high loads on bearings, which tends to squeeze out the oil film. These loads cause the bearings to flex, which produces fine cracks in the bearing face (fatigue failure). Eventually the bearing material will loosen in pieces and tear away from the steel backing. Short trip driving leads to corrosion of bearings because insufficient engine heat is produced to drive off the condensed water and corrosive gases. These products collect in the engine

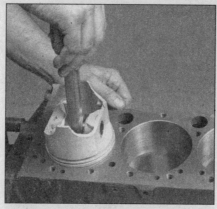

21.3 When checking piston ring end gap, the ring must be square in the cylinder bore (this is done by pushing the ring down with the top of a piston as shown)

oil, forming acid and sludge. As the oil is carried to the engine bearings, the acid attacks and corrodes the bearing material.

7   Incorrect bearing refitting during engine assembly will lead to bearing failure as well. Tight fitting bearings leave insufficient oil clearance and will result in oil starvation. Dirt or foreign particles trapped behind a bearing insert result in high spots on the bearing which lead to failure.

20   Engine overhaul - reassembly sequence

1   Before beginning engine reassembly, make sure you have all the necessary new parts, gaskets and seals as well as the following items on hand:

Common hand tools
Torque wrench (1/2-inch drive)
Piston ring refitting tool
Piston ring compressor
Vibration damper refitting tool
Short lengths of rubber or plastic hose to fit over connecting rod bolts
Plastigage
Feeler gauges
Fine-tooth file
New engine oil
Engine assembly lube or moly-base grease
Gasket sealant
Thread locking compound

2   In order to save time and avoid problems, engine reassembly must be done in the following general order:

Four-cylinder petrol engine
Crankshaft and main bearings
Rear main oil seal housing
Piston/connecting rod assemblies
Oil pump
Sump
Timing chain housing
Timing chain and sprockets
Silent shaft chain and sprockets
Intake and exhaust manifolds
Cylinder head, camshaft and rocker arms

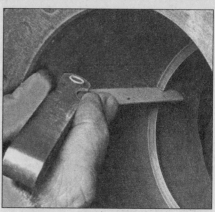

21.4 With the ring square in the cylinder, measure the end gap with a feeler gauge

Valve cover
Flywheel/driveplate

V6 engines
Crankshaft and main bearings
Rear main oil seal housing
Piston/connecting rod assemblies
Oil pump
Sump
Timing belt cover
Timing belt and sprockets
Cylinder heads, camshafts and rocker arms
Intake and exhaust manifolds
Valve covers
Flywheel/driveplate

Four-cylinder diesel engines
Piston cooling jets
Crankshaft and main bearings
Rear main oil seal housing
Piston/connecting rod assemblies
Oil filter bracket assembly
Oil pump and front cover assembly
Sump
Silent shaft belt and sprockets
Timing belt and sprockets
Cylinder head and camshaft
Timing belt covers
Valve cover

21   Piston rings - refitting

Refer to illustrations 21.3, 21.4, 21.5, 21.9a, 21.9b, 21.11 and 21.12

1   Before refitting the new piston rings, the ring end gaps must be checked. It's assumed the piston ring side clearance has been checked and verified correct (see Section 17).

2   Lay out the piston/connecting rod assemblies and the new ring sets so the ring sets will be matched with the same piston and cylinder during the end gap measurement and engine assembly.

3   Insert the top (number one) ring into the first cylinder and square it up with the cylinder walls by pushing it in with the top of the piston **(see illustration)**. The ring should be near the bottom of the cylinder, at the lower limit of ring travel.

21.5 If the end gap is too small, clamp a file in a vice and file the ring ends (from the outside in only) to enlarge the gap slightly

21.9a Installing the spacer/expander in the oil control ring groove

21.9b DO NOT use a piston ring refitting tool when fitting the oil ring side rails

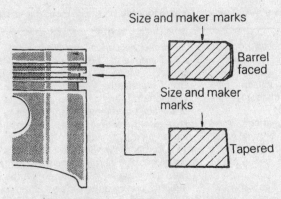

21.11 The number 1 (top) and number 2 compression rings have different cross-sections - be sure to refit them in the correct locations with the marks facing UP

21.12 Fitting the compression rings with a ring expander - the mark (arrow) must face up

2E

4   To measure the end gap, slip feeler gauges between the ends of the ring until a gauge equal to the gap width is found **(see illustration)**. The feeler gauge should slide between the ring ends with a slight amount of drag. Compare the measurement to this Chapter's Specifications. If the gap is larger or smaller than specified, double-check to make sure you have the correct rings before proceeding.5

If the gap is too small, it must be enlarged or the ring ends may come in contact with each other during engine operation, which can cause serious engine damage. The end gap can be increased by filing the ring ends very carefully with a fine file. Mount the file in a vice equipped with soft jaws, slip the ring over the file with the ends contacting the file teeth and slowly move the ring to remove material from the ends. When performing this operation, file only from the outside in **(see illustration)**.

6   Excess end gap isn't critical unless it's greater than 1.0 mm. Again, double-check to make sure you have the correct rings for the engine.

7   Repeat the procedure for each ring that will be fitted in the first cylinder and for each ring in the remaining cylinders. Remember to keep rings, pistons and cylinders matched up.

8   Once the ring end gaps have been checked/corrected, the rings can be refitted on the pistons.

9   The oil control ring (lowest one on the piston) is usually fitted first. It's composed of three separate components. Slip the spacer/expander into the groove **(see illustration)**. If an anti-rotation tang is used, make sure it's inserted into the drilled hole in the ring groove. Next, fit the lower side rail. Don't use a piston ring refitting tool on the oil ring side rails, as they may be damaged. Instead, place one end of the side rail into the groove between the spacer/expander and the ring land, hold it firmly in place and slide a finger around the piston while pushing the rail into the groove **(see illustration)**. Next, fit the upper side rail in the same manner.

10   After the three oil ring components have been fitted, check to make sure both the upper and lower side rails can be turned smoothly in the ring groove.

11   The number two (middle) ring is fitted next. It's usually stamped with a mark, which must face up, toward the top of the piston

(see illustration). **Note:** *Always follow the instructions printed on the ring package or box - different manufacturers may require different approaches. Don't mix up the top and middle rings, as they have different cross sections.*

12   Use a piston ring refitting tool and make sure the identification mark is facing the top of the piston, then slip the ring into the middle groove on the piston **(see illustration)**. Don't expand the ring any more than necessary to slide it over the piston.

13   Fit the number one (top) ring in the same manner. Make sure the mark is facing up. Be careful not to confuse the number one and number two rings.

14   Repeat the procedure for the remaining pistons and rings.

22   Crankshaft - refitting and main bearing oil clearance check

Refer to illustrations 22.3, 22.11, 22.13 and 22.15

1   Crankshaft refitting is the first step in engine reassembly. It's assumed at this point

that the engine block and crankshaft have been cleaned, inspected and repaired or reconditioned.

2   Position the engine with the bottom facing up.

3   Remove the main bearing cap bolts and lift out the caps. Lay them out in the proper order to ensure correct refitting **(see illustration)**.

4   If they're still in place, remove the original bearing inserts from the block and the main bearing caps. Wipe the bearing surfaces of the block and caps with a clean, lint-free cloth. They must be kept spotlessly clean.

Main bearing oil clearance check

Note: *Don't touch the faces of the new bearing inserts with your fingers. Oil and acids from your skin can etch the bearings.*

5   Clean the back sides of the new main bearing inserts and lay one in each main bearing saddle in the block. If one of the bearing inserts from each set has a large groove in it, make sure the grooved insert is fitted in the block. Lay the other bearing from each set in the corresponding main bearing cap. Make sure the tab on the bearing insert fits into the recess in the block or cap. **Caution:** *The oil holes in the block must line up with the oil holes in the bearing inserts. Do not hammer the bearing into place and don't nick or gouge the bearing faces. No lubrication should be used at this time.*

6   The flanged thrust bearing must be refitted in the number two position on four cylinder petrol engines. On all other engines, it is refitted in the centre position.

7   Clean the faces of the bearings in the block and the crankshaft main bearing journals with a clean, lint-free cloth.

8   Check or clean the oil holes in the crankshaft, as any dirt here can go only one way - straight through the new bearings.

9   Once you're certain the crankshaft is clean, carefully lay it in position in the main bearings.

10   Before the crankshaft can be permanently fitted, the main bearing oil clearance must be checked.

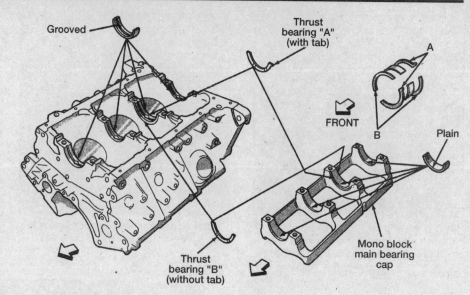

22.3 The V6 engine uses a thrust bearing (shim) located on the number 3 journal

11   Cut several pieces of the appropriate size Plastigage (they should be slightly shorter than the width of the main bearings) and place one piece on each crankshaft main bearing journal, parallel with the journal axis **(see illustration)**.

12   Clean the faces of the bearings in caps and fit the caps in their original locations (don't mix them up) with the arrows pointing toward the front of the engine. Don't disturb the Plastigage.

13   Starting with the centre main and working out toward the ends, tighten the main bearing cap bolts, in three steps, to the torque figure listed in this Chapter's Specifications. Don't rotate the crankshaft at any time during this operation. **Note:** *On V6 engines, torque bolts on the mono-block in the proper sequence* **(see illustration)**.

14   Remove the bolts and carefully lift off the main bearing caps. Keep them in order. Don't disturb the Plastigage or rotate the crankshaft. If any of the main bearing caps are difficult to remove, tap them gently from side-to-side with a soft-face hammer to loosen them.

15   Compare the width of the crushed Plastigage on each journal to the scale printed on the Plastigage envelope to obtain the main bearing oil clearance **(see illustration)**. Check the Specifications at the beginning of this Chapter to make sure it's correct.

16   If the clearance is not as specified, the bearing inserts may be the wrong size (which means different ones will be required). Before deciding different inserts are needed, make

22.11 Lay the Plastigage strips on the main bearing journals, parallel to the crankshaft centerline

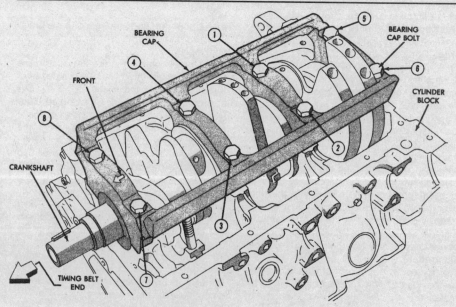

22.13 Tightening sequence for the V6 main bearing caps

sure no dirt or oil was between the bearing inserts and the caps or block when the clearance was measured. If the Plastigage was wider at one end than the other, the journal may be tapered (see Section 18).

17   Carefully scrape all traces of the Plastigage material off the main bearing journals and/or the bearing faces. Use your fingernail or the edge of a credit card - don't nick or scratch the bearing faces.

Final crankshaft refitting

18   Carefully lift the crankshaft out of the engine.

22.15 Compare the width of the crushed Plastigage to the scale on the envelope to determine the main bearing oil clearance (always take the measurement at the widest point of the Plastigage); be sure to use the correct scale - standard and metric ones are included

19   Clean the bearing faces in the block, then apply a thin, uniform layer of moly-base grease or engine assembly lube to each of the bearing surfaces. Be sure to coat the thrust faces as well as the journal face of the thrust bearing.

20   Make sure the crankshaft journals are clean, then lay the crankshaft back in place in the block.

21   Clean the faces of the bearings in the caps, then apply lubricant to them.

22   Fit the caps in their original locations with the arrows pointing toward the front of the engine.

23   Fit the bolts.

24   Tighten all except the thrust bearing cap bolts to the torque listed in this Chapter's Specifications (work from the centre out and approach the final torque in three steps).

25   Tighten the thrust bearing cap bolts to 10-to-12 ft-lbs.

26   Tap the ends of the crankshaft forward and backward with a lead or brass hammer to line up the main bearing and crankshaft thrust surfaces.

27   Retighten all main bearing cap bolts to the torque listed in this Chapter's Specifications, starting with the centre main and working out toward the ends.

28   Rotate the crankshaft a number of times by hand to check for any obvious binding.

29   The final step is to check the crankshaft endplay with feeler gauges or a dial indicator as described in Section 13. The endplay should be correct if the crankshaft thrust faces aren't worn or damaged and new bearings have been fitted.

30   Refer to Section 24 and fit the new rear main oil seal.

23 Crankshaft refitting - 2.8L diesel engine

Refer to illustrations 23.1, 23.2, 23.3, 23.4, 23.5, 23.6 and 23.9

Note: *This Chapter contains information specific to the 2.8L diesel engine. Refer to Section 22 for complete information on crankshaft refitting procedures. The selection and refitting of the various crankshaft assembly components used on the 2.8L diesel engine requires special equipment and expertise. Unless you are very experienced and well equipped, these procedures are best left to a professional.*

1   If it was removed during servicing, drive the oil slinger onto the rear of the crankshaft with a driver or a length of pipe of a suitable diameter **(see illustration)**. Likewise, refit the drive gear to the front of the crankshaft after heating it in boiling water.

2E

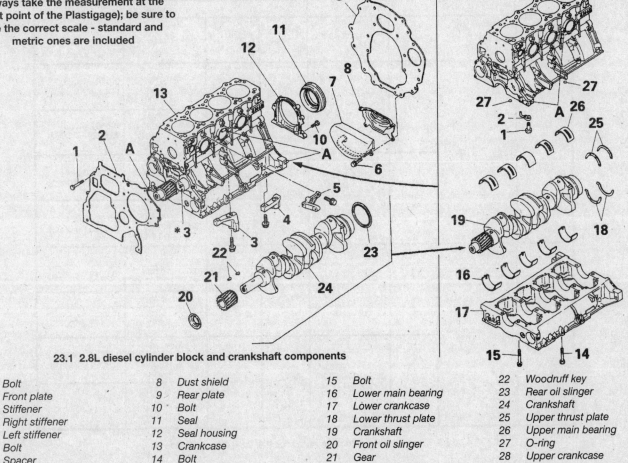

23.1 2.8L diesel cylinder block and crankshaft components

1	Bolt	8	Dust shield	15	Bolt	22	Woodruff key
2	Front plate	9	Rear plate	16	Lower main bearing	23	Rear oil slinger
3	Stiffener	10	Bolt	17	Lower crankcase	24	Crankshaft
4	Right stiffener	11	Seal	18	Lower thrust plate	25	Upper thrust plate
5	Left stiffener	12	Seal housing	19	Crankshaft	26	Upper main bearing
6	Bolt	13	Crankcase	20	Front oil slinger	27	O-ring
7	Spacer	14	Bolt	21	Gear	28	Upper crankcase

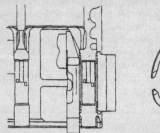

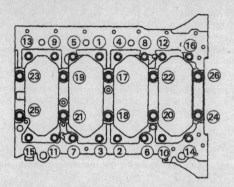

23.3 Main bearing cap and lower crankcase bolt tightening sequence. Main bearing cap bolts numbered from 17 through 26 are tightened first. After the entire sequence has been completed, tighten bolts numbered from 1 through 16

23.2 Thrust plates of the correct thickness must be used in order to obtain the proper crankshaft endplay

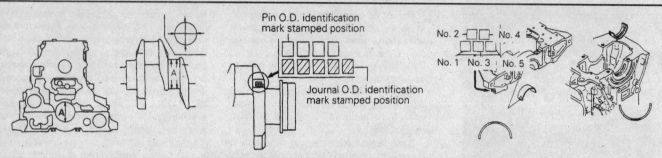

23.4 Typical measuring points and identification mark locations

4M4 ENGINE – Crankshaft and Crankcase

Unit: mm (in.)

Crankshaft		Crankcase			Main bearing			
Identification color (Identification mark)	Journal O.D.	Size mark	Bearing mounting hole I.D.	Identification color (L/U)	Journal No.		Plate Thickness	Oil Clearance
None (1)	68 (2.68) −0.022 (−0.0009) −0.030 (−0.0012)	A	72 (2.83) +0.019 (0.0007) +0.010 (0.0004)	Black/ Black	No. 1,2,4,5	2 (0.08)	−0.004 (−0.0002) −0.008 (−0.0003)	0.040 − 0.065 (0.0016 − 0.0026)
					No.3	2 (0.08)	−0.014 (−0.0006) −0.018 (0.0007)	0.060 − 0.085 (0.0024 − 0.0033)
		B	72 (2.83) +0.010 (+0.0004) +0 (+0)	Blue/Blue	No. 1,2,4,5	2 (0.08)	−0.008 (−0.0003) −0.012 (−0.0005)	0.038 − 0.064 (0.0015 − 0.0025)
					No.3	2 (0.08)	−0.018 (−0.007) −0.022 (−0.0009)	0.058 − 0.084 (0.0023 − 0.0033)
Blue (2)	68 (2.68) −0.030 (−0.0012) −0.039 (−0.0015)	A	72 (2.83) +0.019 (0.0007) +0.010 (0.0004)	Yellow/ Yellow	No. 1,2,4,5	2 (0.08)	−0 (−0) −0.004 (−0.0002)	0.040 − 0.066 (0.0016 − 0.0026)
					No. 3	2 (0.08)	−0.010 (−0.0004) −0.014 (−0.0006)	0.060 − 0.086 (0.0024 − 0.0034)
		B	72 (2.83) +0.010 (+0.0004) +0 (+0)	Black/ Black	No. 1,2,4,5	2 (0.08)	−0.004 (−0.0002) −0.008 (−0.0003)	0.038 − 0.065 (0.0015 − 0.0026)
					No. 3	2 (0.08)	−0.014 (−0.006) −0.018 (−0.007)	0.058 − 0.085 (0.0023 − 0.0033)

23.5 Main bearing selection chart for the 2.8L diesel engine

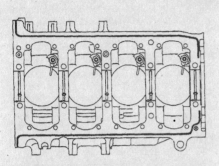

23.6 Apply a bead of RTV silicone sealer to the bottom of the engine block in this manner immediately prior to the final refitting of the lower crankcase. Make certain to clean all sealing surfaces with acetone or lacquer thinner before using the RTV

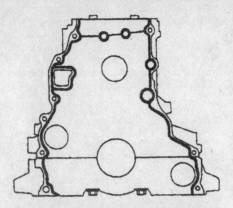

23.9 Apply a bead of RTV silicone sealer to the front of the engine block in this manner immediately prior to the refitting of the front cover. Make certain to clean all sealing surfaces with acetone or lacquer thinner before using the RTV

24.1 To remove the old seal, support the housing on a pair of wood blocks and drive out the seal with a punch or screwdriver and hammer - make sure you don't damage the seal bore

2   Refit the thrust plates to the number 5 (rear) journal **(see illustration)**. Make certain that the oil grooves face toward the rear of the engine. If the crankshaft endplay is excessive using the original thrust plates, refit thicker ones. If it is necessary to use oversize thrust plates, use the same thickness plates on the top and bottom. You need not use the same size plates on each side of the crankshaft.

3   Refit the lower crankcase to the cylinder block and tighten all of the fasteners to the recommended torque's in the proper sequence **(see illustration)**. Refer to the Specifications in this Chapter for the correct torque's. Do not refit the crankshaft at this time. Using a dial bore gauge, precisely measure the inside diameter of the main bearing bores in the crankcase in the vertical direction.

4   Using a micrometer, precisely measure the outside diameter of the crankshaft main bearing journals. Note any identifying paint marks or stampings on any components **(see illustration)**.

5   Refer to the chart to select the correct main bearing thickness for each position **(see illustration)**. **Note:** *The bearings must be refitted as shown. The number 3 bearings are a different thickness than the others. The upper main bearing on journal number 3 has a different shape than the others. Use the Plastigage method outlined in Section 22 to check the clearances.*

6   Refit the correct thrust plates, main bearings and crankshaft. Thoroughly read Section 22 for more details. Apply a bead of RTV seal around the lower crankcase **(see illustration)**.

7   Tighten the main bearing caps to the torque listed in the specifications in this Chapter. Follow the proper sequence for each tightening operation.

8   When all of the main bearing caps have been tightened, then proceed to tighten the outer crankcase bolts in the same manner

(see illustration 23.3). Verify that the endplay is correct and that the crankshaft rotates smoothly by hand.

9   Apply a bead of RTV sealer around the front of the block **(see illustration)** and then refit the front cover.

24 Rear main oil seal - refitting

Refer to illustrations 24.1, 24.2 and 24.3
Note: *The crankshaft must be refitted and the main bearing caps bolted in place before the new seal and housing assembly can be bolted to the block.*

1   Remove the old seal from the housing with a hammer and punch by driving it out from the back side **(see illustration)**. Be sure to note how far it's recessed into the housing bore before removing it; the new seal will have to be recessed an equal amount. Be very careful not to scratch or otherwise damage the bore in the housing or oil leaks could develop.

2   Make sure the housing is clean, then apply a thin coat of engine oil to the outer edge of the new seal. The seal must be pressed squarely into the housing bore, so hammering it into place isn't recommended. If you don't have access to a press, sandwich the housing and seal between two smooth pieces of wood and press the seal into place with the jaws of a large vice. If you don't have a vice big enough, lay the housing on a workbench and drive the seal into place with a block of wood and hammer **(see illustration)**. The pieces of wood must be thick enough to distribute the force evenly around the entire circumference of the seal. Work slowly and make sure the seal enters the bore squarely.

3   Lubricate the seal lips with moly-based grease or engine assembly lube before you slip the seal/housing over the crankshaft and bolt it to the block. Apply anaerobic sealer on

24.2 To fit he new rear seal in the housing, simply lay the housing on a clean, flat workbench, lay a block of wood on the seal and carefully tap it into place with a hammer

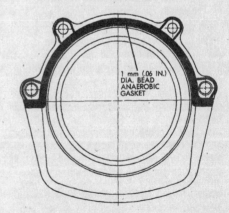

24.3 Apply anaerobic sealer onto the upper portion of the retainer

the upper portion of the retainer **(see illustration)** before refitting the housing.

4   Tighten the housing bolts a little at a time until they're all snug.

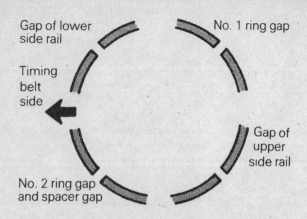

25.5 Position the ring gaps as shown here before refitting the piston/connecting rod assemblies in the engine

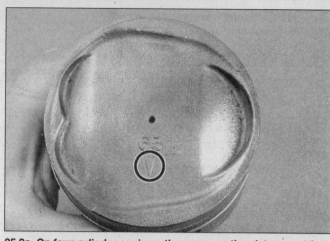

25.9a On four-cylinder engines, the arrow on the piston must face the front of the engine

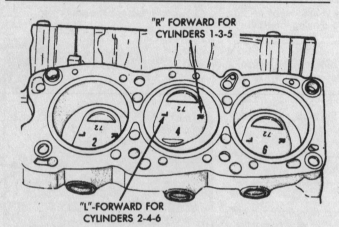

25.9b On the V6 engine, the proper letter must be positioned towards the front of the engine (R for cylinders 1, 3 and 5; L for cylinders 2, 4 and 6)

25.11 Drive the piston gently into the cylinder bore with the end of a wooden or plastic hammer handle

25 Pistons and connecting rods - refitting and rod bearing oil clearance check

Refer to illustrations 25.5, 25.9a, 25.9b, 25.11, 25.13, 25.14 and 25.17

1   Before refitting the piston/connecting rod assemblies, the cylinder walls must be perfectly clean, the top edge of each cylinder must be chamfered, and the crankshaft must be in place.

2   Remove the cap from the end of the number one connecting rod (check the marks made during removal). Remove the original bearing inserts and wipe the bearing surfaces of the connecting rod and cap with a clean, lint-free cloth. They must be kept spotlessly clean.

Connecting rod bearing oil clearance check

Note: *Don't touch the faces of the new bearing inserts with your fingers. Oil and acids from your skin can etch the bearings.*

3   Clean the back side of the new upper bearing insert, then lay it in place in the con-

necting rod. Make sure the tab on the bearing fits into the recess in the rod. Don't hammer the bearing insert into place and be very careful not to nick or gouge the bearing face. Don't lubricate the bearing at this time.

4   Clean the back side of the other bearing insert and fit it in the rod cap. Again, make sure the tab on the bearing fits into the recess in the cap and don't apply any lubricant. It's critically important that the mating surfaces of the bearing and connecting rod are perfectly clean and oil free when they're assembled.

5   Position the piston ring gaps at 120-degree intervals around the piston **(see illustration)**.

6   Slip a section of plastic or rubber hose over each connecting rod cap bolt.

7   Lubricate the piston and rings with clean engine oil and attach a piston ring compressor to the piston. Leave the skirt protruding about 6.35 mm to guide the piston into the cylinder. The rings must be compressed until they're flush with the piston.

8   Rotate the crankshaft until the number one connecting rod journal is at BDC (bottom dead centre) and apply a coat of engine oil to the cylinder walls.

9   With the mark or notch on top of the piston facing the front of the engine **(see illustrations)**, gently insert the piston/connecting rod assembly into the number one cylinder bore and rest the bottom edge of the ring compressor on the engine block.

10   Tap the top edge of the ring compressor to make sure it's contacting the block around its entire circumference.

11   Gently tap on the top of the piston with the end of a wooden or plastic hammer handle **(see illustration)** while guiding the end of the connecting rod into place on the crankshaft journal. The piston rings may try to pop out of the ring compressor just before entering the cylinder bore, so keep some downward pressure on the ring compressor. Work slowly, and if any resistance is felt as the piston enters the cylinder, stop immediately. Find out what's hanging up and fix it before proceeding. Do not, for any reason, force the piston into the cylinder - you might break a ring and/or the piston.

12   Once the piston/connecting rod assembly is fitted, the connecting rod bearing oil clearance must be checked before the rod cap is permanently bolted in place.

13   Cut a piece of the appropriate size Plas-

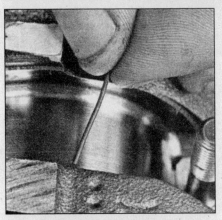

25.13 Lay the Plastigage strips on each rod bearing journal, parallel to the crankshaft centerline

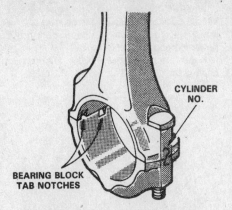

25.14 Match up the cylinder number marks and the bearing tab notches when refitting the connecting rod caps

25.17 Measuring the width of the crushed Plastigage to determine the rod bearing oil clearance (be sure to use the correct scale - standard and metric ones included)

tigage slightly shorter than the width of the connecting rod bearing and lay it in place on the number one connecting rod journal, parallel with the journal axis **(see illustration)**.

14 Clean the connecting rod cap bearing face, remove the protective hoses from the connecting rod bolts and fit the rod cap. Make sure the mating mark on the cap is on the same side as the mark on the connecting rod **(see illustration)**.

15 Fit the nuts and tighten them to the torque listed in this Chapter's Specifications. Work up to it in three steps. **Note:** Use a thin-wall socket to avoid erroneous torque readings that can result if the socket is wedged between the rod cap and nut. If the socket tends to wedge itself between the nut and the cap, lift up on it slightly until it no longer contacts the cap. Do not rotate the crankshaft at any time during this operation.

16 Remove the nuts and detach the rod cap, being very careful not to disturb the Plastigage.

17 Compare the width of the crushed Plastigage to the scale printed on the Plastigage envelope to obtain the oil clearance **(see illustration)**. Compare it to this Chapter's Specifications to make sure the clearance is correct.

18 If the clearance is not as specified, the bearing inserts may be the wrong size (which means different ones will be required). Before deciding different inserts are needed, make sure no dirt or oil was between the bearing inserts and the connecting rod or cap when the clearance was measured. Also, recheck the journal diameter. If the Plastigage was wider at one end than the other, the journal may be tapered (see Section 18).

Final connecting rod refitting

19 Carefully scrape all traces of the Plastigage material off the rod journal and/or bearing face. Be very careful not to scratch the bearing - use your fingernail or the edge of a credit card.

20 Make sure the bearing faces are perfectly clean, then apply a uniform layer of

clean moly-base grease or engine assembly lube to both of them. You'll have to push the piston into the cylinder to expose the face of the bearing insert in the connecting rod - be sure to slip the protective hoses over the rod bolts first.

21 Slide the connecting rod back into place on the journal, remove the protective hoses from the rod cap bolts, fit the rod cap and tighten the nuts to the torque specified in this Chapter. Again, work up to the torque in three steps. **Note:** Again, make sure the mating mark on the cap is on the same side as the mark on the connecting rod **(see illustration 25.14)**.

22 Repeat the entire procedure for the remaining pistons/connecting rods.

23 The important points to remember are . . .

a) Keep the back sides of the bearing inserts and the insides of the connecting rods and caps perfectly clean when assembling them.

b) Make sure you have the correct piston/rod assembly for each cylinder.

c) The arrow or mark on the piston must face the front (timing chain end) of the engine.

d) Lubricate the cylinder walls with clean oil.

e) Lubricate the bearing faces when refitting the rod caps after the oil clearance has been checked.

24 After all the piston/connecting rod assemblies have been properly refitted, rotate the crankshaft a number of times by hand to check for any obvious binding.

25 As a final step, the connecting rod endplay must be checked. Refer to Section 12 for this procedure.

26 Compare the measured endplay to this Chapter's Specifications to make sure it's correct. If it was correct before disassembly and the original crankshaft and rods were refitted, it should still be right. If new rods or a new crankshaft were fitted, the endplay may be inadequate. If so, the rods will have to be removed and taken to an automotive machine shop for resizing.

2.8L diesel engine piston protrusion measurement

27 It is very important to calculate the distance which the pistons protrude above the block deck. This is used to choose the correct head gasket thickness for safe and efficient engine operation.

28 Refer to Chapter 2D for more information on this procedure.

26 Initial start-up and break-in after overhaul

Warning: Have a fire extinguisher handy when starting the engine for the first time.

1 Once the engine has been refitted in the vehicle, double-check the engine oil and coolant levels.

2 With the spark plugs or glow plugs out of the engine and the ignition system disabled (see Section 3), crank the engine until oil pressure registers on the gauge or the light goes out.

3 Refit the spark plugs glow plugs, hook up the plug wires and restore the ignition system functions (see Section 3).

4 Start the engine. It may take a few moments for the fuel system to build up pressure, but the engine should start without a great deal of effort. **Note:** If backfiring occurs through the carburettor or throttle body, recheck the valve timing and ignition timing. On diesel engines, the injection timing and pre-heat systems should be checked and then the timing sprocket positions checked.

5 After the engine starts, it should be allowed to warm up to normal operating temperature. While the engine is warming up, make a thorough check for fuel, oil and coolant leaks.

6 Shut the engine off and recheck the engine oil and coolant levels.

7 Drive the vehicle to an area with minimum traffic, accelerate from 50 to 80 kph, then allow the vehicle to slow to 50 kph with

2E

the throttle closed. Repeat the procedure 10 or 12 times. This will load the piston rings and cause them to seat properly against the cylinder walls. Check again for oil and coolant leaks.

8   Drive the vehicle gently for the first 1000 kilometres (no sustained high speeds) and keep a constant check on the oil level. It isn't unusual for an engine to use oil during the break-in period.

9   At approximately 1000 kilometres, change the oil and filter.

10   For the next few hundred kilometres, drive the vehicle normally. Don't pamper it or abuse it.

11   After 3000 kilometres, change the oil and filter again and consider the engine broken in.

Chapter 3
Cooling, heating and air conditioning systems

Contents

Specifications

General

Coolant type and capacity	See Chapter 1
Thermostat opening temperature	88-degrees C
Radiator cap pressure rating	65 kPa
Refrigerant capacity	Approx. 992 grams

Torque specifications

	Nm
Cooling fan bolts	
Four-cylinder	10 to 12
V6	20 to 27
Coolant temperature switch	10 to 12
Coolant temperature sensor	
Petrol	20 to 40
Diesel	30 to 39
Fan clutch bolts	
Petrol engines	10 to 12
Diesel engines	24
Oil cooler	
2.5L diesel engine	
Line banjo bolts	30 to 34
Tube-to-hose fittings	40 to 49
2.8L diesel engine	
Bypass valve plug	45
Cooler-to-housing nuts	20
Relief valve plug	45
Water drain plug	30
Thermo switch	6 to 9
Water pump bolts	
Four-cylinder petrol	9 to 11
V6	24
Diesel	12 to 15
Water pump pulley plate bolts, 2.8L diesel	24

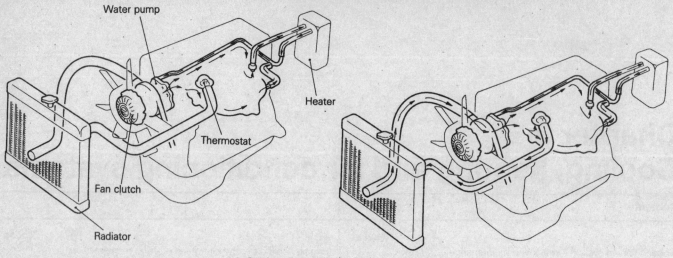

1.2 Coolant flow with the engine cold and hot

1   General information

Refer to illustration 1.2

Engine cooling system

All vehicles covered by this manual employ a pressurised engine cooling system with thermostatically controlled coolant circulation. An impeller-type water pump mounted on the front of the block pumps coolant through the engine. The coolant flows around each cylinder and toward the rear of the engine. Cast-in coolant passages direct coolant around the intake and exhaust ports, near the spark plug areas and in close proximity to the exhaust valve guides.

A wax pellet-type thermostat is located in a housing near the front of the engine. During warm-up, the closed thermostat prevents coolant from circulating through the radiator. As the engine nears normal operating temperature, the thermostat opens and allows hot coolant to travel through the radiator, where it's cooled before returning to the engine **(see illustration)**.

The cooling system is sealed by a pressure type radiator cap, which raises the boiling point of the coolant and increases the cooling efficiency of the radiator. If the system pressure exceeds the cap pressure relief value, the excess pressure in the system forces the spring-loaded valve inside the cap off its seat and allows the coolant to escape through the overflow tube into a coolant reservoir. When the system cools the excess coolant is automatically drawn from the reservoir back into the radiator.

The coolant reservoir does double duty as both the point at which fresh coolant is added to the cooling system to maintain the proper fluid level and as a holding tank for overheated coolant.

This type of cooling system is known as a closed design because coolant that escapes past the pressure cap is saved and reused.

Heating system

The heating system consists of a blower fan and heater core located in the heater box, the hoses connecting the heater core to the engine cooling system and the heater/air conditioning control head on the dashboard. Hot engine coolant is circulated through the heater core. When the heater mode is activated, a flap door opens to expose the heater box to the passenger compartment. A fan switch on the control head activates the blower motor, which forces air through the core, heating the air.

Air conditioning system

The air conditioning system consists of a condenser mounted in front of the radiator, an evaporator mounted adjacent to the heater core, a compressor mounted on the engine, a receiver/drier which contains a high-pressure relief valve and the plumbing connecting all of the above components.

A blower fan forces the warmer air of the passenger compartment through the evaporator core (sort of a radiator-in-reverse), transferring the heat from the air to the refrigerant. The liquid refrigerant boils off into low pressure vapour, taking the heat with it when it leaves the evaporator.

2   Antifreeze - general information

Warning: *Do not allow antifreeze to come in contact with your skin or painted surfaces of the vehicle. Rinse off spills immediately with plenty of water. If consumed, antifreeze can be fatal; children and pets are attracted by its sweet taste, so wipe up garage floor and drip pan coolant spills immediately. Keep antifreeze containers covered and repair leaks in your cooling system as soon as they are noticed.*

The cooling system should be filled with a water/ethylene glycol-based antifreeze solution, which will prevent freezing down to at -29-degrees C, or lower if local climate requires it. It also provides protection against corrosion and increases the coolant boiling point.

The cooling system should be drained, flushed and refilled at the specified intervals (see Chapter 1). Old or contaminated antifreeze solutions are likely to cause damage and encourage the formation of rust and scale in the system. Use distilled water with the antifreeze.

Before adding antifreeze, check all hose connections, because antifreeze tends to leak through very minute openings. Engines don't normally consume coolant, so if the level goes down, find the cause and correct it.

The exact mixture of antifreeze-to-water which you should use depends on the relative weather conditions. The mixture should contain at least 50 percent antifreeze, but should never contain more than 70 percent antifreeze. Consult the mixture ratio chart on the antifreeze container before adding coolant. Hydrometers are available at most auto parts stores to test the coolant. Use antifreeze which meets the vehicle manufacturer's specifications.

3   Thermostat - check and renewal

Warning: *Do not remove the radiator cap, drain the coolant or renew the thermostat until the engine has cooled completely.*

Check

1   Before assuming the thermostat is to blame for a cooling system problem, check the coolant level, water pump (see Section 7), drivebelt tension (see Chapter 1) and temperature gauge (or light) operation.

2   If the engine seems to be taking a long time to warm up (based on heater output or temperature gauge operation), the thermostat is probably stuck open. Renew the thermostat.

3.10a Removing the thermostat housing

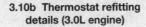

3.10b Thermostat refitting details (3.0L engine)

1 *Upper radiator*
2 *Thermostat housing*
3 *Gasket*
4 *Thermostat*

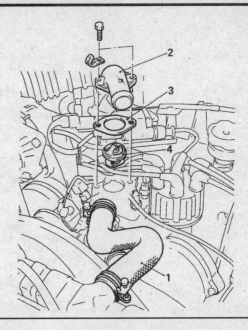

3   If the engine runs hot, use your hand to check the temperature of the upper radiator hose. If the hose isn't hot, but the engine is, the thermostat is probably stuck closed, preventing the coolant inside the engine from escaping to the radiator. Renew the thermostat. **Caution:** *Don't drive the vehicle without a thermostat. The computer may stay in open loop and emissions and fuel economy will suffer.*

4   If the upper radiator hose is hot, it means that the coolant is flowing and the thermostat is open. Consult the *Troubleshooting* Section at the front of this manual for cooling system diagnosis.

Renewal

Refer to illustrations 3.10a, 3.10b and 3.13

5   Disconnect the negative battery cable from the battery.

6   Drain the cooling system (see Chapter 1). If the coolant is relatively new or in good condition (see Chapter 1), save it and reuse it.

7   Follow the upper radiator hose to the engine to locate the thermostat housing. **Note:** *On 2.5L diesel engines, the lower radiator hose connects to the thermostat housing.*

8   Loosen the hose clamp, then detach the hose from the fitting. If it's stuck, grasp it near the end with a pair of Channelock pliers and twist it to break the seal, then pull it off. If the hose is old or deteriorated, cut it off and fit a new one.

9   If the outer surface of the large fitting that mates with the hose is deteriorated (corroded, pitted, etc.) it may be damaged further by hose removal. If it is, the thermostat housing cover will have to be renewed.

10   Remove the bolts and detach the housing cover **(see illustrations)**. If the cover is stuck, tap it with a soft-face hammer to jar it loose. Be prepared for some coolant to spill as the gasket seal is broken.

11   Note how it's fitted (which end is facing up), then remove the thermostat.

12   Stuff a rag into the engine opening, then remove all traces of old gasket material and sealant from the housing and cover with a gasket scraper. Remove the rag from the opening and clean the gasket mating surfaces with lacquer thinner or acetone.

13   Fit the new thermostat in the housing. Make sure the correct end faces up - the spring end is normally directed into the engine **(see illustration)**.

14   Apply a thin, uniform layer of RTV sealant to both sides of the new gasket and position it on the housing.

15   Fit the cover and bolts. Tighten the bolts securely.

16   Reattach the hose to the fitting and tighten the hose clamp securely.

17   Refill the cooling system (see Chapter 1).

18   Start the engine and allow it to reach normal operating temperature, then check for leaks and proper thermostat operation (as described in Steps 2 through 4).

4   Radiator - removal and refitting

Refer to illustration 4.6

Warning: *Wait until the engine is completely cool before beginning this procedure.*

1   Disconnect the negative battery cable from the battery.

2   Drain the cooling system (see Chapter 1). If the coolant is relatively new or in good condition, save it and reuse it. If necessary for clearance, remove the air duct.

3   Loosen the hose clamps, then detach the radiator hoses from the fittings. If they're stuck, grasp each hose near the end with a pair of adjustable pliers and twist it to break the seal, then pull it off - be careful not to distort the radiator fittings! If the hoses are old or deteriorated, cut them off and fit new ones.

4   Disconnect the reservoir hose from the radiator filler neck.

5   If equipped, remove the screws that attach the upper fan shroud to the radiator and slide the shroud toward the engine. Remove the lower shroud, on models so equipped.

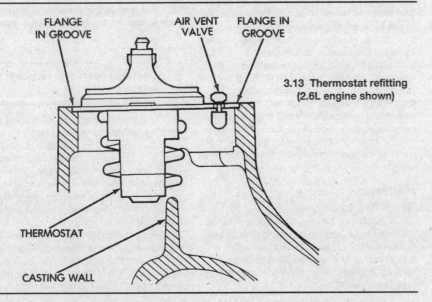

3.13 Thermostat refitting (2.6L engine shown)

FLANGE IN GROOVE
AIR VENT VALVE
FLANGE IN GROOVE
THERMOSTAT
CASTING WALL

3

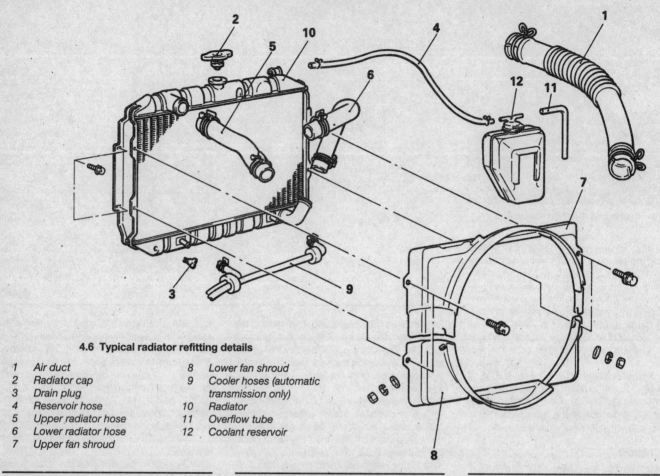

4.6 Typical radiator refitting details

1	Air duct	8	Lower fan shroud
2	Radiator cap	9	Cooler hoses (automatic
3	Drain plug		transmission only)
4	Reservoir hose	10	Radiator
5	Upper radiator hose	11	Overflow tube
6	Lower radiator hose	12	Coolant reservoir
7	Upper fan shroud		

6   If the vehicle is equipped with an automatic transmission, disconnect the cooler hoses from the radiator (see illustration). Use a drip pan to catch spilled fluid.

7   Plug the lines and fittings.

8   Remove the radiator mounting bolts.

9   Carefully lift out the radiator. Don't spill coolant on the vehicle or scratch the paint.

10   With the radiator removed, it can be inspected for leaks and damage. If it needs repair, have a radiator shop or dealer service department perform the work as special techniques are required.

11   Bugs and dirt can be removed from the radiator with compressed air and a soft brush. Don't bend the cooling fins as this is done.

12   Check the radiator mounts for deterioration and make sure there's nothing in them when the radiator is refitted.

13   Refitting is the reverse of the removal procedure.

14   After refitting, fill the cooling system with the proper mixture of antifreeze and water. Refer to Chapter 1 if necessary.

15   Start the engine and check for leaks. Allow the engine to reach normal operating temperature, indicated by the upper radiator hose becoming hot. Recheck the coolant level and add more if required.

16   If you're working on an automatic transmission equipped vehicle, check and add fluid as needed.

5   Engine cooling fan and clutch - check and renewal

Warning: *To avoid possible injury or damage, DO NOT operate the engine with a damaged fan. Do not attempt to repair fan blades - renew a damaged fan with a new one.*

Check

1   Disconnect the negative battery cable and rock the fan back and forth by hand to check for excessive bearing play.

2   With the engine cold, turn the fan blades by hand. The fan should turn freely.

3   Visually inspect for substantial fluid leakage from the clutch assembly. If problems are noted, renew the clutch assembly.

4   With the engine completely warmed up, turn off the ignition switch and disconnect the negative battery cable from the battery. Turn the fan by hand. Some drag should be evident. If the fan turns easily, renew the fan clutch.

Renewal

Refer to illustration 5.6

5   Disconnect the negative battery cable. Remove the fan shroud mounting screws and detach the shroud (see illustration 4.6).

6   Remove the bolts/nuts attaching the fan/clutch assembly to the water pump hub (see illustration).

7   Lift the fan/clutch assembly (and shroud, if necessary) out of the engine compartment.

8   Carefully inspect the fan blades for damage and defects. Renew it if necessary.

9   At this point, the fan may be unbolted from the clutch, if necessary. If the fan clutch is stored, position it with the radiator side facing down.

10   Refitting is the reverse of removal Be sure to tighten the fan and clutch mounting nuts/bolts evenly and securely.

6   Coolant reservoir - removal and refitting

1   The coolant reservoir is located on the right fenderwell. It should be removed periodically and checked for cracks and other damage, and flushed with clean water. **Note:** *On 1991 and later models, the reservoir is located to the left of the radiator.*

2   To remove the reservoir, carefully prise off the cap with the hose attached and lay the cap aside.

3   Pull out the reservoir and simultaneously pull up and slide the reservoir off its mount.

4   To refit the reservoir, line it up with the mount and push down until it is properly seated. Don't forget to refit the cap.

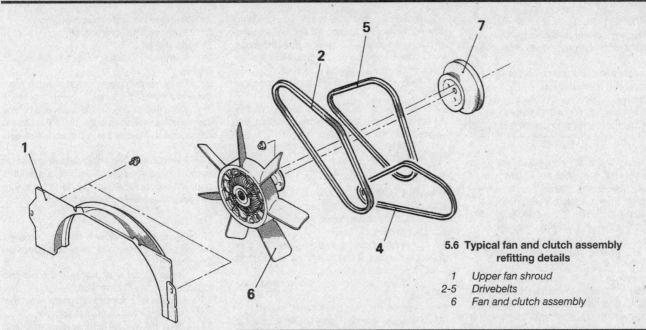

5.6 Typical fan and clutch assembly refitting details

1   Upper fan shroud
2-5 Drivebelts
6   Fan and clutch assembly

7   Water pump - check

Refer to illustration 7.5
1   A failure in the water pump can cause serious engine damage due to overheating.
2   There are three ways to check the operation of the water pump while it's installed on the engine. If the pump is defective, it should be renewed with a new or rebuilt unit.
3   With the engine running at normal operating temperature, squeeze the upper radiator hose. If the water pump is working properly, a pressure surge should be felt as the hose is released. **Warning:** *Keep your hands away from the fan blades!*
4   Water pumps are equipped with weep or vent holes. If a failure occurs in the pump seal, coolant will leak from the hole. In most cases you'll need a flashlight to find the hole on the water pump from underneath to check for leaks.
5   If the water pump shaft bearings fail,

there may be a howling sound at the front of the engine while it's running. Shaft wear can be felt if the water pump pulley is rocked up and down **(see illustration)**. Don't mistake drivebelt slippage, which causes a squealing sound, for water bearing failure.

8   Water pump - renewal

Four-cylinder engines

Removal
Refer to illustration 8.8
Warning: *Wait until the engine is completely cool before beginning this procedure.*
1   Disconnect the negative battery cable from the battery.
2   Drain the cooling system (see Chap-

ter 1). If the coolant is relatively new or in good condition, save it and reuse it.
3   Remove the cooling fan and clutch assembly (see Section 5).
4   Disconnect and remove the lower radiator hose and heater hose.
5   Remove the drivebelts (see Chapter 1).
Note: *To remove the air conditioning belt, completely remove the adjustment bracket assembly.*
6   Remove the cooling fan and water pump pulley.
7   Remove the alternator bracket from the water pump. (If required)
8   Remove the bolts and detach the water pump from the engine. Note the locations of the various lengths and different types of bolts as they're removed to ensure correct refitting **(see illustration)**.

7.5 Grasp the water pump flange and try to rock the shaft back and forth to check for play (fan and pulley shown removed for clarity)

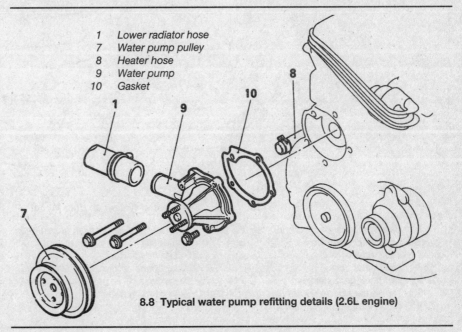

1   Lower radiator hose
7   Water pump pulley
8   Heater hose
9   Water pump
10 Gasket

8.8 Typical water pump refitting details (2.6L engine)

Refitting

9   Clean the bolt threads and the threaded holes in the engine to remove corrosion and sealant.

10   Compare the new pump to the old one to make sure they're identical.

11   Remove all traces of old gasket material from the engine with a gasket scraper.

12   Clean the engine and new water pump mating surfaces with lacquer thinner or acetone.

13   On engines that use gaskets, apply a thin coat of RTV sealant to the engine side of the gasket and to the gasket mating surface of the new pump, then carefully mate the gasket and the pump. Slip a couple of bolts through the mounting holes to hold the gasket in place. On engines that use an O-ring instead of a gasket, apply no sealers or lubricants to the O-ring. Refit it dry.

14   Carefully attach the pump and gasket to the engine and thread the bolts into the holes finger tight. Note that, on some engines the bolt on the left side of the pump (that attaches the alternator brace) is longer than the other four bolts. Be sure to refit the bolt(s) with the correct length into the corresponding water pump holes.

15   Place the alternator bracket in position, refit the bolts and tighten all the bolts to the torque listed in this Chapter's Specifications in 1/4-turn increments. Don't overtighten them or the pump may be distorted.

16   Refit all parts removed for access to the pump.

17   Refill the cooling system and check the drivebelt tension (see Chapter 1). Run the engine and check for leaks.

V6 engines

Removal

Warning: *Wait until the engine is completely cool before beginning this procedure.*

18   Disconnect the negative battery cable from the battery.

19   Drain the cooling system (see Chapter 1). If the coolant is relatively new or in good condition, save it and reuse it.

20   Remove the radiator fan shroud (see Section 4).

21   Remove the drivebelts (see Chapter 1).

22   Remove the air conditioner tensioner pulley.

23   Remove the fan and fan clutch (see Section 5).

24   Remove the water pump pulley.

25   Remove the crankshaft pulleys (see Chapter 2, Part B).

26   Remove the timing belts (see Chapter 2, Part B).

27   Remove the lower radiator hose from the water pump. If it's stuck, grasp it near the end with a pair of adjustable pliers and twist it to break the seal, then pull it off. If the hose is old or deteriorated, cut it off and fit a new one.

28   Remove the bolts and detach the water pump. Note the locations and various lengths and different types of bolts as they're removed to ensure correct refitting.

Refitting

29   Clean the bolt threads and the threaded holes in the engine to remove any corrosion and sealant.

30   Compare the new pump to the old one to make sure they're identical.

31   Remove all traces of old gasket material from the engine with a gasket scraper.

32   Clean the engine and new water pump mating surfaces with lacquer thinner or acetone.

33   Fit a new O-ring in the groove at the

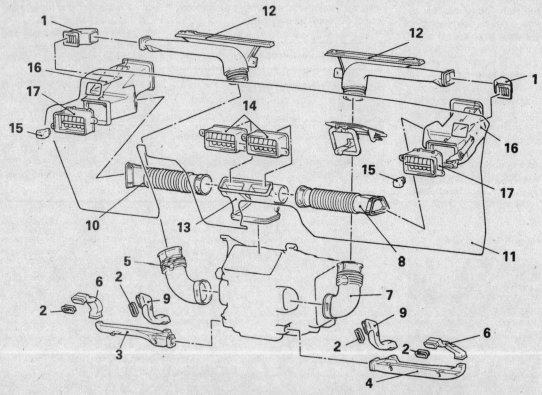

10.4 Heater system air duct layout

1	Demister grille	8	Right hand air duct (air conditioned models)
2	Lap heater garnish		
3	Lap heater duct B	9	Lap heater duct A
4	Lap heater duct C	10	Left hand air duct (air conditioned models)
5	Left hand defroster duct		
6	Lap heater duct A	11	Instrument panel
7	Right hand defroster duct		

12	Defroster duct
13	Centre ventilator duct
14	Centre air outlet
15	Knob
16	Air duct
17	Side air outlet

front end of the coolant pipe and lubricate the O-ring with coolant.

34   Apply a thin coat of RTV sealant to the engine side of the new gasket and to the gasket mating surface of the new pump, then carefully mate the gasket and the pump. Slip a couple of bolts through the pump mounting hole to hold the gasket in place.

35   Carefully attach the pump and gasket to the engine and thread the bolts into the holes finger tight. Be sure to refit the bolts with the correct length into the corresponding water pump holes.

36   Tighten all bolts to the torque listed in this Chapter's Specifications in 1/4-turn increments. Don't overtighten them or the pump may be distorted.

37   Refer to Chapter 2, part B for the refitting of the timing belt(s).

38   Refitting of all parts removed is the reverse of removal.

39   Refill the cooling system and check the drivebelt tension (see Chapter 1). Run the engine and check for leaks.

9   Coolant temperature gauge sending unit - check and renewal

Warning: *Wait until the engine is completely cool before beginning this procedure.*

1   The coolant temperature indicator system is composed of a light or temperature gauge mounted in the instrument panel and a coolant temperature sending unit mounted on the engine. Some vehicles have more than one sending unit, but only one is used for the indicator system.

2   If an overheating indication occurs, check the coolant level in the system and then make sure the wiring between the light or gauge and the sending unit is secure and all fuses are intact.

3   When the ignition switch is turned on and the starter motor is turning, the indicator light should be on (overheated engine indication).

4   If the light is not on, the bulb may be burned out, the ignition switch may be faulty or the circuit may be open. Test the circuit by connecting the sending unit wire to earth while the ignition is on (engine not running for safety). If the gauge deflects full scale or the light comes on, renew the sending unit.

5   As soon as the engine starts, the light should go out and remain out unless the engine overheats. Failure of the light to go out may be due to a shorted wire between the light and the sending unit, a defective sending unit or a faulty ignition switch. Check the coolant to make sure it's the proper type. Plain water may have too low a boiling point to activate the sending unit.

6   If the sending unit must be renewed, simply unscrew it from the engine and fit the new one. Use sealant on the threads. Make sure the engine is cool before removing the defective sending unit. There will be some coolant loss as the unit is removed, so be prepared to catch it. Check the level after the new one has been fitted.

10   Heating system - general information

Refer to illustration 10.4

The main components of the heating system include the heater unit (which contains the heater core and cable-operated valves) the blower motor, the control assembly (mounted in the dash) and the air ducts which deliver the air to the various outlet locations.

Either outside air or interior (recirculated) air (depending on the settings) is drawn into the system through the blower unit. From there the blower motor forces the air into the heater unit.

The lever settings on the control assembly operate the valves in the heater unit, which determines the mix of heated and outside air by regulating how much air passed through the heater core. The hotter the setting the more air is passed through core.

The air ducts carry the heated air from the heater unit to the desired location **(see illustration)**. Again, valves within the duct system regulate where in the vehicle the air will be delivered.

The heater core is heated by engine coolant passing through it. The heater hoses carry the coolant from the engine to the heater core and then back again.

11   Blower motor - removal and refitting

Refer to illustration 11.3

1   Remove the lap heater duct and the glove box.

2   Detach the air selection control wire and duct for access to the blower

3   Remove the three bolts attaching the motor to the heater assembly, unplug the electrical connectors, then lower the motor and fan **(see illustration)**.

4   Refitting is the reverse of removal.

12   Heater core - removal and refitting

1990 and earlier models

Refer to illustrations 12.7, 12.8a, 12.8b 12.10, 12.13a, 12.13b, and 12.13c

1   To gain access to the heater core, the heater assembly must be removed from the vehicle.

2   Disconnect the negative battery cable from the battery.

3   Drain the cooling system (see Chapter 1).

4   Remove the centre console (see Chapter 11).

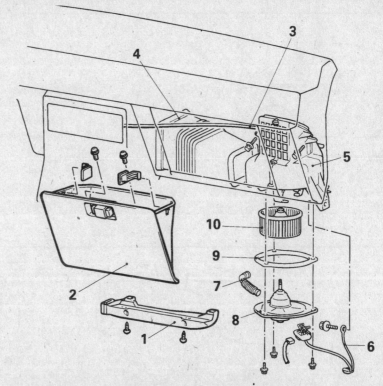

11.3 Blower motor refitting details

1	Lap heater duct		6	Resistor block
2	Glove box		7	Hose
3	Air selection wire connection		8	Blower motor
4	Duct		9	Packing
5	Blower assembly		10	Fan

5   Remove the centre panel and the instrument panel.

6   Disconnect the heater control cables at the heater assembly (not at the control assembly).

7   Working inside the engine compartment, disconnect the heater hoses from the heater unit **(see illustration)**. Place rags under the hose connections to catch spilled coolant. After disconnecting the hoses, plug them and the heater unit tubes.

8   Remove the water valve cover, then detach the clamps, link and hoses **(see illustrations)**. Plug the hoses and the inlets and outlets on the heater core.

9   Unplug the blower motor wiring connectors.

10   Remove the FOOT/DEF damper link from the positioning lever, move the lever out of the way and remove the heater core **(see illustration)**. It may be necessary to remove the lever to provide room to slide the heater core out.

11   Repair and cleaning of the heater core should be done by a radiator repair shop, or renew it.

12   Refitting is the reverse of removal.

13   Adjust the heater control cables **(see illustrations)**.

14   After the heater assembly is in place, fill the cooling system (see Chapter 1).

15   Place the heater control in the HOT position. Start the engine and allow it to run

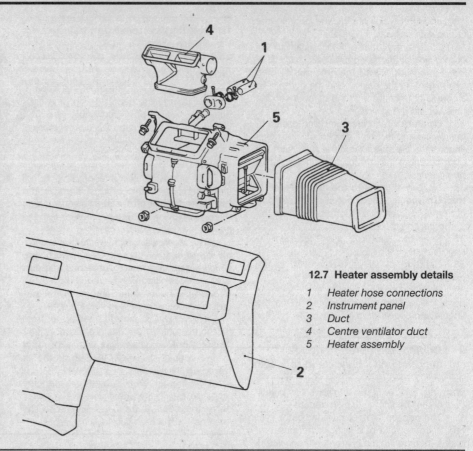

12.7 Heater assembly details

1   *Heater hose connections*
2   *Instrument panel*
3   *Duct*
4   *Centre ventilator duct*
5   *Heater assembly*

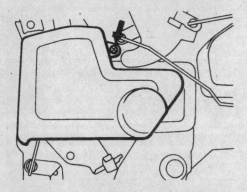

12.8a Remove the screw (arrow) and detach the water valve cover

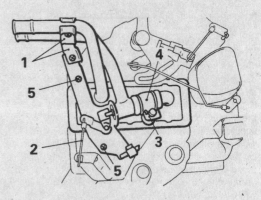

12.8b Water valve connection details

1   *Pipe clamp*
2   *Water valve link*
3   *Clamp*
4   *Hose*
5   *Set screws*

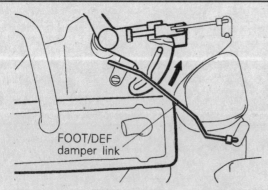

12.10 Detach the damper link and move the lever out of the way so the heater core can be removed

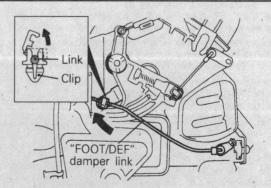

12.13a To adjust the FOOT/DEFROSTER damper, disconnect the link and move the lever in the direction of the arrow

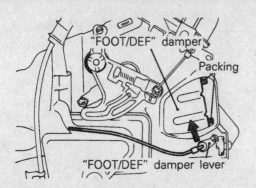

12.13b Pull the FOOT/DEFROSTER lever up, then move the fully damper up (arrow), making sure the packing is in contact with the case

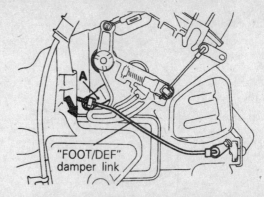

12.13c Pull the FOOT/DEFROSTER lever (A) in the direction of the arrow and connect the link

to circulate the coolant to eliminate any air from the cooling system.

16   Add coolant as the level drops. Once the level has stabilised, refit the radiator pressure cap and check for leaks.

1991 and later models

17   Remove the instrument panel (see Chapter 11).

18   Remove the main duct.

19   Remove the centre ventilator duct.

20   Remove the defroster duct.

21   Unbolt the centre reinforcements (four bolts at the bottom and four nuts at the top) and remove the heater unit

22   If the heater unit is a split-type, remove the clips that hold the two halves of the heater unit together, then separate the halves and remove the heater core.

23   If the heater unit cannot be split, remove the bolt from the joint hose clamp, cut off the joint hose and remove the heater core.

24   Refitting is the reverse of removal.

25   After the heater assembly is in place, fill

the cooling system (see Chapter 1).

26   Place the heater control in the HOT position. Start the engine and allow it to run to circulate the coolant to eliminate any air from the cooling system.

27   Add coolant as the level drops. Once the level has stabilised, refit radiator pressure cap and check for leaks.

13 Air conditioning system - general information

Refer to illustration 13.3

Warning: *The air conditioning system is under high pressure. Do not loosen any hose fitting or remove any components until after the system has been discharged by a service station or automotive air conditioning shop. Always wear eye protection when disconnecting air conditioning fittings.*

The air conditioning system used in these vehicles maintains proper temperature

by cycling the compressor on and off according to the pressure within the system, and by maintaining a mix of cooled, outside and heated air, using the same blower, heater core and outlet duct system that the heating system uses.

A fast-idle control device regulates idle speed when the air conditioner is operating.

The main components of the system include a belt-driven compressor, a condenser (mounted in front of the radiator), a receiver/drier and an evaporator **(see illustration)**.

The system operates by air (outside or recirculated) entering the evaporator core by the action of the blower motor, where it receives cooling. When the air leaves the evaporator, it enters the heater/air conditioner duct assembly and, by means of a manually controlled deflector, either passes through or bypasses the heater core in the correct proportions to provide the desired vehicle temperature.

Distribution of this air into the vehicle is regulated by a manually operated deflector, and is directed either to the floor vents, dash vents or defroster vents according to settings.

14 Air conditioning system - check and maintenance

Refer to illustrations 14.7 and 14.8

Warning: *The air conditioning system is under high pressure. Do not loosen any fittings or remove any components until after the system has been discharged. Air conditioning refrigerant should be properly discharged into an EPA-approved container at a dealer service department or an automotive air conditioning repair facility. Always wear eye protection when disconnecting air conditioning system fittings.*

Note: *1993 and earlier model air conditioning systems use R-12 refrigerant. In 1994, the refrigerant system was changed to use the new, "environmentally friendly," R-134a refrigerant. Each system uses similar components and locations, but components are NOT interchangeable. All discharging of*

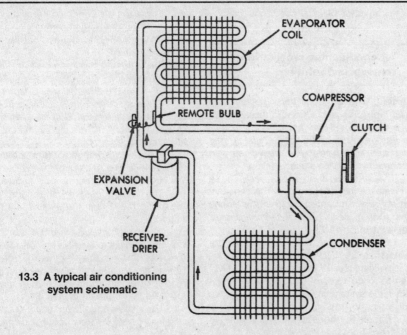

13.3 A typical air conditioning system schematic

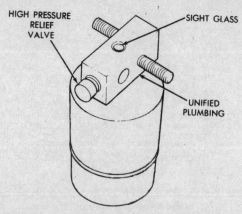

14.7 Watch the receiver/drier sight glass and see if it looks clear inside (which is normal) - if it's foamy inside, the system needs recharging

14.8 Place a thermometer in the right-side dashboard vent to monitor cooling

refrigerant, for parts renewal or maintenance, should be done by an approved air conditioning facility with the proper refrigerant recovery equipment.

1   The following maintenance checks should be performed on a regular basis to ensure that the air conditioner continues to operate at peak efficiency.

a) *Check the compressor drivebelt. If it's worn or deteriorated, renew it (see Chapter 1).*

b) *Check the drivebelt tension and, if necessary, adjust it (see Chapter 1).*

c) *Check the system hoses. Look for cracks, bubbles, hard spots and deterioration. Inspect the hoses and all fittings for oil bubbles and seepage. If there's any evidence of wear, damage or leaks, renew the hose(s).*

d) *Inspect the condenser fins for leaves, bugs and other debris. Use a "fin comb" or compressed air to clean the condenser.*

e) *Make sure the system has the correct refrigerant charge.*

2   It's a good idea to operate the system for about 10 minutes at least once a month, particularly during the winter. Long term non-use can cause hardening, and subsequent failure, of the seals.

3   Because of the complexity of the air conditioning system and the special equipment necessary to service it, in-depth troubleshooting and repairs are not included in this manual. However, simple checks and component renewal procedures are provided in this Chapter. For more complete information on the air conditioning system, refer to the *Haynes automotive heating and air conditioning* manual.

4   The most common cause of poor cooling is simply a low system refrigerant charge. If a noticeable drop in cool air output occurs, the following quick check will help you determine if the refrigerant level is low.

5   Warm the engine up to normal operating temperature.

6   Place the air conditioning temperature selector at the coldest setting and put the blower at the highest setting. Open the doors (to make sure the air conditioning system doesn't cycle off as soon as it cools the passenger compartment.

7   With the compressor engaged - the clutch will make an audible click and the centre of the clutch will rotate - inspect the sight glass, if equipped, which is located on the receiver/drier **(see illustration)**. If the refrigerant looks foamy, it's low. Have a dealer service department or licensed air conditioning repair facility charge the system.

8   If there's no sight glass, feel the inlet and outlet pipes at the compressor. One side should be cold and one hot. If there's no perceptible difference between the two pipes, there's something wrong with the compressor or the system. It might be a low charge - it might be something else **(see illustration)**. Take the vehicle to a dealer service department or an automotive air conditioning shop.

15 Air conditioning receiver/drier - removal and refitting

Warning: *The air conditioning system is under high pressure. DO NOT disassemble any part of the system (hoses, compressor, line fittings, etc.) until after the system has been depressurised by a dealer service department or service station.*

1   The receiver/drier, which acts as a reservoir for the refrigerant, is the canister-shaped object mounted either in the engine compartment or in front of the condenser **(see illustration 14.7)**.

2   Before removing the receiver/drier, the system must be discharged by an conditioning technician (see **Warning** above). DO NOT attempt to do this yourself; the refrigerant used in the system can cause serious injuries and respiratory irritation.

3   Loosen the hose clamps and remove both hoses from the receiver/drier.

4   loosen the clamp and pull up on the receiver/receiver to remove it from its mount.

5   When refitting the receiver/drier, lubricate the inside surfaces of the hoses and the outside of the fittings with refrigerant oil. Be sure the hose clamps are properly located by the clamp finders and securely tightened.

6   Have the system evacuated, recharged and leak tested by the shop that discharged it.

16 Air conditioning compressor - removal and refitting

Refer to illustration 16.5

Warning: *The air conditioning system is under high pressure. DO NOT disassemble any part of the system (hoses, compressor, line fittings, etc.) until after the system has been depressurised by a dealer service department or service station.*

1   Have the air conditioning system discharged (see **Warning** above).

2   Disconnect the negative battery cable from the battery.

3   Disconnect the compressor clutch wiring harness.

4   Remove the drivebelt (see Chapter 1).

5   Disconnect the refrigerant lines from the rear of the compressor. Plug the open fittings to prevent entry of dirt and moisture **(see illustration)**.

6   Unbolt the compressor from the mounting brackets and lift it out of the vehicle.

7   If a new compressor is being fitted, follow the directions with the compressor regarding the draining of excess oil prior to refitting.

8   The clutch may have to be transferred from the original to the new compressor.

9   Refitting is the reverse of removal. Renew all O-rings with new ones specifically made for air conditioning system use and lubricate them with refrigerant oil.

10   Have the system evacuated, recharged and leak tested by the shop that discharged it.

17 Air conditioning condenser - removal and refitting

Warning: *The air conditioning system is under high pressure. DO NOT disassemble any part of the system (hoses, compressor, line fittings, etc.) until after the system has been depressurised by a dealer service department or service station.*

1   Have the air conditioning system discharged (see **Warning** above).

2   Remove the battery (see Chapter 5).

3   Drain the cooling system (see Chapter 1).

4   Remove the radiator (see Chapter 3).

5   Disconnect the refrigerant lines from the condenser **(see illustration 16.5)**.

6   Remove the mounting bolts from the condenser brackets.

7   Lift the condenser out of the vehicle and plug the lines to keep dirt and moisture out.

8   If the original condenser will be refitted, store it with the line fittings on top to prevent oil from draining out.

9   If a new condenser is being fitted, pour a small amount of refrigerant oil into it prior to refitting.

10   Refit the components in the reverse order of removal. Be sure the rubber pads are in place under the condenser.

11   Have the system evacuated, recharged and leak tested by the shop that discharged it.

18 Air conditioning evaporator - removal and refitting

Refer to illustrations 18.1, 18.9a and 18.9b

Warning: *The air conditioning system is under high pressure. DO NOT disassemble any part of the system (hoses, compressor, line fittings, etc.) until after the system has been depressurised by a dealer service department or service station.*

1   The air conditioner evaporator is combined with the heater assembly and is mounted under the vehicle dashboard **(see illustration)**.

2   Before removing the evaporator, the system must be depressurised by an air conditioning technician. DO NOT attempt to do this yourself; the refrigerant used in the system can cause serious injuries and respiratory irritation.

3   Remove the glove box (see Chapter 11).

4   Loosen the hose clamps and remove the hoses from the evaporator fittings inside the engine compartment.

5   Disconnect the control cable from the damper lever at the right side of the evaporator.

6   Slide back the hose clamp and remove the drain hose from the spigot at the rear of the evaporator.

7   Peel off the sealing compound around the evaporator inlet and outlet tubes at the vehicle fire wall

8   Remove the bolts attaching the evapo-

16.5 Air conditioning compressor, receiver/drier and condenser refitting details

1   Receiver/drier mounting bolt
2   Receiver/driver
3   Condenser fan
4   Blower motor mounting bolt
5   Blower motor
6   Condenser mounting bolt
7   Condenser
8   Compressor clutch coil electrical connector
9   Drivebelt
10   Refrigerant line mounting bolt
11   Compressor clutch mounting bolt
12   Compressor clutch assembly

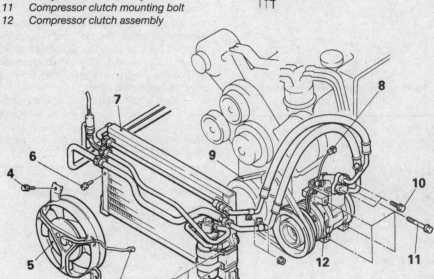

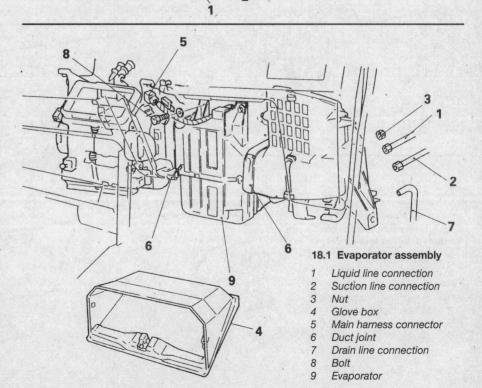

18.1 Evaporator assembly

1   Liquid line connection
2   Suction line connection
3   Nut
4   Glove box
5   Main harness connector
6   Duct joint
7   Drain line connection
8   Bolt
9   Evaporator

rator to the dashboard and firewall and carefully move it down and out from the dashboard. Do not misplace the plastic duct that fits between the heater assembly and the evaporator.

9   Use a flat-bladed screwdriver to remove the clips from the evaporator housing and remove the evaporator **(see illustrations)**.

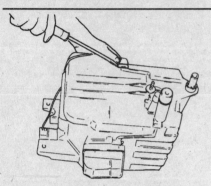

18.9a Use a screwdriver to detach the evaporator case clips

10   Refitting is the reverse of removal. Be sure to position the plastic ducts before slipping the evaporator into place. When refitting the hoses, lubricate their surfaces and the outside of the fittings with refrigerant oil. The hoses must be positioned properly with the clamp finders and tightened securely. Do not forget to fit the drain hose and the sealing compound.

11   Have the system evacuated and recharged by the shop that discharged it.

19   Heater/air conditioning control assembly - removal and refitting

Refer to illustration 19.1

1   Remove the screws and detach the lap heater duct under the dash and remove the stoppers and the glove box **(see illustration)**.

2   Pull off the heater fan control knob and the heater control lever ends. Remove the nut from the fan control knob.

3   Use a small screwdriver to prise out the plugs for access to the panel attaching screws.

4   Remove the screws from the centre bezel and lift it out of place.

18.9b Evaporator assembly details

1   *Air conditioning relay*
2   *Thermostat*
3   *Screw*
4   *Clip*
5   *Upper evaporator case*
6   *Lower evaporator case*
7. *Evaporator assembly*
8   *Expansion valve*

5   Disconnect the electrical connectors and the control cable from the heater (not from the control assembly.

7   Remove the four screws attaching the control assembly and remove it from the dashboard.

8   Minor repairs, such as cleaning and lubrication of the pivots and cables, can be performed on the heater control assembly. But it would be a good idea to renew it if it is not operating properly.

9   Refitting is the reverse of the removal. Remember to plug in the electrical connectors before refitting the instrument cluster trim panel.

20   Oil cooler - removal and refitting

Remote-mounted style

Removal

Refer to illustration 20.4

1   The remote mounted oil cooler is used on all models except those vehicles equipped with the 2.8L diesel engine. Refer to Step 9 for information about the engine-mounted oil cooler used on the 2.L engine. The remote-mounted oil cooler is secured in front of the radiator and behind the grille on all other models.

2   Remove the grille (refer to Chapter 11).

3   Place some rags beneath the oil cooler to catch spills.

4   Disconnect the two banjo bolts which attach the oil cooler lines to the oil cooler **(see illustration)**. **Caution:** *Hold the stationary fitting on the oil cooler with a spanner while you loosen the banjo bolt with another in order to avoid damaging the cooler.*

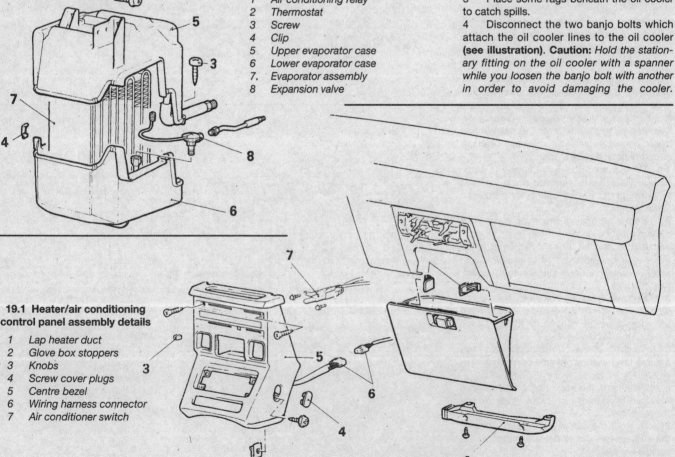

19.1 Heater/air conditioning control panel assembly details

1   *Lap heater duct*
2   *Glove box stoppers*
3   *Knobs*
4   *Screw cover plugs*
5   *Centre bezel*
6   *Wiring harness connector*
7   *Air conditioner switch*

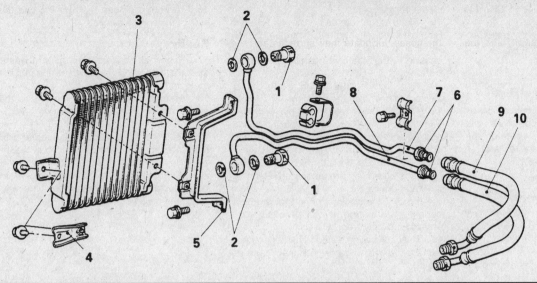

20.4 Remote-mounted oil cooler details

1　Banjo bolt
2　Gasket
3　Cooler
4　Bracket
5　Bracket
6　Tube fittings
7　Return tube
8　Supply tube
9　Return hose
10　Supply hose

3

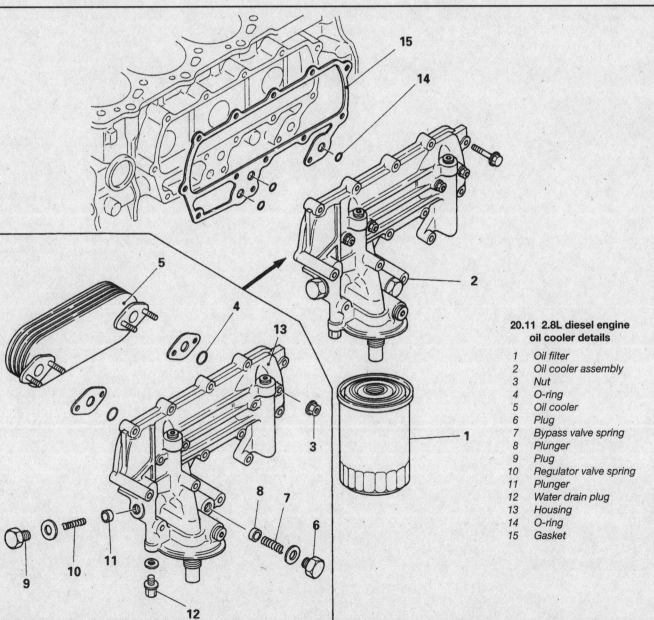

20.11 2.8L diesel engine oil cooler details

1　Oil filter
2　Oil cooler assembly
3　Nut
4　O-ring
5　Oil cooler
6　Plug
7　Bypass valve spring
8　Plunger
9　Plug
10　Regulator valve spring
11　Plunger
12　Water drain plug
13　Housing
14　O-ring
15　Gasket

Remove the sealing washers from each fitting.

5   Unbolt the oil cooler from the mounting brackets and lift it from the vehicle.

Refitting

6   Bolt the oil cooler to the mounting brackets.

7   Renew all the sealing washers on the oil lines. Attach the lines to the cooler with the banjo bolts. **Note:** *There are marks on the ends of the lines which must face upward.*

8   The remainder of the refitting is the reverse of removal.

2.8L diesel engine-mounted style

Removal

Refer to illustration 20.10

9   Remove any interfering engine compartment components.

10   Place rags beneath the oil cooler. Remove the oil filter (refer to Chapter 1).

11   Remove the bolts securing the oil cooler housing to the side of the engine **(see illustration)**.

12   Remove the nuts securing the cooler element to the oil cooler housing.

13   Remove the regulator and bypass plugs from the housing. Remove the washer, spring and plunger from the bore beneath each plug. Lay all of the components neatly in order so they can be returned to the same positions after they are inspected. Remove the water drain plug.

14   Inspect the cooler element for signs of damage and sludge. It can be cleaned, if required, using solvent.

15   Check the bypass and regulator components for wear and damage. Renew parts as required.

16   Thoroughly clean the housing and the side of the engine block.

Refitting

17   Renew all gaskets, O-rings and washers. Lubricate the O-rings with oil and refit the three on the engine block.

18   Assemble the oil cooler element to the cooler housing using new gaskets and O-rings.

19   Refit the three plugs in the cooler with their internal components using new washers.

20   Fill the oil filter with fresh engine oil before installing it. The remainder of the refitting is the reverse of removal.

Chapter 4
Fuel and exhaust systems

Contents

4

Specifications

Accelerator cable freeplay

Carburetted and diesel engines	1 mm
Fuel-injected petrol engines	1 to 2 mm

Fuel pressure

Carburetted models	20 to 30 kPa at idle
Fuel-injected petrol models	
Vacuum hose connected to pressure regulator	270 kPa at curb idle
Vacuum hose disconnected from regulator	330 to 370 kPa at curb idle
Fuel injector (petrol) resistance	13 to 16 ohms

Idle speed

Four-cylinder petrol engine	
1983 and 1984 models	850 + 50 rpm
1985 and 1986 models	
Manual transmission	750 + 50 rpm
Automatic transmission	800 + 50 rpm
1987 through 1991 models	800 + 50 rpm
Idle-up (throttle opener) engine speed	
(Air-conditioned models)	850 to 950 rpm

Float level .... 20 mm

Dashpot speed
Manual transmission	2000 rpm
Automatic transmission	1500 rpm

Fast idle throttle valve-to-bore gap opening
Manual	0.8 mm
Automatic	0.7 mm

Choke valve-to-choke bore clearance
Unloader opening	1.9 to 2.0 mm
Choke breaker gap	1.5 mm

Idle Speed Control (ISC) servo coil resistance
	28 to 33 ohms

Diesel injection pump adjustment
Setting position (degrees after TDC)	Refer to underhood decal or owner's manual
Plunger stroke reading	0.97 to 1.03 mm

Diesel fuel cut solenoid resistance
	8 to 10 ohms

Glow plug resistance (at room temperature)
2.5L engine	0.22 to 0.28 ohms
2.8L engine	
Metal type	1.0 ohms
Ceramic type	0.5 ohms

Glow plug relay resistance
2.5L engine	20 ohms
2.8L engine	3 ohms

Diesel coolant temperature sensor resistance
At 0-degrees C	8.6 Kohms
At 20-degrees C	3.25 Kohms
At 40-degrees C	1.5 Kohms
At 80-degrees C	300 ohms

Turbocharger maximum boost
2.5L engine	85 kPa
2.8L engine	95 kPa

Turbocharger wastegate operating pressure
2.5L engine	82 kPa
2.8L engine	89 kPa

Torque specifications
	Nm
Air intake plenum mounting bolts	18
Carburettor mounting bolts/nuts	15 to 22
Diesel fuel supply tube nuts	
2.5L engine	30
2.8L engine	29
Diesel fuel injectors	50 to 58
Diesel fuel injection pump-to-engine	19
Diesel fuel injection pump sprocket nut	59 to 69
Diesel fuel return nuts-to-injectors	30 to 39
Electric fuel pump flange nuts	3
Exhaust manifold bolts	18
Exhaust pipe-to-manifold nuts	35
Fuel high-pressure hose attaching bolts	5
Glow plugs	15 to 19
Glow plug nuts	1 to 1.5
Mechanical (petrol) fuel pump bolts	19
Turbocharger mounting nuts	60

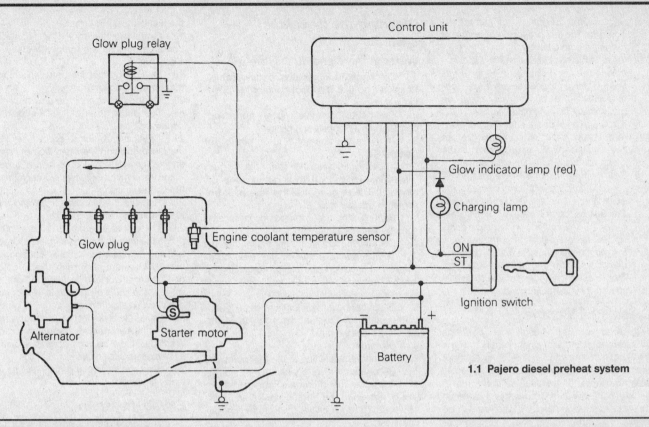

1.1 Pajero diesel preheat system

1 General information, precautions and diesel fuel system cleaning

Diesel fuel system

Refer to illustration 1.1

The fuel system is comprised of a fuel tank, a fuel injection pump, an engine compartment-mounted fuel filter, fuel supply and return lines and four fuel injectors **(see illustration)**.

The injection pump is driven at the front of the engine. Fuel is drawn from the fuel tank through the filter by the injection pump, which then distributes the fuel under very high pressure to the injectors via separate lines. Some vehicles are equipped with a turbocharger and an intercooler to improve power.

The injectors are spring loaded mechanical valves which open when the pressure of the fuel supplied to them exceeds a specific limit. Fuel is then sprayed into the combustion chamber. The high compression developed by the rising piston superheats the mixture to the point of combustion.

The basic injection timing is set by the position of the injection pump on the engine. When the engine is running, the pump is advanced and retarded by the pump itself. It is influenced primarily by the accelerator position and engine speed.

The engine is stopped by means of a fuel cut solenoid which interrupts the flow of fuel to the injection pump when it is de-energized.

The engine idle speed can be raised by using a hand throttle which is located on the dash.

Petrol fuel system

The fuel system consists of the fuel tank, a mechanical or electric fuel pump, an air cleaner, either a carburettor or a fuel injection system and the hoses and lines which connect these components.

All four-cylinder models are carburetted. These models have a mechanical fuel pump mounted on the cylinder head. The pump is driven by an eccentric on the camshaft.

All V6 models are fuel-injected. A multi-point (one injector per cylinder) Electronic Fuel Injection (EFI) system is used. All fuel-injected models use an in-tank electric fuel pump. For more information regarding the EFI system, refer to Section 15.

Precautions

Many of the operations described in this Chapter involve the disconnection of fuel lines which may cause fuel to leak. Before commencing work, refer to the Warnings and Cautions given below and the information in Safety first at the beginning of this manual.

Warning 1: *Fuel is flammable, so take extra precautions when you work on any part of the fuel system. Don't smoke or allow open flames or bare light bulbs near the work area. Don't work in a garage where a natural gas appliance such as a water heater or a clothes dryer is present. Since diesel fuel is carcinogenic, wear latex gloves when there is a possibility of being exposed to fuel. If you spill fuel on your skin, rinse it immediately with soap and water. Mop up any spills immediately and do not store fuel-soaked rags where they could ignite. When you perform any work on the fuel system, wear safety glasses and keep a Class B type fire extinguisher on hand.*

Warning 2: *Fuel injectors operate at extremely high pressures and the jet of fuel produced at the nozzle is capable of piercing the skin with potentially fatal results. Never work with pressurized injectors - any pressure testing of the fuel system must be done by a diesel fuel systems specialist.*

Caution: *Under no circumstance should fuel be allowed to come in contact with coolant hoses - wipe off accidental spillage immediately. Hoses that have been contaminated with fuel for an extended period should be renewed. Diesel fuel systems are particularly sensitive to contamination from dirt, air and water. Pay particular attention to cleanliness when working on any part of the fuel system to prevent the entry of dirt. Thoroughly clean the area around fuel fittings before disconnecting them. Store dismantled components in sealed containers to prevent contamination and the formation of condensation. Use only lint-free rags and clean fuel for cleaning. Avoid using compressed air when cleaning components in place.*

Diesel fuel contamination

Before you renew an injection pump or some other expensive component, find out what caused the failure. If water contamination is present, buying a new pump or other component won't do much good. The following procedure will help you pinpoint whether water contamination is present:

4

a) *Remove the fuel filter and inspect the contents for the presence of water or petrol (refer to Chapter 1).*

b) *If the vehicle has been stalling, performance has been poor or the engine has been knocking loudly, suspect fuel contamination. Petrol or water must be removed by flushing (see below).*

c) *If you find a lot of water in the fuel filter, remove the injection pump fuel return line and check for water there. If the pump has water in it, flush the system.*

d) *Small quantities of surface rust won't create a problem. If contamination is excessive, the vehicle will probably stall.*

e) *Sometimes, contamination in the system becomes severe enough to cause damage to the internal parts in the pump. If the damage reaches this stage, have the damaged parts renewed and the pump rebuilt by an authorized fuel injection shop or buy a rebuilt pump.*

Diesel fuel storage

Good quality diesel fuel contains inhibitors to stop the formation of rust in the fuel lines and the injectors. So long as there are no leaks in the fuel system, it is generally safe from water contamination. Diesel fuel is usually contaminated from water as a result of careless storage. There is little you can do about the storage practices of service stations where you buy diesel fuel, but if you keep a small supply of diesel fuel on hand at home, as many diesel owners do, follow these simple rules:

a) *Diesel fuel "ages" and goes stale. Don't store containers of diesel fuel for long periods of time. Use it up regularly and replace it with fresh fuel.*

b) *Keep fuel storage containers out of direct sunlight. Variations in heat and humidity promote condensation inside fuel containers.*

c) *Don't store diesel fuel in galvanized containers. It may cause the galvanizing to flake off, contaminating the fuel and clogging filters when the fuel is used.*

d) *Label containers properly as containing diesel fuel.*

Fighting fungi and bacteria in diesel fuel with biocides

If there is water in the fuel, fungi and/or bacteria can form in diesel fuel in warm or humid weather. Fungi and bacteria plug fuel lines, fuel filters and injection nozzles; they can also cause corrosion in the fuel system.

If you've had problems with water in the fuel system and you live in a warm and humid climate, have your dealer correct the problem. Then use a diesel fuel biocide to sterilize the fuel system in accordance with the manufacturer's instructions. Biocides are available from your dealer, service stations and auto parts stores. Consult your dealer for advice on using biocides in your area and for recommendations on which ones to use.

Cleaning the diesel fuel system

Water in the diesel fuel system

1 Disconnect the negative battery cable. Position it so that it cannot contact the positive cable.

2 Drain the fuel tank into an approved container and dispose of it properly.

3 Remove the fuel sending unit (refer to Chapter 4A).

4 Thoroughly clean the fuel tank. If it is rusted inside, send it to a repair shop or renew it. Clean or renew the fuel pick-up screen in the fuel tank.

5 Reinstall the fuel tank but do not connect the fuel lines to it yet.

6 Remove the fuel filter (refer to Chapter 1).

7 Temporarily disconnect the fuel return line at the injection pump and again, using low air pressure, blow out the lines toward the rear of the vehicle.

8 Reconnect the main fuel and return lines at the tank. Fill the tank to a fourth of its capacity. Refit the cap.

9 Discard the fuel filter.

10 Connect the fuel line to the fuel pump.

11 Reconnect the battery cable.

12 Purge the fuel pump and pump-to-filter line by cranking the engine until clean fuel runs out. Catch the fuel in a closed metal container.

13 Fit a new fuel filter.

14 Refit a hose from the fuel return line (from the injection pump) to a closed metal container with a capacity of at least eight litres.

15 Crank the engine until clear fuel appears at the return line. Don't crank the engine for more than 30 seconds at a time. If it is necessary to crank it again, allow a three minute interval before resuming.

17 Crank the engine until clear fuel appears at each nozzle. Don't crank the engine for more than 30 seconds at a time. If it is necessary to crank it again, allow a three minute interval before resuming.

Petrol in the diesel fuel system

Warning: *Diesel fuel is flammable, so take extra precautions when you work on any part of the fuel system. Don't smoke or allow open flames or bare light bulbs near the work area. Don't work in a garage where a natural gas appliance such as a water heater or a clothes dryer is present. Since diesel fuel is carcinogenic, wear latex gloves when there is a possibility of being exposed to fuel. If you spill fuel on your skin, rinse it immediately with soap and water. Mop up any spills immediately and do not store fuel-soaked rags where they could ignite. When you perform any work on the fuel system, wear safety glasses and keep a Class B type fire extinguisher on hand.*

If petrol has been accidentally pumped into the fuel tank, it should be drained immediately. Petrol in the fuel in small amounts, up to 30 percent, isn't usually noticeable. At higher ratios, the engine may make a knocking noise which will get louder as the ratio of petrol increases. Here is how to rid the fuel system of petrol:

18 Drain the fuel tank into an approved container and fill the tank with clean, fresh diesel fuel.

19 Detach the fuel line between the fuel filter and the injection pump.

20 Connect a short pipe and hose to the fuel filter outlet and run it to a closed metal container.

21 Crank the engine to purge petrol out of the fuel pump and fuel filter. Do not crank the engine for more than 30 seconds at a time. Allow three minutes between interval to allow the starter to cool.

22 Remove the pipe and hose and refit the fuel line previously removed.

23 Try to start the engine. If it doesn't start, purge the injection pump and lines: Crack the fuel line fittings open a little, just enough for fuel to leak out. Depress the accelerator pedal to the floor and, holding it there, crank the engine until all petrol is removed, i.e. diesel fuel leaks from the fittings. Tighten the fittings. Limit cranking to 30 seconds with three minute intervals between cranking. **Warning:** *Avoid sources of ignition and have a fire extinguisher nearby.*

24 Start the engine and run it at idle for fifteen minutes.

Exhaust system

The exhaust system consists of the exhaust manifold(s), exhaust pipes, catalytic converter and muffler. For information regarding the removal and refitting of the exhaust manifold(s), refer to Chapter 2, Part A. For information regarding exhaust system and catalytic converter servicing, refer to the last Section in this Chapter. For further information regarding the catalytic converter, refer to Chapter 6.

---

2 Fuel pressure relief procedure (fuel-injected petrol models)

Refer to illustration 2.1

1 Disconnect the electrical connector for the fuel pump harness on top of the fuel tank under a cover **(see illustration)**.

2 Start the engine, let it run until it stalls and turn off the ignition switch.

3 Detach the cable from the negative terminal of the battery and re-connect it after repairs are complete.

---

3 Fuel pump/fuel pressure (petrol models) - check

Warning: *Petrol is extremely flammable, so take extra precautions when you work on any part of the fuel system. Don't smoke or allow open flames or bare light bulbs near the work area, and don't work in a garage where a natural gas-type appliance (such as a water heater or clothes drier) with a pilot light is present. If you spill any fuel on your skin, rinse it off immediately with soap and water. When*

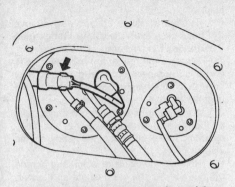

2.1 The electrical connector (arrow) for the fuel pump harness is located on the top of the fuel tank

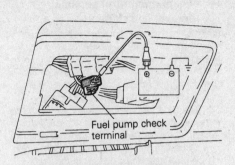

3.11a Fuel pump driving terminal (check connector) location on 1989 and 1990 models

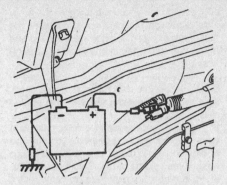

3.11b The check connector on 1991 and later models is located at the right centre of the engine firewall

you perform any kind of work on the fuel system, wear safety glasses and have a Class B type fire extinguisher on hand.

Carburetted models

1   Before deciding that the fuel pump is defective, it should be tested for correct pressure while still in the vehicle.
2   To check the fuel pump pressure, you will need a 'T' fitting, a length of hose (with the same inside diameter as the fuel hoses), a fuel pressure gauge and a tachometer.

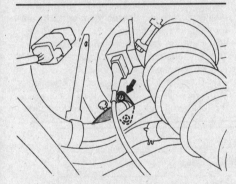

3.13 To disconnect the fuel high-pressure hose flange, remove these two bolts (arrow)

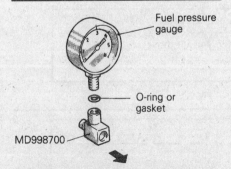

3.14 To measure the fuel pressure on a fuel-injected petrol engine, you'll need to attach a special hose (MD998753 or equivalent) to the adapter as shown - be sure to seal both hose flanges with O-rings or gaskets as shown

3   Loosen the hose clamp and pull the fuel hose off the fuel pump outlet fitting. Insert one end of the 'T' fitting into the hose that was disconnected from the pump and tighten the hose clamp. Cut a short length of hose, slip one end over the 'T' fitting and the other end onto the fuel pump outlet fitting.
4   Connect another length of hose (approximately 15 cm long) between the fuel pressure gauge and the remaining end of the 'T' fitting. Refit hose clamps on all the connections.
5   Loosen the hose clamp and disconnect the fuel return hose, which returns fuel to the fuel tank from the carburettor. Slip a short length of hose, which has been plugged, onto the fitting and refit the hose clamp.
6   Connect the tachometer according to the instructions provided by the manufacturer.
7   Start the engine and allow it to run for a few moments before taking the pressure reading. This will allow any air in the pump to be vented, which will ensure an accurate reading.
8   Make sure the engine idle speed is correct, then note the pressure reading on the gauge and compare it to this Chapter's Specifications.
9   Stop the engine and observe the gauge. The pressure should remain constant or return to zero slowly.
10   If the pressure was higher or lower than specified, or if it dropped to zero instantly

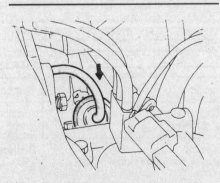

3.18 Fuel pressure regulator/vacuum hose (arrow)

when the engine was shut off, the fuel pump is defective and should be renewed.

Fuel-injected models

Fuel pump check
Refer to illustrations 3.11a and 3.11b
11   Turn the ignition switch to Off, open the fuel tank filler cap, apply battery voltage directly to the check connector for the fuel pump **(see illustrations)** and listen for the whirring sound of the electric pump through the filler port. Now squeeze the fuel high-pressure hose - you should be able to feel pressure in the hose. If you cannot hear whirring, the fuel pump or its circuit is defective. If you can hear whirring, but pressure does not develop in the fuel high-pressure hose, the fuel pump is defective.

Fuel pressure check
Refer to illustrations 3.13, 3.14, 3.18, 3.22 and 3.23
12   Relieve the system fuel pressure (see Section 2), detach the cable from the negative battery terminal and reconnect the electrical connector for the fuel pump.
13   Disconnect the fuel high-pressure hose at the delivery pipe **(see illustration)**. Cover the connection with shop rags to absorb any fuel that leaks out.
14   Attach your fuel pressure gauge (it must have a range through 350 kPa) to the special adapter (MD998700 or equivalent) and attach special hose (MD998753 or equivalent) to the adapter as shown as shown **(see illustration)**.
15   Attach the gauge with adapter to the fuel delivery pipe.
16   Reconnect the battery terminal.
17   Apply battery voltage to the fuel pump check connector **(see illustrations 3.11a and 3.11b)** and activate the fuel pump. Make sure there's no fuel leaking from the pressure gauge/adapter setup.
18   Start the engine and run it at curb idle speed, measure the fuel pressure with the vacuum hose connected to the pressure regulator **(see illustration)** and compare your reading to the pressure listed in this Chapter's Specifications.

4

19   Detach the vacuum hose from the pressure regulator, plug the hose, measure the fuel pressure again and compare this reading to the pressure listed in this Chapter's Specifications.

20   Race the engine two or three times in quick succession, then recheck the fuel pressure to verify it doesn't fall when the engine runs at idle.

21   Gently squeeze the fuel return hose with your fingers while repeatedly racing the engine to verify fuel pressure in the return hose. If the volume of fuel flow is insufficient, there won't be any fuel pressure in the return hose.

22   If the results of your readings aren't within the specified values, use the accompanying table (see illustration) to determine the probable cause and make the necessary repairs.

23   Stop the engine and verify that the reading on the fuel pressure gauge doesn't drop. If it does drop, note the rate of drop and use the accompanying table (see illustration) to determine the cause and make the necessary repairs.

24   Relieve the system fuel pressure (see Section 2).

25   Cover the fuel high-pressure hose connection with a shop towel to absorb leaking fuel, disconnect the fuel high-pressure hose, remove the fuel gauge/adapter assembly, fit a new O-ring in the groove in the end of the high-pressure hose fitting and reconnect the hose. Tighten the attaching screws for the fuel high-pressure hose fitting to the torque listed in this Chapter's Specifications.

26   Apply battery voltage to the fuel pump terminal, operate the pump and check the fuel high-pressure hose for leaks.

---

4   Fuel pump (petrol engines) - removal and refitting

Warning: *Petrol is extremely flammable, so take extra precautions when you work on any part of the fuel system. Don't smoke or allow open flames or bare light bulbs near the work area, and don't work in a garage where a natural gas-type appliance (such as a water heater or clothes dryer) with a pilot light is present. If you spill any fuel on your skin, rinse it off immediately with soap and water. When you perform any kind of work on the fuel system, wear safety glasses and have a Class B type fire extinguisher on hand.*

Carburetted engines

Refer to illustration 4.6

1   The fuel pump is mounted on the cylinder head immediately in front of the carburettor. It is held in place with two nuts.

2   Pull the coil high-tension lead out of the distributor and connect it to the engine block with a jumper wire. Remove the spark plugs and place your thumb over the number one cylinder spark plug hole.

3   Rotate the crankshaft in a clockwise direction (with a spanner on the large bolt attaching the pulley to the front of the crankshaft) until you can feel the compression pressure rising in the number one cylinder.

4   Continue rotating the crankshaft until the notch on the crankshaft pulley lines up with the 'T' on the timing mark tab on the timing chain case. At this point, the lift of the fuel pump drive cam is reduced to a minimum, which will make the pump easier to remove.

5   Refit the spark plugs and hook up the wires. Do not forget the coil high-tension

lead.

6   Loosen the hose clamps and remove the fuel hoses from the pump fittings (see illustration). Plug the ends of the hoses.

7   Remove the fuel pump mounting bolts and pull the pump off the engine. You may have to tap the pump body with a soft-faced hammer to break the gasket seal.

8   If the pump is difficult to remove, take off the valve cover (see Chapter 2) and guide the pump rocker arm out of the head from the inside.

9   Remove the insulator block and scrape off all traces of the old gaskets and sealer. Clean the mating surfaces on the head and insulator block with lacquer thinner or acetone.

10   Before fitting the new pump ensure that the rocker arm moves up and down without binding or sticking.

11   Coat both sides of the new gaskets with silicone-type gasket sealer before refitting.

12   Slip the first gasket, the insulator block and the second gasket (in that order) onto the fuel pump mounting studs.

13   Refit the fuel pump. It may be necessary to guide the rocker arm into place from inside the head. Work slowly; there is not much clearance between the rocker arm and the valve gear.

14   Once the fuel pump is properly seated, refit the mounting nuts and tighten them evenly. Do not overtighten them or the insulator block may be cracked.

15   Refit the valve cover if it was removed.

16   Refit the hoses (after inspecting them for cracks) and the hose clamps.

17   Start the engine and check for fuel leaks at the hose fittings. Check for oil leaks where the fuel pump mounts on the cylinder head.

Symptom	Probable cause	Remedy
Fuel pressure is lower than standard value	Clogged fuel strainer	Replace fuel strainer
	Faulty pressure regulator	Replace pressure regulator
	Faulty fuel pump	Replace fuel pump
Fuel pressure is higher than standard value	Faulty pressure regulator	Replace pressure regulator
	Clogged fuel return hose or pipe	Clean or replace hose or pipe
Fuel pressure does not vary even if the vacuum hose is connected	Leakage around vacuum hose	Replace the vacuum hose

3.22 Fuel pressure troubleshooting table for fuel-injected engines

Symptom	Probable cause	Remedy
Fuel pressure drops slowly after engine is stopped	Faulty injector (leaks)	Replace injector
Fuel pressure drops sharply immediately after engine is stopped	Faulty fuel pump (pump inside check valve binding)	Replace fuel pump

3.23 Fuel pressure drop troubleshooting table for fuel-injected engines

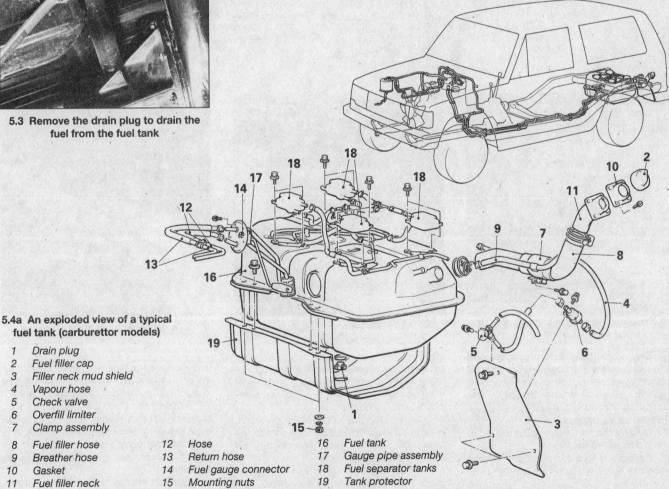

4.6 An exploded view of the mechanical pump used on carburetted engines

1 *Air cleaner housing*
2 *Fuel hose*
3 *Fuel pump*
4 *Push rod*
5 *Gasket*
6 *Insulator*
7 *Gasket*

Fuel-injected engines

18 Remove the fuel tank (see Section 5).
19 Remove the six fuel pump retaining nuts and pull the pump assembly out of the fuel tank **(see illustration 5.4b)**.
20 Refitting is the reverse of removal. Be sure the gasket between the fuel pump assembly and the fuel tank is in good shape. If not, renew it.
21 Refit the fuel tank (see Section 5).

5   Fuel tank - removal and refitting

Refer to illustrations 5.3, 5.4a, 5.4b, 5.6, 5.7a, 5.7b and 5.8

Warning: *Petrol is extremely flammable, so take extra precautions when you work on any part of the fuel system. Don't smoke or allow open flames or bare light bulbs near the work area, and don't work in a garage where a natural gas-type appliance (such as a water heater or clothes dryer) with a pilot light is present. If you spill any fuel on your skin, rinse it off immediately with soap and water. When you perform any kind of work on the fuel system, wear safety glasses and have a Class B type fire extinguisher on hand.*

5.3 Remove the drain plug to drain the fuel from the fuel tank

5.4a An exploded view of a typical fuel tank (carburettor models)

1   *Drain plug*
2   *Fuel filler cap*
3   *Filler neck mud shield*
4   *Vapour hose*
5   *Check valve*
6   *Overfill limiter*
7   *Clamp assembly*
8   *Fuel filler hose*
9   *Breather hose*
10 *Gasket*
11 *Fuel filler neck*
12 *Hose*
13 *Return hose*
14 *Fuel gauge connector*
15 *Mounting nuts*
16 *Fuel tank*
17 *Gauge pipe assembly*
18 *Fuel separator tanks*
19 *Tank protector*

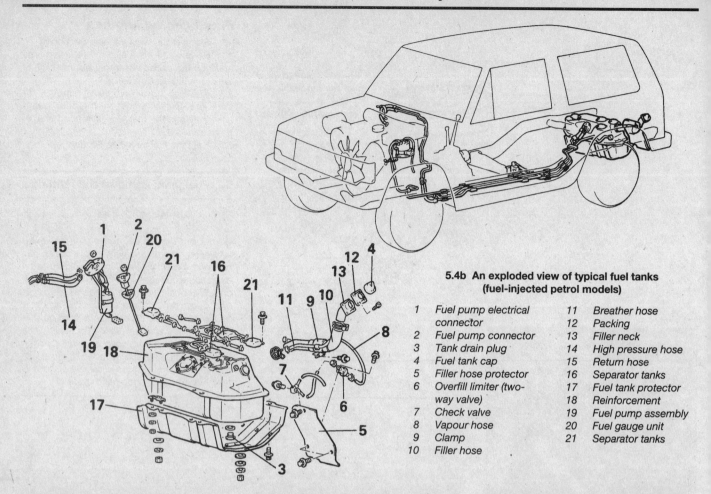

5.4b An exploded view of typical fuel tanks (fuel-injected petrol models)

1	Fuel pump electrical connector	11	Breather hose
2	Fuel pump connector	12	Packing
3	Tank drain plug	13	Filler neck
4	Fuel tank cap	14	High pressure hose
5	Filler hose protector	15	Return hose
6	Overfill limiter (two-way valve)	16	Separator tanks
7	Check valve	17	Fuel tank protector
8	Vapour hose	18	Reinforcement
9	Clamp	19	Fuel pump assembly
10	Filler hose	20	Fuel gauge unit
		21	Separator tanks

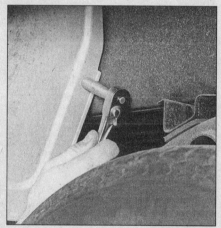

5.6 Remove the filler neck mud shield

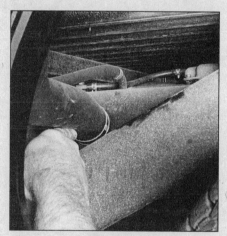

5.7a Filler connecting hose clamp location

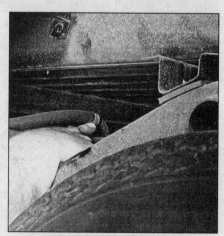

5.7b Breather hose clamp location

1   Before doing any work around the fuel tank, make sure that the ignition switch is off and remove the key from the ignition lock. Block the front wheels to keep the vehicle from rolling, then raise the rear of the vehicle and set it on jack stands.

2   Remove the tank filler cap so any pressure in the tank can escape.

3   Position a suitable container (large enough to hold the fuel that it is in the tank) under the tank. Remove the drain plug **(see illustration on page 4-7)** and allow the fuel to drain into the container. Be very careful when working around petrol; it is highly explosive. After the fuel has drained completely, refit the drain plug.

4   Loosen the hose clamps on the main, return and vapour fuel hoses, then pull the hoses off the tank **(see illustrations on pages 4-7 and 4-8)**.

5   Unplug the electrical wires from the fuel pump (fuel-injected models) and fuel level sending unit.

6   Remove the filler neck mud shield from the inside of the left rear wheel well. It is held in place with three bolts **(see illustration)**.

7   Loosen the hose clamps on the filler connecting hose (large) and the breather hose (small) where they attach to the tank **(see illustrations)**. Pull the hoses off the tank. (Be careful not to damage them in the process).

8   Support the fuel tank, preferably with a portable jack and a block of wood. Remove

5.8 Remove the fuel tank mounting nuts while supporting the tank securely

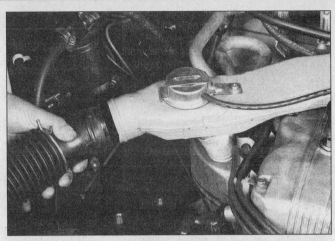

7.2 Slide back the hose clamp and remove the snorkel tube (carburetted engines)

7.3 Pull off the crankcase breather hose (carburetted engines)

7.4 Remove the large hose leading to the secondary air supply system reed valve (carburetted engines)

7.5 Remove the hose that leads to the purge control valve (carburetted engines)

the four mounting nuts **(see illustration)**, lower the tank carefully and move it out from under the vehicle.

9 Check the tank interior for rust and corrosion. If the tank is not extremely corroded, it can be cleaned and reused. Special solvents made especially for cleaning fuel tanks are available. If you use one, be sure to follow the directions on the container. The inside of the tank is plated with zinc so be sure to use a cleaner that will not harm it in any way.

10 If the tank is severely corroded, renew it.

11 Look for evidence of leaks and cracks. If any are found, take the tank to a repair shop to have it fixed.

12 Inspect all fuel and breather hoses for cracks and deterioration. Check all hose clamps for damage and proper operation.

13 Refitting of the tank is basically the reverse of removal. Be sure to double check all hoses for proper routing. Also, if you have not already done so, be sure to tighten the drain plug securely.

14 Fill the tank with fuel and check for leaks. After the engine has been run, make a second check for leaks, particularly at the hose fittings that were removed.

6 Fuel tank cleaning and repair - general information

1 All repairs to the fuel tank or filler neck should be carried out by a professional who has experience in this critical and potentially dangerous work. Even after cleaning and flushing of the fuel system, explosive fumes can remain and ignite during repair of the tank.

2 If the fuel tank is removed from the vehicle, it shouldn't be placed in an area where sparks or open flames could ignite the fumes coming out of the tank. Be especially careful inside garages where a natural gas-type appliance is located, because the pilot light could cause an explosion.

7 Air cleaner assembly - removal and refitting

1 The air cleaner assembly must be removed in order to perform many maintenance repair and adjustment procedures. It is

very important to remove and refit it carefully and correctly to ensure proper engine operation.

Carburetted engines

Refer to illustrations 7.2, 7.3, 7.4, 7.5, 7.7, 7.8a and 7.8b

2 Remove the snorkel tube (connected between the air cleaner and the headlight brace) from the air cleaner **(see illustration)**.

3 Pull off the crankcase breather hose (if equipped) from the front of the air cleaner housing **(see illustration)**.

4 Remove the large hose leading to the secondary air supply system valve **(see illustration)**.

5 Slide back the hose clamp and remove the hose that leads to the purge control valve from the air cleaner housing **(see illustration)**.

6 Remove the top cover (it is held in place with four spring clips and a wing nut) and lift out the filter element.

7 Remove the two nuts, lock washers and flat washers attaching the air cleaner housing to the valve cover **(see illustration)**.

4

7.7 Remove the two nuts, lock washers and flat washers (carburetted engines)

7.8a Disconnect the hot air duct (carburetted engines)

7.8b Remove the vacuum hose (carburetted engines)

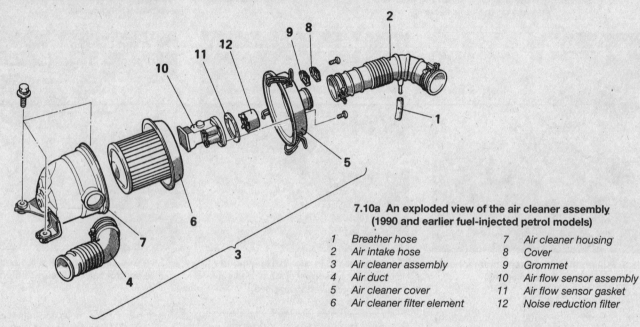

7.10a An exploded view of the air cleaner assembly (1990 and earlier fuel-injected petrol models)

1	Breather hose	7	Air cleaner housing
2	Air intake hose	8	Cover
3	Air cleaner assembly	9	Grommet
4	Air duct	10	Air flow sensor assembly
5	Air cleaner cover	11	Air flow sensor gasket
6	Air cleaner filter element	12	Noise reduction filter

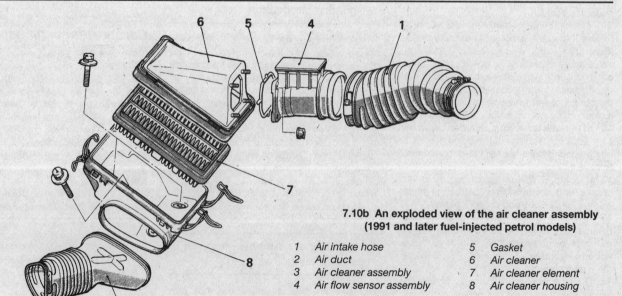

7.10b An exploded view of the air cleaner assembly (1991 and later fuel-injected petrol models)

1	Air intake hose	5	Gasket
2	Air duct	6	Air cleaner
3	Air cleaner assembly	7	Air cleaner element
4	Air flow sensor assembly	8	Air cleaner housing

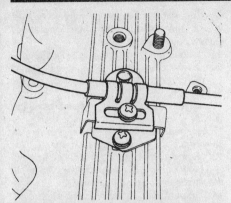

8.2 Detach this accelerator cable clamp from the valve cover to renew the cable - or loosen the screw and slide the clamp back and forth to adjust the cable (earlier carburetted engines)

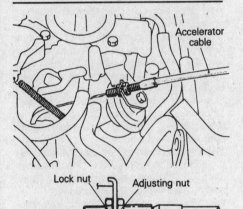

8.3 Typical accelerator cable support bracket with locknut and adjusting nut arrangement (used on later model carburetted engines and on fuel-injected engines)

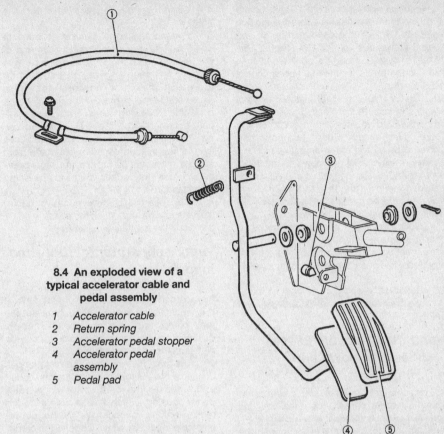

8.4 An exploded view of a typical accelerator cable and pedal assembly

1 *Accelerator cable*
2 *Return spring*
3 *Accelerator pedal stopper*
4 *Accelerator pedal assembly*
5 *Pedal pad*

8   Carefully lift up on the housing and disconnect the hot-air duct between the exhaust manifold and air cleaner housing **(see illustration)** and the vacuum hose leading to the air bleed valve in the housing. (The hose is colour coded white) **(see illustration)**.

9   Refit the air cleaner by reversing the removal procedure. Be sure to line up the arrows on the top cover and the housing before setting the cover in place.

Fuel-injected petrol engines

Refer to illustrations 7.10a and 7.10b

10   Remove the air intake hose **(see illustrations)**.

11   Unplug the electrical connector for the air flow sensor assembly.

12   On 1991 and later models, remove the mounting nuts and remove the air flow sensor (on 1990 and earlier models, the air flow sensor is an integral part of the air cleaner housing mounted on the inside of the air cleaner cover).

13   Remove the air cleaner housing mounting bolts and remove the housing.

14   Refitting is the reverse of removal.

---

8   Accelerator cable and hand throttle cable - renewal and adjustment

---

Refer to illustrations 8.2, 8.3 and 8.4

Accelerator cable removal and refitting

1   Remove the air cleaner housing (see Section 7).

2   On carburetted engines, loosen the cable clamp on top of the valve cover **(see illustration)** and detach the cable from the valve cover. On 3.0L engines, remove the two cable adjusting bolts from the air intake plenum and detach the cable from the plenum. On diesel engines, loosen the adjustment nuts and cable clamp. Disconnect the inner and outer cables from the injection pump.

3   If the cable has a support bracket at the carburettor or throttle body, loosen the locknut at the bracket **(see illustration)** and detach the cable from the bracket.

4   Working inside the vehicle, under the dash, unhook the throttle return spring and disconnect the accelerator cable from the accelerator pedal assembly **(see illustration)**.

5   Detach the cable guide from the firewall. Earlier guides are threaded into the firewall; later units are attached to the firewall with two bolts.

6   Disconnect the cable from the throttle lever at the carburettor or throttle body and remove the cable.

7   Refitting is the reverse of removal.

Accelerator cable adjustment

8   To adjust the cable on carburetted and diesel engines, loosen the cable clamp on the valve cover (earlier engines) or the locknut at the cable support bracket (later engines). Move the cable toward or away until there's just enough freeplay to allow the throttle valve to close freely when the accelerator pedal is released, with a little bit of slack. Pull the cable (clamp-type) or turn the adjustment nut (support bracket type) until the cable starts to lift the throttle lever off its stop, then let the cable come back slightly (clamp-type) or back off the adjustment nut one turn (support bracket type). To ensure the correct gap between the throttle lever and its stopper, insert a feeler gauge between the lever and the stopper. The correct gap is listed in this Chapter's Specifications. Tighten the clamp bolts or support bracket locknut.

9   Before adjusting the accelerator cable freeplay on fuel-injected petrol engines, turn off the air conditioner and all lights, warm up the engine, verify the idle speed is correct (see Section 13), stop the engine (ignition switch off) and make sure there are no sharp

4

bends in the accelerator cable. Then, before checking the cable freeplay, turn the ignition switch to On (with the engine stopped) and keep it in that position for 15 seconds. This 15-second key-on/engine off interval fully extends the probe for the idle speed control actuator.

10 The cable on fuel-injected petrol engines is adjusted basically the same way as carburetted engines with a clamp on the valve cover, except it uses two bolts and slotted clips on top of the air intake plenum. To ensure the correct gap between the throttle lever and its stopper, insert a feeler gauge between the lever and the stopper. The correct gap is listed in this Chapter's Specifications. Tighten adjustment bolts securely.

11 Now check the accelerator pedal: It should operate smoothly and the throttle valve must open fully by the time the accelerator pedal has been depressed as far as it will go.

12 Periodically, apply a thin coat of multi-purpose grease to the accelerator pedal pivot points.

Hand throttle cable (diesel engines) - removal and refitting

13 Disconnect the inner and outer cables from the injection pump. Loosen the mounting screws only enough the remove the cable.

14 Working inside the vehicle, loosen the small screw on the side of the hand throttle knob and remove the knob.

15 Loosen the mounting nuts and pull the cable assembly from the mounting bracket. The cable can now be pulled through the ties in the engine compartment and through the bulkhead.

16 Refitting is the reverse of removal.

9 Fuel hoses and vapour separator - renewal

Warning: *Fuel is extremely flammable, so take extra precautions when you work on any part of the fuel system. Don't smoke or allow open flames or bare light bulbs near the work area, and don't work in a garage where a natural gas-type appliance (such as a water heater or clothes dryer) with a pilot light is present. If you spill any fuel on your skin, rinse it off immediately with soap and water. When you perform any kind of work on the fuel system, wear safety glasses and have a Class B type fire extinguisher on hand.*
Note: *Since the fuel injection system is under considerable pressure, always renew all clamps released or removed with new ones.*

Fuel hoses

1 Periodically, check all rubber fuel hoses and metal fuel lines for cracks, bends, deformation, deterioration or clogging.

2 Remove the air cleaner assembly.

3 On fuel-injected engines, relieve the fuel system pressure (see Section 2).

4 Disconnect the negative cable from the battery.

5 Loosen the hose clamps or bolts (if equipped), wrap a cloth around each end of the hose to catch the residual fuel and twist and pull (clamped on type), pull straight off (bolted-on type) or unscrew the hose (screwed-in type) to remove the hose.

6 When renewing hoses, always use original equipment-type renewal hose and use new hose clamps or O-rings. Pressure hoses for the fuel injection system are made from special materials to handle the high pressures - use only hoses made to the same high standards.

7 Connect the battery negative cable, start the engine and check for leaks.

8 Refit the air cleaner assembly.

Vapour separator (carburetted models)

9 The vapour separator is the small canister mounted high on the left front fenderwell. It is mounted in the fuel system between the fuel pump and the carburettor and is designed to prevent vapour lock caused by high underhood temperatures.

10 The main fuel line from the fuel pump is connected to the middle fitting (colour-coded red) leads to the carburettor accelerator pump housing (which is also colour-coded red). The hose connected to the bottom fitting (colour coded yellow) leads to the carburettor fuel inlet (also colour-coded yellow).

11 The colour-coded lines and fittings reduce the possibility of incorrect hose refitting during carburettor servicing.

12 If the vapour separator is somehow damaged or begins to leak, it must be renewed. When fitting a new vapour separator, position it so that the red fitting is at the top.

10 Carburettor - servicing

1 A thorough road test and check of carburettor adjustment should be done before any major carburettor service. Specifications for some adjustments are listed on the Vehicle Emissions Control Information label found in the engine compartment.

2 Some performance complaints directed at the carburettor are actually a result of loose, misadjusted or malfunctioning engine or electrical components. Others develop when vacuum hoses leak, are disconnected or are incorrectly routed. The proper approach to analysing carburettor problems should include a routine check of the following areas:

3 Inspect all vacuum hoses and actuators for leaks and proper refitting (see Chapter 6).

4 Tighten the inlet manifold nuts and carburettor mounting nuts evenly and securely.

5 Perform a cylinder compression test (see Chapter 2).

6 Clean or renew the spark plugs as necessary.

7 Test the resistance of the spark plug wires (see Chapter 5).

8 Inspect the ignition primary wires and check the vacuum advance operation. Renew any defective parts.

9 Check the ignition timing with the vacuum advance line disconnected and plugged.

10 Set the carburettor idle mixture (see Section 13).

11 Check the fuel pump pressure (see Section 3).

12 Inspect the heat control valve in the air cleaner for proper operation (see Chapter 6).

13 Remove the carburettor air filter element and blow out any dirt with compressed air. If the filter is extremely dirty, renew it.

14 Inspect the crankcase ventilation system (see Chapter 6).

15 Carburettor problems usually show up as flooding, hard starting, stalling, severe backfiring, poor acceleration and lack of response to idle mixture screw adjustments. A carburettor that is leaking fuel and/or covered with wet-looking deposits definitely needs attention.

16 Diagnosing carburettor problems may require that the engine be started and run with the air cleaner removed. While running the engine without the air cleaner it is possible that it could backfire. A backfiring situation is likely to occur if the carburettor is malfunctioning, but removal of the air cleaner alone can lean the air/fuel mixture enough to produce an engine backfire.

17 Once it is determined that the carburettor is indeed at fault, it should be disassembled, cleaned and reassembled using new parts where necessary. Before dismantling the carburettor, make sure you have a carburettor rebuild kit, which will include all necessary gaskets and internal parts, carburettor cleaning solvent and some means of blowing out all the internal passages of the carburettor. To do the job properly, you will also need a clean place to work and plenty of time and patience.

11 Carburettor - removal and refitting

Refer to illustrations 11.5 and 11.6
Warning: *Petrol is extremely flammable, so take extra precautions when you work on any part of the fuel system. Don't smoke or allow open flames or bare light bulbs near the work area, and don't work in a garage where a natural gas-type appliance (such as a water heater or clothes dryer) with a pilot light is present. If you spill any fuel on your skin, rinse it off immediately with soap and water. When you perform any kind of work on the fuel tank, wear safety glasses and have a Class B type fire extinguisher on hand.*

Removal

1 Remove the fuel filler cap to relieve fuel tank pressure and disconnect the negative cable from the battery.

2 Remove the air cleaner from the carburettor. Be sure to label all vacuum hoses attached to the air cleaner housing (see Sec-

11.5 Removing the float bowl vent tube from the carburettor

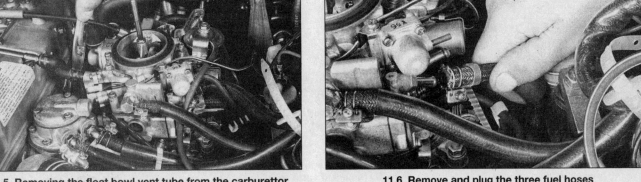

11.6 Remove and plug the three fuel hoses

tion 7).

3   Disconnect the accelerator cable from the throttle lever on the carburettor (see Section 8).

4   If the vehicle is equipped with an automatic transmission, disconnect the TV (kickdown) cable from the throttle lever.

5   Clearly label all vacuum and coolant hoses and fittings, then disconnect the hoses **(see illustration)**.

6   Disconnect the fuel lines from the carburettor **(see illustration)**.

7   Label the wires and terminals, then unplug all electrical connectors.

8   Remove the nuts (there are five on most models) and lock washers attaching the carburettor to the inlet manifold. Removal of the idle speed adjusting screws (SAS) from the carburettor body will make access to the left rear mounting nut less restricted. Remove the carburettor mounting gasket. Stuff a shop rag into the inlet manifold openings.

Refitting

9   Use a gasket scraper to remove all traces of gasket material and sealant from the inlet manifold (and the carburettor, if it's being refitted), then remove the shop rag from the manifold openings. Clean the mating surfaces with lacquer thinner or acetone.

10   Place a new gasket on the inlet manifold.

11   Position the carburettor on the gasket and refit the mounting nuts.

12   To prevent carburettor distortion or damage, tighten the nuts in a criss-cross pattern, 1/4-turn at a time, to the torque listed in this Chapter's Specifications.

13   The remaining refitting steps are the reverse of removal.

14   Check and, if necessary, adjust the idle speed (see Section 13).

15   If the vehicle is equipped with an automatic transmission, refer to Chapter 7B for the TV (kickdown) cable adjustment procedure.

16   Start the engine and check carefully for fuel leaks.

12 Carburettor - overhaul

Warning: *Petrol is extremely flammable, so take extra precautions when you work on any part of the fuel system. Don't smoke or allow* open flames or bare light bulbs near the work area, and don't work in a garage where a natural -type appliance (such as a water heater or clothes dryer) with a pilot light is present. If you spill any fuel on your skin, rinse it off immediately with soap and water. When you perform any kind of work on the fuel system, wear safety glasses and have a Class B type fire extinguisher on hand.

Note: *The following overhaul procedure is for an early model carburettor. The procedure for carburettors installed on later models is essentially the same, but slight detail changes made to these models may slightly affect the disassembly and reassembly sequence.*

Disassembly

Refer to illustrations 12.1a, through 12.28

1   Remove the carburettor (see Section 11). Remove the air cleaner hold-down stud **(see illustration)** and the air cleaner gasket from the top of the carburettor. Pull back the hose clamp and remove the coolant hose from the back of the carburettor **(see illustration)**.

2   Remove the spring clip and carefully prise the throttle opener actuating rod out of the primary throttle shaft lever (air conditioned models only) **(see illustration)**.

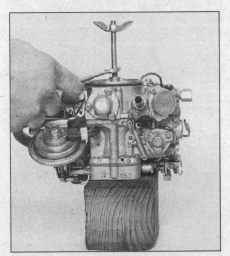

12.1a Remove the air cleaner hold-down stud

12.1b Slide back the hose clamps and remove the coolant hose

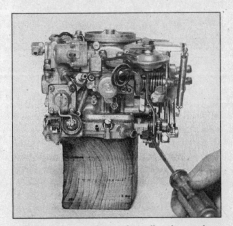

12.2a Remove the spring clip, then prise the throttle opener rod out of the throttle lever (air conditioned models only)

12.2b The throttle opener is held in place with two screws

12.3a Remove the fuel cut-off solenoid earth wire

12.3b Remove the solenoid retaining screw

12.3c Carefully lift the solenoid away from the carburettor

12.4a Unscrew the idle mixture screw . . .

12.4b . . . and remove the screw, spring, washer and rubber seal

12.5a Prise the spring clip off the sub-EGR valve linkage pin

12.5b Sub-EGR linkage pin

Remove the throttle opener from the carburettor body; it is held in place with two screws **(see illustration)**.

3   Disconnect the fuel cut-off solenoid earth wires from the carburettor body **(see illustration)**. Remove the solenoid retaining screw **(see illustration)** and lift the solenoid away from the carburettor **(see illustration)**. Do not lose the O-ring on the solenoid body.

4   Unscrew and remove the idle mixture screw, the spring, the washer and rubber seal **(see illustrations)**.

5   Disconnect the linkage at the sub EGR

valve by levering off the spring clip **(see illustration)** and removing the pin **(see illustration)**. Slide the linkage out of position and remove the spring and ball from the end of the sub EGR plunger. Using a screwdriver, unsnap the accelerator pump linkage from the throttle shaft arm **(see illustration)** and remove the accelerator pump from the carburettor body. It is held in place with four screws **(see illustration)**. Disassemble the pump and inspect the parts **(see illustration)**.

6   Remove the four screws holding the ASV housing in place **(see ilustration)** and

lift off the housing. Remove the spring, the spring cap, the spring guide and the diaphragm. Lay the parts out on a clean surface in the order of disassembly **(see illustration)**.

7   Remove the screw attaching the ASV body to the carburettor **(see illustration)** and carefully lift off the ASV body **(see illustration)**.

8   Remove the vent system earth wire **(see illustration)** and the three screws holding the solenoid to the carburettor body **(see illustration)**. Carefully lift the solenoid and the

12.5c Unsnap the accelerator pump linkage from the throttle shaft arm

12.5d Remove the accelerator pump from the carburettor body

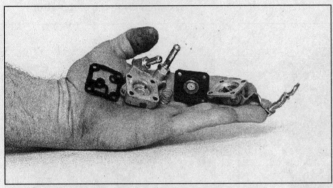

12.5e Accelerator pump components

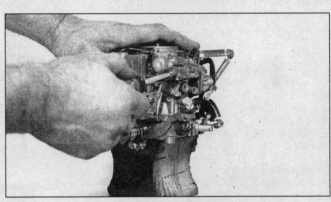

12.6a Remove the ASV housing screws

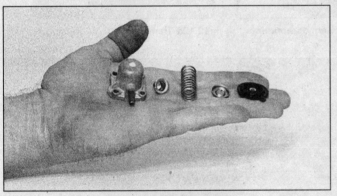

12.6b ASV components

12.7a Remove the ASV body attaching screws

12.7b The ASV body

12.8a Remove the vent system earth wire

4

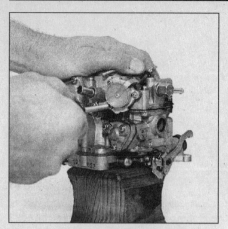

12.8b Remove the screws attaching the solenoid to the carburettor body

12.8c The solenoid and spring

12.9 Remove the screw holding the vent system body to the carburettor

12.10 Vent system components

12.11 Enrichment system components

12.12a Remove the CAV housing screws

12.12b CAV components

12.12c Remove the choke unloader diaphragm plate screws

spring inside it away from the carburettor **(see illustration)**.

9   Remove the one remaining screw holding the vent system body to the carburettor **(see illustration)** and lift it off (don't forget to remove the rubber gasket from the carburettor body).

10   To disassemble the vent valve, remove the spring clip, the washer, the valve seal from the end of the plunger. Slip the O-ring

off the body. The diaphragm and plunger (one piece) can now be withdrawn from the valve body. Lay the parts out on a clean surface in the order of disassembly **(see illustration)**.

11   Remove the enrichment system diaphragm housing. It is held in place by three screws. Remove the gasket, separate the two halves of the housing, and lift out the spring and the diaphragm **(see illustration)**.

12   Remove the CAV housing. It is held in place by three screws **(see illustration)**. Lift out the spring guide, the springs, the spring cap and the diaphragm. Lay the parts out on a clean surface in the order of disassembly **(see illustration)**. Remove the three screws holding the choke unloader diaphragm plate to the carburettor body **(see illustration)**. Lift off the plate and remove the spring **(see illustration)**.

12.12d Choke unloader diaphragm plate and spring

12.13a Prise the secondary diaphragm link out of the secondary throttle lever

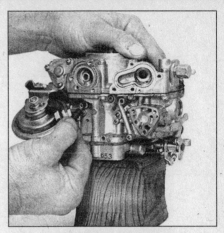

12.13b Pull the hose off the carburettor body

12.13c Remove the secondary diaphragm mounting screws

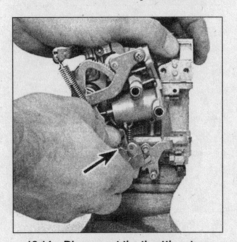

12.14a Disconnect the throttle return spring from the primary throttle lever

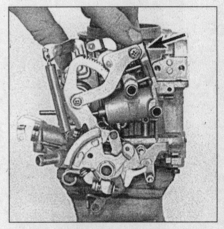

12.14b Note the reference lines on the upper choke pinion gear assembly mount

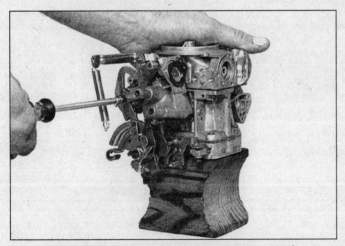

12.15 Remove the two screws holding the choke pinion gear assembly to the carburettor

12.16 Remove the screws attaching the choke plate to the choke shaft

13 Carefully prise the secondary diaphragm link out of the secondary throttle lever **(see illustration)** and pull the hose off the carburettor body **(see illustration)**. Remove the two mounting screws and lift off the diaphragm assembly **(see illustration)**.

14 Disconnect the throttle return spring from the primary throttle lever **(see illustration)**. The upper choke pinion gear assembly mount has a series of lines scribed on it. Note which one is lined up with the dot on the body **(see illustration)**.

15 Remove the two screws holding the choke pinion gear assembly to the carburet-

tor body and carefully pull it free **(see illustration)**.

16 Separate the choke plate from the choke shaft. It is held in place with two small screws **(see illustration)**.

17 Remove the spring clip and carefully prise the manual choke unloader linkage rod

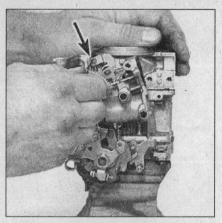

12.17 Remove the spring clip from the manual choke unloader linkage rod

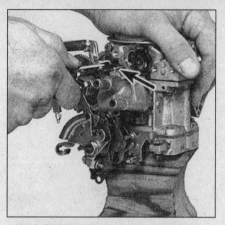

12.18 Pull out the pin holding the choke unloader diaphragm in alignment

12.19 Remove the throttle return spring mount

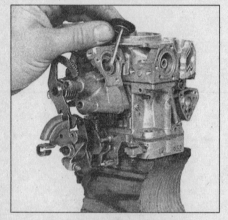

12.20a Pull out the choke unloader diaphragm and linkage

12.20b Withdraw the choke shaft

12.21a Unhook the secondary return spring

12.21b Remove the two choke mechanism housing screws

12.21c Lift the choke mechanism housing away from the carburettor body

out of the choke lever **(see illustration)**.

18   Using small pliers, pull out the pin holding the choke unloader diaphragm in alignment **(see illustration)**.

19   Remove the throttle return spring mount. It is held in place with one bolt **(see illustration)**.

20   Pull out the choke unloader diaphragm and linkage **(see illustration)**, then withdraw the choke shaft from the carburettor body

(see illustration).

21   Unhook the secondary return spring from the choke mechanism housing **(see illustration)**. Remove the two screws **(see illustration)** and lift the choke mechanism housing away from the carburettor body **(see illustration)**. Separate the spacer and small O-ring from the housing **(see illustration)**.

22   Remove the four remaining screws **(see illustration)** and lift the top cover off the car-

burettor. Be careful not to bend or otherwise damage the float mechanism **(see illustration)**.

23   Before removing the float, invert the top cover and measure the distance from the float seam to the gasket surface of the top cover **(see illustration)**. Record the measurement for future reference.

24   Carefully slide out the pivot pin and separate the float and inlet needle from the top

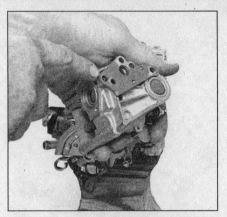

12.21d Separate the spacer and O-ring from the housing

12.22a Remove the top cover screws

12.22b Lift the top cover off; don't bend the float arm

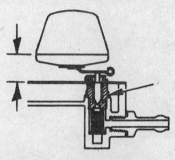

12.23 Measure the distance from the float seam to the gasket surface of the top cover

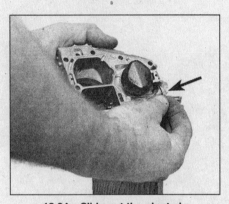

12.24a Slide out the pivot pin

12.24b Separate the float and needle from the top cover

12.24c Remove the inlet needle seat

12.25 Remove the top cover gasket

12.26a Accelerator pump discharge plunger bore

cover **(see illustration)**. Slip the needle out of its mount on the float **(see illustration)**. Unscrew and remove the inlet needle seat and washer **(see illustration)**.

25   Remove the top cover gasket from the carburettor body **(see illustration)**.

26   Hold your finger over the accelerator pump discharge plunger bore **(see illustration)**. Tip the carburettor upside down and let the steel ball from the anti-overflow mechanism in the bottom of the float bowl fall out **(see illustration)**. Next, remove the accelerator pump steel check ball and weight **(see illustration)**. Draw a simple diagram showing the sizes (stamped on the jets) and the loca-

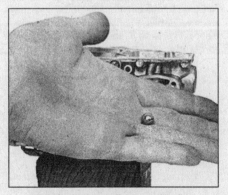

12.26b Anti-overflow mechanism steel ball

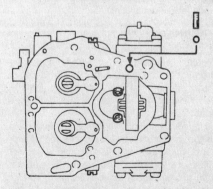

12.26c Accelerator pump steel check ball and weight location

12.26d Remove the primary main jet

12.26e Remove the secondary main jet

12.26f Remove the idle jets

12.27a Remove the two screws attaching the throttle body to the carburettor body

12.27b Separate the throttle body from the carburettor body (don't disassemble the throttle shafts and linkages at this time)

tions of the primary and secondary main jets, then unscrew and remove them from the carburettor body **(see illustrations)**.

27   Remove the two attaching screws **(see illustration)** and separate the throttle body from the carburettor body **(see illustration)**. Do not remove any plugs or fittings from the carburettor body that have been sealed with white paint.

28   Slip off the rubber boot and slide the sub-EGR valve plunger out of the throttle body **(see illustration)**.

Inspection

29   Once the carburettor has been completely disassembled, the parts should be thoroughly cleaned and inspected. There are many commercial carburettor cleaning solvents available which can be used with good results.

30   The diaphragms and some plastic parts of the carburettor can be damaged by solvents; avoid placing these parts in any liquid. Clean the external surfaces of these parts with a clean cloth or soft brush. Shake or wipe dirt and other foreign material from the stem plunger side of the diaphragm. Compressed air can be used to remove loose dirt,

but should not be connected to the vacuum diaphragm fitting.

31   If the commercial solvent or cleaner recommends the use of water as a rinse, hot water will produce the best results. After rinsing, all traces of water must be blown from the passages using compressed air. Never clean jets with a wire, drill bit or other objects. The orifices may be enlarged, making the mixture too rich for proper performance.

32   When checking parts removed from the carburettor, it is often difficult to be sure they are serviceable. It is therefore recommended that new parts be fitted, if available, when the carburettor is disassembled. The required parts should be included in the carburettor rebuild kit.

33   After all the parts have been cleaned and dried, check the throttle valve shaft and choke shaft for proper operation. If sticking or binding occurs, clean the shafts with solvent and lubricate them with engine oil.

34   Check the jets for damage or clogging. Renew them if damage is evident.

35   Inspect the idle mixture adjusting screw. The tapered portion of the screw must be straight and smooth. If the tapered portion is grooved or ridged renew the screw with a

12.28 Slide the sub-EGR plunger out of the throttle body

new one.

36   Check the strainer screen for clogging and damage.

37   Check the vacuum chamber. Push the vacuum chamber rod in, seal off the nipple and release the rod. If the rod does not return, the vacuum chamber is most likely in

good condition. If the rod returns when released, the diaphragm is defective. The vacuum chamber should be renewed if this condition exists.

38 To check the fuel cut-off solenoid, connect a jumper lead to the positive (+) terminal of a 12-volt battery and the wire lead of the solenoid. Connect a second jumper lead to the negative (-) terminal of the battery and the solenoid earth wire. The needle should move in toward the solenoid when the battery is connected and out when the battery is disconnected. If it does, the fuel cut-off solenoid is good.

Reassembly

Note: *The reassembly process will be easier if the sequenced photos in the disassembly section are followed in reverse.*

39 Using a new gasket, assemble the throttle body to the carburettor body and tighten the mounting screws securely.
40 Refit the main and pilot jets in the carburettor body. Make sure they are installed in the correct bores.
41 Place the anti-overflow ball in place in the bottom of the float bowl and insert the accelerator pump steel check ball and weight into the accelerator pump bore.
42 Fit the new inlet needle seat in place in the carburettor top cover; (don't forget to include a new washer). Assemble the new inlet needle to the float and attach the float to the top cover.
43 Invert the top cover and measure the distance from the float seam to the gasket surface of the top cover (**see illustration 12.23**). If the measured distance is more or less than it was during disassembly, remove the float from the top cover, unscrew the inlet needle seat and add or remove washers (as necessary) to change the float height. Reassemble the inlet needle and float and recheck the measurement. Repeat the procedure as required until the distance is the same as it was during disassembly. When checking the float level on 1984 and later models, hold the measure the distance from the bottom of the float to the gasket surface of the float chamber and compare this figure to the one in this Chapters Specifications Section.
44 Gently lay the top cover in place using a new gasket and refit the mounting screws. Tighten them evenly and securely.
45 Refit the choke mechanism housing and tighten the screws securely. Make sure the manual choke unloader rod is facing in the proper direction.
46 Slide the choke shaft into place and refit the choke plate. It is a very good idea to use a thread locking compound on the choke plate attaching screws.
47 Insert the manual choke unloader rod into the choke lever.
48 Refit the choke unloader/diaphragm and push the pin into place.
49 Refit the throttle return spring mount and tighten the screw securely.

50 Engage the spring loop on the choke pinion gear assembly, hold the choke plate closed and engage the plastic gear teeth of the choke pinion gear with the gear teeth on the choke set lever. Refit the screws, move the pinion gear assembly to line up the marks exactly as they were before disassembled, then tighten the screws securely.
51 Refit the secondary diaphragm assembly and hook up the hose. Slip the diaphragm link into the secondary throttle lever.
52 Refit the choke unloader diaphragm plate and tighten the screws.
53 Refit the CAV internal parts and housing then tighten the mounting screws evenly and securely.
54 Assemble the enrichment system components and refit the housing in place on the carburettor body. (The wire clamp fits over the upper left mounting screw). Tighten the mounting screws securely.
55 Assemble the vent valve. Lubricate the O-ring on the valve body and slide the valve into place in the carburettor body. Tighten the mounting screws securely.
56 Refit the vent valve solenoid and tighten the mounting screws. Attach the earth wire to the carburettor body.
57 Refit the ASV housing (with the wire clamp on the longest screw) and tighten the mounting screws finger-tight. Assemble the ASV internal parts, refit the housing and tighten the mounting screws.
58 Refit the accelerator pump and hook the linkage to the throttle shaft arm.
59 Slip the small steel ball and the spring into place in the end of the sub-EGR valve plunger Refit the rubber boot and push the plunger into place in the throttle body. Hold the linkage in place, refit the pin and snap the spring clip into place on the end of the pin.
60 Make sure the O-ring is in place on the fuel cut-off solenoid body, then refit the solenoid and tighten the mounting screws. Remove the short screw on the ASV body. Refit the fuel cut-off solenoid earth wire and tighten both ASV body mounting screws securely.
61 Insert the throttle opener actuating rod into the primary throttle shaft lever. Refit the spring clip and mount the throttle opener on the carburettor (air-conditioned models only).
62 Refit the coolant hose and slide the hose clamps into place.
63 Double check all screws to make sure they are tight and the carburettor reassembly is complete.

13 Carburettor - adjustments

Idle speed and mixture

Refer to illustration 13.6

1 An exhaust analyser must be used to adjust the idle mixture. Since the average home mechanic doesn't have access to such equipment, we recommend the idle speed and mixture adjustments be done by a dealer service department or a suitably-equipped

automotive tune-up facility perform.
2 However, you can do the basic adjustments for the idle speed and mixture without an exhaust gas analyser if you follow the steps outlined here. Just remember that final adjustment must be done with the proper equipment to ensure compliance with emission standards.
3 Before making the idle speed and mixture adjustments, check the ignition system, including the ignition timing. Look for cracked or disconnected vacuum lines. Make sure the inlet manifold and carburettor mounting nuts are tightened evenly and securely; any intake leaks must be fixed before proceeding. Also, the engine must be at normal operating temperature so the choke is completely open. Place the transmission in Neutral and set the parking brake. The air conditioner, lights and all accessories must be off.
4 Hook up a tachometer in accordance with the instructions provided by its manufacturer.
5 Remove the air hose from the inlet of the secondary air supply system reed valve and plug the reed valve inlet.
6 With the engine running, carefully turn the idle mixture adjusting screw (MAS) **(see illustration)** clockwise, preferably by hand, until the engine starts to slow down or misfire. When this happens, slowly turn the MAS in the opposite direction (counter-clockwise). The engine should start to speed up again. Then, as the MAS is turned further, it should begin to slow down or misfire.
7 These two points are sometimes difficult

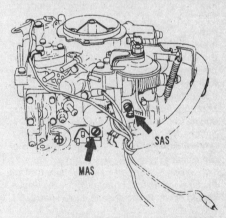

13.6 Idle speed (SAS) and mixture (MAS) adjustment screw locations

to discern, so keep a close eye on the tachometer. The MAS should be turned approximately 1/16 of a turn each time, allowing about ten seconds for the engine speed to stabilise between adjustments.
8 Once you have determined how the engine reacts to changes of the MAS position, slowly turn it clockwise or counter-clockwise, as necessary, until the smoothest, fastest idle speed is obtained. Next turn the idle speed adjusting screw (SAS) until the idle speed listed in this Chapter's Specifications

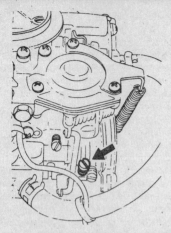

13.13 Throttle opener (idle-up) adjusting screw location (air-conditioned models)

is obtained. Recheck the MAS to make sure it is still providing the smoothest, fastest idle speed at that position.

9   Unplug the reed valve inlet and hook up the air hose.

10   If the idle speed changes, return it to the specified rpm by turning the SAS in or out as necessary.

11   If the engine misfires badly, repeat the procedure, turning the MAS further counter-clockwise initially.

Air-conditioned models

Refer to illustration 13.13

12   After the idle mixture and speed have been adjusted, an additional adjustment must be made to all air-conditioned models.

13   Turn off all accessories. Put the trans-mission in Neutral and apply the parking brake. If the vehicle has power steering, put the wheels in the straight ahead position so the power steering pump isn't loaded. Now turn the air conditioner control switch to On (this activates the throttle opener on the car-burettor). Adjust the idle speed to the idle-up engine speed listed in this Chapter's Specifi-cations by turning the throttle opener (idle-up) adjusting screw **(see illustration)** in or out as necessary.

14   When the speed has been set, turn off the air conditioner control switch - the engine should return to the specified idle speed.

Automatic choke

15   The choke valve is automatically oper-ated by a wax element that senses the coolant temperature. This element allows the choke valve to close under spring pressure at low coolant temperatures and opens it through a set lever and a rack and pinion gear setup as the coolant temperature increases.

16   The wax element plunger pushes against an adjustable screw on the choke set lever. This screw is pre-set at the factory to provide for proper choke closing and opening and sealed with white paint. Do not tamper with it, as choke operation will be adversely affected.

17   The choke should not require any adjustment as long as the rack and pinion gears are properly oriented and the choke pinion gear assembly is adjusted so that the choke plate is lightly seated in the closed position when the choke linkage is refitted.

14   Multi-Point Injection (MPI) - general information

All V6 models are equipped with an electronic fuel injection system known as Multi-Point Injection (MPI). Aside from slight differences in some emissions-related com-ponents, the earlier and later MPI systems are virtually identical. Both are computerised, electronically controlled fuel, ignition and emission control systems. Their important sub-systems include air induction, fuel deliv-ery, fuel control, emission control and the engine control unit. Each system differs slightly in the type and location of these com-ponents.

Air induction system

The air induction system includes the air cleaner assembly, the throttle body, the duct-work between the air cleaner and the throttle body, the Throttle Position Sensor (TPS) and the Idle Speed Control (ISC) servo.

Fuel delivery system

The fuel delivery system provides fuel from the fuel tank into the fuel control sys-tem. It also returns any excess fuel back into the fuel tank. The system includes an in-tank electric fuel pump, fuel filter and return line.

Fuel control system

The fuel control system includes the fuel pressure regulator, the fuel rail and the fuel injectors. On MPI systems, the inlet manifold supplies air only; fuel is sprayed directly into the ports by the fuel injectors.

Emission controls and the engine control unit

The oxygen sensor, airflow sensor, intake air temperature sensor, engine coolant temperature sensor, Throttle Position Sensor (TPS), idle position switch, crank angle sen-sor and barometric pressure sensor are all important to the proper operation of the MPI system, but they're more closely related to emissions than to fuel. If you'd like to know more about related emission control sys-tems, particularly the information sensors and the engine control unit, refer to Chap-ter 6.

15   Fuel injection system - check

Note: *The following procedure is based on the assumption that the fuel pressure is ade-quate (see Section 3).*

1   Check all earth wire connections for tightness. Check all wiring harness connec-tors related to the MPI system. Loose con-nectors and poor connections can cause many problems that resemble more serious malfunctions. Also check all vacuum connec-tions and make sure all vacuum hoses are in good condition and not hardened, cracked or plugged.

2   Verify that the battery is fully charged; the engine control unit and the information sensors depend on an accurate supply volt-age to function properly.

3   Check the air filter element - a dirty or partially blocked filter will severely impede performance and economy (see Chapter 1).

4   Check for blown fuses. If a blown fuse is found, renew it and see if it blows again. If it does, search the circuit for a short.

5   Look for leaks in the air intake duct between the air cleaner housing and the throttle body and at the gasket between the throttle body and the air intake plenum. Air leaks cause an excessively lean mixture. Also inspect all vacuum hoses connected to the throttle body and inlet manifold.

6   Remove the air intake duct from the throttle body and check for dirt, carbon or other residue build-up. If the throttle body is dirty (pay particular attention to the area just inside the throttle plate), clean it with carbu-rettor cleaner and a toothbrush.

7   With the engine running, place a screw-driver against each injector, one at a time, and listen through the handle for the clicking sound made by the solenoid inside. This sound should be clearly audible at idle.

16   Throttle body - removal and refitting

Refer to illustration 16.2

1   Disconnect the negative cable from the battery. Disconnect the accelerator cable (see Section 8).

2   Detach the vacuum hose(s) **(see illus-tration)**.

3   Loosen the hose clamp and detach the air intake hose.

4   Unplug the Throttle Position Sensor (TPS) electrical connector.

5   Unplug the Idle Speed Control (ISC) servo electrical connector.

6   Place some absorbent shop towels under the connections for the coolant hoses, then detach both hoses. Some coolant will be lost.

7   Remove the throttle body mounting bolts, the throttle body and the gasket. Using a scraper, remove all traces of old gasket material from the throttle body and air intake plenum mating surfaces. Clean the surfaces with a rag soaked in lacquer thinner or ace-tone.

8   Refitting is the reverse of removal. Be sure to tighten the throttle body mounting bolts to the torque listed in this Chapter's Specifications. Adjust the accelerator cable

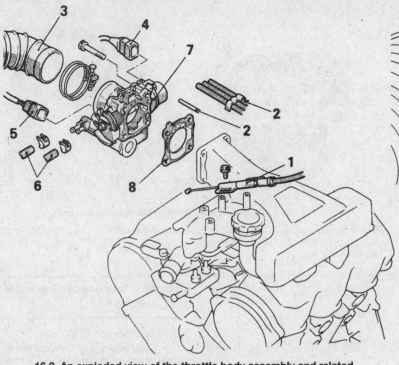

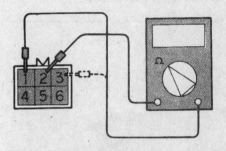

17.1 The ISC servo is located under the throttle body

16.2 An exploded view of the throttle body assembly and related components (3.0L engine)

1	*Accelerator cable*
2	*Vacuum hose(s) (California models have extra hoses)*
3	*Air intake hose*
4	*Throttle Position Sensor (TPS) electrical connector*

5	*Idle Speed Control (ISC) electrical connector*
6	*Coolant hose*
7	*Throttle body*
8	*Gasket*

17.4 Using an ohmmeter or multimeter, check the continuity of the ISC servo connector at the indicated terminals and compare your measurements with the resistance listed in this Chapter's Specifications

when you're through (see Section 8), and add coolant to renew the coolant lost when you disconnected the coolant hoses from the throttle body. Connect the negative battery cable.

17 Idle Speed Control (ISC) servo - check and renewal

Check

Refer to illustrations 17.1, 17.4 and 17.8

1   Listen to the ISC servo **(see illustration)** while an assistant turns the ignition switch to On (not to Start). The servo should make an audible sound.

2   If the servo is silent, inspect the electrical circuit. If the circuit is in good shape, the likely cause is a malfunction of the servo or the engine control unit.

3   Unplug the ISC servo electrical connector.

4   Measure the resistance between terminals 2 and 1, and between terminals 2 and 3 **(see illustration)** and compare your reading to the resistance listed in this Chapter's Specifications.

5   Measure the resistance between terminals 5 and 6, and between terminals 5 and 4 and compare your reading to the resistance

listed in this Chapter's Specifications.

6   Remove the throttle body (see Section 16).

7   Remove the ISC servo (see below).

8   Hook up the positive terminal of a 6V DC battery to terminals 2 and 5 **(see illustration)**.

9   Holding the ISC servo as shown in the preceding illustration, hook up the negative terminal of the 6V DC battery to each terminal of the connector in the following sequence and note whether there's any vibration (a very

slight shaking of the servo) as the motor is activated.

1) *Connect the battery negative terminal to connector terminals 3 and 6.*

2) *Connect the battery negative terminal to connector terminals 1 and 6.*

3) *Connect the battery negative terminal to connector terminals 1 and 4.*

4) *Connect the battery negative terminal to connector terminals 3 and 4.*

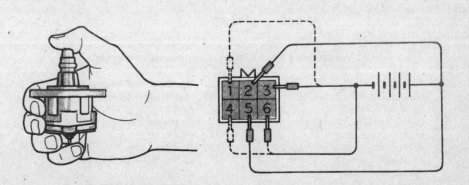

17.8 Holding the ISC servo as shown, power it up with a 6V DC battery by touching the terminals of the electrical connector in the sequence described in the accompanying text

5) Connect the battery negative terminal to connector terminals 3 and 6.

6) Repeat the above five steps in the reverse sequence (5 through 1).

10   If the servo vibrates slightly during these tests, it's okay; if it doesn't, renew it.

Renewal

Refer to illustration 17.12

11   Unplug the ISC servo electrical connector, if you haven't already done so.

12   Remove the ISC servo mounting screws **(see illustration)**. The threads of these screws have been coated with adhesive, so make sure you don't strip out the heads trying to loosen them.

13   Remove the ISC servo unit.

14   Refitting is the reverse of removal. Be sure to tighten the screws to the torque listed in this Chapter's Specifications.

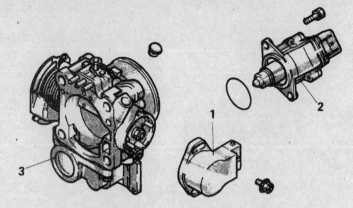

17.12 An exploded view of the throttle body assembly

1   *Throttle Position Sensor (TPS)/idle position switch assembly*
2   *Idle Speed Control (ISC) servo assembly*
3   *Throttle body*

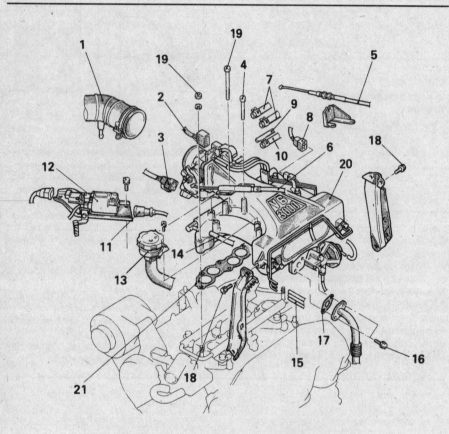

18.1 An exploded view of the air intake plenum assembly

1	*Air intake hose*	10	*Brake booster vacuum hose*
2	*Throttle Position Sensor (TPS)* *electrical connector*	11	*High tension cable*
3	*Idle Speed Control (ISC) servo* *electrical connector*	12	*Ignition coil*
		13	*Engine oil filler neck bracket*
4	*Accelerator cable adjusting bolt*	14	*PCV hose*
5	*TV (kickdown) cable*	15	*Vacuum hoses*
6	*Accelerator cable*	16	*EGR pipe attaching bolt*
7	*Coolant hoses*	17	*Gasket*
8	*EGR temperature sensor electrical* *connector*	18	*Plenum stay-to-plenum bolt*
		19	*Bolt and nut*
9	*Vacuum hose*	20	*Air intake plenum assembly*
		21	*Plenum gasket*

18 Air intake plenum - removal and refitting

Refer to illustration 18.1

1   If you're planning to renew the air intake plenum assembly, remove the throttle body (see Section 16); if you're only removing the plenum to renew a gasket or service the cylinder head (i.e. if you intend to refit the same plenum assembly), the throttle body can remain attached. Detach all hoses, cables and connectors from the throttle body as if you were going to remove it, but leave it bolted to the plenum **(see illustration)**.

2   Unplug the electrical connector for the EGR temperature sensor.

3   Detach the brake booster vacuum hose, all other vacuum hoses and the PCV hose from the plenum.

4   Remove the ignition coil (see Chapter 5). Detach the accelerator and TV (kickdown) cable brackets from the plenum.

5   Detach the bracket for the engine oil filler neck.

6   Remove the EGR pipe attaching bolts and detach the EGR pipe from the plenum.

7   Unbolt and remove the plenum stays. Remove the mounting bolts for the plenum assembly.

8   Remove the plenum and gasket.

9   Using a scraper, remove all traces of old gasket material from the plenum and inlet manifold mating surfaces. Wipe the mating surfaces clean with a rag soaked in lacquer thinner or acetone.

10   Refitting is the reverse of removal. Use a new gasket and tighten the plenum mounting bolts in several stages, working from the centre out, to the torque listed in this Chapter's Specifications.

19 Fuel rail assembly - removal and refitting

Refer to illustrations 19.5 and 19.10

Warning: *Petrol is extremely flammable, so*

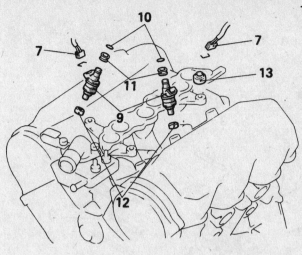

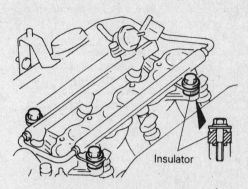

19.5 An exploded view of the fuel rail assembly

1 Air intake plenum assembly
2 Fuel high-pressure hose
3 Fuel return hose
4 Vacuum hose
5 Fuel pressure regulator
6 O-ring
7 Fuel injector wiring harness electrical connector
8 Fuel rail assembly
9 Fuel injector
10 O-ring
11 Grommet
12 Insulator
13 Insulator

19.10 After refitting the fuel rail and mounting bolts, verify that all four insulators are properly seated before tightening the bolts

take extra precautions when you work on any part of the fuel system. Don't smoke or allow open flames or bare light bulbs near the work area, and don't work in a garage where a natural gas-type appliance (such as a water heater or clothes dryer) with a pilot light is present. If you spill any fuel on your skin, rinse it off immediately with soap and water. When you perform any kind of work on the fuel system, wear safety glasses and have a Class B type fire extinguisher on hand.

1 Relieve the fuel system pressure (see Section 2).

2 Disconnect the negative cable from the battery.

3 Disconnect all hoses, cables and connectors from the throttle body (see Section 16)

4 Remove the throttle body and air intake plenum as an assembly (see Section 18).

5 Cover the connection for the fuel high-pressure hose with a shop rag to absorb any spilled fuel (there's still residual pressure in the line, even after the fuel pressure has been relieved). Remove the fuel high-pressure hose attaching bolts (see illustration) and disconnect the hose. Discard the O-ring.

6 Loosen the hose clamp and disconnect the fuel return hose.

7 Detach the vacuum hose from the fuel pressure regulator and any other vacuum hoses in the way.

8 Pull up the retaining clip on each injector electrical connector and unplug the connector from the injector.

9 Remove the fuel rail mounting bolts and remove the fuel rail and the insulators. Pull gently up on the rail, using a rocking motion. Discard the insulators.

10 Refitting is the reverse of removal. Be sure to use new insulators for the fuel rail (see illustration) and fuel injectors. Also, use a new O-ring for the fuel high-pressure hose connection and coat the O-ring with petrol before refitting. Tighten the fuel high-pressure hose attaching bolts to the torque listed in this Chapter's Specifications.

20 Fuel injector(s) petrol engines - check, removal and refitting

Warning: Petrol is extremely flammable, so take extra precautions when you work on any part of the fuel system. Don't smoke or allow open flames or bare light bulbs near the work area, and don't work in a garage where a natural gas-type appliance (such as a water heater or clothes dryer) with a pilot light is present. If you spill any fuel on your skin, rinse it off immediately with soap and water. When you perform any kind of work on the fuel system, wear safety glasses and have a Class B type fire extinguisher on hand.

Check

Refer to illustration 20.2

1 With the engine running or cranking, listen to the sound from each injector with an automotive stethoscope and verify the injectors are all clicking the same. If you don't have a stethoscope, place the tip of a screw-

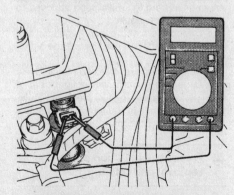

20.2 If the injector is malfunctioning, check the resistance across the terminals and compare your measurement to the resistance listed in this Chapters Specifications - if the indicated resistance is outside specifications, renew the injector

driver against the injectors and press your ear against the handle of the screwdriver. Also feel the operation of each injector with your finger. It should sound/feel smooth and uniform and its sound/feel should rise and fall with engine RPM. If an injector isn't operating, or sounds/feels erratic, check the injector connector and the wire harness connector. If the connectors are snug, check for voltage to the injector, using a special injector harness test light (available at most auto parts stores).

2 If there's voltage to the injector but it isn't operating, or if it sounds or feels erratic, check the injector's resistance (see illustration). Compare your measurement to the resistance listed in this Chapter's Specifications. If the indicated resistance is outside the specified range, renew the injector.

Removal and refitting

Refer to illustration 20.5

3 Remove the air intake plenum assembly (see Section 18) and the fuel rail assembly (see Section 19).

4 Place the fuel rail assembly on a clean work surface so the fuel injectors are accessible. To remove an injector from the fuel rail, gently pull it straight out. Twisting it slightly as you pull may help. Discard the old O-ring and grommet.

5 Refitting is the reverse of removal. Fit a new O-ring and grommet onto each injector (see illustration). Apply a light coat of fresh

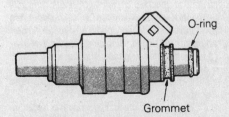

20.5 Make sure you fit a new grommet and O-ring at the correct location on each injector

4

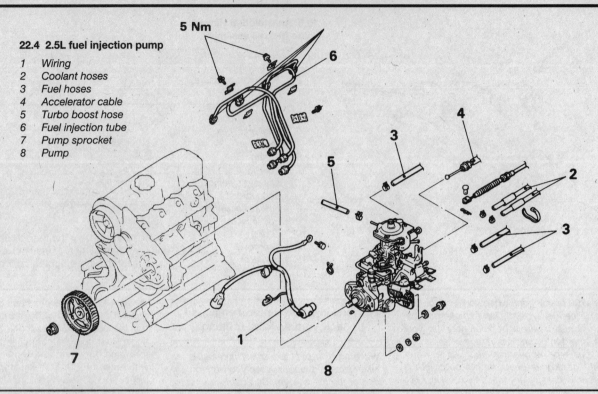

5 Nm

22.4 2.5L fuel injection pump

1　Wiring
2　Coolant hoses
3　Fuel hoses
4　Accelerator cable
5　Turbo boost hose
6　Fuel injection tube
7　Pump sprocket
8　Pump

petrol to the O-ring to facilitate refitting. To refit an injector into the fuel rail, push it straight into its bore in the fuel rail, gently twisting it to the left and right as you push. Once the injector is fully seated, try to rotate it back and forth. It should turn smoothly if it's properly fitted. If it doesn't, the O-ring may be pinched or jammed; remove the injector and check the O-ring. If it's okay, refit the injector; if the O-ring is damaged, renew it before refitting the injector.

6　Refit the fuel rail assembly with the injectors installed in the fuel rail (see Section 19). Refit the air intake plenum assembly (see Section 18).

21　Fuel pressure regulator (petrol models) - removal and refitting

Warning: *Petrol is extremely flammable, so take extra precautions when you work on any part of the fuel system. Don't smoke or allow open flames or bare light bulbs near the work area, and don't work in a garage where a natural gas-type appliance (such as a water heater or clothes dryer) with a pilot light is present. If you spill any fuel on your skin, rinse it off immediately with soap and water. When you perform any kind of work on the fuel system, wear safety glasses and have a Class B type fire extinguisher on hand.*

1　Relieve the system fuel pressure (see Section 2).
2　Disconnect the cable from the negative battery terminal.
3　Remove the air intake plenum (see Section 18).
4　Detach the vacuum line from the fuel pressure regulator **(see illustration 19.5).**

5　Loosen the hose clamp, slide it back on the fuel return hose and disconnect the fuel return hose from the metal tube attached to the fuel pressure regulator.
6　Unbolt the fuel pressure regulator and detach it from the fuel rail. Discard the old O-ring.
7　Refitting is the reverse of removal. Use a new O-ring and coat it with a light coat of fresh petrol. Tighten the fuel pressure regulator mounting bolts to the torque listed in this Chapter's Specifications.

22　Diesel fuel injection pump - removal and refitting

Warning: *Diesel fuel is flammable, so take extra precautions when you work on any part of the fuel system. See* **Warnings** *in Section 1.*
Caution: *Do not attempt to disassemble the injection pump. All repairs to the pump should be carried out by a dealer service department or a diesel engine specialist.*

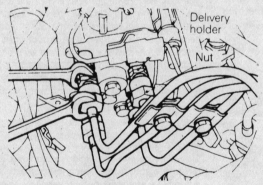

Delivery holder

Nut

22.5 Whenever loosening or tightening fuel line fittings, always use two spanners to avoid twisting the fuel lines

2.5L engine

Removal
Refer to illustrations 22.4 and 22.5
Caution: *Do not remove or handle the pump by the accelerator or the fast-idle levers. Do not attempt to remove either of these levers.*

1　Disconnect the negative battery cable. Position it so that it cannot contact the positive cable.
2　Disconnect the wiring harness from the pump.
3　Place a container or rags under the injection pump. Remove the intercooler if so equipped.
4　Disconnect both suction and discharge hoses from the pump **(see illustration)**. Plug both fittings to avoid contamination of the pump.
5　Disconnect and remove all of the injector tubes from the engine. Be certain to hold the injection pump valve holder with a spanner to keep it from rotating **(see illustration)**.
6　Disconnect the throttle cable from the pump arm (refer to Section 3). Disconnect the

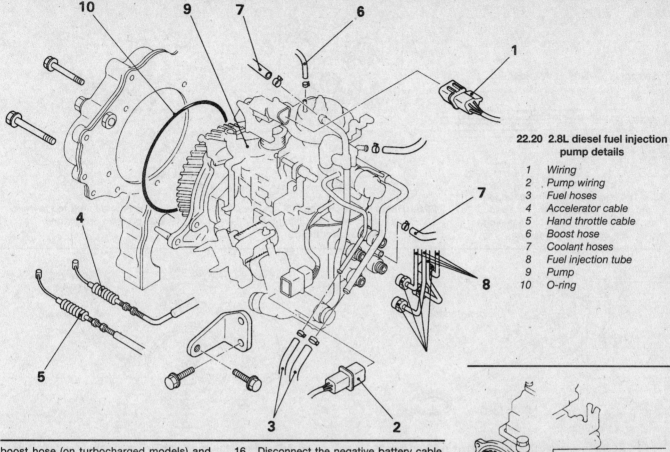

22.20 2.8L diesel fuel injection pump details

1 Wiring
2 Pump wiring
3 Fuel hoses
4 Accelerator cable
5 Hand throttle cable
6 Boost hose
7 Coolant hoses
8 Fuel injection tube
9 Pump
10 O-ring

boost hose (on turbocharged models) and the vacuum hoses.

7   Position the number one cylinder at TDC on the compression stroke (refer to Chapter 2).

8   Remove the timing belt upper cover (refer to Chapter 2).

9   Remove the nut and its washer from the injection pump sprocket. **Caution:** *Do not drop either part into the engine while removing them.*

10   Using a gear puller, remove the sprocket. Do not turn the engine after this procedure is completed.

11   Remove the mounting nuts and bolts and lift the pump from the engine.

Refitting

12   Renew the mounting O-ring.

13   Refitting is the reverse of removal. Make certain that all sprockets are correctly aligned with respective marks (refer to Chapter 2). To set the injection pump timing, refer to Section 23. Adjust the timing belt tension (refer to Chapter 2).

14   Tighten all fasteners to the torque listed in the Specifications in this Chapter.

15   Bleed the fuel system (refer to Chapter 1). Adjust the idle speed (refer to Chapter 1).

2.8L engine

Removal

Refer to illustrations 22.20 and 22.28

Caution: *Do not remove handle the pump by the accelerator or the fast-idle levers. Do not attempt to remove either of these levers.*

16   Disconnect the negative battery cable. Position it so that it cannot contact the positive cable.

17   Drain the engine coolant (refer to Chapter 1). Remove the intercooler, if so equipped.

18   Position the engine at TDC for number one cylinder on the compression stroke (refer to Section 3).

19   Clean the pump area of debris that could fall into the front cover when the pump is removed.

20   Disconnect the wiring harness from the pump **(see illustration)**.

21   Disconnect the water hoses and fuel hoses at the pump.

22   Disconnect the cables (refer to Section 8).

23   Disconnect the boost hose on turbocharged models.

24   Disconnect all of the fuel injection tubes. Be sure to hold the stationary part of the connection with a spanner to prevent it from rotating.

25   Remove the nut from the injection pump sprocket. Using a puller, remove the sprocket from the pump.

26   Remove the mounting fasteners and lift the pump from the engine.

Refitting

Refer to illustration 22.27

27   Refitting is the reverse of removal. The notch on the pump drive gear must align with the T mark for turbocharged vehicles or the N for non-turbocharged vehicles on the plate

22.27 When installing the 2.8L fuel pump, align the notch on the gear with the appropriate letter on the plate - T for turbocharged, N for non-turbocharged

(see illustration).

28   To set the injection pump timing, refer to Section 23.

29   Tighten all fasteners to the torque's listed in the Specifications in this Chapter. Be certain to hold the stationary parts of the connections with a spanner as you tighten them.

30   Bleed the fuel system (refer to Chapter 1). Adjust the idle speed (refer to Chapter 1).

23   Diesel fuel injection pump timing adjustment

Refer to illustrations 23.4, 23.5a, 23.5b, 23.5c and 23.6

Note: *This procedure involves special measuring instruments. If you do not have access to these special tools, take the vehicle to a properly equipped diesel specialist.*

4

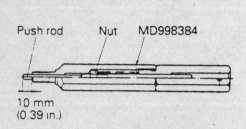

23.4 The special dial indicator adaptor must be adjusted so that the end protrudes 10 mm prior to beginning the checking procedure

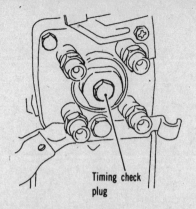

23.5a Remove this plug on 2.5L engines to gain access for installing the dial indicator fixture

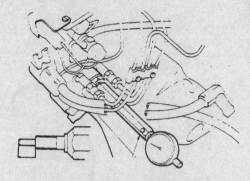

23.5b The fixture is refitted in the 2.5L pump in this manner

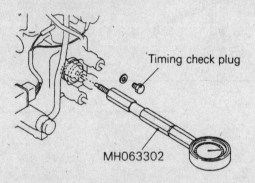

23.5c 2.8L engine injection pump fixture refitting details

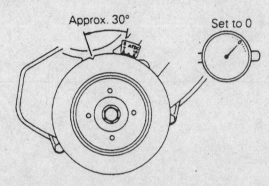

23.6 After setting the engine to TDC on number one cylinder on the compression stroke, back the crankshaft counter-clockwise 30-degrees to set the dial indicator to zero

1   Set the engine at TDC for number one cylinder on the compression stroke (refer to Chapter 2).
2   Loosen all of the fuel supply tubes at the discharge side of the injection pump. Be certain to hold the stationary parts of the connections with a spanner to prevent them from rotating.
3   Loosen the fasteners which secure the pump to the engine.
4   Obtain the required special tool (pre-stroke measuring adaptor MD998384 or its equivalent). Set the push rod so that it protrudes 10 mm from the end (see illustration).
5   Remove the timing check plug from the center of the injection pump (see illustrations). Attach the prestroke measuring tool and a dial indicator.
6   Rotate the engine so that the notch on the crankshaft pulley is at approximately thirty degrees before TDC (see illustration). Set the dial indicator to zero.
7   Rock the crankshaft back and forth and verify that the dial indicator needle does not move. If it does set the engine to thirty degrees before TDC more accurately.
8   Rotate the engine clockwise until the notch is at the position listed on the under-bonnet information decal or the owner's manual (each model uses a slightly different setting, however all are several degrees AFTER TDC). The dial indicator should read the value listed in the Specifications in this Chapter.

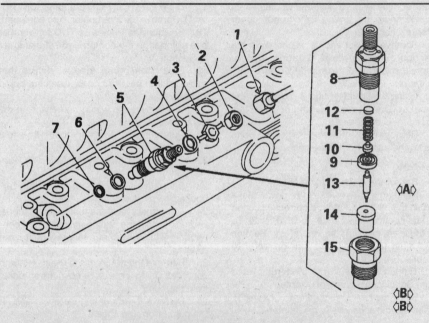

24.5 Typical diesel fuel injector details

1	Fuel tube	6	Nozzle holder	11	Spring
2	Nut	7	Gasket	12	Shim
3	Leak-off tube	8	Body	13	Needle valve
4	Gasket	9	Spacer	14	Tip
5	Nozzle assembly	10	Pushrod	15	Nut

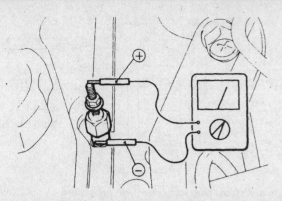

27.2 Connect an ohmmeter to check glow plug resistance

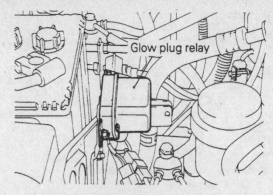

Glow plug relay

28.1 Typical glow plug relay location

9   If the reading is not within specifications, rotate the pump housing until it is correct. Tighten the fasteners and then re-check the reading.

10   Remove the dial indicator and the adaptor, then refit the plug, using a new gasket.

11   Tighten the injector tubes or the glow plugs to the torque listed in the Specifications in this Chapter.

24 Fuel injectors (diesel) - removal and refitting

Refer to illustration 24.5

Note: *Disassembly and testing of fuel injectors should be left to a shop with the proper equipment.*

1   Disconnect the negative battery cable. Position it so that it cannot contact the positive cable.

2   Remove any interfering components such as the air cleaner assembly, the intercooler, etc.

3   Disconnect the fuel return hose.

4   Disconnect the fuel return tube. Be certain to hold the stationary part of the connection with a spanner to prevent it from rotating while you loosen the nut.

5   Use a deep socket and a ratchet to remove the injectors from the cylinder head **(see illustration). Note:** *Remove the injector gaskets from the cylinder heads.*

6   Refitting is the reverse of removal. Tighten the injectors to the value listed in the Specifications in this Chapter.

25 Fuel cut solenoid - check and renewal

Check

1   Turn the ignition OFF.

2   Put a stethoscope to the fuel cut solenoid. If a stethoscope is not available, a long screwdriver can be used. Hold the tip against the solenoid and the handle against your ear.

3   Have an assistant turn the ignition ON. **Warning:** *Do not allow the engine to start while your body is near rotating components.*

4   Listen for a click as the ignition is energised. If no click is heard, disconnect the wiring harness from the solenoid and use test leads to apply earth and fused twelve volts. If no click is heard, renew the solenoid. If a click is heard, check the wiring circuit to the solenoid.

5   If the solenoid checks good, disconnect the wiring harness and use an ohmmeter to measure the resistance across he solenoid terminals. Compare your rearing to that listed ion the Specifications in this Chapter.

Renewal

6   Disconnect the negative battery cable. Position it so that it cannot contact the positive cable.

7   Disconnect the wiring from the solenoid.

8   Remove the fuel cut solenoid from the injection pump.

9   Refitting is the reverse of removal.

26 Preheat system - general information

To assist cold starting, diesel engines are equipped with a preheat system. This is comprised of a glow plug for each cylinder, a preheat control module, a coolant temperature sensor, a relay and a light on the instrument panel.

The glow plugs are small electrical heating elements, encapsulated in a metal or ceramic case with a probe at one end and an electrical connector at the other. Each cylinder has a glow plug threaded into it. When the glow plug is energized, the air and fuel passing over it is heated, allowing its optimum combustion temperature to be achieved more readily.

The duration of the preheating is governed by the preheat control unit which monitors the temperature of the engine via the coolant temperature sensor. It alters the preheating conditions to suit the engine temperature.

Preheating is triggered by the ignition key being turned ON. A dash-mounted lamp informs the driver that preheating is taking place. The lamp turns off when sufficient preheating has taken place to allow the engine

to start. The control unit will switch off the glow plug's power if the engine is not started within a short time to prevent battery drain and glow plug burn-out.

After the engine has been started, the glow plugs continue to operate for a period of time. This helps to improve fuel combustion while the engine is warming up. This results in quieter, smoother running and reduced exhaust emissions. Refer to Section 1 for a diagram of the preheat system.

27 Glow plugs - check and renewal

Check

Refer to illustration 27.2

1   Remove any interfering components such as the intercooler. Remove the glow plug electrical connection plate from all of the glow plugs.

2   Use an ohmmeter to check the resistance between the uppermost tip of the glow plug and the base (earth) **(see illustration).** Compare your readings to that listed in the Specifications in this Chapter.

3   Renew any that are not within specifications.

Renewal

4   With the glow plug plate removed, clean any debris from around the glow plugs. Compressed air works best, but a rag will suffice.

5   Unscrew the glow plugs from the cylinder head. Be careful to not drop anything into the holes in the cylinder head. Seal the holes with tape to prevent any accidents.

6   Fit new glow plugs as required. Tighten them to the value listed in the Specifications in this Chapter.

7   Refit the glow plug plate.

28 Glow plug relay - check and renewal

Check

Refer to illustrations 28.1, 28.2a and 28.2b

1   Disconnect the wiring from the relay **(see illustration).**

4

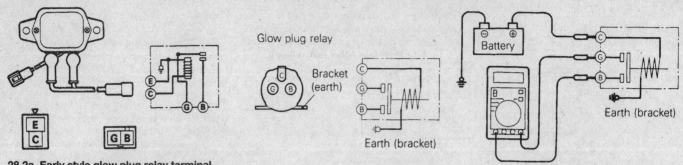

28.2a Early style glow plug relay terminal arrangement

28.2b Typical late style glow plug relay checking procedure

2   Use an ohmmeter to check the continuity between terminal C and terminal E (earth). If there is no terminal E, use the bracket for an earth connection **(see illustrations)**.

| 4 | 3 | ✕ | 2 | 1 |
| 9 | 8 | 7 | 6 | 5 |

29.4a Typical 2.5L diesel glow control unit harness-side connector as seen from the terminal side

Control unit inspection terminal	Inspection item	Inspection conditions			Standard value
1	Ignition switch (IG power supply)	Ignition switch	"OFF" → "ON"		Battery voltage
			"ON" → "OFF"		0 – 0.5V
3	Pre-heat display lamp	Ignition switch	"OFF" → "ON"		0 – 1V After approx. 6 seconds [when engine coolant temperature is 20°C (68°F)] 11 – 13V
4	Alternator L-terminal	Ignition switch	"OFF" → "ON"		1 – 4V
		Idle			More than 11V
5	Glow plug relay 1	Ignition switch	"OFF" → "ON"		9 – 12V After approx. 36 seconds [when engine coolant temperature is 20°C (68°F)] 0 – 0.5V
6	Ignition switch (ST power supply)	Ignition switch	"OFF" → "START"		More than 8V
8	Start display lamp	Ignition switch	After "OFF" → "ON" After approx. 6 seconds have passed [when engine coolant temperature is 20°C (68°F)]		0 – 1V After approx. 30 seconds [when engine coolant temperature is 20°C (68°F)] 11 – 13V
9	Engine coolant temperature sensor	Ignition switch "OFF" → "ON"	When engine coolant temperature is – 20°C (– 4°F)		4.3 – 4.5V
			When engine coolant temperature is 0°C (32°F)		3.7 – 3.9V
			When engine coolant temperature is 20°C (68°F)		2.8 – 3.0V
			When engine coolant temperature is 40°C (104°F)		1.9 – 2.1V
			When engine coolant temperature is 80°C (176°F)		0.5 – 0.7V

29.4b Use this chart if your glow plug control unit connector is as shown in illustration 29.4a. The connector must be connected while testing. Connect terminal 7 to earth

29.4c The connector must be connected while testing. Connect terminal 10 to earth

3   Compare your readings to that listed in the Specifications in this Chapter. There should be a small amount of resistance (neither an open circuit or a short).
4   Use fused test leads to connect terminal C to positive twelve volts at the battery. Connect terminal E to the negative battery terminal. If there is no terminal E, connect the negative battery terminal to the relay bracket.
5   Use an ohmmeter to check the continuity between terminals B and G on the relay.

With power applied to the relay, there should be continuity (near zero resistance). When the test leads are disconnected, there should not be continuity (near infinite resistance).
6   if the relay fails either test, renew it.

Renewal

7   With the wiring disconnected, remove the mounting bolts and lift the relay from the engine compartment.
8   Refitting is the reverse of removal.

29   Glow control unit - check and renewal

Check

Refer to illustrations 29.4a, 29.4b, 29.4c and 29.4d
1   The glow control unit itself cannot be checked, but the voltage inputs into it can be checked. Also, the wiring harness can be checked for continuity. By performing these checks, the glow control unit can be diagnosed by process of elimination.
2   If the engine has been having trouble starting, especially when cold, check for voltage at the glow plug plate with the ignition ON. Voltage at the glow plug plate should be very low with the ignition OFF, approximately 10 volts with the ignition ON, approximately 6 volts while cranking and approximately 12 volts after starting. After warm-up, voltage should go to zero again. If no voltage is present, check the glow plug fuse. If the fuse is good, check the glow plug control unit using the following procedure.
3   If all the tests are good, check the glow plug relay, the glow plugs, and the coolant temperature sensor.
4   Refer to the accompanying charts and check for voltage or continuity on the indicated terminals of the electrical connector. If all of the checks are as indicated, renew the control unit. **Note:** *Compare the electrical connector on your vehicle with those shown in the accompanying charts, then perform the checks shown in that chart.*

Renewal

5   Unplug the electrical connector, remove the bolts and detach the unit from the chassis. Refitting is the reverse of removal.

Glow control unit inspection terminal	Inspection item	Inspection condition		Standard value
13	Engine coolant temperature sensor (Engine coolant temperature detection)	Ignition switch "OFF" → "ON"	Engine coolant temperature: –20°C	4.3 – 4.5V
			Engine coolant temperature: 0°C	3.7 – 3.9V
			Engine coolant temperature: 20°C	2.8 – 3.0V
			Engine coolant temperature: 40°C	1.9 – 2.1V
			Engine coolant temperature: 80°C	0.5 – 0.7V
2	Ignition switch (power supply)	Ignition switch "OFF" → "START"		8V or more
7	Glow plug relay (glow time control)	Ignition switch "OFF" → "ON" Engine coolant temperature: 40° or less (Pre-glow function inspection)		9 – 12V ↓ 0 – 0.5V after approx. 12 sec. (when engine coolant temperature is 20°C)
3	Glow indicator lamp	Ignition switch "OFF" → "ON" Engine coolant temperature: 40° or less		0 – 1V ↓ 11 – 13V after approx. 4 sec. (when engine coolant temperature is 20°C)
6	Alternator charging signal ("L" terminal)	Ignition switch "OFF" → "ON"		1 – 4V
		Engine is idling		11V or more
10	Earth	—		—

29.4d Glow plug control unit continuity chart

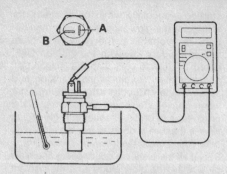

30.4 Ohmmeter connection details for checking the coolant temperature sensor

30 Coolant temperature sensor (diesel) - check and renewal

Check

Refer to illustration 30.4

1   Allow the engine to cool completely. Drain sufficient coolant from the radiator (refer to Chapter 1).
2   Remove the coolant temperature sensor from the engine.
3   Put the sensor into a pan of water on a stove. Place a thermometer into the pan to monitor the water temperature.
4   Connect an ohmmeter to terminal B and the body of the sensor **(see illustration)**. Observe the resistance and the water temperature as the pan is heated. Compare your readings to the values listed in the Specifications in this Chapter. If the values differ greatly, renew the sensor.

Renewal

5   Wait until the vehicle has completely cooled.
6   Place a container and rags under the sensor to catch coolant spillage. Alternatively, some coolant can be drained from the engine (refer to Chapter 1).
7   Apply sealer to the threads of the new sensor and place it close at hand.
8   Disconnect the wiring, then remove the sensor from the thermostat housing.
9   To minimize coolant loss, quickly fit the new sensor.
10   Tighten it to the torque listed in this Chapter's Specifications.

31 Turbocharger and intercooler - general information

Only the diesel engines are available with turbochargers.

The turbocharger and intercooler increase power by using an exhaust gas driven turbine to pressurise the fuel/air mixture before it enters the combustion chambers. The amount of boost (inlet manifold pressure) is controlled by the wastegate (exhaust bypass valve). The wastegate is operated by a spring-loaded actuator assembly which controls the maximum boost level by allowing some of the exhaust gas to bypass the turbine.

After the inlet fuel/air mixture has been compressed by the turbocharger, its temperature rises greatly. It is then passed through an intercooler on some models to cool and condense it, thus providing more power. An intercooler works exactly like a radiator, using ambient air passing through a heat exchanger to cool the inlet charge.

A boost pressure signal is also supplied to the fuel injection pump so that it can alter the injection timing based upon boost pressure.

32 Turbocharger - check

General checks

1   While it is a simple device, the turbocharger is also a precision component which can be severely damaged by an interrupter oil or coolant supply as well as loose or damaged ducts.
2   Due to the specialised equipment and techniques required, checking and diagnosis of suspected problems dealing with the turbocharger should be left to a dealer service department. The home mechanic can, however, check the connections and linkages for security, damage and other obvious problems. Also, the home mechanic can check items that control the turbocharger, such as the wastegate. Refer to the wastegate check later in this Section.
3   Because each turbocharger has its own distinctive whine, a change in the noise level can be a sign of potential problems.
4   a high pitched whistling sound is a symptom of an inlet air or exhaust gas leak.
5   If the unusual sound comes from the area of the exhaust turbine housing, the turbocharger can be removed and the turbine wheel inspected. **Caution:** *All checks must be made with the engine OFF and cool to the touch. The turbocharger must be stopped or personal injury could result. Operating the engine without all of the turbocharger ducts and filters connected is also dangerous and can result in damage to the turbine wheel blades.*
6   With the engine turned OFF and completely cool, reach inside the inlet compressor housing and turn the compressor/turbine wheel to make sure that it spins very freely. If it doesn't, it's possible that the cooling and lubricating oil has sludged or clogged from overheating. Push in on the wheel and check for binding. The inlet compressor/exhaust turbine wheels should rotate freely with no binding or rubbing on the housing. If they do, the bearings are worn out.
7   Check the exhaust system for cracks and loose connections.
8   Because the turbocharger wheels rotate at speeds up to 140,000 rpm, severe damage can result from the interruption of coolant or lubrication to the bearings. Check for leaks in the oil and coolant lines. Also check that the oil return (drain-back) line is completely clear. If it is clogged, it can cause severe oil loss through the turbocharger seals. Burned oil on the turbocharger housing is a sign of this. **Caution:** *It is important to allow the engine to idle for a period of time before turning it OFF if it has been operated at high speed immediately prior. If it is raced and then turned OFF, the turbocharger will be left spinning extremely fast when its lubrication stops. This can result in turbocharger failure. Additionally, if the engine has been rebuilt or had the oil removed for some other reason, be certain to prime the turbocharger with clean oil before starting the engine. Alternatively, you can operate the starter (while making certain that the engine will not start) until oil is supplied to the turbocharger.*
9   A boost level check can be made by connecting a pressure gauge to the wastegate hose using a tee fitting. Make certain that all connections are held securely with hose clamps, as substantial pressure is generated.
10   Carefully route the test hose and gauge through the engine compartment keeping clear of exhaust and rotating components. Run the gauge into the passenger area of the vehicle.
11   Have an assistant monitor the gauge while you make a full-throttle test in low gear. Maximum boost should occur at approximately 3,000 rpm. Compare your readings to those listed in the Specifications in this Chapter.
12   If the engine produces excessive boost, then there is a problem with the wastegate.
13   If there is not sufficient boost, the problem could be due to a turbocharger system leak, an engine problem, a clogged intercooler, a wastegate malfunction or a defect in the turbocharger itself. Also check for a restricted exhaust system

Wastegate check

14   Disconnect the small hose from the wastegate. Connect a manual testing vacuum/pressure pump to the wastegate.
15   Slowly apply pressure to the wastegate and observe when the actuator begins to move. **Caution:** *Do not apply more than 90 kPa or damage could result.*
16   Compare your reading with that listed in the Specifications in this Chapter. If the wastegate operates at too low a pressure, then the engine will not produce enough power. If the wastegate begins to open at too high a pressure, then engine damage could result.

33 Turbocharger - removal and refitting

2.5L engine

Removal

Refer to illustration 33.7

1   Disconnect the negative battery cable. Position it so that it cannot contact the positive cable.

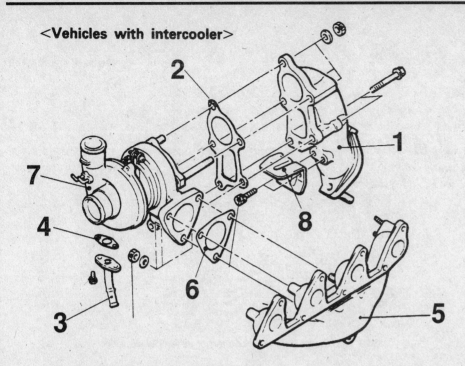

<Vehicles with intercooler>

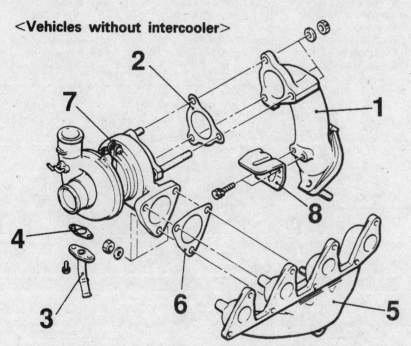

<Vehicles without intercooler>

33.7 2.5L diesel engine turbocharger assembly exploded view

1	Exhaust adaptor	5	Exhaust manifold
2	Gasket	6	Gasket
3	Oil return line	7	Turbocharger
4	Gasket	8	Heat shield

2   Drain the engine coolant (refer to Chapter 1).

3   Remove the air cleaner cover and the air inlet hose.

4   Remove the intercooler (refer to Section 34).

5   Remove the master cylinder heat shield if it interferes.

6   Disconnect the exhaust pipes.

7   Remove the interfering heat shields as you progress with this procedure **(see illustration)**.

8   Disconnect the boost hose and the wastegate.

9   On vehicles equipped with EGR, remove the EGR tube and the EGR valve.

10   Remove the inlet manifold (refer to Chapter 2).

11   Disconnect the coolant connections.

12   Disconnect the oil supply and return lines.

13   Remove the turbocharger.

14   Place rags in all open inlet and exhaust ports to prevent the entry of debris. Seal all coolant and oil lines as well.

Refitting

15   Refitting is the reverse of removal. Make certain that all oil and coolant lines and ports are perfectly clean prior to assembly. Pour fresh oil into the turbocharger oil housing before attaching the oil lines.

2.8L engine

Removal

Refer to illustration 33.22

16   Disconnect the negative battery cable. Position it so that it cannot contact the positive cable.

17   Drain the engine coolant (refer to Chapter 1).

18   Remove the air cleaner cover and the air inlet hose.

19   Remove the intercooler (refer to Section 34).

20   Remove the master cylinder heat shield if it interferes.

21   Disconnect the front exhaust pipe. Drain the engine oil (if fresh, it may be saved and reused).

22   Remove the interfering heat shields as you progress with this procedure **(see illustration)**.

23   Remove the two boost hoses.

24   On vehicles equipped with EGR, remove the EGR tube.

25   Disconnect the oil supply and return lines.

26   Disconnect the coolant connections.

27   Disconnect the oil supply and return lines.

28   Remove the turbocharger along with the exhaust adaptor.

29   With the assembly on the work bench, you can now disassemble the wastegate, the heat shields and then remove the exhaust adaptor from the turbocharger.

30   Place rags in all open inlet and exhaust ports to prevent the entry of debris. Seal all coolant and oil lines as well.

Refitting

31   Refitting is the reverse of removal. Make certain that all oil and coolant lines and ports are perfectly clean prior to assembly. Pour fresh oil into the turbocharger oil housing before attaching the oil lines.

34 Intercooler - removal and refitting

Refer to illustrations 34.1a and 34.1b

1   Disconnect the air temperature sensor wiring harness and the wiring to the intercooler fan motor **(see illustrations)**.

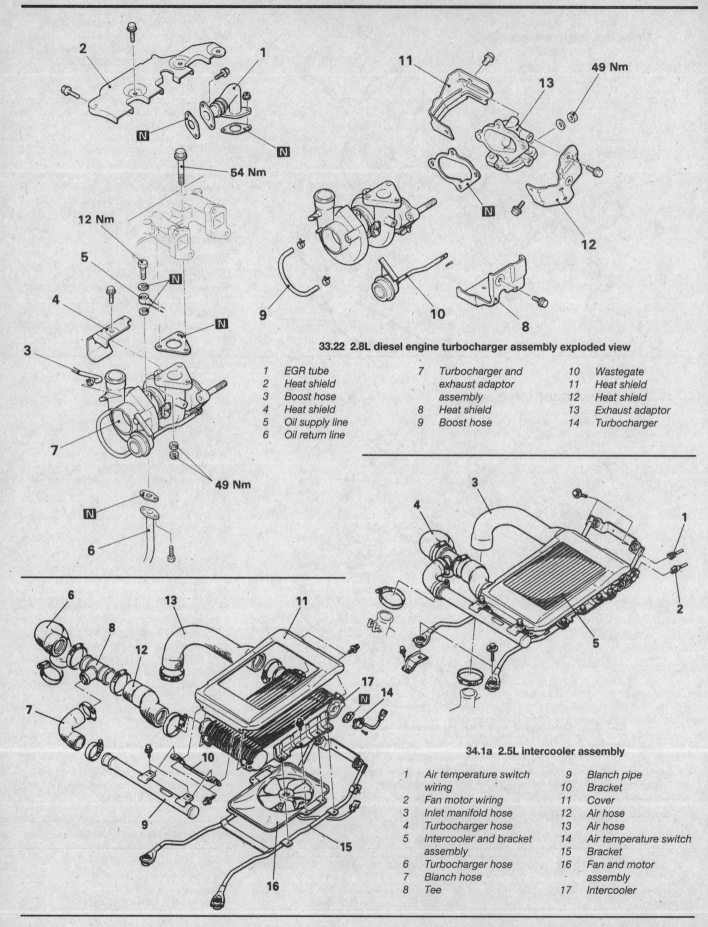

33.22 2.8L diesel engine turbocharger assembly exploded view

1	EGR tube	7	Turbocharger and	10	Wastegate
2	Heat shield		exhaust adaptor	11	Heat shield
3	Boost hose		assembly	12	Heat shield
4	Heat shield	8	Heat shield	13	Exhaust adaptor
5	Oil supply line	9	Boost hose	14	Turbocharger
6	Oil return line				

34.1a 2.5L intercooler assembly

1	Air temperature switch	9	Blanch pipe		
	wiring	10	Bracket		
2	Fan motor wiring	11	Cover		
3	Inlet manifold hose	12	Air hose		
4	Turbocharger hose	13	Air hose		
5	Intercooler and bracket	14	Air temperature switch		
	assembly	15	Bracket		
6	Turbocharger hose	16	Fan and motor		
7	Blanch hose		assembly		
8	Tee	17	Intercooler		

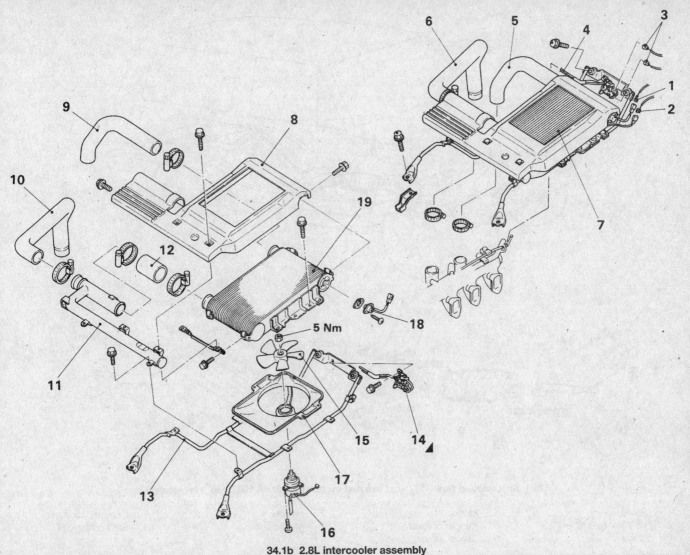

34.1b 2.8L intercooler assembly

1	Air temperature switch wiring	7	Intercooler and bracket assembly	14	Not used
2	Fan motor wiring	8	Cover	15	Fan
3	Not used	9	Air hose	16	Fan motor
4	Not used	10	Air hose	17	Fan shroud
5	Inlet manifold hose	11	Branch pipe	18	Air temperature switch
6	Turbocharger hose	12	Branch hose	19	Intercooler
		13	Bracket		

2   Disconnect the inlet and outlet air ducts at the turbocharger and inlet manifold.

3   Remove the intercooler along with the support assembly and the various ducts and set it on a clean work bench.

4   On 2.8L engines, remove the intercooler cover. Remove the hoses and tubes attached to the intercooler assembly. It is important to make marks on each component as it is removed to indicate where it was refitted and in what orientation.

5   Remove the air temperature sensor, the bracket and the fan and motor assembly. The intercooler can now be serviced or inspected.
Note: *If the inside of the intercooler has become partially clogged with sludge due to turbocharger wear, it can be cleaned at a radiator shop.*

6   Refitting is the reverse of removal.

35 Exhaust system servicing - general information

Refer to illustration 35.1
Warning: *Inspection and repair of exhaust system components should be done only with the engine and exhaust components completely cool. Also, when working under the vehicle, make sure it's securely supported on jackstands.*

1   The exhaust system **(see illustration)** consists of the exhaust manifold(s), the catalytic converter, the muffler, the tailpipe and all connecting pipes, brackets, hangers and clamps. The exhaust system is attached to the body with mounting brackets and rubber hangers. If any of the parts are improperly fit-

ted, excessive noise and vibration will be transmitted to the body.

2   Conduct regular inspections of the exhaust system to keep it safe and quiet. Look for any damaged or bent parts, open seams, holes, loose connections, excessive corrosion or other defects which could allow exhaust fumes to enter the vehicle. Deteriorated exhaust system components shouldn't be repaired; they should be renewed with new parts.

3   If the exhaust system components are extremely corroded or rusted together, welding equipment will probably be required to remove them. The convenient way to accomplish this is to have a muffler repair shop remove the corroded sections with a cutting torch. If, however, you want to save money by doing it yourself (and you don't have a

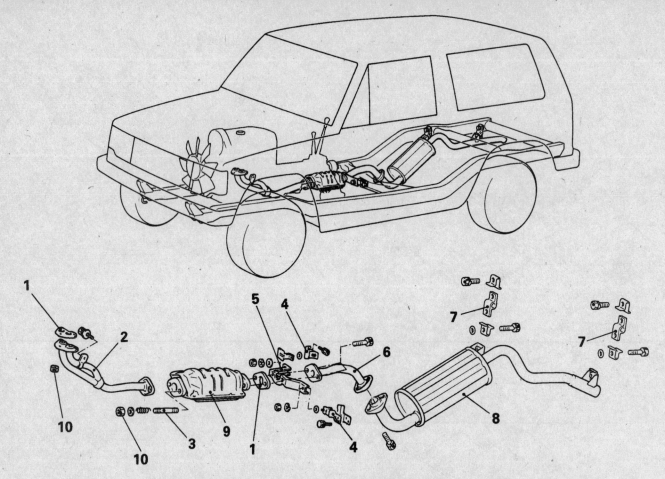

35.1 An exploded view of typical exhaust systems used on 1987 and later models

1	Gasket	4	Mount	7	Hanger	9	Catalytic converter
2	Front exhaust pipe	5	Hanger bracket	8	Main muffler	10	Self-locking nut
3	Spring	6	Centre exhaust pipe				

welding outfit with a cutting torch), simply cut off the old components with a hacksaw. If you have compressed air, special pneumatic cutting chisels can also be used. If you do decide to tackle the job at home, be sure to wear safety goggles to protect your eyes from metal chips and work gloves to protect your hands.

4   Here are some simple guidelines to follow when repairing the exhaust system:

a) Work from the back to the front when removing exhaust system components.
b) Apply penetrating oil to the component fasteners to make them easier to remove.
c) Use new gaskets, hangers and clamps when refitting exhaust system components.

d) Apply anti-seize compound to the threads of all exhaust system fasteners during reassembly.
e) Be sure to allow sufficient clearance between newly fitted parts and all points on the underbody to avoid overheating the floor pan and possibly damaging the interior carpet and insulation. Pay particularly close attention to the catalytic converter and heat shields.

Chapter 5
Engine electrical systems

Contents

5

Specifications

Distributor pick-up air gap (four-cylinder engines)

1983 models	Not adjustable
1984 and later	0.8 mm
Pick-up coil resistance	920 to 1,120 ohms

Ignition coil

Primary resistance
Four cylinder engine	1.1 to 1.3 ohms
3.0l V6 engine	0.72 to 0.88 ohms
3.5L V6 engine	0.69 to 0.85 ohms

Secondary resistance
Four cylinder engine
1985 and earlier	7.10 to 9.60 K-ohms
1986	11.6 to 15.8 K-ohms
1987 and later	14.88 to 20.12 K-ohms
3.0L V6 engine	12.1 ohm
3.5L V6 engine	15.3 to 2.0 K-ohms
Ballast resistor resistance	1.2 to 1.5 ohms

1 General information

The engine electrical systems include all ignition, charging and starting components. Because of their engine-related functions, these components are discussed separately from chassis electrical devices such as the lights, the instruments, etc. (which are included in Chapter 12).

Always observe the following precautions when working on the electrical systems:

a) *Be extremely careful when servicing engine electrical components. They are easily damaged if checked, connected or handled improperly.*
b) *Never leave the ignition switch on for long periods of time with the engine off.*
c) *Don't disconnect the battery cables while the engine is running.*
d) *Maintain correct polarity when connecting a battery cable from another vehicle during jump starting.*
e) *Always disconnect the negative cable first and hook it up last or the battery may be shorted by the tool being used to loosen the cable clamps.*

It's also a good idea to review the safety-related information regarding the engine electrical systems located in the *Safety first!* section near the front of this manual before beginning any operation included in this Chapter.

2 Battery - emergency jump starting

Refer to the *Booster battery (jump) starting* procedure at the front of this manual.

3 Battery - removal and refitting

Refer to illustration 3.1

1 **Caution:** *Always disconnect the negative cable first and hook it up last or the battery may be shorted by the tool being used to loosen the cable clamps. Disconnect both cables from the battery terminals* **(see illustration).**
2 Remove the battery hold-down clamp.
3 Lift out the battery. Be careful - it's heavy.
4 While the battery is out, inspect the carrier (tray) for corrosion (see Chapter 1).
5 If you are renewing the battery, make sure that you get one that's identical, with the same dimensions, amperage rating, cold cranking rating, etc.
6 Refitting is the reverse of removal.

4 Battery cables - check and renewal

1 Periodically inspect the entire length of each battery cable for damage, cracked or

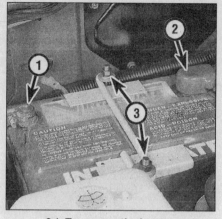

3.1 To remove the battery

1 *Detach the cable from the negative terminal*
2 *Detach the cable from the positive terminal*
3 *Remove the nuts and detach the hold-down clamp*

burned insulation and corrosion. Poor battery cable connections can cause starting problems and decreased engine performance.
2 Check the cable-to-terminal connections at the ends of the cables for cracks, loose wire strands and corrosion. The presence of white, fluffy deposits under the insulation at the cable terminal connection is a sign that the cable is corroded and should be renewed. Check the terminals for distortion, missing mounting bolts and corrosion.
3 When removing the cables, always disconnect the negative cable first and hook it up last or the battery may be shorted by the tool used to loosen the cable clamps. Even if only the positive cable is being renewed, be sure to disconnect the negative cable from the battery first (see Chapter 1 for further information regarding battery cable removal).
4 Disconnect the old cables from the battery, then trace each of them to their opposite ends and detach them from the starter solenoid and earth terminals. Note the routing of each cable to ensure correct refitting.
5 If you are renewing either one or both of the cables, take them with you when buying new cables. It is vitally important that you renew the cables with identical parts. Cables have characteristics that make them easy to identify: positive cables are usually red, larger in cross section and have a larger diameter battery post clamp; earth cables are usually black, smaller in cross-section and have a slightly smaller diameter clamp for the negative post.
6 Clean the threads of the solenoid or earth connection with a wire brush to remove rust and corrosion. Apply a light coat of battery terminal corrosion inhibitor, or petroleum jelly, to the threads to prevent future corrosion.
7 Attach the cable to the solenoid or earth connection and tighten the mounting nut/bolt securely.

8 Before connecting a new cable to the battery, make sure that it reaches the battery post without having to be stretched.
9 Connect the positive cable first, followed by the negative cable.

5 Ignition system - general information and precautions

When working on the ignition system, take the following precautions:

a) *Do not keep the ignition switch on for more than 10 seconds if the engine will not start.*
b) *Always connect a tachometer in accordance with the manufacturer's instructions. Some tachometers may be incompatible with this ignition system. Consult a dealer service department before buying a tachometer for use with this vehicle.*
c) *Never allow the primary terminals of the ignition coil to become earthed.*
d) *Do not disconnect the battery when the engine is running.*

The ignition system includes the ignition switch, the battery, the coil, the primary (low voltage) and secondary (high voltage) wiring circuits, the distributor and the spark plugs. On later distributors not using a vacuum or centrifugal advance, the ignition timing is controlled by the Electronic Control Unit (ECU).

A distributorless ignition system (DIS) is used on 3.5L V6 engines. This system consists of the crankshaft position sensor, camshaft position sensor, ignition power transistor and separate ignition coils mounted on each spark plug.

6 Ignition system - check

Refer to illustration 6.2
Warning: *Because of the very high voltage generated by the ignition system, extreme care should be taken when this check is performed.*
1 If the engine turns over but won't start, disconnect the spark plug wire from any spark plug and attach it to a calibrated ignition tester (available at most auto parts stores). **Note:** *Be sure to purchase the correct tester for either an electronic distributor or points distributor, depending which system the vehicle is equipped with.*
2 Connect the clip on the tester to a bolt or metal bracket on the engine **(see illustration).** If you're unable to obtain a calibrated ignition tester, remove the wire from one of the spark plugs and, using an insulated tool, hold the end of the wire about 6.4 mm from a good earthing point.
3 Crank the engine and watch the end of the tester or spark plug wire to see if bright blue, well-defined sparks occur. If you're not using a calibrated tester, have an assistant crank the engine for you. **Warning:** *Keep*

6.2 To use a calibrated ignition tester (available at most auto parts stores), simply disconnect a spark plug wire, attach the wire to the tester and clip the tester to a good earthing point - if there is enough power to fire the plug, sparks will be clearly visible between the electrode tip and the tester body as the engine is turned over

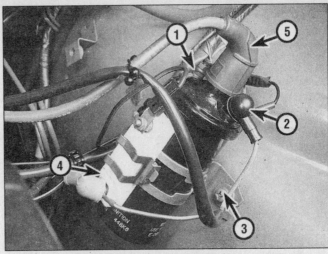

7.2 To remove a typical coil from the engine compartment, disconnect the primary wires and the high-voltage lead, then unbolt the bracket

1 Negative primary wire
2 Positive primary wire
3 Bracket
4 Ballast resistor
5 High-voltage lead

7.4a To check the coil primary resistance on an earlier type coil, touch the leads of an ohmmeter to the positive and negative primary terminals (arrows) and compare your reading with the coil primary resistance listed in this Chapter's specifications

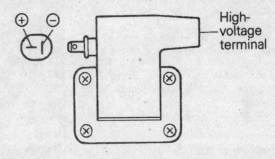

7.4b To check the coil primary resistance on a later type coil, touch the leads of an ohmmeter to the positive and negative primary terminals and compare your reading with the coil primary resistance listed in this Chapter's Specifications

clear of drivebelts and other moving engine components that could injure you.

4 If sparks occur, sufficient voltage is reaching the plug to fire it (repeat the check at the remaining plug wires to verify the wires, distributor cap, rotor and coil are not defective. However, the plugs themselves may be fouled, so remove them and check them as described in Chapter 1.

5 If no sparks or intermittent sparks occur, remove the distributor cap and check the cap and rotor as described in Chapter 1. If moisture is present, dry out the cap and rotor, then refit the cap.

6 If there is still no spark, detach the coil secondary wire from the distributor cap and hook it up to the tester (reattach the plug wire to the spark plug), then repeat the spark check. Again, if you don't have a tester, hold the end of the wire about 6 mm from a good earthing point. If sparks occur now, the distributor cap, rotor or plug wire(s) may be defective.

7 If no sparks occur, check the wire connections at the coil to make sure they're clean and tight. Check for voltage to the coil. Make any necessary repairs, then repeat the check again.

8 If there's still no spark, the coil-to-cap wire may be bad (check the resistance with an ohmmeter - it should be 7000 ohms per 30 cm or less). If a known good wire doesn't make any difference in the test results, the ignition coil, module or pick-up coil may be defective.

7 Ignition coil and ballast resistor - check and renewal

Ignition coil

Refer to illustrations 7.2, 7.4a, 7.4b, 7.5a and 7.5b

1 Detach the cable from the negative bat-

tery terminal.

2 Mark the wires and terminals with pieces of numbered tape, then remove the primary wires and the high-voltage lead from the coil (see illustration). Disconnect the coil mounting bracket, remove the coil/bracket assembly, clean the outer case and check it for cracks and other damage. The ignition coils used DIS (direct ignition system) models are mounted directly on each spark plug and held in place by a bolt. The checking procedure is the same as for single ignition coils.

3 Clean the coil primary terminals and check the coil tower terminal for corrosion. Clean it with a wire brush if any corrosion is found.

4 Check the coil primary resistance by attaching the leads of an ohmmeter to the positive and negative primary terminals (see illustrations). Compare your readings to the primary resistance listed in this Chapter's Specifications.

5 Check the coil secondary resistance by

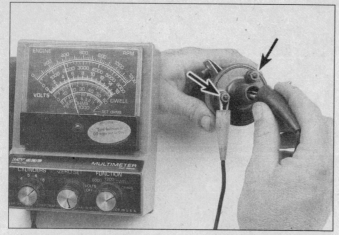

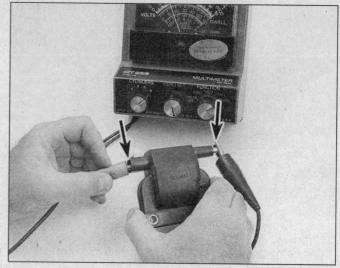

7.5a To check the coil secondary resistance on an earlier type coil, touch one lead of the ohmmeter to one of the primary terminals and the other lead to the high-tension terminal (arrows), then compare your reading to the coil secondary resistance listed in this Chapter's Specifications

7.5b Checking the coil secondary resistance on a later-type coil

hooking one of the ohmmeter leads to one of the primary terminals and the other ohmmeter lead to the large centre terminal **(see illustrations)**. Compare your readings to the secondary resistance listed in this Chapter's Specifications.

6   If the measured resistances are not as specified, the coil is probably defective and should be renewed.

7   For proper ignition system operation, all coil terminals and wire leads must be kept clean and dry.

8   Refit the coil in the vehicle and hook up the wires.

Ballast resistor

9   Some earlier models use a ballast resistor **(see illustration 7.2)** to protect the coil from excessive voltage during low-speed operation.

10   To check the ballast resistor, detach it from the coil or firewall, unplug the leads, touch the probes of an ohmmeter to the terminals of the resistor and compare your readings to the resistance listed in this Chapter's Specifications. If the resistance is not as specified, renew the resistor.

8   Distributor - removal and refitting

Removal

Refer to illustrations 8.6a and 8.6b

1   Detach the cable from the negative battery terminal.

2   Unplug the coil high-voltage lead from the distributor cap.

3   Detach the vacuum hose(s) from the advance unit (if equipped).

4   Look for a raised "1" on the distributor cap. This marks the location for the number one cylinder spark plug wire terminal. If the cap does not have a mark for the number one terminal, locate the number one spark plug

8.6a Before removing the distributor, paint or scribe an alignment mark on the edge of the distributor base directly beneath the rotor tip - DO NOT use a lead pencil

8.6b Also paint an alignment mark on the engine and the distributor base to ensure the correct timing after the distributor is fitted

and trace the wire back to the terminal on the cap.

5   Remove the distributor cap (see Chapter 1) and turn the engine over until the rotor is pointing toward the number one spark plug terminal (see the locating TDC procedure in Chapter 2).

6   Make a mark on the edge of the distributor base directly below the rotor tip and in line with it **(see illustration)**. Also, mark the distributor base and the engine block to ensure that the distributor is fitted correctly **(see illustration)**.

7   Remove the distributor hold-down nut and washer, then pull the distributor straight out to remove it. **Caution:** *DO NOT turn the crankshaft while the distributor is out of the engine, or the alignment marks will be useless.*

8   Detach the primary wiring from the distributor.

Refitting

Note: *If the crankshaft has been moved while the distributor is out, the number one piston must be repositioned at TDC. This can be done by feeling for compression pressure at the number one plug hole as the crankshaft is turned. Once compression is felt, align the TDC marks on the drivebelt pulley and the timing cover.*

9   Insert the distributor into the engine in exactly the same relationship to the block that it was in when removed.

10   To mesh the helical gears on the camshaft and the distributor, it may be necessary to turn the rotor slightly. Recheck the alignment marks between the distributor base and the block to verify that the distributor is in the same position it was in before removal. Also check the rotor to see if it's aligned with the mark you made on the edge of the distributor base.

11   Loosely refit the nut.

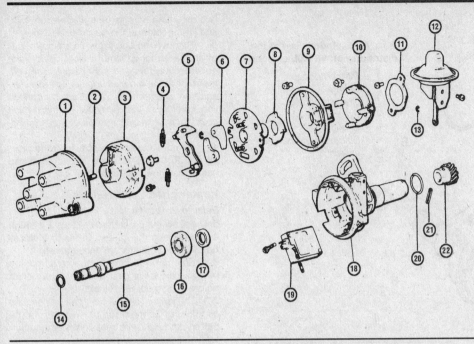

9.7a An exploded view of the distributor used on earlier four-cylinder models

1   Cap
2   Contact carbon
3   Rotor assembly
4   Centrifugal advance spring
5   Centrifugal advance plate
6   Centrifugal advance weight
7   Centrifugal advance base
8   Reluctor
9   Pick-up coil
10 Breaker plate
11 Plate
12 Vacuum control unit
13 E-ring
14 Washer
15 Shaft
16 Ball bearing
17 Oil seal
18 Housing
19 Oil seal
20 O-ring
21 Spring pin
22 Drive gear

9.7b An exploded view of the distributor on later four-cylinder models

1   Breather
2   Cap
3   Contact carbon
4   Rotor
5   Cable assembly
6   Earthing point wire
7   Igniter
8   Dowel pin
9   Signal rotor
10 Advance plate
11 Vacuum advance unit
    (dual-diaphragm type)
12 Vacuum advance unit
    (single-diaphragm type)
13 Rotor shaft
14 Spring retainers
15 Centrifugal advance springs
16 Centrifugal advance weights
17 Distributor shaft
18 Oil seal
19 Packing
20 Housing
21 O-ring
22 Washer
23 Driven gear
24 Pin

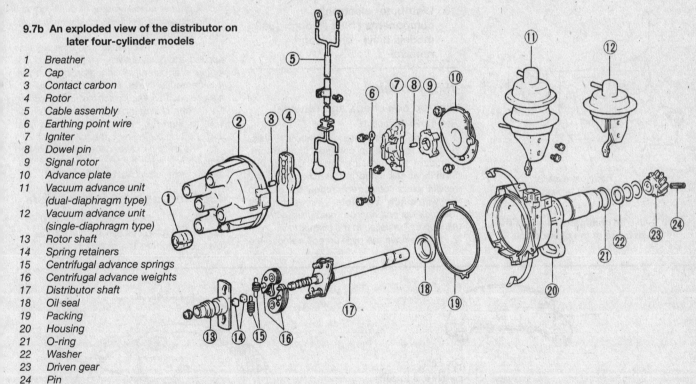

5

12   Reconnect the electrical leads.
13   Refit the distributor cap.
14   Reattach the vacuum line(s) to the advance unit (if equipped).
15   Reattach the spark plug wires to the plugs (if removed).
16   Connect the cable to the negative terminal of the battery.
17   Check the ignition timing (see Chapter 1) and tighten the distributor hold-down nut securely.

9   Centrifugal advance assembly - check and renewal

Refer to illustrations 9.7a, 9.7b and 9.7c
1   Detach the vacuum line(s) from vacuum advance unit on the distributor and plug them.
2   Connect a timing light according to it's manufacturer's instructions.
3   Start the engine.

4   While watching the timing marks with the use of the timing light, raise the engine speed while watching the timing marks advance.
5   The timing should advance smoothly.
6   If the timing does not advance smoothly, check the advance weights, springs and plate for damage or binding.
7   Renew parts as needed **(see illustrations)**.

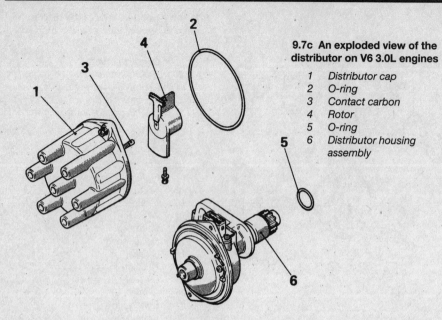

9.7c An exploded view of the distributor on V6 3.0L engines

1   Distributor cap
2   O-ring
3   Contact carbon
4   Rotor
5   O-ring
6   Distributor housing assembly

two mounting screws **(see illustration 9.7a)** and lift the rotor off the governor assembly.
3   Remove the bolt from the shaft and pull off the governor assembly. **Note:** *Before the governor weights and springs are removed, make marks on the pins and springs for reference on assembly. Also, handle the springs very carefully to avoid any deformation which could cause changes in the advance characteristics.*
4   Remove the screws attaching the pick-up coil to the distributor. The coil and cap gasket can now be lifted out.

Igniter check and renewal

Refer to illustration 10.7

5   Follow the procedure in Steps 2 through 4 and remove the igniter. **Refer to illustration 9.7a** if problems are encountered.
6   Be sure to mark the relationship between the drive gear and distributor shaft before driving out the roll pin.
7   The igniter (control unit) can be checked as follows. Connect jumper wires from the battery and a 12-volt test light to the igniter terminals **(see illustration)**.
8   Connect an ohmmeter or small dry cell to the remaining terminals as shown (this will apply a small signal to the igniter).
9   If the test light glows when the signal is applied and goes out when it is removed, the igniter is apparently working properly. If not, it is defective. **Note:** *Even if the test results are as specified, the igniter may be defective.*
10   When reassembling the distributor, be sure to align the mating marks on the gear and shaft before refitting the roll pin.
11   The air gap between the signal rotor and pick-up coil must be adjusted after the distributor is reassembled (see Section 11).

1984 through 1989 Mitsubishi type

12   The pick-up coil can be checked as follows. Disconnect the electrical connectors

---

10   Distributor electronic components (1983 through 1989 models only) - check and renewal

1983 models

Pick-up coil check and renewal

Refer to illustration 10.1

1   Using an ohmmeter, measure the resistance of the pick-up coil **(see illustration)**. Compare the measured resistance to the Specifications listed in this Chapter. If the resistance is not correct, renew the pick-up coil with a new unit. **Note:** *The resistance of the pick-up coil can be measured with the pick-up coil installed in the distributor.*
2   To remove the pick-up coil, remove the

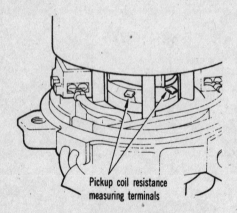

Pickup coil resistance measuring terminals

10.1 Use an ohmmeter to check the resistance of the pick-up coil

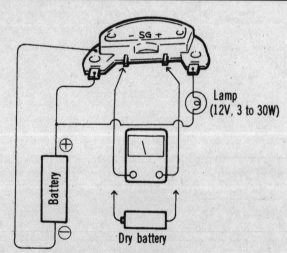

10.7 Set-up for checking the igniter used on earlier model four-cylinder distributors

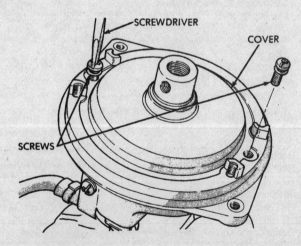

SCREWDRIVER

COVER

SCREWS

10.18 To get at the photo-optic sensing unit on a 3.0L distributor, remove these two screws (arrows) and this protective cover

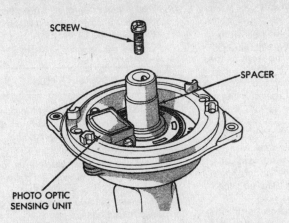

10.19 Remove the screw (arrow) from the spacer and remove the spacer

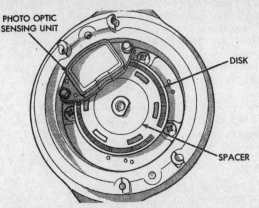

10.20a Carefully remove the upper disk spacer, the disk and the lower disk spacer (underneath the disk, not visible in this illustration)

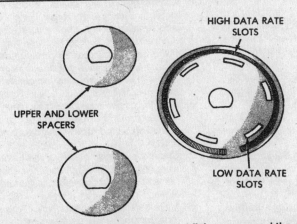

10.20b Note how the upper and lower disk spacers and the disk itself are keyed to prevent incorrect reassembly

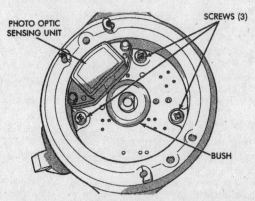

10.22 Remove the bush (arrow) from the photo-optic sensing unit, remove these three screws (arrows) and remove the photo-optic sensing unit

5

from the coil. Connect an ohmmeter to the electrical terminals and check the resistance.

13 The resistance should be within the range listed in this Chapter's Specifications. If the test results are not within this range, renew the pick-up coil with a new unit.

14 To remove the pick-up coil, follow the procedure in Steps 3 through 6, but note that later model distributors differ in certain details. **Refer to illustration 9.7b** if problems are encountered.

15 The air gap between the signal rotor and pick-up coil must be adjusted after the distributor is reassembled (see Section 11).

Photo-optic sensing unit (3.0L V6 engine)

Refer to illustrations 10.18, 10.19, 10.20a, 10.20b and 10.22

16 Remove the distributor (see Section 8).
17 Remove the rotor (see Chapter 1).
18 Remove the protective cover from the distributor housing **(see illustration)**.
19 Remove the screw from the spacer **(see illustration)** and remove the spacer.
20 Carefully remove the upper disk spacer, the disk and the lower disk spacer **(see illustration)**. **Note:** *The disk and spacers are*

keyed to ensure proper reassembly **(see illustration)**.

21 Check the disk for warpage, cracks or damaged slots. If any damage is evident, renew the disk.

22 Remove the bush from the photo-optic sensing unit, remove the three screws from the sensing unit **(see illustration)** and remove the sensing unit.

23 Reassembly is the reverse of disassembly.

24 Refit the distributor (see Section 8) and refit the rotor and cap (see Chapter 1).

11 Distributor pick-up air gap - check and adjustment

Refer to illustration 11.2
Note: This procedure does not apply to V6 engines.

1 Anytime you disturb the pick-up air gap in the distributor it must be properly adjusted.
2 Loosen the pick-up mounting screws. Place a feeler gauge of the thickness listed in this Chapter's Specifications between one of the projections on the signal rotor and the pick-up **(see illustration)**.

11.2 To adjust the air gap between the pick-up and the signal rotor, loosen the pick-up mounting screws, insert a feeler gauge of the specified thickness between the pick-up and one of the signal rotor projections, push the pick-up against the gauge and tighten the mounting screws

3 Gently push the pick-up toward the signal rotor until it's a snug - not tight - fit against the feeler gauge.
4 Tighten the pick-up mounting screws.
5 Check the adjustment by noting the

amount of drag on the feeler gauge when you pull it out of the gap between the signal rotor and the pick-up. You should feel a slight amount of drag. If you feel excessive drag on the gauge, the gap is probably too small. If you don't feel any drag on the gauge when you pull it out, the air gap is too large.

12 Vacuum advance unit - check and renewal

Check

1   Remove the vacuum line from the vacuum advance unit and plug the line. If there are two lines, disconnect and plug the outer (furthest from the distributor) line.
2   Connect a timing light to the vehicle.
3   Attach a vacuum pump to the advance unit.
4   With the engine running, gradually apply vacuum to the advance unit while watching the timing marks with the timing light.
5   The timing should gradually advance. If it doesn't advance, but the unit holds vacuum, the advance plate in the distributor is binding. If it doesn't advance, and the unit does not hold vacuum, renew the unit.

Renewal

Refer to illustrations 12.7 and 12.8

6   Remove the distributor cap and rotor (see Chapter 1).
7   Remove the vacuum unit mounting screws **(see illustration)**.
8   Remove the vacuum unit link from the pin on the breaker base, then detach the vacuum unit **(see illustration)**.
9   Refitting is the reverse of removal.

13 Charging system - general information and precautions

The charging system includes the alternator, with an integral voltage regulator, the battery, the fusible link(s) and wiring between all the components. The charging system supplies electrical power for the ignition system, the lights, the radio, etc. The alternator is driven by a drivebelt at the front of the engine.

The purpose of the voltage regulator is to limit the alternator's voltage to a preset value. This prevents power surges, circuit overloads, etc., during peak voltage output.

The fusible link can be either a short length of insulated wire integral with the engine compartment wiring harness or a fuse-like device fitted in the underbonnet electrical panel. See Chapter 12 for additional information regarding fusible links.

The charging system doesn't ordinarily require periodic maintenance. However, the drivebelt, battery and wires and connections should be inspected at the intervals outlined in Chapter 1.

The dashboard warning light should come on when the ignition key is turned to Start, then go off immediately. If it remains on, there is a malfunction in the charging system (see Section 14).

Be very careful when making electrical circuit connections to a vehicle equipped with an alternator and note the following:

a) When reconnecting wires to the alternator from the battery, be sure to note the polarity.
b) Before using arc welding equipment to repair any part of the vehicle, disconnect the wires from the alternator and the battery terminals.
c) Never start the engine with a battery charger connected.
d) Always disconnect both battery leads before using a battery charger.
e) The alternator is turned by an engine drivebelt which could cause serious injury if your hands, hair or clothes become entangled in it with the engine running.
f) Because the alternator is connected directly to the battery, it could arc or cause a fire if overloaded or shorted out.

g) Wrap a plastic bag over the alternator and secure it with rubberbands before steam cleaning the engine.

14 Charging system - check

1   If a malfunction occurs in the charging circuit, don't automatically assume that the alternator is causing the problem. First check the following items:

a) Check the drivebelt tension and condition (Chapter 1). Renew it if it's worn or deteriorated.
b) Make sure the alternator mounting and adjustment bolts are tight.
c) Inspect the alternator wiring harness and the connectors at the alternator. They must be in good condition and tight.
d) Check the fusible link(s). If burned, determine the cause, repair the circuit and renew the link (the vehicle won't start and/or the accessories won't work if the fusible link blows). Sometimes a fusible link may look good, but still be bad. If in doubt, remove it and check for continuity.
e) Start the engine and check the alternator for abnormal noises (a shrieking or squealing sound indicates a bad bearing).
f) Check the specific gravity of the battery electrolyte. If it's low, charge the battery (doesn't apply to maintenance free batteries).
g) Make sure the battery is fully charged (one bad cell in a battery can cause overcharging by the alternator).
h) Disconnect the battery cables (negative first, then positive). Inspect the battery posts and the cable clamps for corrosion. Clean them thoroughly if necessary (see Chapter 1). Reconnect the cable to the positive terminal.
i) With the key off, connect a test light between the negative battery post and the disconnected negative cable clamp.
   1) If the test light does not come on, reattach the clamp and proceed to the next step.
   2) If the test light comes on, there is a short (drain) in the electrical system of the vehicle. The short must be repaired before the charging system can be checked.
   3) Disconnect the alternator wiring harness.
      (a) If the light goes out, the alternator is bad.
      (b) If the light stays on, pull each fuse until the light goes out (this will tell you which component is shorted).

2   Using a voltmeter, check the battery voltage with the engine off. If should be approximately 12-volts.
3   Start the engine and check the battery voltage again. It should now be approximately 14-to-15 volts.

12.7 To detach the vacuum unit from the distributor, remove the two screws (arrows) . . .

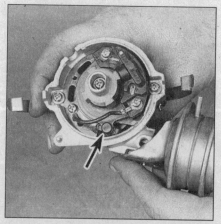

12.8 . . . then tilt it down, detach it from the pin (arrow) on the breaker base and pull it out

15.3 Loosen the adjustment bolt (arrow) and the pivot bolts to remove the drivebelt from the alternator pulley

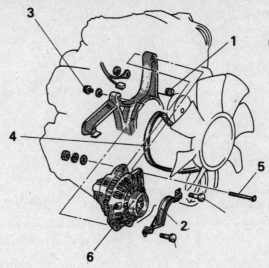

15.4a An exploded view of the mounting hardware for a typical V6 alternator refitting

1 Alternator adjustment bolt
2 Alternator cover
3 Alternator brace bolt
4 Alternator drive belt
5 Alternator support bolt
6 Alternator

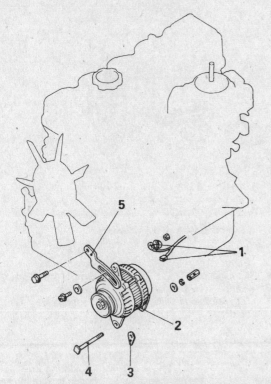

15.4b An exploded view of the mounting hardware for a typical alternator refitting on a four-cylinder engine without air conditioning

1	Electrical connector	4	Alternator support
2	Alternator		bolt
3	Shim	5	Bracket

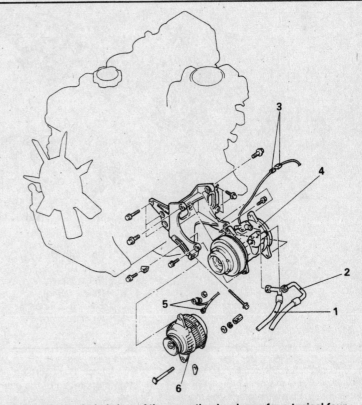

15.4c An exploded view of the mounting hardware for a typical four-cylinder engine alternator refitting with air conditioning

1	Compressor high pressure hose	4	Compressor
2	Compressor low pressure hose	5	Alternator electrical connector
3	Compressor electrical connector	6	Alternator

4 Turn on the headlights. The voltage should drop, and then come back up, if the charging system is working properly.

5 If the voltage reading is more than the specified charging voltage, renew the voltage regulator (refer to Section 16). If the voltage is less, the alternator diode(s), stator or rectifier may be bad or the voltage regulator may be malfunctioning.

15 Alternator - removal and refitting

Refer to illustrations 15.3, 15.4a, 15.4b and 15.4c

1 Detach the cable from the negative terminal of the battery.

2 Detach the electrical connector(s) from

the alternator. Be sure to label each wire to avoid confusion during refitting.

3 Loosen the alternator adjustment and pivot bolts and detach the drivebelt **(see illustration)**.

4 Remove the adjustment and pivot bolts and separate the alternator from the engine **(see illustrations)**.

5 If you're renewing the alternator, take

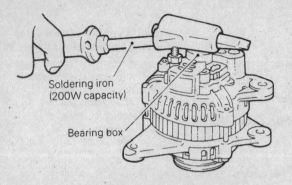

16.5a Heating the rear bearing box of the alternator will make splitting the alternator easier

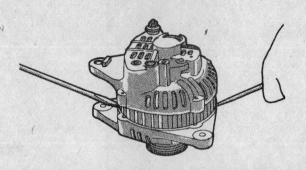

16.5b Use two screwdrivers to split the alternator

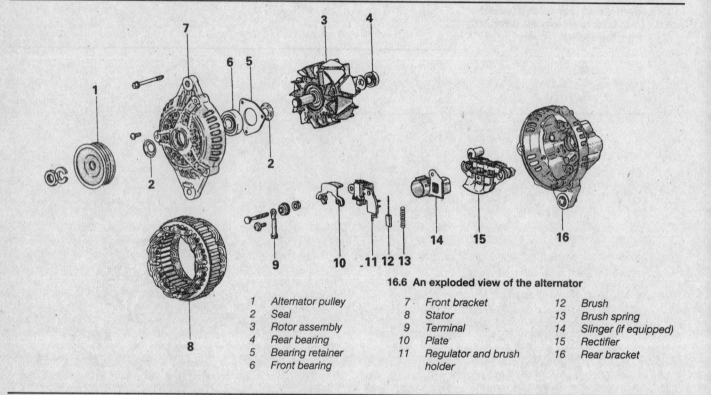

16.6 An exploded view of the alternator

1	Alternator pulley	7	Front bracket	12	Brush
2	Seal	8	Stator	13	Brush spring
3	Rotor assembly	9	Terminal	14	Slinger (if equipped)
4	Rear bearing	10	Plate	15	Rectifier
5	Bearing retainer	11	Regulator and brush	16	Rear bracket
6	Front bearing		holder		

the old one with you when purchasing a new unit. Make sure the new/rebuilt unit looks identical to the old alternator. Look at the terminals - they should be the same in number, size and location as the terminals on the old alternator. Finally, look at the identification numbers - they will be stamped into the housing or printed on a tag attached to the housing. Make sure the numbers are the same on both alternators.

6   Many new/rebuilt alternators DO NOT have a pulley fitted, so you may have to switch the pulley from the old unit to the new/rebuilt one. When buying an alternator, find out the shop's policy regarding pulleys - some shops will perform this service free of charge.

7   Refitting is the reverse of removal.

8   After the alternator is refitted, adjust the drivebelt tension (see Chapter 1).

9   Check the charging voltage to verify proper operation of the alternator (see Section 14).

16   Voltage regulator/alternator brushes - renewal

Refer to illustrations 16.5a, 16.5b, 16.6, 16.7a, 16.12b, 16.8 and 16.9

1   Remove the alternator (see Section 15).

2   Remove the bolts retaining the two halves of the alternator together.

3   Mount the front of the alternator face down in a vice. Using rags as a cushion, clamp to the front case portion of the alternator.

4   Remove all nuts from the back of the alternator.

5   Using a 200-watt soldering iron, heat the rear bearing area (bearing box) of the rear case **(see illustration)**. Insert two standard screwdrivers carefully between the two halves of the alternator (not too deep or you will damage the stator) and lever the rear case off the alternator **(see illustration).Caution:** *Lever gently or you'll break the delicate aluminium case.*

6   Unsolder the regulator/brush holder **(see illustration)**. **Note:** *While applying heat to electrical components, it's a good idea to use a pair of needle-nose pliers as a heat sink. Don't apply heat for more than about five seconds.*

7   Inspect the brushes for excessive wear **(see illustration)** and renew them if necessary by unsoldering **(see illustration)**.

8   When fitting new brushes, solder the pigtails so the brush limit line will be about 2

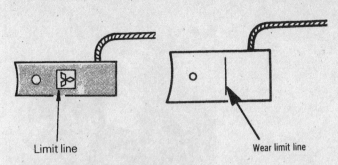

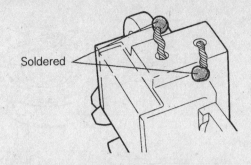

Soldered

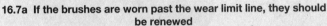

Limit line

Wear limit line

16.7a If the brushes are worn past the wear limit line, they should be renewed

16.7b If the brushes are being renewed, unsolder and solder the pigtails at the area shown

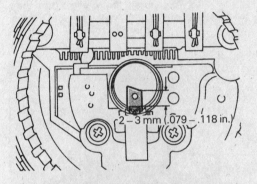

2 – 3 mm (.079 – .118 in.)

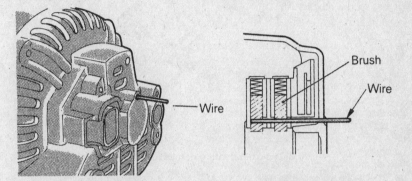

Wire

Brush

Wire

16.8 When fitting new brushes, they should extend out of the holder the proper amount

16.9 When placing the two covers together, use a piece of wire through the rear case and into the brush holder to retain the brushes in the holder

to 3 mm above the end of the brush holder **(see illustrations).**

9   To reassemble, compress the brushes into their holder and retain them with a straight piece of wire that can be pulled from the back of the alternator when reassembled **(see illustration).**

10   To reassemble, reverse disassembly procedure.

17 Starting system - general information and precautions

The sole function of the starting system is to turn over the engine quickly enough to allow it to start.

The starting system consists of the battery, the starter motor, the starter solenoid and the wires connecting them. The solenoid is mounted directly on the starter motor.

The solenoid/starter motor assembly is fitted on the transmission bellhousing.

When the ignition key is turned to the Start position, the starter solenoid is actuated through the starter control circuit. The starter solenoid then connects the battery to the starter. The battery supplies the electrical energy to the starter motor, which does the actual work of cranking the engine.

Always observe the following precautions when working on the starting system:

a) *Excessive cranking of the starter motor*

can overheat it and cause serious damage. Never operate the starter motor for more than 30 seconds at a time without pausing to allow it to cool for at least two minutes.

b) *The starter is connected directly to the battery and could arc or cause a fire if mishandled, overloaded or shorted out.*

c) *Always detach the cable from the negative terminal of the battery before working on the starting system.*

18 Starter motor - in-vehicle check

Note: *Before diagnosing starter problems, make sure the battery is fully charged.*

1   If the starter motor does not turn at all when the switch is operated, make sure that the shift lever is in Neutral or Park (automatic transmission) or that the clutch pedal is depressed (manual transmission).

2   Make sure that the battery is charged and that all cables, both at the battery and starter solenoid terminals, are clean and secure.

3   If the starter motor spins but the engine is not cranking, the overrunning clutch in the starter motor is slipping and the starter motor must be renewed.

4   If, when the switch is actuated, the starter motor does not operate at all but the solenoid clicks, then the problem lies with

either the battery, the main solenoid contacts or the starter motor itself (or the engine is seized).

5   If the solenoid plunger cannot be heard when the switch is actuated, the battery is bad, the fusible link is burned (the circuit is open) or the solenoid itself is defective.

6   To check the solenoid, connect a jumper lead between the battery (+) and the ignition switch wire terminal (the small terminal) on the solenoid. If the starter motor now operates, the solenoid is not defective and the problem is in the ignition switch, neutral start switch or the wiring.

7   If the starter motor still does not operate, remove the starter/solenoid assembly for disassembly, testing and repair.

8   If the starter motor cranks the engine at an abnormally slow speed, first make sure that the battery is charged and that all terminal connections are tight. If the engine is partially seized, or has the wrong viscosity oil in it, it will crank slowly.

9   Run the engine until normal operating temperature is reached. Disconnect the coil wire from the distributor cap and connect it to an earthing point using a jumper wire.

10   Connect a voltmeter positive lead to the positive battery post and connect the negative lead to the negative post.

11   Crank the engine and take the voltmeter readings as soon as a steady figure is indicated. Do not allow the starter motor to turn for more than 30 seconds at a time. A reading

5

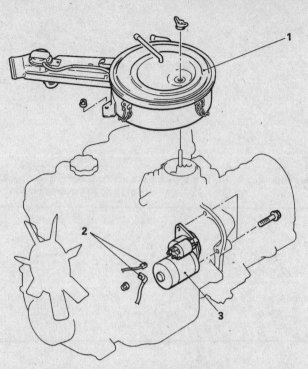

19.3 Typical mounting details for the starter motor

1	Air cleaner housing	3	Starter motor
2	Electrical connections		

20.3 To separate the solenoid from the starter motor, remove the nut and detach the lead (arrow) . . .

20.4 . . . then remove the solenoid mounting screws (arrows) and pull the solenoid straight off the starter flange

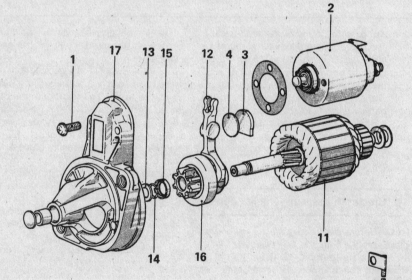

20.5 Direct drive starter motor components

1	Mounting screw	10	Housing
2	Solenoid	11	Armature
3	Packing	12	Lever
4	Plate	13	Washer
5	Screw	14	Snap-ring
6	Through bolt	15	Stop-ring
7	Rear bracket	16	Over running clutch
8	Rear bearing	17	Front bracket
9	Brush holder assembly		

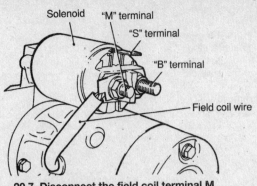

20.7 Disconnect the field coil terminal M

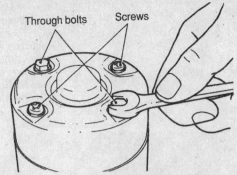

20.8a Remove the through bolts from the starter housing

of 9 volts or more, with the starter motor turning at normal cranking speed, is normal. If the reading is 9 volts or more but the cranking speed is slow, the solenoid contacts are burned, there is a bad connection or the motor is faulty. If the reading is less than 9 volts and the cranking speed is slow, the starter motor is bad or the battery is discharged.

19 Starter motor - removal and refitting

Refer to illustration 19.3
1   Detach the cable from the negative terminal of the battery.
2   Clearly label, then disconnect the wires

from the terminals on the starter solenoid.
3   Remove the mounting bolts **(see illustration)** and remove the starter.
4   Refitting is the reverse of removal.

20 Starter motor/solenoid/gear reduction assembly - renewal

1   Disconnect the cable from the negative terminal of the battery.
2   Remove the starter motor (see Section 19).

Direct drive type
Refer to illustrations 20.3, 20.4 and 20.5
3   Remove the field terminal nut, disconnect the field terminal lead and remove the

washer **(see illustration)**.
4   Remove the solenoid mounting screws **(see illustration)**.
5   Work the solenoid off the shift fork and detach it from the drive end housing **(see illustration)**.
6   Refitting is the reverse of removal.

Gear reduction type
Refer to illustrations 20.7, 20.8a, 20.8b and 20.9
7   If you're renewing the starter motor or solenoid, disconnect the field coil wire from the solenoid terminal **(see illustration)**; if you're renewing the gear reduction assembly, skip this step and proceed to the next step.
8   To detach the starter motor from the gear reduction assembly, simply remove the

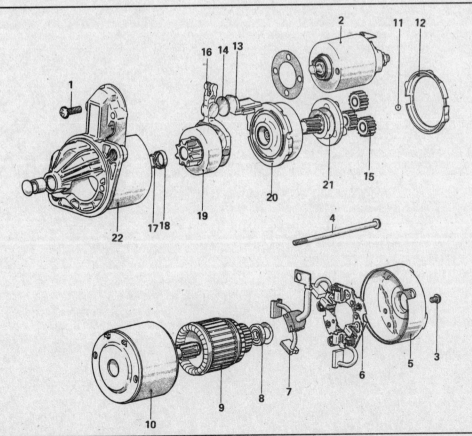

20.8b Gear reduction starter motor components (later model shown)

1   Mounting screw
2   Solenoid
3   Screw
4   Screw
5   Rear bracket
6   Brush holder
7   Brush
8   Rear bearing
9   Armature
10   Housing
11   Ball
12   Packing A
13   Packing B
14   Plate
15   Planetary gear
16   Lever
17   Snap-ring
18   Stop-ring
19   Over running clutch
20   Integral gear
21   Planetary gear holder
22   Front bracket

5

20.9 Remove the screws to separate the solenoid from the gear reduction assembly

two long through-bolts and pull off the starter **(see illustrations)**.

9   To detach the solenoid from the gear reduction assembly, remove the starter, then remove the two Phillips screws from the gear reduction assembly and pull off the solenoid **(see illustration)**.

10   Refitting is the reverse of removal.

Chapter 6
Emissions and engine control systems

Contents

Specifications

Dashpot adjustment (four-cylinder engine)
Engine set speed	1700 + 100 rpm
Dashpot drop time	Three to six seconds

Throttle position sensor
Output voltage	0.4 to 1.0 volts
Resistance (at closed throttle)	3.5 to 6.5 K-ohms

EGR control solenoid valve resistance
36 to 44 ohms

Engine coolant temperature sensor resistance
0-degrees C	5.9 K-ohms
20-degrees C	2.5 K-ohms
40-degrees C	1.1 K-ohms
80-degrees C	0.3 K-ohms
Oxygen sensor output voltage	0.6 to 1 volt

Purge control solenoid valve resistance
36 to 44 ohms @ 20-degrees C

Torque specifications
	Nm
EGR valve bolts	17 to 26
EGR temperature sensor	6 to 9
Engine coolant temperature sensor	29

6

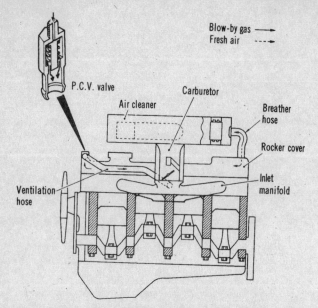

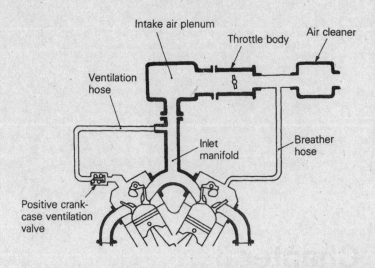

2.1a Typical four-cylinder engine Positive Crankcase Ventilation (PCV) system

2.1b Typical V6 Positive Crankcase Ventilation (PCV) system

1   General information

To prevent pollution of the atmosphere from incompletely burned and evaporating gases, and to maintain good driveability and fuel economy, a number of emission control systems are incorporated on petrol models. The principal systems are:

Catalytic converter
Deceleration system
Evaporative emission control system
Exhaust Gas Recirculation (EGR) system
Heated air inlet system
Multi-Port Injection (MPI) system
Oxygen sensor
Positive Crankcase Ventilation (PCV) system
Secondary Air Supply (SAS) system

The Sections in this Chapter include general descriptions, checking procedures within the scope of the home mechanic and component renewal procedures (when possible) for each of the systems listed above.

Before assuming an emissions control system is malfunctioning, check the fuel and ignition systems carefully. The diagnosis of some emission control devices requires specialised tools, equipment and training. If checking and servicing become too difficult or if a procedure is beyond your ability, consult a dealer service department. Remember, the most frequent cause of emissions problems is simply a loose or broken vacuum hose or wire, so always check the hose and wiring connections first **(see illustrations)**.

This doesn't mean, however, that emission control systems are particularly difficult to maintain and repair. You can quickly and easily perform many checks and do most of the regular maintenance at home with common tune-up and hand tools.

Pay close attention to any special precautions outlined in this Chapter. It should be noted that the illustrations of the various systems may not exactly match the system fitted on your vehicle because of changes made by the manufacturer during production or from year-to-year.

A Vehicle Emissions Control Information label is located in the engine compartment (usually on the underside of the bonnet). This label contains important emissions specifications and adjustment information. When servicing the engine or emissions systems, the VECI label in your particular vehicle should always be checked for up-to-date information.

2   Positive Crankcase Ventilation (PCV) system

Refer to illustrations 2.1a and 2.1b

1   A closed-type crankcase ventilation system is utilised to prevent blow-by gases from escaping into the atmosphere. This system has a small orifice fixed at the inlet manifold or at the valve cover **(see illustrations)**.
2   The blow-by gas is led through a rubber hose from the front of the valve cover into the air cleaner and through another hose from the rear of the cover into the inlet manifold through the orifice. At narrow throttle openings, the blow-by gas is drawn from the rear of the cover into the inlet manifold with fresh air entering from the air cleaner through the front of the valve cover. At wide open throttle, the blow-by gas is drawn through both passages.
3   Very little maintenance is required for the crankcase emission control system. Check the hoses for cracks and kinks. Renew them if they are deteriorated. Make sure that the orifice isn't clogged or poor crankcase ventilation will result.

3   Evaporative emissions control system

Refer to illustration 3.2

1   To prevent fuel vapours from escaping into the atmosphere from the fuel tank (due to normal vaporisation) the vehicles in this manual are equipped with an evaporative emissions control system.
2   The evaporative emissions control system consists of one or two vapour/liquid separators (not used on all models), an overfill limiter (two-way valve), a fuel check valve, a purge control valve (carburetted models) or purge control solenoid valve (fuel-injected models), a charcoal-filled canister and lines and hoses connecting the components **(see illustration)**. No routine maintenance is required, but if the element appears to be clogged or dirty, renew it.
3   The charcoal-filled canister is fitted between the fuel tank and the air cleaner. Petrol vapours are routed to this canister for temporary storage. While the engine is running, outside air is drawn through the canister, purging the vapours from the charcoal. This air/vapour mixture is then routed to the engine combustion chambers (through the air cleaner) and burned.
4   The purge control valve is kept closed at idle speeds to prevent fuel vapour from entering the air cleaner and causing high-idle carbon monoxide emissions.
5   The carburettor itself is vented internally or through the charcoal canister, depending on the temperature, which prevents the escape of petrol vapours into the atmosphere from the carburettor.
6   When the engine is not running, petrol vapours produced in the fuel tank (by an increase in atmospheric temperatures) are

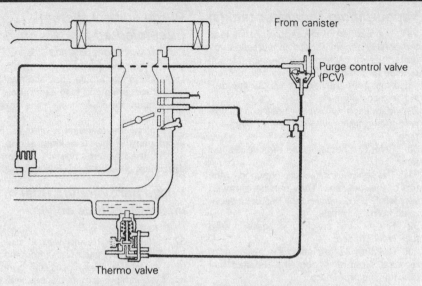

3.2 Typical evaporative emissions control system

routed to the separator tank in which liquid petrol formed by condensation of the vapours is separated. The remaining fuel vapour is led into a two-way valve. The two-way pressure valve is designed to open at a predetermined pressure, admitting the fuel vapours into the charcoal-filled canister, the vapours are trapped by the charcoal, preventing the discharge of raw hydrocarbons into the atmosphere.

7   While the engine is running, a vacuum is built above the canister (on the carburettor side) causing outside air to be drawn into the canister through the inlet holes in the case, then passing through the filter and the charcoal. As the outside air flows through, the vapours trapped by the char- charcoal are carried away, passing through the passage at the centre of the canister into the air cleaner, the carburettor and ultimately the engine cylinders where they are burned.

8   During engine operation, vapours originating in the fuel tank are also routed directly into the canister (through the passage in the centre of the canister) and fed into the engine for combustion.

9   As the fuel is used, a vacuum is produced inside the fuel tank. The two-way vacuum valve opens momentarily, drawing outside air through the air inlet hose of the canister into the fuel tank, thus maintaining normal pressure in the tank.

10   During filling of the fuel tank, the air in the tank flows through the leveling pipe and out into the atmosphere, venting the tank. When the fuel entering the tank has sealed off the leveling pipe opening in the tank, further filling cannot be done because of the air pressure inside the tank. If filling is continued, overflow of fuel will result.

Charcoal canister

11   Because of the fact that the canister inlet air hose and filter can become clogged over a long period of time, it is recommended that the canister be renewed according to the

time/distance intervals listed in Chapter 1.
12   Also, carefully inspect the rubber hoses attached to the canister. If they are cracked or otherwise deteriorated, renew them when the canister is renewed.
13   Refer to Chapter 1 for canister removal and refitting procedures.

Purge control valve

Refer to illustration 3.17
14   The purge control valve is connected by hoses to the top of the canister, the air cleaner and the carburettor.
15   It is a simple spring-loaded close valve, and its operation is controlled by negative pressure, generated at a port provided slightly above the carburettor throttle valve, which acts on a diaphragm in the valve. When the engine is idling, the valve and evaporated gas passage are closed. When the engine is running at 1500 rpm or more the valve is opened and the fuel vapours stored in the canister are drawn into the carburettor.
16   When inspecting the valve, the engine must be at normal operating temperature.

17   Disconnect the purge hose from the air cleaner **(see illustration)** and blow into it. If the valve is not open, it is in good condition. Next, start the engine and increase the engine speed to 1500 or 2000 rpm and blow into the purge hose again. If the valve is open, it is operating properly.
18   If the valve does not check out as described, renew it.

Fuel check valve

19   The fuel check valve, located just to the left of the fuel tank, is designed to prevent fuel leaks should the vehicle roll over during an accident. The check valve contains two balls. Under normal conditions the petrol vapour passage in the valve is open, but if a roll-over occurs, either of the two balls will close the fuel passage and prevent fuel leaks.
20   Remove the hose clamps and disconnect the hoses from the check valve.
21   Remove the bolt attaching the fuel check valve to the rear body mount bracket.
22   Check the hoses for cracks and renew them if they are deteriorated.
23   Refitting is the reverse of removal.

Two-way valve

Refer to illustration 3.27
24   The two-way valve, located just to the left of the fuel tank, is composed of a pressure valve and a vacuum valve. The pressure valve is designed to open when the fuel tank internal pressure has increased over the normal pressure, which allows the fuel vapours to enter the charcoal canister for storage, and the vacuum valve opens when a vacuum has been produced in the tank.
25   Removal of the valve is quite simple. Loosen the hose clamps and pull off the two hoses, then remove the valve mounting bolt.
26   Blow lightly into the valve inlet. If there is an initial resistance followed by passage of air, the valve is in good condition. Repeat the check by blowing into the outlet.
27   Refitting is the reverse of removal. The valve must tilt approximately 7-degrees **(see illustration)** in relation to the fuel tank when it is in place.

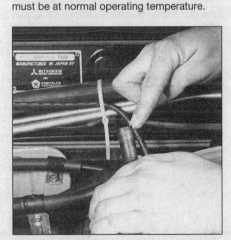

3.17 To check the operation of the purge control valve, disconnect the hose from the air cleaner housing and blow into it

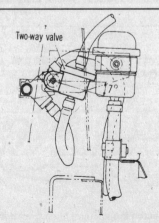

3.27 Refit the two-way valve at a seven-degree angle (in relation to the tank)

6

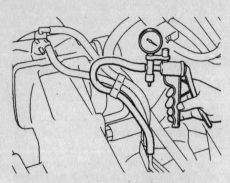

3.34 Detach the vacuum hose with the red stripes from the throttle body and attach it to a hand vacuum pump (plug the vacuum pipe from which the hose was detached)(fuel-injected models only)

Vapour/liquid separator tank(s)

28 The function of the separator tank is to temporarily accommodate an increased volume of petrol caused by expansion at high outside air temperatures. They also prevent liquid fuel from entering the vapour line during hard cornering.

29 Mark each fuel/vapour hose and its corresponding fitting with numbered pieces of tape.

30 Refer to Chapter 4 and remove the fuel tank.

31 The separator tanks are attached to the top of the fuel tank. They can be removed very easily once the fuel tank has been separated from the vehicle.

32 Renew any cracked or deteriorated fuel/vapour hoses.

33 Refitting is basically the reverse of removal. Chapter 4 contains detailed fuel tank refitting procedures.

Purge control system (fuel-injected models only)

Refer to illustrations 3.34 and 3.35

34 Detach the vacuum hose with the red stripes from the throttle body and attach it to a hand vacuum pump **(see illustration)**. Plug the vacuum pipe from which the hose was detached.

35 Follow the sequence of tests in the accompanying chart **(see illustration)**.

36 If the system doesn't perform as described, proceed to the following tests.

Purge port vacuum (fuel-injected models only)

Refer to illustration 3.38

37 Start the engine and warm it up.

38 Detach the vacuum hose from the throttle body purge hose nipple and connect a hand vacuum pump in its place **(see illustration)**.

39 Start the engine and verify that, after the engine rpm is raised by racing the engine, vacuum remains fairly constant.

40 If there's no vacuum created, the throttle body port may be clogged and require cleaning.

Purge control solenoid valve (fuel-injected models only)

Refer to illustration 3.41

41 Detach the vacuum hose with the red stripe from the solenoid valve and attach a hand-held vacuum pump in its place **(see illustration)**.

42 Unplug the electrical connector from the solenoid valve.

43 Apply battery voltage (or any 12V DC source) to the purge control solenoid valve, apply a vacuum and verify that the valve leaks vacuum when voltage is applied; when voltage is discontinued, the valve should maintain vacuum.

44 Measure the resistance between the terminals of the solenoid valve and compare your reading to the range of acceptable resistance listed in this Chapter's Specifications.

45 If the purge control solenoid valve fails either of these tests, renew it.

When engine is cold

Engine operating condition	Applying vacuum	Result
Idling	50 kPa (14 in. Hg)	Vacuum is maintained
3,000 rpm		

When engine is warm

Engine operating condition	Applying vacuum	Result
Idling	50 kPa (14 in. Hg)	Vacuum is maintained
Within 3 minutes after engine start 3,000 rpm	Try applying vacuum	Vacuum leaks
After 3 minutes have passed after engine start 3,000 rpm	50 kPa (14 in. Hg)	Vacuum will be maintained momentarily after which it will leaks.

3.35 Follow the sequence of tests in this chart to diagnose the purge control system (fuel-injected models only)

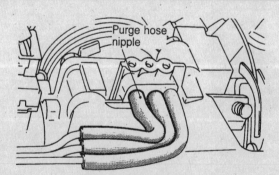

3.38 Detach the vacuum hose from the throttle body purge hose nipple and connect a hand-held vacuum pump in its place (fuel-injected models)

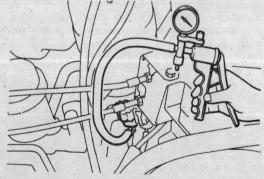

3.41 Detach the vacuum hose with the red strip from the solenoid valve and attach a hand-held vacuum pump in its place (fuel-injected models)

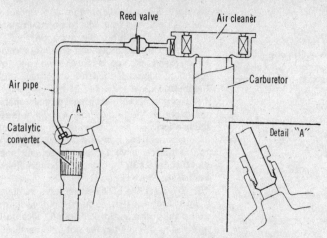

5.1 Secondary Air Supply (SAS) system (typical)

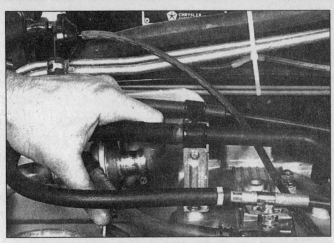

5.4 To check the operation of the SAS reed valve, place your finger over the valve inlet with the engine running

4 Catalytic converter

1 The catalytic converter provides for the oxidising of hydrocarbons and carbon monoxide in the exhaust system, which reduces the levels of these pollutants in the exhaust.
2 Its ceramic monolithic element, coated with a catalytic agent, is pressed into the exhaust manifold on early models. On later models it is a renewable component located under the vehicle in the exhaust system.
3 The catalytic converter requires the use of the unleaded fuel only. Leaded petrol will destroy the effectiveness of the catalyst as an emission control device.
4 Under normal operating conditions, the catalytic converter will not require maintenance. However, it is important to keep the engine properly tuned. If the engine is not properly tuned, engine misfiring may cause overheating of the catalyst, which may damage the converter or other vehicle components. Heat damage can also occur during diagnostic testing if spark plug wires are removed and the engine is allowed to idle for a prolonged period of time.
5 **Caution:** *Vehicle operation, including idling, should be avoided if engine misfiring occurs. Under these conditions the exhaust system will operate at an abnormally high*

temperature and may cause damage to the catalyst or other underbody parts of the vehicle. Alteration or deterioration of the ignition or fuel systems, or any type of operating condition which results in engine misfiring, must be corrected to avoid overheating the catalytic converter.

5 Secondary Air Supply (SAS) system (carburetted models only)

Description

Refer to illustration 5.1
1 The SAS system **(see illustration)** consists of reed valves and air pipes that supply secondary air into the exhaust manifold and exhaust pipe (at a point beyond the catalytic converter) for the purpose of promoting oxidation (or complete burning) of any remaining unburned fuel. The system used on later models is somewhat more complex; it utilises a secondary air control valve and a solenoid valve to control the flow of air through the reed valve and into the exhaust manifold.
2 The SAS is actuated by exhaust vacuum generated from pulsations in the exhaust manifold. Air is drawn through the air cleaner and directed into the manifold by the valve motion corresponding to the exhaust pulses.

Check

Refer to illustrations 5.4 and 5.5
3 Check the air hose and air pipe for damage and cracks. Check the air pipe connections for leakage.
4 Start and run the engine at idle. Disconnect the rubber air hose from the reed valve and place your hand over the inlet port of the valve **(see illustration)**. If suction is felt, the reed valve is operating properly. If no suction is felt, or if pressure is felt, renew the reed valve.
5 To check the air control valve diaphragm on later models, remove it and hook up a hand-operated vacuum pump to the valve fitting with a short section of hose and apply a vacuum of approximately 500 mm-Hg **(see illustration)**. The pump gauge needle should remain stable.
6 Now apply a vacuum of 35 kPa to the air control valve with the pump and make sure that air passes from air cleaner side to the exhaust manifold side but not from the exhaust manifold to the air cleaner side.

Renewal

7 Removal of the reed valve is very simple. Pull the rubber hose off the inlet and unscrew the valve from the air pipe. Be sure to use a backup spanner on the pipe so it doesn't become twisted when the valve is unscrewed.
8 Refitting is the reverse of removal.

6 Exhaust Gas Recirculation (EGR) system

Description

Carburetted models
Refer to illustration 6.3
1 The vehicles covered in this manual utilise an Exhaust Gas Recirculation (EGR) system to reduce oxides of nitrogen in the exhaust.
2 Oxides of nitrogen emission standards require high rates of EGR flow, which adversely affects driveability of the vehicle.

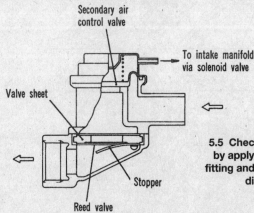

5.5 Check the air control valve diaphragm by applying vacuum to the inlet manifold fitting and making sure the air passes in the direction of the arrows only

6

To solve this problem, it is necessary to increase EGR flow during high load vehicle operation and decrease EGR flow to improve driveability during low load operation.

3   With this system, the exhaust gas is partially recirculated from an exhaust port in the cylinder head, through the EGR control valve, to a port located in the inlet manifold below the carburettor **(see illustration)**.

4   EGR flow is controlled by the EGR control valve and is varied according to engine load. The flow is increased during high load vehicle operation and decreased to preserve driveability of the vehicle during low load operation.

5   With this arrangement, the EGR control valve is activated by carburettor vacuum, drawn from slightly above the throttle valve, so the EGR flow is modulated to attain effective oxides of nitrogen reduction and is suspended at idle and wide-open throttle conditions.

6   The vacuum to be applied on the EGR control valve is controlled by a thermal valve, which senses the coolant temperature and cuts off the vacuum when the engine is cold and a vacuum valve which respond to vehicle load by detecting engine manifold vacuum which responds to vehicle load by detecting engine manifold vacuum.

Fuel-injected models

Refer to illustration 6.7

7   The EGR system on fuel-injected models is essentially the same as the one on carburetted models. However, the EGR valve is computer-controlled via the EGR control solenoid valve **(see illustration)**.

Check

Refer to illustrations 6.13 and 6.15

Carburetted models

8   Check all vacuum hoses for cracks and correct refitting.

9   Start the engine (it must be completely cool) and run it at idle speed.

10   Touch the underside of the secondary EGR valve diaphragm and increase the engine speed from idle to approximately 3500 rpm. No movement of the secondary EGR diaphragm should be felt. If it does move, which means the secondary EGR valve is opening, renew the thermo valve.

Warning: *The valve may be very hot - wear a glove or use a rag to prevent your hand from burns.*

11   Allow the engine to warm up until the coolant temperature exceeds 80-degrees C.

12   Again, touch the underside of the sec-ondary EGR valve diaphragm and increase the engine speed from idle to approximately 3500 rpm. This time, the secondary EGR diaphragm should move. If it does not move, which means the secondary EGR valve is not opening, inspect the EGR control valve and the thermo valve.

13   To check the thermo valve, disconnect the green-striped hose from the valve **(see illustration)**.

14   Connect the hand-held vacuum pump to the thermo valve and apply vacuum **(see illustration 6.13)**. If no vacuum can be held, the thermo valve is good.

15   To check the EGR control valve, remove it and connect it to a hand-held vacuum pump **(see illustration)**. Apply 67 kPa and make sure the valve does not lose vacuum. With 5.3 kPa applied, air should pass through the air passage but when 35 kPa applied, it should not.

16   To check the vacuum regulator valve, disconnect the green-striped hose from the valve, connect a hand-held vacuum pump and apply a vacuum of 50 kPa to the valve. If no vacuum can be held with the engine off, the regulator valve is good.

17   Start the engine and increase the engine speed from idle to approximately 3500 rpm. The vacuum should not hold. If the regulator valve fails either test, it should be renewed.

Fuel-injected models

EGR system inspection

Refer to illustrations 6.18 and 6.21

18   Disconnect the vacuum hose with the green stripe from the EGR valve and connect a hand-operated vacuum pump/gauge into the line with a three-way terminal **(see illustration)**.

19   Start the engine. While it's still cold, press down on the accelerator pedal abruptly and race the engine - there should be no vacuum indicated (atmospheric pressure).

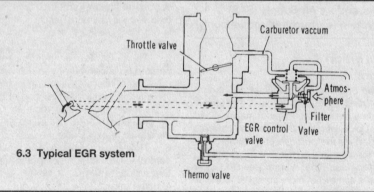

6.3 Typical EGR system

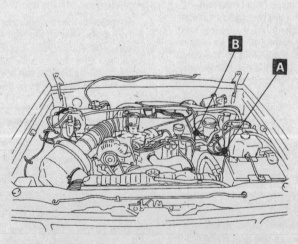

6.7 Typical EGR system component locations (V6 engine)

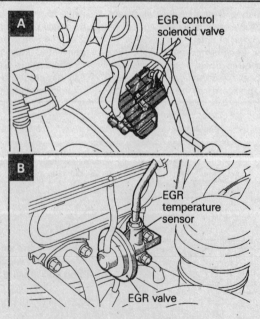

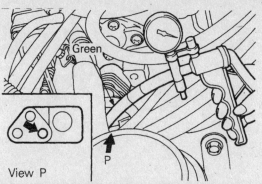

6.13 Disconnect the green-striped hose from the Thermo and apply a vacuum to the thermo valve

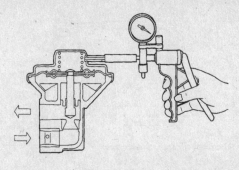

6.15 To check for proper operation of the EGR control valve, hook up a hand-operated vacuum pump/gauge to the carburettor side of the valve

20   After the engine is warmed up, press down suddenly on the accelerator again - the indicated vacuum should rise momentarily to about 20 kPa.

21   Disconnect the vacuum pump from the three-way terminal, remove the terminal and connect the vacuum pump directly to the EGR valve **(see illustration)**. With the engine at idle, apply a vacuum of 35 kPa and note whether the engine stalls or idles roughly (it should).

22   If there's a problem, proceed to the next Step.

EGR valve control vacuum

Refer to illustration 6.23

23   The engine should be warmed up for this test. Disconnect the vacuum hose from the throttle body EGR vacuum nipple **(see illustration)** and hook up a hand vacuum pump in its place.

24   Start the engine, race the engine and verify that vacuum rises in proportion to the rise in engine speed.

25   If it doesn't, the port in the throttle body may be clogged and require cleaning.

EGR valve

Refer to illustration 6.28

26   Remove the EGR valve and, through the open portion underneath, check the diaphragm for sticking. Look for carbon deposits inside the valve. If the valve is dirty,

or the diaphragm is stuck, clean the valve with solvent and check it again. If it's still sticking, or clogged, renew it.

27   Hook up a hand-operated vacuum pump to the EGR valve, apply a vacuum of 500 mm-Hg and note whether the diaphragm leaks (the valve should hold the vacuum).

28   Release the vacuum applied in the previous Step. Apply less than 15 kPa and try to blow through the valve - you shouldn't be able to; now apply 35 or more kPa and try to blow through the valve again - this time you should be able to **(see illustration)**.

29   Refit the EGR valve. Use a new gasket and tighten the EGR valve mounting bolts to the torque listed in this Chapter's Specifications.

6.18 Disconnect the vacuum hose with the green stripe from the EGR valve and connect a hand-operated vacuum pump/gauge into the line with a three-way terminal

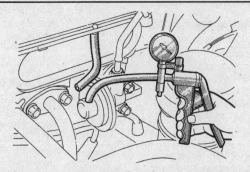

6.21 Disconnect the vacuum pump from the three-way terminal, remove the terminal and connect the vacuum pump directly to the EGR valve

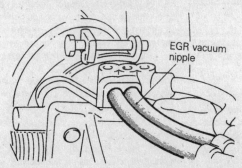

6.23 Disconnect the vacuum hose from the throttle body EGR vacuum nipple and hook up a hand-held vacuum pump in its place

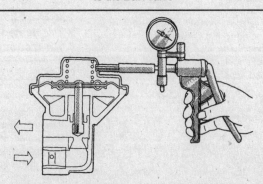

6.28 Apply less than 68 kPa and try to blow through the valve - you shouldn't be able to; now apply a 35 or more kPa and try to blow through the valve again - this time you should be able to do so

6

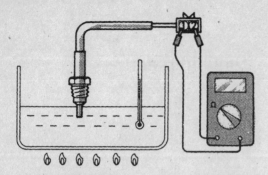

6.31 Measure the resistance of the temperature sensor at the temperatures specified in the text

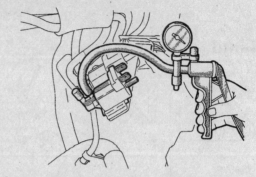

6.34 Disconnect the vacuum hose with the yellow and green stripes from the solenoid valve and connect a hand-operated vacuum pump in its place

EGR temperature sensor

Refer to illustration 6.31

30   Remove the EGR temperature sensor and place it in a pot of water. Use a thermometer to monitor the water temperature.

31   As you bring the water to a boil, measure the resistance between terminals 1 and 2 **(see illustration)**. Up to about 20-degrees C, the resistance between the terminals should be about 2.5 K-ohms; at 80-degrees C, the resistance should be between 290 and 322 ohms.

32   If the temperature sensor doesn't perform as described, renew it.

33   When you refit the temperature sensor, coat the threads with sealant or Teflon tape and tighten the sensor to the torque listed in this Chapter's Specifications.

EGR control solenoid valve

Refer to illustration 6.34

34   Disconnect the vacuum hose with the red (early models) or yellow and green stripes (later models) from the solenoid valve and connect a hand-operated vacuum pump in its place **(see illustration)**.

35   Unplug the wiring harness electrical connector.

36   Apply battery voltage and vacuum to the EGR control solenoid simultaneously. With vacuum and voltage applied, the solenoid should maintain vacuum. When voltage is interrupted, the solenoid should leak vacuum.

37   Measure the resistance between the terminals of the solenoid valve and compare your reading to the value listed in this Chapter's Specifications.

38   If the solenoid valve doesn't perform as described, renew it.

Component renewal

EGR control valve

39   The EGR valve is attached to the lower part of the inlet manifold, directly under the carburettor.

40   Mark the vacuum hose and fittings with pieces of numbered tape, then disconnect the vacuum hoses from the EGR valve.

41   Remove the bolts attaching the EGR valve to the inlet manifold and the valve can be lifted away. You may have to tap gently on

the EGR body with a soft-faced hammer to break the gasket seal.

42   When refitting the EGR valve, use a new gasket and tighten the mounting bolts evenly and securely. Also, be sure to refit the vacuum hoses properly.

Thermal valve

43   The thermal valve is located just in front of the carburettor and is threaded into the coolant passage in the inlet manifold.

44   Removal of the thermal valve is quite simple. Pull off the vacuum hoses that are connected to the thermal valve fittings, then unscrew the valve from the manifold.

45   When refitting the thermal valve, be sure to use thread-sealing tape on the threads.

---

7   Heated air inlet system (carburetted models only)

Description

Refer to illustration 7.1

1   Carburetted models are equipped with a temperature-regulated air cleaner **(see illustration)** so that the carburettor can be calibrated leaner to reduce carbon monoxide and hydrocarbon emissions. Improved engine warm-up characteristics and minimised carburettor icing can also be attained with this system.

2   The air cleaner is equipped with an air control valve inside the snorkel to modulate the temperature of carburettor inlet air which

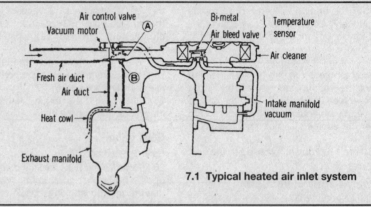

7.1 Typical heated air inlet system

flows through the intake. The air control valve is controlled by a vacuum motor/temperature sensor combination system which responds to the inlet manifold vacuum and temperature inside the air cleaner.

3   When the bimetal senses a temperature inside the air cleaner below about 30-degrees C, the air bleed valve of the temperature sensor assembly remains closed, causing inlet manifold vacuum to be applied to the diaphragm of the vacuum motor. This in turn opens the air control valve and allows the preheated inlet air to flow through the heat cowl and air duct into the air cleaner.

4   When the bimetal senses that the temperature inside the air cleaner is above about 45-degrees C, the air bleed valve is fully open. As a result, the inlet air to the carburettor comes directly through the fresh air duct, since the air control valve is positioned at 'B', as shown in **illustration 7.1**, regardless of the inlet manifold vacuum.

5   At intermediate temperatures, the air entering the carburettor is a blend of fresh and preheated air as regulated by the thermostatically-actuated air control valve.

Check

Refer to illustrations 7.10 and 7.11

6   Make sure all vacuum hoses and the heat cowl-to-air cleaner air duct are properly attached and in good condition.

7   With the engine completely cold and the outside air temperature less than 61-degrees C, remove the rubber tube from the end of the air cleaner snorkel. Start the engine and look

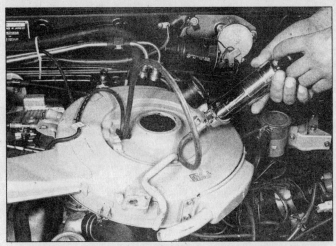

7.10 To check the temperature sensor for the heated air inlet system, apply vacuum to the sensor - the air control valve should be in the "up" (heat on) position

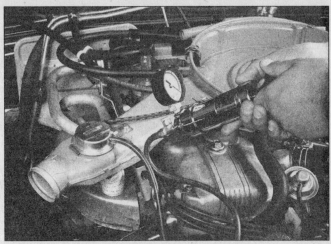

7.11 To check the vacuum motor for the heated air inlet system, apply a vacuum to the motor inlet fitting - the air control valve should be in the "up" (heat on) position

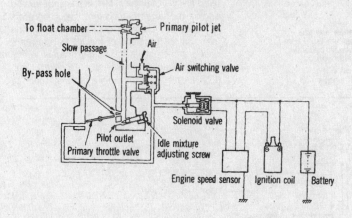

8.2 The fuel cut system Air Switching Valve (ASV) and solenoid valve operation

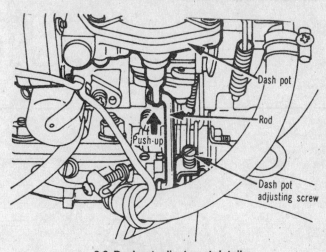

8.6 Dashpot adjustment details

into the snorkel (be careful when working around moving engine parts). The air control valve should be in the 'Up' (Heat on) position.

8   With the engine running at normal operating temperatures, check the temperature of the air entering the end of the air cleaner snorkel. If the temperature is 45-degrees C or higher, the air control valve should be in the "down" (heat off) position.

9   To check the operation of the sensor and vacuum motor, you will need a hand-held vacuum pump.

10   Remove the air cleaner from the engine (see Chapter 4) and allow it to cool to below 61-degrees C. Hook the vacuum pump to the sensor hose and apply a vacuum to the sensor **(see illustration)**. The air control valve should be in the "up" (heat on) position. If it is not, check the vacuum motor for proper operation.

11   To check the vacuum motor, apply a vacuum directly to the motor inlet fitting **(see illustration)**. The air control valve should be in the "up" (heat on) position. If it is not, check to be sure it is not sticking. If the valve

moves freely but will not operate properly when a vacuum is applied, the air cleaner housing will have to be renewed.

12   If the vacuum motor operates properly but the valve does not operate when vacuum is applied to the sensor, the sensor should be removed and renewed.

8   Deceleration systems (carburetted models only)

Description

Refer to illustration 8.2

1   The deceleration or fuel cut system decreases hydrocarbon emission during vehicle deceleration. It includes the Air Switching Valve (ASV) and the fuel cut-off solenoid, which is built into the carburettor.

2   The fuel cut system ASV **(see illustration)** is activated by carburettor ported vacuum and improves fuel economy by supplying additional air into the idle circuit slow passage.

3   In order to maintain smooth vehicle deceleration, and to prevent stalling, operation of the ASV is suspended by opening the solenoid valve (when the engine speed sensor detects engine speed at or below a specified value).

Dashpot systems

4   The dashpot delays the closing of the throttle valve during vehicle deceleration and reduces the hydrocarbon emissions.

Dashpot adjustment

Refer to illustration 8.6

5   Before adjusting the dashpot, make sure the idle speed is set correctly. Use a tachometer connected according to the manufacturer's instructions.

6   Push the dashpot rod up through its entire stroke until it comes to a stop **(see illustration)**.

7   Check the engine speed (set speed) at this point and compare it to the specifications. If it is not correct, turn the dashpot

adjusting screw, as necessary, until the set speed is as specified **(see illustration 8.6)**.
8   Raise the engine speed, then release the throttle. If the engine speed drops too quickly (see this Chapter's Specifications), the dashpot should be renewed.

9   Vacuum delay valve (carburetted models only)

Refer to illustration 9.1

1   Some later vehicles with an automatic transmission are equipped with a vacuum delay valve **(see illustration)**, which delays the opening of the secondary throttle valve

and reduces CO and HC emissions during acceleration.
2   Periodically check the vacuum hoses for cracks, leaks and correct refitting. The delay valve itself should be open when a vacuum is applied to one end and restricted when vacuum is applied to the other end.

10   Throttle opener (carburetted models only)

Refer to illustration 10.1

1   The throttle opener system **(see illustration)** is fitted on all vehicles with air conditioning. It consists of a throttle opener

assembly, a solenoid valve, an engine speed sensor and the compressor switch for the air conditioner.
2   The throttle opener opens the throttle slightly when the air conditioning system is turned on (which prevents stalling and increases emission due to the increased engine load).
3   The throttle opener adjustment is part of the idle speed adjustment procedure (see Chapter 4).
4   Maintenance consists of checking the vacuum hoses and wires for damage and correct refitting and making sure the linkage is not binding in any way.

11   Multi-Point Injection (MPI) system

Refer to illustrations 11.1 and 11.3

1   A Multi-Point Injection (MPI) system is used on all V6 models. MPI is a computerised engine management system which controls all emission, fuel and ignition functions. The fuel control functions of the MPI system are covered in Chapter 4. The information in this Section concerns the electronic control unit (ECU), the information sensors it uses to

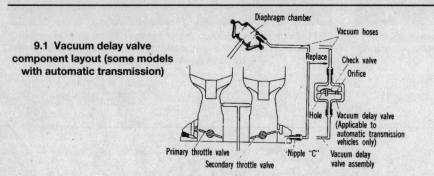

9.1 Vacuum delay valve component layout (some models with automatic transmission)

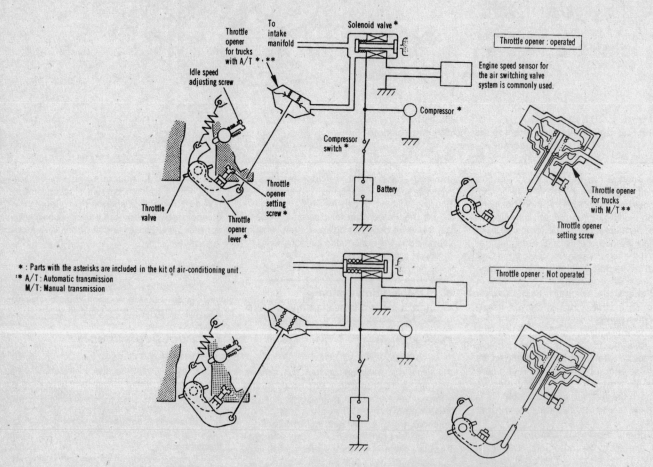

10.1 Throttle opener system component layout (models with air conditioning)

monitor the MPI system and the emission devices it uses to adjust the system **(see illustration)**.

2   The ECU is the "brain" of the MPI system. Its sophisticated network of information sensors monitor engine operation and transmit digital voltage signals to the ECU. The ECU analyses this data, compares it to the "map" (program) stored in its memory and fine-tunes variables such as ignition timing, spark advance, fuel injector pulse width and idle speed by readjusting various devices such as the fuel injectors, the idle speed control servo, the purge control solenoid valve, etc. The result is an always correct air-fuel ratio under all driving conditions that lowers exhaust emissions and maintains good driveability.

3   Numerous sensors transmit data to the ECU; they include:

Air conditioner switch
Air-flow sensor
Barometric pressure sensor
Coolant temperature sensor
Crank angle sensor
Idle position switch
Ignition switch
Inhibitor switch (models equipped with an automatic transmission)
Inlet air temperature sensor
Oxygen sensor
Throttle position sensor
Top dead centre sensor
Vehicle speed sensor

You can locate these sensors and switches by referring to the accompanying illustration **(see illustration)**.

4   The ECU also monitors most of its own input and output circuits. If it detects a fault somewhere in the MPI system, it stores this information in its memory. You can often determine the location of a problem, or at least which circuit it's in, by outputting stored malfunction codes with a voltmeter. To learn how to output this information and display it on a voltmeter, refer to Section 12.

5   Your first step should be a thorough visual inspection of the vacuum hoses and electrical connectors in the part of the MPI system that's malfunctioning. Make sure everything is properly connected and/or plugged in. The most common cause of a problem in an MPI system is a loose or corroded electrical connector or a loose vacuum line. If that doesn't solve the problem, you'll find simple tests of the important information sensors in Section 13.

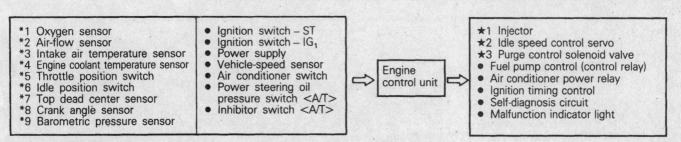

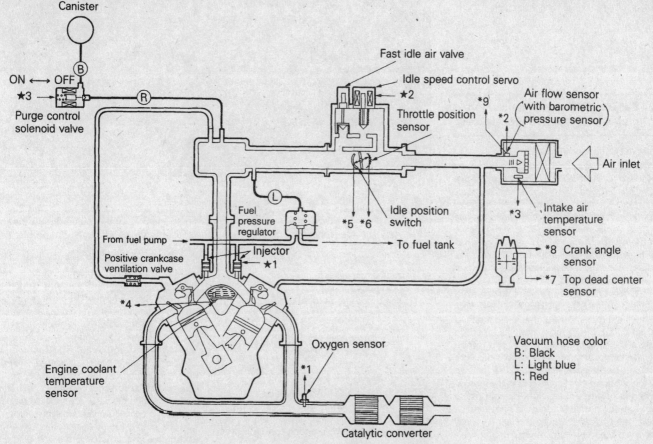

11.1 Multi-Point Injection (MPI) system (3.0L models)

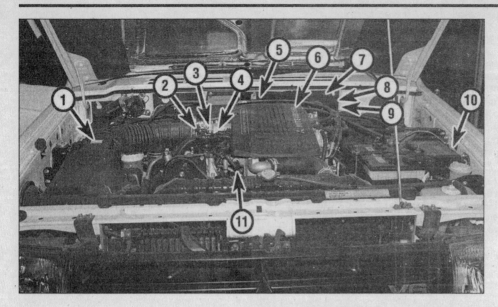

11.3a MPI system engine compartment component locations

1   Air flow sensor
2   Idle speed control (ISC) servo
3   Throttle position sensor (with idle position switch)
4   Ignition coil (power transistor)
5   Oxygen sensor
6   Fuel injectors
7   Crank angle sensor
8   Fuel pump check terminal
9   Ignition timing adjustment terminal
10   Air conditioner compressor power relay
11   Engine coolant temperature sensor

11.3b MPI system interior component locations

12   Air conditioner switch
13   Vehicle speed sensor
14   Self-diagnosis connector
15   Engine control relay
16   Engine control unit

12   Self-diagnosis and malfunction codes (fuel-injected models only)

Refer to illustrations 12.6 and 12.7
Note: *To access the code information on 1994 and later models, it is necessary to use a the MUT-II Scan Tool and additional support test equipment. These tools are very expensive and are not recommended for use by the home mechanic. If you suspect a problem with the emission related components on a 1994 and later model, have the system tested by a dealer service department or other repair shop.*

1   When a malfunction in the MPI system is detected by the ECU, a CHECK ENGINE light on the instrument panel comes on. If the ECU detects that the trouble has disappeared before the ignition switch has been turned off, the light goes out. And even if the light remains on, it goes out when the ignition switch is turned off. The next time the ignition switch is turned on, the light doesn't come back on again unless the ECU has "memorised" the code(s) it stored the last time you operated the vehicle, or it detects the malfunction again. The light does, however, come on for five seconds - then goes out - every time you turn on the ignition switch, to

indicate that the CHECK ENGINE light circuit is operating normally.

2   The CHECK ENGINE light will come on when any of the following components develop a problem:

   Air flow sensor
   Crank angle sensor
   Engine control unit
   Engine coolant temperature sensor
   Fuel injector(s)
   Fuel pump
   Intake air temperature sensor
   No. 1 cylinder TDC sensor
   Oxygen sensor
   Throttle position sensor

3   To check the CHECK ENGINE light, verify that the light comes on for five seconds when you turn on the ignition switch. If the light doesn't come on, check the indicator light circuit and the light bulb.

4   If the CHECK ENGINE light comes on - and stays on - when you start the car, or if it

comes on while you're driving - and doesn't go off, drive the vehicle home and discontinue operation until you've output the malfunction code(s), identified the problem and fixed it.

5   Any malfunction codes memorised and stored by the ECU will remain in its memory even when the ignition switch is turned off, because the computer memory is battery-powered when the engine electrical system is shut off. But if the battery is disconnected, or the ECU is unplugged, memory is erased and any codes stored are lost. Because the ECU's memory is battery-powered when the engine is turned off, the battery must be fully charged and in good condition. If battery voltage is low, the ECU is unable to detect a malfunction or memorise and store a code.

6   To output the malfunction codes, hook up an analog voltmeter to the self-diagnosis connector as shown **(see illustration)**.

7   Turn the ignition switch to On. The ECU

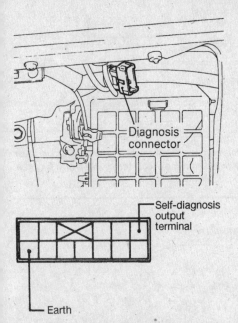

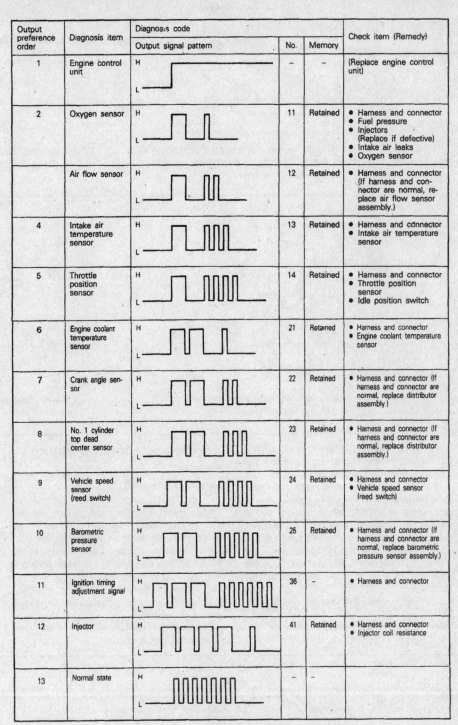

12.6 The self-diagnosis connector is located in the right (driver's) end of the instrument panel to put the ECU in the malfunction code output mode, simply hook up an analog voltmeter to the indicator terminal of the connector

Output preference order	Diagnosis item	Diagnosis code		No.	Memory	Check item (Remedy)
		Output signal pattern				
1	Engine control unit	H —⎍ L		–	–	(Replace engine control unit)
2	Oxygen sensor	H L		11	Retained	• Harness and connector • Fuel pressure • Injectors (Replace if defective) • Intake air leaks • Oxygen sensor
	Air flow sensor	H L		12	Retained	• Harness and connector (If harness and connector are normal, replace air flow sensor assembly.)
4	Intake air temperature sensor	H L		13	Retained	• Harness and connector • Intake air temperature sensor
5	Throttle position sensor	H L		14	Retained	• Harness and connector • Throttle position sensor • Idle position switch
6	Engine coolant temperature sensor	H L		21	Retained	• Harness and connector • Engine coolant temperature sensor
7	Crank angle sensor	H L		22	Retained	• Harness and connector (If harness and connector are normal, replace distributor assembly.)
8	No. 1 cylinder top dead center sensor	H L		23	Retained	• Harness and connector (If harness and connector are normal, replace distributor assembly.)
9	Vehicle speed sensor (reed switch)	H L		24	Retained	• Harness and connector • Vehicle speed sensor (reed switch)
10	Barometric pressure sensor	H L		25	Retained	• Harness and connector (If harness and connector are normal, replace barometric pressure sensor assembly.)
11	Ignition timing adjustment signal	H L		36	–	• Harness and connector
12	Injector	H L		41	Retained	• Harness and connector • Injector coil resistance
13	Normal state	H L		–	–	

12.7 Malfunction code and diagnosis table

will begin displaying the contents of its memory immediately. Now refer to the accompanying malfunction code and diagnosis table **(see illustration)**. If the MPI system is operating normally and there are no problems, the needle on the voltmeter indicates a normal pattern of deflection; in other words, it deflects on and off at a regular rate - the "on" and "off" segments are equal in duration (see the "normal state" output signal pattern). However, if the ECU outputs a malfunction code, the deflection of the voltmeter needle will be long or short (sort of like Morse code). For example, if the oxygen sensor is malfunctioning, the needle will make one long deflection, followed by a one short deflection; if the air flow sensor is bad, the needle will make one long deflection, then two short ones; and so on.

8   Note that the actual malfunction code number on the accompanying table is not the same number as the output preference order (far left column on the chart). That's because the ECU outputs any stored codes in a specific order to simplify your task of identifying each sequence of needle deflection patterns.

9   After you've output all stored codes and identified the general source of the problem(s), go to the next Section, or the indicated Chapter, check the suspected bad component or circuit and make the necessary repairs or renew the component.

10   After you've fixed the problem, check your work: Repeat the procedure above and verify that the malfunction code for the problem you fixed is no longer displayed. If the

code is still displayed, you haven't fixed the problem (or the ECU itself is faulty, but don't renew an ECU until you're positive that everything in a circuit or system is functioning normally).

11   To erase the ECU's memory of any stored codes once the problem is fixed, simply disconnect the negative terminal of the battery for at least 10 seconds.

13 Information sensors (fuel-injected models only)

Intake air temperature sensor

Refer to illustrations 13.2a, 13.2b, 13.3a and 13.3b

1   Unplug the electrical connector from the

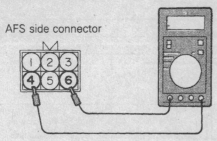

13.2a To check the inlet air temperature sensor on 1990 and earlier models, measure the resistance between terminals 4 and 6 of the air flow sensor

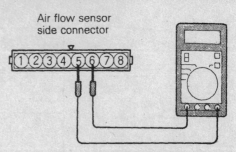

13.2b To check the inlet air temperature sensor on 1991 and later models, measure the resistance between terminals 5 and 6 of the air flow sensor

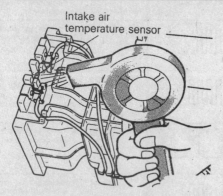

13.3a Heating the inlet air temperature sensor on a 1990 and earlier model

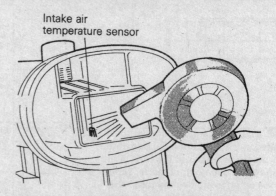

13.3b Heating the inlet air temperature sensor on a 1991 and later model

intake air temperature sensor.

2   Measure the resistance between the indicated terminals **(see illustrations)**.

3   While heating the sensor with a hair drier **(see illustrations)**, measure the resistance and note how the resistance changes as the sensor heats up. At 0-degrees C the resistance should be 6 K-ohms; at 2-degrees C it should be 2.7 K-ohms; at 80-degrees C, it should be 0.4 K-ohms. In other words, as the temperature goes up, the resistance should go down.

4   If your readings deviate significantly from these figures, renew the sensor. Don't forget to plug in the electrical connector.

Engine coolant temperature sensor

Refer to illustration 13.5

5   Unplug the electrical connector from the engine coolant temperature sensor, remove the sensor from the inlet manifold and immerse its temperature sensing tip in a container of water. Place a thermometer in the water so you can monitor the temperature and hook up an ohmmeter to the terminals of the sensor. As the water heats up, measure the resistance across the sensor terminals **(see illustration)**. Compare your measurements with the resistance values listed in this Chapter's Specifications.

6   If your readings deviate significantly from these figures, renew the sensor. Be sure to apply thread sealant or Teflon tape to the threads of the new unit to prevent leaks. Tighten the coolant temperature sensor to the torque listed in this Chapter's Specifications. Plug in the electrical connector.

Throttle position sensor

Refer to illustrations 13.8, 13.13, 13.14, 13.15 and 13.19

7   Unplug the electrical connector from the throttle position sensor.

8   Measure the resistance between terminals 1 and 4 **(see illustration)** and compare

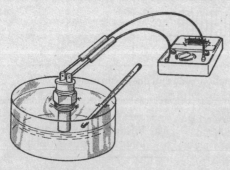

13.5 To check the engine coolant temperature sensor, immerse the sensing tip in a container of water and, as the water heats up, measure the resistance across the terminals

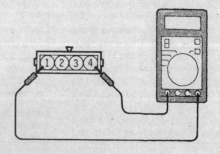

13.8 To check the throttle position sensor, measure the resistance between terminals 1 and 4

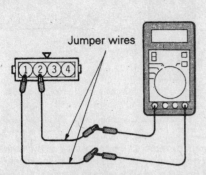

13.13 Hook up an ohmmeter between terminals 1 and 2 with a pair of jumper wires

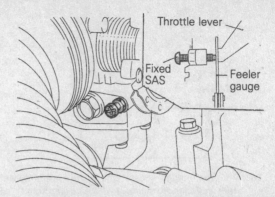

13.14 Insert feeler gauges with a combined thickness of 0.0256 in between the fixed SAS and the throttle lever (3.0L models)

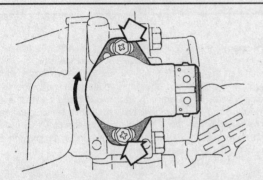

13.15 The TPS is located on the side of the throttle body - it's secured by two screws

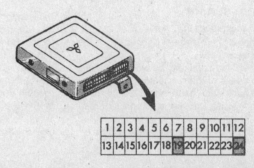

13.19 Hook up a voltmeter between terminals 19 (throttle position sensor output voltage) and terminal 24 (earth) of the engine control unit

your measurement with the resistance value listed in this Chapter's Specifications. If the indicated resistance is outside this specification, renew the throttle position sensor.

9   Using an analog ohmmeter hooked up to terminals 1 and 3, slowly open the throttle valve from its idle position all the way to the fully open position and verify that the resistance rises smoothly in proportion to the throttle valve opening angle.

10   If the indicated resistance doesn't fall within the specified values or operate as described above, renew the throttle position sensor.

11   Loosen the accelerator cable (see Chapter 4).

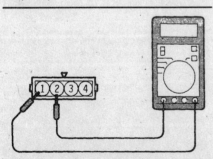

13.27 To check the idle position switch, check the continuity between terminal 1 (sensor earth) and terminal 2 (idle position switch) of the electrical connector for the throttle position sensor

12   Unplug the electrical connector for the throttle position sensor.

13   Hook up an ohmmeter between terminals 1 and 2 with a pair of jumper wires **(see illustration)**.

14   Insert feeler gauges with a total combined thickness of 0.0256 in between the fixed SAS and the throttle lever **(see illustration)**.

15   Loosen the throttle position sensor mounting screws **(see illustration)**.

16   Turn the sensor clockwise as far as it will go, then check the continuity between terminals 1 and 2.

17   Slowly turn the throttle position sensor in the counterclockwise direction to the point at which there's no longer any continuity. Tighten the sensor mounting screws securely at this point.

18   Plug in the electrical connector for the throttle position sensor.

19   Hook up a voltmeter between terminal 19 (throttle position sensor output voltage) and terminal 24 (earth) of the engine control unit **(see illustration)**.

20   Turn the ignition switch to On (but don't start the engine), check the output voltage of the throttle position sensor and compare your reading to the standard value listed in this Chapter's Specifications.

21   If the indicated resistance is outside the specified value, check the throttle position sensor and the wiring harness.

22   Remove the feeler gauge.

23   Turn the ignition switch to Off.

24   Adjust the tension of the accelerator cable (see Chapter 4).

Idle position switch

Refer to illustration 16.27

25   With the accelerator pedal released, verify that the throttle valve lever or the fixed SAS is pushed. If it isn't, adjust the fixed SAS (see Chapter 4).

26   Unplug the electrical connector from the throttle position sensor.

27   Check the continuity between terminal 1 (sensor earth) and terminal 2 (idle position switch) of the throttle position sensor connector **(see illustration)**. With the accelerator pedal pushed down, there shouldn't be any continuity (infinite resistance); with the pedal released, there should be continuity (zero resistance). If there is no continuity when the accelerator pedal is returned, loosen the throttle position sensor mounting screws, turn the sensor as far as it will go in the clockwise direction and check again. If the throttle position sensor still fails either test, renew it (the idle position switch is inside the throttle position sensor, so you have to renew the throttle position sensor to renew the idle position switch).

28   If you fit a new throttle position sensor/idle position switch unit, adjust it (see Steps 12 through 24) before tightening the throttle position sensor mounting screws securely.

29   Plug in the electrical connector.

6

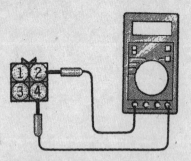

13.31 To check the oxygen sensor, check the continuity between terminal 2 and terminal 4 of the connector

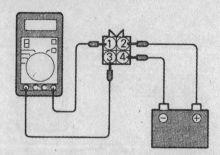

13.34 Connect terminal 2 and terminal 4 of the connector to the positive and negative battery terminals, respectively, with jumper wires, hook up a digital voltmeter to terminal 1 and terminal 3 of the connector, race the engine several times and measure the output voltage of the oxygen sensor

Oxygen sensor

Refer to illustrations 16.31 and 16.34

30   Unplug the electrical connector for the oxygen sensor.

31   Check the continuity between terminal 2 and terminal 4 of the connector **(see illustration)**. There should be about 20 ohms of resistance when the sensor is cool (approximately 20-degrees C).

32   If there's no continuity, renew the oxygen sensor (see Chapter 1).

33   Warm up the engine to normal operating temperature.

34   Connect terminal 2 and terminal 4 of the connector to the positive and negative battery terminals, respectively, with jumper wires **(see illustration)**. **Caution:** *Connecting the terminals on the connector to the battery terminals in the reverse order can damage the oxygen sensor.*

35   Hook up a digital voltmeter to terminal 1 and terminal 3 of the connector.

36   Race the engine several times and measure the output voltage of the oxygen sensor. Compare your measurement with the output voltage listed in this Chapter's Specifications. If the indicated voltage isn't within the specified voltage range, renew the oxygen sensor (see Chapter 1).

Chapter 7 Part A
Manual transmission

Contents

Specifications

General

Lubricant type.. See Chapter 1

Torque specifications   Nm

Transmission-to-engine bolts
    Four-cylinder engine 54
    V6 engines.. 81

1   General information

All vehicles covered in this manual come equipped with either a four-speed or five-speed manual transmission or an automatic transmission. All information on the manual transmissions is included in this part of Chapter 7. Information on the automatic transmission and transfer case can be found in Parts B and C of this Chapter.

The manual transmission used in these models is a four-speed or a five-speed unit, with fifth gear being an overdrive.

Due to the complexity, unavailability of new parts and the special tools necessary, internal repair by the home mechanic is not recommended. The information in this Chapter is limited to general information and removal and refitting of the transmission.

Depending on the expense involved in having a faulty transmission overhauled, it may be a good idea to renew the unit with either a new or rebuilt one. Your local dealer or transmission shop should be able to supply you with information concerning cost, availability and exchange policy. Regardless of how you decide to remedy a transmission problem, you can still save a lot of money by removing and refitting the unit yourself.

2   Oil seals - renewal

Refer to illustrations 2.5 and 2.13

1   Oil leaks frequently occur due to wear of the extension housing oil seal and/or the speedometer drive gear oil seal and O-ring. Renewal of these seals is relatively easy, since the repairs can usually be performed without removing the transmission or transfer case from the vehicle.

2   The housing oil seals are located at the extreme front and rear of the transfer case, where the driveshafts are attached. If leakage at the seal is suspected, raise the vehicle and support it securely on jackstands. If the seal is leaking, transmission lubricant will be built up on the front of the driveshaft and may be dripping from the front or rear of the transfer case.

3   Refer to Chapter 8 and remove the driveshaft.

4   Using a soft-faced hammer, carefully tap the dust shield (if equipped) to the rear and remove it from the transfer case. Be careful not to distort it.

5   Using a screwdriver or lever, carefully lever the oil seal out of the rear of the transfer case **(see illustration)**. Do not damage the splines on the output shaft.

6   If the oil seal cannot be removed with a screwdriver or lever, a special oil seal

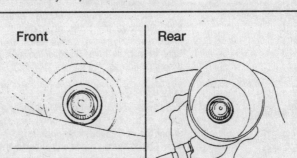

2.5 A screwdriver can be used to remove the front and rear transfer case oil seals

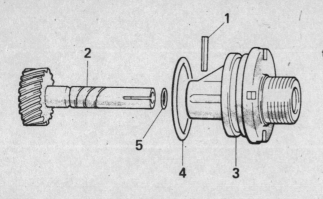

2.13 Exploded view of the speedometer driven gear assembly

1   Spring pin
2   Driven gear
3   Housing
4   O-ring
5   O-ring

removal tool (available at auto parts stores) will be required.

7   Using a large section of pipe or a very large deep socket as a drift, fit the new oil seal. Drive it into the bore squarely and make sure it's completely seated.

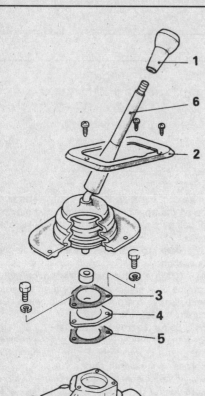

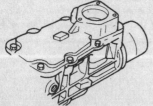

3.3 Shift lever details

1   Shift knob
2   Shifter boot plate
3   Gasket
4   Stopper plate
5   Gasket
6   Shift lever

8   Refit the dust shield (if equipped) by carefully tapping it into place. Lubricate the splines of the transmission output shaft and the outside of the driveshaft sleeve yoke with lightweight grease, then refit the driveshaft. Be careful not to damage the lip of the new seal.

9   The speedometer gear housing is located on the side of the extension housing. Look for transmission lubricant around the housing to determine if the O-rings are leaking.

10   Unscrew the speedometer cable casing from the speedometer gear housing.

11   Mark the relationship of the speedometer gear housing to the extension housing.

12   Remove the bolt and withdraw the housing.

13   Fit a new O-ring on the driven gear shaft and on the housing, then refit the housing **(see illustration)**.

3   Shift lever - removal and refitting

Refer to illustration 3.3

Removal

1   Disconnect the negative cable from the battery.

2   If your vehicle is equipped with a centre console, remove it (see Chapter 11).

3   Remove the screws that attach the shifter boot plate to the tunnel **(see illustration)**. Lift off the plate and pull back the rubber boot. It has a lip that fits over the sheet-metal of the tunnel; take care not to tear the boot as you pull it back.

4   Place the shift lever in the Neutral position. Remove the bolts attaching the shift lever assembly to the transmission and carefully lift out the lever. Plug or cover the hole with a clean rag.

Refitting

5   Apply a thin coat of RTV sealant to both sides of the two gaskets (one over and one under the shift lever stopper plate).

6   Apply multi-purpose grease to the shift lever bush and all shift lever sliding surfaces.

7   The remainder of refitting is the reverse of removal. Tighten the fasteners securely.

4   Transmission mount - check and renewal

Refer to illustration 4.3

Check

1   Insert a large screwdriver or lever into the space between the transmission extension housing and the crossmember and try to prise up slightly.

2   The transmission should not move from the crossmember. If there is any cracking or separation of the rubber from the mounting plate, renew the mount.

Renewal

3   Support the transmission with a jack. Place a block of wood on the jack head to serve as a cushion. Remove the fasteners attaching the mount to the crossmember and the transmission **(see illustration)**.

4   Raise the transmission slightly with the jack and remove the mount.

5   Refitting is the reverse of removal. Be sure to tighten the nuts/bolts securely.

4.3 Transmission mount

5   Manual transmission - removal and refitting

Removal

1   Disconnect the negative battery cable from the battery.

2   Remove the air cleaner assembly (see Chapter 4), then remove the starter (see Chapter 5).

3   Raise the vehicle and support it securely on jackstands. Place a drain pan under the transmission, remove the drain plug and allow the transmission to lubricant to drain.

4   Remove the driveshaft(s) (see Chapter 8).

5   Remove the shift lever (see Section 3).

6   Disconnect the speedometer cable where it enters the transmission. Bend back the retaining strap (if equipped) that holds the speedometer cable housing to the frame crossmember and pull the speedometer

cable away from the engine and transmission. Lay it on top of the left frame rail to keep it out of the way.

7   Push forward on the parking brake lever and. disengage the cable from the lever. Loosen the parking brake cable housing clamp in front of the frame crossmember and slide the cable housing forward to free it from the support bracket on the crossmember. Lay the cable on top of the left frame rail to keep it out. of the way. Remove the pin attaching the rear parking brake cable balancer to the parking brake lever.

8   Unplug the electrical connector for the back-up light switch (just behind the steering box). Disconnect the clutch cable from the clutch control lever at the transmission bellhousing. Back off the clutch cable adjuster and put as much freeplay as possible in the cable. Pull the rubber dust cover from the end of the clutch cable and slip the cable through the mounting boss on the transmission bellhousing. Lay the clutch cable on top of the left frame rail to keep it out of the way.

9   Remove the splash shield from the front of the transmission. It is attached to the engine with two bolts and to the transmission with two bolts.

10 Remove the bolt attaching the exhaust pipe bracket to the transmission.

11 Support the engine with a hoist or, if a hoist isn't available, a floor jack placed under the engine sump (place a wood block on the jack head to serve as a cushion). Remove the bolts that attach the transmission bellhousing to the engine block.

12 Remove the two nuts that attach the transmission to the transmission support crossmember.

13 Support the transmission with a sturdy jack (preferably one equipped with wheels or casters). Remove the transmission support crossmember.

14 Carefully move the transmission/transfer case assembly straight back and away from the engine by moving the transmission supporting jack toward the rear of the vehicle. It would be very helpful to have an assistant at this point. You must pull the transmission/transfer case straight back until it is completely free from the engine or damage to the input shaft may result.

15 Slowly lower the jack and move the transmission/transfer case out from under the vehicle.

Refitting

16 Refitting is the reverse of removal. Be sure to check the clutch disc to make sure it is centre (see Chapter 8) before sliding the transmission into place. Also, before refitting, apply a coat of lithium-based grease to the end of the transmission input shaft and the splines.

17 With the help of an assistant, line up the clutch with the transmission input shaft. Make sure the engine and transmission/transfer case are in a straight line, not angled in relation to each other. Carefully slide the transmission forward until the bell-

housing contacts the engine block. To properly engage the clutch disc and the transmission input shaft, you may have to rotate the crankshaft slightly (with a spanner on the bolt holding the pulley to the front of the crankshaft). Do not force the input shaft into the clutch. If the transmission does not move forward smoothly, either the clutch disc/input shaft splines are not lined up, or the transmission is cocked at an angle.

18 Once the transmission/transfer case assembly is in place, support it securely and tighten all of the mounting bolts to the torque listed in this Chapter's Specifications.

19 Don't forget to fill the transmission to the proper level with the recommended lubricant (see Chapter 1).

20 Be sure to adjust the clutch as described in Chapter 8.

6 Manual transmission overhaul - general information

Refer to illustrations 6.4a, 6.4b and 6.4c

Overhauling a manual transmission is a difficult job for the do-it-yourselfer. It involves the disassembly and reassembly of many small parts. Numerous clearances must be precisely measured and, if necessary, changed with select fit spacers and snap-rings. As a result, if transmission problems arise, it can be removed and refitted by a competent do-it-yourselfer, but overhaul should be left to a transmission repair shop. Rebuilt transmissions may be available - check with your dealer parts department and auto parts stores. At any rate, the time and money involved in an overhaul is almost sure to exceed the cost of a rebuilt unit.

Nevertheless, it's not impossible for an inexperienced mechanic to rebuild a transmission if the special tools are available and the job is done in a deliberate step-by-step manner so nothing is overlooked.

The tools necessary for an overhaul include internal and external snap-ring pliers, a bearing puller, a slide hammer, a set of pin punches, a dial indicator and possibly a hydraulic press. In addition, a large, sturdy workbench and a vise or transmission stand will be required.

During disassembly of the transmission, make careful notes of how each piece comes off, where it fits in relation to other pieces and what holds it in place.

Before taking the transmission apart for repair, it will help if you have some idea what area of the transmission is malfunctioning. Certain problems can be closely tied to specific areas in the transmission, which can make component examination and renewal easier. Refer to the *Troubleshooting* Section at the front of this manual for information regarding possible sources of trouble.

7A

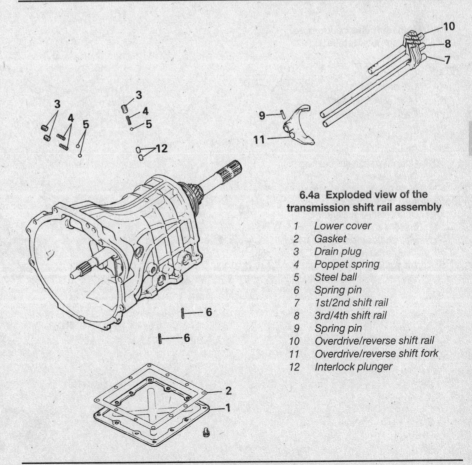

6.4a Exploded view of the transmission shift rail assembly

1   *Lower cover*
2   *Gasket*
3   *Drain plug*
4   *Poppet spring*
5   *Steel ball*
6   *Spring pin*
7   *1st/2nd shift rail*
8   *3rd/4th shift rail*
9   *Spring pin*
10 *Overdrive/reverse shift rail*
11 *Overdrive/reverse shift fork*
12 *Interlock plunger*

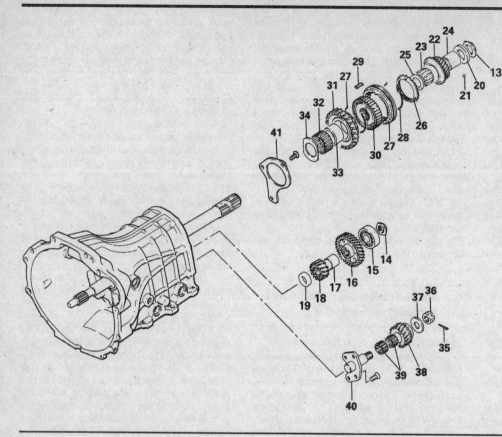

6.4b Exploded view of the transmission mainshaft assembly

13 Mainshaft locknut
14 Countershaft locknut
15 Countershaft rear bearing
16 Countershaft overdrive gear
17 Spacer
18 Reverse idler gear
19 Spacer
20 Sleeve
21 Steel ball
22 Overdrive gear
23 Needle bearing
24 Bearing sleeve
25 Bearing spacer
26 Synchroniser key
27 Synchroniser hub
28 Synchroniser spring
29 Synchroniser key
30 Synchroniser hub
31 Reverse gear
32 Needle bearing
33 Bearing sleeve
34 Spacer
35 Split pin
36 Slotted nut
37 Thrust washer
38 Reverse idler gear
39 Needle bearing
40 Reverse idler gear shaft
41 Rear bearing retainer

6.4c Mainshaft and countergear assembly details

42 Mainshaft bearing
43 Spacer
44 Countergear
45 Front bearing retainer
46 Front bearing retainer gasket
47 Spacer
48 Oil seal
49 Spacer
50 Countergear front bearing outer race
51 Main drive gear assembly
52 1st/2nd shift fork
53 Countershaft assembly
54 3rd/4th shift fork
55 Mainshaft assembly
56 Needle bearing
57 Transmission case

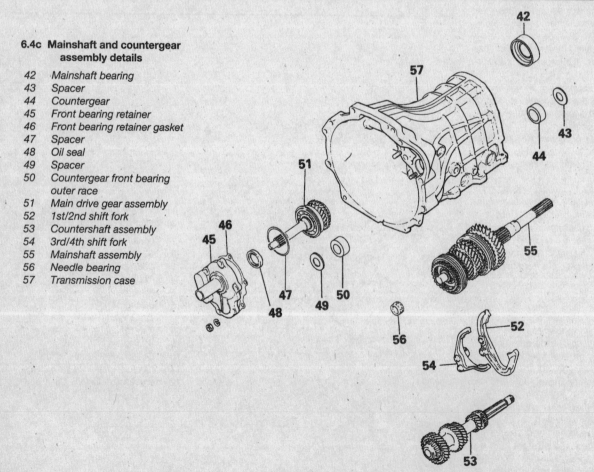

Chapter 7 Part B
Automatic transmission

Contents

Specifications

Torque specifications

	Nm
Torque converter-to-driveplate bolts	34
Transmission drain plug	20
Transmission-to-engine bolts	
Transmission-to-engine bolts	
Four-cylinder engine	
10X40 mm and 10X65 mm bolts	50
10X65 mm bolts	30
8X25 and 8X60 mm bolts	25
V6 engines	
12X40, 12X35 and 12X50 mm bolts	75
12X55 mm bolts	90
10X55 mm bolts	31
10X40 mm bolts	36
10X30 mm bolts	42

7B

1 General information

All vehicles covered in this manual come equipped with either a five-speed manual transmission or an automatic transmission. All information on the automatic transmission is included in this, Part B, of Chapter 7. Information on the manual transmission can be found in Part A of this Chapter.

Due to the complexity of the automatic transmissions covered in this manual and the need for specialised equipment to perform most service operations, this Chapter contains only general diagnosis, adjustment and removal and installation procedures.

If the transmission requires major repair work, it should be left to a dealer service department or an automotive or transmission repair shop. You can, however, remove and install the transmission yourself and save the expense, even if the repair work is done by a transmission shop.

2 Diagnosis - general

Note: *Automatic transmission malfunctions may be caused by five general conditions: poor engine performance, improper adjustments, hydraulic malfunctions, mechanical malfunctions or malfunctions in the computer or its signal network. Diagnosis of these problems should always begin with a check of the* easily repaired items: fluid level and condition (see Chapter 1), shift linkage adjustment and throttle linkage adjustment. Next, perform a road test to determine if the problem has been corrected or if more diagnosis is necessary. If the problem persists after the preliminary tests and corrections are completed, additional diagnosis should be done by a dealer service department or transmission repair shop. Refer to the Troubleshooting Section at the front of this manual for information on symptoms of transmission problems.

Preliminary checks

1 Drive the vehicle to warm the transmission to normal operating temperature.

2   Check the fluid level as described in Chapter 1:

a) If the fluid level is unusually low, add enough fluid to bring the level within the designated area of the dipstick, then check for external leaks (see below).

b) If the fluid level is abnormally high, drain off the excess, then check the drained fluid for contamination by coolant. The presence of engine coolant in the automatic transmission fluid indicates that a failure has occurred in the internal radiator walls that separate the coolant from the transmission fluid (see Chapter 3).

c) If the fluid is foaming, drain it and refill the transmission, then check for coolant in the fluid or a high fluid level.

3   Check the engine idle speed. **Note:** If the engine is malfunctioning, do not proceed with the preliminary checks until it has been repaired and runs normally.

4   Check the throttle control cable for freedom of movement. Adjust it if necessary (see Section 4). **Note:** The throttle cable may function properly when the engine is shut off and cold, but it may malfunction once the engine is hot. Check it cold and at normal engine operating temperature.

5   Inspect the shift linkage (see Section 3). Make sure that it's properly adjusted and that the linkage operates smoothly.

Fluid leak diagnosis

6   Most fluid leaks are easy to locate visually. Repair usually consists of renewing a seal or gasket. If a leak is difficult to find, the following procedure may help.

7   Identify the fluid. Make sure it's transmission fluid and not engine oil or brake fluid (automatic transmission fluid is a deep red colour).

8   Try to pinpoint the source of the leak. Drive the vehicle several miles, then park it over a large sheet of cardboard. After a minute or two, you should be able to locate the leak by determining the source of the fluid dripping onto the cardboard.

9   Make a careful visual inspection of the suspected component and the area immediately around it. Pay particular attention to gasket mating surfaces. A mirror is often helpful for finding leaks in areas that are hard to see.

10   If the leak still cannot be found, clean the suspected area thoroughly with a degreaser or solvent, then dry it.

11   Drive the vehicle for several miles at normal operating temperature and varying speeds. After driving the vehicle, visually inspect the suspected component again.

12   Once the leak has been located, the cause must be determined before it can be properly repaired. If a gasket is renewed but the sealing flange is bent, the new gasket will not stop the leak. The bent flange must be straightened.

13   Before attempting to repair a leak, check to make sure that the following conditions are corrected or they may cause

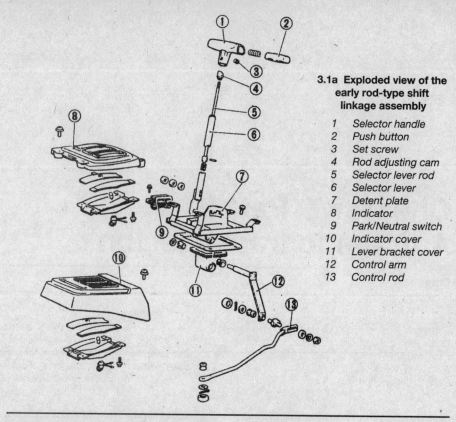

3.1a   Exploded view of the early rod-type shift linkage assembly

1   Selector handle
2   Push button
3   Set screw
4   Rod adjusting cam
5   Selector lever rod
6   Selector lever
7   Detent plate
8   Indicator
9   Park/Neutral switch
10   Indicator cover
11   Lever bracket cover
12   Control arm
13   Control rod

another leak. **Note:** Some of the following conditions cannot be fixed without highly specialised tools and expertise. Such problems must be referred to a transmission repair shop or a dealer service department.

Gasket leaks

14   Check the pan periodically. Make sure the bolts are tight, no bolts are missing, the gasket is in good condition and the pan is flat (dents in the pan may indicate damage to the valve body inside).

15   If the pan gasket is leaking, the fluid level or the fluid pressure may be too high, the vent may be plugged, the pan bolts may be too tight, the pan sealing flange may be warped, the sealing surface of the transmission housing may be damaged, the gasket may be damaged or the transmission casting may be cracked or porous. If sealant instead of gasket material has been used to form a seal between the pan and the transmission housing, it may be the wrong sealant.

Seal leaks

16   If a transmission seal is leaking, the fluid level or pressure may be too high, the vent may be plugged, the seal bore may be damaged, the seal itself may be damaged or improperly installed, the surface of the shaft protruding through the seal may be damaged or a loose bearing may be causing excessive shaft movement.

17   Make sure the dipstick tube seal is in good condition and the tube is properly seated. Periodically check the area around the speedometer gear or sensor for leakage.

If transmission fluid is evident, check the O-ring for damage.

Case leaks

18   If the case itself appears to be leaking, the casting is porous and will have to be repaired or renewed.

19   Make sure the oil cooler hose fittings are tight and in good condition.

Fluid comes out vent pipe or fill tube

20   If this condition occurs, the transmission is overfilled, there is coolant in the fluid, the case is porous, the dipstick is incorrect, the vent is plugged or the drain-back holes are plugged.

---

3   Shift linkage - check and adjustment

Refer to illustrations 3.1a, 3.1b, 3.3, 3.5 and 3.9

Rod-type

1   The control rod is adjusted where it connects to the control arm **(see illustrations)**.

2   Raise the front of the vehicle and support it securely on jackstands. Loosen the adjusting locknut on the control rod-to-control arm joint.

3   Place the shift control lever (on the left side of the transmission) in the neutral position. Place the selector lever (inside the vehicle) in the neutral position also **(see illustration)**.

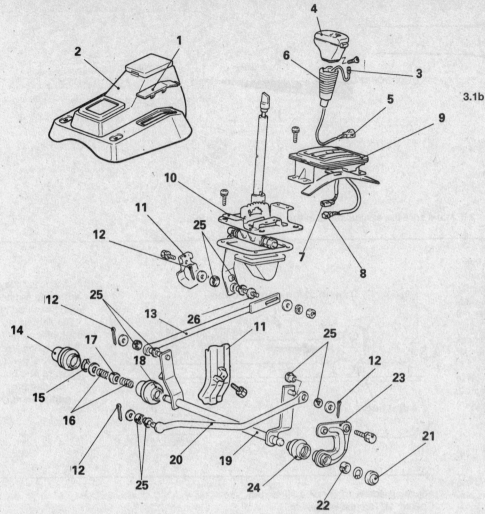

3.1b Exploded view of the later rod-type shift linkage assembly

1 Screw cover
2 Console
3 Overdrive switch
4 Knob
5 Electrical connector
6 Cover
7 Inhibitor switch and harness
8 Shift position indicator connector
9 Indicator plate
10 Bracket
11 Insulator
12 Split pin
13 Control rod
14 Dust cover
15 Snap-ring
16 Spring
17 Cross shaft bush
18 Cross shaft boot
19 Selector cross shaft
20 Control rod
21 Cap
22 Bush
23 Bracket
24 Boot
25 Bush
26 Pin

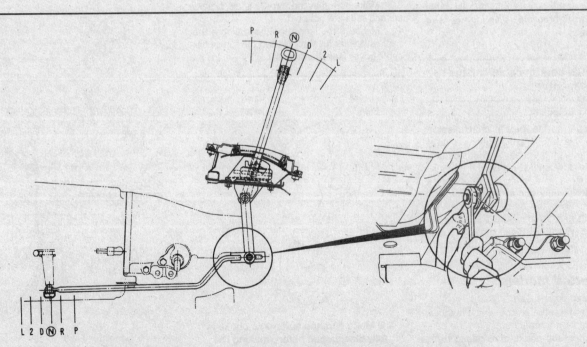

3.3 Place the shift control lever and the selector lever in the "N" position

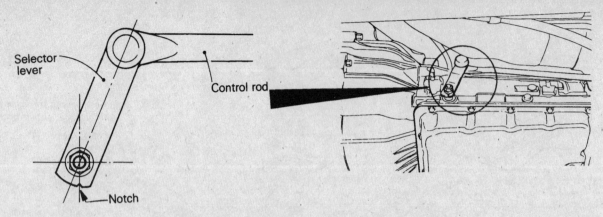

3.5 Make sure the engine starts in the "N" and "P" positions

4   At this point, the control rod adjustment is made automatically. Tighten the control rod-to-control arm adjusting locknut securely.

5   Set the parking brake. Apply the brakes, then check to make sure the engine does not start while the shift lever is in the "D", "L", "2", or "R" position. At the same time check to be sure that the engine starts in the "N" and "P" positions (see illustration).

6   Set the shifter lever in the "R" position to check that the backup lights are illuminated, and not illuminated in any other position (make this check with the engine off).

Cable-type

7   Loosen the adjusting nut at the shift lever end of the cable.

8   Put the shift lever in the vehicle and the control lever (on the left side of the transmission), in the "N" position.

9   To adjust the cable, lightly pull the cable forward and tighten the adjusting nut (see illustration).

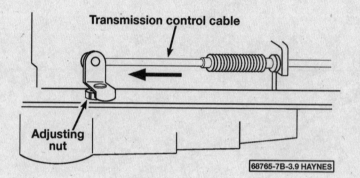

3.9 After the adjusting nut has been loosened and the shifter has been placed in the "N" positions, pull the cable gently forward and then tighten the adjusting nut

adjusting screw to the specified rpm (see Chapter 1). Turn the engine off.

3   Make sure that the throttle lever, brackets and rods are not bent.

4   Measure the length between where the cable stops (at full throttle) and the top of the cable cover (see illustration).

---

4   Throttle control cable/linkage - adjustment

1   The throttle control linkage adjustment is very important to proper transmission operation. This adjustment positions a valve which controls shift speed, shift quality and part-throttle downshift sensitivity. If the linkage is adjusted so it is too short, slippage between shifts may occur. If the linkage is adjusted so it is too long, shifts may be delayed and part-throttle downshifts may be very erratic. **Warning:** *When working under the vehicle be sure to support it on sturdy jackstands.*

Carburetted models

Refer to illustrations 4.2 and 4.4

2   Start and run the engine until it reaches normal operating temperature. With the carburettor automatic choke disengaged from the fast idle cam (see illustration), adjust the engine idle speed (by turning the speed

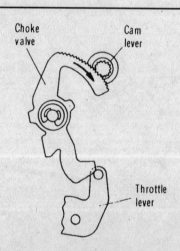

4.2 Make sure the automatic choke is fully disengaged before making the throttle control linkage adjustment

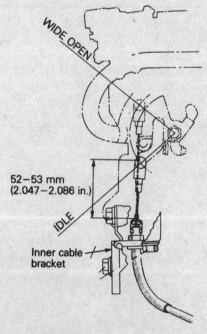

4.4 Throttle control cable adjustment details (1987 and 1988 models)

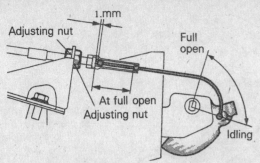

4.7 When the engine is idling, the throttle control lever on the transmission should be within the range shown (1 mm)

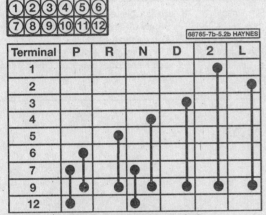

Note: ●——● indicate that there is a continuity between the terminals.

Terminal	P	R	N	D	2	L
1					●	
2						●
3				●		
4			●			
5		●				
6	●					
7	●		●			
9	●	●	●	●	●	●
12	●		●			

68765-7b-5.2b HAYNES

5.2b Park/Neutral safety switch continuity table and terminal guide - 1991 and later models

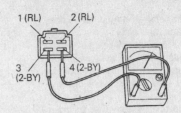

	Terminals	1	2	3	4
Select lever position					
P				○——○	
R		○——○			
N				○——○	

5.2a Park/Neutral safety switch continuity table and terminal guide - 1990 and earlier models

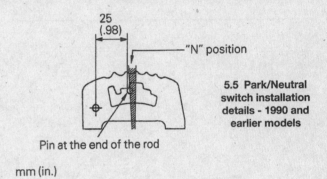

Pin at the end of the rod

5.5 Park/Neutral switch installation details - 1990 and earlier models

mm (in.)

---

5   If it is out of adjustment, adjust the cable bracket by moving it up or down.

Fuel injected models

Refer to illustration 4.7

6   Be sure the throttle lever and bracket are not bent or distorted.

7   Move the throttle to the full-open position and adjust the space between the cable stop and housing to 1 mm (see illustration).

5   Park/Neutral safety switch - check and renewal

Refer to illustrations 5.2a, 5.2b and 5.5

Check

1   The Park/Neutral safety switch completes the circuit from the ignition switch to the starter when the shift lever is in the Park or Neutral positions.

2   To check the switch, disconnect the electrical connector and using an ohmmeter, check for continuity on the indicated terminals with the shift lever in the indicated positions (see illustrations).

Renewal

1990 and earlier models

3   Remove the centre console (see Chapter 11).

4   Disconnect the electrical connector, remove the mounting screws and remove the switch from the shift lever assembly.

5   Install the new switch leaving the mounting screws loose. Position the shift lever with the pin on the end of the rod positioned as shown (see illustration).

6   Connect an ohmmeter to terminals 3 and 4 of the Park/Neutral switch connector (see illustration 5.2a). Move the switch back and forth until continuity is indicated on the meter. Position the switch with 2.5 mm of clearance between the switch and the shift lever and tighten the mounting screws.

7   Install the centre console. Verify the engine starts in Park and Neutral only.

1991 and later models

8   Apply the parking brake securely and position the shift lever in the Neutral position. Raise the vehicle and support it securely on jackstands.

9   Disconnect the electrical connector from the Park/Neutral switch.

10   Remove the nut, washer and lever from the selector shaft.

11   Remove the mounting bolts and slide the switch off the selector shaft.

12   Install the switch leaving the mounting bolts loose. Install the shift lever, washer and nut. Tighten the nut securely.

13   Move the switch back and forth until the two raised bosses are aligned with the edges of the selector shaft (with the transmission in Neutral) and tighten the mounting bolts securely.

14   Adjust the shift cable (see Section 3).

15   Lower the vehicle and verify the engine starts in Park and Neutral only.

6   Automatic transmission - removal and installation

Refer to illustrations 6.6 and 6.11

Removal

1   Disconnect the negative cable from the battery.

2   Remove the knob from the transfer case shift lever.

3   Raise the vehicle and support it securely

7B

on jackstands.

4   Drain the transmission fluid (see Chapter 1), then reinstall the pan.

5   Remove the torque converter cover.

6   Mark the relationship of the torque converter to one of the studs so they can be installed in the same position **(see illustration)**.

7   Remove the torque converter-to-driveplate nuts. Turn the crankshaft for access to each nut. Turn the crankshaft in a clockwise direction only (as viewed from the front).

8   Remove the starter motor (see Chapter 5).

9   Remove the driveshaft(s) (see Chapter 8).

10 Disconnect the speedometer cable.

11 Detach the electrical connectors from the transmission **(see illustration)**.

12 Remove any exhaust components which will interfere with transmission removal (see Chapter 4).

13 Disconnect the throttle control linkage

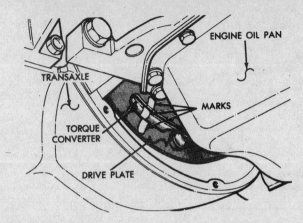

6.6 Mark the relationship to the torque converter to the driveplate

rod or cable.

14 Disconnect the shift linkage.

15 Support the engine with a jack. Use a block of wood under the sump to spread the load.

16 Support the transmission with a jack -

preferably a jack made for this purpose. Safety chains will help steady the transmission on the jack.

17 Remove the rear mount to crossmember bolts and the two crossmember-to-frame bolts.

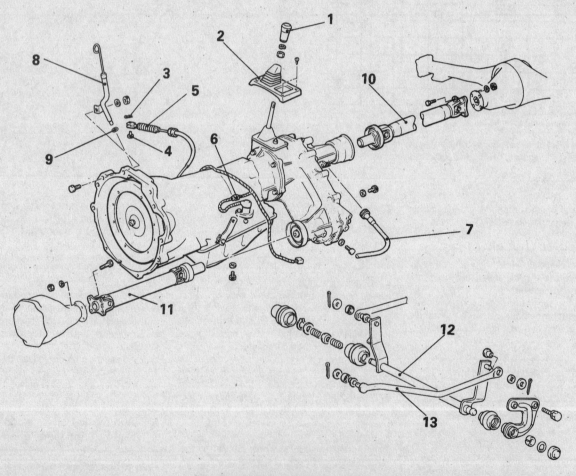

6.11 Transmission installation details

1	Transfer case lever	6	Overdrive solenoid harness
2	Console	7	Speedometer cable
3	Clip	8	Dipstick tube assembly
4	Clevis pin	9	O-ring
5	Throttle control cable	10	Rear driveshaft

11	Front driveshaft
12	Shifter cross shaft
13	Transmission control rod

18   Remove the two engine rear support-to-transmission extension housing bolts.
19   Raise the transmission enough to allow removal of the crossmember.
20   Remove the bolts securing the transmission to the engine.
21   Lower the transmission slightly and disconnect and plug the transmission fluid cooler lines.
22   Remove the transmission dipstick tube.
23   Move the transmission to the rear to disengage it from the engine block dowel pins and make sure the torque converter is detached from the driveplate. Secure the torque converter to the transmission so it won't fall out during removal.

Installation

24   Prior to installation, make sure the torque converter hub is securely engaged in the pump.
25   With the transmission secured to the jack, raise it into position. Be sure to keep it level so the torque converter does not slide forward.
26   Turn the torque converter to line up the studs with the holes in the driveplate. The mark on the torque converter and the stud made in Step 5 must line up.
27   Move the transmission forward carefully until the dowel pins and the torque converter are engaged.
28   Install the transmission housing-to-engine bolts. Tighten them securely.
29   Install the torque converter-to-driveplate nuts. Tighten the nuts to the torque listed in this Chapter's Specifications.
30   Connect the transmission fluid cooler lines. Install the transmission mount crossmember and through-bolts. Tighten the bolts and nuts securely.
31   Remove the jacks supporting the transmission and the engine.
32   Install the dipstick tube.
33   Install the starter motor (see Chapter 5).
34   Connect the shift and throttle control cable/linkage.
35   Plug in the transmission electrical connectors.
36   Install the torque converter cover.
37   Install the driveshaft(s).
39   Connect the speedometer cable.
40   Adjust the shift linkage.
41   Install any exhaust system components that were removed or disconnected.
42   Lower the vehicle.
43   Fill the transmission with the proper type and amount of fluid (see Chapter 1), run the engine and check for fluid leaks.

7B

Notes

Chapter 7 Part C
Transfer case

Contents

7C

Specifications

Torque specifications

	Nm
4WD indicator light switch	30
Transfer case-to-transmission nuts and bolts	30

---

1 General information

These models are equipped with a transfer case mounted on the transmission housing. Drive is passed through the transmission and transfer case to the front and rear axles by the driveshafts.

The transfer case is combined with the transmission to form one unit. The transfer case can't be removed without first removing the transmission from the vehicle. Because of the special tools and techniques required, disassembly and overhaul of the transfer case should be left to a dealer service department or properly equipped shop. You can, however, remove and refit the transmission/transfer case yourself and save the expense, even if the repair work is done by a specialist.

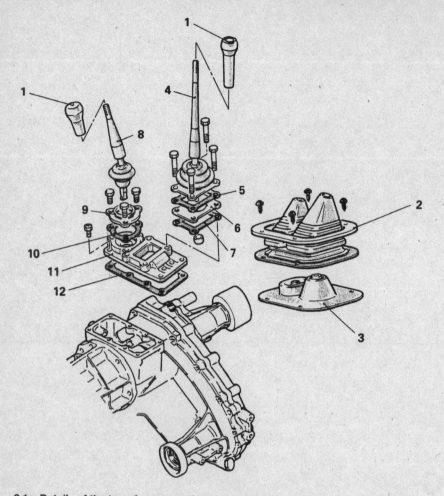

2.1a Details of the transfer case and transmission shift levers (manual transmission)

1	Shift lever knob	7	Gasket
2	Dust cover retaining plate	8	Transfer case shift lever
3	Shift lever cover	9	Control housing cover
4	Transmission shift lever	10	Gasket
5	Gasket	11	Control housing
6	Stopper plate	12	Gasket

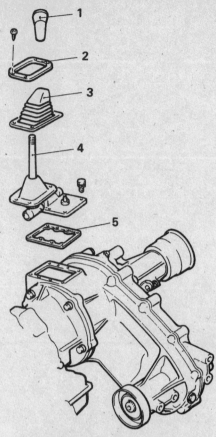

2.1b Details of the transfer case shift lever (automatic transmission)

1   *shift lever knob*
2   *Dust cover retaining plate*
3   *Shift lever cover*
4   *Transfer case shift lever*
5   *Control housing gasket*

2   Shift lever - removal and refitting

Refer to illustrations 2.1a and 2.1b

The procedure for removing the transfer case shift lever is essentially the same as for removing the manual transmission shift lever **(see illustrations)**. Refer to Chapter 7 Part A, Section 3, and follow the procedure outlined there.

3   4WD indicator light switches - removal and refitting

Refer to illustration 3.2

1   Raise the vehicle and support it securely on jackstands.
2   The 4WD indicator light switches are located on the right-hand side of the transfer case housing **(see illustration)**.

3   Unscrew the switch and remove the steel ball.
4   Refitting is the reverse of removal. Be sure to apply Teflon tape or a small amount of RTV sealant to the threads. Tighten the switch to the torque listed in this Chapter's Specifications.
7   Lower the vehicle.

4   Transfer case overhaul - general information

On these models the transmission/transfer case assembly is designed to be overhauled as a unit. Consequently, overhaul should be left to a repair shop specialising in both transmission and transfer cases. Rebuilt units may be available - check with your dealer parts department and auto parts stores. At any rate, some cost savings can be

3.2 Location of the 4WD indicator light switches (arrows)

realised by removing the transmission/transfer case unit and taking it to the shop (see Part A or B of this Chapter).

Chapter 8
Clutch and driveline

Contents

Specifications

Clutch
Hydraulic system fluid type	See Chapter 1
Clutch disc minimum lining thickness	0.3 mm
Clutch pedal freeplay	See Chapter 1

Driveline
U-joint journal endplay	0.06 mm
Brake contact surface depth	11.8 to 12.2 mm
Driveaxle axial play	0.2 to 0.5 mm

Torque specifications
	Nm
Front hub turning force (measured with spring scale)	4 to 18
Clutch pressure plate-to-flywheel bolts	12 to 14

Torque specifications (continued)

	Nm
Driveline	
U-joint flange bolts	
All but 1996 limited slip models	
Front or rear driveshaft	50 to 60
1996 limited slip differential models	
Rear driveshaft	98 to 108
Rear axle	
Bearing retainer/brake backing plate-to-axle housing nuts	50 to 60
Differential pinion shaft nut	190 to 250
Front axle	
Differential carrier bolts	60 to 70
Free-wheeling hub body assembly bolts	50 to 60
Manual free-wheeling hub cover bolts	50 to 60
Differential pinion shaft nut	
Four-cylinder engine	160 to 220
V6 engine	190 to 250
Right front driveaxle flange bolts	50 to 60 Nm

1 General information

The information in this Chapter deals with the components from the rear of the engine to the front and rear wheels, except for the transmission and transfer case, which are dealt with in the previous Chapter. For the purposes of this Chapter, these components are grouped into four categories: clutch, driveshaft, front axle and rear axle. Separate Sections within this Chapter offer general descriptions and checking procedures for each of these groups.

Since nearly all the procedures covered in this Chapter involve working under the vehicle, make sure it's securely supported on sturdy jackstands or on a hoist where the vehicle can be easily raised and lowered.

2 Clutch - description and check

Refer to illustrations 2.1a and 2.1b

1   All models equipped with a manual transmission feature a single dry-plate, diaphragm spring-type clutch **(see illustrations)**. The actuation is through a hydraulic system.

2   When the clutch pedal is depressed, hydraulic fluid (under pressure from the clutch master cylinder) flows into the release cylinder. Because the release cylinder is connected to the clutch fork, the fork moves the release bearing into contact with the pressure plate release fingers, disengaging the clutch disc.

3   Terminology can be a problem regarding the clutch components because common names have in some cases changed from that used by the manufacturer. For example, the driven plate is also called the clutch plate or disc, the clutch release bearing is sometimes called a throwout bearing, the release cylinder is sometimes called the operating or slave cylinder.

4   Due to the slow wearing qualities of the

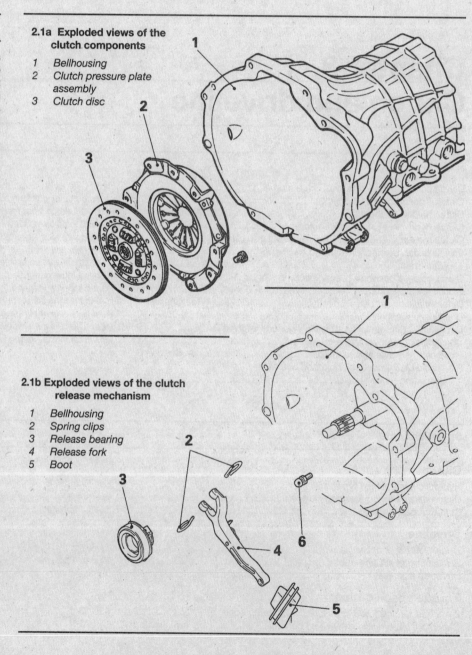

2.1a Exploded views of the clutch components

1   *Bellhousing*
2   *Clutch pressure plate assembly*
3   *Clutch disc*

2.1b Exploded views of the clutch release mechanism

1   *Bellhousing*
2   *Spring clips*
3   *Release bearing*
4   *Release fork*
5   *Boot*

clutch, it is not easy to decide when to go to the trouble of removing the transmission in order to check the wear on the friction lining. The only positive indication that something should be done is when it starts to slip or when squealing noises during engagement indicate that the friction lining has worn down to the rivets. In such instances it can only be hoped that the friction surfaces on the flywheel and pressure plate have not been badly worn or scored.

5   A clutch will wear according to the way in which it is used. Much intentional slipping of the clutch while driving - rather than the correct selection of gears - will accelerate wear. It is best to assume, however, that the disc will need renewal at 64,000 kilometres.

6   Because of the clutch's location between the engine and transmission, it cannot be worked on without removing either the engine or transmission. If repairs which would require removal of the engine are not needed, the quickest way to gain access to the clutch is by removing the transmission as described in Chapter 7.

7   Other than to renew components with obvious damage, some preliminary checks should be performed to diagnose a clutch system failure.

a) *The first check should be of the fluid level in the clutch master. If the fluid level is low, add fluid as necessary and re-test. If the master cylinder runs dry, or if any of the hydraulic components are serviced, bleed the hydraulic system as described in Section 8.*

b) *To check "clutch spin down time", run the engine at normal idle speed with the transmission in Neutral (clutch pedal up - engaged). Disengage the clutch (pedal down), wait nine seconds and shift the transmission into Reverse. No grinding noise should be heard. A grinding noise would indicate component failure in the pressure plate assembly or the clutch disc.*

c) *To check for complete clutch release, run the engine (with the brake on to prevent movement) and hold the clutch pedal approximately 12 mm from the floor mat. Shift the transmission between 1st gear and Reverse several times. If the shift is not smooth, component failure is indicated. Measure the hydraulic release cylinder pushrod travel (hydraulically actuated models). With the clutch pedal completely depressed the release cylinder pushrod should extend substantially. If the pushrod will not extend very far or not at all, check the fluid level in the clutch master cylinder. The system may need to be bled (see Section 8).*

d) *Visually inspect the clutch pedal bush at the top of the clutch pedal to make sure there is no sticking or excessive wear.*

e) *Under the vehicle, check that the release fork is solidly mounted on the ball stud.*

Note: *Because access to the clutch compo-*

nents is an involved process, any time either the engine or transmission is removed, the clutch disc, pressure plate assembly and release bearing should be carefully inspected and, if necessary, renewed with new parts. Since the clutch disc is normally the item of highest wear, it should be renewed as a matter of course if there is any question about its condition.

---

3   Clutch components - removal, inspection and refitting

Refer to illustrations 3.10 and 3.12
Warning: *Dust produced by clutch wear and deposited on clutch components contains asbestos, which is hazardous to your health. DO NOT blow it out with compressed air and DO NOT inhale it. DO NOT use petrol or petroleum-based solvents to remove the dust. Brake system cleaner should be used to flush the dust into a drain pan. After the clutch components are wiped clean with a rag, dispose of the contaminated rags and cleaner in a covered container.*

Removal

1   Access to the clutch components is normally accomplished by removing the transmission, leaving the engine in the vehicle. If, of course, the engine is being removed for major overhaul, then the opportunity should always be taken to check the clutch for wear and renew worn components as necessary. The following procedures assume that the engine will stay in place.

2   Remove the release cylinder without disconnecting the hydraulic line (see Section 8). Support the cylinder out of the way by a piece of wire from the undercarriage.

3   Referring to Chapter 7 Part A, remove the transmission from the vehicle. Support the engine while the transmission is out. Preferably, an engine hoist should be used to support it from above. However, if a jack is used underneath the engine, make sure a

piece of wood is used between the jack and sump to spread the load. **Caution:** *The pickup for the oil pump is very close to the bottom of the sump. If the pan is bent or distorted in any way, engine oil starvation could occur.*

4   To support the clutch disc during removal, install a clutch alignment tool through the clutch disc hub.

5   Carefully inspect the flywheel and pressure plate for indexing marks. The marks are usually an X, an O or a white letter. If they cannot be found, apply marks yourself so the pressure plate and the flywheel will be in the same alignment during refitting.

6   Turning each bolt only 1/2-turn at a time, slowly loosen the pressure plate-to-flywheel bolts. Work in a diagonal pattern and loosen each bolt a little at a time until all spring pressure is relieved. Then hold the pressure plate securely and completely remove the bolts, followed by the pressure plate and clutch disc.

Inspection

7   Ordinarily, when a problem occurs in the clutch, it can be attributed to wear of the clutch disc assembly. However, all components should be inspected at this time.

8   Inspect the flywheel for cracks, heat checking, grooves or other signs of obvious defects. If the imperfections are slight, a machine shop can machine the surface flat and smooth, which is highly recommended regardless of the surface appearance. Refer to Chapter 2 for the flywheel removal and refitting procedure.

9   Inspect the pilot bearing (if equipped) (Section 5).

10   Inspect the lining on the clutch disc. There should be at least 1 mm of lining above the rivet heads. Check for loose rivets, warpage, cracks, distorted springs or damper bushes and other obvious damage **(see illustration)**. As mentioned above, ordinarily the clutch disc is renewed as a matter of course, so if in doubt about the condition, renew it with a new one.

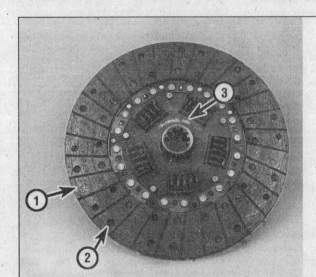

3.10 The clutch disc

1   **Lining** - This will wear down in use
2   **Marks** - "Flywheel side" or something similar
3   **Rivets** - These secure the lining and will damage the pressure plate if allowed to contact it

8

 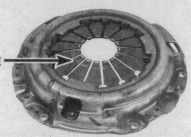 

NORMAL FINGER WEAR   **EXCESSIVE FINGER WEAR**   **BROKEN OR BENT FINGERS**

EXCESSIVE WEAR

3.12 Renew the pressure plate if the diaphragm spring fingers exhibit these signs of wear

11   Ordinarily, the release bearing is also renewed along with the clutch disc (see Section 4).

12   Check the machined surfaces of the pressure plate and the diaphragm spring fingers **(see illustration)**. If the surface is grooved or otherwise damaged, renew the pressure plate. Also check for obvious damage, distortion, cracking, etc. Light glazing can be removed with medium grit emery cloth. If a new pressure plate is indicated, new or factory-rebuilt units are available.

Refitting

13   Before refitting, carefully wipe the flywheel and pressure plate machined surfaces clean with a rubbing-alcohol dampened rag. It's important that no oil or grease is on these surfaces or the lining of the clutch disc. Handle these parts only with clean hands.

14   Position the clutch disc and pressure plate with the clutch held in place with an alignment tool. Make sure it's fitted properly (most renewal discs will be marked "flywheel side" or something similar - if not marked, refit the clutch with the damper springs or bushes toward the transmission.

15   Tighten the pressure plate-to-flywheel bolts only finger tight, working around the pressure plate.

16   Centre the clutch disc by ensuring the alignment tool is through the splined hub and into the pilot bearing in the crankshaft. Wiggle the tool up, down or side-to-side, as needed, to bottom the tool in the pilot bearing. Tighten the pressure plate-to-flywheel bolts a little at a time, working in a criss-cross pattern to prevent distorting the cover. After all of the bolts are snug, tighten them to the torque listed in this Chapter's Specifications. Remove the alignment tool.

17   Using high temperature grease, lubricate the inner groove of the release bearing (refer to Section 4). Also place grease on the fork fingers.

18   Refit the clutch release bearing as described in Section 4.

19   Refit the transmission, release cylinder and all components removed previously, tightening all fasteners to the proper torque specifications.

4   Clutch release bearing - removal and refitting

Removal

1   Disconnect the negative cable from the battery.

2   Remove the transmission (Chapter 7).

3   Detach the spring clip(s), then slide the release bearing off the transmission input shaft **(see illustration 2.1b)**.

4   Detach the fork from the ballstud by pulling it straight off.

5   Hold the bearing and turn the inner portion. If the bearing doesn't turn smoothly or if it's noisy, renew it with a new one. Wipe the bearing with a clean rag and inspect it for damage, wear and cracks. Don't immerse the bearing in solvent - it's sealed for life and to do so would ruin it.

Refitting

6   Lubricate the clutch fork ends where they contact the bearing lightly with moly-based grease. Apply a thin coat of the same grease to the inner diameter of the bearing and also to the transmission input shaft bearing retainer.

7   Refit the release bearing on the clutch fork so that both of the fork ends fit into the bearing tabs. Make sure the spring clip seats securely.

8   Lubricate the clutch release fork ball socket with moly-based disulfide grease and push the fork onto the ball stud until it's firmly seated. Check to see that the bearing slides back and forth smoothly on the input shaft bearing retainer.

9   The remainder of the refitting is the reverse of the removal procedure, tightening all bolts to the specified torques.

5   Pilot bearing - inspection, removal and refitting

1   The clutch pilot bearing is a ball-type bearing used on some models which is pressed into the rear of the crankshaft. Its primary purpose is to support the front of the transmission input shaft. The pilot bearing should be inspected whenever the clutch components are removed from the engine. Due to its inaccessibility, if you are in doubt as to its condition, renew it with a new one. **Note:** *If the engine has been removed from the vehicle, disregard the following steps which do not apply.*

2   Remove the transmission (refer to Chapter 7 Part A).

3   Remove the clutch components (Section 3).

4   Using a clean rag, wipe the bearing clean and inspect for any excessive wear, scoring or obvious damage. A flashlight will be helpful to direct light into the recess.

5   Check to make sure the pilot bearing turns smoothly and quietly. If the transmission input shaft contact surface is worn or damaged, renew the bearing with a new one.

6   Removal can be accomplished with a special puller but an alternative method also works very well.

7   Find a solid steel bar which is slightly smaller in diameter than the bearing. Alternatives to a solid bar would be a wood dowel or a socket with a bolt fixed in place to make it solid.

8   Check the bar for fit - it should just slip into the bearing with very little clearance.

9   Pack the bearing and the area behind it (in the crankshaft recess) with heavy grease. Pack it tightly to eliminate as much air as possible.

10   Insert the bar into the bearing bore and lightly hammer on the bar, which will force the grease to the backside of the bearing and push it out. Remove the bearing and clean all grease from the crankshaft recess.

11   To fit the new bearing, lubricate the outside surface with oil then drive it into the recess with a hammer and a socket with an outside diameter that matches the bearing outer race.

12   Pack the bearing with lithium base grease (NLGI No.2). Wipe off all excess grease so the clutch lining will not become contaminated.

13   Refit the clutch components, transmission and all other components removed to gain access to the pilot bearing.

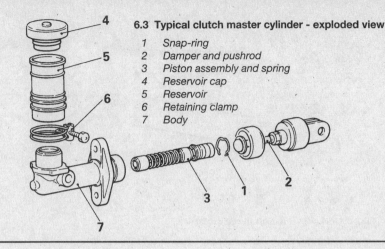

6.3 Typical clutch master cylinder - exploded view

1   Snap-ring
2   Damper and pushrod
3   Piston assembly and spring
4   Reservoir cap
5   Reservoir
6   Retaining clamp
7   Body

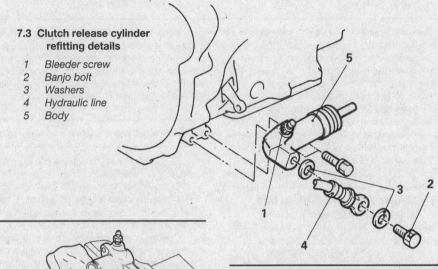

7.3 Clutch release cylinder refitting details

1   Bleeder screw
2   Banjo bolt
3   Washers
4   Hydraulic line
5   Body

7.6a   With the cylinder padded to catch the piston, use compressed air to force the piston out of the bore - make sure your hands are not in the way of the piston

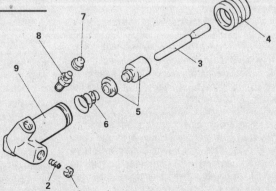

7.6b   An exploded view of the clutch release cylinder

1   Valve plate
2   Spring
3   Pushrod
4   Boots
5   Piston and cup assembly
6   Conical spring
7   Cap
8   Bleeder screw
9   Cylinder body

---

6   Clutch master cylinder - removal, overhaul and refitting

Refer to illustration 6.3

Caution: *Do not allow brake fluid to contact any painted surfaces of the vehicle, as damage to the finish may result.*

Removal

1   Disconnect the hydraulic line from the master cylinder and drain the fluid into a suitable container.

2   Remove the master cylinder flange mounting nuts and withdraw the unit from the engine compartment.

Overhaul

3   Remove the retaining clamp and pull off the reservoir **(see illustration)**.
4   Push the piston down and remove the snap-ring with a pair of snap-ring pliers or a small screwdriver.
5   Pull out the piston assembly and spring.
6   Examine the inner surface of the cylinder bore. If it is scored or exhibits bright wear areas, the entire master cylinder should be renewed.
7   If the cylinder bore is in good condition, obtain a clutch master cylinder rebuild kit, which will contain all of the necessary renewal parts.
8   Prior to refitting any parts, first dip them in brake fluid to lubricate them.
9   Refitting of the parts in the cylinder is the reverse of removal.

Refitting

10   Position the clutch master cylinder against the firewall, inserting the pedal pushrod into the piston. Refit the nuts, tightening them securely.
11   Bleed the clutch hydraulic system following the procedure in Section 8, then check the pedal height and freeplay as described in Chapter 1.

---

7   Clutch release cylinder - removal, overhaul and refitting

Refer to illustrations 7.3, 7.6a and 7.6b

Removal

1   The clutch release cylinder is located on the side of the transmission bellhousing.
2   Raise the vehicle and support it securely on jackstands.
3   Disconnect the hydraulic line from the release cylinder. This is done by removing the bolt from the banjo fitting on the cylinder body **(see illustration)**.
4   Remove the bolt(s) and pull off the release cylinder.

Overhaul

5   Pull off the dust boot and pushrod.
6   Mount the release cylinder body in a padded vise and use compressed air to force the piston and spring out of the bore **(see illustrations)**.
7   Unscrew and remove the bleeder screw.
8   Examine the surfaces of the piston and cylinder bore for scoring or bright wear areas. If any are found, discard the cylinder and purchase a new one.
9   If the components are in good condition, wash them in clean brake fluid. Remove the piston cup and discard it, noting carefully which way the cup lips face.
10   Obtain a repair kit which will contain all the necessary new items.

8

Front propeller shaft

Rear propeller shaft

9.1 Front and rear driveshafts used on these models

1	Snap-ring	3	Journal bearing	5	Flange yoke
2	Grease fitting	4	Journal	6	Sleeve yoke

11   Fit the new piston cup using your fingers only to manipulate it into position. Be sure the lips face in the proper direction.

12   Dip the piston assembly in clean brake fluid before refitting it and the spring into the cylinder.

13   Refit the bleeder screw.

14   Complete the reassembly by refitting the pushrod and the dust cover. Be sure the dust cover is secure on the cylinder housing.

Refitting

15   Refitting is the reverse of the removal procedure. Use new sealing washers at the banjo fitting. After the cylinder has been refitted, bleed the clutch hydraulic system as described in Section 8.

8   Clutch hydraulic system - bleeding

Caution: *Do not allow the brake fluid to contact any painted surface of the vehicle, as damage to the finish will result.*

1   Bleeding will be required whenever the hydraulic system has been dismantled and reassembled and air has entered the system.

2   First fill the fluid reservoir with clean brake fluid which has been stored in an airtight container. Never use fluid which has drained from the system or has bled out previously, as it may contain grit and moisture.

3   Attach a rubber or plastic bleed tube to the bleeder screw on the release cylinder and immerse the open end of the tube in a glass jar containing 25 to 50 mm of fluid.

4   Open the bleeder screw about half a turn and have an assistant quickly depress the clutch pedal completely. Tighten the screw and then have the clutch pedal slowly released with the foot completely removed. Repeat this sequence of operations until air bubbles are no longer ejected from the open end of the tube beneath the fluid in the jar.

5   After two or three strokes of the pedal, make sure the fluid level in the reservoir has not fallen too low. Keep it full of fresh fluid,

otherwise air will be drawn into the system.

6   Tighten the bleeder screw on a pedal down stroke (do not overtighten it), remove the bleed tube and jar, top-up the reservoir and refit the cap.

7   If an assistant is not available, alternative 'one-man' bleeding operations can be carried out using a bleed tube equipped with a one-way valve or a pressure bleed kit, both of which should be used in accordance with the manufacturer's instructions.

9   Driveshafts, differentials and axles - general information

Refer to illustration 9.1

These models use two driveshafts **(see illustration)**; the primary shaft runs between the transfer case and the front differential and the rear driveshaft runs between the transfer case and the rear differential.

All universal joints are of the solid type and can be renewed separately from the driveshaft. The driveshafts are finely balanced during production and whenever they are removed or disassembled, they must be reassembled and refitted in the exact manner and positions they were originally in, to avoid excessive vibration.

The rear axle is of the semi-floating type, having a 'banjo' design axle housing, which is held in proper alignment with the body by the rear suspension.

Mounted in the centre of the rear axle is the differential, which transfers the turning force of the driveshaft to the rear axleshafts, on which the rear wheels are mounted.

The axleshafts are splined at their inner ends to fit into the splines in the differential gears; outer support for the shaft is provided by the rear wheel bearing.

The front axle consists of a frame-mounted differential assembly and two driveaxles. The driveaxles incorporate two constant velocity (CV) joints each, enabling them to transmit power at various suspension angles independent from each other.

Because of the complexity and critical nature of the differential adjustments, as well as the special equipment needed to perform the operations, we recommend any disassembly of the differential be done by a dealer service department or other repair shop.

10   Driveline inspection

1   Raise the rear of the vehicle and support it securely on jackstands.

2   Slide under the vehicle and visually inspect the condition of the driveshaft. Look for any dents or cracks in the tubing. If any are found, the driveshaft must be renewed.

3   Check for any oil leakage at the front and rear of the driveshaft. Leakage where the driveshaft enters the transmission indicates a defective rear transmission seal. Leakage where the driveshaft enters the differential indicates a defective pinion seal.

4   While still under the vehicle, have an assistant turn the rear wheel so the driveshaft will rotate. As it does, make sure that the universal joints are operating properly without binding, noise or looseness. Listen for any noise from the centre bearing, indicating it is worn or damaged. Also check the rubber portion of the centre bearing for cracking or separation, which will necessitate renewal.

5   The universal joint can also be checked with the driveshaft motionless, by gripping your hands on either side of the joint and attempting to twist the joint. Any movement at all in the joint is a sign of considerable wear. Lifting up on the shaft will also indicate movement in the universal joints.

6   Finally, check the driveshaft mounting bolts at the ends to make sure they are tight.

7   The above driveshaft checks should be repeated on the front driveshaft. In addition, check for grease leakage around the sleeve yoke, indicating failure of the yoke seal.

8   Check for leakage at each connection of the driveshafts to the transfer case and front differential. Leakage indicates worn oil seals.

9   At the same time, check for looseness in the joints of the front driveaxles.

11.1 Mark the front driveshaft-to-differential flange relationship

11.3 Typical front driveshaft refitting details

11 Driveshafts - removal and refitting

Front driveshaft

Refer to illustrations 11.1 and 11.3

1   Raise the front of the vehicle and place it on jackstands. Mark the relationship of the front driveshaft flange to the front differential companion flange so they can be realigned upon refitting **(see illustration)**.
2   Lock the driveshaft from turning with a large screwdriver or lever, then remove the four nuts and bolts from the front flange.
3   Detach the flange from the front differential, withdraw the shaft from the transfer case and lower the driveshaft from the vehicle **(see illustration)**.
4   Refitting is the reverse of removal. Be sure to align all marks and tighten the flange bolts to the torque listed in this Chapter's Specifications.

Rear driveshaft

Refer to illustration 11.7

5   Raise the rear of the vehicle and support it on jackstands.
6   Remove the nuts holding the centre support bearing bracket to the frame (three-joint type).
7   Mark the edges of the driveshaft rear flange and the differential companion flange so they can be realigned upon refitting **(see illustration)**.
8   Remove the four nuts and bolts.
9   Push the shaft forward slightly to disconnect the rear flange.
10   Pull the yoke from the transmission/transfer case while supporting the driveshaft with your hands.
11   While the driveshafts are removed, insert a plug in the transmission/transfer case to prevent lubricant leakage.
12   Refitting is the reverse of the removal procedure. During refitting, make sure all flange marks line up.

12 Universal joints - renewal

Refer to illustrations 12.4 and 12.11

Note: *Selective fit snap-rings are used to retain the universal joint spiders in the yokes. In order to maintain the driveshaft balance, you must use renewal snap-rings of the same size as originally used.*

1   Clean away all dirt from the ends of the bearings on the yokes so the snap-rings can be removed with a pair of snap-ring pliers or long-nose pliers.
2   Support the universal joint in a vise equipped with soft jaws and remove the snap-rings. If they are very tight, tap the end of the bearing with a hammer to relieve the pressure.
3   You will need two sockets to remove the bearings from the yokes. One should be large enough to fit into the yoke where the snap-rings were fitted and the other should have an inside diameter just large enough for the bearings to fit into when they are forced out of the yoke.
4   Mount the universal joint in the vise with the large socket on one side of the yoke and the small socket on the other side, pushing against the bearing. Carefully tighten the vise until the bearing is pushed out of the yoke and into the large socket **(see illustration)**. If it can't be pushed all the way out, remove the universal joint from the vise and use a pair of pliers to finish removing the bearing.
5   Reverse the sockets and push out the bearing on the other side of the yoke. This time, the small socket will be pushing against the cross-shaped universal joint journal end.

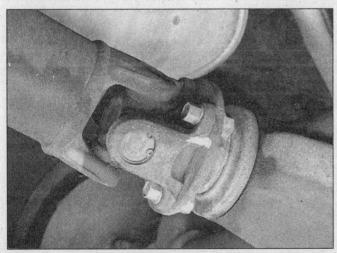

11.7 Mark the rear driveshaft-to-differential flange relationship

12.4 To press the universal joint out of the driveshaft, set it up in a vise with the small socket (on the left) pushing the joint and bearing cap into the large socket

8

6　Before pressing out the two remaining bearings, mark the universal joint journal (the cross) so it can be refitted in the same position during reassembly. Also mark the relationship of the yokes to each other.

7　The two remaining universal joints can be disassembled following the same procedure. Be sure to mark all components for each universal joint so they can be kept together and reassembled in the proper position.

8　When reassembling the universal joints, renew all needle bearings and dust seals with new ones.

9　Before reassembly, pack each grease cavity in the universal joint journals with a small amount of grease. Also, apply a thin coat of grease to the new needle bearing rollers and the roller contact areas on the universal joint journal.

10　Apply a thin coat of grease to the dust seal lips and fit the bearings and universal joint journals into the yoke using the vise and sockets that were used to remove the old bearings. Work slowly and be very careful not to damage the bearings as they are being pressed into the yokes.

11　Once the bearings are in place and properly seated, refit the snap-rings and check the clearance (U-joint journal endplay) with a feeler gauge (see illustration). This is done with both snap-rings in place and the bearings and journal pressed toward one side of the yoke. Measure the clearance at the opposite side of the yoke. Compare this measurement with those in the Specifications Section at the beginning of this Chapter. If the measurement is greater than specified, fit a snap-ring of a different thickness and recheck the clearance. Repeat the procedure until the correct clearance is obtained. If possible, use snap-rings of the same thickness on each side of the yoke so the driveshaft balance isn't affected.

13　Rear axle assembly - removal and refitting

1　Loosen the rear wheel lug nuts, raise the vehicle and support it securely on jackstands placed underneath the frame. Remove the wheels.

2　Support the rear axle assembly with a floor jack placed underneath the differential.

3　Remove the shock absorber lower mounting nuts, detach the lower part of the shocks from the axle brackets and compress the shocks to get them out of the way (see Chapter 10).

4　Disconnect the driveshaft from the differential companion flange and hang it with a piece of wire from the underbody (see Section 11).

5　Disconnect the parking brake cables from the parking brake lever at each rear wheel (see Chapter 9).

6　Disconnect the rear flexible brake hose from the brake line above the rear axle housing. Disconnect the rear axle breather hose on top of the axle housing (if equipped). Plug the ends of the line and hose or wrap plastic bags tightly around them to prevent excessive fluid loss and contamination.

7　Support the rear axle assembly with a jack.

Leaf spring models

8　Remove the U-bolt nuts from the leaf spring seats and raise the axle assembly slightly with the jack.

9　Remove the rear spring shackle bolts and lower the rear of each leaf spring to the floor.

Coil spring models

10　Remove the stabiliser bar bolts.

11　Remove the rear suspension lower arms and lateral rod.

All models

12　Carefully lower the axle assembly to the floor with the jack, then remove it from under the vehicle. It would be a good idea to have an assistant on hand, as the assembly is very heavy.

13　Refitting is the reverse of the removal procedure. Be sure to tighten the bolts and nuts and the driveshaft companion flange bolts to the torques listed in this Chapter and the Specifications in Chapter 10. Bleed the brakes (see Chapter 9).

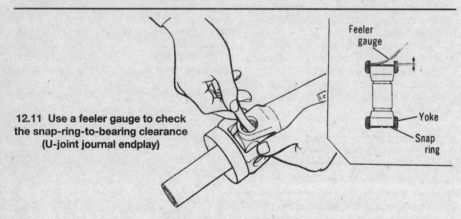

12.11　Use a feeler gauge to check the snap-ring-to-bearing clearance (U-joint journal endplay)

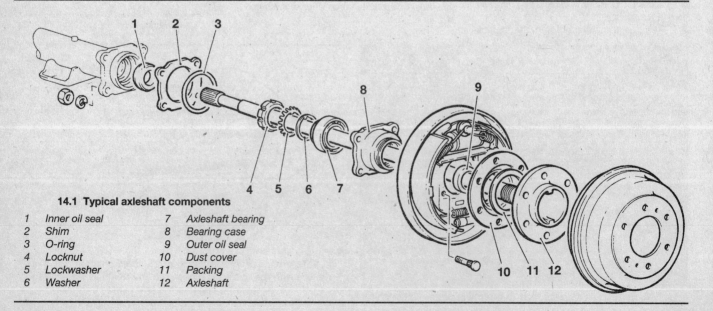

14.1　Typical axleshaft components

1	Inner oil seal	7	Axleshaft bearing
2	Shim	8	Bearing case
3	O-ring	9	Outer oil seal
4	Locknut	10	Dust cover
5	Lockwasher	11	Packing
6	Washer	12	Axleshaft

14.9 Use a hooked tool to remove the oil seal from the axle housing

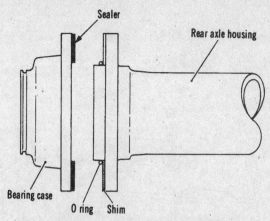

14.15 Apply a thin, even coat of silicone sealer to the area shown on the bearing case

14 Rear axle oil seal - renewal

Refer to illustrations 14.1, 14.9, 14.15 and 14.17

1 The axleshafts can be removed without disturbing the differential assembly. They must be removed in order to renew the oil seals and when removing the differential carrier from the rear axle housing **(see illustration)**. **Note:** *Read this entire procedure before starting work.*

2 Raise the rear of the vehicle and support it securely on jackstands. Block the front wheels to keep the vehicle from rolling.

3 Remove the rear wheels and release the parking brake.

4 Remove the drain plug and drain the differential lubricant into a suitable container. When the draining is complete, finger-tighten the drain plug in place.

5 On drum brake models, remove the brake drum from the end of the axle and the metal brake line from the wheel cylinder by referring to Chapter 9. The brakes do not have to be disassembled to remove the axles. On later models with rear disc brakes, refer to Chapter 9 for brake disassembly.

6 Remove the parking brake cables from the vehicle as described in Chapter 9. Do not disconnect the cables from the levers in the rear brake assemblies. If only one axle shaft is being removed, remove only the cable on the side of the vehicle that the axle shaft is being removed from. If both axle shafts are being removed, both parking brake cables must also be removed.

7 Remove the four nuts and lock washers attaching the bearing case and brake backing plate to the axle housing and withdraw the axle, the bearing case, the brake backing plate and brake assembly from the axle housing. A slide hammer-type axle puller may be required to dislodge the bearing housing from the axle housing. Do not prise between the two flanges, as damage to the gasket sealing surfaces will result. Support the axle shaft as it is removed from the axle housing to prevent damage to the old seal in the end of the axle housing.

8 Remove the O-ring and shim (or shims) from the rear axle housing flange. Retain the shims for reassembly.

9 Prise or pull the oil seal out of the housing with a screwdriver or a slide hammer-type seal puller **(see illustration)**.

10 Thoroughly clean the seal mounting area, and fit a new seal (with the rubber side facing out) using a hammer and a block of wood or other suitable tool. Tap the seal carefully into place around its entire circumference and make sure it is properly seated in the axle housing.

11 At this point, the axleshaft assembly should be taken to a dealer service department or a automotive machine shop if the outer oil seal or wheel bearing has to be renewed.

12 Before beginning the assembly procedure, remove all old gasket sealer and any rust from the mating surfaces of the bearing case and the axle housing. Also, thoroughly pack the bearing case and axle housing end with high-temperature wheel bearing grease and lubricate the lip of the oil seal in the axle housing.

13 If both axle shafts have been removed, the left-side shaft should be refitted first during reassembly

14 Fit a 1.0 mm shim and a new O-ring into place on the left end of the axle housing.

15 Apply a thin, even coat of silicone-type gasket sealer to the mating surface of the bearing case and carefully refit the left-side axle/brake assembly into the rear axle housing **(see illustration)**. (Do not damage the oil seal in the process). It may be necessary to turn the axle slightly to engage its inner splines with the differential. You may have to tap gently on the axle hub with a soft-faced hammer to seat the bearing case in the end of the axle housing.

16 Refit the four lock washers and nuts attaching the bearing case and brake backing plate to the axle housing. Tighten the nuts to the torque listed in this Chapter's Specifications.

17 Refit the right-side axle into the housing without a shim or O-ring in place, and temporarily tighten the attaching nuts to a torque of 6 Nm. When the axle is refitted in this manner, a gap will exist between the bearing case and the axle housing end flange, which must be measured with a feeler gauge **(see illustration)**.

18 Separate the axle shaft from the housing and select a shim with a thickness equal to the gap measured in the previous step. Also, select a shim with a thickness of from 0.05 to 0.020 mm. A list of available preload adjusting shims is included in the Specifications Section at the beginning of this Chapter.

8

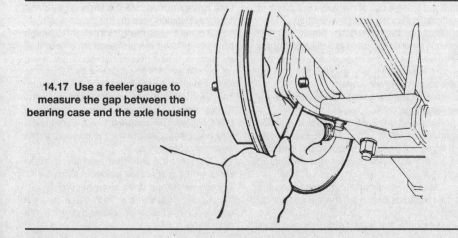

14.17 Use a feeler gauge to measure the gap between the bearing case and the axle housing

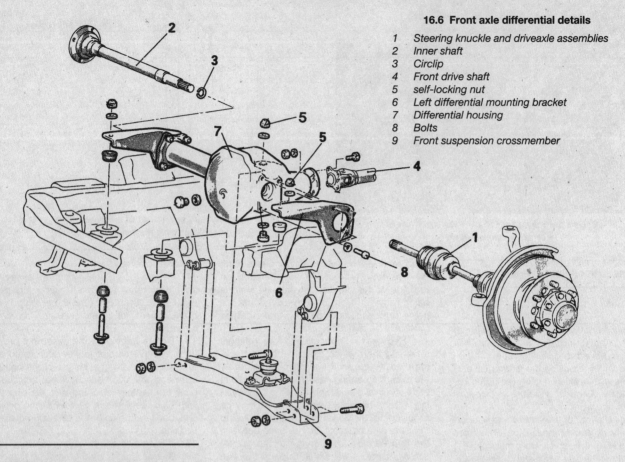

16.6 Front axle differential details

1   *Steering knuckle and driveaxle assemblies*
2   *Inner shaft*
3   *Circlip*
4   *Front drive shaft*
5   *self-locking nut*
6   *Left differential mounting bracket*
7   *Differential housing*
8   *Bolts*
9   *Front suspension crossmember*

19   Refit the previously selected shims and a new O-ring into place on the end of the axle housing.

20   Apply a thin, even coat of silicone-type gasket sealer to the mating surface of the bearing case and carefully refit the axle assembly into the housing. Refit the lock washers and nuts and tighten the nuts to the torque listed in this Chapter's Specifications.

21   Using a dial indicator, check the axial play of the axle shaft by pulling out and pushing in on the axle shaft hub. If the play is more or less than specified, remove the right-side axle again and renew the shims with shims that are thicker or thinner, as required.

22   Refit the axle and recheck the axial play. If necessary, repeat the procedure until the correct amount of play is obtained.

23   Refit the parking brake cables, hook up the brake lines and refit the brake drums by referring to Chapter 9. Also, bleed the brakes at the rear wheel cylinder as described in Chapter 9.

24   Tighten the rear axle housing drain plug to the torque specified in Chapter 1 and fill the housing to the proper level with the recommended gear lubricant (see the *Recommended Lubricants and Fluids* Section at the front of Chapter 1). Refit the filler plug and tighten it to the specified torque.

25   Refit the wheels, lower the vehicle to the ground and test drive it. Check for leaks where the wheel bearing case attaches to the rear axle housing.

15   Pinion bearing oil seal - renewal

1   It isn't uncommon for front or rear bearing oil seal to fail, resulting in gear lubricant leaking past the seal and onto the driveshaft flange yoke. The seal can be easily renewed without removing the differential.

2   Raise the vehicle and support it securely on jackstands.

3   Remove the drain and fill plugs and drain the lubricant into a suitable container. After the lubricant has drained, refit the plugs finger tight.

4   Separate the driveshaft from the differential and hang it out of the way by a piece of wire from the underbody (see Section 11).

5   Remove the differential pinion nut. On the front differential, have an assistant apply the brakes to lock the front wheels from turning. On rear differentials, engage the parking brake to lock the rear wheels.

6   Use a gear puller tool to detach the differential flange yoke.

7   Carefully prise off the dust cover for access to the seal. Note which side of the seal faces out and prise it out of the differential, taking care not to damage the pinion shaft splines.

8   Clean the seal outside diameter and the contact surfaces of the differential and pinion shaft.

9   Lubricate the seal lip with moly-base grease and place it in position in the differential. Working around the circumference, a little at a time, tap the seal evenly into the differential using a hammer and block of wood until it's fully seated.

10   Refit the seal dust cover.

11   Clean the contact surface of the differential end yoke and apply a thin coat of moly-base grease. Fit the yoke onto the pinion shaft, rotating it as necessary to line up the splines.

12   Tap the yoke fully into place with a soft face hammer, then refit the large washer and a new self-locking nut on the pinion shaft.

13   To help seat the pinion shaft bearings properly, release the brakes (front differential) or parking brake (rear differential) and snug up the nut while holding one of the wheels to keep the shaft from turning as it is tightened.

14   Tighten the nut to the torque in the Specifications Section at the beginning of this Chapter. This torque figure is very important because it determines the preload on the pinion shaft bearings.

15   Connect the driveshaft and fill the differential with the specified lubricant (Chapter 1). Tighten the fill and drain plugs securely.

16   Lower the vehicle, test drive it, then check for evidence of leakage around the pinion and yoke.

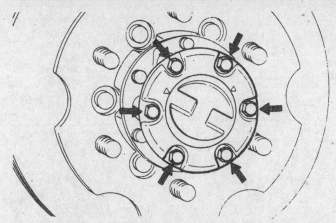

17.3a On manual locking hubs, the cover is held in place by bolts (arrows)

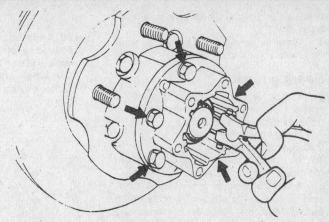

17.3b On manual locking hubs, remove the snap-ring, then the bolts (arrows)

17.4a On automatic free-wheeling hubs, the cap can be unscrewed by hand or with a spanner such as this oil filter wrench

17.4b Lock the hub from turning with a large screwdriver and use a socket with the proper head to remove the bolts

16 Front differential assembly - removal and refitting

Refer to illustration 16.6

1   Loosen the wheel lug nuts, raise the front of the vehicle and support it securely on jackstands. Remove the wheels.
2   Drain the lubricant from the differential (Chapter 1).
3   Remove the driveaxles and pull the inner shaft out of the right side axle tube (a slide hammer-type tool with a flange adaptor may be required to remove the inner shaft from the differential).
4   Remove the front driveshaft (see Section 11).
5   Support the differential assembly with a floor jack.
6   Remove the left differential mounting bracket and the bolt holding the right bracket to the frame **(see illustration)**.
7   Remove the front crossmember-to-frame bolts and carefully lower the differential and crossmember as a unit.
8   Refitting is the reverse of the removal

procedure. Be sure to tighten the bolts/nuts securely and refill the differential with the recommended lubricant (Chapter 1).

17 Front hub assembly - removal, bearing repack, refitting and adjustment

Refer to illustrations 17.3a, 17.3b, 17.4a, 17.4b, 17.6, 17.9, 17.21, 17.23, 17.25 and 17.26
Note: *Special tools and a great deal of care are required to remove and refit the hub, so be sure to read through the entire procedure before beginning work. It may be a good idea to leave the job to a dealer service department or repair shop.*

Removal

1   Raise the front of the vehicle and support it securely on jackstands.
2   Refer to Chapter 9 and remove the brake caliper/pad assembly. Do not disconnect the hose from the caliper and do not

allow the caliper to hang by the hose - support it with a section of stiff wire so there is no strain on the hose.
3   On manual free-wheeling hub models, turn the control handle to the free position and remove the hub cover **(see illustration)**. Remove the snap-ring from the end of the driveaxle with snap-ring pliers, then remove the bolts and separate the free-wheeling hub assembly from the wheel hub by pulling it straight out **(see illustration)**.
4   On automatic free-wheeling hub models, unscrew the free-wheeling hub cover (if it cannot be done by hand, wrap a rag around it and use an oil filter wrench, large pipe spanner or similar tool to loosen it) **(see illustration)**. Remove the O-ring from the hub cover, then remove the snap-ring and spacer/shim from the end of the driveaxle. Loosen and remove the bolts (a special tool is needed for this), then detach the free-wheeling hub from the wheel hub by pulling straight out on it **(see illustration)**.
5   On all models, remove the screws and detach the lockwasher from the hub.
6   Using the special socket (available from your dealer or most auto parts stores) and a

breaker bar, remove the locknut **(see illustration)**.

7   Carefully remove the hub from the spindle (don't drop the outer bearing).

Bearing repack

8   Use a screwdriver to prise the grease seal out of the rear of the hub. As this is done, note how the seal is fitted.

9   Remove the inner wheel bearing from the hub **(see illustration)**.

10   Use solvent to remove all traces of the old grease from the bearings, hub and spindle. A small brush may prove helpful; however make sure no bristles from the brush embed themselves inside the bearing rollers. Allow the parts to air dry.

11   Carefully inspect the bearings for cracks, heat discolouration, worn rollers, etc. Check the bearing races inside the hub for wear and damage. If the bearing races are defective, the hubs should be taken to a machine shop with the facilities to remove the old races and press new ones in. Note that the bearings and races come as matched sets and old bearings should never be fitted on new races.

12   Use high-temperature front wheel bearing grease to pack the bearings. Work the grease completely into the bearings, forcing it

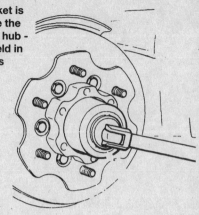
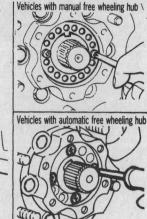

17.6 A special socket is required to remove the locknut and free the hub - lockwashers are held in place by screws

between the rollers, cone and cage from the back side.

13   Apply a thin coat of grease to the spindle at the outer bearing seat, inner bearing seat, shoulder and seal seat.

14   Put a small quantity of grease behind each bearing race inside the hub. Using your finger, form a dam at these points to provide for extra grease and to keep thinned grease from flowing out of the bearing.

15   Place the grease-packed inner bearing

into the rear of the hub and put a little more grease outside of the bearing.

16   Place a new seal over the inner bearing and tap the seal evenly into place with a hammer and block of wood until it's flush with the hub.

17   Apply a thin coat of grease to the seal lip.

Refitting and adjustment

18   Slide the hub into place on the wheel spindle (be careful not to damage the seal), then refit the outer wheel bearing and adjust the bearing preload as follows:

19   Using the special tool and a torque wrench, tighten the locknut to 130 to 200 Nm while turning the hub by hand.

20   Loosen the locknut to relieve the pressure on the bearing, then retighten it to 25 Nm.

21   On manual free-wheeling hub models, back the nut off 30-degrees, then refit the lockwasher. If the holes in the lockwasher and locknut do not line up, loosen the locknut (20-degrees maximum). Attach a spring scale to one of the wheel nut studs and pull on the scale to see how much force is required to turn the hub **(see illustration)**. It should take one to four pounds of force. If it doesn't, repeat the locknut tightening procedure. Apply grease to the inner surfaces of the freewheeling hub assembly and coat the mating surfaces of the hubs with semi-drying gasket

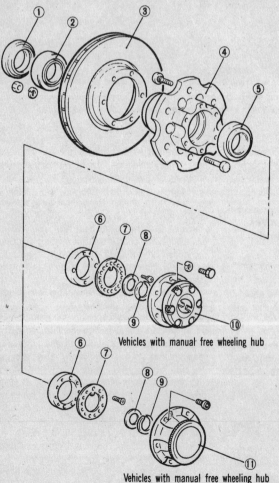

17.9 Typical free-wheeling hub components - exploded view

1	Seal
2	Inner wheel bearing
3	Brake disc
4	Hub
5	Outer wheel bearing
6	Locknut
7	Lockwasher
8	Shim/spacer
9	Snap-ring
10	Manual locking hub
11	Automatic locking hub

Vehicles with manual free wheeling hub

Vehicles with manual free wheeling hub

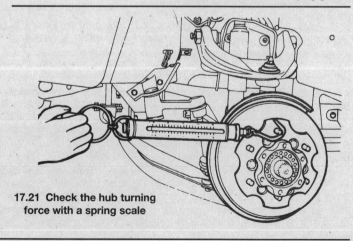

17.21 Check the hub turning force with a spring scale

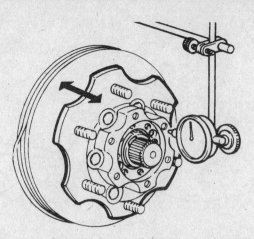

17.23 Use a dial indicator to check the hub axial play

17.25 Apply sealant to the shaded area of the hub mounting surface (manual hub models)

sealant, then refit the free-wheeling hub and tighten the bolts in a criss-cross pattern. Check the axial play of the driveaxle and make sure it is within the specified range (see the driveaxle refitting procedure in Section 19), then refit the hub cover assembly with the control handle and clutch in the free position. Tighten the bolts in a criss-cross pattern.

22 On 1984 models, loosen the locknut about 30 to 40 degrees, then check the force required to turn the hub as described in Step 21 (it should be one to five Nm). Refit the lockwasher. On models with automatic free-wheeling hubs, adjust the brake contact surface depth by adding or removing shims (see this Chapter's Specifications).

23 On 1985 and later models, loosen the locknut about 30 to 40-degrees, then check the force required to turn the hub as described in Step 21 (it should be one to five Nm). Check the axial play of the wheel hub as shown in the **accompanying illustration** (see this Chapter's Specifications), then refit the lockwasher. If the holes in the lockwasher and locknut do not line up, loosen the locknut slightly (40-degrees maximum).

24 On later models with free-wheeling hubs, refit the hub assembly.

25 On models with a manual hub, apply grease to the inner surfaces of the free-wheeling hub assembly and coat the mating surfaces of the hubs with semi-drying gasket sealant, then refit the free-wheeling hub and tighten the bolts in a criss-cross pattern **(see illustration)**. On models with manual hubs only, check the axial play of the driveaxle and make sure it is within the specified range (see the driveaxle refitting procedure in Section 18). On all models, refit the hub cover assembly with the control handle and clutch in the Free position. Tighten the bolts in a criss-cross pattern.

26 On models with an automatic hub, apply semi-drying gasket sealant to the hub mating surfaces, then align the key of Brake B with the keyway in the spindle as shown in the **accompanying illustration** and refit the hub assembly. Make sure the free-wheeling hub and the wheel hub make contact when light pressure is applied to the free-wheeling hub (if they don't, turn the hub as required). Refit the mounting bolts and tighten them in a criss-cross pattern. Refit the shim/spacer and snap-ring on the end of the driveaxle. Recheck the hub turning force and compare it to the figure obtained before the free-wheeling hub was refitted. The difference should be less than 4 Nm - if it isn't, the free-wheeling hub is probably fitted incorrectly

(remove and refit it). Check the driveaxle axial play and compare it to the Specifications at the beginning of this Chapter (see Section 18 for the driveaxle refitting procedure).

27 On later models with an automatic hub, recheck the hub turning force with a spring scale, then align the key of brake B with the slot in the spindle and refit the hub assembly **(see illustration 17.26)**. Make sure the free-wheeling hub and the wheel hub make contact when light pressure is applied to the free-wheeling hub (if they don't, turn the hub as required). Refit the mounting bolts and tighten them in a criss-cross pattern, then refit the shim and snap-ring on the end of the driveaxle. Recheck the hub turning force and compare it to the figure obtained before the free-wheeling hub was refitted. The difference should be less than three pounds - if it isn't, the free-wheeling hub is either assembled or fitted incorrectly (remove and refit it and/or disassemble and reassemble it). Remove the free-wheeling hub and apply semi-drying gasket sealant to the hub mating surfaces. Then refit it and tighten the bolts in a criss-cross pattern.

28 On later models with an automatic hub, apply grease to the cover O-ring and attach it to the cover. Refit the cover and tighten it securely.

29 On all models, refit the brake caliper and wheel and lower the vehicle to the ground.

18 Front driveaxles - removal and refitting

Refer to illustrations 18.6 and 18.12

Removal

1 Raise the front of the vehicle and support it securely with jackstands, then remove the wheels and the brake caliper assemblies (see Chapter 9). Do not disconnect the hoses from the calipers and do not allow the calipers to hang by the hoses - suspend them with pieces of stiff wire so there is no strain on the hoses.

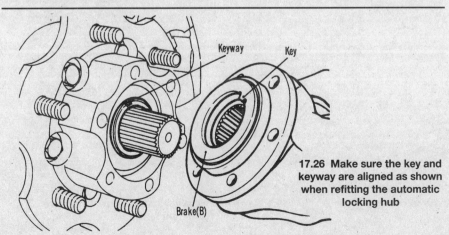

Keyway   Key

Brake(B)

17.26 Make sure the key and keyway are aligned as shown when refitting the automatic locking hub

8

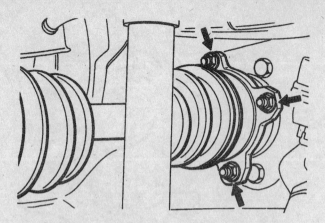

18.6 The right driveaxle is attached to the inner shaft with bolts and nuts (arrows)

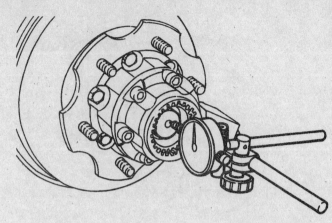

18.12 Check the driveshaft axial (end) play with a dial indicator

2   Detach the free-wheeling hub cover assemblies and remove the snap-rings from the end of the driveaxles. Manual hub covers are held in place with several bolts, while automatic hub covers can be unscrewed from the hub (see Section 17).

3   Remove each steering knuckle and front hub assembly as a unit (see Chapter 10).

4   Grasp the inner and outer joints and pull the left driveaxle out of the differential. Be careful not to damage the differential oil seal with the driveaxle inner splines as it is removed.

5   Use a jack to raise the right lower suspension arm, then remove the nuts and detach the shock absorber from the upper mount. **Caution:** *Do not lower the jack until after the shock absorber has been reattached.*

6   Remove the nuts and bolts that attach the right driveaxle flange to the inner shaft **(see illustration)**, then carefully pull out the driveaxle. Remove the circlip from the inner end of the left driveaxle and renew it with a new one.

Refitting

7   Attach the right driveaxle to the inner shaft flange, refit the bolts and nuts and tighten them to the torque listed in this Chapter's Specifications.

8   Attach the right shock absorber to the upper mount bracket and tighten the nuts.

9   Refit the left driveaxle in the differential and seat it by tapping on the outer end with a soft-face hammer.

10   Refit each steering knuckle and hub assembly and attach the balljoints, then adjust the driveaxle play as follows:

11   Refit the snap-ring on the end of the driveaxle, but do not refit the spacer/shim.

12   Mount a dial indicator on the front hub or brake disc and position the stem of the dial indicator against the end of the driveaxle as shown in the **accompanying illustration**.

13   Move the driveaxle in and out and note the reading on the indicator. This is the axial (end) play. **Note:** *On vehicles with automatic locking hubs, turn the driveaxle in both directions until resistance is felt (this is the centre of the turning stroke), then check the driveaxle play with the dial indicator.*

14   If the axial play is not as specified, select a shim/spacer from the sizes available that will produce the correct play.

19   Front driveaxle boot renewal and Constant Velocity (CV) joint overhaul

Refer to illustrations 19.2, 19.4, 19.5, 19.6, 19.7, 19.14 and 19.19

Note 1: *If the CV joints exhibit signs of wear indicating need for an overhaul (usually due to torn boots), explore all options before beginning the job. Complete rebuilt driveaxles are available on an exchange basis, which eliminates much time and work. Whichever route you choose to take, check on the cost and availability of parts before disassembling the vehicle.*

Note 2: *Obtain a new rubber boot kit for each joint on the driveaxle before beginning disassembly. Do not disassemble the Birfield (outer) joints - if they are worn or damaged, new driveaxles are in order.*

1   Remove the boot bands by levering up the ends with a screwdriver or by cutting them off (new bands must be used during reassembly).

2   Use a screwdriver to remove the large

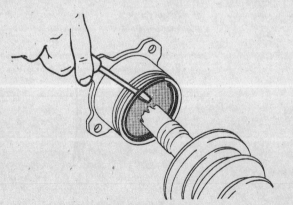

19.2 Remove the DOJ outer race circlip with a screwdriver

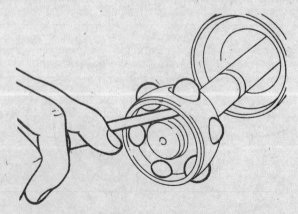

19.4 Raise the balls with a screwdriver to remove them from the cage

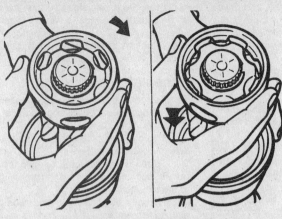

19.5 Turn the cage 30-degrees to disengage the inner race, then slide it down the driveaxle shaft

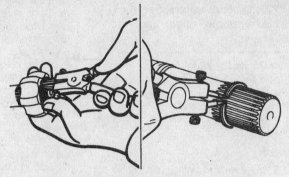

19.6 Remove the snap-ring, the inner race and the circlip from the shaft

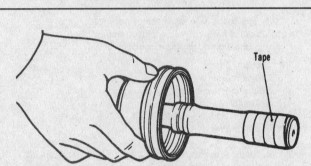

19.7 Wrap the splines with tape to prevent damage to the boot as it is removed

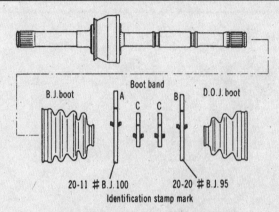

19.14 Boot and band refitting details

circlip from the DOJ outer race **(see illustration)**.

3   Pull the driveaxle out the DOJ outer race and wipe away as much of the grease as possible.

4   Push the balls in the DOJ cage up with a screwdriver and remove them **(see illustration)**.

5   Separate the cage from the inner race by turning it 30-degrees and sliding it down the driveaxle **(see illustration)**.

6   Remove the snap-ring from the driveaxle with snap-ring pliers, then pull off the inner race and slide the cage off the shaft **(see illustration)**.

7   Remove the circlip and the boots from the driveaxle. Wrap tape around the splines on the DOJ end of the shaft so the boots are not damaged by the splines **(see illustration)**.

8   Remove the dust covers with a large screwdriver.

9   Clean all of the components with solvent, then check the dust covers for damage and wear. Look for water, rust, foreign material and damage in the Birfield joints.

10   Inspect the driveaxle shafts for distortion and worn splines. Check all circlips for distortion and cracks.

11   Check the rubber boots for damage and cracks. **Note:** *Renew the boots, even if they appear to be in good condition.*

12   Check the cage, inner race, outer race and balls of each DOJ joint for wear and damage.

13   Drive new dust covers onto the joints with a section of pipe and a hammer. For Birfield joints, the pipe must be 68.9 mm outside diameter with a 2.3 mm wall thickness. For DOJ joints, the pipe must be 75 mm outside diameter with a wall thickness 4 mm.

14   Wrap tape around the driveaxle splines, then fit the new boots and bands on the shaft. The Birfield and DOJ boots are different sizes and shapes, so make sure they are correctly positioned on the shaft **(see illustration)**.

15   Slip the DOJ cage onto the shaft, smaller diameter first. Refit the circlip and make sure it is seated in the shaft groove, then refit the inner race and snap-ring. Make sure the snap-ring is seated in the groove.

16   Apply the specified grease (included with the boot kit) to the DOJ inner race and cage. Slip the cage into place on the inner race and turn it 30-degrees to align the ball races, then refit the balls and lubricate them with the grease.

17   Pack the DOJ outer race with 50 to 80 grams of the specified grease, then slide it onto the driveaxle while aligning the balls and races.

18   Pack an additional 50 to 80 grams of grease into the outer race, behind the inner

race and cage, then Refit the circlip (make sure it is seated in the groove).

19   Slip the boot over the outer race and adjust the joint until the dimension shown in the **accompanying illustration** is achieved. Slip a screwdriver between the joint and boot to equalize the pressure, then refit the band clamps (follow the directions in the boot kit).

20   Pack the grease supplied with the boot kit into the Birfield joint to renew the grease that was wiped off, then refit the boot (the clamping instructions are supplied with the boot kit).

21   Repeat the procedure for the remaining driveaxle.

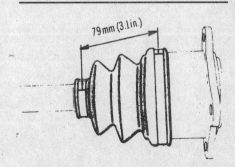

19.19 The DOJ boot dimension must be as shown when the band clamps are refitted

20 Front axle disconnect solenoid and actuator - check and renewal

Refer to illustration 20.1

1   The front axle is engaged into four-wheel drive by a vacuum-operated solenoid valve assembly and actuator which operates a free-wheeling clutch assembly **(see illustration)**.

Check

2   With the engine running, disconnect the hose from the vacuum source and check for strong vacuum.

3   Disconnect the electrical connectors from the solenoid valve assembly and check for 12 volts at the connector's blue-yellow wire. Check for continuity to earth at the yellow-green wire (with four-wheel drive engaged).

4   With the solenoid valves disconnected, check the resistance across the solenoid terminals. The resistance should be 36 to 46 ohms at 15-degrees C. If not within these specifications, renew the solenoid valve assembly.

5   Turn off the engine and check the vacuum hoses and pipes from the solenoid valve assembly to the actuator for kinks, cracks, or other damage.

6   Disconnect the vacuum hoses at the actuator and, with a hand vacuum pump, apply vacuum to one side and then the other of the actuator (be sure to cap the other side when applying vacuum). The actuator should shift the free-wheeling clutch in and out. If it doesn't, renew the actuator.

Renewal

7   To renew the solenoid valve assembly, remove the vacuum hoses and electrical connectors from the solenoid valves.

8   Remove the fasteners and renew the solenoid valve assembly.

9   To renew the actuator, remove the vacuum hoses and pin connecting the shift rod to the actuator.

10   Remove the fasteners and renew the actuator assembly.

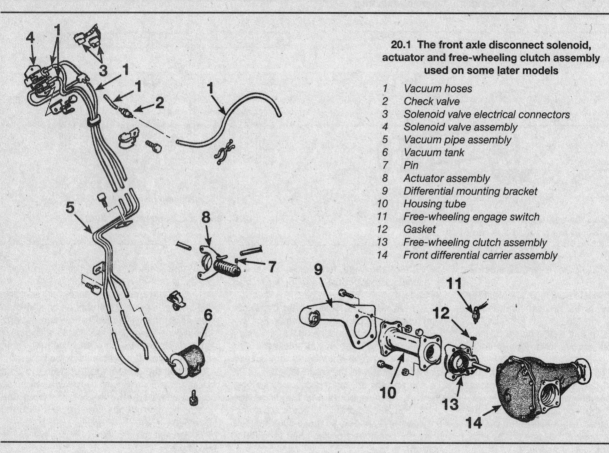

20.1 The front axle disconnect solenoid, actuator and free-wheeling clutch assembly used on some later models

1   *Vacuum hoses*
2   *Check valve*
3   *Solenoid valve electrical connectors*
4   *Solenoid valve assembly*
5   *Vacuum pipe assembly*
6   *Vacuum tank*
7   *Pin*
8   *Actuator assembly*
9   *Differential mounting bracket*
10   *Housing tube*
11   *Free-wheeling engage switch*
12   *Gasket*
13   *Free-wheeling clutch assembly*
14   *Front differential carrier assembly*

Chapter 9 Brakes

Contents

Specifications

General

Brake fluid type	See Chapter 1
Brake booster pushrod-to-master cylinder piston clearance (with vacuum applied to booster)	0.05 to 0.30 mm

Disc brakes

Minimum brake pad thickness	See Chapter 1
Disc minimum thickness*	
Front	
1990 and earlier	18.4 mm
1991 on	22.4 mm
Rear	16.4 mm
Disc runout	
Front	
1990 and earlier	0.15 mm
1991 on	0.10 mm
Rear	0.08 mm

* Refer to the marks stamped on the disc (they supersede information printed here)

9

Disc brakes (continued)
Drum brakes
    Minimum brake shoe lining thickness .... See Chapter 1
Brake drums
    Rear drum brakes
        Standard drum diameter .... 254 mm
        Maximum drum diameter* .... 256 mm
    Rear disc (parking) brake
        Standard drum diameter .... 197 mm
        Maximum drum diameter* .... 198 mm
* *Refer to the marks stamped on the drum (they supersede information printed here)*

Torque specifications   Nm
Brake caliper mounting bolts
    Sliding caliper .... 51 to 65
    Floating caliper
        Upper mounting bolt .... 39 to 48
        Lower mounting bolt .... 23 to 30
Caliper mounting bracket bolts .... 78 to 97
Caliper inlet fitting .... 13 to 17
Disc-to-hub bolts .... 50 to 60
Wheel cylinder mounting bolts .... 18 to 21
Master cylinder mounting nuts .... 8 to 12
Power brake booster mounting nuts .... 12 to 14
Wheel lug nuts .... See Chapter 1
Vacuum pump oil line banjo bolts 17

1   General information

The vehicles covered by this manual are equipped with hydraulically operated front and rear brake systems. The front brakes are disc-type. Earlier models use a sliding caliper while later models use a floating caliper.

The rear brakes on earlier models are drum-type while later models use four-wheel disc brakes. Some later models are equipped with anti-lock brakes (ABS).

These models are equipped with a dual master cylinder which allows the operation of half of the system if the other half fails. This system also incorporates a blend proportioning valve which limits pressure to the rear brakes under heavy braking to prevent rear wheel lock-up. Later models have a Load Sensing Proportioning Valve (LSPV) mounted to the frame and connected to the rear axle by a link.

All models are equipped with a power brake booster which utilises engine vacuum to assist in application of the brakes. The parking brake operates the rear brakes only, through cable actuation.

There are some notes and cautions involving the brake system on this vehicle:

a) *Use only DOT 3 brake fluid in this system.*
b) *The brake pads and linings contain asbestos fibres which are hazardous to your health if inhaled. Whenever you work on the brake system components, carefully clean all parts with brake cleaner. Do not allow the fine asbestos dust to become airborne.*
c) *Safety should be paramount whenever any servicing of the brake components is performed. Do not use parts or fasteners which are not in perfect condition, and be sure that all clearances and torque specifications are adhered to. If you are at all unsure about a certain procedure, seek professional advice. Upon completion of any brake system work, test the brakes carefully in a controlled area before putting the vehicle into normal service. If a problem is suspected in the brake system, do not drive the vehicle until the fault is corrected.*
d) *Tyres, load and front end alignment are factors which also affect braking performance.*

2   Disc brake pads - renewal

Warning: *Disc brake pads must be renewed on both front wheels at the same time - never renew the pads on only one wheel. Also, the dust created by the brake system may contain asbestos, which is harmful to your health. Never blow it out with compressed air and don't inhale any of it. An approved filtering mask should be worn when working on the brakes. Do not, under any circumstances, use petroleum-based solvents to clean brake parts. Use brake cleaner or denatured alcohol only!*
Note 1: *When servicing the disc brakes, use only high-quality, nationally recognised name brand pads.*
Note 2: *The vehicles covered by this manual are equipped with either sliding or floating*

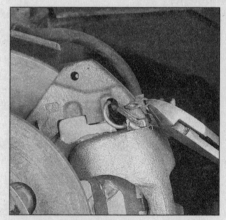

2.3 Use pliers to remove the spigot pins

calipers. To determine which type of caliper your vehicle has, look at the caliper with the wheel removed. If there are spigot pins like the one **shown in illustration 2.3,** *you have sliding calipers. If there are no spigot pins, you have floating calipers.*
Note 3: *This procedure applies to both front and rear disc brakes.*

1   Remove the master cylinder reservoir cap and siphon out approximately half of the fluid into a container. Be careful not to spill fluid onto any of the painted surfaces - it will damage the paint.

2   Loosen the front wheel lug nuts, raise the front of the vehicle and support it securely on jackstands. Remove the wheels. Work on one brake assembly at a time, using the assembled brake for reference if necessary.

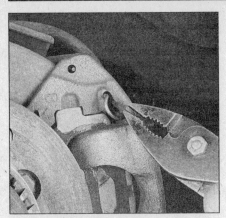

2.4a Pull the stopper plug out with the pliers, followed by . . .

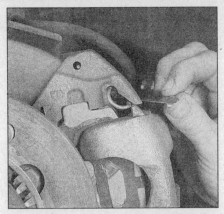

2.4b . . . the pad support plate

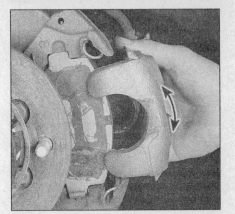

2.4c Work the caliper up-and-down while pulling it off the brake bracket

Sliding caliper

Refer to illustrations 2.3, 2.4a, 2.4b, 2.4c, 2.5a, 2.5b, 2.6 and 2.9

3   Remove the two spigot pins from the stopper plugs (see illustration). Each caliper has two stopper plugs and each plug has two spigot pins.

4   Pull the stopper plugs and pad support plates out from the caliper (see illustrations). Move the caliper assembly up-and-down to separate it from the caliper mounting bracket as you pull it off the bracket (see illustration). If the caliper bracket interferes with the brake line, remove the upper bolt. Hang the caliper out of the way on a piece of wire.

5   Remove the pads from the caliper bracket (see illustration). Separate the shim from the outer pad. Remove the inner and outer pad clips and the pad clips labeled "B" from the caliper mounting bracket (see illustration).

6   With the shim fitted on the outer pad, slip the new pads into place (see illustration).

7   Use a wood dowel or hammer handle to push the piston back into its bore to make room for the new, thicker, pads. If the piston does not move easily, loosen the bleeder screw and push again (be to sure bleed the brakes as described in Section 9 after refit-

2.5a Rotate the pads out of the brake bracket

ting). Lubricate the contact surfaces of the caliper and support plates with a thin coat of multi-purpose grease. Refit the pad clips on the bracket (see illustration 2.5b).

8   Slide the caliper assembly into position over the new pads and seat it on the mounting bracket. If removed, refit and tighten the upper caliper bracket bolt.

9   Refit the pad support plates, stopper plugs and spigot pins (see illustration). Repeat the procedure on the other wheel.

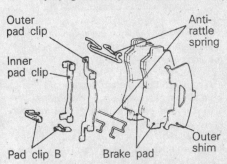

2.5b Typical brake pad components

Outer pad clip — Anti-rattle spring — Inner pad clip — Pad clip B — Brake pad — Outer shim

Floating caliper

Refer to illustrations 2.10, 2.11a, 2.11b, 2.12, 2.13a and 2.13b

Note: *Some later models are equipped with dual-piston calipers on the front wheels. Although the photographs in this procedure show pad renewal on a single-piston caliper, the procedure is the same for dual-piston calipers.*

10   Using a large C-clamp, bottom the piston back into the caliper bore. The frame end of the C-clamp should be positioned on the backside of the caliper body and the screw should bear on the outer brake pad (see illustration).

2.6 It's a good idea to apply a coat of brake anti-squeal compound to the backs of the shims

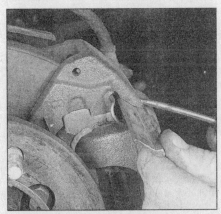

2.9 Prise the caliper up with a screwdriver and then insert the stopper plate

2.10 Use a C-clamp to bottom the piston in the bore

9

2.11a Unscrew the caliper bolt with a box-end spanner or socket so the bolt head will not be rounded off

2.11b Rotate the caliper up for access to the pads

2.12 Slide the pads away from the disc, out of the caliper bracket

11   Remove the caliper lower mounting bolt and rotate the caliper up to allow removal of the pads **(see illustrations)**.
12   Remove the anti-rattle springs (if equipped) and pull the brake pads and shims from the caliper bracket **(see illustration)**.
13   Remove the retaining clips from the bracket **(see illustrations)**.
14   Clean the mounting surfaces of the caliper and bracket, removing any dirt or corrosion. Fit new retaining clips in the bracket.
15   Coat the shims with disc brake grease and refit the pads and shims into the caliper bracket. Refit the anti-rattle springs (if equipped).
16   Refit the wear indicator (if equipped), then swing the caliper down over the pads. Refit the lower mounting bolt, tightening it to the torque listed in this Chapter's Specifications.
17   Repeat the procedure on the other wheel.

All models

18   Refit the wheels and lower the vehicle. Firmly depress the brake pedal a few times to bring the pads into contact with the disc. Check the fluid level in the master cylinder, topping it up if necessary.
19   Road test the vehicle carefully before placing it into normal use.

---

3   Disc brake caliper - removal, overhaul and refitting

Warning: *Dust created by the brake system may contain asbestos, which is harmful to your health. Never blow it out with compressed air and don't inhale any of it. An approved filtering mask should be worn when working on the brakes. Do not, under any circumstances, use petroleum-based solvents to clean brake parts. Use brake cleaner or denatured alcohol only!*
Note: *If an overhaul is indicated (usually because of fluid leakage), explore all options before beginning the job. New and factory rebuilt calipers are available on an exchange*

2.13a Remove the lower . . .

basis, which makes this job quite easy. If it's decided to rebuild the calipers, make sure that a rebuild kit is available before proceeding. Always rebuild the calipers in pairs - never rebuild just one of them.

Removal

1   Remove the cap from the brake fluid reservoir, siphon off two-thirds of the fluid into a container and discard it.
2   Loosen the wheel lug nuts, raise the front of the vehicle and support it securely on jackstands. Remove the wheels.
3   Remove the brake hose inlet fitting bolt and detach the hose. Have a rag handy to catch spilled fluid and wrap a plastic bag tightly around the end of the hose to prevent fluid loss and contamination.
4   Remove the caliper (see Section 2). On floating calipers, remove the upper mounting bolt, then detach the caliper from the bracket.

Overhaul

Refer to illustrations 3.6, 3.7a, 3.7b and 3.8
5   Clean the exterior of the caliper with brake cleaner or denatured alcohol. Never use petrol, kerosene or petroleum-based cleaning solvents. Place the caliper on a clean workbench.
6   On floating calipers, remove the sleeves

2.13b . . . and the upper pad retaining clips from the bracket

and dust boots **(see illustration). Note:** *On later models with four-wheel disc brakes, the front disc brakes are floating, dual-piston calipers. The overhaul procedure for the dual-piston caliper is the same as for the single-piston caliper; simply repeat the procedure for each piston. In Step 8, since only one piston will be ejected at a time, block the first-ejected piston loosely back in place while you apply air pressure again to eject the second piston.*
7   Using a small screwdriver, prise the piston boot ring from the caliper. Then prise out the boot **(see illustrations)**.
8   Position a wooden block or several shop rags in the caliper as a cushion, then use compressed air to remove the piston from the caliper **(see illustration)**. Use only enough air pressure to ease the piston out of the bore. If the piston is blown out, even with the cushion in place, it may be damaged.
Warning: *Never place your fingers in front of the piston in an attempt to catch or protect it when applying compressed air, as serious injury could occur.*
9   Using a wood or plastic tool, remove the piston seal from the groove in the caliper bore. Metal tools may cause bore damage.
10   Clean all components in brake cleaner or clean brake fluid and blow dry with compressed air. Check the cylinder bore and pistons for signs of wear, corrosion or surface

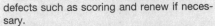

3.7a Prise the ring boot out . . .

3.7b . . . then the boot itself

3.6 Floating caliper - exploded view

1	Lower mounting bolt	6	Dust boot
2	Upper mounting bolt	7	Dust boot
		8	Boot ring
3	Caliper support	9	Piston boot
4	Sleeve	10	Piston
5	Sleeve	11	Piston seal

defects such as scoring and renew if necessary.

11   The dust seal and piston seal must always be renewed when the caliper is overhauled.

12   To reassemble the caliper, lubricate the piston seal and piston with brake lube (usually supplied with the overhaul kit) or brake fluid, refit it in the groove in the caliper bore, then lubricate the seal and the bore.

13   Carefully insert the piston into the caliper using only finger pressure.

14   Apply brake lube to the piston and then refit the boot in the piston and caliper. Insert the boot ring into the boot.

15   On floating calipers, apply brake lube into the sleeve and dust boots **(see illustration 3.6)**. Then refit the sleeve dust boot to the caliper and insert the sleeve into the dust boot. Apply brake lube into the upper mounting bolt hole and then refit the dust boot to the caliper.

Refitting

16   On sliding calipers, refer to Steps 8 and 9, Section 2 for the refitting procedure.

17   On floating calipers, refit the upper mounting bolt, swing the caliper down into position and tighten the upper mounting bolt and lower mounting bolt to the torque listed in the Specifications Section at the beginning of this Chapter.

18   Refit the flexible brake hose to the caliper. Be sure the hose does not interfere with any suspension or steering components.

19   Refit the wheel and tyre.

20   Bleed the brake system (see Section 9).

21   Lower the vehicle to the ground. Test the brakes carefully before placing the vehicle into normal operation.

4   Brake disc - inspection, removal and refitting

Refer to illustrations 4.4a, 4.4b, 4.5 and 4.7

Note: *The following procedure applies to both front and rear disc brakes.*

Inspection

1   Loosen the wheel lug nuts, raise the vehicle and support it securely on jackstands. Remove the wheel. On rear disc brakes, reverse and refit two wheel lugs nuts to hold the disc securely in place.

2   Remove the brake caliper as outlined in Sections 2 and 3. It's not necessary to disconnect the brake hose. After removing the caliper, suspend the caliper out of the way with a piece of wire from the underbody.

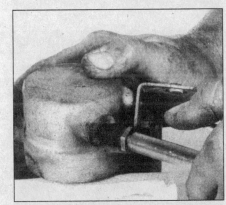

3.8 Apply compressed air to the brake fluid hose connection in the caliper body - position a wood block between the piston and the caliper to prevent damage

Don't let the caliper hang by the hose and don't stretch or twist the hose.

3   Visually check the disc surface for score marks and other damage. Light scratches and shallow grooves are normal after use and may not always be detrimental to brake operation, but deep score marks - over 0.38 mm - require disc removal and refinishing by an automotive machine shop. Be sure to check both sides of the disc. If pulsating has been noticed during application of the brakes, suspect excessive disc runout.

4   To check disc runout, place a dial indicator at a point about 12 mm from the outer edge of the disc **(see illustration)**. Set the

4.4a Check the disc runout with a dial indicator positioned approximately 12 mm from the edge of the disc - if the reading exceeds the allowable runout, the disc will have to be resurfaced

9

4.4b Using a swirling motion, remove the glaze from the disc with emery cloth

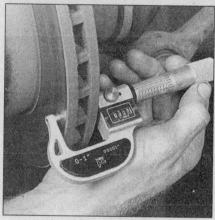

4.5 Use a micrometer to measure the thickness of the disc

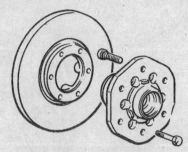

4.7 Remove the bolts from the disc/hub assembly, then separate the two components (it may be necessary to tap the disc off with a hammer and block of wood)

indicator to zero and turn the disc. The indicator reading should not exceed the limit listed in this Chapter's Specifications. If it does, the disc should be refinished by an automotive machine shop. **Note:** *Professionals recommend resurfacing of brake discs regardless of the dial indicator reading (to produce a smooth, flat surface, that will eliminate brake pedal pulsations and other undesirable symptoms related to questionable discs).* At the very least, if you elect not to have the discs resurfaced, deglaze the brake pad surface with medium-grit emery cloth (use a swirling motion to ensure a non-directional finish) **(see illustration)**.

5   The disc must not be machined to a thickness less than the specified minimum thickness. The minimum thickness is cast into the inside of the disc. The disc thickness can be checked with a micrometer **(see illustration)**.

Removal

6   Remove the caliper mounting bracket bolts and lift the bracket off.

7   On front disc brakes, remove the front hub/disc assembly. Unbolt the disc from the hub **(see illustration)**. On rear disc brakes, remove the retaining screws (if fitted) and/or the lug nuts previously fitted and lift off the disc.

Refitting

8   On front disc brakes, refit the disc to the hub, tightening the bolts to the torque listed in this Chapter's Specifications in a criss-cross pattern.

9   On front disc brakes, refit the front disc and hub assembly and adjust the wheel bearing (see Chapter 8).

10   On rear-disc brakes, slide the disc back into place. It's not necessary to refit the retaining screw.

11   Refit the caliper mounting bracket, tightening the mounting bolts to the torques listed in this Chapter's Specifications. Position the pads in the bracket and refit the caliper (refer to Section 3 for the caliper refitting procedure, if necessary). Tighten the caliper bolts

to the torque listed in this Chapter's Specifications.

12   Refit the wheel, then lower the vehicle to the ground. Depress the brake pedal a few times to bring the brake pads into contact with the disc. Bleeding of the system will not be necessary unless the brake hose was disconnected from the caliper. Check the operation of the brakes carefully before placing the vehicle into normal service.

5   Drum brake shoes - renewal

Refer to illustrations 5.2a, 5.2b, 5.4, 5.5, 5.6, 5.7a, 5.7b, 5.7c, 5.12, 5.14, 5.15, 5.16a and 5.16b

Warning: *Drum brake shoes must be renewed on both rear wheels at the same time - never renew the shoes on only one wheel. Also, the dust created by the brake system may contain asbestos, which is harmful to your health. Never blow it out with compressed air and don't inhale any of it. An approved filtering mask should be worn when working on the brakes. Do not, under any circumstances, use petroleum-based solvents to clean brake parts. Use brake cleaner or denatured alcohol only!*

Caution: *Whenever the brake shoes are*

5.2a Thread two bolts into the brake drum to draw it off the axle flange

renewed, the retractor and hold-down springs should also be renewed. Due to the continuous heating/cooling cycle that the springs are subjected to, they lose their tension over a period of time and may allow the shoes to drag on the drum and wear at a much faster rate than normal. When renewing the brake shoes, use only high-quality nationally recognised brand-name parts.

Note: *The brakes on your vehicle are either duo-servo or leading/trailing type. If you're not sure which type your vehicle has, study the brake assembly with the drum removed and compare it to* **illustration 5.4**.

1   Loosen the wheel lug nuts, raise the vehicle and support it securely on jackstands. Remove the wheel(s).

2   Pull off the brake drum. If you have difficulty removing it, screw an 8 mm bolt into each of the two threaded holes in the drum **(see illustration)**. Tighten each bolt one-half turn at a time to back the drum off the axle flange. It may be necessary to retract the brake shoes away from the inside of the drum. This is accomplished by removing the rubber plug in the backing plate and turning the adjuster star wheel with a screwdriver until the shoes no longer contact the drum **(see illustration)**.

3   Before removing anything, clean the brake assembly with brake cleaner - DO NOT use compressed air to blow the dust from the brake assembly! Take a long, close look at

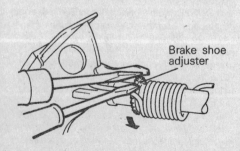

Brake shoe adjuster

5.2b Use one screwdriver to hold the adjuster lever out of the way and turn the starwheel with a second screwdriver

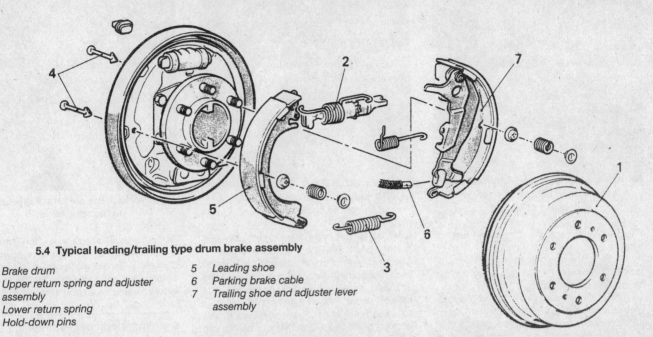

5.4 Typical leading/trailing type drum brake assembly

1   Brake drum
2   Upper return spring and adjuster
    assembly
3   Lower return spring
4   Hold-down pins

5   Leading shoe
6   Parking brake cable
7   Trailing shoe and adjuster lever
    assembly

the relationship between the parts before disassembling the brake assembly.

4   Use pliers to detach the upper return
spring (see illustration).

5   Remove the leading brake shoe hold-
down spring and pin (see illustration). This is
accomplished by grasping the spring cup
with a special tool or a pair of pliers, pushing
down and rotating it 90-degrees, disengaging
it from the pin. Place a finger behind the pin
to prevent it from being pushed out.

6   Remove the leading brake shoe and disconnect the lower spring (see illustration).

7   Remove the trailing shoe hold-down
spring and pin, remove the shoe, disconnect
the parking brake cable from the adjuster lever
and remove the shoe (see illustrations).

**5.5 Use pliers or a special tool like this
one to remove the hold-down spring**

**5.6 Rotate the leading show down and
unhook the return spring**

5.7a Remove the trailing shoe hold-down spring . . .

5.7b . . . rotate the trailing shoe and adjuster assembly . . .

9

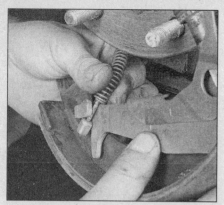

5.7c . . . then unhook the parking brake cable

5.12 Lubricate the contact surfaces of the backing plate

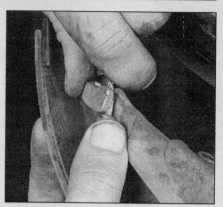

5.14 Hook the parking brake cable to the adjuster lever

8   Detach the adjuster assembly from the shoe.

9   Check the wheel cylinders for signs of leaking fluid, renewing or rebuilding them if necessary (see Section 6).

10   Check the brake drum for hard spots, cracks, score marks and grooves. Hard spots will appear as small discoloured areas. If they can't be removed with emery cloth or if any of the other conditions listed above exist, the drum must be taken to an automotive machine shop to have it turned (machined on a lathe). **Note:** *Professional mechanics recommend resurfacing the drums whenever a*

5.15 Connect the leading shoe to the lower return spring and rotate the shoe up into position

5.16a Use needle-nose pliers to connect the upper return spring

brake job is performed. Resurfacing will eliminate the possibility of out-of-round drums.

11   Unscrew the brake adjuster, clean it and apply a little high-temperature grease to the adjuster screw threads. Assemble the adjuster screw, turning it in completely.

12   Lubricate the contact surfaces of the backing plate and wheel cylinder clevis with high-temperature grease **(see illustration)**. Be careful not to get any grease on the brake shoe surfaces.

13   Refit the adjuster assembly to the trailing shoe.

14   Connect the parking brake cable to the lever and position the shoe against the backing plate **(see illustration)**. Refit the hold-down pin and spring.

15   Connect the leading shoe to the lower spring and rotate it up into position **(see illustration)**. Refit the hold-down pin and spring.

16   Refit the upper return spring **(see illustrations)**.

17   Wiggle the brake shoe assembly to centre it on the backing plate. Make sure the tops of the shoes are seated in the slots of the wheel cylinder clevis' and the bottoms of the shoes are resting under the tabs of the anchor plate.

18   Adjust the brakes by turning the star wheel on the adjuster assembly until the drum will just fit over the shoe assembly.

Refit the drum and wheel. Don't forget to tighten the lug nuts to the torque specified in Chapter 1. Repeat the operation on the other wheel, then road test the vehicle carefully before placing it into normal service.

6   Wheel cylinder - removal, overhaul and refitting

Refer to illustration 6.7

Note: *If an overhaul is indicated (usually because of fluid leakage or sticky operation), explore all options before beginning the job. New wheel cylinders are available, which make this job quite easy. If it's decided to rebuild the wheel cylinder, make sure that a rebuild kit is available before proceeding. Never overhaul only one wheel cylinder - always rebuild both of them at the same time.*

Removal

1   Raise the rear of the vehicle and support it securely on jackstands. Block the front wheels to keep the vehicle from rolling.

2   Remove the brake shoe assembly (see Section 5).

3   Remove all dirt and foreign material from around the wheel cylinder.

4   Disconnect the brake line using a flare-nut spanner. Don't pull the brake line away from the wheel cylinder.

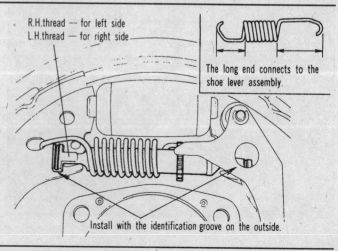

5.16b Upper return spring and adjuster details

R.H.thread — for left side
L.H.thread — for right side

The long end connects to the shoe lever assembly.

Install with the identification groove on the outside.

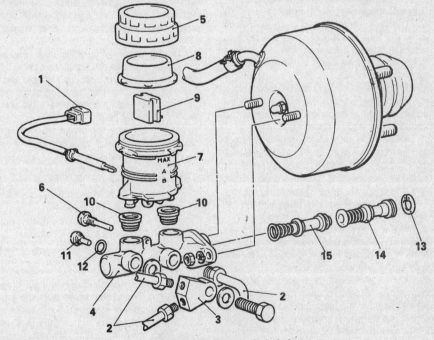

6.7 Wheel cylinder-exploded view

1	Boots	3	Pistons
2	Piston assemblies	4	Piston cups

5   Wheel cylinder body

5   Remove the wheel cylinder mounting bolts.

6   Detach the wheel cylinder from the brake backing plate and place it on a clean workbench. Immediately plug the brake line to prevent fluid loss and contamination.

Overhaul

7   Remove the bleeder screw, piston cups, pistons, boots and piston assemblies from the wheel cylinder body **(see illustration)**.

8   Clean the wheel cylinder with brake fluid, denatured alcohol or brake system cleaner. **Warning:** *Do not, under any circumstances, use petroleum-based solvents to clean brake parts!*

9   Use compressed air to remove excess fluid from the wheel cylinder and to blow out the passages.

10   Check the cylinder bore for corrosion and score marks. Crocus cloth can be used to remove light corrosion and stains, but the cylinder must be renewed with a new one if the defects cannot be removed easily, or if the bore is scored.

11   Lubricate the new piston cups with brake fluid.

12   Assemble the brake cylinder components. Make sure the lips on the piston cups face in.

Refitting

13   Place the wheel cylinder in position and refit the bolts.

14   Connect the brake line and refit the brake shoe assembly.

15   Bleed the brakes (see Section 9).

7   Master cylinder - removal, overhaul and refitting

Refer to illustration 7.11

Note: *Before deciding to overhaul the master cylinder, check on the availability and cost of a new or factory rebuilt unit and also the availability of a rebuild kit.*

Removal

1   The master cylinder is located in the engine compartment, mounted to the power brake booster.

2   Remove as much fluid as you can from the reservoir with a syringe.

3   Place rags under the fluid fittings and prepare caps or plastic bags to cover the ends of the lines once they are disconnected. **Caution:** *Brake fluid will damage paint. Cover all body parts and be careful not to spill fluid during this procedure.*

4   Loosen the tube nuts at the ends of the brake lines where they enter the master cylinder. To prevent rounding off the flats on these nuts, the use of a flare-nut spanner, which wraps around the nut, is preferred.

5   Pull the brake lines slightly away from the master cylinder and plug the ends to prevent contamination. On models with a remotely mounted fluid reservoir, disconnect the fluid hoses from the master cylinder and plug the ends to prevent fluid loss.

6   Remove the mounting nuts and pull the master cylinder off the studs and out of the engine compartment. Again, be careful not to spill the fluid as this is done.

Overhaul

7   Before attempting the overhaul of the master cylinder, obtain the proper rebuild kit, which will contain the necessary new parts and also any instructions which may be specific to your model.

8   Inspect the reservoir or inlet grommet(s) for indications of leakage near the base of the reservoir. If the reservoir is attached to the master cylinder, remove the mounting screw(s) and remove the reservoir.

9   Place the cylinder in a vice and use a punch or Phillips screwdriver to fully depress the pistons until they bottom against the other end of the master cylinder. Hold the pistons in this position and remove the stop bolt(s) on the side of the master cylinder. Remove the two check valves or connector block and the copper gaskets.

10   Depress the pistons once again, then carefully remove the snap-ring at the end of the master cylinder. Snap-ring pliers are needed on later models.

11   The internal components can now be removed from the cylinder bore **(see illustration)**. Make a note of the proper order of the

7.11 Master cylinder - exploded view

1	Fluid level sensor connector	6	Stop bolt	11	Stop bolt
2	Brake lines	7	Reservoir	12	Gasket
3	Connector block	8	Diaphragm	13	Stopper ring
4	Master cylinder	9	Fluid level sensor float	14	Primary piston
5	Reservoir cap	10	Reservoir seal	15	Secondary piston

9

components so they can be returned to their original locations. Also note which direction the lip of each seal faces so the new seals can be fitted the same way. **Note:** *The two springs are of different tension, so pay particular attention to their order.*

12   Carefully inspect the bore of the master cylinder. Any deep scoring or other damage will mean a new master cylinder is required.

13   Renew all parts included in the rebuild kit, following any instructions in the kit. Clean all reused parts with clean brake fluid or denatured alcohol. Do not use any petroleum-based cleaners. During assembly, lubricate all parts liberally with clean brake fluid. Be sure to tighten all fittings and connections securely.

14   Push the assembled components into the bore, compressing them with the screwdriver or punch and refit the stop bolt(s).

15   Compress the piston assemblies and fit the new snap-ring, making sure it is seated properly in the groove.

16   Before fitting the new master cylinder it should be bench bled. Because it will be necessary to apply pressure to the master cylinder piston and, at the same time, control flow from the brake line outlets, it is recommended that the master cylinder be mounted in a vice, with the jaws of the vice clamping on the mounting flange.

17   Insert threaded plugs into the brake line outlet holes and snug them down so that there will be no air leakage past them, but not so tight that they cannot be easily loosened.

18   Fill the reservoir with brake fluid of the recommended type (see Chapter 1).

19   Remove one plug and push the piston assembly into the master cylinder bore to expel the air from the master cylinder. A large Phillips screwdriver can be used to push on the piston assembly.

20   To prevent air from being drawn back into the master cylinder the plug must be fitted and snugged down before releasing the pressure on the piston assembly.

21   Repeat the procedure until only brake fluid is expelled from the brake line outlet hole. When only brake fluid is expelled, repeat the procedure with the other outlet hole and plug. Be sure to keep the master cylinder reservoir filled with brake fluid to prevent the introduction of air into the system.

22   Since high pressure is not involved in the bench bleeding procedure, an alternative to the removal and refitting of the plugs with each stroke of the piston assembly is available. Before pushing in on the piston assembly, remove the plug as described in Step 19. Before releasing the piston, however, instead of refitting the plug, simply put your finger tightly over the hole to keep air from being drawn back into the master cylinder. Wait several seconds for brake fluid to be drawn from the reservoir into the piston bore, then depress the piston again, removing your finger as brake fluid is expelled. Be sure to put your finger back over the hole each time before releasing the piston, and when the bleeding procedure is complete for that out-

let, install the plug and snug it before going on to the other port.

Refitting

23   Refit the master cylinder over the studs on the power brake booster and tighten the attaching nuts only finger tight at this time.

24   Thread the brake line fittings into the master cylinder. Since the master cylinder is still a bit loose, it can be moved slightly in order for the fittings to thread in easily. Do not strip the threads as the fittings are tightened.

25   Fully tighten the mounting nuts and the brake fittings.

26   Fill the master cylinder reservoir with fluid, then bleed the master cylinder (only if the cylinder has not been bench bled; see Steps 16 through 22) and the brake system as described in Section 9. To bleed the cylinder on the vehicle, have an assistant pump the brake pedal several times and then hold the pedal to the floor. Loosen the fitting nuts to allow air and fluid to escape. Repeat this procedure on both fittings until the fluid is clear of air bubbles. Test the operation of the brake system carefully before placing the vehicle in normal service.

---

8   Brake lines and hoses - inspection and renewal

1   About every six months the flexible hoses which connect the steel brake lines with the front and rear brakes should be inspected for cracks, chafing of the outer cover, leaks, blisters, and other damage (Chapter 1).

2   Spare steel and flexible brake lines are commonly available from dealer parts departments and auto parts stores. Do not, under any circumstances, use anything other than genuine steel lines or approved flexible brake hoses as renewal items.

3   When refitting the brake line, leave at least 19 mm clearance between the line and any moving or vibrating parts.

4   When disconnecting a hose and line, first remove the spring clip. Then, using a normal spanner to hold the hose and a flare-nut spanner to hold the tube, make the disconnection. Use the spanners in the same manner when making a connection, then fit a new clip. **Note:** *Make sure the tube passes through the centre of its grommet.*

5   When disconnecting two hoses, use normal spanners on the hose fittings. When connecting two hoses, make sure they are not bent, twisted or strained.

6   Steel brake lines are usually retained along their span with clips. Always remove these clips completely before removing a fixed brake line. Always refit these clips, or new ones if the old ones are damaged, when renewing a brake line, as they provide support and keep the lines from vibrating, which can eventually break them.

7   Remember to bleed the hydraulic system after renewing a hose or line.

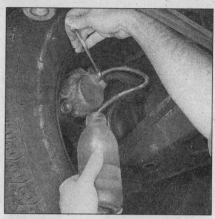

9.8 When bleeding the brakes, a hose is connected to the bleeder valve at the caliper or wheel cylinder and then submerged in brake fluid - air will be seen as bubbles in the hose and container when the valve is opened - all air must be expelled before moving the next wheel

---

9   Brake system - bleeding

Refer to illustration 9.8

Warning: *Wear eye protection when bleeding the brake system. If the fluid comes in contact with your eyes, immediately rinse them with water and seek medical attention.*

Note: *Bleeding the hydraulic system is necessary to remove any air that manages to find its way into the system when it's been opened during removal and refitting of a hose, line, caliper, wheel cylinder or master cylinder.*

1   It will probably be necessary to bleed the system at all four brakes if air has entered the system due to low fluid level, or if the brake lines have been disconnected at the master cylinder.

2   If a brake line was disconnected only at a wheel, then only that caliper or wheel cylinder must be bled.

3   If a brake line is disconnected at a fitting located between the master cylinder and any of the brakes, that part of the system served by the disconnected line must be bled.

4   Remove any residual vacuum from the brake power booster by applying the brake several times with the engine off.

5   Remove the master cylinder reservoir cover and fill the reservoir with brake fluid. Refit the cover. **Note:** *Check the fluid level often during the bleeding operation and add fluid as necessary to prevent the fluid level from falling low enough to allow air bubbles into the master cylinder.*

6   Have an assistant on hand, as well as a supply of new brake fluid, a clear container partially filled with clean brake fluid, plastic, rubber or vinyl tubing to fit over the bleeder valve and a spanner to open and close the bleeder valve.

7   Beginning at the right rear wheel, loosen the bleeder valve slightly, then tighten it to a point where it is snug but can still be loosened quickly and easily.

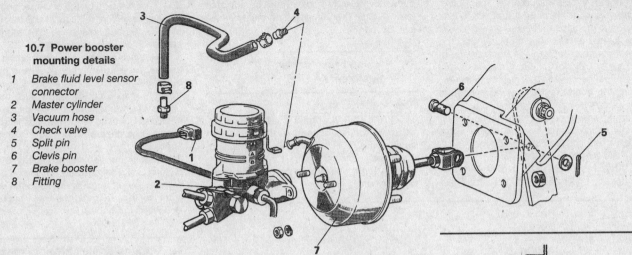

10.7 Power booster mounting details

1   Brake fluid level sensor connector
2   Master cylinder
3   Vacuum hose
4   Check valve
5   Split pin
6   Clevis pin
7   Brake booster
8   Fitting

8   Place one end of the tubing over the bleeder valve and submerge the other end in brake fluid in the container **(see illustration)**.

9   Have the assistant pump the brakes slowly a few times to get pressure in the system, then hold the pedal firmly depressed.

10   While the pedal is held depressed, open the bleeder valve just enough to allow a flow of fluid to leave the valve. Watch for air bubbles to exit the submerged end of the tube. When the fluid flow slows after a couple of seconds, close the valve and have your assistant release the pedal.

11   Repeat Steps 9 and 10 until no more air is seen leaving the tube, then tighten the bleeder valve and proceed to the left rear wheel, the right front wheel and the left front wheel, in that order, and perform the same procedure. Be sure to check the fluid in the master cylinder reservoir frequently.

12   Never use old brake fluid. It contains moisture which will lower the boiling point of the brake fluid and also deteriorate the brake system rubber components.

13   Refill the master cylinder with fluid at the end of the operation.

10   Power brake booster - check, removal and refitting

Refer to illustrations 10.7, 10.14a and 10.14b

Operating check

1   Depress the brake pedal several times with the engine off and make sure that there is no change in the pedal reserve distance.

2   Depress the pedal and start the engine. If the pedal goes down slightly, operation is normal.

Airtightness check

3   Start the engine and turn it off after one or two minutes. Depress the brake pedal several times slowly. If the pedal goes down farther the first time but gradually rises after the second or third depression, the booster is airtight.

4   Depress the brake pedal while the engine is running, then stop the engine with the pedal depressed. If there is no change in the pedal reserve travel after holding the pedal for 30 seconds, the booster is airtight.

Removal

5   Power brake booster units should not be disassembled. They require special tools not normally found in most service stations or shops. They are fairly complex and, because of their critical relationship to brake performance, it is best to renew a defective booster unit with a new or rebuilt one.

6   To remove the booster, first remove the brake master cylinder as described in Section 7. On some vehicles it is not necessary to disconnect the brake lines from the master cylinder, as there is enough room to reposition the cylinder to allow booster removal.

7   Locate the pushrod clevis connecting the booster to the brake pedal **(see illustration)**. This is accessible from the interior in front of the driver's seat.

8   Remove the clevis pin retaining clip with pliers and pull out the pin.

9   Holding the clevis with pliers, disconnect the clevis locknut with a spanner. The clevis is now loose.

10   Disconnect the hose leading from the engine to the booster. Be careful not to damage the hose when removing it from the booster fitting.

11   Remove the four nuts and washers holding the brake booster to the firewall. You may need a light to see these, as they are up under the dash area.

12   Slide the booster straight out from the firewall until the studs clear the holes and pull the booster, brackets and gaskets from the engine compartment area.

Refitting

13   Refitting procedures are basically the reverse of those for removal. Tighten the booster mounting nuts to the torque listed in this Chapter's Specifications. Tighten the clevis locknut securely.

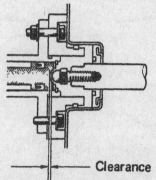

10.14a The clearance between the booster pushrod and the master cylinder piston must be within the specified range. If there's excessive clearance, the brake pedal travel will be excessive; if there's no clearance, the brakes may drag

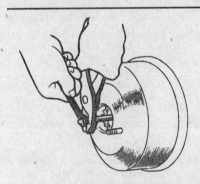

10.14b To adjust the length of the booster pushrod, hold the serrated portion of the rod with a pair of pliers and then turn the adjusting nut in or out, as necessary, to achieve the desired setting

14   If the power booster unit is being renewed, the clearance between the master cylinder piston and the pushrod in the vacuum booster must be measured and, if necessary, adjusted **(see illustration)**. Using a depth micrometer or vernier calipers, measure the distance from the seat (recessed area) in the master cylinder to the master cylinder mounting flange. Next, connect a

9

hand held vacuum pump to the power booster vacuum fitting and apply 68 kPa of vacuum to the booster. Measure the distance from the end of the vacuum booster pushrod to the mounting face of the booster (where the master cylinder mounting flange seats). Determine the clearance from the measurements and compare it to the value listed in this Chapter's Specifications. Turn the adjusting screw on the end of the power booster pushrod until the clearance is within the specified limit **(see illustration)**.

15   Refit the master cylinder.

16   After the final refitting of the master cylinder and brake hoses and lines, the brake pedal height and freeplay must be adjusted (see Chapter 1) and the system must be bled (see Section 9).

11   Parking brake cables - adjustment

Refer to illustration 11.3

1   If the parking brake doesn't keep the vehicle from rolling when the handle is applied 4 to 6 clicks on parking brake lever, adjust the cable.

2   Raise the vehicle and support it securely on jackstands.

3   Turn the nuts on the equaliser end of the cables. Make sure the equaliser is maintained at a 90-degree angle to the joint as the nuts are tightened **(see illustration)**.

4   Remove all slack from the parking brake cables. After adjustment apply the parking brake several times and check that handle travel is 4 to 6 clicks. Make sure the rear brakes don't drag when the parking brake is released. Check to see that the parking brake light on the dash glows when the handle is applied.

6   Lower the vehicle and verify that the parking brake will hold the vehicle on a moderate incline. If it still won't keep the vehicle from rolling, inspect the rear brakes as described in Chapter 1.

12   Parking brake cable(s) - renewal

Refer to illustrations 12.3a and 12.3b

1   Raise the vehicle and support it securely on jackstands.

2   Disassemble the rear brakes and remove the ends of the parking brake cables from the parking brake levers (Section 5).

3   Remove the return spring (if equipped), separate the parking brake cables at the adjuster, then remove the bolts and the cables **(see illustrations)**.

4   Refitting is the reverse of the removal procedure.

5   Following refitting, adjust the parking brake (see Section 11).

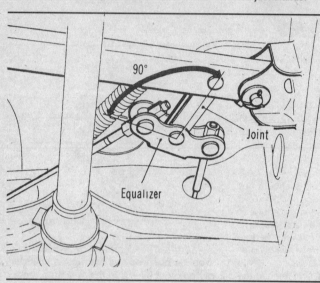

11.3 The equaliser and joint on the parking brake assembly must be at right angles to each other as the parking brake adjustment is made

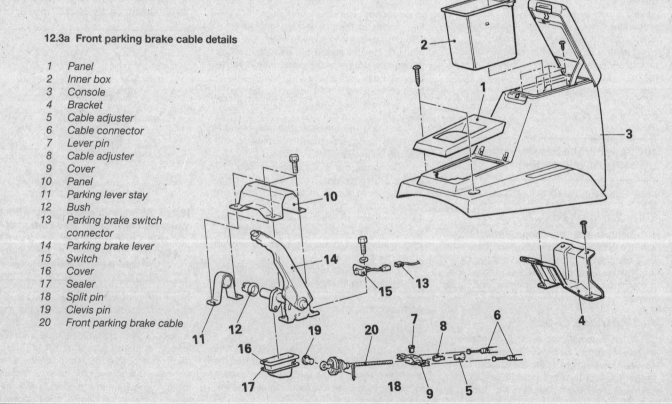

12.3a Front parking brake cable details

1   Panel
2   Inner box
3   Console
4   Bracket
5   Cable adjuster
6   Cable connector
7   Lever pin
8   Cable adjuster
9   Cover
10   Panel
11   Parking lever stay
12   Bush
13   Parking brake switch connector
14   Parking brake lever
15   Switch
16   Cover
17   Sealer
18   Split pin
19   Clevis pin
20   Front parking brake cable

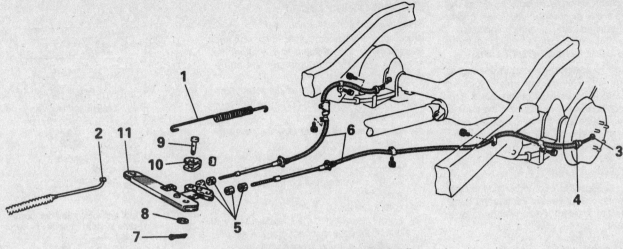

12.3b   Rear parking brake cable details

1	Return spring	4	Cable-to-brake shoe lever	6	Rear cable	9	Clevis pin
2	Cable end		connector	7	Split pin	10	Spacer
3	Stopper	5	Adjusting nut	8	Washer	11	Lever assembly

13   Parking brake shoes (models with rear disc brakes) - renewal

Refer to illustration 13.1

1   Loosen rear wheel lug nuts, raise the rear of the vehicle and support it securely on jackstands. Remove the wheels and brake disc (see Section 4). Work on the brake assemblies one side at a time, using the assembled brake for reference, if necessary (see illustration).

2   Remove the brake caliper as described in Section 2.

3   Release the parking brake lever and rotate the brake disc (rotor). If the disc does not turn freely, or will not pull off, remove the adjustment hole rubber plug (located on the back side of the backing plate). Turn the star-wheel counter clockwise with a flat-bladed screwdriver approximately 3 to 4 clicks to retract the shoes and allow for the disc/drum

assembly to slide off. Pull disc/drum assembly off.

4   Remove the adjusting wheel spring.

5   Remove the parking brake shoe hold-down spring, washer and pin.

6   Remove the adjuster and the anchor-to-shoe springs, then remove the strut and strut-to-shoe spring.

7   Remove the brake shoes.

8   Disconnect the parking brake cable.

9   Remove the lever assembly from the rear brake shoe.

10   Refitting is the reverse of removal. Repeat the operation on the other wheel. Don't forget to tighten the lug nuts to the torque specified in Chapter 1. Road test the vehicle carefully on a level road, away from traffic, before placing it into normal service again.

14   Anti-lock Brake System (ABS) - general description and diagnosis

The anti-lock brake system prevents wheel lock-up by sensing the drop in wheel speed and modulating hydraulic pressure to the brakes accordingly. It consists of several components:

Control unit

The function of the control unit is to accept and process information received from the speed sensors, G-sensor and brake light switch to control the hydraulic pressure through the modulator to prevent wheel lock up. The control unit also constantly monitors the system, even under normal driving conditions, to find faults within the system.

If a problem develops within the system, the BRAKE warning light will glow on the dashboard. A diagnostic code will also be

13.1   Parking brake shoe assembly details (later models with rear disc brakes)

A	Caliper assembly	G	Adjuster star wheel assembly
B	Rear brake disc	H	Anchor-to-shoe springs
C	Adjuster star wheel spring	I	Strut
D	Shoe hold-down washer	J	Strut-to-shoe spring
E	Shoe hold-down spring	K	Parking brake cable clip
F	Shoe hold-down pin	L	Parking brake shoes

9

stored, which, when retrieved will indicate the problem areas or component. These codes can be retrieved using an analog voltmeter.

Modulator and control unit

The modulator is located in the engine compartment. The control unit is located behind the right rear quarter trim panel. The modulator receives a signal from the control unit, it then regulates the hydraulic pressure to the rear wheels as necessary to prevent full wheel lock-up.

G-sensor

The G-sensor is located behind the centre console. The G-sensor senses the force and speed of deceleration and sends a signal to the control unit.

Speed sensors

The speed sensors are located at each wheel, behind the brake disc. The speed sensor sends a signal to the control unit indicating the wheel rotational speed.

Brake light switch

The brake light switch powers the control unit when the brake pedal is applied. Without this signal the anti-lock system would not activate.

Diagnosis and repair

Refer to illustrations 14.1 and 14.2

Warning: *If a dashboard light comes on and stays on while the vehicle is in operation, the anti-lock system requires immediate attention!*

Before checking the self-diagnosis connector for codes, you can perform a few preliminary checks.

a) *Check the brake fluid level in the reservoir.*
b) *Verify that the control unit electrical connectors are securely connected.*
c) *Check the electrical connectors at the modulator.*
d) *Check the fuses.*
e) *Follow the wiring to the speed sensor and check that the connections are secure and that the wiring is not damaged.*

Code retrieval

1   Turn ignition switch off and connect an analog voltmeter to the self-diagnosis check connector terminals **(see illustration)**.
2   Turn ignition switch to the on position and read the failure code signal pattern **(see illustration)**.
3   To clear codes after repairs have been completed turn ignition switch off and disconnect the battery for 10 seconds.

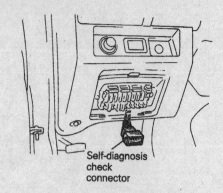

Self-diagnosis check connector

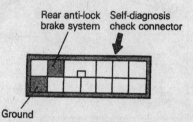

Rear anti-lock   Self-diagnosis
brake system   check connector

Ground

14.1 The self-diagnosis connector is located in the console. To access the anti-lock system diagnostic mode, simply hook an analog voltmeter to the indicated terminals of the connector

Diagnostic code	Output signal pattern	Component or system	Probable cause
---		Normal operation	System is operating normally
11		Right front wheel speed sensor or circuit	Defective right front wheel speed sensor, open or short circuit, defective ABS ECU
12		Left front wheel speed sensor or circuit	Defective left front wheel speed sensor, open or short circuit, defective ABS ECU
13		Right rear wheel speed sensor or circuit	Defective right rear wheel speed sensor, open or short circuit, defective ABS ECU
14		Left rear wheel speed sensor or circuit	Defective left rear wheel speed sensor, open or short circuit, defective ABS ECU
15		Wheel speed sensor circuits	Defective or mismatched tyres, loose wheel speed sensor, broken or defective sensor rotor, defective ABS ECU

14.2 Anti-lock brake system codes and diagnosis tables

Diagnostic code	Output signal pattern	Component or system	Probable cause
16		ABS ECU battery power circuit	Problem with the circuit supplying power to the ABS ECU
21		Right front wheel speed sensor or circuit	Defective right front wheel speed sensor, open or short circuit, defective sensor rotor or excessive sensor gap, defective ABS ECU
22		Left front wheel speed sensor or circuit	Defective left front wheel speed sensor, open or short circuit, defective sensor rotor or excessive sensor gap, defective ABS ECU
23		Right rear wheel speed sensor or circuit	Defective right rear wheel speed sensor, open or short circuit, defective sensor rotor or excessive sensor gap, defective ABS ECU
24		Left rear wheel speed sensor or circuit	Defective left rear wheel speed sensor, open or short circuit, defective sensor rotor or excessive sensor gap, defective ABS ECU
25		Free-wheel engage switch circuit	Open or short circuit in the free-wheel engage switch circuit, defective free-wheel engage switch, 4WD indicator control unit or ABS ECU
26		Centre differential lock detection switch circuit	Open or short circuit in the centre differential lock detection switch circuit, defective centre differential lock detection switch, 4WD indicator control unit or ABS ECU
27		Rear differential lock detection switch circuit	Open or short circuit in the rear differential lock detection switch circuit, defective rear differential lock detection switch, 4WD indicator control unit or ABS ECU
31		G-sensor battery power circuit	Open or short in the G-sensor battery power circuit or defective ABS ECU
32		G-sensor	Open or short in the G-sensor circuit, defective G-sensor or ABS ECU
33		Brake light switch	Open or short in the brake light switch circuit, defective brake light switch or ABS ECU
41		ABS hydraulic unit solenoid valve no. 1	Open or short in the ABS hydraulic unit circuit, defective ABS hydraulic unit or ABS ECU
43		ABS hydraulic unit solenoid valve no. 2	Open or short in the ABS hydraulic unit circuit, defective ABS hydraulic unit or ABS ECU

14.2 Anti-lock brake system codes and diagnosis tables (continued)

9

Diagnostic code	Output signal pattern	Component or system	Probable cause
45		ABS hydraulic unit solenoid valve no. 3	Open or short in the ABS hydraulic unit circuit, defective ABS hydraulic unit or ABS ECU
51		ABS system bulb relay circuit	Open or short in the ABS hydraulic unit circuit, defective bulb relay, ABS hydraulic unit or ABS ECU
52		ABS system motor relay	Open or short in the ABS hydraulic unit circuit, defective motor relay, ABS hydraulic unit or ABS ECU
63		Defective ABS ECU	Replace the ABS ECU
64		Defective ABS ECU	Replace the ABS ECU

14.2 Anti-lock brake system codes and diagnosis tables (continued)

15 Vacuum pump (diesel engines) - removal and refitting

Removal

1   Remove the intercooler assembly and any other interfering upper engine compartment component.

2   Disconnect the vacuum hose from the pump.
3   Remove the oil pressure switch, the sealing washers and the oil line to the vacuum pump.
4   Unbolt and remove the vacuum pump from the front of the engine. Remove the O-rings from the pump.

Refitting

5   Renew both of the O-rings on the pump. Bolt the pump to the engine.
6   Renew the sealing washers on the oil line/oil pressure switch assembly.
7   The remainder of the refitting is the reverse of removal.

Chapter 10
Suspension and steering systems

Contents

Specifications

General

Bump stop base-to-bracket clearance (A in illustration 4.10a) 1990 and earlier models	71 mm
Bump stop tip-to-bracket clearance (A in illustration 4.10b) 1991 and later	21 to 23 mm

Torque specifications

Front suspension — Nm

	Nm
Upper balljoint-to-steering knuckle nut	75
Upper arm shaft-to-frame bolt	110
Lower balljoint-to-steering knuckle nut	150
Lower balljoint-to-lower arm bolt	25
Lower arm shaft-to-crossmember nut or bolt	150
Lower arm pivot shaft	150
Upper shock absorber nut	15
Lower shock absorber bolts	70
Torsion bar locknut	45
Torsion bar anchor arm bolt B	108
Stabiliser bar mounting bracket bolts	24
Stabiliser bar link bolts 1993 and earlier models	15
1994 and later models Upper	93
Lower	33

10

Torque specifications

	Nm
Rear suspension	
Leaf spring type	
Rear shackle pin nuts	53
Front shackle pin nut	53
U-Bolt nuts	110
Rear shock absorber nuts	22
Coil spring type	
Trailing arm-to-frame nut	140
Trailing arm-to-axle bolts	235
Lateral rod nuts	235
Stabiliser bar bracket bolts	
1993 and earlier models	35
1994 and later models	15
Lower shock absorber bolt	
1993 and earlier models	120
1994 and later models	216
Upper shock absorber nut	15
Steering	
Steering gear-to-frame bolts	30 to 35
Flexible coupling-to-steering gear pinch bolt	35
Pitman arm-to-steering gear nut	30 to 35
Pitman arm-to-relay rod nut	15
Idler arm bracket-to-frame bolts	55 to 65
Idler arm-to-pivot shaft nut	32
Tie-rod end-to-relay rod nut	45
Tie-rod end-to-steering knuckle nut	45
Steering wheel nut	40
Wheel lug nuts	See Chapter 1

1.1 Typical front suspension layout

1	Steering relay rod	4	Tie rod	7	Tie-rod end
2	Stabiliser bar	5	Torsion bar	8	Upper control arm
3	Lower control arm	6	Lower balljoint	9	Steering gear

1.2 Typical leaf spring type rear suspension layout

1	Upper shock absorber mount	3	Spring U-bolt	5	Lower shock bolt
2	Leaf spring	4	Spring through bolt		

1 General information

Refer to illustrations 1.1 and 1.2

The front suspension on the vehicles covered by this manual is an independent type, made up of upper and lower arms, torsion), balljoint-mounted steering knuckles and shock absorbers **(see illustration)**. Some models are equipped with a stabiliser bar to limit body roll during cornering.

The rear suspension consists of the rear axle housing, leaf springs and shock absorbers **(see illustration)**. Later models use coil springs with a trailing arm and track rod arrangement to locate the axle. Information regarding axles and the rear axle housing can be found in Chapter 8.

The steering system is composed of a steering column, steering gear, Pitman arm, relay rod, two tie-rod assemblies and an idler arm. Later models feature power assisted steering, which includes a belt-driven pump and associated hoses to provide hydraulic pressure to the steering gear.

Frequently, when working on the suspension or steering system components, you may come across fasteners which seem impossible to loosen. These fasteners on the underside of the vehicle are continually sub-

jected to water, road grime, mud, etc., and can become rusted or "seized," making them extremely difficult to remove. In order to unscrew these stubborn fasteners without damaging them (or other components), be sure to use lots of penetrating oil and allow it to soak in for a while. Using a wire brush to clean exposed threads will also ease removal of the nut or bolt and prevent damage to the threads. Sometimes a sharp blow with a hammer and punch is effective in breaking the bond between a nut and bolt threads, but care must be taken to prevent the punch from slipping off the fastener and ruining the threads. Heating the stuck fastener and surrounding area with a torch sometimes helps too, but isn't recommended because of the obvious dangers associated with fire. Long breaker bars and extension, or "cheater," pipes will increase leverage, but never use an extension pipe on a ratchet - the ratcheting mechanism could be damaged. Sometimes, turning the nut or bolt in the tightening (clockwise) direction first will help to break it loose. Fasteners that require drastic measures to unscrew should always be renewed.

Since most of the procedures that are dealt with in this Chapter involve jacking up the vehicle and working underneath it, a good pair of jackstands will be needed. A hydraulic

floor jack is the preferred type of jack to lift the vehicle, and it can also be used to support certain components during various operations. **Warning:** *Never, under any circumstances, rely on a jack to support the vehicle while working on it. Whenever any of the suspension or steering fasteners are loosened or removed they must be inspected and, if necessary, renewed with new ones of the same part number or of original equipment quality and design. Torque specifications must be followed for proper reassembly and component retention. Never attempt to heat or straighten any suspension or steering component. Always renew them.*

2 Front stabiliser bar - removal and refitting

Refer to illustration 2.2

Warning: *Whenever any of the suspension or steering fasteners are loosened or removed, they must be inspected and, if necessary, renewed with new ones of the same part number or of original equipment quality and design. Torque specifications must be followed for proper reassembly and component retention.*

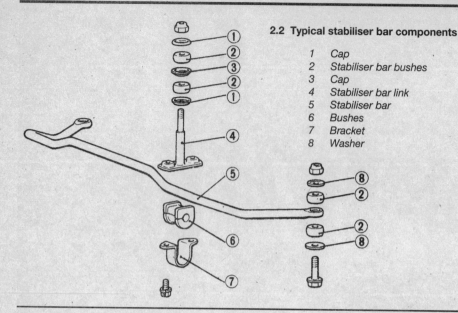

2.2 Typical stabiliser bar components

1   Cap
2   Stabiliser bar bushes
3   Cap
4   Stabiliser bar link
5   Stabiliser bar
6   Bushes
7   Bracket
8   Washer

3.3 Remove the locking and mounting nuts on the upper end of the shock absorber shaft

Removal

1   Raise the front of the vehicle and support it securely on jackstands. Apply the parking brake.
2   Remove the stabiliser bar-to-lower arm link nuts and bolts, noting how the spacers, washers and bushes are positioned **(see illustration)**.
3   Remove the stabiliser bar bracket bolts and detach the bar from the vehicle.
4   Pull the brackets off the stabiliser bar and inspect the bushes for cracks, hardening and other signs of deterioration. If the bushes are damaged, split them.

Refitting

5   Position the stabiliser bar bushes on the bar. Push the brackets over the bushes and raise the bar up to the frame. Install the bracket bolts but don't tighten them completely at this time.
6   Install the stabiliser bar-to-lower arm bolts, washers, spacers and rubber bushes and tighten the nuts securely.
7   Tighten the bracket, bolts and link nuts securely. Lower the vehicle and release the parking brake.

3   Front shock absorber - removal and refitting

Refer to illustrations 3.3 and 3.5
Warning: *Whenever any of the suspension or steering fasteners are loosened or removed, they must be inspected and, if necessary, renewed with new ones of the same part number or of original equipment quality and design. Torque specifications must be followed for proper reassembly and component retention.*

1   Jack up the front of the vehicle and place it securely on jackstands.
2   Remove the front wheels.
3   Remove the nuts holding the shock

absorber to the upper mount **(see illustration)**. Clamp a pair of locking pliers to the flats at the top of the shock rod to prevent it from turning. **Note:** *If the vehicle has remote-controlled variable shock absorbers, the actuator assembly is bolted to the top of the shock absorber stud end. To remove the actuator, loosen the two bolts that hold the actuator to the mounting bracket, then remove the upper shock absorber hold-down nut and actuator mounting bracket. Remove the lower shock absorber hold-down nut and actuator washer assembly with the stud pin. Be careful not to bend the stud pin on the washer assembly.*
4   Remove the upper washer and rubber cushion from the shaft of the shock absorber.
5   Remove the two shock absorber-to-lower control arm bolts (accessible from the upper surface of the arm), then fully compress the shock absorber and lift it up and over the arm to remove it **(see illustration)**.
6   Refitting is the reverse of the removal procedure. Make sure the washers and bushes are assembled in the proper order. Tighten the bolts and nuts securely.

4   Torsion bar - removal, refitting and adjustment

Refer to illustrations 4.2, 4.3, 4.4, 4.10a and 4.10b
Warning: *Whenever any of the suspension or steering fasteners are loosened or removed, they must be inspected and, if necessary, renewed with new ones of the same part number or of original equipment quality and design. Torque specifications must be followed for proper reassembly and component retention.*

Removal

1   Loosen the wheel lug nuts, raise the front of the vehicle and support it securely on

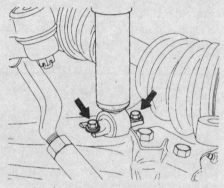

3.5 The lower shock absorber mounting bolts (arrows) are accessible from the top of the lower control arm

jackstands, then remove the wheel and the brake caliper assembly (see Chapter 9).
2   Remove the anchor arm dust covers **(see illustration)**.
3   Mark the torsion bar directly opposite the mark on the anchor arm **(see illustration)**. **Caution:** *Do not punch or scratch the torsion bar - use paint to make the mark.*
4   With the rebound stop on the upper arm in contact with the frame, make sure the distance from the underside of the adjusting bolt head to the bottom face of the nut on the left side ('A' in the accompanying illustration) and the right side ('B' in the illustration) is as specified (see this Chapter's Specifications).
5   Loosen the jam nut and adjusting nut at the anchor arm assembly until the torsion bar can be slipped out of the anchor arms.

Refitting and adjustment

6   When refitting the torsion bar, apply grease to the torsion bar and anchor arm splines, the adjusting bolt threads and the inside of the dust boots.
7   If both bars have been removed, the right torsion bar can be distinguished from the left by checking the end of the bar. Look for an L or an R stamped into the end of each bar (R is right, L is left).
8   Position the marked end of the bar into

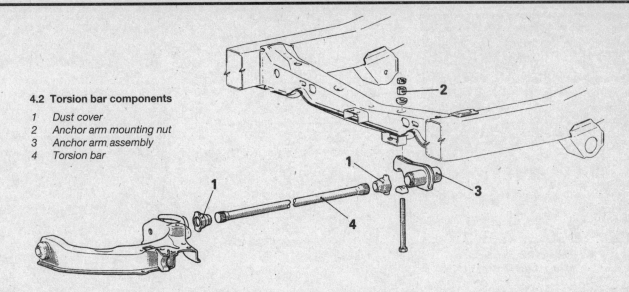

4.2 Torsion bar components

1   Dust cover
2   Anchor arm mounting nut
3   Anchor arm assembly
4   Torsion bar

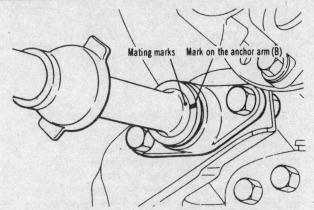

4.3 Mark the torsion bar before removing it, but **DO NOT** scratch it or make a mark with a centre-punch

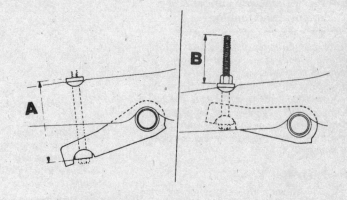

4.4 Make sure the adjusting bolt measurements A and B are as specified as the torsion bar is installed

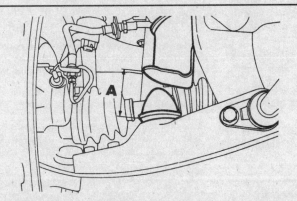

4.10a On 1990 and earlier models, the distance A from the bump stop base to the bracket must be as specified with the vehicle weight on the suspension, or the torsion bars may require further adjustment

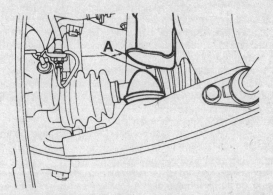

4.10b On 1991 and later models, measure the distance A from the bump stop tip to the bracket with the vehicle weight on the suspension, if it isn't as specified, the torsion bars may require further adjustment

10

the anchor arm with the mating marks aligned (if a new bar is installed, align the white spline with the mark on the anchor arm).

9   Assemble the torsion bar and the rear anchor arm and tighten the adjusting nut until the distance from the adjusting nut bottom face to the top of the bolt is the same as the measurements made in Step 4 **(see illustration 4.4)**.

10   Reinstall the hub, wheel and brake caliper, then lower the vehicle and measure the distance from the bump stop to the bracket with the vehicle unloaded **(see illustrations)**. Compare this measurement to the Specifications Section at the beginning of this Chapter. If necessary, tighten the adjusting nut on the anchor arm until the distance is as specified.

11   After assembly, take the vehicle to an alignment shop to have the ride height and front end alignment checked.

5.2 Loosen the torsion bar anchor nuts (arrow)

5 Front suspension upper arm - removal and refitting

Refer to illustrations 5.2 and 5.4

Warning: *Whenever any of the suspension or steering fasteners are loosened or removed, they must be inspected and, if necessary, renewed with new ones of the same part number or of original equipment quality and design. Torque specifications must be followed for proper reassembly and component retention.*

Removal

1   Loosen the wheel lug nuts, raise the front of the vehicle and support it securely on jackstands. Apply the parking brake. Remove the wheel.

2   Support the lower arm with a jack. The support point must be as close to the balljoint as possible to give maximum leverage on the lower arm. Release the torsion bar tension by fully loosening the anchor nut(s) **(see illustration).**

3   Remove the split pin and nut and separate the upper balljoint from the steering knuckle, but be careful not to let the steering knuckle/brake caliper assembly fall outward, as this may damage the brake hose (see Section 8).

4   On all models, remove the upper arm-to-frame bolts, noting the positions of any alignment shims. They must be reinstalled in the same locations to maintain wheel alignment **(see illustration).**

5   Detach the upper arm from the vehicle. Inspect the bushes for deterioration, cracks and other damage, renewing them, if necessary. On later models, it may be necessary to loosen the body mount nuts and raise the front of the body with a jack to provide sufficient clearance to allow removal of the upper arm.

Refitting

6   Position the arm on the frame and install

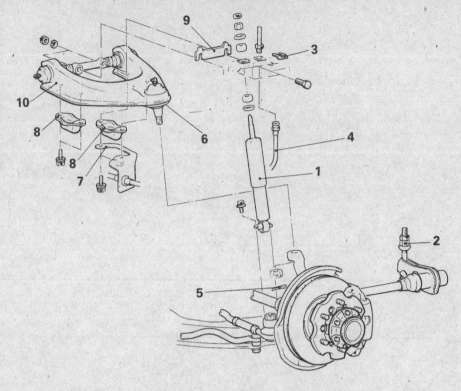

5.4 Upper suspension arm details

1	Shock absorber		6	Upper balljoint
2	Torsion bar anchor nut		7	Brake hose bracket
3	Brake hose clip		8	Rebound bumper
4	Brake hose		9	Alignment shims
5	Split pin		10	Upper suspension arm

the bolts. Install any alignment shims that were removed. Tighten the bolts to the torque listed in this Chapter's Specifications.

7   Connect the balljoint to the steering knuckle and tighten the nut to the torque listed in this Chapter's Specifications.

8   Tighten the torsion bar anchor bolt(s) and adjust the bumper stop-to-bracket clearance as described in Section 4, Step 10.

9   Install the wheel and lug nuts and lower the vehicle. Tighten the lug nuts to the torque specified in Chapter 1.

10   Drive the vehicle to an alignment shop to have the front end alignment checked and, if necessary, adjusted.

6 Front suspension lower arm - removal and refitting

Refer to illustration 6.2

Warning: *Whenever any of the suspension or steering fasteners are loosened or removed, they must be inspected and, if necessary, renewed with new ones of the same part number or of original equipment quality and design. Torque specifications must be followed for proper reassembly and component retention.*

Removal

1   Loosen the wheel lug nuts, raise the front of the vehicle and support it securely on jackstands. Remove the wheel.

2   Remove the torsion bar (see Section 4 and unbolt the lower balljoint from the control arm. Remove the lower arm pivot nuts and shafts and lower the arm from the vehicle **(see illustration).**

Refitting

3   Inspect the lower arm bushes for deterioration, cracking and other damage. If the bushes is in need of renewal, take the lower arm to an automotive machine shop to have the old bushes pressed out and a new one pressed in.

4   Connect the balljoint to the lower arm and install the bolts and nuts. Position the arm at normal ride height and tighten the pivot shaft nuts to torque listed in the Specifications Section at the beginning of this Chapter. Install the torsion bar (see Section 4).

5   Install the wheel and lug nuts. Lower the vehicle and tighten the lug nuts to the torque specified in Chapter 1.

6   Drive the vehicle to an alignment shop to have the front end alignment checked and, if necessary, adjusted.

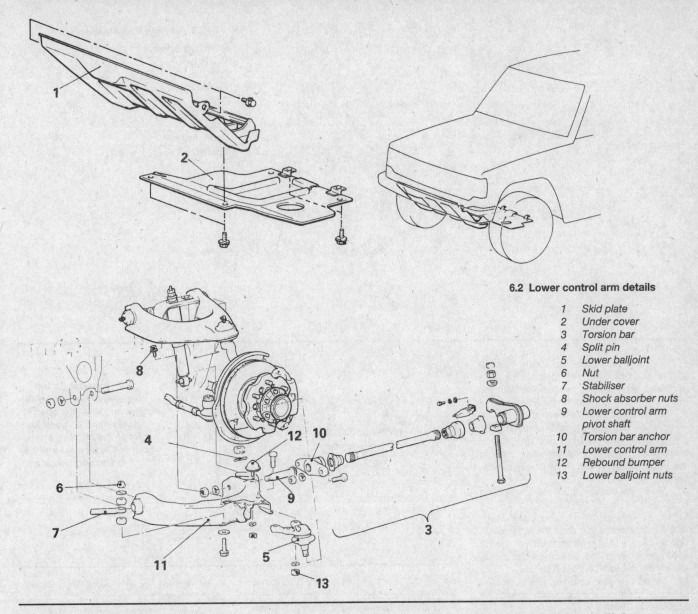

6.2 Lower control arm details

1   Skid plate
2   Under cover
3   Torsion bar
4   Split pin
5   Lower balljoint
6   Nut
7   Stabiliser
8   Shock absorber nuts
9   Lower control arm
     pivot shaft
10   Torsion bar anchor
11   Lower control arm
12   Rebound bumper
13   Lower balljoint nuts

7   Balljoints - check and renewal

Warning: *Whenever any of the suspension or steering fasteners are loosened or removed, they must be inspected and, if necessary, renewed with new ones of the same part number or of original equipment quality and design. Torque specifications must be followed for proper reassembly and component retention.*

Check

1   Raise the vehicle and support it securely on jackstands.
2   Visually inspect the rubber seal for cuts, tears or leaking grease. If any of these conditions are noticed, the balljoint should be renewed.
3   Place a large lever under the balljoint and attempt to push the balljoint up. Next, position the lever between the steering knuckle and the arm and apply downward pressure. If any movement is seen or felt during either of these checks, a worn out balljoint is indicated.
4   Have an assistant grasp the tyre at the top and bottom and shake the top of the tyre in an in-and-out motion. Touch the balljoint stud castellated nut. If any looseness is felt, suspect a worn out balljoint stud or a widened hole in the steering knuckle boss. If the latter problem exists, the steering knuckle should be renewed as well as the balljoint.

Renewal

Upper control arm balljoint

5   The balljoints on upper control arms are pressed into place. Consequently, renewal requires removing the upper arm and taking it to a dealer or other properly equipped shop to have the balljoint pressed out and a new one installed.

Lower control arm balljoint

6   With the vehicle raised and supported, position a floor jack under the lower arm - it must stay there throughout the entire operation. Remove the wheel. Remove the balljoint split pin and loosen the castellated nut a couple of turns, but don't remove it (it will prevent the balljoint and steering knuckle from separating violently).
7   Using a balljoint separating tool, separate the balljoint from the steering knuckle. There are several types of balljoint tools available, but the kind that pushes the balljoint stud out of the knuckle boss works the best **(see illustration 8.7)**. The wedge, or "pickle fork" type works fairly well, but it tends to damage the balljoint seal. Some two-jaw pullers will do the job, also.
8   Remove the castellated nut and disconnect the balljoint from the steering knuckle. If necessary, remove the steering knuckle (see Section 8) and the driveaxle (see Chapter 8).

10

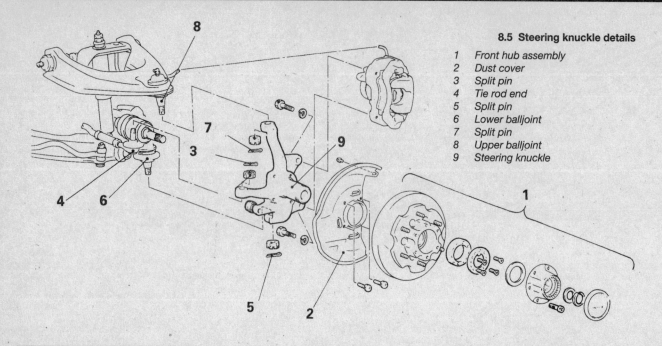

8.5 Steering knuckle details

1   Front hub assembly
2   Dust cover
3   Split pin
4   Tie rod end
5   Split pin
6   Lower balljoint
7   Split pin
8   Upper balljoint
9   Steering knuckle

9   The balljoint is retained to the suspension arm by bolts and nuts. Remove the bolts and nuts, then detach the balljoint from the arm. Take note of how the balljoint is positioned on the arm - the new one must be installed the same way **(see illustration 6.2)**.

10   Position the new balljoint on the arm and install the nut or bolts, tightening them to the torque listed in this Chapter's Specifications.

11   Insert the balljoint stud into the steering knuckle boss, install the castellated nut and tighten it to the specified torque. Install a new split pin. If necessary, tighten the nut an additional amount to line up the slots in the nut with the hole in the balljoint stud (never loosen the nut to align the hole).

12   Install the wheel and lug nuts. Lower the vehicle and tighten the lug nuts to the torque specified in Chapter 1.

8   Steering knuckle - removal and refitting

Warning: *Whenever any of the suspension or steering fasteners are loosened or removed, they must be inspected and, if necessary, renewed with new ones of the same part number or of original equipment quality and design. Torque specifications must be followed for proper reassembly and component retention.*

Removal

Refer to illustrations 8.5 and 8.7

1   Loosen the wheel lug nuts, raise the vehicle and support it securely on jackstands placed under the frame. Apply the parking brake. Remove the wheel.

2   Remove the brake caliper and place it

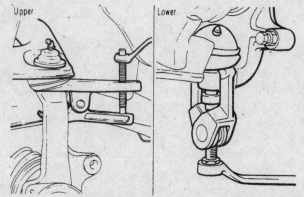

8.7 To separate the suspension arms from the steering knuckle, special tools must be used to force the balljoint studs out of the tapered holes in the steering knuckle

on top of the upper arm or wire it up out of the way. Remove the caliper mounting bracket from the steering knuckle (see Chapter 9 if necessary).

3   Remove the front hub assembly and brake disc (see Chapter 9).

4   Separate the tie-rod end from the knuckle arm (see Section 16).

5   Remove the split pins from the upper and lower balljoint studs and back off the nuts one turn each **(see illustration)**.

6   Remove the shock absorber (see Section 3).

7   Using a special tool, separate the suspension arms from the steering knuckle **(see illustration)**. There are several types of tools available, but the kind that pushes the balljoint stud out of the knuckle boss works the best. The wedge, or "pickle fork" type works fairly well, but it tends to damage the balljoint seal. Some two-jaw pullers will do the job, also. Once the balljoints have been released from the tapered holes in the knuckle, remove the nuts completely and carefully detach the knuckle. Be careful not

to damage the CV joint boots when detaching the driveaxle.

Refitting

8   Place the knuckle between the upper and lower suspension arms and insert the balljoint studs into the knuckle, beginning with the lower balljoint. Install the nuts and tighten them to the torque listed in this Chapter's Specifications. Install new split pins, tightening the nuts slightly to align the slots in the nuts with the holes in the balljoint studs, if necessary.

9   Install the shock absorber.

10   Connect the tie-rod end to the knuckle arm and tighten the nut to the torque listed in this Chapter's Specifications. Be sure to use a new split pin.

11   Install the strut rod and connect the stabiliser bar.

12   Install the brake caliper mounting bracket and caliper (see Chapter 9).

13   Install the wheel and lug nuts. Lower the vehicle to the ground and tighten the nuts to the torque specified in Chapter 1.

9.3 The lower mounting nut on the rear shock absorber (arrow)

9.4 The upper rear shock absorber mounting nut (arrow)

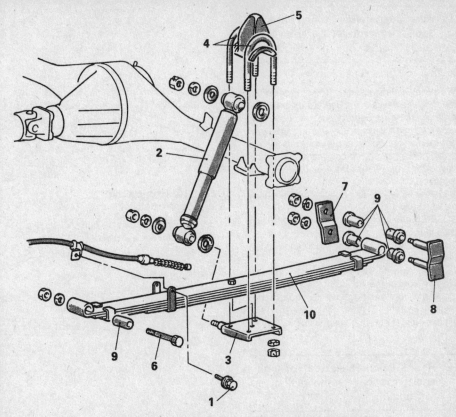

10.6 Exploded view of the rear leaf spring components

1	Parking brake cable attaching bolt	6	Shackle pin
2	Shock absorber	7	Shackle plate
3	Spring seal	8	Shackle pin plate
4	U-bolts	9	Bushes
5	Bump stop	10	Leaf spring

9 Rear shock absorber - removal and refitting

Refer to illustrations 9.3 and 9.4
Warning: *Whenever any of the suspension or steering fasteners are loosened or removed, they must be inspected and, if necessary, renewed with new ones of the same part number or of original equipment quality and design. Torque specifications must be followed for proper reassembly and component retention.*

1 If the shock absorber is to be renewed with a new one, it is recommended that both shocks on the rear of the vehicle be renewed at the same time.
2 Raise and support the rear of the vehicle according to the jacking and towing procedures at the front of this manual. Use a jack to raise the differential until the tyres clear the ground, then place jackstands under the axle housing. Do not attempt to remove the shock absorbers with the vehicle raised and the axle unsupported.
3 Unscrew and remove the lower shock absorber mounting nut to disconnect it at the spring seat **(see illustration).**
4 Unscrew and remove the upper mounting nut at the frame and remove the shock

absorber **(see illustration). Note:** *If the vehicle is equipped with remote-controlled variable shock absorbers, remove the actuator assembly before removing the shock absorber.*
5 If the unit is defective, it must be renewed. Renew worn rubber bushes.
6 Install the shocks in the reverse order of removal, but let the vehicle be free standing on the ground before tightening the mounting nuts.
7 Bounce the rear of the vehicle a couple of times to settle the bushes into place, then tighten the nuts securely.

10 Rear leaf spring - removal and refitting

Refer to illustration 10.6
Warning: *Whenever any of the suspension or steering fasteners are loosened or removed, they must be inspected and, if necessary, renewed with new ones of the same part number or of original equipment quality and design. Torque specifications must be followed for proper reassembly and component retention.*

1 Jack up the vehicle and support the frame securely on jackstands.
2 Remove the rear wheels and tyres.
3 Place a jack under the rear differential housing.
4 Lower the axle housing until the leaf spring tension is relieved, and lock the jack in this position.
5 Disconnect the shock absorber from the spring seat (see Section 9).
6 Remove the U-bolt mounting nuts **(see illustration).**
7 Remove the U-bolts and spring seat.
8 Remove the bolt and detach the parking brake cable from the spring. Remove the nuts and the shackle pin assemblies, then lower the spring from the vehicle.
9 If the bushes in the spring or frame are deteriorated, renew them. If you need to renew the bushes in the spring, take the spring to an automotive machine shop to have the old bushes pressed out and new ones pressed in.
10 Refitting is the reverse of the removal procedure. Lubricate the shackle pins and bushes with lithium-based grease. When fitting the U-bolt and shackle pin nuts, tighten them to the specified torque values (see this Chapter's Specifications).

10

11   Rear suspension trailing arms (coil spring models) - removal and refitting

Refer to illustration 11.2

Warning: *Whenever any of the suspension or steering fasteners are loosened or removed, they must be inspected and, if necessary, renewed with new ones of the same part number or of original equipment quality and design. Torque specifications must be followed for proper reassembly and component retention.*

1   Raise the vehicle and support it securely on jackstands

2   Remove the parking brake cable bolt **(see illustration).**

3   Remove the nuts and bolts and detach the trailing arm from the vehicle.

4   Refitting is the reverse of removal. Tighten the nuts and bolts to the torques listed in the Specifications Section at the beginning of this Chapter before lowering the vehicle weight onto the suspension.

12   Rear suspension lateral rod (coil spring models) - removal and refitting

Refer to illustration 12.2

Warning: *Whenever any of the suspension or steering fasteners are loosened or removed, they must be inspected and, if necessary, renewed with new ones of the same part number or of original equipment quality and design. Torque specifications must be followed for proper reassembly and component retention.*

1   Raise the vehicle and support it securely on jackstands

2   Remove the left side parking brake cable bolt **(see illustration).**

3   Remove the left side lower shock absorber bolt.

4   Remove the left side trailing arm bolts (see Section 11).

5   Remove the nuts and detach the lateral rod.

6   Refitting is the reverse of removal. Tighten the nuts and bolts to the torques listed in the Specifications Section at the beginning of this Chapter before lowering the vehicle weight onto the suspension.

13   Rear suspension coil spring - removal and refitting

Refer to illustration 13.3

Warning: *Whenever any of the suspension or steering fasteners are loosened or removed, they must be inspected and, if necessary, renewed with new ones of the same part number or of original equipment quality and design. Torque specifications must be fol-*

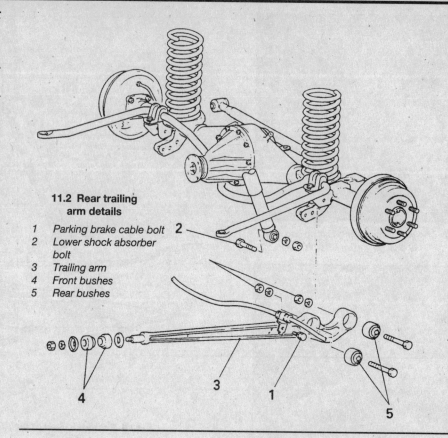

11.2 Rear trailing arm details

1   Parking brake cable bolt
2   Lower shock absorber bolt
3   Trailing arm
4   Front bushes
5   Rear bushes

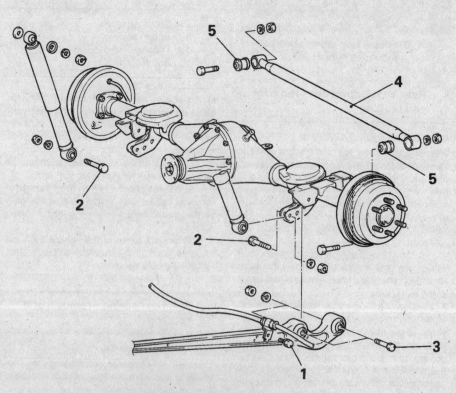

12.2 Rear suspension lateral rod details

1 Parking brake cable bolt	4 Lateral rod
2 Lower shock absorber bolt	5 Lateral rod bushes
3 Lower trailing arm bolt	

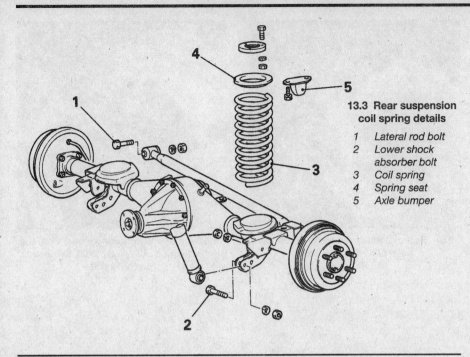

13.3 Rear suspension coil spring details

1 Lateral rod bolt
2 Lower shock absorber bolt
3 Coil spring
4 Spring seat
5 Axle bumper

number or of original equipment quality and design. Torque specifications must be followed for proper reassembly and component retention.

1 Raise the vehicle and support it securely on jackstands

2 Remove the parking brake cable attaching bolt **(see illustration)**.

3 Remove the lower left shock absorber bolt.

4 Remove the stabiliser bar bracket bolts and detach the brackets and bushes.

5 Remove the stabiliser link bolts and detach the bar from the vehicle.

6 Refitting is the reverse of removal. Before lowering the vehicle weight onto the suspension, tighten the bracket bolts to the torque listed in the Specifications Section at the beginning of this Chapter. Tighten the nuts on the stabiliser link bolts securely.

15 Steering wheel - removal and refitting

Refer to illustrations 15.3, 15.4 and 15.6

Warning: *Whenever any of the suspension or steering fasteners are loosened or removed, they must be inspected and, if necessary, renewed with new ones of the same part number or of original equipment quality and design. Torque specifications must be followed for proper reassembly and component retention.*

Removal

1 Disconnect the cable from the negative battery terminal.

2 Using a small screwdriver, prise off the horn button or centre pad and unplug the

lowed for proper reassembly and component retention.

1 Raise the vehicle and support it securely on jackstands

2 Support the axle with a jack.

3 Remove the right side lateral rod bolt **(see illustration)**.

4 Remove the lower left shock absorber bolt.

5 Lower the axle and remove the springs and seats.

6 Refitting is the reverse of removal. Tighten the nuts and bolts to the torques

listed in the Specifications Section at the beginning of this Chapter before lowering the vehicle weight onto the suspension.

14 Rear stabiliser bar (coil spring models) - removal and refitting

Refer to illustration 14.2

Warning: *Whenever any of the suspension or steering fasteners are loosened or removed, they must be inspected and, if necessary, renewed with new ones of the same part*

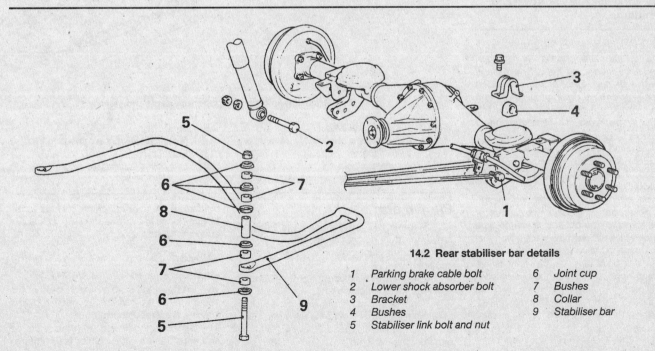

14.2 Rear stabiliser bar details

1 Parking brake cable bolt
2 Lower shock absorber bolt
3 Bracket
4 Bushes
5 Stabiliser link bolt and nut
6 Joint cup
7 Bushes
8 Collar
9 Stabiliser bar

10

15.3 Use a socket and extension to remove the steering wheel nut

15.4 Remove the screws and lift off the horn plate (if equipped)

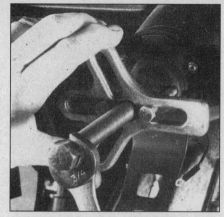

15.6 Remove the steering wheel from the shaft with a puller - DO NOT hammer on the shaft!

horn switch connector.

3   Unscrew the steering wheel nut **(see illustration)**.

4   Remove the horn plate (if equipped) **(see illustration)**.

5   Mark the steering wheel hub and the column shaft with paint to ensure correct repositioning during reassembly.

6   Remove the wheel using a puller **(see illustration)**. **Caution:** *Do not hammer on the wheel or the shaft to separate them.*

Refitting

7   Realign the steering wheel and the column shaft using the paint marks. Install and tighten the retaining nut to the torque listed in this Chapter's Specifications, then attach the horn plate and button or centre pad.

8   Hook up the negative battery cable.

16 Steering linkage - removal and refitting

Warning: *Whenever any of the suspension or steering fasteners are loosened or removed, they must be inspected and, if necessary, renewed with new ones of the same part number or of original equipment quality and design. Torque specifications must be followed for proper reassembly and component retention.*

1   All steering linkage removal and refitting procedures should be performed with the front end of the vehicle raised and placed securely on jackstands.

2   Before removing any steering linkage components, obtain a balljoint separator. It may be a screw-type puller or a wedge-type (pickle fork) tool, although the wedge-type tool tends to damage the balljoint seals. It is possible to jar a balljoint taper pin free from its eye by striking opposite sides of the eye simultaneously with two large hammers, but the space available to do so is usually very limited.

3   After fitting any of the steering linkage components, the front wheel alignment should be checked by a reputable front end alignment shop.

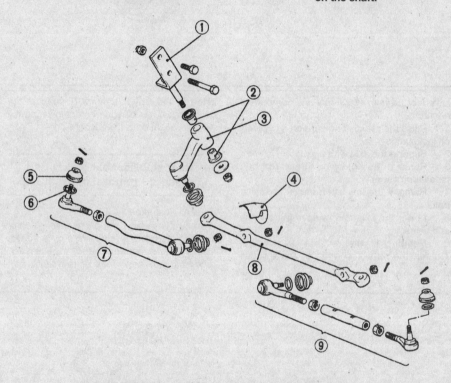

16.10 Steering linkage components - exploded view

1	Idler arm bracket	6	O-ring
2	Idler arm bushes	7	Right side tie-rod assembly
3	Idler arm	8	Relay rod
4	Heat shield	9	Left side tie-rod assembly
5	Dust cover		

Pitman arm

4   Remove the nut securing the Pitman arm to the steering gear sector shaft.

5   Scribe or paint match marks on the arm and shaft.

6   Using a puller, disconnect the Pitman arm from the shaft splines.

7   Remove the split pin and castle nut securing the Pitman arm to the relay rod.

8   Using a puller, disconnect the Pitman arm from the relay rod.

9   Refitting is the reverse of the removal procedure. Be sure to tighten the nuts to the torques listed in this Chapter's Specifications and install a new split pin.

Tie-rod

Refer to illustrations 16.10 and 16.11

10   Remove the split pins and castle nuts securing the tie-rod to the relay rod and knuckle arm **(see illustration)**.

11   Separate the tie-rod from the relay rod and knuckle arm with a puller **(see illustration)**.

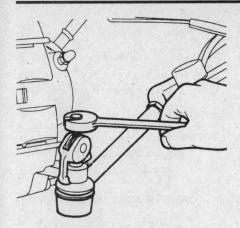

16.11 Use a puller to separate the tie-rod end from the steering knuckle

12   If a tie-rod end is to be renewed, loosen the jam nut and mark the relationship of the tie-rod end to the tie-rod with white paint. When fitting the new rod end, thread it onto the tie-rod until it reaches the mark, then turn the jam nut until it contacts the rod end. Don't tighten it fully at this time.

13   Turn the tie-rod ends so they are at approximately 90-degree angles to each other, then tighten the jam nuts to lock the ends in position.

14   The remaining refitting steps are the reverse of those for removal. Make sure to tighten the castle nuts to the torques listed in this Chapter's Specifications.

Idler arm

15   Remove the nut securing the idler arm to the bracket **(see illustration 16.10)**.

16   Remove the split pin and castle nut securing the idler arm to the relay rod.

17   Using a puller, disconnect the idler arm from the relay rod.

18   Slide the idler arm off the bracket shaft and remove it from the vehicle.

19   Refitting is the reverse of the removal procedure. Be sure to tighten the nuts to the specified torque and install a new split pin.

17   Steering gear - removal and refitting

Warning: *Whenever any of the suspension or steering fasteners are loosened or removed, they must be inspected and, if necessary, renewed with new ones of the same part number or of original equipment quality and design. Torque specifications must be followed for proper reassembly and component retention.*

Note: *If you find that the steering gear is defective, it is not recommended that you overhaul it. Because of the special tools needed to do the job, it is best to let your dealer service department overhaul it for you (or renew it with a factory rebuilt unit). However, you can remove and install it yourself by*

18.6 Loosen the locknut with a spanner and use a screwdriver to turn the adjusting screw - when tightening the locknut, be sure to hold the screw to keep it from turning

following the procedure outlined here. The removal and refitting procedures for manual steering and power steering gear housings are identical except that the inlet and outlet lines must be removed from the steering gear housing on power steering-equipped models before the housing can be removed. The steering system should be filled and power steering systems should be bled after the gear is reinstalled (see Section 20).

1   Raise the front of the vehicle and place it securely on jackstands. Apply the parking brake.

2   Place an alignment mark on the steering shaft flexible coupling and the gear housing worm shaft to assure correct reassembly, then remove the coupling pinch bolt.

3   Disconnect the power steering line connections from the steering gear. Plug the lines so the fluid will not drain.

4   Disconnect the Pitman arm and the left tie-rod from the relay rod (see Section 16).

5   Remove the bolts securing the gear housing to the chassis and lower the gear from the vehicle.

6   Refitting is the reverse of the removal procedure. Be sure to tighten all nuts and bolts to the torques listed in this Chapter's Specifications.

18   Steering freeplay - adjustment

Refer to illustration 18.6

1   Raise the vehicle with a jack so that the front wheels are off the ground and place the vehicle securely on jackstands.

2   Point the wheels straight ahead.

3   Using a spanner, loosen the locknut on the steering gear.

4   Turn the adjusting screw clockwise to decrease wheel freeplay and counterclockwise to increase it. **Note:** *Turn the adjusting screw in small increments, checking the steering wheel freeplay between them.*

5   Turn the steering wheel halfway around

in both directions, checking that the freeplay is correct and that the steering is smooth.

6   Hold the adjusting screw so that it will not turn and tighten the locknut **(see illustration)**.

7   Remove the jackstands and lower the vehicle.

19   Power steering pump - removal and refitting

Warning: *Whenever any of the suspension or steering fasteners are loosened or removed, they must be inspected and, if necessary, renewed with new ones of the same part number or of original equipment quality and design. Torque specifications must be followed for proper reassembly and component retention.*

Note: *If you find that the steering pump is defective, it is not recommended that you overhaul it. Because of the special tools needed to do the job, it is best to let your dealer service department overhaul it for you (or renew it with a factory rebuilt unit). However, you can remove it yourself using the procedure which follows.*

Removal

1   Position a container to catch the pump fluid. Disconnect the hoses from the pump body. As each is disconnected, cap or tape over the hose opening and then secure the end in a raised position to prevent leakage and contamination. Cover or plug the pump openings to so dirt won't enter the unit.

2   Loosen the pump belt adjustment until the drivebelt can be removed from the pump pulley (see Chapter 1, if necessary).

3   Remove the pump mounting bolts and lift the pump out of the engine compartment.

Refitting

4   Refitting is the reverse of the removal procedure. When fitting the pressure line, make sure there is sufficient clearance between the line and the exhaust manifold.

5   To adjust the drivebelt tension, see Chapter 1.

6   Fill the power steering fluid reservoir with the specified fluid and bleed the power steering system (see Section 20).

7   Check for fluid leaks.

20   Power steering system - bleeding

1   Check the fluid in the reservoir and add fluid of the specified type if it is low.

2   Jack up the front of the vehicle and place it securely on jackstands.

3   With the engine off, turn the steering wheel fully in both directions two or three times.

4   Recheck the fluid in the reservoir and add more fluid if necessary.

5   Start the engine and turn the steering wheel fully in both directions two or three

10

times. The engine should be running at 1000 rpm or less.

6   Remove the jackstands and lower the vehicle completely.

7   With the engine running at 1000 rpm or less, turn the steering wheel fully in both directions two or three times.

8   Return the steering wheel to the centre position.

9   Check that the fluid is not foamy or cloudy.

10   Measure the fluid level with the engine running.

11   Turn off the engine and again measure the fluid level. It should rise no more than 0.20 in (5 mm) when the engine is turned off.

12   If a problem is encountered, repeat Steps 7 through 11.

13   If the problem persists, remove the pump (see Section 19), and have it repaired by a dealer service department.

21 Front end alignment - general information

Refer to illustration 21.1

A front end alignment refers to the adjustments made to the front wheels so they are in proper angular relationship to the suspension and the ground. Front wheels that are out of proper alignment not only affect steering control, but also increase tyre wear. The front end adjustments normally required are camber, caster and toe-in **(see illustration)**.

Getting the proper front wheel alignment is a very exacting process, one in which complicated and expensive machines are necessary to perform the job properly. Because of this, you should have a technician with the proper equipment perform these tasks. We will, however, use this space to give you a basic idea of what is involved with front-end alignment so you can better understand the process and deal intelligently with the shop that does the work.

Toe-in is the turning in of the front wheels. The purpose of a toe specification is to ensure parallel rolling of the front wheels. In a vehicle with zero toe-in, the distance between the front edges of the wheels will be the same as the distance between the rear edges of the wheels. The actual amount of toe-in is normally only a small number of millimetres. Toe-in adjustment is controlled by the tie-rod end position on the inner tie-rod.

Incorrect toe-in will cause the tyres to wear improperly by making them scrub against the road surface.

Camber is the tilting of the front wheels from the vertical when viewed from the front of the vehicle. When the wheels tilt out at the top, the camber is said to be positive (+). When the wheels tilt in at the top the camber is negative (-). The amount of tilt is measured in degrees from the vertical and this measurement is called the camber angle. This angle affects the amount of tyre tread which contacts the road and compensates for changes in the suspension geometry when the vehicle is cornering or travelling over an undulating surface.

Caster is the tilting of the front steering axis from the vertical. A tilt toward the rear is positive caster and a tilt toward the front is negative caster. Caster angle affects the self-centering action of the steering, which governs straight-line stability. Caster is adjusted by moving shims from one end of the upper arm mount to the other.

22 Wheels and tyres - general information

Wheels can be damaged by an impact with a curb or other solid object. If the wheels are bent, the result is a hazardous condition that must be corrected. To check the wheels, raise the vehicle and set it on jackstands. Visually inspect the wheels for obvious signs of damage such as cracks and deformation.

Tyre and wheel balance is very important to the overall handling, braking and ride performance of the vehicle. Whenever a tyre is dismounted for repair or renewal, the tyre and wheel assembly should be balanced before being installed on the vehicle.

Wheels should be periodically cleaned, especially on the inside, where mud and road salts accumulate and eventually cause rust and, ultimately, possible wheel failure.

Tyres are extremely important from a safety standpoint. The tread should be checked periodically to see that the tyres have not worn excessively, a condition which can be dangerous, especially in wet weather.

To equalise wear and add life to a set of tyres, it is recommended that they be rotated periodically. When rotating, check for signs of abnormal wear and foreign objects in the tread or sidewalls (refer to Chapter 1, Routine Maintenance).

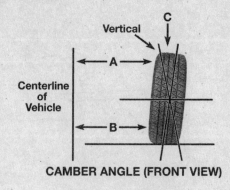

CAMBER ANGLE (FRONT VIEW)

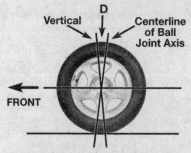

CASTER ANGLE (SIDE VIEW)

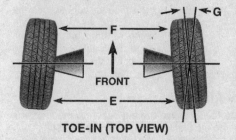

TOE-IN (TOP VIEW)

21.1 Front end alignment details

1   A minus B = C (degrees camber)
2   E minus F = toe-in (measured in millimetres)
3   G = toe-in (expressed in degrees)

Proper tyre inflation is essential for maximum life of the tread and for proper handling and braking. Tyres that are wearing in an abnormal way are an indication that their inflation is incorrect or that the front end components are not adjusted properly. Take the vehicle to a reputable front-end alignment and repair shop to correct the situation.

Chapter 11   Body

Contents

1   General information

These models feature a separate boxed steel frame and body. Certain components are particularly vulnerable to accident damage and can be unbolted and renewed. Among these parts are the body mouldings, doors, bumpers, bonnet and all glass.

Only general body maintenance practices and body panel repair procedures within the scope of the do-it-yourselfer are included in this Chapter.

2   Body - maintenance

1   The condition of your vehicle's body is very important, because the resale value depends a great deal on it. It's much more difficult to repair a neglected or damaged body than it is to repair mechanical components. The hidden areas of the body, such as the wheel wells, the frame and the engine compartment, are equally important, although they don't require as frequent attention as the rest of the body.

2   Once a year, or every 19,000 kilometres, it's a good idea to have the under-side of the body steam cleaned. All traces of dirt and oil will be removed and the area can then be inspected carefully for rust, damaged brake lines, frayed electrical wires, damaged cables and other problems. The front suspension components should be greased after completion of this job.

3   At the same time, clean the engine and the engine compartment with a steam cleaner or water soluble degreaser.

4   The wheel wells should be given close attention, since undercoating can peel away and stones and dirt thrown up by the tyres can cause the paint to chip and flake, allowing rust to set in. If rust is found, clean down to the bare metal and apply an anti-rust paint.

5   The body should be washed about once a week. Wet the vehicle thoroughly to soften the dirt, then wash it down with a soft sponge and plenty of clean soapy water. If the surplus dirt is not washed off very carefully, it can wear down the paint.

6   Spots of tar or asphalt thrown up from the road should be removed with a cloth soaked in solvent.

7   Once every six months, wax the body and chrome trim. If a chrome cleaner is used to remove rust from any of the vehicle's plated parts, remember that the cleaner also removes part of the chrome, so use it sparingly.

3   Vinyl trim - maintenance

Don't clean vinyl trim with detergents, caustic soap or petroleum-based cleaners. Plain soap and water works just fine, with a soft brush to clean dirt that may be ingrained. Wash the vinyl as frequently as the rest of the vehicle. After cleaning, application of a high-quality rubber and vinyl protectant will help prevent oxidation and cracks. The protectant can also be applied to weatherstripping, vacuum lines and rubber hoses, which often fail as a result of chemical degradation, and to the tyres.

4   Upholstery and carpets - maintenance

1   Every three months remove the floor mats and clean the interior of the vehicle (more frequently if necessary). Use a stiff whisk broom to brush the carpeting and loosen dirt and dust, then vacuum the upholstery and carpets thoroughly, especially along seams and crevices.

2   Dirt and stains can be removed from carpeting with basic household or automotive carpet shampoos available in spray cans.

Follow the directions and vacuum again, then use a stiff brush to bring back the "nap" of the carpet.

3   Most interiors have cloth or vinyl upholstery, either of which can be cleaned and maintained with a number of material-specific cleaners or shampoos available in auto supply stores. Follow the directions on the product for usage, and always spot-test any upholstery cleaner on an inconspicuous area (bottom edge of a back seat cushion) to ensure that it doesn't cause a colour shift in the material.

4   After cleaning, vinyl upholstery should be treated with a protectant. **Note:** *Make sure the protectant container indicates the product can be used on seats - some products may make a seat too slippery.* **Caution:** *Do not use protectant on vinyl-covered steering wheels.*

5   Leather upholstery requires special care. It should be cleaned regularly with saddlesoap or leather cleaner. Never use alcohol, petrol, nail polish remover or thinner to clean leather upholstery.

6   After cleaning, regularly treat leather upholstery with a leather conditioner, rubbed in with a soft cotton cloth. Never use car wax on leather upholstery.

7   In areas where the interior of the vehicle is subject to bright sunlight, cover leather seating areas of the seats with a sheet if the vehicle is to be left out for any length of time.

5   Body repair - minor damage

See photo sequence

Repair of scratches

1   If the scratch is superficial and does not penetrate to the metal of the body, repair is very simple. Lightly rub the scratched area with a fine rubbing compound to remove loose paint and built up wax. Rinse the area with clean water.

These photos illustrate a method of repairing simple dents. They are intended to supplement *Body repair - minor damage* in this Chapter and should not be used as the sole instructions for body repair on these vehicles.

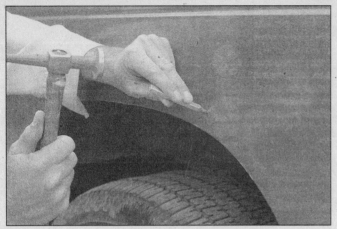

1   If you can't access the backside of the body panel to hammer out the dent, pull it out with a slide-hammer-type dent puller. In the deepest portion of the dent or along the crease line, drill or punch hole(s) at least one inch apart . . .

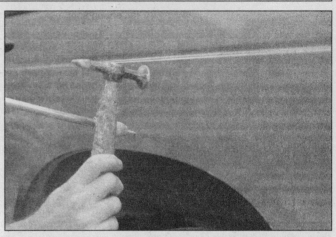

2   . . . then screw the slide-hammer into the hole and operate it. Tap with a hammer near the edge of the dent to help 'pop' the metal back to its original shape. When you're finished, the dent area should be close to its original contour and about 1/8-inch below the surface of the surrounding metal

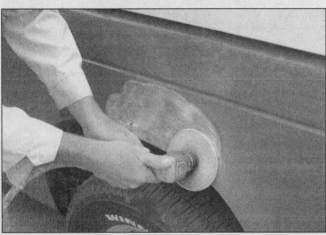

3   Using coarse-grit sandpaper, remove the paint down to the bare metal. Hand sanding works fine, but the disc sander shown here makes the job faster. Use finer (about 320-grit) sandpaper to feather-edge the paint at least one inch around the dent area

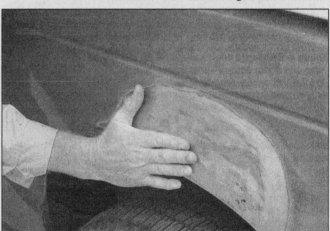

4   When the paint is removed, touch will probably be more helpful than sight for telling if the metal is straight. Hammer down the high spots or raise the low spots as necessary. Clean the repair area with wax/silicone remover

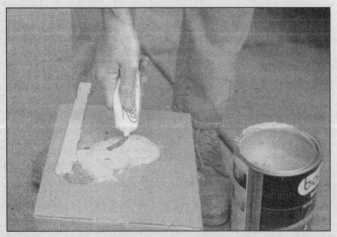

5   Following label instructions, mix up a batch of plastic filler and hardener. The ratio of filler to hardener is critical, and, if you mix it incorrectly, it will either not cure properly or cure too quickly (you won't have time to file and sand it into shape)

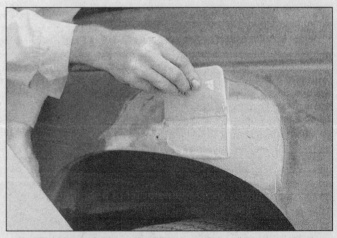

6   Working quickly so the filler doesn't harden, use a plastic applicator to press the body filler firmly into the metal, assuring it bonds completely. Work the filler until it matches the original contour and is slightly above the surrounding metal

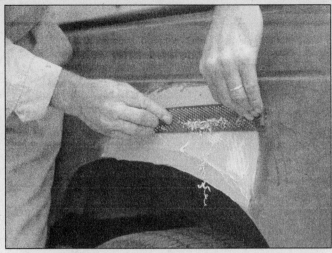

7   Let the filler harden until you can just dent it with your fingernail. Use a body file or Surform tool (shown here) to rough-shape the filler

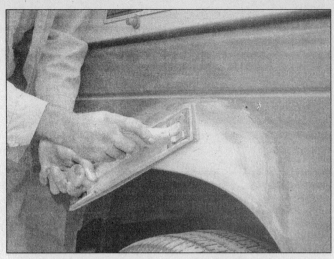

8   Use coarse-grit sandpaper and a sanding board or block to work the filler down until it's smooth and even. Work down to finer grits of sandpaper - always using a board or block - ending up with 360 or 400 grit

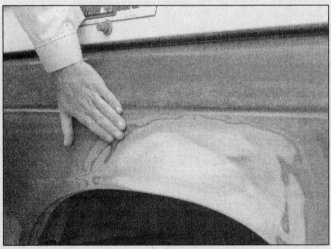

9   You shouldn't be able to feel any ridge at the transition from the filler to the bare metal or from the bare metal to the old paint. As soon as the repair is flat and uniform, remove the dust and mask off the adjacent panels or trim pieces

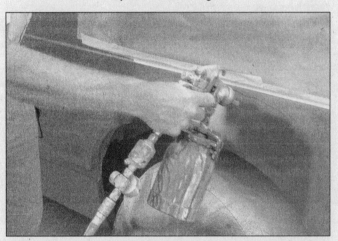

10   Apply several layers of primer to the area. Don't spray the primer on too heavy, so it sags or runs, and make sure each coat is dry before you spray on the next one. A professional-type spray gun is being used here, but aerosol spray primer is available inexpensively from auto parts stores

11   The primer will help reveal imperfections or scratches. Fill these with glazing compound. Follow the label instructions and sand it with 360 or 400-grit sandpaper until it's smooth. Repeat the glazing, sanding and respraying until the primer reveals a perfectly smooth surface

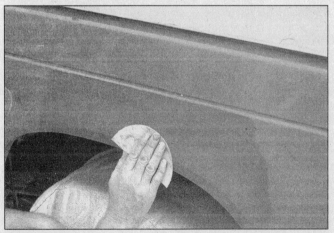

12   Finish sand the primer with very fine sandpaper (400 or 600-grit) to remove the primer overspray. Clean the area with water and allow it to dry. Use a tack rag to remove any dust, then apply the finish coat. Don't attempt to rub out or wax the repair area until the paint has dried completely (at least two weeks)

2   Apply touch-up paint to the scratch, using a small brush. Continue to apply thin layers of paint until the surface of the paint in the scratch is level with the surrounding paint. Allow the new paint at least two weeks to harden, then blend it into the surrounding paint by rubbing with a very fine rubbing compound. Finally, apply a coat of wax to the scratch area.

3   If the scratch has penetrated the paint and exposed the metal of the body, causing the metal to rust, a different repair technique is required. Remove all loose rust from the bottom of the scratch with a pocket knife, then apply rust inhibiting paint to prevent the formation of rust in the future. Using a rubber or nylon applicator, coat the scratched area with glaze-type filler. If required, the filler can be mixed with thinner to provide a very thin paste, which is ideal for filling narrow scratches. Before the glaze filler in the scratch hardens, wrap a piece of smooth cotton cloth around the tip of a finger. Dip the cloth in thinner and then quickly wipe it along the surface of the scratch. This will ensure that the surface of the filler is slightly hollow. The scratch can now be painted over as described earlier in this section.

Repair of dents

4   When repairing dents, the first job is to pull the dent out until the affected area is as close as possible to its original shape. There is no point in trying to restore the original shape completely as the metal in the damaged area will have stretched on impact and cannot be restored to its original contours. It is better to bring the level of the dent up to a point which is about 3 mm below the level of the surrounding metal. In cases where the dent is very shallow, it is not worth trying to pull it out at all.

5   If the back side of the dent is accessible, it can be hammered out gently from behind using a soft-face hammer. While doing this, hold a block of wood firmly against the opposite side of the metal to absorb the hammer blows and prevent the metal from being stretched.

6   If the dent is in a section of the body which has double layers, or some other factor makes it inaccessible from behind, a different technique is required. Drill several small holes through the metal inside the damaged area, particularly in the deeper sections. Screw long, self tapping screws into the holes just enough for them to get a good grip in the metal. Now the dent can be pulled out by pulling on the protruding heads of the screws with locking pliers.

7   The next stage of repair is the removal of paint from the damaged area and from 2.5 cm or so of the surrounding metal. This is easily done with a wire brush or sanding disk in a drill motor, although it can be done just as effectively by hand with sandpaper. To complete the preparation for filling, score the surface of the bare metal with a screwdriver or the tang of a file or drill small holes in the affected area. This will provide a good grip for the filler material. To complete the repair, see the Section on filling and painting.

Repair of rust holes or gashes

8   Remove all paint from the affected area and from 2.5 cm or so of the surrounding metal using a sanding disk or wire brush mounted in a drill motor. If these are not available, a few sheets of sandpaper will do the job just as effectively.

9   With the paint removed, you will be able to determine the severity of the corrosion and decide whether to renew the whole panel, if possible, or repair the affected area. New body panels are not as expensive as most people think and it is often quicker to fit a new panel than to repair large areas of rust.

10   Remove all trim pieces from the affected area except those which will act as a guide to the original shape of the damaged body, such as headlight shells, etc. Using metal snips or a hacksaw blade, remove all loose metal and any other metal that is badly affected by rust. Hammer the edges of the hole inward to create a slight depression for the filler material.

11   Wire brush the affected area to remove the powdery rust from the surface of the metal. If the back of the rusted area is accessible, treat it with rust inhibiting paint.

12   Before filling is done, block the hole in some way. This can be done with sheet metal riveted or screwed into place, or by stuffing the hole with wire mesh.

13   Once the hole is blocked off, the affected area can be filled and painted. See the following subsection on filling and painting.

Filling and painting

14   Many types of body fillers are available, but generally speaking, body repair kits which contain filler paste and a tube of resin hardener are best for this type of repair work. A wide, flexible plastic or nylon applicator will be necessary for imparting a smooth and contoured finish to the surface of the filler material. Mix up a small amount of filler on a clean piece of wood or cardboard (use the hardener sparingly). Follow the manufacturer's instructions on the package, otherwise the filler will set incorrectly.

15   Using the applicator, apply the filler paste to the prepared area. Draw the applicator across the surface of the filler to achieve the desired contour and to level the filler surface. As soon as a contour that approximates the original one is achieved, stop working the paste. If you continue, the paste will begin to stick to the applicator. Continue to add thin layers of paste at 20-minute intervals until the level of the filler is just above the surrounding metal.

16   Once the filler has hardened, the excess can be removed with a body file. From then on, progressively finer grades of sandpaper should be used, starting with a 180-grit paper and finishing with 600-grit wet or dry paper. Always wrap the sandpaper around a flat rubber or wooden block, otherwise the surface of the filler will not be completely flat. During the sanding of the filler surface, the wet-or-dry paper should be periodically rinsed in water. This will ensure that a very smooth finish is produced in the final stage.

17   At this point, the repair area should be surrounded by a ring of bare metal, which in turn should be encircled by the finely feathered edge of good paint. Rinse the repair area with clean water until all of the dust produced by the sanding operation is gone.

18   Spray the entire area with a light coat of primer. This will reveal any imperfections in the surface of the filler. Repair the imperfections with fresh filler paste or glaze filler and once more smooth the surface with sandpaper. Repeat this spray-and-repair procedure until you are satisfied that the surface of the filler and the feathered edge of the paint are perfect. Rinse the area with clean water and allow it to dry completely.

19   The repair area is now ready for painting. Spray painting must be carried out in a warm, dry, windless and dust free atmosphere. These conditions can be created if you have access to a large indoor work area, but if you are forced to work in the open, you will have to pick the day very carefully. If you are working indoors, dousing the floor in the work area with water will help settle the dust which would otherwise be in the air. If the repair area is confined to one body panel, mask off the surrounding panels. This will help minimise the effects of a slight mismatch in paint colour. Trim pieces such as chrome strips, door handles, etc., will also need to be masked off or removed. Use masking tape and several thicknesses of newspaper for the masking operations.

20   Before spraying, shake the paint can thoroughly, then spray a test area until the spray painting technique is mastered. Cover the repair area with a thick coat of primer. The thickness should be built up using several thin layers of primer rather than one thick one. Using 600-grit wet-or-dry sandpaper, rub down the surface of the primer until it is very smooth. While doing this, the work area should be thoroughly rinsed with water and the wet-or-dry sandpaper periodically rinsed as well. Allow the primer to dry before spraying additional coats.

21   Spray on the top coat, again building up the thickness by using several thin layers of paint. Begin spraying in the centre of the repair area and then, using a circular motion, work out until the whole repair area and about 5.0 cm of the surrounding original paint is covered. Remove all masking material 10 to 15 minutes after spraying on the final coat of paint. Allow the new paint at least two weeks to harden, then use a very fine rubbing compound to blend the edges of the new paint into the existing paint. Finally, apply a coat of wax.

---

6   Body repair - major damage

1   Major damage must be repaired by an auto body shop specifically equipped to perform unibody repairs. These shops have the

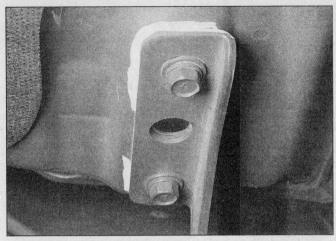

9.2 Use a scribe or marking pen to mark the hinge locations

9.7 Loosen the bolts on the catch assembly (arrows) to adjust the position - be sure to mark the edges first so it can be returned to the original location

specialised equipment required to do the job properly.

2   If the damage is extensive, the body must be checked for proper alignment or the vehicle's handling characteristics may be adversely affected and other components may wear at an accelerated rate.

3   Due to the fact that all of the major body components (bonnet, fenders, etc.) are separate units, any seriously damaged components should be renewed rather than repaired. Sometimes the components can be found in a wrecking yard that specialises in used vehicle components, often at considerable savings over the cost of new parts.

7   Hinges and locks - maintenance

Once every 5000 kilometres, or every three months, the hinges and latch assemblies on the doors, bonnet and cargo door should be given a few drops of light oil or lock lubricant. The door latch strikers should also be lubricated with a thin coat of grease to reduce wear and ensure free movement. Lubricate the door and cargo door locks with spray-on graphite lubricant.

8   Windscreen and fixed glass - renewal

Renewal of the windscreen and fixed glass requires the use of special fast-setting adhesive/caulk materials and some specialised tools and techniques. These operations should be left to a dealer service department or a shop specialising in glass work.

9   Bonnet - removal, refitting and adjustment

Refer to illustrations 9.2, 9.7, 9.10 and 9.11
Note: *The bonnet is heavy and somewhat*

awkward to remove and refit - at least two people should perform this procedure.

Removal and refitting

1   Use blankets or pads to cover the cowl area of the body and the fenders. This will protect the body and paint as the bonnet is lifted off.

2   Scribe or mark alignment marks around the hinge plate to insure proper alignment during refitting **(see illustration)**.

3   Disconnect any cables or wire harnesses which will interfere with the removal.

4   Have an assistant support the weight of the bonnet. Remove the hinge-to-bonnet nuts or bolts.

5   Lift off the bonnet.

6   Refitting is the reverse of removal.

Adjustment

7   Fore-and-aft and side-to-side adjustment of the bonnet is done by moving the bonnet in relation to the hinge plate after loosening the bolts and by loosening the catch adjusting screws and repositioning it **(see the accompanying illustration and illustration 9.2)**.

8   Scribe a line or paint the edges around

the entire hinge plate so you can judge the amount of movement.

9   Loosen the bolts and move the bonnet into correct alignment. Move it only a little at a time. Tighten the hinge bolts and carefully lower the bonnet to check the alignment.

10   If necessary after refitting, the entire bonnet latch assembly can be adjusted in-and-out as well as from side-to-side on the bonnet so the bonnet closes securely and is flush with the fenders. To do this, scribe a line around the bonnet latch mounting bolts to provide a reference point for the side-to-side movement. Then loosen the bolts and reposition the latch assembly as necessary to adjust the side-to-side movement and use a screwdriver to turn the height adjustment screw to adjust the bonnet up-and-down **(see illustration)**. Following adjustment, retighten the mounting bolts and adjustment screw locknut.

11   Finally, adjust the bonnet bumpers on the bonnet so the bonnet, when closed, is flush with the fenders **(see illustration)**.

12   The bonnet latch assembly, as well as the hinges, should be periodically lubricated with white lithium-base grease to prevent sticking and wear.

9.10 Loosen the mounting bolts (arrows) and adjust the latch assembly

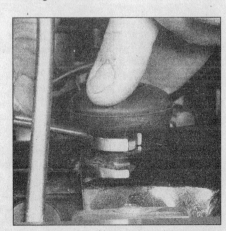

9.11 On early models it may be necessary to loosen the jam nuts before adjusting the bonnet bumper height

11

10　Radiator grille - removal and refitting

Refer to illustration 10.1

1　The radiator grille is held in place by clips and, on some models, screws. Remove any screws and disengage the grille retaining clips with a small screwdriver **(see illustration)**.

2　Once all the retaining clips are disengaged, pull the grille out and remove it.

3　To refit the grille, press it in place until the clips lock it in position.

11　Bumpers - removal and refitting

Refer to illustrations 11.3a and 11.3b

1　Disconnect any wiring or other components that would interfere with bumper removal.

2　Support the bumper with a jack or jackstand. Alternatively, have an assistant support the bumper as the bolts are removed.

3　Remove the retaining bolts and detach the bumper **(see illustrations)**.

4　Refitting is the reverse of removal.

5　Tighten the retaining bolts securely.

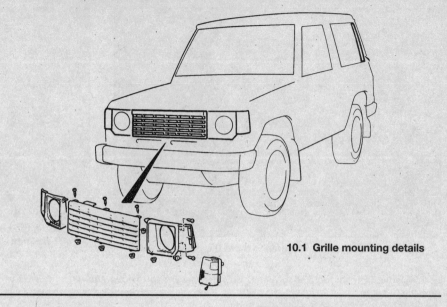

10.1　Grille mounting details

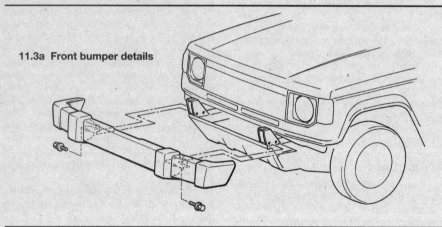

11.3a　Front bumper details

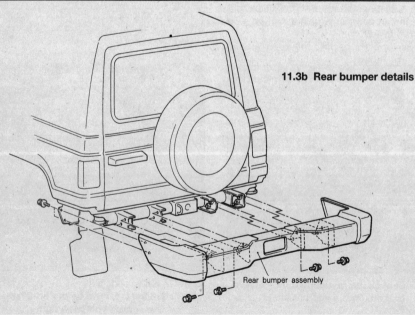

11.3b　Rear bumper details

Rear bumper assembly

12　Door trim panel - removal and refitting

Refer to illustrations 12.2a, 12.2b, 12.2c, 12.3 and 12.4

1　Disconnect the negative cable from the battery.

2　Remove all door trim panel retaining screws and door pull/armrest assemblies **(see illustrations)**.

3　Remove the window crank, using a wire hook or crank removal tool (or a rag) to pull out the retaining clip **(see illustration)**.

4　Insert a putty knife between the trim panel and the door and disengage the retaining clips **(see illustration)**. Work around the outer edge until the panel is free.

5　Once all of the clips are disengaged, detach the trim panel, unplug any wire harness connectors and remove the trim panel from the vehicle.

6　For access to the inner door, carefully peel back the plastic watershield **(see illustration 12.2a)**.

7　Prior to refitting of the door panel, be sure to refit any clips in the panel which may have come out during the removal procedure and remain in the door itself.

8　Plug in the wire harness connectors and place the panel in position in the door. Press the door panel into place until the clips are seated and refit the armrest/door pulls. Refit the clip and press the manual regulator window crank onto the shaft until it locks.

13　Door - removal, refitting and adjustment

Refer to illustration 13.4

1　Remove the door trim panel. Disconnect any wire harness connectors and push them through the door opening so they won't interfere with door removal.

2　Place a jack or jackstand under the door

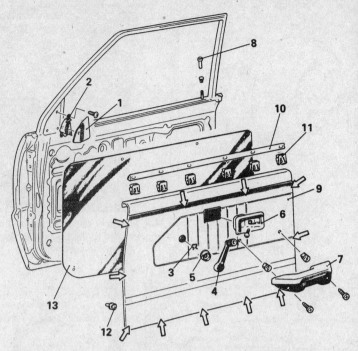

12.2a Typical front door trim panel and details

1	Inner trim panel	6	Inside handle	10	Inner weatherstrip
2	Bracket		cover	11	Clip
3	Clip	7	Arm rest	12	Trim clip
4	Regulator handle	8	Lock knob	13	Plastic
5	Escutcheon	9	Door trim		watershield

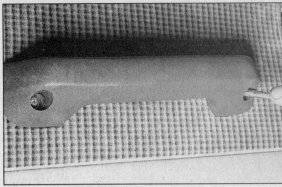

12.2b Remove the screws from the armrest

12.2c Remove the screw from the inside handle cover

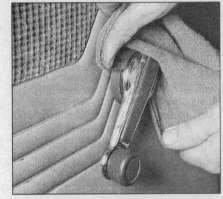

12.3 Use a rag to force the horseshoe shaped clip off the shaft

or have an assistant on hand to support it when the hinge bolts are removed. **Note:** *If a jack or jackstand is used, place a rag between it and the door to protect the door's painted surfaces.*

3   Scribe around the door hinges.

4   Remove the hinge-to-door bolts and carefully lift off the door **(see illustration)**.

5   Refitting is the reverse of removal.

6   Following refitting of the door, check the alignment and adjust it, if necessary. The door lock striker can be adjusted both up-

13.4 Front door hinge details

1	Door opening trim (power window)	8	Door lower hinge
2	Cowl side trim	9	Door lower hinge shim
3	Wiring harness connector (power window)	10	Striker
		11	Striker shim
4	Spring pin	12	Door switch cap
5	Door	13	Door switch
6	Door upper hinge		
7	Door upper hinge shim		

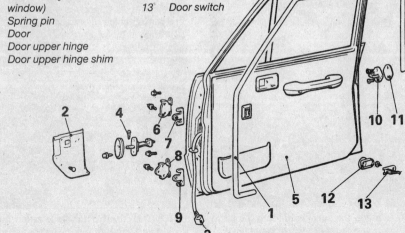

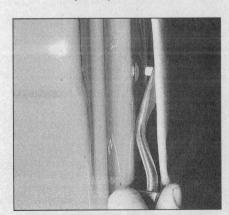

12.4 Carefully prise the door panel off the door

11

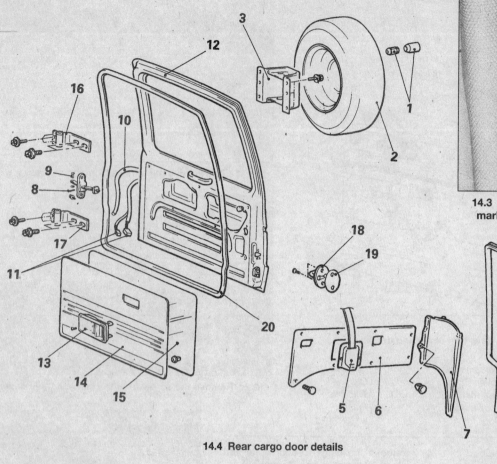

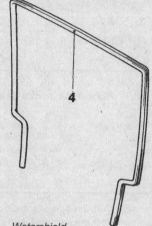

14.3 Scribe or use a marker to make marks around the bolts and hinges on the cargo door

14.4 Rear cargo door details

1	Spare tyre lock cylinder	8	Split pin	15	Watershield
2	Spare tyre	9	Clevis pin	16	Door upper hinge
3	Spare tyre carrier	10	Washer tube	17	Door lower hinge
4	Rear opening trim	11	Wiring harness connectors	18	Striker
5	Retractor cover	12	Back door	19	Striker shim
6	Quarter trim	13	Inside handle cover	20	Weatherstrip
7	Rear pillar lower trim	14	Back door trim		

and-down and sideways to provide positive engagement with the lock mechanism. This is done by loosening the mounting screws and moving the striker as necessary.

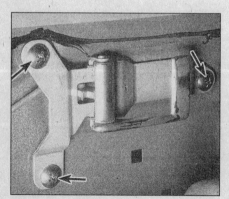

15.4 Remove the interior door handle screws (arrows) from the body

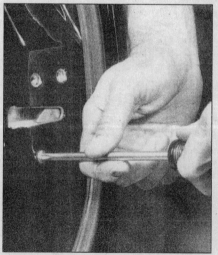

15.7 Remove the screws holding the latch assembly to the door

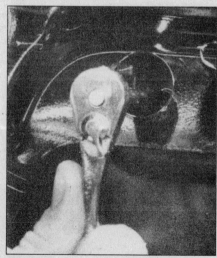

15.8 The exterior handle is attached to the door with two bolts that are accessible from the inside

14 Rear cargo door - removal, refitting and adjustment

Refer to illustrations 14.3 and 14.4

Removal and refitting

1   Disconnect any wire harness connectors and push them through the door opening so they won't interfere with door removal.
2   Place a jack or jackstand under the door or have an assistant on hand to support it when the hinge bolts are removed. **Note 1:** *If a jack or jackstand is used, place a rag between it and the door to protect the door's painted surfaces.* **Note 2:** *Remove the spare tyre to help lighten the door weight.*
3   Scribe around the door bolts **(see illustration)**.
4   Remove the hinge-to-door bolts and carefully lift off the door **(see illustration)**.
5   Refitting is the reverse of removal.

Adjustment

6   Following refitting of the door, check the alignment and adjust it if necessary as follows:

a) *Up-and-down and side-to-side adjustments are made by loosening the hinge-to-body bolts and moving the door as necessary.*

b) *The door lock striker can also be adjusted both up-and-down and sideways to provide positive engagement with the lock mechanism. This is done by loosening the mounting screws and moving the striker as necessary.*

15 Door latch, lock cylinder and handles - removal, refitting and adjustment

Front door

Refer to illustrations 15.4, 15.7, 15.8 and 15.9

Removal and refitting

1   Remove the door trim panel as described in Section 12.
2   Remove the plastic watershield, taking care not to tear it.
3   Remove the inside lever link clip and

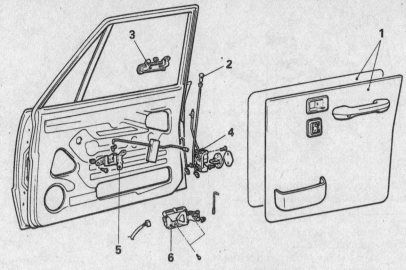

15.9 Front door lock and handle details

1	Door trim and watershield	4	Door latch
2	Inside lock knob	5	Inside handle
3	Outside handle	6	Door lock actuator (power lock)

detach the link from the door lock assembly.
4   Remove the screws that retain the interior handle assembly and lift it out **(see illustration)**.
5   Remove the glass run channel.
6   Disengage the door lock rod from the door latch assembly.
7   Remove the door latch assembly mounting screws **(see illustration)** and lift out the door latch assembly.
8   If necessary, remove the two nuts retaining the exterior handle and lift it out **(see illustration)**.
9   Remove the door lock cylinder through the outside of the door **(see illustration)**.
10   Refitting is the reverse of removal. **Note:** *During refitting, apply grease to the sliding surface of all levers and springs.*

Adjustment

Refer to illustration 15.11

11   To adjust the outside door handle freeplay, remove the retaining clip from the actuating rod and turn the connector up or down to remove the freeplay **(see illustration)**.

Cargo door

Refer to illustration 15.14

Removal and refitting

12   Remove the door trim panel as described in Section 12.
13   Remove the plastic watershield, taking care not to tear it.
14   Remove the inside lever link clip and detach the link from the door lock assembly **(see illustration)**.

15.14 Cargo door lock and handle details

1   *Trim and watershield*
2   *Garnish bracket*
3   *Garnish*
4   *Outside handle*
5   *Inside handle*
6   *Door lock assembly*
7   *Door lock actuator (power door lock)*

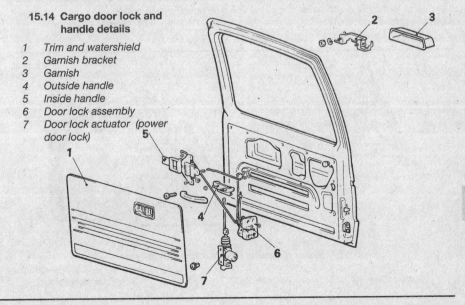

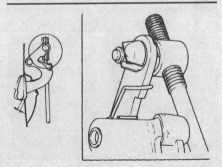

15.11 Adjusting the freeplay on the exterior handle

11

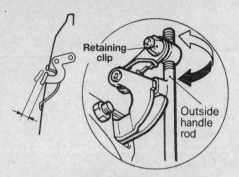

15.21 Adjusting the freeplay on the exterior handle of the rear cargo door

15   Remove the screws that retain the interior handle assembly and lift it out.
16   Disengage the door lock rod from the door lock assembly.
17   Remove the door lock assembly mounting screws and lift out the door lock assembly.
18   If necessary, remove the two nuts retaining the exterior handle and lift it out.
19   Squeeze the retaining clip with pliers and push the door lock cylinder through to the outside of the door and remove it.
20   Refitting is the reverse of removal. **Note:** *During refitting, apply grease to the sliding surface of all levers and springs.*

Adjustment

Refer to illustration 15.21

21   To adjust the outside door handle freeplay, remove the retaining clip from the actuating rod and turn the connector up or down to remove the freeplay **(see illustration).**

16 Door window and regulator - removal and refitting

Refer to illustration 16.2
1   Remove the door trim panel and plastic watershield (see Section 12).

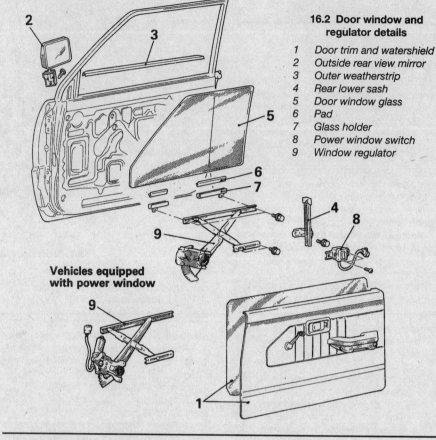

16.2 Door window and regulator details

1   *Door trim and watershield*
2   *Outside rear view mirror*
3   *Outer weatherstrip*
4   *Rear lower sash*
5   *Door window glass*
6   *Pad*
7   *Glass holder*
8   *Power window switch*
9   *Window regulator*

Vehicles equipped with power window

2   Remove the screws from the window bottom channel assembly and lower the window glass **(see illustration).**
3   Prise the two glass seals from the window opening. Remove the window glass by tilting it to detach the regulator arm from the glass channel and then sliding the glass up and out of the door.
4   Remove the regulator retaining screws.
5   Detach the regulator and guide it out of the opening in the door.
6   Refitting is the reverse of removal.

17 Outside mirror - removal and refitting

Refer to illustrations 17.1 and 17.3
1   On high-mount type mirrors, open the door and use a small screwdriver to prise the screw cover off the mirror base **(see illustration).**
2   Remove the screws and lift the mirror off the door
3   On low-mounted mirrors, remove the screws and detach the mirror from the door **(see illustration).**
4   Refitting is the reverse of removal.

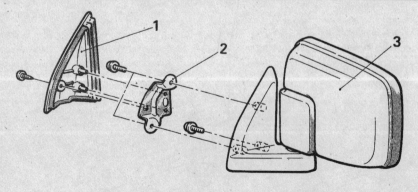

17.1 Mirror mounting details (high-mount type)

1   *Screw cover*   2   *Bracket*   3   *Rear view mirror*

17.3 On low-mount mirrors, remove the screws (arrows) from the outside area of the door

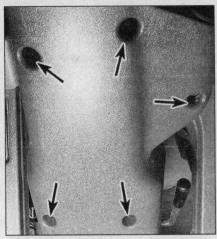

18.9 Remove the screws (arrows) and separate the steering column trim panel

18 Instrument panel and related trim - removal and refitting

Refer to illustrations 18.9 and 18.11

1   Disconnect the cable from the negative battery terminal.

2   Remove the centre console, if equipped (see Section 19).

3   Remove the insulation panels from under the instrument panel.

4   Remove the fuel filler door release cable and the bonnet release cable brackets from the instrument panel.

5   Remove the glove box assembly.

6   Remove the radio and the heater/air conditioning control panel.

7   Remove the centre trim panel.

8   Remove the instrument cluster bezel and the instrument cluster. Remove the speedometer cable adapter, if equipped.

9   Remove the steering column covers **(see illustration)**.

10   Remove the clock, rear view mirror control switch, front speakers, lights dimmer and rear wiper switch, if equipped.

11   Remove the heater ducts, defroster grilles and ventilation control cables **(see illustration)**.

12   Remove the fuse panel and disconnect any remaining wiring harness connectors.

13   Remove the steering wheel (see Chapter 10). Remove the bolts securing the steering column to the instrument panel brace.

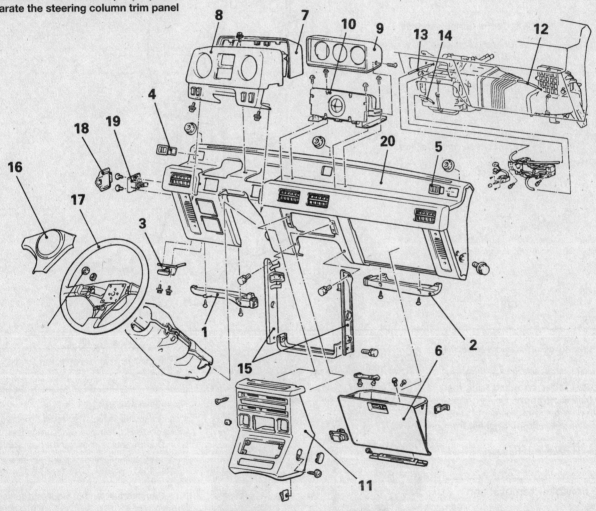

18.11 Instrument panel details

1 Lap heater duct A	8 Instrument cluster bezel	14 Water valve control cable
2 Lap heater duct B	9 Combination meter pad	15 Centre reinforcement
3 Bonnet release cable bracket	10 Combination meter case	16 Horn pad
4 Demister grille (left)	11 Centre panel	17 Steering wheel
5 Demister grille (right)	12 Recirculation/fresh air changeover cable	18 Fuse box cover
6 Glove box	13 Mode selection control cable	19 Fuse box assembly
7 Instrument cluster		20 Instrument panel

11

19.2 Centre console details

1 Front floor console
2 Shift plate
3 Rear console panel
4 Inner box
5 Lid
6 Floor console
7 Rear floor console
8 Console inner bracket
9 Floor console inner bracket

Lower the steering column and support it securely.

14   Remove the nuts/bolts securing the instrument panel to the cowl and reinforcement braces **(see illustration)**. On early models remove the center reinforcement brace. Carefully remove the instrument panel from the passenger compartment.

15 Refitting is the reverse of removal.

19 Centre console - removal and refitting

Refer to illustration 19.2

1   Remove the shift knob from the shift lever.

2   Remove the panel screws from the console base **(see illustration)**.

3   Lift the console from the passenger compartment.

4   Refitting is the reverse of removal.

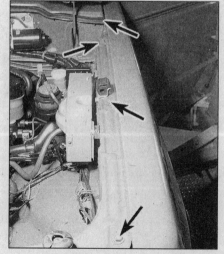

20.3 Remove the bolts (arrows) from the front fender

20 Front fender - removal and refitting

Refer to illustration 20.3

1   Raise the vehicle, support it securely on jackstands and remove the front wheel.

2   Disconnect the aerial and all light bulb wiring harness connectors and other components that would interfere with fender removal.

3   Remove the fender mounting bolts **(see illustration)**.

4   Detach the fender. It's a good idea to have an assistant support the fender while it's being moved away from the vehicle to prevent damage to the surrounding body panels.

5   Refitting is the reverse of removal.

6   Tighten all nuts, bolts and screws securely.

Chapter 12
Chassis electrical system

Contents

1 General information

The electrical system is a 12-volt, negative earth type. Power for the lights and all electrical accessories is supplied by a lead/acid-type battery which is charged by the alternator.

This Chapter covers repair and service procedures for the various electrical components not associated with the engine. Information on the battery, alternator, distributor and starter motor can be found in Chapter 5.

It should be noted that when portions of the electrical system are serviced, the negative battery cable should be disconnected from the battery to prevent electrical shorts and/or fires.

2 Electrical troubleshooting - general information

A typical electrical circuit consists of an electrical component, any switches, relays, motors, fuses, fusible links or circuit breakers related to that component and the wiring and connectors that link the component to both the battery and the chassis. To help you pin-point an electrical circuit problem, wiring diagrams are included at the end of this book.

Before tackling any troublesome electrical circuit, first study the appropriate wiring diagrams to get a complete understanding of what makes up that individual circuit. Trouble spots, for instance, can often be narrowed down by noting if other components related to the circuit are operating properly. If several components or circuits fail at one time, chances are the problem is in a fuse or earth connection, because several circuits are often routed through the same fuse and earth connections.

Electrical problems usually stem from simple causes, such as loose or corroded connections, a blown fuse, a melted fusible link or a bad relay. Visually inspect the condition of all fuses, wires and connections in a problem circuit before troubleshooting it.

If testing instruments are going to be utilised, use the diagrams to plan ahead of time where you will make the necessary connections in order to accurately pinpoint the trouble spot.

The basic tools needed for electrical troubleshooting include a circuit tester or voltmeter (a 12-volt bulb with a set of test leads can also be used), a continuity tester, which includes a bulb, battery and set of test leads, and a jumper wire, preferably with a circuit breaker incorporated, which can be used to bypass electrical components. Before attempting to locate a problem with test instruments, use the wiring diagram(s) to decide where to make the connections.

Voltage checks

Voltage checks should be performed if a circuit is not functioning properly. Connect one lead of a circuit tester to either the negative battery terminal or a known good earth. Connect the other lead to a connector in the circuit being tested, preferably nearest to the battery or fuse. If the bulb of the tester lights, voltage is present, which means that the part of the circuit between the connector and the battery is problem free. Continue checking the rest of the circuit in the same fashion. When you reach a point at which no voltage is present, the problem lies between that point and the last test point with voltage. Most of the time the problem can be traced to a loose connection. **Note:** *Keep in mind that some circuits receive voltage only when the ignition key is in the accessory or run position.*

12

Finding a short

One method of finding shorts in a circuit is to remove the fuse and connect a test light or voltmeter in its place to the fuse terminals. There should be no voltage present in the circuit. Move the wiring harness from side-to-side while watching the test light. If the bulb goes on, there is a short to earth somewhere in that area, probably where the insulation has rubbed through. The same test can be performed on each component in the circuit, even a switch.

Earth check

Perform an earthing point test to check whether a component is properly earthed. Disconnect the battery and connect one lead of a self-powered test light, known as a continuity tester, to a known good earth. Connect the other lead to the wire or earth connection being tested. If the bulb goes on, the earth is good. If the bulb does not go on, the earth is not good.

Continuity check

A continuity check is done to determine if there are any breaks in a circuit - if it is passing electricity properly. With the circuit off (no power in the circuit), a self-powered continuity tester can be used to check the circuit. Connect the test leads to both ends of the circuit (or to the "power" end and a good earth), and if the test light comes on the circuit is passing current properly. If the light doesn't come on, there is a break somewhere in the circuit. The same procedure can be used to test a switch, by connecting the continuity tester to the switch terminals. With the switch turned On, the test light should come on.

Finding an open circuit

When diagnosing for possible open circuits, it is often difficult to locate them by sight because oxidation or terminal misalign-

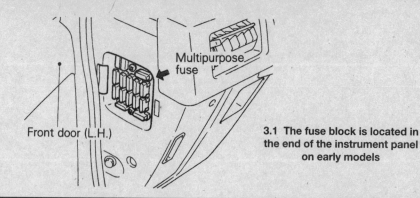

Front door (L.H.)

Multipurpose fuse

3.1 The fuse block is located in the end of the instrument panel on early models

ment are hidden by the connectors. Merely wiggling a connector on a sensor or in the wiring harness may correct the open circuit condition. Remember this when an open circuit is indicated when troubleshooting a circuit. Intermittent problems may also be caused by oxidised or loose connections.

Electrical troubleshooting is simple if you keep in mind that all electrical circuits are basically electricity running from the battery, through the wires, switches, relays, fuses and fusible links to each electrical component (light bulb, motor, etc.) and to an earthing point, from which it is passed back to the battery. Any electrical problem is an interruption in the flow of electricity to and from the battery.

3 Fuses - general information

Refer to illustrations 3.1 and 3.3

1   The electrical circuits of the vehicle are protected by a combination of fuses, circuit breakers and fusible links. The fuse block is located in the end of the instrument panel under a cover on the right (RHD) or left (LHD) side of the **(see illustration)**. On later models the fuse blocks are located under the dash on the right and left side. Later models also have a combination fuse/relay block in the engine compartment.

2   Each of the fuses is designed to protect a specific circuit, and the various circuits are identified on the fuse panel itself.

3   Miniaturised fuses are employed. These compact fuses, with blade terminal design, allow fingertip removal and refitting. If an electrical component fails, always check the fuse first. A blown fuse is easily identified through the clear plastic body. Visually inspect the element for evidence of damage **(see illustration)**. If a continuity check is called for, the blade terminal tips are exposed in the fuse body.

4   Be sure to renew blown fuses with the correct type. Fuses of different ratings are physically interchangeable, but only fuses of the proper rating should be used. Renewing a fuse with one of a higher or lower value than specified is not recommended. Each electrical circuit needs a specific amount of protection. The amperage value of each fuse is moulded into the fuse body.

5   If the renewed fuse immediately fails, don't renew it again until the cause of the problem is isolated and corrected. In most cases, the cause will be a short circuit in the wiring caused by a broken or deteriorated wire.

4 Fusible links - general information

Refer to illustration 4.1

Some circuits are protected by fusible links. The links are used in circuits which are not ordinarily fused, such as the ignition circuit **(see illustration)**.

State of fuse blown due to overcurrent

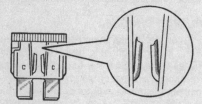

State of fuse blown due to thermal fatigue

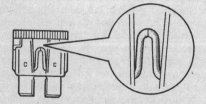

3.3 Miniaturised fuses are used - overcurrent or thermal fatigue can cause them to fail

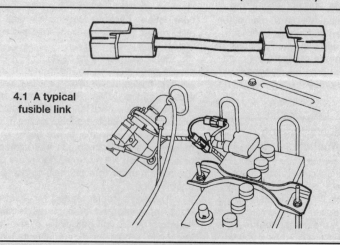

4.1 A typical fusible link

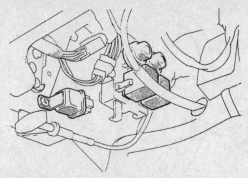

6.2 This group of relays is located under the driver's side of the instrument panel

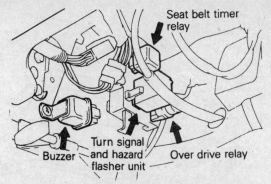

7.1 Turn signal/hazard flasher location

Although the fusible links appear to be a heavier gauge than the wire they are protecting, the appearance is due to the thick insulation. All fusible links are four wire gauges smaller than the wire they are designed to protect.

Fusible links cannot be repaired, but a new link of the same size wire can be put in its place. The procedure is as follows:
a) *Disconnect the negative cable from the battery.*
b) *Disconnect the fusible link from the wiring harness.*
c) *Plug in the connectors at each end of the new fusible link.*
d) *Connect the battery negative cable. Test the circuit for proper operation.*

5 Circuit breakers - general information

Circuit breakers protect components such as power windows, power door locks and headlights. Some circuit breakers are located in the fuse box.

On some models the circuit breaker resets itself automatically, so an electrical overload in a circuit breaker protected system will cause the circuit to fail momentarily, then come back on. If the circuit does not come back on, check it immediately. Once the condition is corrected, the circuit breaker will resume its normal function. Some circuit breakers must be reset manually.

6 Relays - general information

Refer to illustration 6.2

1   Several electrical accessories in the vehicle use relays to transmit the electrical signal to the component. If the relay is defective, that component will not operate properly.
2   The various relays are grouped together in several locations **(see illustration)**.
3   If a faulty relay is suspected, it can be removed and tested by a dealer service department or a repair shop. Defective relays must be renewed as a unit.

7 Turn signal and hazard flashers - check and renewal

Refer to illustration 7.1

Turn signal flasher

1   The turn signal flasher, a small box or canister-shaped unit located under the driver's side of the instrument panel **(see illustration)**, flashes the turn signals.
2   When the flasher unit is functioning properly, an audible click can be heard during its operation. If the turn signals fail on one side or the other and the flasher unit does not make its characteristic clicking sound, a faulty turn signal bulb is indicated.
3   If both turn signals fail to blink, the problem may be due to a blown fuse, a faulty flasher unit, a broken switch or a loose or open connection. If a quick check of the fuse box indicates that the turn signal fuse has blown, check the wiring for a short before fitting a new fuse.
4   To renew the flasher, simply pull it out and press in a new one.
5   Make sure that the renewed unit is identical to the original. Compare the old one to the new one before fitting it.
6   Refitting is the reverse of removal.

Hazard flasher

7   The hazard flasher on most models is integral with the turn signal flasher unit.
8   The hazard flasher is checked in a fashion similar to the turn signal flasher (see Steps 2 and 3).
9   To renew the hazard flasher, pull it from the back of fuse block.
10   Make sure the renewed unit is identical to the one it replaces. Compare the old one to the new one before fitting it.
11   Refitting is the reverse of removal.

8 Ignition switch and lock cylinder - removal and refitting

Refer to illustration 8.2

1   Disconnect the negative battery cable from the battery.
2   Remove the steering column cover to gain access to the ignition switch/lock cylinder **(see illustration)**.
3   Using wire cutters, remove the cable band.

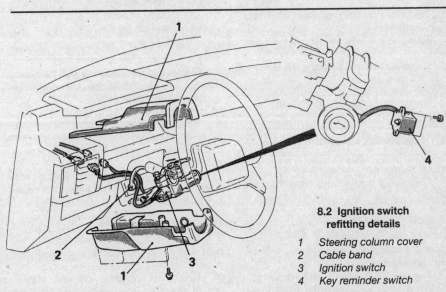

8.2 Ignition switch refitting details

1   *Steering column cover*
2   *Cable band*
3   *Ignition switch*
4   *Key reminder switch*

12

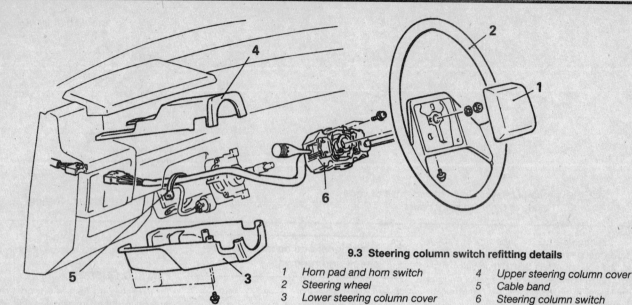

9.3 Steering column switch refitting details

1	Horn pad and horn switch	4	Upper steering column cover
2	Steering wheel	5	Cable band
3	Lower steering column cover	6	Steering column switch

4   Remove the screw retaining the ignition switch to the steering column.

5   Unbolt and remove the key reminder switch, if necessary. On 1991 and later models the lock cylinder can be removed separately with the switch assembly in place. Turn the key to the ACC position, insert a small screwdriver or similar tool into the hole at the bottom of the casting to depress the release pin and pull the lock cylinder out.

6   Refitting is the reverse of removal.

9   Steering column switch - removal and refitting

Refer to illustration 9.3

1   Disconnect the negative battery cable from the battery.

2   Remove the steering wheel (see Chapter 10).

3   Remove the steering column covers **(see illustration)**.

4   Using wire cutters to remove the cable band.

5   Remove the screws holding the steering column switch.

6   Remove the steering column switch.

7   Refitting is the reverse of removal.

10   Headlights - renewal

Refer to illustrations 10.2 and 10.4

1   Disconnect the negative cable from the battery.

Sealed-beam type

2   Remove the retaining screws and detach the radiator grille and headlight bezel **(see illustration)**.

3   Remove the headlight retainer screws, taking care not to disturb the adjustment screws **(see illustration 10.2)**.

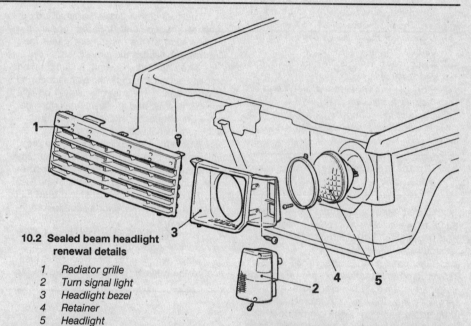

10.2 Sealed beam headlight renewal details

1	Radiator grille
2	Turn signal light
3	Headlight bezel
4	Retainer
5	Headlight

4   Remove the retainer and pull the headlight out enough to allow the connector to be unplugged **(see illustration)**.

5   Remove the headlight.

6   To refit the headlight, plug the connector in, place the headlight in position and refit the retainer and screws. Tighten the screws securely.

7   Place the headlight bezel in position and refit the retaining screws. Connect the negative battery cable.

Halogen bulb type

8   Disconnect electrical connector at the bulb, then pull out the socket cover and connector.

9   Detach the spring retainer and rotate it out of the way, then withdraw the bulb assembly from the headlight housing.

10.4 Unplugging the electrical connector (sealed-beam type)

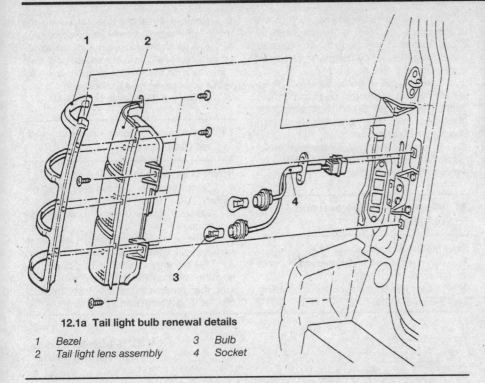

12.1b To remove a rear light bulb, push it in and rotate it 90-degrees counter-clockwise

12.1a Tail light bulb renewal details

1 Bezel
2 Tail light lens assembly
3 Bulb
4 Socket

10   Insert the new bulb assembly into the headlight housing, secure it with the spring retainer, refit the socket cover and plug in the connector. **Note:** *To renew the left side bulb it's necessary to remove the engine coolant reservoir.* **Caution:** *Never hold a halogen bulb with your bare hands, a dirty rag, etc. The oils on the glass will cause the bulb to create a hot spot and fail prematurely. If any oil or dirt gets on the glass, clean it thoroughly with lacquer thinner or alcohol before refitting.*

11 Headlights - adjustment

Note: *The headlights must be aimed correctly. If adjusted incorrectly they could blind the driver of an oncoming vehicle and cause a serious accident or seriously reduce your ability to see the road. The headlights should be checked for proper aim every 12 months and any time a new headlight is fitted or front end body work is performed. It should be emphasised that the following procedure is only an interim step which will provide temporary adjustment until the headlights can be adjusted by a properly equipped shop.*

1   Headlights have two spring loaded adjusting screws, one on the top controlling up-and-down movement and one on the side controlling left-and-right movement.
2   There are several methods of adjusting the headlights. The simplest method requires a blank wall 8 meters in front of the vehicle and a level floor.
3   Position masking tape vertically on the wall in reference to the vehicle centerline and the centerlines of both headlights.
4   Position a horizontal tape line in reference to the centerline of all the headlights.

Note: *It may be easier to position the tape on the wall with the vehicle parked only a few centimetres away.*

5   Adjustment should be made with the vehicle sitting level, the fuel tank half-full and no unusually heavy load in the vehicle.
6   Starting with the low beam adjustment, position the high-intensity zone so it's five centimeters below the horizontal line and five centimeters to the side of the headlight vertical line, away from oncoming traffic. Adjustment is made by turning the top adjustment screw clockwise to raise the beam and counterclockwise to lower it. The adjusting screw

on the side is used in the same manner to move the beam left or right.
7   With the high beams on, the high-intensity zone should be vertically centred with the exact centre just below the horizontal line. **Note:** *It may not be possible to position the headlight aim exactly for both high and low beams. If a compromise must be made, keep in mind that the low beams are the most used and have the greatest effect on driver safety.*
8   Have the headlights adjusted by a dealer service department or service station at the earliest opportunity.

12 Bulb - renewal

Refer to illustrations 12.1a, 12.1b, 12.1c, 12.1d, 12.1e and 12.1f
1   The lenses of many lights are held in place by screws, which makes it a simple procedure to gain access to the bulbs **(see illustrations).**

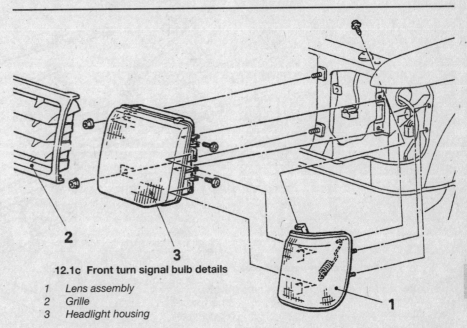

12.1c Front turn signal bulb details

1   Lens assembly
2   Grille
3   Headlight housing

12.1d Remove the screw, then pull off the side marker lens

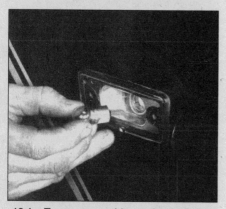

12.1e To remove a side-marker bulb like the one shown, push it in and rotate it 90-degrees counter-clockwise

2   On some lights the lenses, such as the interior dome light lens, are held in place by clips. The lenses can be removed either by unsnapping them or by using a small screwdriver to prise them off.

3   Several types of bulbs are used. Some are removed by pushing in and turning them counter-clockwise. Others can simply be unclipped from the terminals or pulled straight out of the socket.

4   To gain access to the instrument panel lights, the instrument cluster will have to be removed first (see Section 15).

13 Wiper motor - removal and refitting

Refer to illustrations 13.3 and 13.4

1   Remove the negative battery cable from the battery.

2   Unplug the electrical connector leading from the wiper motor.

3   Remove the three bolts attaching the motor to the vehicle firewall **(see illustration)**.

4   Pull up on the wiper arm until the actuator arm joint is visible in the access hole, then prise the motor out of the actuator arm joint with a screwdriver **(see illustration)**.

5   Refitting is the reverse of removal.

14 Instrument cluster - removal and refitting

Refer to illustration 14.3

1   Disconnect the negative cable from the battery.

2   Remove any screws and detach the cluster cover.

3   Remove the bolts holding the instrument cluster in place **(see illustration)**.

4   Pull the instrument cluster out, disconnect the speedometer and electrical connectors, then remove the cluster from the vehicle. Refitting is the reverse of removal.

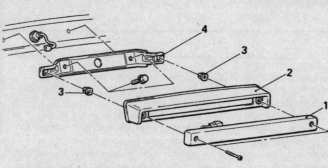

12.1f High-level brake light refitting details

1   *High level brake light lens*
2   *High level brake light housing*
3   *Plastic nuts*
4   *Mounting bracket*

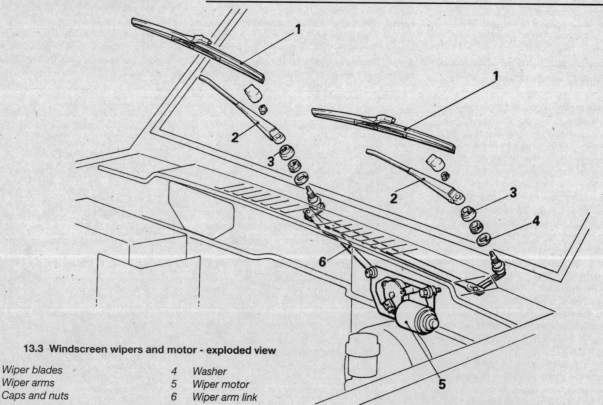

13.3 Windscreen wipers and motor - exploded view

1	Wiper blades	4	Washer
2	Wiper arms	5	Wiper motor
3	Caps and nuts	6	Wiper arm link

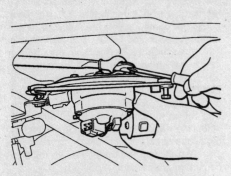

13.4 Use a screwdriver to detach the wiper link from the motor

15   Instrument cluster - disassembly and reassembly

Refer to illustration 15.1

1   Remove the nuts holding the cover in place **(see illustration)**.

2   Turn the cluster over, remove any screws or nuts and separate the components from the case **(see illustration 15.1)**.

3   Remove the bulb holders from the printed circuit board by turning them counter-clockwise.

4   Reassembly is the reverse of disassembly.

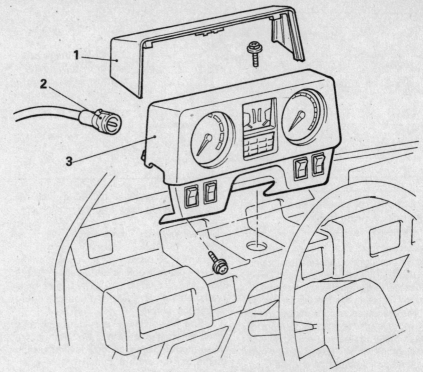

14.3 Instrument cluster details

1 Instrument cluster cover	3 Instrument cluster
2 Speedometer cable	

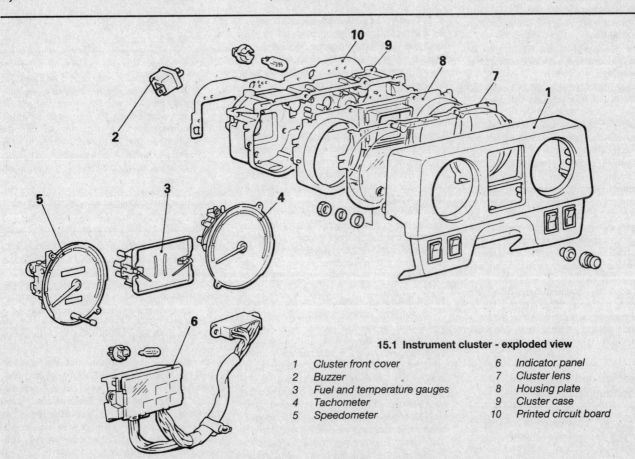

15.1 Instrument cluster - exploded view

1	Cluster front cover	6	Indicator panel
2	Buzzer	7	Cluster lens
3	Fuel and temperature gauges	8	Housing plate
4	Tachometer	9	Cluster case
5	Speedometer	10	Printed circuit board

12

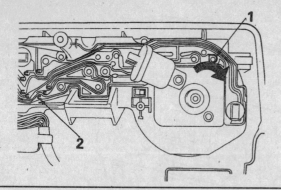

16.7 Check the speed sensor by turning the shaft while checking for continuity at terminals 1 and 2

16   Cruise control system - description and check

Refer to illustration 16.7

1   The cruise control system maintains vehicle speed with a vacuum actuated servo motor located in the engine compartment, which is connected to the throttle linkage by a cable. The system consists of the electronic control module, brake switch, control switches, a relay, the vehicle speed sensor and associated wiring. Listed below are some general procedures that may be used to locate common cruise control problems.

2   Locate and check the fuse (see Section 3).

3   Have an assistant operate the brake lights while you check their operation (voltage from the brake light switch deactivates the cruise control).

4   If the brake lights don't come on or don't shut off, correct the problem and retest the cruise control.

5   Inspect the cable linkage between the cruise control actuator and the throttle linkage.

6   Visually inspect the wires connected to the cruise control actuator and check for damage and broken wires.

7   The vehicle speed sensor is located in the instrument cluster on the back of the speedometer. Remove the cluster, unplug the electrical connector use an ohmmeter to determine that the continuity and discontinuity alternates between terminals 1 and 2 four times when the speedometer shaft is rotated **(see illustration)**. If the continuity doesn't vary as the shaft rotates, the sensor is defective.

8   Test drive the vehicle to determine if the cruise control is now working. If it isn't, take it to a dealer service department or an automotive electrical specialist for further diagnosis and repair.

17   Power window system - description and check

1   The power window system consists of the control switches, the motors, glass mechanisms (regulators), and associated wiring.

2   Power windows are wired so they can be lowered and raised from the master control switch by the driver or by remote switches located at the individual windows. Each window has a separate motor which is reversible. The position of the control switch determines the polarity and therefore the direction of operation. The system is equipped with a relay that controls current flow to the motors.

3   The power window system operates when the ignition switch is ON. In addition, these models have a window lockout switch at the master control switch which, when activated, disables the switches at the rear windows and, sometimes, the switch at the passenger's window also. Always check these items before troubleshooting a window problem.

4   These procedures are general in nature, so if you can't find the problem using them, take the vehicle to a dealer service department or other qualified repair shop.

5   If the power windows don't work at all, check the fuse or circuit breaker.

6   If only the rear windows are inoperative, or if the windows only operate from the master control switch, check the rear window lockout switch for continuity in the unlocked position. Renew it if it doesn't have continuity.

7   Check the wiring between the switches and fuse panel for continuity. Repair the wiring, if necessary.

8   If only one window is inoperative from the master control switch, try the other control switch at the window. **Note:** *This doesn't apply to the drivers door window.*

9   If the same window works from one switch, but not the other, check the switch for continuity.

10   If the switch tests OK, check for a short or open in the wiring between the affected switch and the window motor.

11   If one window is inoperative from both switches, remove the trim panel from the affected door and check for voltage at the motor while the switch is operated.

12   If voltage is reaching the motor, disconnect the glass from the regulator (see Chapter 11). Move the window up and down by hand while checking for binding and damage. Also check for binding and damage to the regulator. If the regulator is not damaged and

the window moves up and down smoothly, renew the motor (see Chapter 11). If there's binding or damage, lubricate, repair or renew parts, as necessary.

13   If voltage isn't reaching the motor, check the wiring in the circuit for continuity between the switches and motors. Check that the relay is earthed properly and receiving voltage from the switches. Also check that the relay sends voltage to the motor when the switch is turned on. If it doesn't, renew the relay.

14   Test the windows after you are done to confirm proper repairs.

18   Power door lock system - description and check

The power door lock system operates the door lock actuators mounted in each door. The system consists of the switches, actuators and associated wiring. Since special tools and techniques are required to diagnose the system, it should be left to a dealer service department or a repair shop. However, it is possible for the home mechanic to make simple checks of the wiring connections and actuators for minor faults which can be easily repaired. These include:

a) *Check the system fuse and/or circuit breaker.*

b) *Check the switch wires for damage and loose connections.*

c) *Check the switches for continuity.*

d) *Remove the door panel(s) and check the actuator wiring connections to see if they're loose or damaged. Inspect the actuator rods (if equipped) to make sure they aren't bent or damaged. Inspect the actuator wiring for damaged or loose connections. The actuator can be checked by applying battery power momentarily. A discernible click indicates that the solenoid is operating properly.*

19   Speedometer cable - renewal

Refer to illustrations 19.2 and 19.4

1   Disconnect the negative cable from the battery.

2   Disconnect the speedometer cable from the transmission **(see illustration)**.

3   Detach the cable from the routing clips in the engine compartment and pull it up to provide enough slack to allow disconnection from the speedometer.

4   Remove the instrument cluster screws, pull the cluster out (see Section 14) and disconnect the speedometer cable from the back of the cluster **(see illustration)**. **Note:** *On later models with a ratio adapter, after removing the instrument cluster, rotate the adapter to the left or right to release the locks and pull the adapter out.*

5   Remove the cable from the vehicle.

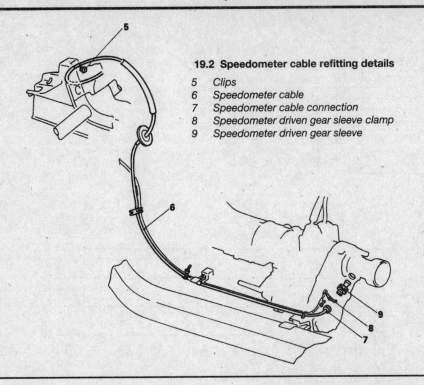

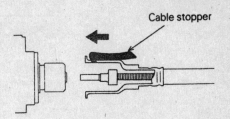

Cable stopper

19.2 Speedometer cable refitting details

5 *Clips*
6 *Speedometer cable*
7 *Speedometer cable connection*
8 *Speedometer driven gear sleeve clamp*
9 *Speedometer driven gear sleeve*

19.4 On most models, when attaching or detaching the speedometer cable from the speedometer, press down on the end of the cable stopper

4 Unplug the centre panel wiring harness.
5 Detach the radio panel, remove the bracket screws and detach the radio from the bracket.
6 Lift the radio and unplug the electrical connectors.
7 Refitting is the reverse of removal.

21 Wiring diagrams - general information

Since it isn't possible to include all wiring diagrams for every year covered by this manual, the following diagrams are those that are typical and most commonly needed.

When checking a circuit, make sure that all connectors are clean, with no broken or loose terminals. When unplugging a connector, do not pull on the wires. Pull only on the connector housings themselves.

6 Prior to refitting, lubricate the speedometer end of the cable with spray-on speedometer cable lubricant (available at auto parts stores).
7 Refitting is the reverse of removal. Prior to troubleshooting any circuits, check the fuse and circuit breakers (if equipped) to make sure they're in good condition. Make sure the battery is properly charged and check the cable connections (see Chapter 1).

20 Radio - removal and refitting

Refer to illustration 20.2
1 Disconnect the negative cable from the battery.
2 Pull off the radio knobs **(see illustration).**
3 Remove the centre console (see Chapter 11).

20.2 Radio refitting details

1 *Knob*
2 *Screw cover plug*
3 *Console assembly*
4 *Wiring harness connector*
5 *Radio panel*
6 *Bracket*
7 *Radio*
8 *Optional tape box*
9 *Radio unit*

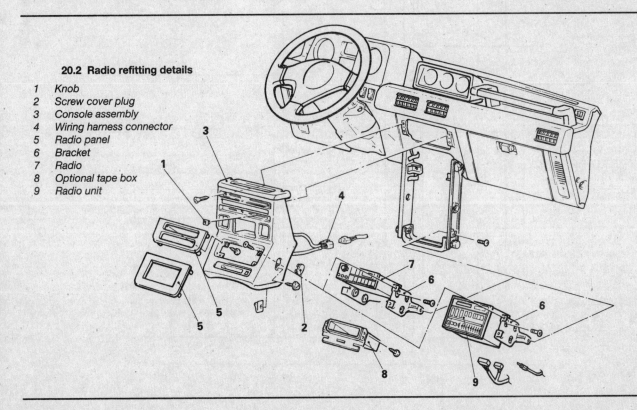

12

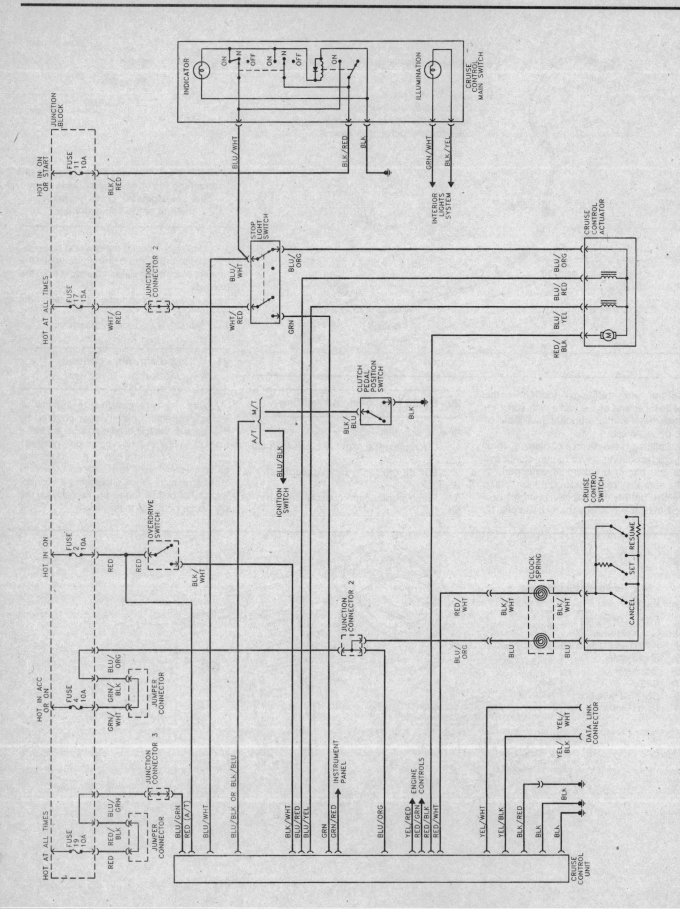

1991 and later model cruise control system

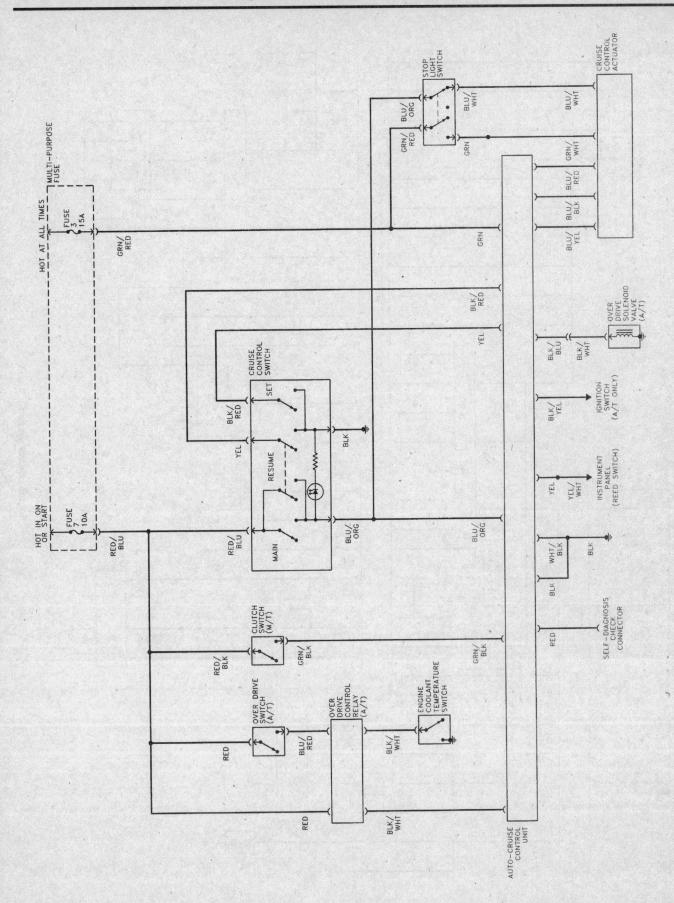

1990 and earlier model cruise control system

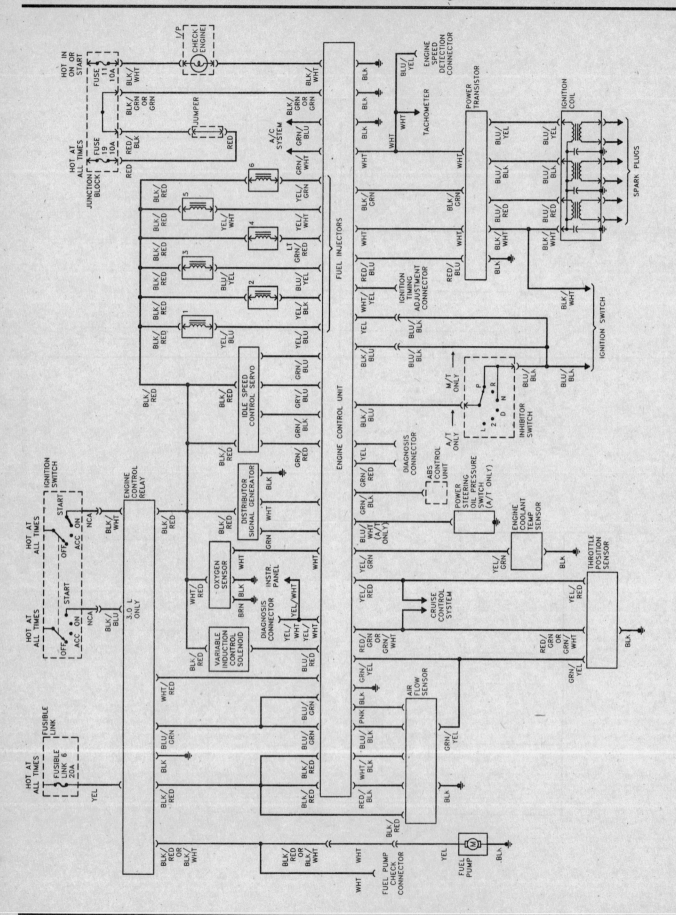

Engine control system

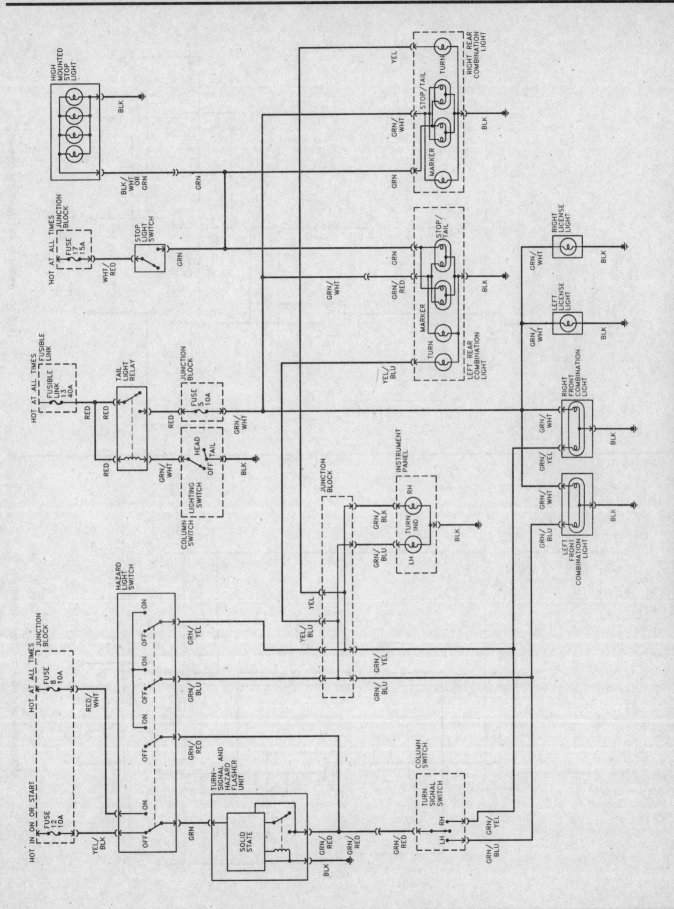

1991 and later model exterior lighting system (except headlight)

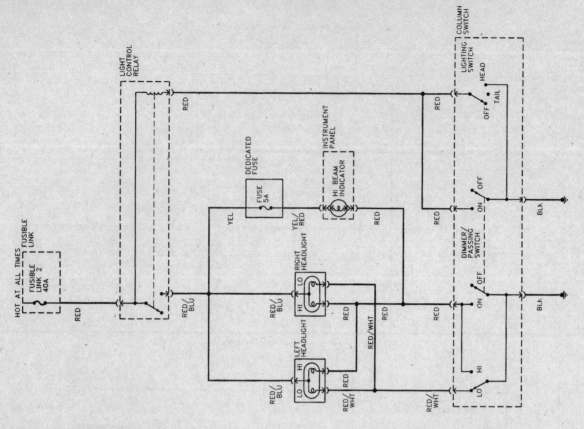

1990 and earlier model headlight system

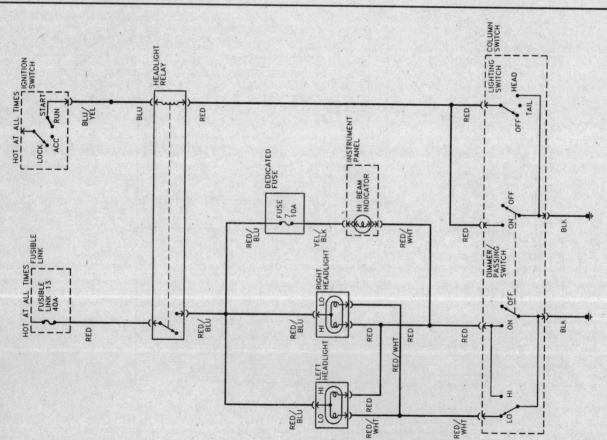

1991 and later model headlight system

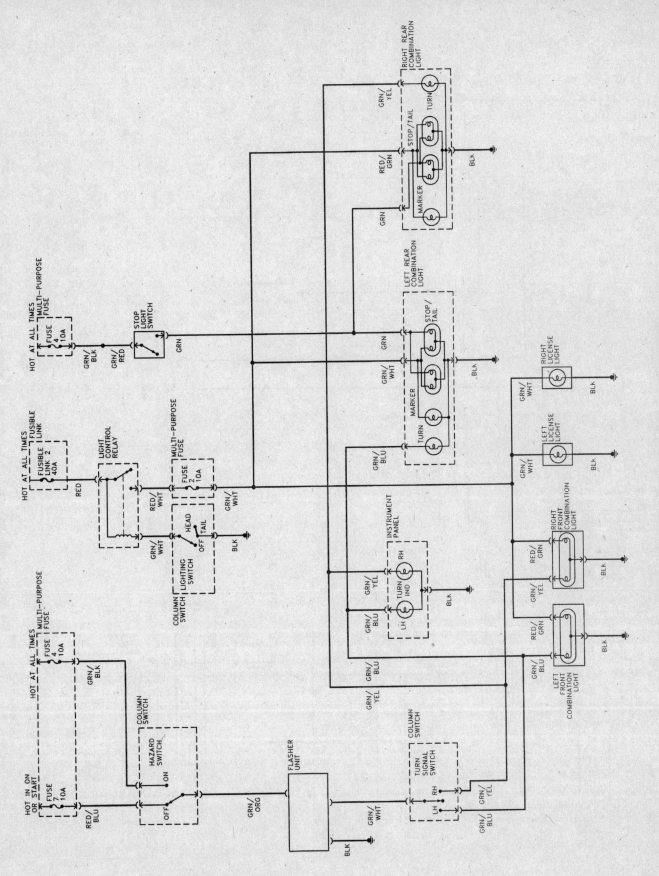

1990 and earlier model exterior lighting system (except headlights)

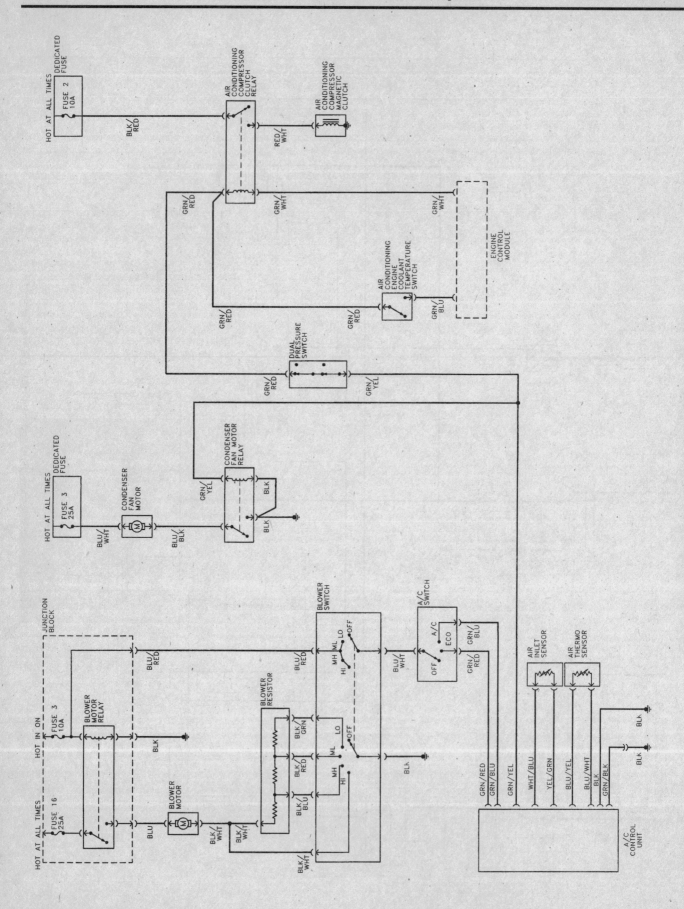

1991 and later model heating, air conditioning and engine cooling system

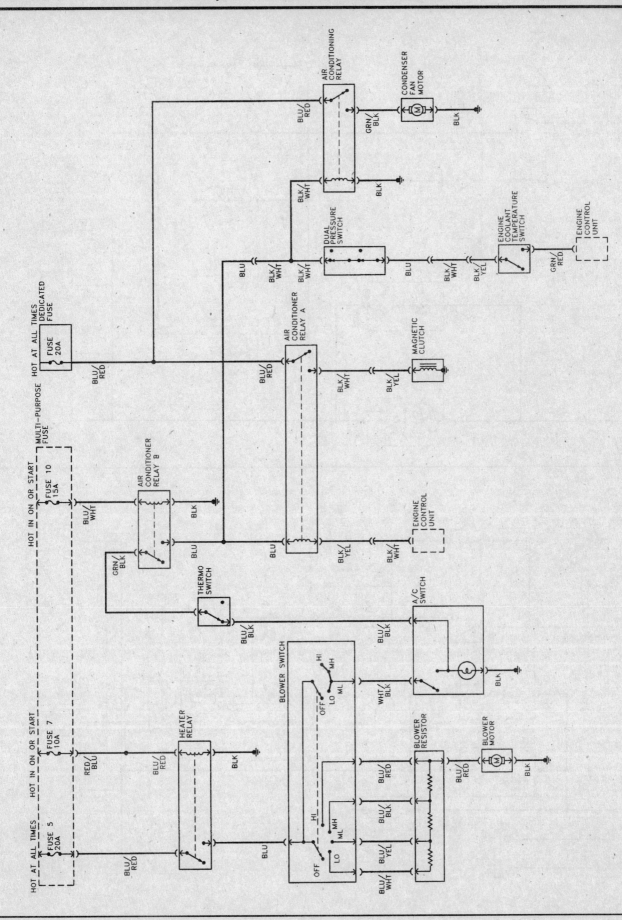

1990 and earlier model heating, air conditioning and engine cooling system

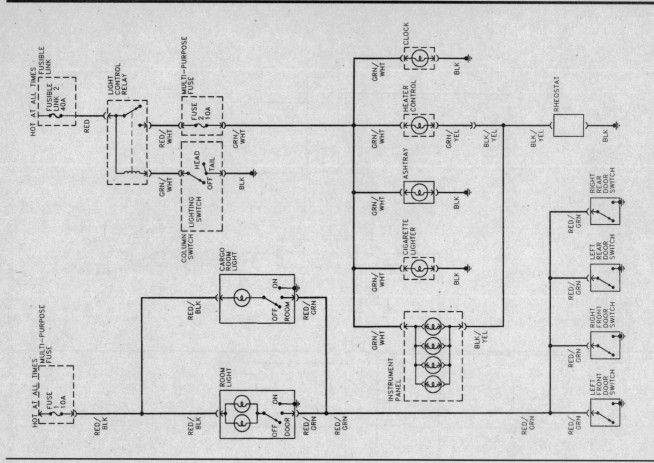

1990 and earlier model interior illumination system

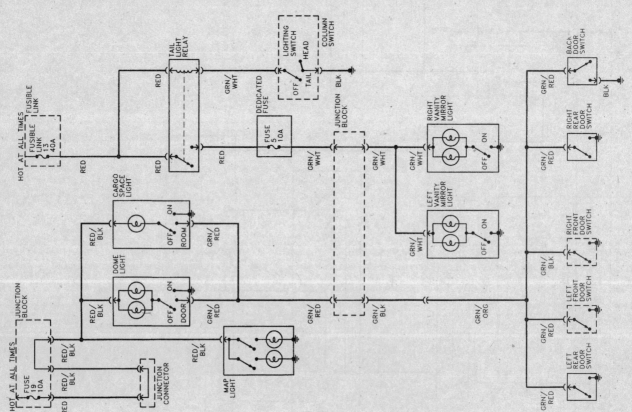

1991 and later model courtesy light system

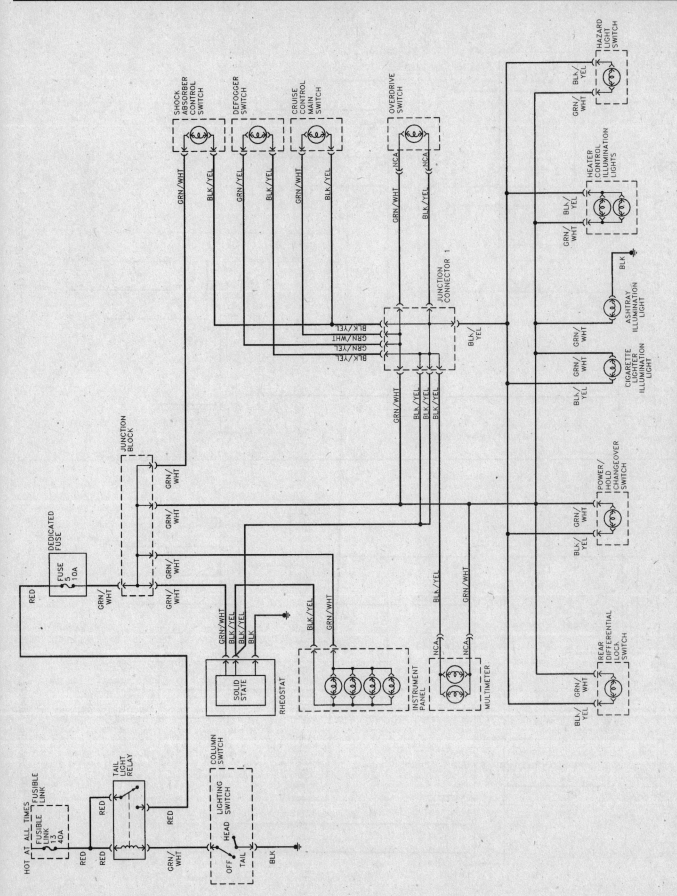

1991 and later model interior illumination system

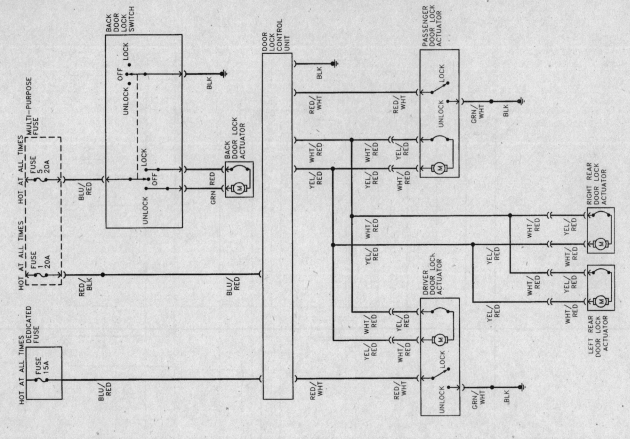

1990 and earlier model power door lock system

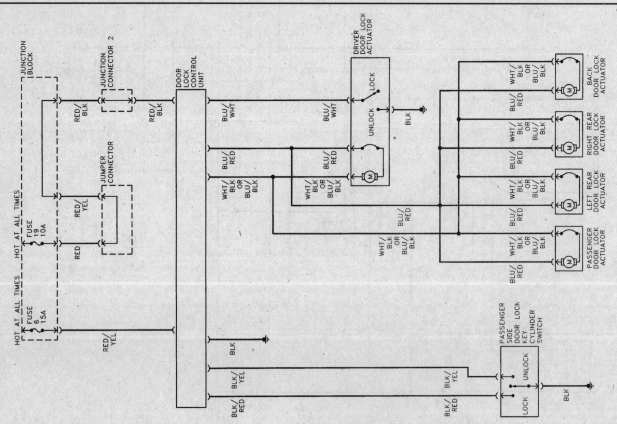

1991 and later model power door lock system

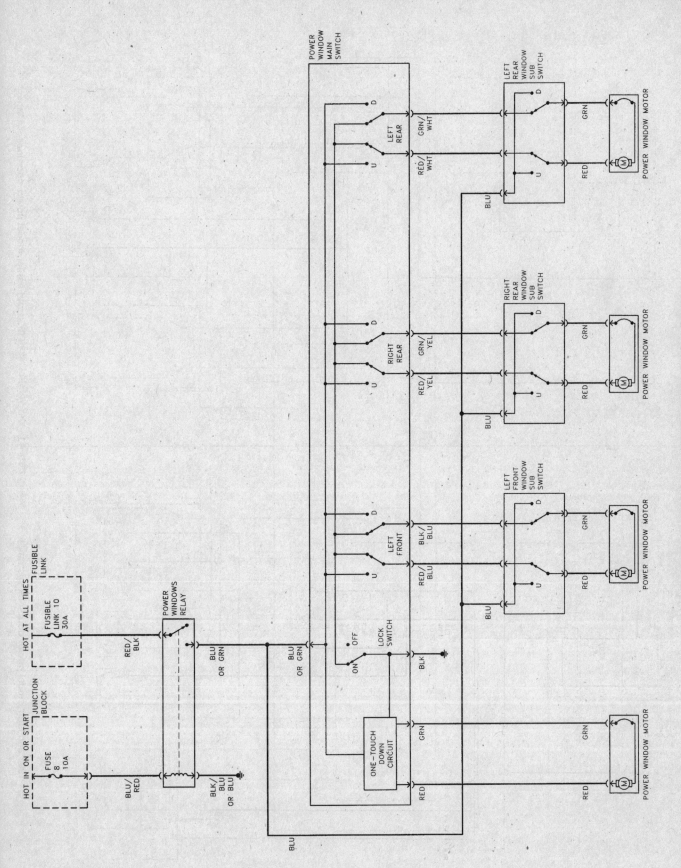

1991 and later model power window system wiring diagram

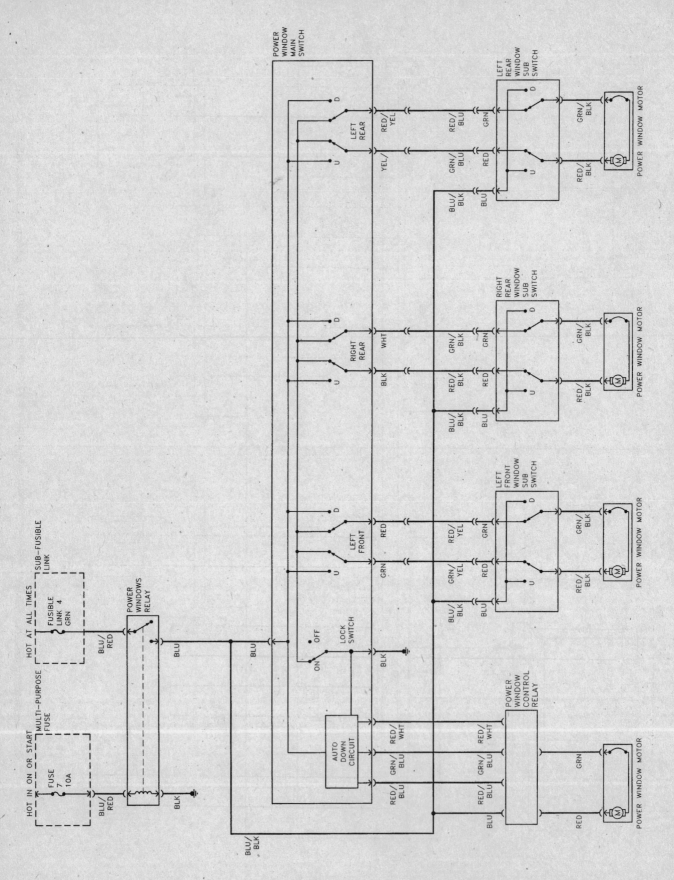

1990 and earlier model power window system

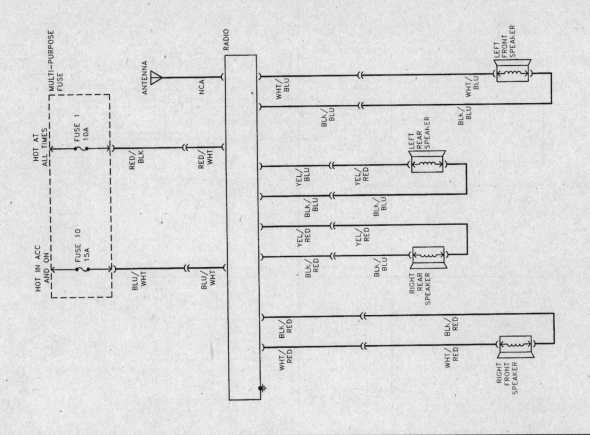

1990 and earlier model radio system

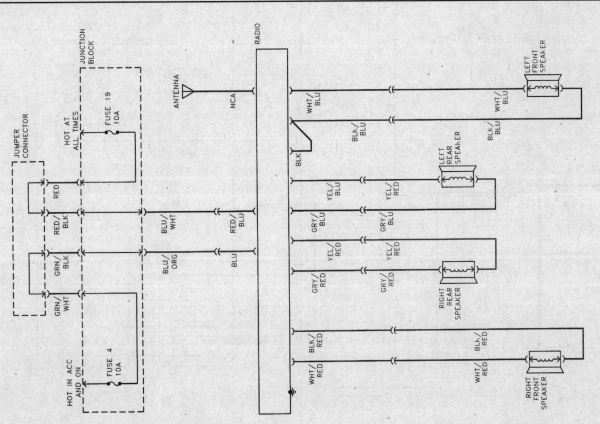

1991 and later model radio system

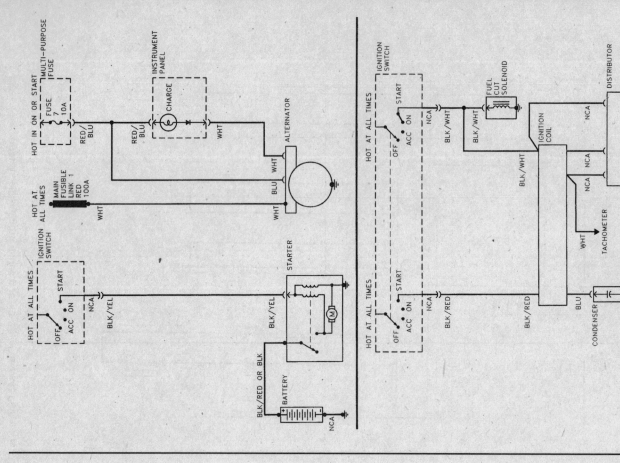

1989 and earlier model starting, charging and ignition system

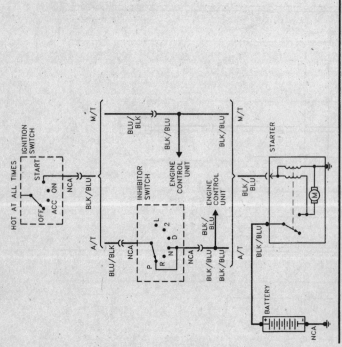

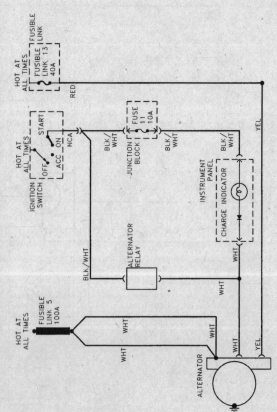

1990 and later model starting and charging system

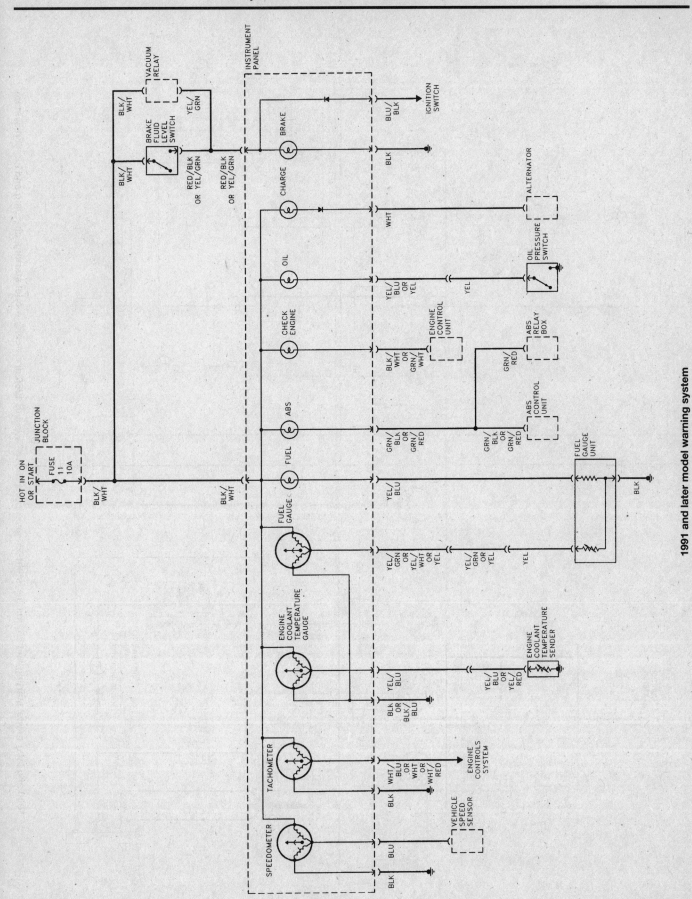

1991 and later model warning system

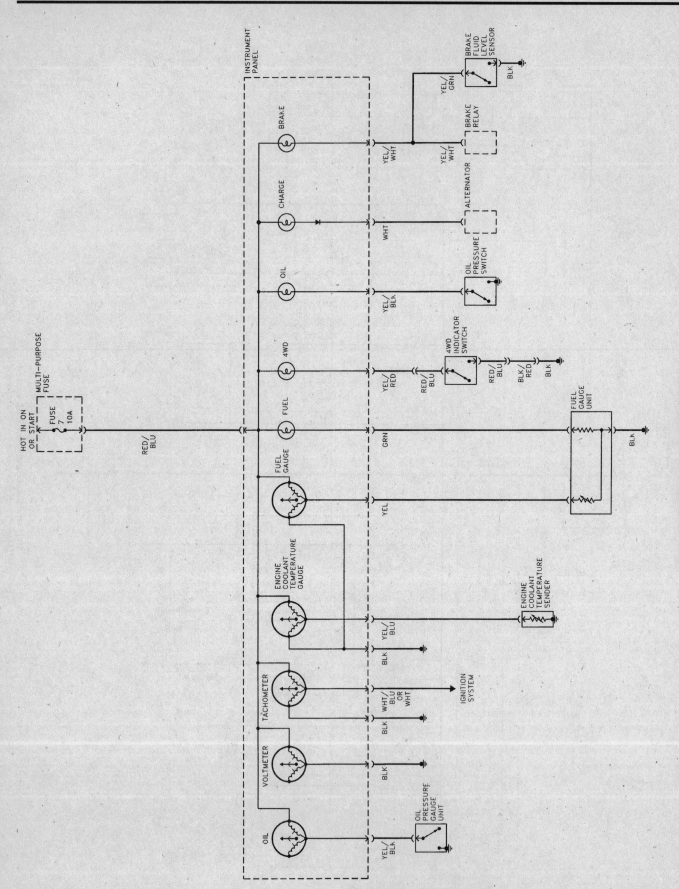

1990 and earlier model warning system

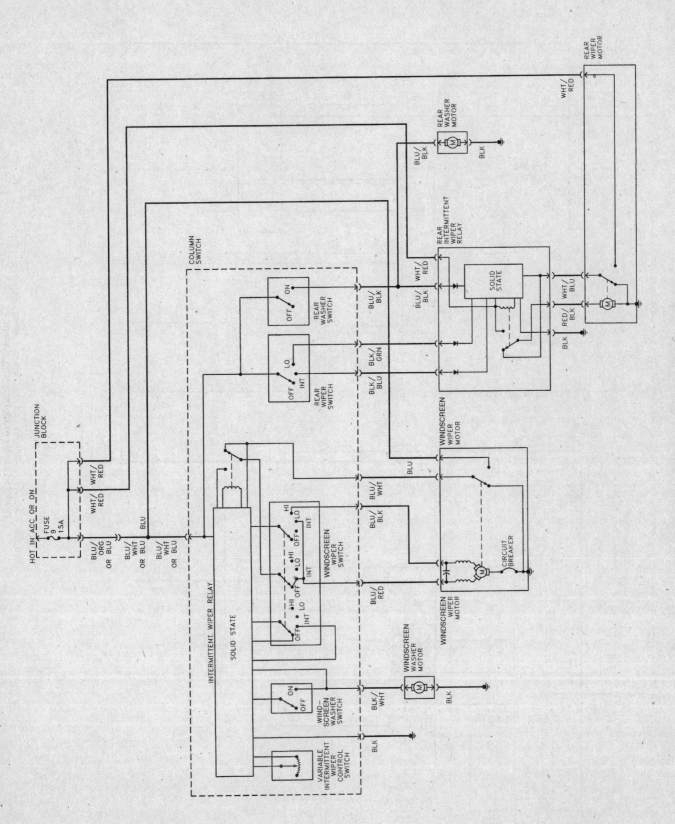

1991 and later model front and rear wiper/washer system

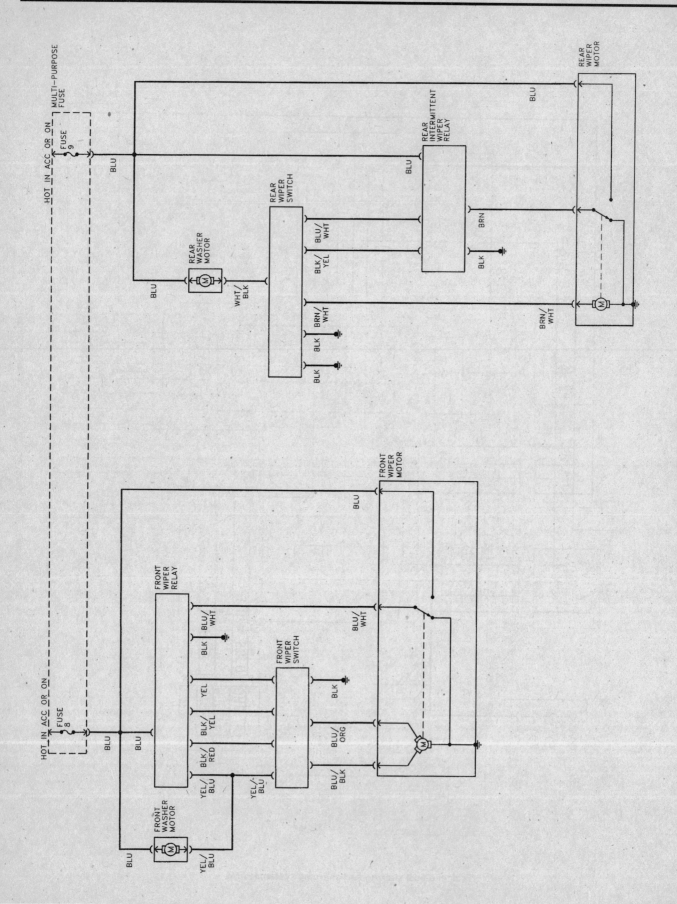

1990 and earlier model front and rear wiper/washer system

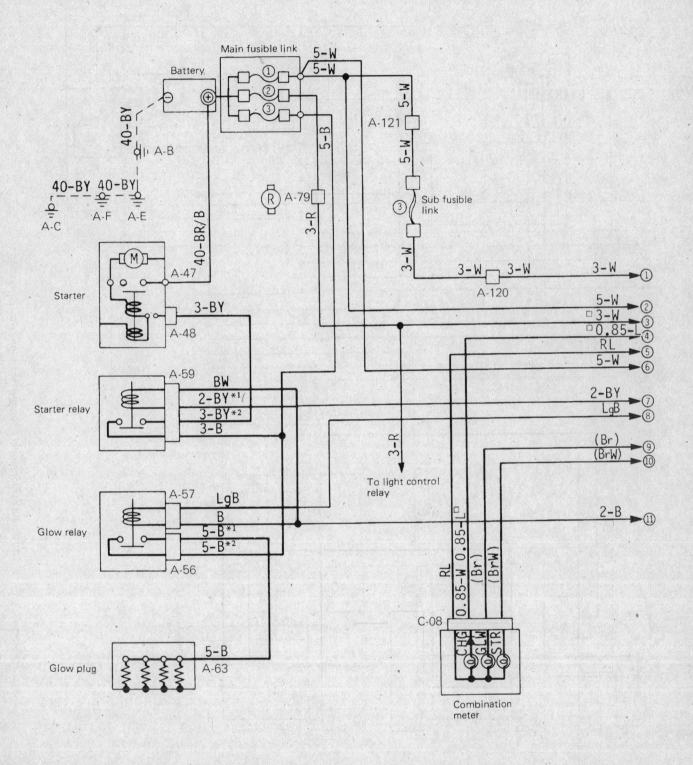

Typical diesel starting and charging system (1 of 2)

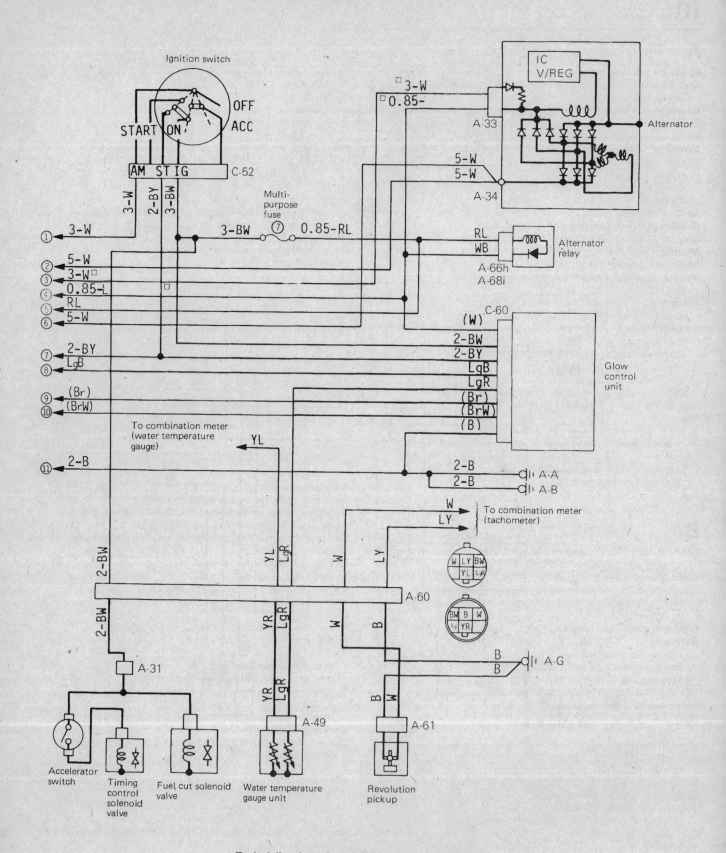

Typical diesel starting and charging system (2 of 2)

Index